ROUTLEDGE LIBRARY EDITIONS:
WORLD EMPIRES

Volume 3

THE GERMAN EMPIRE 1867–1914

THE GERMAN EMPIRE 1867–1914

And the Unity Movement (Volume One)

WILLIAM HARBUTT DAWSON

First published in 1919 by George Allen & Unwin Ltd

This edition first published in 2018
by Routledge
2 Park Square, Milton Park, Abingdon, Oxon OX14 4RN

and by Routledge
711 Third Avenue, New York, NY 10017

Routledge is an imprint of the Taylor & Francis Group, an informa business

British Library Cataloguing in Publication Data
A catalogue record for this book is available from the British Library

ISBN: 978-1-138-47911-1 (Set)
ISBN: 978-1-351-00226-4 (Set) (ebk)
ISBN: 978-1-138-48149-7 (Volume 3) (hbk)
ISBN: 978-1-351-05943-5 (Volume 3) (ebk)

Publisher's Note
The publisher has gone to great lengths to ensure the quality of this reprint but points out that some imperfections in the original copies may be apparent.

Disclaimer
The publisher has made every effort to trace copyright holders and would welcome correspondence from those they have been unable to trace.

THE GERMAN EMPIRE
1867–1914
AND THE UNITY MOVEMENT

BY

WILLIAM HARBUTT DAWSON

IN TWO VOLUMES.—VOL. I

London

GEORGE ALLEN & UNWIN LTD

RUSKIN HOUSE . MUSEUM STREET

FIRST PUBLISHED 1919
SECOND IMPRESSION 1966

PRINTED IN THE UNITED STATES OF AMERICA

PREFACE

It has been my desire to make this survey of the modern political history of Germany something more than a compendium of facts or a work of reference, and the public which I have had in mind in writing it is less the limited circle of scholars and students than those "general readers," the number of whom, one may believe, is steadily increasing, who wish to form their opinions on foreign politics independently, intelligently, and therefore on adequate information.

Inasmuch as my chief concern is with the German Empire as established in **1867–1871**, only so much attention has been given to the earlier phases of the national unity movement as seemed needful in order to make the later developments intelligible. Hence in dealing with the first half of last century I have concentrated attention upon capital events and tendencies, and in referring to the actors in these have refrained from dragging out of obscurity and oblivion personalities and reputations which, tried by the test of time, have proved to have had significance only for their own day, or even for their own narrow political circles.

In discharging my task, an old reflection has repeatedly returned to me: How comes it that in normal conditions German politics make so slight an appeal to the outside world? Why does German political life at any time so little interest observers in this country in particular? The reason lies, I think, in the fact that the German political system encourages in—almost one might say, imposes upon—the nation in general an attitude of quiescence and inertia. In German parliamentary life there is no serious struggle; such struggles as do occur are histrionic and unreal, since the combatants engaged in them know in advance that they can seldom lead to practical results. This would appear to be an inevitable consequence of constitutions under which the work of government is the business and the rightful prerogative of a small handful of men, set above and apart from the rest of the nation. The effect of this arrangement is that parliamentary politicians are as a rule little more than supernumeraries, performing more or less mutely their unimportant parts in the background of the stage, while to the people at large is assigned merely the right to look on. It is a fact of profound significance that during nearly the whole of the thirty years from 1860 to 1890 a single figure dominated German political life. How many of Bismarck's political contemporaries seriously count in the history of their country? How many have left any lasting impression, or any impression at all, upon the political thought and movements of their time?

Rightly or wrongly, I have not written this History impersonally, nor have I tried so to write it. Had I adhered more faithfully to conventional forms, the work of writing it would have lost half its interest for me, and it may be that the result for the reader would have been less helpful. I shall be satisfied if it should be held that I have succeeded in preserving the mean between a colourless formalism and excessive subjectivity. It has also seemed to me natural to give special prominence to points of contact with my own country, yet without writing from the British standpoint, and this inclination I have not unduly restrained.

Although it has necessarily been treated very summarily, I confess that the first half of the period covered by my survey has attracted me more than the second. For Germany the years following 1860, marking the maturity of the unity movement, are naturally the palmy era—the *Glanzzeit*—of their country's modern annals. An outsider may be forgiven the avowal that to him the most sympathetic part of the history of that movement is that dating from Prussia's fall at Jena to the middle of the century. The immediate results of the unity struggle during that epoch were small; the efforts of the nationalists and constitutionalists alike were requited by manifold disappointments, reverses, and disillusionments. None the less, it was a time of intense moral earnestness and persistent upward striving; in it the political idealism of the German nation reached its zenith; never before or since did that nation in general reach a higher elevation of spirit. It is customary to judge the episode of the ill-fated Frankfort National Assembly in particular as amongst the most humiliating in the history of national unity: I prefer to regard it as one of the few epical incidents of that history.

Preface

The story is an epic of failure, it is true, yet of a failure more heroic and honourable than many brilliant successes.

Naturally a large part of this History is occupied with events in which Germany's most distinguished statesman and son played a leading and determining part. In recording these events, and later in estimating Bismarck's character, I have not hesitated to speak the whole truth as I know it. It were doing an ill-service to the fame of that great man to pretend that all the motives and acts of his public life were above reproach. The comfortable doctrine of the literary panegyrist, that history and biography should be written politely, and that of the dead no harsh word should be spoken, is responsible for much misrepresentation of fact and perversion of opinion, not least in Germany, as those best know who have had occasion to study German sources. Some of the most pretentious German histories of the new Empire are not histories at all, but political tracts written for the greater glorification of the Empire's rulers and its chief builder. In their pages one looks in vain for healthy, independent criticism, or even for a straightforward, unvarnished statement of facts. Nowhere is there so much talk of the "historical sense" as in Germany, yet no writers exhibit less trace of this admirable gift than the authors of these euphonic productions.

Let the doctrine that Sovereigns, Governments, and popular statesmen cannot err be left to the historians of the country in which it has originated. There were times when Bismarck, who was no moral coward, was utterly straightforward and unsparingly candid with himself. There is no justification whatever for falling behind him in the honesty that looks facts fairly in the face and calls wrong things by their right names. The only condition is that nothing in his deflections from strict rectitude should be exaggerated, and that nothing should be set down against him in malice. "I leave it all to history," were the words which he once addressed to myself, at the close of a long conversation in which he had discussed not a few episodes of his political career. "And history," I rejoined, "will tell the truth." Still I see the grave face which was turned to me as he repeated the words—"Yes, history will tell the truth." And when the truth has all been told, with no attempt to hide his shortcomings, the magnitude of his achievements will remain undiminished and the lustre of his reputation undimmed. Greatness was the mark of the man, and it was inevitable that this attribute should be conspicuous in his faults as in his virtues, though it is but just to remember that even the faults were those of a passionate and unselfish patriotism, of which the worst that can be said is that it was insufficiently discriminating in its choice of means.

None the less, Bismarck's career offers a fascinating study for the casuist. In judging the policies and acts by which great national movements and events have been consummated, how far is it true, or is it true at all, that the end sanctifies the means and that success is its own justification? Is the consoling thought permissible that History is merely a secular name for Providence, or is it only, in Lord Acton's words, "the conscience of mankind"—conscience, that broken light of the human soul, that unstable guide of human action, so capricious in its judgments, so variable in its perceptions of right and wrong? Such questions almost inevitably force themselves upon the mind which has occupied itself closely with the part played by Bismarck in the story of German unity. Little more than half a century ago the German races were still disunited; they neither formed a nation nor had they any immediate hope of becoming such. The age-long aspirations after unity had hitherto been frustrated by particularist jealousies, the factions of parties, the short-sightedness of Sovereigns; above all, by obscurity of purpose and uncertainty as to the means by which unity might be attained. Different lines of advance had been followed, but always without success. Were the ways already tried wrong, was it necessary to discard them altogether, because they had hitherto failed to lead to the desired goal? In the making of States and nations need the builders work to a time-limit?

But now a statesman comes forward who is at least perfectly clear as to his aims. With an iron resolution and a matchless concentration of purpose he overbears opposition, moulds to his own ends the plastic wills of weaker men, and marches forward with undeviating steps to his objective. In so doing he arrogantly defies the accepted norms of public probity, and, extolling force as the master-key to State policy, makes wars with cold deliberation and glories in the act. Unity is achieved; the nation finds itself; and the world applauds. Is success, then, the seal that ratifies and closes the transaction? Is applause the last word? If not, how many issues in the lives of nations remain open, still awaiting the judge's summing up and the jury's verdict!

It is true that not a few of the violent convulsions recorded by history have been due to procrastinating statesmanship. Golden opportunities of accommodation and conciliation have been allowed to pass unimproved, and hence the solution of problems apparently amenable, in some at least of their stages, to peaceful adjustment has passed from the decision of reason to that of will. Was the consummation of German unity by "blood and iron" similarly inevitable, and if it was not inevitable, what is the verdict that should be passed upon the statecraft which wrought with these ugly implements? It is a question which has been discussed for half a century, and it may well be that it will excite far more controversy in the future than in the past. Never was it so pregnant with gravity as now, when fate holds in suspense the decision of the question whether the German nation stands before the climax or the *débâcle* of its political aspirations. That even for Germany herself unity gained in Bismarck's way has not proved an unmixed blessing cannot for a moment be doubted. Granting that the hope of attaining unity by political liberty seemed unrealizable when Bismarck appeared upon the scene, it is not less true that the price of a unity attained by force was that political liberty receded more and more from the nation's view.

The whole of these chapters have been written during the time of war, though some of them are based on materials which had accumulated during a period of twenty-five years. When a further twenty-five years have passed away—perhaps long before—those who look back upon the present troublous times will view the events incidental to them in a very different perspective from that in which they appear to-day. Some events which now occupy a large place in the minds and judgments of most of us will then take a minor place. On the other hand, it may well happen that events to which now a small significance is attached, or which are ignored altogether, will receive an unanticipated prominence. Writing of the affairs of a nation with which we are in conflict, there is a danger lest, under the influence of honourable feelings, facts should be unconsciously perverted, acts of policy be interpreted unfairly in the light of later knowledge, sinister motives be attributed or suspected where they did not exist, and that in this way history should be falsified in the name of patriotism, just as the pious scriveners of the monastery were wont to falsify history in the name of religion.

Compelled by the conditions of my task to record, and in some measure to pronounce upon, events which are in a certain sense *sub judice*, I have honestly tried to preserve a dispassionate judgment, and to estimate known facts at their rightful value and significance. I frankly own to having written with more of the critic's freedom and less of the indulgence of the friend than might have been the case in other circumstances. It is doubtful, indeed, whether for a very long time, if ever, the history of German unity will be written again out of Germany with enthusiasm. Yet the only bias of which I am conscious has been a bias towards scrupulous investigation and candour of utterance, for history that is not entirely honest is entirely contemptible, degrading to the writer and fraudulent and pernicious in its influence upon public opinion. None the less, without design on my part, it will be seen that many passages in the earlier part of my story have a vital bearing upon recent developments of German politics, and that to some of these they seem to offer a direct clue.

Several points of literary *technique* may be noted in conclusion. My sources—for the most part German and French, and only in a minor degree, and chiefly when dealing with questions immediately affecting this country, English—have been far too numerous to justify the addition of a bibliography, but I may fairly claim that no essential authority has been overlooked. The reader who wishes to carry his studies further may be referred for guidance to the excellent bibliographies appended to the volumes of Sir Adolphus Ward's *Germany*. To that scholarly work—published after this History was completed—I cannot deny myself the pleasure of paying a tribute of sincere respect. Where in footnote references to foreign books the titles are given in the original, quotations from these books have been made at first hand. Many of the quotations from translations, however, have been compared with the originals.

The close student of Bismarck's career will not be surprised if I own to having used his monumental *Gedanken und Erinnerungen* with a certain discrimination. It is needful to remember that in writing that book Bismarck had in mind an international public—the universal republic of letters—and was conscious that he was addressing himself to the tribunal of history, that *Weltgericht* of which Schiller spoke as the final arbiter of events and reputations. While, therefore, the opinions and dicta recorded in his Memoirs—not a few of which revise earlier utterances—are those by which he would wish to be judged, it does not follow that they can be accepted in all cases as faithful clues to his attitude *at the time* towards the events to which they relate. It is needful to receive these last words and confessions subject to this important reservation.

Preface

The treatment of foreign Christian names is a standing difficulty, and the choice between the original forms and the English equivalents would appear to be regarded as a matter of taste. While admitting that "Frederick Schiller" or "Henry Treitschke" would read no less quaintly in English than "Wilhelm Shakespeare" or "Johann Milton" in German, I have nevertheless followed the rule of translating the names of German Sovereigns; it is an arbitrary compromise, and, like most compromises, it cannot be altogether defended.

It seems desirable to add for the benefit of critics who judge books, not by what their authors say, but by what they do not say, that as this History is in substance a political essay I have deliberately refrained from dealing with such phases of German national life—e.g. letters, art, and science—as are comprised in reason, and upon the further and conclusive ground of want of the term *Kulturgeschichte*, or History of Civilization. For the same technical knowledge, in what I have said about the three wars which preceded German unity I have not attempted to invade the special province of the military writer.

My cordial thanks are due to Mr. G. P. Gooch, the historian, who has kindly read these volumes in proof-sheet form, thereby performing the most valuable service that one author can render to another: of his criticisms and suggestions I have not failed to make profitable use. Dr. K. Breul, Schroeder Professor of German in the University of Cambridge, has likewise placed me under a similar obligation, to acknowledge which is no less a pleasure than a duty.

W. H. D.

BECKENHAM, KENT,
August, 1918.

CONTENTS OF CHAPTERS

CHAPTER I

(1806–1848)

THE GERMANIC FEDERATION

CHAPTER II

(1848–1851)

THE FRANKFORT NATIONAL ASSEMBLY

Contents of Chapters

CHAPTER III

(1851–1861)

BISMARCK—THE FIRST PHASE

CHAPTER IV

(1858–1863)

THE PRUSSIAN CONSTITUTIONAL CONFLICT

CHAPTER V

(1846–1865)

THE ELBE DUCHIES AND THE DANISH WAR

CHAPTER VI

(1865–1866)

THE EXTRUSION OF AUSTRIA

Contents of Chapters

CHAPTER VII

(1866–1867)

THE NORTH GERMAN CONFEDERATION

CHAPTER VIII

(1867–1870)

THE HOHENZOLLERN CANDIDATURE

CHAPTER IX

(1870–1871)

THE WAR WITH FRANCE

CHAPTER X

(1870–1874)

THE NEW EMPIRE

CHAPTER XI

(1868–1883)

CHURCH AND STATE

THE GERMAN EMPIRE

CHAPTER I

(1806–1848)

THE GERMANIC FEDERATION

At the opening of the nineteenth century the Holy Roman Empire of the German Nation still existed, after a thousand years of chequered life. Long decadent, it was now moribund, however, and perpetuated only in name an august sovereignty which at one time extended over a large part of the European Continent. Diverse in race, language, religion, and political forms, having no common bond in administration, law, justice, or military organization, the many parts of the imperial dominion were kept together in firm union only so long as they were subject to a strong rule, and when once the centre of authority had become weakened, decline and disintegration ran their certain course.

The first powerful impetus to this process was given by the Peace of Westphalia, which secured to the German Princes a large degree of territorial sovereignty. Now for a century and a half these Sovereigns had steadily encroached upon the imperial jurisdiction and disputed its claims, local autonomy had spread and strengthened, until the might and majesty of Charlemagne's and Barbarossa's sway had come at last to be represented by a loose and incoherent political system, composed of States which had little in common save a desire to magnify themselves at the expense of the Emperor and of each other. Of these States there were three hundred, for the most part petty and as political organizations contemptible, each with its Court and Government, army and bureaucracy, customs and taxes, coinage, weights, and measures. Giants amongst pigmies, Austria and Prussia overshadowed all the rest.

The German Empire

For over five hundred years the Austrian reigning house had borne the imperial title, yet for a long time it had been Prussia and not Austria which had been gaining in power at home and repute abroad. As a member of the old Empire, Prussia had long gone her own way; never had the Emperors succeeded in asserting an effectual authority over her masterful rulers. More and more the northern kingdom had disputed the superiority claimed, in virtue of a sovereignty that had become little more than titular, by its older but less vigorous rival on the Danube. From the time when Frederick the Great established the Prussian military State, whose foundations had been laid by his father, and challenged the power of the house of Habsburg in its citadel by the rape of Silesia, an act of aggression which he had to defend by seven years of continuous warfare, the precedence of Austria in the Empire had been definitely threatened.

Frederick the Great had almost doubled his territory; he had increased the population under his sway from two and a half to six millions and his army from 82,000 to 200,000. As his master-thought in life had been conquest, so his supreme concern at the last—he died in 1786—was that the gains which he had won, some by fair, others by unfair means, should be consolidated and preserved. "My last wishes when my breath expires," he wrote in his will, "will be for the happiness of my country. May it ever be ruled with justice, wisdom, and decision; may it be the happiest of States because of the clemency of its laws, the best managed financially, and the most bravely defended, because of the honourable and worthy fame of its army."

The immediate successors of the greatest of the Hohenzollerns failed to live up to his reputation, or to improve or even rightly value the inheritance which he had committed to their keeping. Frederick William II, known as William the Fat, was, with all his amiability, a man of small intelligence and weak character. He neither ruled well himself nor had he the wit to choose men able to do his work well for him, and he became the creature of scheming flatterers. A frank libidinist, his notorious amours were only made more vulgar by the bouts of religious extravagance which alternated with them. More than once he made a feeble show of challenging Austria's reviving pretensions, but when it came to supporting words by acts, his courage failed him. The administration of his country, energetic and efficient at his accession, he left weak and corrupt; the army had diminished in numbers and in spirit; debt had accumulated though taxation had increased; in civil life, public spirit and private virtue had decayed.

It was due to this King even more than to his successor, Frederick William III, a weakling likewise, though free from his coarseness and private vices, that twelve years after the death of Frederick the Great the fame of that ruler's martial triumphs had been sacrificed and Prussia's prestige in Europe for a time suffered eclipse. Even in Germany the once powerful northern kingdom had ceased to be either feared or respected. The Alliance of Princes (*Fürstenbund*) which Frederick had concluded, with himself as its centre, had been dissolved, and States which, like Saxony, had been accustomed to look to Prussia for support had gravitated instead to Austria.

The German household, divided against itself, its chief members indifferent custodians of the common interest of security, was unable to stand the shock of Napoleon's onslaught. After Austria, already vanquished in Italy, had been compelled to conclude on behalf of the Empire the Peace of Lunéville in 1801, the subjugation of all Germany followed swiftly. Meanwhile, Bavaria, Würtemberg, and Baden had sought safety by joining the enemy of the larger fatherland. State after State fell beneath the hammer-blows of the mighty Thor, and soon from the Rhine to the Elbe ancient sovereignties lay in ruins, heap on heap. The climax came in 1806, when at the battle of Jena (October 14th) the kingdom of Prussia, which Frederick had raised to such a dizzy height of power, was shattered and overthrown; while by the succeeding Peace of Tilsit (July 7, 1807) its area was reduced to the four eastern provinces of Brandenburg, Silesia, West Prussia, and East Prussia, and its population from ten to five millions. Two months before Jena, Napoleon had declared the Holy Roman Empire dissolved, in order that he might himself claim succession to Charlemagne, and on August 6th, at his bidding, Francis II not unwillingly laid down the imperial office.[1] So it was that a dominion which had been created by warlike emprise, and many acts of masterly if cunning statecraft, succumbed in helpless impotence, unhonoured and unregretted.

If Napoleon found delight in putting down the mighty from their seats, he was no less fond of exalting the humble and meek. As far as was consistent with his political designs, he lightened

[1] In 1804 the Emperor took the title "Emperor of Austria," being Francis I in the new line.

the sorrows of many of his German victims, for in his rare deeds of magnanimity, as well as in those of heartless cruelty, there was always a deep, calculated purpose. To some he gave new territories for those taken away, to others he gave titles; to two reigning houses he deigned to give his relatives in marriage. There was a systematic readjustment of princely rank amongst the rulers who passed into his service or under his protection. The duke, for reward or consolation, was made a grand duke, the grand duke an elector, the elector a king. Three of the four kingdoms comprised within the present German Empire, Bavaria, Würtemberg, and Saxony, owed their higher status to the favour of Napoleon.

The fall of the Empire and the consequent re-arrangement of the map of Germany seemed to mark the occultation of the German national idea. Even in its moribund condition, the Empire had to the last, in some sort, symbolized the substantial unity of the German peoples. Now not only the substance but almost the shadow of unity appeared to have passed away.

In place of the dissolved Empire Napoleon created (July 17, 1806), the Confederation of the Rhine, composed at first of sixteen of the southern and western States, which he had allowed to retain their independence, and which acknowledged him as protector and overlord. The most important of these vassal States were Bavaria, Würtemberg, Baden, Hesse-Darmstadt, and Nassau. To the original members of the union others were added after the battle of Jena, and chiefly Saxony, the Mecklenburgs, Anhalt, and Oldenburg. The Confederation was to have had a representative assembly, meeting at Frankfort, but this was never convened. At that time, therefore, old Germany consisted in the main of Austria, Prussia, and the Rhenish Confederation; of the petty octavo and duodecimo States, some had been absorbed by France, others thrown together with larger ones, and others again merged in a brand-new kingdom of Westphalia, formed for the purpose of supplying Napoleon's brother Jerome with a crown.

The fate which Germany suffered at Napoleon's hands was a bitter one, but it was hardly worse than she deserved. Had the States at the outset coalesced loyally and met the invader with united and unselfish will, disaster might conceivably have been averted; and even had military defeat still befallen them, honour would have been saved though all else had been lost. So disunited was Germany, however, that Napoleon was able to deal with the States one by one and apportion to each its fate in turn. Thus Prussia, instead of going to Austria's assistance betimes, dallied and prevaricated until it was too late either to help Austria or to save herself. So little conscious was her King of the duty of the German States to one another, that he concluded a bargain with the usurper by which he received Hanover in return for Prussian territory (December 15, 1805). Frederick William III hated the idea of war, and clung to the hope of staving it off by concessions and capitulations, only to find too late that the more he surrendered the greater were Napoleon's demands. By 1806 Prussia had fallen to such a depth of impotence that further decline seemed impossible.

It had been the chief boast of Prussia's later rulers that theirs was a military State, yet in the hour of need the army itself proved incapable. It was not the standing army organized by Frederick the Great but a militia, a voluntary *levée en masse* of the people, that later saved both State and Crown. The aristocracy, as a class, failed no less ignominiously to rise to its responsibilities. There were many brilliant exceptions, but on the whole the crisis found most of the men who had claimed to be the natural leaders of the nation lacking in public spirit, and content to accept with weak resignation whatever fate might have in store for their country. It is a significant fact that of the six most eminent soldiers and statesmen who at the beginning of last century devoted themselves to Prussia's renewal, Blücher, Scharnhorst, Gneisenau, Stein, Hardenberg, and Wilhelm von Humboldt, only the last was a Prussian.[1] Of the spiritual harbingers of Germany's rebirth, Prussia could claim Arndt, Schenkendorf, and Schleiermacher, but most of them—Fichte, Körner, Niebuhr, the younger Eichhorn, and the rest—were likewise sons of another soil.

The officials of the higher bureaucracy had long been taught to regard themselves as the King's meek creatures, and as such they had been treated; hence in that time of appeal to manly virtue it was inevitable that there could be no response where every trace of manliness had been extinguished. "Like the soulless machine it was," writes a German historian, "the administration quietly went on its way, caring little under which Sovereign it lived, whether Frederick William or Napoleon; and, accustomed to look above for remedies, the high officials even

[1] Blücher was of Mecklenburg extraction, Scharnhorst and Hardenberg were Hanoverians, Gneisenau was a Saxon, and Stein a Nassauer.

repressed the aspirations of the healthy, energetic spirit which still lived on in the so-called common people."[1] A district governor in Silesia pressed upon Napoleon's troops supplies which they neither sought nor wanted, and introduced the Emperor's decrees with "We Napoleon by the grace of God," until Napoleon himself rebuked his foolery. In Berlin a general refused to obey the King's orders to convey to the fortresses the ammunition then lying in the city. When Napoleon arrived in that capital, seven Ministers of the Crown and a crowd of officials promptly took the oath of allegiance to him. Writing of the demoralization prevalent in Prussia at the time, the same German historian says: "Not only did the Junkers, who had hitherto boasted that they were the chief pillars of the State, break like dried reeds in the wind; the other 'pillars'—the bureaucracy, the learned classes, and the higher society down to the burgher class, covered themselves with shame in those days." In every rank of society faithlessness and cowardice were shown in their unloveliest forms. Jews sold themselves into Napoleon's pay, and in servile newspapers proclaimed his fame and denounced everything Prussian, yet when the usurper had been overthrown the same men arrogantly claimed that they had saved the country. One Hebrew writer asserted that at Waterloo fifty-five officers of his race had fallen, though the number of officers lost in the entire Prussian army was only twenty-four.

But Prussia had no monopoly of sycophancy and treachery in those days. The rulers of Bavaria, Saxony, Würtemberg, and Baden all danced attendance upon the conqueror, enrolled themselves in his retinue, and seemed happy in their new service. What was right in the ruler was more than pardonable in the ruled. The professors of Leipzig effusively greeted Napoleon as the hero of his age. Even Goethe, the honoured leader of the nation's intellectual life, could watch from his Weimar home the fall and rise of Germany at that time without emotion; he philosophized and wondered, but was unperturbed. His admirers excused this apparent apathy by his age, yet when Napoleon partitioned a large part of Germany amongst his favourites the author of *Faust* was only fifty-six. Nowhere was the old rule thrown off more lightly and the new rule accepted more readily than in the Rhineland, whose populations had already changed sovereignty and form of government so often. It is

[1] W. Pierson, *Preussische Geschichte*, vol. i., pp. 496, 497.

difficult for men to be patriotic who are not certain to what country they belong to-day or to what country they will belong to-morrow, and though the Rhenish peoples have been reproached for the facility with which they changed their allegiance, their indifference may be excused, at least in part, by the tragedy of their position. No greater shame ever fell upon countries or nations than that which the German Princes brought upon their own lands and peoples over a hundred years ago.

The facts thus briefly stated will help the reader to visualize the German question as it presented itself at the beginning of the nineteenth century. There remained no longer a Germany, but only the disjointed members of a Germany that had been. To bring these members together, to kindle a new national consciousness, to weld the many races into a political unity, was a task to be achieved by efforts long continued and means the most diverse—by statecraft and diplomacy, by parliaments, universities, and schools, by commerce and railways, by customs unions and military conventions, by revolution and war, above all by a stern political discipline which should subordinate the individual State and citizen to the needs and interests of a larger commonwealth and a new nation. Hardly might it have seemed possible that a German Empire could be recreated out of elements so unpromising, yet it was in that time of national abasement and humiliation that the spirit of unity originated. Periods of progress were to alternate with periods of stagnation, periods of buoyant confidence with those of depression and disillusionment, before the ideal, passing through all the gradations of doubt, hope, and probability, could reach the firm ground of certitude; yet if the way was to be long, so much surer was the goal.

In 1813–14 a supreme effort was made, under Prussia's leadership, to throw off the French yoke, and it succeeded. Yet in the campaign which sealed Napoleon's fate the King of Saxony fought in the Corsican's army and King Frederick of Würtemberg wrote to wish him "a happy return" to Germany. All Europe, Princes and people alike, breathed again freely after 1814, and most relieved of all were those German Sovereigns who had bartered themselves into Napoleon's service, had taken their orders from him, marched under his banners, fought his battles against their own countrymen, and had been proud to receive their crowns at his hand. Now began the work of internal reconstruction. The old States were restored, but not in every case the old frontiers. On November 1, 1814, the Congress of Vienna assembled in order to decide on the future constitution of Germany. Prince Metternich, the Austrian Chancellor, who was destined to exert a baneful influence on the development of German political life for over a generation, was the President and almost the dictator of the assembly. The Princes marked their patriotism by indulging in a greedy scramble for territory, bartering souls like chattels, and rectifying boundaries like the fences of their forests and parks. Every German State strong enough to press its claims wished to be enlarged at the expense of its weaker neighbours. Prussia wanted the whole of Saxony, while Austria, England, and France, supported by Bavaria and other States of the dissolved Rhenish Federation, opposed the demand.[1] Nevertheless, Prussia did well for herself, for she obtained a large slice of the Saxon kingdom—the present province of that name—most of Westphalia, some territory on the left bank of the Rhine, and Swedish Pomerania, while the territory of which Napoleon had robbed her was restored. Bavaria received Ansbach and Bayreuth, and Hanover received East Friesland.

Though the Confederation of the Rhine and the kingdom of Westphalia had disappeared, they left behind them traces and traditions important for the future development of German political life. Westphalia had been given a constitutional system of government, and in the States united in the Rhenish Confederation the principles of the French Revolution, in their good as in their less attractive aspects, had been applied, though in most of them the earlier constitutional arrangements, such as they were, were for the time suspended. Hence, during the

[1] For a long time Prussia never forgave England for having successfully placed herself at the head of the opposition to her extreme demands. Lord Castlereagh, the British Plenipotentiary at Vienna, had to meet at home attacks from all sides upon his action in the Saxon question. In a speech in the House of Lords in March 1815 he stated the case against Saxony in the words, "Saxony was a conquered country in the strictest sense of the word; though it is true that the Saxon army, on the third day of the battle of Leipzig, did join the Allies, and perhaps decide the victory, yet the House must know that Saxony, until that moment, which did not depend upon the voice of the Sovereign, had been a Power whose army and resources were devoted to the cause of the common enemy against whom we were fighting." Explaining, on the other hand, why he had not assented to the entire annexation of the country by Prussia, he continued: "I was persuaded that the public feeling not merely of the people of Germany, but of other countries, would have been wounded by so great and complete a sacrifice of an ancient family; that the general opinion of mankind would have revolted at such a proceeding, and that Prussia would be prejudiced in the general estimation of Europe by the annexation" (*Memoirs and Correspondence of Viscount Castlereagh*, vol. i., pp. 50, 51).

time that the seal of France rested upon it, Western Germany received political impressions which were never wholly removed; a break with the Empire was made in political thought and life; and when the detached territories went back to the old allegiance their populations retained much French influence, and Paris for a time interested them more than Berlin or capitals nearer home. Above all, they gained a fixed bias towards Liberalism and an appreciation of free institutions which have never ceased to single them out from the rest of the country; without being denationalized, they had become singularly open to progressive influences from the outside.

"When a man like Napoleon falls he falls altogether," wrote the Russian diplomat Count Nesselrode, after the battle of Leipzig (October 18, 1813). So good an apothegm deserved to be true, but it miscarried. At that great "battle of the peoples" the conqueror's dream of world dominion was, indeed, shattered, yet though Napoleon was sent a captive to Elba six months later, the end was not yet. Before the Congress of Vienna had completed its work, the dethroned Emperor returned to France (March 1, 1815), and the war was resumed. It is characteristic of the selfish particularism which ruled even in that time of danger that the Prussian general Gneisenau, than whom no soldier was more a politician or fonder of committing his immature political ideas to paper, drew up a memorial proposing that unless the Allies granted Prussia's territorial demands beforehand she should withdraw and enter into an alliance with Napoleon. Gneisenau gave this document to the Chancellor Hardenberg, and asked that it might be offered for the King's consideration. The discreet Minister, however, returned it to its author with the comment that what it proposed was a "moral enormity" which could not be even whispered in the royal ear.

After Waterloo had been fought (June 18, 1815), and the disturber of Europe had been sent to his "sullen isle," St. Helena, there to gaze upon the sea which he had vainly hoped to conquer,[1] the Congress of Vienna faced the larger problem of the future of Germany. Here opinions were hopelessly divided. Baron vom Stein, believing that the surest pledge of national unity and of the continuity of the German name lay in the inti-

[1] Then haste thee to thy sullen isle,
And gaze upon the sea:
That element may meet thy smile—
It ne'er was ruled by thee.
Byron, *Ode to Napoleon.*

mate association of the small with the two major States, was ready to welcome the revival of the Empire, still under the house of Habsburg, as the best means of securing this end. Hanover favoured this course, and in so doing almost stood alone. The King of Prussia, usually slow to make up his mind upon political questions, was quick to recognize the danger and fatuity of Stein's view, and in rejecting it he was supported by Hardenberg and Humboldt, the former opposing the idea of restoration from Prussia's standpoint and the latter holding it to be contrary to the interests of Germany as a whole. Public opinion in the monarchy was urgent upon one point, viz. that the undisputed primacy in Germany which Austria had held in the past should no longer be conceded.

Nor were the rest of the States, even the small ones, more willing than Prussia to resume the old position of subordination in the Empire, for at its dissolution they had gained complete sovereignty, and this sovereignty neither Princes nor peoples were now willing to renounce. Of the secondary States, none was more jealous of its new independence and higher political status than Bavaria, whose unfortunate position it was to be too small to rank with Austria and Prussia as a Great Power, but too large in area, population, and still more in self-esteem, to be willing to associate with the petty principalities on equal terms.

Yet the prospect of the Empire's revival was never a hopeful one, for Austria herself was opposed to any such futile attempt to call back the past. Remembering how she had for so long a time shone as the one star of the first magnitude in the German constellation, she was determined that, whatever form German union might take, the leadership should fall to her in the future as in the past. Nevertheless, the Emperor Francis had no desire to hold again the imperial office. Not only was he doubtful whether the German Princes would be willing in general to return to the imperial fold, but he was conscious that the office had lost in dignity and would no longer carry authority. In this prudent attitude he was unreservedly supported by his Chancellor, Prince Metternich.

It was from Prussia that the solution of the problem of Germany's future organization came in the proposal of a loose union of States. It was a solution defective and inadequate, a makeshift in every sense of the word, yet in the circumstances the only one that seemed practicable. As early as November, 1813, there had been conferences at Frankfort at which the

Princes agreed to surrender so much of their independence as might be necessary to the creation of a constitution for all Germany, but no details were arranged. The choice was between a federal State (*Bundesstaat*) and a federation of States (*Staatenbund*), and it was soon seen that the latter represented the utmost concession to national unity that was to be hoped for. In order to bring matters to a practical issue, Hardenberg in the following year laid before Metternich a draft constitution, under which all the States were to be united *in æternum* in an association to be called the *Deutscher Bund*, or Germanic Federation, whose purpose was to be the maintenance of Germany's security within and without and of the independence and inviolability of the federated States. There was to be a directory of Sovereigns at the head, with an upper and a lower house, the former composed of delegates of the Princes and the latter of delegates of the Princes and estates jointly. For Austria the scheme went too far, and at Metternich's suggestion it was modified, and thereafter was discussed by the Governments of the six kingdoms preparatory to its submission to the whole of the States.

Accepted as a basis of negotiation, and subjected to repeated revision, the outcome of this scheme was the Federal Act of the Congress, dated June 8, 1815. By this Act or treaty the sovereign Princes and Free Cities of Germany united in a permanent federation of States, which came into existence in November of the following year, Austria and Prussia joining for all their territories which belonged to the dissolved Empire, the King of Denmark for the duchies of Holstein and Lauenburg, the King of the Netherlands for the grand duchy of Luxemburg and for Limburg, and the King of England for Hanover.[1] The dissolved Holy Roman Empire had contained more than three hundred separate sovereignties, but, to the benefit of Germany, the great majority of these had disappeared. The original number of States now federated was forty-one, though the number fell eventually to thirty-three, owing to the extinction or absorption of certain of the smaller principalities. Austria was given the presidency in virtue of her headship of the old Empire. Within the union the States retained independent sovereignty. Such powers as they devolved to the Bund were vested in and exercised by the Federal Diet or

[1] The kingdom of Hanover was finally separated from England in 1837, on the accession of Queen Victoria.

Assembly, a standing council composed of plenipotentiaries of the Sovereigns and Free Cities, whose meeting-place was the old imperial city of Frankfort. The jurisdiction of the Diet was very limited. Strictly speaking, the Diet was an executive council. It made no binding laws ; it could vote ordinances, but they were only valid when adopted by each State independently ; and it had no power to conclude treaties, for the Governments reserved this right to themselves. In contrast to the narrowness and jealousy of the faint-hearted rulers of those days, fearful lest one whit of their sovereignty should be threatened by concessions to liberal ideas, a statesmanlike utterance of the Hanoverian plenipotentiary at the Congress of Vienna (October 21, 1814) stands out, conspicuous for its sobriety and sanity. "As for all this clinging to the word 'sovereignty,'" he said, "the King of Great Britain is just as indisputably a Sovereign as any other Prince in Europe, and yet his throne is not undermined but rather strengthened by the liberty of his people." Such a sentiment was hopelessly untimely, even if it was understood.

The Diet transacted most of its business as a council of seventeen, the eleven larger States having one vote each and the other States being grouped in six *curiæ*, each with one vote. Before any resolution could be voted on, each member had to take the instructions of his Government, and in the case of the curial votes the States concerned had first to agree amongst themselves. For the determination of certain fundamental or organic questions, such as the modification of the basis and organization of the Federation, the admission of new members, the amendment of the constitution, or the cession of federal territory, except to federals, the Diet sat as a plenary body (*im Plenum*), i.e. the States had individual though unequal representation. In this event the six kingdoms, Austria, Prussia, Bavaria, Saxony, Würtemberg, and Hanover, had four votes each, Baden, Electoral Hesse, Hesse-Darmstadt, Holstein, and Luxemburg three each, Brunswick, Mecklenburg-Schwerin, and Nassau two each, and the rest of the States one vote each, giving a total of seventy.

In the inner council most questions were decided by absolute majority of votes, but in the plenary body a two-thirds majority was needed in the case of questions relating to peace and war, and for the rest no resolution was valid unless adopted unanimously. In practice, therefore, the principle of *liberum veto* applied in the Plenum, so that the smallest State or Free City in the Federation was able, theoretically, to obstruct the will of all the rest. Apart from this right of veto, the small States had it in their power at all times, by acting together, to determine the policy of the Federation altogether according to their will, and the only effective restraint was the danger of arousing the resentment of their powerful allies.

In one respect the power of the Diet was far-reaching and even ominous. As the main concern of the Federation was peace and tranquillity at home, it was given the right to interfere in constitutional disputes occurring in the federal States. Disputes between members of the Federation might also be referred for settlement to the Diet, which was able to enforce its decisions, like its resolutions generally, by means of a federal execution. This consisted of the military occupation of the contumelious State by troops of one or more of the Governments commissioned to execute the Diet's will.

For the treaty contained provision for a federal army, to which each State was to be required to contribute a "contingent" or quota proportionate to its population. With a shortsightedness which half a century later was to bring about a severe retribution, Austria, concerned far more to exercise imperial power than to recognize imperial responsibilities, opposed Prussia's proposal to place the federal army on a strong and efficient foundation. Had Prussia had her way, the army would have been equal to 1 per cent. of the population, a ratio which would have given a force of 300,000 men, and the obligation of the federal States in relation thereto would have been real instead of nominal. Austria, however, was lukewarm in the matter, and the other States, particularly those of the South, were suspicious of an arrangement which, if faithfully carried out, would have placed at the disposal of the two major Powers so preponderant an armed force. The contingents were never forthcoming in the allotted numbers, with the consequence that the duty of providing for Germany's safety was left primarily to Prussia.

Such as it was, however, the federal army proved a singularly heterogeneous formation, devised on no common plan, clad in uniforms of as many colours as Joseph's coat—an army without uniformity of system, training, equipment, or administration, or even a commander-in-chief, for this officer, who should have been the symbol of unity and efficiency, was only to be chosen in the event of war, and then by the Diet and subject to the orders of the Committee on Military Affairs. Five towns were created federal fortresses—Luxemburg, Mayence, Landau, Ulm, and Rastatt. Equally impotent was the Diet in the matter of taxation: the power to levy taxes was denied to it, and its necessary expenditure was met by "matricular contributions," or levies upon the States proportionately to population, a principle of assessment taken over from the old Empire.

With the constitution as thus devised the rulers were on the whole well pleased, for it left Germany as divided as before, but the peoples at large received it with disappointment and disgust. While the Congress of Vienna was sitting, writes Friedrich von Gentz, its secretary, "deputies from every part of Germany" were in the Austrian capital, "agitating day and night for a federal constitution." For the nation had hoped to see its liberation confirmed and assured by political unity. In the proclamation of Kalisch, dated March 25, 1813, following the treaty of alliance concluded there between the King of Prussia and the Czar on February 28th, the German nation had been called to the struggle on behalf of a reconstituted Empire, in which its "ancient and native spirit" was to be revived, an Empire in which Germany should be rejuvenated, vigorous, and free. So in the darkest hours of humiliation it had been cheered, and its heaviest sacrifices had been lightened, by the thought that it was fighting not only to free Germany from foreign oppression, but to win for itself unity, by the creation of ties stronger and more intimate than those which held the old Empire together. It had been cherishing an illusion. Germany was not yet ready to become either an Empire or a federal State, and even if it had been ready the Sovereigns were not willing to forgo any substantial part of their independence. Austria, above all, was bent on maintaining the old divisions under new sanctions, as the surest guarantee of her continued domination.

"Poor, faithful German nation," wrote the patriot-poet Ernst Moritz Arndt in bitterness of soul, "thou art to have no Emperor! Thy Princes wish themselves to play the Emperor. Instead of one lord, thou art to have two dozen [in point of fact, there were over three dozen] who will never be able to agree upon German questions." But what else could have been expected? The Congress of Vienna was exclusively an affair of the Princes and Governments. They alone decreed, appointed, and composed it, and only their interests and wishes had voice or hearing in its deliberations. It was a typical creation and expression of the old diplomacy. In this august areopagus, in which the elect of the diplomatic world of Europe was assembled —Blücher, fresh from the battlefield, where niceties of language are disregarded, called it a "council of thrice-accursed constables and lazy-bones"—the German nation had no part or lot whatever, though its political destinies were being determined for an indefinite period; it had no share in its deliberations; its opinion was not once given, because it was never sought; nowhere was the nation as such mentioned in the Act under which the new union was constituted.

The Germanic Federation began its career handicapped by distrust and odium, and it lived up to its first reputation. For practical purposes it proved a replica of the Holy Alliance which was created in 1815 under the influence of Czar Alexander I, and its purpose was to do for Germany what the Alliance was intended to do for the Continent—to counteract all democratic movements and to preserve the existing political order unchanged, if need be, by forcible measures. For just fifty years it maintained an undistinguished existence, its Diet chiefly useful as a coward's castle from which the liberties of the people could be safely assailed, and as affording an arena in which Austria and Prussia were able to contend for the hegemony of Germany.

From the standpoint of national unity in particular it was a cruel mockery. Designed to renew the earlier union of the States, in effect it emphasized only their dissensions and discords. The Empire, at the time of its extinction, had indeed become the pale reflection of a reality majestic and imposing in the days of its full vigour and vitality; yet almost to the last, even when fallen into impotence and decay, it was impressive, and conveyed, to the imagination at least, ideas at once grandiose and inspiring. For the Bund no such distinction could be claimed. The creation of artifice, compromise, and expediency, it never possessed inherent strength or outward dignity; to the smaller Princes it afforded a city of refuge, in which they were immune against arbitrary treatment by their powerful neighbours, since the security of each was the concern of all; but because it was unable to commend itself to the German peoples by public utility or any recognition of common national interests, it failed entirely to win either their enthusiasm or their attachment. If the Empire had represented a condition of disorganized union, the new Bund represented one of organized disunion.

The leading European Governments accredited ambassadors to the pompous Frankfort Diet, but the compliment was not returned; only seldom did the Diet appoint envoys for special purposes. On the other hand, the federal States themselves had their own envoys at foreign Courts, and exercised their power to conclude treaties and alliances, so long as these were not directed against the Federation. As the Diet inevitably served as a cockpit in which the two rival Powers disputed for position and influence, the secondary and petty States constantly ranged themselves on one side or the other. If Austria and Prussia were in agreement its proceedings went smoothly; if not, bickering, discord, and intrigue ran riot.

It was not the Bund and the Princes but the nation which kept alive the desire and the hope for a more real unity during the succeeding half century. Throughout this period the political life of Germany was dominated by two great parallel movements. One had as its object national unity, the other aimed at constitutional liberty. It is impossible to separate the history of these movements, so closely were they related; though not identical, they proceeded from the same source, and derived their strength from the same spiritual impulses.

Article 13 of the Federal Act of June 8, 1815, declared that each federal State should receive an assembly or representation of the estates (*landständische Verfassung*). It was a pious affirmation, intended to mean much or little or nothing at all, according to the will of the Sovereigns concerned. There was no suggestion of parliaments or legislatures as understood in constitutional countries. Interpreted literally, the most shadowy concession to the representative principle would have enabled an unwilling Prince to plead that he had duly honoured his bond. But more sinister was the fact that the Act allowed each of the signatories to decide at his discretion when this shadowy representation should take effect. In the original draft, Article 13 stipulated that constitutions "shall be" introduced within a year. The word "shall" was later altered to "will," and the time-limit was expunged. The omission of a date was not accidental; on the contrary, it was a plain intimation that in a matter upon which they were greatly divided in opinion the rulers did not intend to be unduly hurried. As the provision ran, they would have been within their rights had they delayed the issue of constitutions until the eve of doomsday. Taken literally, therefore, this provision of the Act did not imply a formal pledge or promise; it was at the most the voluntary assertion of a vague and indeterminate principle, and an admission that this principle ought at some convenient season—to be chosen by each ruler for himself—to be applied. There is no need, and perhaps no justification, to assume that the provision was given an illusory form in bad faith; the fact remains, however, that it afforded a convenient loophole for the evasion of a disagreeable surrender to popular expectations and that many of the Princes made a perfidious use of it.

For more than a decade the German peoples had been engaged in repelling an arbitrary dictatorship imposed from without. Henceforth they were to contend against the despotisms which still lingered at home. Nowhere was this struggle so severe as in Prussia. War, besides being a great leveller, is a great educator, and the War of Liberation wrought a surprising change in the political ideas of the Prussian people. Their active participation in the struggle gave to them the consciousness of a new position and stake in the country; the men who had before been subjects now felt and thought as citizens; Prussia had become their fatherland in a fuller and deeper sense than before. In country and in town a new sense of freedom had come to the people—in the former with the promulgation of Stein's Edict of Emancipation of October, 1807, abolishing serfdom and other feudal institutions, in the latter with the introduction of his Municipal Ordinance of 1808, establishing a liberal system of self-government in the old provinces of the kingdom. Moreover, the fact that a law of September 3, 1814, imposed upon the manhood of the nation the obligatory duty of military service seemed to justify the people's claim that with this duty should go, hand in hand, the right to share in the government of the country which they were expected to defend.

Thus it was that liberation from an outside yoke gave an impetus to the desire for liberation at home. Hence as soon as the tumult of war had died down there arose on every hand a call for greater political freedom, and the concession of the constitutional privileges which were enjoyed already by Western nations. The eyes of the reformers of that day were turned particularly to England. Stein, Schön, and other Prussian statesmen had carefully and admiringly studied the political institutions of that country, and while not wishing to follow them slavishly, they had English parliamentary life in view in all their proposals to supersede autocratic by constitutional government. So it was with all the popular leaders of the day. Dahlmann, the historian, who identified himself devotedly with the reform movement, saw in England, and not in revolutionary France, the ideal State. "Here," he wrote in 1815, "are most purely developed and preserved the foundations of the constitution towards which all new European nations are striving." The poet Rückert, in an outburst of political enthusiasm, sang—

> O build we now a temple
> On Albion's example!

Not without cause did England become for the reactionaries of Prussia from that time forward the hated symbol of political progress; honest in their prejudices, they have ever seen in her only a disturber of their country's peace and a menace to its conservative traditions.

Earnest and insistent as was the call for a new start in political life, the call fell in most of the States upon ears deaf to the dictates either of duty or of wisdom. Directly the danger was overpast, most of the Sovereigns ignored their pledges. The only exceptions occurred amongst those of the South and West, the portions of Germany which under French influence had imbibed Liberal ideas. Thus it was not to the Great Powers but to the minor States that Germany owed the first measure of release from political despotism and the beginnings of constitutional life. The ruler of Weimar, the enlightened Karl August, led the way in 1816, and Würtemberg, Bavaria, Nassau and Baden followed soon afterwards. It was in the smaller States also that the strongest desire for national unity existed.

Nowhere was the restored autocracy more stiffnecked, nowhere were national expectations more cruelly disappointed, than in Prussia. At the close of the War of Liberation, Prussia seemed for a short time to be marked out as the hope of Germany and of the national movement. Every far-seeing friend of unity knew, however, that it was only by meeting Liberal ideas frankly and freely that Prussia would be acceptable to the other States. From Austria, sundered by conflicting races and religious differences, her politics incorporating the worst spirit of reaction, nothing good was to be expected. Thus Prussia seemed to have a golden opportunity of seizing the leadership of Germany by boldly identifying herself with the constitutional cause and national aspirations. Self-interest seemed to point to the wisdom of such a policy. The kingdom had just been extended by the addition of provinces which were not only overwhelmingly Roman Catholic, so modifying the essentially Protestant basis of the State, but which under Napoleon's rule had learned to appreciate the freer spirit of French political institutions. A national parliament would have furnished a rallying-ground upon which internal diversities might have been reconciled for all time. Moreover, the best part of the nation was behind the popular movement, whose leaders and spokesmen were neither violent men nor doctrinaires; among them were, indeed, statesmen like Stein, Hardenberg, Humboldt, Niebuhr, and Vincke, publicists like Arndt, Schön, and Dahlmann, and even generals like Blücher and Gneisenau. The last of these men anticipated in 1814 words which were constantly on the lips of all the most progressive of German statesmen when, over a generation later, Prussia had once more to choose which way she would go: "Prussia must henceforth, by the liberality of her principles, exercise a moral attraction upon the rest of Germany."

States and nations, like individuals, have their opportunities and chances, to take or to leave. Fate, in offering them, has done its duty; it never reasons or compels, and seldom renews a privilege once rejected. At the beginning of last century Prussia might have chosen to become not merely the political but the spiritual leader of all Germany. The call to this high distinction was disregarded, and if Germany suffered as a result, the loss to Prussia herself was greater. It is usually profitless to speculate upon the "might have beens" of political history, yet it is justifiable to believe that if Prussia a hundred years ago, resolutely emancipating herself from Austrian influence, had decided to place herself at the head of the liberal movement in Germany, a whole crop of subsequent problems and disasters might have been avoided. Against a liberalized Prussia the Austria of Metternich could not have competed for that "moral conquest of Germany" which was awaiting the coming of the moral conqueror. But Frederick William III was at heart a despot with a weakling's will; distrustful of his people and not less so of himself, suspecting in every liberal idea the germ of revolution, he allowed the precious opportunity to pass by, and so hardened the tradition of Prussian autocracy that not one of his successors has wholly cast it aside.

His surrender to reaction was the less creditable because it was accompanied by a flagrant breach of faith. During the war he had solemnly promised the nation, in recognition of its unparalleled sacrifices, direct participation in State affairs. Shortly before the signing of the convention of the Princes of June 8, 1815, he had renewed that promise in an explicit form. Yielding to the pressure of Hardenberg and other Liberal advisers who for the moment had influence over him, he issued an edict on May 22nd, ordering that a "representation of the nation" should be formed by the development of the provincial estates. From these was to be elected a national assembly, whose function it should be to "deliberate upon all subjects of legislation affecting the personal and property rights of the citizens, including taxation." The edict also ordered the appointment of a commission for the purpose of organizing the intended assembly and drawing up its constitution, and this body was to meet on September 1st. Here, again, there was no definite promise of a popular legislature, nor yet of a legislature at all in the proper sense of the word, but the issue of the law seemed at least to be a sign that the King was mindful of his pledge. But the hopes thus aroused were destined to be short-lived. In June a commission, consisting of twenty-two members of the Council of State, was appointed to make a grand inquest of the nation. Instead of calling witnesses to Berlin, the King resolved that three Ministers should act as travelling commissioners, visiting the provinces and collecting evidence on the spot, just as the Elector Joachim I had done in 1525, when he was bent on reforming the system of local government. Their inquiries were confined almost exclusively to the landed nobility—in other words, to the representatives of existing conditions, and for the most part these men asked for no change; the provincial assemblies were for them both satisfactory and sufficient. Only the Polish aristocracy recognized the need of a higher form of representation, capable of reflecting the mind of the nation at large.

Yet all the work of the commissioners was wasted. No sooner had their reports been submitted than the King changed his mind. The reactionary influences which, when they did not surround him in the council chamber, lurked in the antechambers, were set busily in motion. The dishonest cry of "The throne in danger!" was raised by unprincipled men whose only concern was to preserve their own illicit influence over the King. Patriotic leaders of the nation were secretly denounced as enemies of the State. The entire popular movement was represented as but a deep design for subverting the monarchy and setting up a republic in its place. Statesmen who had fallen into the background while Liberal tendencies seemed to be in the ascendant, courtiers skilled in exploiting the prejudices and weakness of a ruler who always held the last word as of more account than the first, the spokesmen of an invertebrate bureaucracy, which had no other wish than to be left alone in comfortable indolence—all these and other pillars of a corrupt and discredited political system joined hands in an unseemly plot to incite the King to perfidy and to defeat a loyal nation's ardent desires. They succeeded only too well. An orgy of reaction now set in. Before the close of the year 1815 the King had put out of his mind any idea of a concession to popular aspirations, and was wondering how he could have been so unwise as to contemplate it. The national representation was not created, nor was its constitution drawn up.

In all these sinister movements the master-hand of Metternich was seen. Having successfully thwarted the constitutional aspirations of the time, not by the open and straightforward method of binding the Sovereigns and Governments to an attitude of flat resistance, but more astutely by uniting them in the acceptance of a vague and shadowy promise of concessions which could be lightly ignored, all his efforts were now directed towards the one task of pressing Germany back into the morass of political obscurantism out of which she had seemed for a moment to have rescued herself. Understanding the conditions of this task better than his tools and dupes, he saw that reaction would be the more certain just in proportion as he succeeded in winning the States for a policy of inaction. That may have been the secret of the calculated omission of any reference whatever to times and seasons in the article of the Federal Act of June 8, 1815, which dealt with the future government of Germany. He knew that the nation was tired out, exhausted, incapable of organizing resistance, still less of making resistance effective. Moreover, everywhere material occupations were making urgent calls upon its attention; the lost prosperity had to be retrieved, the harm done by war and long preoccupation with military employments to be made good, trade and industry to be rehabilitated, the decayed towns to be rebuilt and the waste places restored. It was not difficult, therefore, to draw the Governments into the paths of reaction; with few exceptions those which at first were in a mood to hold back yielded to pressure or to their own doubts and apprehensions.

It was not long before the small and even the secondary States were to perceive, to their humiliation and chagrin, how little they counted, how little they were intended to count, in a political union which yet was broadly based on the principle of parity. It is true that each of the States, however petty, had nominally retained complete political independence ; but for that reservation Metternich cared little, so long as he was able to dictate their attitude in the Federation. It was his policy to bring them all into line as members of the Diet, and there make them for federal purposes the servitors of Austria.

Baron von Blittersdorff, Baden's envoy at Frankfort, said : " A hundred times in Vienna I have asked Prince Metternich what it was he really wished to make of the Federation, but could never secure a definite answer." The reason was that the answer could not be put into definite words. Yet the objects of Metternich were never for a moment uncertain. He intended so to rule the Federation as to make it a bulwark against Liberalism and nationalist movements of every kind. It was to be used as a weapon against internal even more than external enemies, against inside political even more than outside military aggression, against intellectual conquests even more than conquests by the sword. Above all, he was determined that the Federation should not prove a step on the way to German unity. There was logic in this attitude, for he knew well that the Empire which he served—and served faithfully according to his lights —made up as it was of so many ethnical elements, would crumble to pieces if ever the ferment of nationalism gained a strong hold upon its inflammable peoples.

Not only, therefore, were popular movements and aspirations to be crushed in the nation, but sympathy with them in the Diet was to be suppressed. Accordingly, Metternich never rested until that body had been purged of all the envoys who failed to fall in with his reactionary aims. The rigid censorship enforced outside was applied to the Diet itself. Books might not be admitted into its library without being first approved by the envoy of the State from which they were issued ; even the right of petition was subjected to the censorship, in order that the Diet might not be troubled by importunate memorials unawares.

From the beginning of 1816 blow after blow rained upon the democratic movement in Germany. Newspapers attached to the constitutional cause were suppressed ; the innocent *Tugend-*

bund, or League of Virtue, of Königsberg, a society of high-minded loyalists, formed for purely ethical purposes, was dissolved ; it became an offence to be a patriot and a crime to advocate national unity. No public reference to the question of unity was allowed ; every symbol of nationality and the national cause was proscribed ; even the display of the tricolour of the old Empire, black, red, and gold, was made a penal offence, and the surest way into prison was to go about the street in a black coat, a red waistcoat, and a straw hat. The tyranny of Napoleon had been destroyed, but another tyranny had taken its place, one far more odious and dangerous than the old, since its victims were the minds and spirits of men.

While the hopes of the ripe manhood of the country, of the men who so recently had borne the burden and stress of the struggle with Napoleon, were thus dashed to the ground, an outrage, even more violent, was done to national aspirations by the forcible suppression of the idealistic movement in favour of unity which began amongst the academic youth of the land in 1815. Fichte had passed away, but his eloquent and fervent *Addresses to the German Nation* had not been spoken in vain. The immediate purpose of the Addresses, the emancipation of the German States from a foreign yoke, had been attained, but the task of uniting these States in a single fatherland remained to be achieved. It was in order to help forward this great work that the students of Germany organized the *Burschenschaft*, emblem at once of the unity of learning and that unity of the nation which it was to be their aim to realize. Each university became, in some degree, a centre of a national movement of moral, as well as political, regeneration. The old students' associations were usually formed on the basis of State or tribe, and represented particularism in its most acute form, so that the students of any one of the larger universities organized themselves in almost as many groups as the political territories from which they came. Moreover, their purposes were in the main social, where they were not outspokenly convivial, and only seldom did they seriously concern themselves with the claims of the higher life.

The *Burschenschaft* was conceived in the idealistic spirit of Fichte. It was an all-German organization, in which the common aspirations after liberty and unity were to find free and powerful expression. It was not deliberately designed as a political society, for its founders were young and naïve enough to think that in their emancipated new Germany liberty and unity were not party but national aims, and hence were outside the sphere of controversy. The heart of the movement was Jena, once the home of Fichte, happy under the rule of the most liberal-minded Prince of his day. To signalize the growing strength of the *Burschenschaft* a national festival of its members was arranged at the Wartburg, and there some hundreds of students, with many of their professors, assembled from all parts of Germany on October 18, 1817. There was much fervid oratory, much exchanging of vows and protestations, and at the end of the day, remembering how Luther had burned the Pope's Bull at Wittenberg, the students did honour to the genius of the place by a bonfire in which various symbols of the powers of darkness against which they were warring were committed to the flames—a pigtail, symbolical of conventionality; a corset, symbolical of stiff-necked pedantry; a corporal's cane, symbolical of tyranny; and a number of books obnoxious to the national party, including the new Prussian Police Code and Kotzebue's *History of the German Empire,* symbolical of the spirit of reaction in general.

This demonstration of the students gave rise to incomprehensible apprehensions and alarms. From all sides vigorous protests reached the easy-going Grand Duke of Weimar, who had permitted the enormity; more than one German Government urged him to make an example of the offenders and to keep a vigilant eye on Jena for the future. Urged by his reactionary advisers, to whom he had more and more handed over his judgment, the King of Prussia now determined that the time had come for ridding himself altogether of his deferred promise of a constitution, and in a Cabinet Order of March 12, 1818, he formally announced that the time was unfavourable for any measure of the kind. The effect of this open proclamation of faithlessness and ingratitude was to create widespread disappointment and resentment in Liberal circles, high and low. Stein had set his heart upon a constitution, for the creation of a national parliament was to have been the fitting crown of the work which he had begun in the reorganization of local government, and the King's repudiation of his pledges deeply distressed him. "The King," he wrote, "regards the present moment as unsuitable; since feelings are excited, it is advisable to wait for a quieter time! But will feelings be quieted by disappointing the just hopes based on Federal Acts, edicts, and promises manifold, or delaying their fulfilment ?" The French, the Belgians, the Swedes, the Poles, he added, were found worthy of constitutions—only the Prussians were not.

Prussia's moral reputation in Germany sank at this time lower than ever before. The Governments of the more backward States were delighted to see Frederick William III dance the Viennese waltz to the music of Metternich. On the other hand, those States in which constitutions had already been introduced deplored the King's act as one of moral treason, and now abandoned any hope of seeing Prussia lead Germany in progressive ways.

Then in March, 1819, there was perpetrated one of those senseless crimes which have so often soiled the fame of good causes and obstructed the path of political advance. This was the assassination of Kotzebue by the Bavarian student Karl Sand at Mannheim. Kotzebue was a voluminous writer of indifferent plays, who had prostituted his talents to political espionage and was known to be in the pay of Russia, while his murderer was a youth of highly-strung temperament and unbalanced judgment, yet of orderly life, an ardent patriot, and an enthusiastic "Burschenschafter." Sand appears to have been convinced that he had a special mission to remove the enemy of the commonwealth, and if he took the life of the obnoxious informer he at least tried to take his own, and mangled himself terribly in the act. He was kept alive in prison for a long time in suffering, and as soon as his doctors could be persuaded to certify his fitness for the scaffold he was duly decapitated. Had the matter ended there, Germany would have been spared much shame. Politically, the only significance of the crime lay in the fact that popular opinion condemned the Governments almost as much as the murderer, and that Sand's fellow-students applauded his act as one of patriotism. The idea that it was part of a deeply laid conspiracy against order was busily exploited, but without the slightest justification.

To Metternich, however, the crime came as a blessing in disguise, for he could point to it as a justification of the measures which had already been taken by the reactionary Governments and use it as a whip wherewith to lash the laggards to heel. Everywhere known or suspected "democrats" were brought under the rigours of a vicious and vindictive police law. Many men of influence and eminence were banished, still more were imprisoned, and others were placed under police control like felons of the lowest order. Arndt, the professor of history, who had done so much to stimulate the patriotic movement in the dark years preceding Napoleon's fall, was kept in prison for three years, while his persecutors tried in vain to discover some offence of which he could be decently convicted. When he was at last liberated for want of incriminating evidence, he was refused permission to return to his university chair at Bonn, and he continued unrobed for twenty years, until a new ruler came to the Prussian throne. The theologian Schleiermacher was similarly removed from his chair at Berlin. Gneisenau, Blücher's valued colleague, was disgraced for daring to hold Liberal sentiments and was placed under police observation. "Father" Jahn, the founder of the German gymnastic clubs, was arrested at his father's deathbed and hurried off to gaol for no offence at all. At the universities, espionage, denunciation, and petty persecution were the lot of professors and students alike. Friedrich List, the economist and the father of modern Protection and the railway system in Germany, fled from his native Würtemberg rather than face imprisonment for a trivial political offence, an honest and much-needed public criticism of the bureaucracy of that State. When he returned, trusting to the clemency of his Sovereign, he was promptly apprehended and kept two years at forced clerical labour—the transcription of accounts. The time soon came when it became a crime to publish in Prussia Fichte's *Addresses to the German Nation*.

Not satisfied with the measures which they took on their own account to suppress Liberal ideas, the Sovereigns and Governments resolved, at a conference held at Carlsbad in August 1819, to organize this campaign of persecution on more systematic and more drastic lines. All the larger States were represented, and the resolutions adopted were soon afterwards presented by Austria and Prussia to the Federal Diet, and by that body were promptly endorsed. The result was the issue of the Carlsbad Decrees for the repression of democratic movements. It rested with the federated Governments to accept and enforce the Decrees with modifications of their own; in many of the States their severity was increased, in few was it relaxed.

Everywhere the Press was subjected to rigorous control; books and pamphlets were placed under an intolerant censorship; political agitation by association, assembly, and public speech was relentlessly suppressed; the *Burschenschaften* were dissolved; and a tribunal was set up for the trial and punishment of treason, only to make itself ridiculous, because it proved impossible to find traitors. So far did interference with intellectual liberty go that it was required that in every university a Government commissary or proctor should be appointed, charged with the duty of spying upon the teaching and opinions of the professors, preventing the formation of student associations, and in general of keeping the educated youth of the nation in order. In a word, despotism set its iron heel upon every manifestation of Liberalism, whether in act or utterance. Furthermore, the provisions of the Final Act of the Vienna Congress relating to the introduction of constitutional assemblies were now, in effect, cancelled.

When the order to enforce the federal resolutions came to the Prussian Ministry from the Diet in Frankfort, Humboldt and two other Ministers of like mind and courage sent a protest to the King, declaring them to be "shameful, unnational, and provocative for a thinking people." The King replied that the resolutions were meant to be enforced, and enforced they should be. A little later Humboldt and his too fastidious colleagues resigned, Humboldt refusing, by way of more emphatic protest, to accept the pension of £300 a year to which he was entitled.

For a long time there were few safe places in Germany for either Liberalism or liberty. The intellectual atmosphere of the country was poisoned by the miasma of political intolerance, bigotry, and dishonesty. The flatterer, the time-server, the apostate, and their kind flourished; upright men hid their heads in shame, or, raising them, were smitten down by the cowardly blow of the renegade and the informer. Prussia, in particular, was overrun with spies, whose business it was to hunt out political disaffection or incite to it. The despicable Schmalz had been decorated by Frederick William III several years before for his activity in this unseemly work. Now the foundations were laid of the vicious system of "denunciation" which became the dishonour of German criminal law, and which still flourishes to-day like a green bay-tree. The whole political development of Germany was demoralized and retarded not only by the clumsy and repressive measures to which the Decrees gave rise, but even more by "the secret political struggle to which the members of the Federation were incited amongst and against themselves" owing to the operation of these vicious edicts.[1]

[1] Duke Ernest II of Saxe-Coburg-Gotha, *Aus meinem Leben und aus meiner Zeit*, vol. i., pp. 33, 34.

The obnoxious Decrees of Carlsbad continued in force for nearly twenty years, and their spirit dominated the home politics of Germany during the whole of that time and long after. The philosophical historian of German political movements, when he appears, may find in the operation of the Decrees the solution to some of the most marked peculiarities of party relationships in Germany. The Decrees helped to consolidate the Liberal party, but they did more. Treitschke, renegade as a historian to his early generous sentiments, is seldom just to German Liberalism and its parliamentary advocates of any epoch, yet he admits that the Liberals were made an anti-Government party against their will. Two courses only were open to them: either to abandon ingloriously the fight for free thought, free opinion, and the ideal of national unity by national liberty, or to rank themselves openly as a party of opposition. They chose the latter way, which ever afterwards proved a way of odium and contumely, except when, in moments of sheer lassitude and exhaustion, they were willing to buy temporary peace and favour by surrender of principle.

Having armed itself with this powerful weapon, henceforth the Diet found little more, and nothing more congenial, to do than to fight against the liberty and unity of the German nation. In his determination to show no quarter to Liberal tendencies, Metternich did not hesitate to manipulate the federal law. On the proposal of individual States the Diet was to be empowered to alter the constitutions of those States, even to the extent of prohibiting the publication of parliamentary proceedings. Here Prussia, herself steeped in reaction, faithfully aided Austria in her dark designs. Thus by a stroke of the pen the independent sovereignty guaranteed to all the allies, great and small, by the Act of Federation was practically annulled. On December 23, 1823, the Diet went to the length of passing a resolution to the effect that even in its own proceedings no appeal should be made to principles and doctrines at variance with the existing basis of the Federation.

Amongst the secondary States, Bavaria and Würtemberg seemed for a time to resent the arrogance of the dictator and his policy. Each of these States regarded itself as the heart of "pure Germany," and both were agreed that neither Austria nor Prussia could be considered German at all. It was at this time that the idea of the Triad, frequently revived in later years, but never realized, originated in Würtemberg. It was a project for the formation of a federation of the secondary States, under Bavaria's leadership, as a counterpoise to Austria and Prussia. Baron von Wangenheim, the Würtemberg envoy, succeeded so far as to create in the Diet a combination—an *entente* or diplomatic group, as it would have been called in later times—which for a time worked independently and was able to exercise a certain amount of effective obstruction. King William of Würtemberg even ventured to take up an attitude of open hostility to the major Powers, but was promptly ostracized by both. The only earnest resistance to the reactionary movement came from some of the smaller States, but, because supported only by moral force, it failed to deter or impress.

When finally all its Liberal members had been either extruded or suppressed, the Diet became more than ever an Austrian committee. The Austrian president even claimed and exercised the right to keep its archives, and these, studiously guarded, were only thrown open for inspection by the other envoys at his discretion. The triumph of Metternich was consummated when the time came for renewing the Carlsbad Decrees, which in the first instance had been promulgated for five years. Without demur the federal Governments agreed to these symbols of darkness being made a permanent part of the armoury of autocracy in its struggle with democracy. Weary of isolation, and wishful to rehabilitate himself in the esteem of his more powerful neighbours, even the King of Würtemberg now made no open protest.

In 1824 the reactionary publicist Gentz could write with truth of the effects of the Austrian Chancellor's policy: "The revolutionary system henceforth can only gain the upper hand in Germany if the Germanic Federation itself succumbs." The arrogance of Metternich reached a height almost sublime when, having obtained from the Diet all that he wanted, he advised it, in 1828, to adjourn indefinitely, since there remained no longer anything for it to do. In the hour of this triumph of reaction Austria's power in Germany seemed to be at its zenith. Well might her Chancellor boast, "If the Emperor doubts that he is Emperor of Germany, he errs greatly." And yet in proportion as Austria was strong in Germany, Germany was weak in Europe. Not in the time of the moribund Empire did she stand lower in the council of the nations or mean less to the life of Europe than during these years of political languor and stagnation.

The retrograde policy followed by Austria and Prussia in

Germany was reflected in their attitude towards European affairs in general. By a convention of November, 1815, the four Powers forming the Grand Alliance—England and Russia, together with the major German States—had agreed to confer periodically upon questions affecting the peace of the Continent. The conferences or congresses of Aix-la-Chapelle (1818), Troppau (1820), Laibach (1821), and Verona (1822) were held in pursuance of this arrangement. On all these occasions the influence of Austria, and of Prussia in sympathy, was exerted wholly on the side of reaction. To Metternich the Concert of the Powers was merely a device for placing Europe under the same system of police surveillance which he had succeeded in imposing upon Germany. To him every stirring of national feeling was a challenge to conflict between the principles of order and revolution as defined by the dominant autocracies. In all the measures, now passive, now active, for the repression of nationalist movements or Liberal aspirations—in Spain and Portugal, in Naples and Greece—Austria was the ringleader, while Prussia meekly did her bidding.

When finally, at the Congress of Verona, Great Britain parted company from her unsympathetic yoke-fellows over the question of Spain, and the Grand Alliance was broken up, there still remained to carry on the crusade against democratic ideas Czar Alexander I's fantastic creation, the Holy Alliance. Formed likewise in 1815, this Alliance professed to pursue aims not merely idealistic but religious; in practice it soon degenerated into a league for the subjection of political thought and the thwarting of constitutional progress. Peace was declared, and truly declared, to be the supreme purpose of the Allies, but the peace which they desired was to be obtained by fastening upon Continental nations the existing political systems and vetoing all changes which would have weakened autocratic power; it was to be a peace purchased at the price of intellectual stagnation and inertia. More and more, after the passing of the Carlsbad Decrees, Eastern Europe, as represented by Russia, Austria, and Prussia, and Western Europe, as represented by Great Britain and France, went apart, the former perpetuating the petrified formulas of autocracy, the latter carrying forward the vital and vivifying doctrines of liberty and progress.

Lord Palmerston, who to the last was never loath to strike a blow at despotism, and who with a justifiable egoism counted amongst his "many good works" the assistance which he gave to down-trodden nations to rid themselves of corrupt government, faithfully defined this fundamental antagonism both of ideas and policies when he wrote in 1836: "Every day brings fresh proof of the complete union of the three (Eastern) Powers in every question of European policy, and affords additional evidence that they are for the present what they told us three years ago they must be considered, viz. a unity. . . . The three Powers fancy their interests lie in a direction opposite to that which we and France conceive ours to be placed. The separation is not of words but of things. . . . The three and the two think differently, and therefore they act differently."

No other serious attempt to redeem the pledges of 1815 was made in Prussia during the reign of Frederick William III. During 1819 Hardenberg himself drew up the outlines of a constitution based on the representation of the existing estates. It is true that the document ended with the excellent sentiment, "Salus publica suprema lex esto!" yet for all that, Stein's reproach that Hardenberg offered "liberal phrases and despotic realities" was well founded. "Why cannot we work together?" Hardenberg had asked of Stein. The reason was that the two were pulling different ways. All that this scheme proposed was that a "general" diet should be elected by the provincial assemblies out of the privileged classes of which they were composed; it was to be allowed to consider and report on legislative proposals put before it by the Ministry, but the King reserved an unconditional veto, as well as undivided executive power. With all its deficiencies, however, the scheme was too liberal for the King, and he refused to proceed with it. Two years later the King, by Cabinet Order, declared that any further proposals of the kind must be left to his "paternal solicitude, to be determined according to time, experience, and the development of events." It was a sign that he had done with the question for good and all. All this time, and to the end of the reign, Prussian policy was dictated by Austria: the astute Metternich was for practical purposes Chancellor in Berlin as well as in Vienna, and the irony of the situation lay in the fact that in Prussia, as Beust remarks, "no one dreamt of finding in that circumstance anything derogatory." [1]

The harsh pressure of the Carlsbad Decrees and the other coercive measures enforced in the same spirit made any effective co-operation for political purposes for many years impossible. Hence it was that the Paris Revolution of July, 1830, received

[1] *Memoirs*, vol. i., p. 27.

at first but little response in Germany. There was popular restlessness in the States of the South, and in Brunswick the illiberal Duke was driven from his palace and deposed; several new constitutions were hastily granted—in Saxony, Hanover, Hesse-Cassel, and elsewhere; but in Prussia, except in the Rhine Province, there was no stirring. But for the provocative action of the Federal Diet the crisis might have passed without further trouble, for all the democrats asked was that constitutional government should be introduced where it did not already exist. Meeting at Frankfort in November, however, the Governments called for the further restriction of the Press, undertook to meet revolutionary movements with a severer hand, and pledged to each other military assistance in quelling every attempt at active disturbance. Other irritating measures of repression succeeded, until finally an open attack made by the Diet upon the constitutional rights of the State legislatures gave the signal for insurrectionary outbreaks in various parts of the country.

A national demonstration, held in May, 1832, at Hambach, in the Bavarian Palatinate, called for the unification of Germany on a democratic basis. In the following April an attempt was made to overthrow the Diet of Frankfort, and the more impetuous members of the revolutionary party united in a secret organization whose purpose was a general rising, which was to issue in the establishment of a republic for all Germany. The answer of the Diet was summary and sharp. Agitation was repressed with a drastic hand, freedom of speech was abrogated, the publication of parliamentary debates was restricted, and the universities were subjected to a humiliating censorship. The example of the Diet was not lost upon individual Sovereigns. When, in 1837, Hanover became separated from the British Crown, the King, Ernest August, celebrated the event by annulling the constitution. Seven Göttingen professors, among them Dahlmann, Gervinus, and the brothers Grimm, publicly protested against the act as an outrage upon the German nation, and were promptly removed from their offices. An appeal to the Frankfort Diet to interfere in the interest of legality and right was treated with disdain.

With the death of Frederick William III in 1840 and the succession of his son Frederick William IV, the repression in Prussia, which had been enforced with a *crescendo* of vigour and rigour ever since 1815, was relaxed. Many of the proscribed patriots who had fallen into disgrace were restored to home and office, amongst them Arndt, who returned to his university work; the Press laws were relaxed; the holding of political opinions which did not bear the official stamp no longer ranked as a crime; and the nation altogether breathed more freely. For a time it even seemed likely that the long-promised constitution was about to be given. But the new King had inherited a bad tradition, and later events did not substantiate the first promise of his reign. Like his father, he was warmly attached to Austria and to Austrian policy in political matters. For some years he played with both the question of constitutional government and that of national unity, and a revolution in Berlin was needed to rouse him to serious action. A man of parts and of the best intentions, Frederick William IV was yet hopelessly unpractical. Idealist, mystic, dreamer, orator, and in everything artist, he was singularly ill-fitted to adorn the royal council chamber; for most of his virtues and all his gifts were just those which a king is better without. His gift of language in particular amounted to a misfortune; wherever he went he made speeches, eloquent, rich in beautiful phrases, but devoid of practical wisdom. He was given also to romanticism, and with this dangerous trait went a weak religiosity. First regarded with lenient toleration, his extravagances in time began to pall upon the taste of his people, who deemed that a Hohenzollern ruler should be made of sterner stuff. Arnold Ruge and Ernst Echtermeyer issued in the *Hallesche Jahrbücher* a "Manifesto against Romanticism," aimed directly at the King and his creatures, and David Strauss ridiculed the royal aberration obliquely yet more vivaciously in a satire entitled *The Romanticist on the Throne of the Cæsars.* In political matters he clung to a mystical belief in monarchy as divine and in Kings as literally vicegerents of the Ruler of the Universe. It was impossible that a mind like his should be receptive of modern ideas. "King and people," said the contemporary Liberal politician Hermann von Beckerath, "spoke wholly different languages and lived in different centuries." He was in truth a complete anachronism; his age, his world, his ideals lay in the past; and he stalked upon the modern stage furtively, uneasily, aimlessly, as though conscious that he was out of place, like a shade that has lost its way.

Frederick William IV could not have succeeded in satisfying the just political expectations of the people, however honestly he had tried; it was inevitable that he should, in perfect good faith, offer to the nation shams for realities and be convinced that he had done his duty. In 1842 he caused to be formed committees of estates which were to serve as a representative assembly, and he was bitterly disappointed that the nation did not share his belief in their sufficiency. To his disgust, some of the provincial Diets, which had seemed to be bulwarks of conservatism, now began to petition for a constitution, for greater freedom for the Press, for trial by jury, and other demands in the charter of popular liberties. "Am I not bound, as an upright man, to fulfil my father's promise?" he asked in 1845 of his Minister von Bülow, in reference to the constitutional question. He had been on the throne five years when this obligation began to trouble him, yet two years more were to pass before he decided to act seriously. In 1847 he moved, and by patent of February 3rd, which was signed by his brother, the Prince of Prussia, and all his Ministers, he convened the United Diet, a pseudo-parliament of two chambers or *curiæ*, one the Diet proper, composed of the members of the Provincial Diets, and the other an upper chamber composed of seventy-two nobles and landed proprietors chosen by the King, chiefly from the Provincial Diets. It was not a legislature and was not intended to be one: it had no powers independently of the royal will; it had no right of decision, it might discuss only the questions referred to it; in fine, it was intended to sit and look at the King while he legislated for the country as before on the old Cabinet Ordinance system.

The King himself opened this assembly on April 11th with a grandiloquent oration in which he declared that "Prussia's destinies can only be directed by one will, and that will must be the King's," and that "No power on earth shall compel me to change the immediate relationship between me and my people into a constitutional relationship." Holding these opinions, it was not clear why the King should have convened the Diet at all. Its creation was, indeed, an unintended admission that the system of autocracy was obsolete and indefensible, but the system proposed in substitution pleased no one. Chagrin and embitterment followed disappointment; Liberalism regarded itself as once more betrayed; and political agitation redoubled in intensity. After the Diet had itself pronounced condemnation upon its insufficiency, nothing could redeem it from discredit and the country lost interest in it. The year before (1846) the King had marked his disapproval of democratic government by joining with Austria and Russia in the destruction of the republic of Cracow, as established by the Congress of Vienna, and its incorporation in the first of these States, without consulting any other Powers. Lord Palmerston strongly criticized the lawless act, but it was not actively challenged.

The accumulated disaffection came to a head in 1848. In February the revolutionary spirit which had slumbered in France since 1830 broke out afresh, and its influence was strongly felt throughout Germany, and most of all in the States nearest to the centre of disturbance. Carl Schurz, a German refugee of that time, later an honoured American citizen, tells how, when the news of the proclamation of the second republic and the flight of Louis Philippe to England reached Bonn, where Schurz was studying, the students of the town assembled in the market-place, many bringing with them their harmless rapiers, having a nebulous idea that something had to be done and ready to take their part in doing it. In many parts of Germany the ferment took a more serious character, and there were risings in Prussia, Hanover, Baden, Würtemberg, Bavaria, Hesse-Nassau, and elsewhere. In Hesse, Baden, and Berlin political emissaries and returned refugees quickly forgathered from all the four winds and busily fanned the flames of rebellion. So suddenly had the thunderbolt fallen that, in spite of all the repressive machinery at their command, the Governments were taken unawares, and before concerted action was possible the revolution had gained the upper hand in the principal seats of disaffection. Prussia, ever stolid and lethargic, responded less readily to the call of Paris than South Germany, yet by the middle of March insurrection had broken out within sight and call of the royal palace in Berlin, where the King and his Ministers, the military, and the police looked on in stupefied inaction while the rebels laid their plans. "When all around everything is seething, I cannot expect that in Prussia alone the popular temper will remain under freezing-point," the King said philosophically to a deputation of loyal but restive citizens which waited on him to urge the wisdom of making concessions in the spirit of the time.

On March 13th, news arrived from Vienna that the revolution had triumphed there and that Metternich had fallen, fighting to the last. Facing disdainfully a body of students who had forced a way into his official rooms, the old man declared to the Archdukes present, "Forty years I have served my country. I have never yielded to an insurrection, nor will I now." This insurrection, however, was not as others, and a little later the Minister who had ruled Austria and Germany so long and so despotically was a fugitive, travelling in disguise to England, the one sure refuge, in those troublous times, of political exiles, revolutionary and reactionary alike.

Disturbed out of his accustomed apathy, the King, on the 18th, issued another patent, promising a Liberal constitution and the reform of the Germanic Federation, and he repeated the promise from the balcony of his castle in the hearing of a large crowd gathered below. The announcement was received with delight, as denoting the "bloodless victory of the revolution," and all might have gone well had not two shots rung out—whence coming or whither going was never made clear. Suspecting the work of traitors, the crowd gave way to transports of anger; at once the fateful cry "To the barricades!" was raised; and in a short time the streets of Berlin were arrayed as for siege. The army of the revolution was composed of many elements of the population—the bad were there as well as the good; but all were inspired by the same firm resolution to fight out the struggle for constitutional liberty in such a way that it would not have to be fought out again. The troops threw themselves into the fray with loyal energy, and for the rest of the day and until far into the night civil war reigned, and a large part of the city had been wrecked before a truce was called. Day-dawn saw upon the walls a proclamation of the King to his "dear Berliners." "Hear the paternal voice of your King, inhabitants of my faithful and beautiful Berlin," ran this document; "forget what has happened, as I from my heart will forget it, for the sake of the great future which will, with God's blessing of peace, open up for Prussia and through Prussia for Germany." The proclamation made no impression upon the incredulous populace, which now had gained the upper hand.

Topsy-turvydom reigned in Berlin in those furious March days. Instead of giving orders, the King received them; instead of commanding, the administrative authorities obeyed. A deputation waited on the King on the 19th, and promised that if the military were withdrawn peace and quiet should be definitely restored. The King agreed, and the entire garrison was sent outside the city. Many officers wept with rage as they rode away. It was a physical as well as a moral victory for rebellion, for now the insurrectionaries came into complete control of the city and all it contained. There was violence but no robbery; some public property was destroyed, but private chattels were left unharmed. More than two hundred people had fallen to the fire of the soldiery and in order to bring home to the King the late murderous work, the bodies, garlanded with flowers, but with their wounds displayed, were paraded before the royal castle. There the attendant mourners sang the dirge " Jesus, lover of my soul," and demanded the appearance of the King, who came forward bareheaded, leading the Queen on his arm, and delivered a sympathetic oration, after which the procession filed away.

On March 21st the King issued another proclamation, addressed this time " to my people and the German nation," declaring for unity under Prussian leadership. " We can only be rescued from our dangers," he said, " by the most intimate union of the German Princes and peoples under one leadership ; I take over this leadership so long as the danger lasts. My people, who do not fear the danger, will not forsake me, and Germany will join me in confidence. I have to-day taken the old German colours, and placed my people under the venerable banner of the German Empire. Prussia henceforth is merged in Germany ! " To make the declaration more impressive the King rode in procession through the streets of Berlin, attended by Ministers and Generals, citizens and students, wearing the imperial tricolour. At suitable places a halt was made and the royal orator made speeches to the wondering crowds. " Make a note of it, gentlemen; write it down," he said to a knot of students who had gathered before the university, " that I usurp nothing and desire nothing save German freedom and unity." Some cheered, some shook their heads, others scoffed. Never was an empire created so speedily and so easily as that which was talked into existence by Frederick William IV of Prussia on that March day of 1848.

Yet the King was quite sincere, so far as he knew himself. He wanted to be right with his people ; he seriously believed that the cause of unity was at that moment in his keeping ; and he was convinced that for Germany a new day had dawned. Unfortunately for the national cause, he laboured under a total misapprehension both of his own powers and of his ability to communicate to others his pathetic faith in words. Had Prussia in 1848 had a ruler or even a statesman of commanding influence, genuinely devoted to the cause of national unity and determined to achieve it, it is at least possible that a new German empire might have been established without the wars of 1864, 1866, and 1870, and that German national life might have been fertilized by liberty instead of blood.

Such a leader was not forthcoming, least of all amongst the Princes, who were as jealous and distrustful of each other as of their peoples. Writing to the Prince Consort of England some months before (October 15, 1847), urging the need of such a change in the relations of the German Sovereigns to their lands as would secure the conditions for "a well-organized national existence," Baron Stockmar had asserted his characteristic faith in reason. "I undertake," he said, "to demonstrate to every Prince who, being of fair intelligence, is also alive to the duties incumbent upon him as a Sovereign, that this desirable measure of self-reform might be carried into effect under conditions which must redound to the welfare of all, and consequently to the advantage of both governors and governed." It was, however, just the Princes' lack of political foresight and of a due sense of responsibility towards their subjects that held Germany back at that time, so opportune as it seemed for a great constitutional forward movement.

In the meantime the Prince of Prussia, who had, perhaps unjustly, been credited with a wish to repress all popular demonstrations by drastic measures, had been despatched to England. It was said that he went on a special mission to Queen Victoria, but in reality he was deemed safer out of the country until public feeling had abated. He was not the only high-born victim of popular odium who sought refuge there in that time of social upheaval, when so many men of mark were marked men: Louis Philippe and Prince Metternich had arrived before him. Bunsen, the Prussian envoy in London, tells how he appeared at the embassy, unexpected and unannounced, early in the morning of March 27th, and has left a picture, in sober colours, of his two months' life of semi-seclusion in the English capital. On one occasion an armchair was placed for him in the position of honour at the breakfast-table, but "the Prince put it away himself and took another, saying, 'One ought to be humble now, for thrones are shaking.'" When he left towards the end of May he told his host that "in no other place or country could he have passed so well the period of distress and anxiety which he had gone through as here, having so much to occupy his mind both in the country and in the nation."[1] One of his first acts on

[1] Count Beust, who was Saxon Minister to England at the time, and had been called to Dresden early in March, writes in his *Memoirs*: "I shall never forget my impressions when I returned to London. After I had heard of nothing day by day and week by week but national uprisings, marching with the times, rupture with the past, sovereignty of the people, etc., I found everything in London precisely as I had left it" (*Memoirs*, vol. i., p. 49).

returning to Berlin in June was to take his seat as an elected member of the United Diet which had just been created, for the purpose of making there public avowal of his acceptance of the constitutional *régime*. This he did in a conciliatory speech, which was received by the Conservatives with applause and by the Liberals with silence, after which he withdrew.

The effect of the revolution upon Prussian constitutional development has here only an incidental interest, and it need not detain us long. Now for the first time the King seemed to be in earnest; the constitution which he had hitherto been so slow to grant was produced with astonishing speed, and a constituent Diet was called together in May to consider the details. Then followed the inevitable relapse. The suppression of the revolution in Vienna encouraged him to believe that the democratic movement might be overcome with equal success in Prussia. In November he formed a strong reactionary Ministry, the "Ministry of the saving deed," and proceeded to curtail the deliberations of the Diet, which was still busy upon a draft constitution. As at Frankfort, the democratic party was in the ascendant, and it was proposing to make short work of the accumulation of privilege which had obstructed political progress. Even a resolution of thanks to the combatants of March 15th and 19th and a declaration that they "deserved well of their country" were lost only by a small number of votes.

Wishing at last to liberate the Diet from the ebullient influence of the Berlin populace, the King declared it removed to Brandenburg. The Liberal majority under Hans von Unruh, however, preferred to continue sitting in the capital, whereupon the King placed Berlin in a state of siege, and on November 13th commissioned General Wrangel, to his unalloyed delight, to eject the deputies from their meeting-place. As the President refused to leave, he was unceremoniously carried into the street upon his chair, the deputies promptly following the symbol of enfeebled authority. Attempts were made to reconstitute the assembly, first in the Town Hall and later in a humble *café*, but from both places it was expelled by the soldiery. Then the outraged politicians shot a last futile bolt by refusing to vote taxes. Nevertheless, the King's high-handed action evoked no violent resentment on the part of the nation at large; the revolution had spent itself, and the people neither rose in protest nor declined to pay their dues. As only a handful of deputies appeared at Brandenburg, the King dissolved the Diet and proceeded to grant a constitution of his own making. This constitution was spoken of as *octroyé* or imposed by the Crown of its free will and motion. It had little in common with the constitutions of free countries, yet as then enacted it continues with hardly a serious modification to the present day.

From this depressing story of the political miscalculations and failures into which the statecraft of Prussia was led under the influence of Metternich, it is a relief to turn to the brighter record of the country's civil and material development. If not startling, this was far from uneventful. One of the most backward of the German States in constitutional life, Prussia was the most advanced in scientific administration. The genius of her rulers and statesmen for order and organization was proverbial, and in grappling with the many difficult problems incidental to a time of national transition and reconstruction in many directions it found a fruitful field of action. Faithless though he was on the constitutional question, Frederick William III was all the more concerned to build up the system of local government. The law establishing provincial Diets, passed in 1823, marked an important break with the old system of administration, which had combined feudal privilege with arbitrary government from above. Metternich had urged the King to restrict his interpretation of article 13 of the Federal Act to the grant of provincial assemblies, and to establish even these in a "circumscribed form." They were so circumscribed, in fact, that the people at large were excluded from direct participation in their affairs; their sessions were held in secret; and even their proceedings were so jealously withheld from public knowledge that only bald summaries of events were published when the assemblies had dispersed. The chief importance of the new provincial Diets lay in the fact that they were part of a comprehensive scheme of administrative devolution. During the next five years a system of circle Diets was created for the various provinces, so that now—the towns having had self-government since the introduction of Stein's Municipal Ordinance of 1808—only the later reforms in the administration of the rural communes were needed in order to complete the edifice of local self-government. Another notable domestic reform of the period was the land legislation passed in the interest of the peasant proprietors. Nothing was done for the rural labourers, however, and the condition of comparative servitude established by the early Labour Ordinances suffered no alleviation; substantially these degrading regulations have remained unchanged to the present day.

It was at this time of awakening also that Prussia and other German States laid the broad foundations of their systems of public and technical schools. This enlightened action was the result of a deliberate recognition of the impossibility of competing with other industrial countries, and particularly England, unless the fullest use were made of the aids offered by education and science. Compulsory elementary education had already been introduced in some of the States, and in the second and third decades of the century technical colleges and schools, in the interest of many trades and crafts, sprang up in all parts of the country. Nothing is more creditable to Prussia than the eagerness with which the new movement was taken up by the industrial towns. When in 1824 Berlin set up a technical school, placing at its head the famous pedagogue K. F. von Klöden, other Prussian towns at once followed suit, e.g. Breslau, Stettin, and Elberfeld. Hearing of Berlin's experiment, Goethe wrote: "We are now assured of the comprehensive care with which the Prussian State is endeavouring to keep pace with the incessant advances in technical methods effected by our neighbours." England, strong in her belief in the "practical man," and scornful of educational enthusiasts, regarded this new departure with cheerful indifference.

Nevertheless, the country's material prosperity was held back by other causes than the presence in the field of earlier and stronger rivals, and one of the principal obstacles was removed when the internal duties and excises, which had acted so injuriously in restraint of trade, were abolished and the enlarged kingdom was made a free market, protected only against undue competition from without by a system of moderate duties.

Here the far-sighted statesmanship of Stein and his associates was abundantly justified by the results. At the beginning of the nineteenth century Prussia was still an agricultural State, no less than 80 per cent. of the inhabitants following pastoral occupations. Hence not only did the country produce food enough for its own use, but it was able to export grain freely. Manufactures were in the main confined to the West, to Silesia, and to Berlin, Magdeburg, and a few other towns, while the most flourishing Prussian ports were Memel, Danzig, Königsberg, and Emden, all but the last situated upon the Baltic. The practice of exclusive trading was carried on as before, and the exchange of merchandise, not only between State and State, but even within the boundaries of the same political territory, was impeded by a grotesque system of duties and dues. There were imposts by land and water, and *octrois* at every town gate, with dues on sales and dues on purchases; and the mischief thus done was aggravated by the monopolies exercised by the Governments and the trade privileges conferred upon corporations and private individuals.

So it was when, after the overthrow of Prussia by Napoleon, Stein and Hardenberg won over a reluctant King to their own firm conviction that Prussia could only be made secure against foreign enemies by being made freer in her own life. From that conviction, and in its spirit, proceeded the series of epoch-making laws and regulations, beginning in 1807, which gave to the economic life of Prussia the relief which it needed, by removing the fetters upon industry, handicraft, trade, and agriculture, and giving scope, for the first time, for the full exercise of the nation's productive powers. "Greater liberty" was Stein's watchword, and the phrase meant for him much more than for Hardenberg except in the fruitful period of his early enthusiasm. Of the two, Stein was unquestionably the more solid economist. He had studied at the University of Göttingen, at that time and later famous as the special home of the cameral sciences, and while a follower of Adam Smith, he sought to apply Liberalistic ideas, not on any slavish model, but according to the special needs of Prussia. The "Instruction to the Royal Governments of the Prussian Provinces" of December 26, 1808, after emphasizing the principle that industry must be free and no man must be restricted in the choice of a calling, proceeded :—

"Together with this liberty, facility of communication and freedom of trade both at home and abroad are also necessary if our industry, trade, and welfare are to thrive. Freedom of trade and of industry creates the greatest possible competition between the producing and consuming public, and protects the consumers most effectively against scarcity and excessive prices."

That was Stein's economic position in theory. In practice he departed from it, like a wise statesman, just as interest and policy dictated. There is a faithful echo of the Glasgow professor of political economy in Stein's doctrine that "It is not necessary to favour trade; it must simply not be obstructed." In harmony with this doctrine the direct State encouragement of industry and trade ceased for a long time. Rightly or wrongly, it was deemed to be incompatible with the ideal of economic freedom and independence. So long as the State exercised the right to control the movements of its citizens by restrictions upon the choice of trade and occupation, upon migration and residence, it recognized the counter-obligation to act in something like a parental relationship towards every class of the community. When, however, these restrictions were cast aside, the State's direct patronage was forfeited as well. There was less prohibition of exports and imports, but there were also no more bounties and subventions. At that time Prussia had two customs tariffs—one for the agricultural East of the monarchy, devised to meet its special economic conditions and sufficiently protective, and the other for the more industrial West, marked by lower duties.

The reforming work of Stein was continued after his resignation. In his spirit was passed the law of May 26, 1818, "on the customs and excise duties on foreign goods and on trade between the provinces of the State," which introduced complete freedom of trade within the kingdom, abolished the last of the old prohibitions, and relaxed the remaining restrictions upon foreign trade. "The duties," so ran the preamble, "shall protect home industry by a suitable taxation of foreign trade and the consumption of foreign goods, and shall secure to the State such a revenue as may be possible without impediment to trade." It was the tariff based on this law which received so warm a commendation from the free trade party in the English House of Commons, where in 1825 Huskisson uttered the hope that "the time would come when England would follow Prussia's example." Yet Prussia's fiscal policy was dictated not by preference for any theories of the schools but by motives of self-interest. Since her agriculturists grew corn enough and to spare and her manufacturers were not yet able to supply the needs of the home market, traffic with other countries was a necessity. Nor can it be doubted that this freer mercantile intercourse greatly helped to regenerate the economic life of the country, depressed and disordered as it was by exhausting wars.

A still larger step forward was taken by the reduction and ultimate unification of the customs system of the German States. The two best-known protagonists of a policy of freer trade at that time were Friedrich List, the professor of Tübingen, and Karl Friedrich Nebenius, a Baden statesman, each of whom devoted to the cause an eloquent tongue and a ready pen. Both regarded complete free trade as the ideal to be aimed at, but wished to attain that goal by stages. List in particular was a consistent advocate of the "infant industry" argument for protection. For the present he worked for freedom of trade within the frontiers of Germany as the first and essential condition of advance towards freer international exchange. He expected far more from the increase of commercial intercourse between the various German States than from the wholesale abolition of the customs barriers dividing them from the outer world. Hence his diligent encouragement of railway enterprise, which owed much to his efforts. Several of the large trunk lines transecting Central and South Germany were projected by him.

The first serious attempt to introduce freedom of internal trade throughout Germany, as reorganized by the Federation of 1815, was made in the Federal Diet by Würtemberg in 1817, but it was not well received. Prussia took up the question a little later on her own account. It was on the question of customs policy that Prussia won her greatest diplomatic success in her early dealings with the other States. The Germanic Federation might not have been intended as a stepping-stone to political unity, but with the increase of commercial intercourse and the development of road and water transport, it was impossible that the States should continue for ever to be independent customs areas, regardless of all considerations of common interest and welfare. Particularism stubbornly held out for a long time, but in the end it was compelled to make to necessity the surrender which it refused to make to patriotism.

Behind the idea of tariff unions and agreements at that time there was not only the pressure of the new industrialism, but the warm advocacy of far-sighted statesmen and men of science. It was owing to the enlightened efforts of Friedrich C. A. Motz, then a provincial lord-lieutenant, that Prussia, in October, 1819, concluded the first tariff convention; and though it was only with the little neighbouring State of Schwarzburg-Sondershausen, it marked a distinct advance. The secondary States were alarmed, and, fearing the extension of Prussian influence, Bavaria invited Würtemberg, Baden, and the two Hesses, with the Thuringian States, to a conference with a view to common action on the same lines, though it led to no immediate practical result. Soon Prussia induced other North German States to join the dual union, and in February, 1828, Motz, now Minister of Finance, scored a triumph when he secured the accession of Hesse-Darmstadt. The month before, Bavaria and Würtemberg had also concluded a customs union of their own.

Now Saxony hatched the ingenious design of coalescing the Mid-German States in a similar union, which was to drive a wedge between north and south and so prevent Prussia from extending her customs conquests further, and this took effect in September of the same year. The design failed of its purpose, however, for, interest proving stronger than jealousy, the northern and southern groups of States concluded, a few months later, a convention in virtue of which reciprocal freedom of trade was introduced within their respective areas. Prussia could now afford to bide her time. She had secured union with the South, and her own large territory and multifarious natural resources and industries made her independent of her small neighbours. It was her policy, therefore, to wait until these hesitant States had convinced themselves that they had greater need of her than she had of them, and that except under Prussia's leadership a customs union of all Germany would be impossible.

Although it may have been shortsighted, the opposition which Prussia had to encounter on this question cannot be regarded as merely perverse. In fairness it should be remembered that the hostile States honestly suspected that Prussia was chiefly concerned for her own material interests, and wished to impose upon them an economic domination which would impede their free development. Moreover, they were unable to distinguish—and how could it have been otherwise ?—between Prussia as a political and as a commercial force, and in politics Prussia represented at that time the powers of darkness and evil. Nor was this fear of Prussian encroachment altogether unjustifiable. Writing at a later date, Motz clearly disclosed the iron hand when he said : " The Prussian State has the capacity and the power to subordinate to its own supreme interests the interests of the federal States, and after the experiences of the last thirteen years we know that the love of these States can only be won through fear and respect for the existing political status." He was for simply destroying the rival Mid-German union, and making its members sue for mercy on bended knees. Nevertheless, Prussia had achieved a feat of which she was justifiably proud, and her success was increased when Electoral Hesse (Cassel) joined the northern union in 1831.

Three years later the separate groups amalgamated in a Prusso-German union, a step which made certain the inclusion of the rest of the States of the Federation, with the exception of Austria, whose presence Prussia did not want. This Customs Union (*Zollverein*) comprised eighteen States with a population of 23,000,000 : only Hanover and Baden of the secondary States still stood aloof. Its motto was " Freedom of trade through unity," yet while the commercial classes looked to the economic advantages which it promised to confer upon the country, the Union was hailed by the Imperialists of that day as more than a victory for the arts of peace and for rational methods of taxation ; they regarded it, as indeed it proved, as an important step on the way to political federation. The Union was first formed for eight years. Before the expiration of that period there had been added to it Hesse-Homburg, Baden, and Nassau in 1835, Frankfort in 1836, Waldeck in 1838, and Brunswick, Lippe, and Luxemburg in 1842 ; Hanover and Oldenburg followed in 1851 and 1852 respectively; and now the only States remaining outside were Austria, the Mecklenburgs, and the Free Cities.

Nor was the pioneer work of Motz in connection with customs unity the only service which he rendered to Prussia and, through Prussia, to Germany. He restored his country's finances, introducing large economies without sacrificing efficiency, raised its credit, did much for the development of the postal and road systems, and gave a great stimulus to internal navigation and shipping. Thanks to him, Prussia was able, in 1824, to conclude with England a valuable navigation treaty, and freedom of traffic on the Rhine was won against the opposition of Holland by the Rhine Navigation Act of 1831, which made that river free to the sea. From the end of the 'thirties forward the railway system was rapidly extended in Prussia and Germany generally.

Thus it was that while the national cause still waited for the cordial support of the Princes and the Governments, material influences of many kinds were slowly but surely helping it forward. It is a fact of much significance that during the political convulsions and dislocations of 1848 and 1849, when the Germanic Federation itself was reduced to impotence, and at one time seemed ready to decree its own extinction, the Customs Union survived unshaken, a sure if solitary symbol of that movement towards union which constitutional reformers and patriotic idealists had once more failed to carry beyond the stage of fervent desire.

CHAPTER II

(1848–1851)

THE FRANKFORT NATIONAL ASSEMBLY

WHILE the King of Prussia had been making one new Germany in Berlin, another was being made at Frankfort. As at the beginning of the century and again in 1830, so now the cause of national unity was intimately bound up with the endeavour of the constitutional party to place the government of the country upon a broader basis. It is an altogether inadequate view that the only motive behind the democratic movements which turned Germany upside-down in 1848 was to increase the power of the people at the expense of the prerogatives of the Sovereigns and their Governments. A genuine and strong desire for closer union existed at that time, and if it was allied with demands for constitutional reform, and on the part of the extreme democrats for a radical change in the form of government itself, these demands derived much of their force and justification from the fact that it was the Sovereigns who, for their own purposes, were keeping Germany disunited.

To the ardent reformers of those days, Liberalism and national unity were merely two aspects of the same question. Without a representative parliament emanating from the free choice of free peoples, and frankly expressing the principle of popular sovereignty, unity had for them neither attraction nor meaning. Herein lay a fundamental difference of principle which hopelessly divided the Sovereigns from the great body of the nation. Many of them were still openly hostile to all constitutional innovations, and chafed sorely under the new restrictions upon their power; such rulers were in no mind to see themselves bound by the fresh restraints which might be expected from the creation of a central parliament.

From the belief, common to the popular parties, that unity

could be brought about only by the resolute will of the nation itself, proceeded a movement which, though unsuccessful at the time, exerted a powerful influence upon the later course of political events and determined some of the main lines upon which the German question was ultimately to be settled. This was the movement whose outcome was the Frankfort Parliament of 1848. The first impetus came from the South, where the democratic tendencies of the early part of the century had always found promptest and most emphatic expression. In the Baden Lower Chamber the Liberal party had actively identified itself with the national cause, and in February a motion proposed by its leader, Friedrich Daniel Bassermann, calling for the assembly of a parliament of all Germany, had evoked great enthusiasm.

For a time it seemed uncertain whether the unity movement, as now revived, would fall into constitutional or revolutionary channels. Early in March the ultra-democrats of Baden, thanks to quick and decisive action, succeeded in obtaining momentary control of the movement in that State and endeavoured to identify it with their extreme political ideas. To their ardent minds the republican cause seemed suddenly to have reached full maturity, and thrones and constitutional monarchies to have become obsolete in a single night. All that remained, therefore, was to inaugurate the new political order, fraught with so much promise, and to this end to create the necessary administrative machinery. Their expectations proved to be short-lived.

Following public meetings held in other towns of the South, a conference of South German democrats met at Heidelberg at the beginning of March in order to discuss the basis of a parliament to be representative of the whole nation. The extremists, chief among them Friedrich K. F. Hecker and Gustav von Struve, called for the immediate establishment of a full-fledged German republic. Moderate men were in a majority, however, and led by Heinrich von Gagern, a Darmstadt Minister, a warm friend of national unity, and a sturdy constitutionalist, they made the counter-proposal of a German Empire with a hereditary head. Between aims so antagonistic compromise was impossible. In the hope of forestalling their opponents, however, the constitutionalists appointed a committee of seven and authorized it to issue a general invitation to members of German legislative bodies and estates to a congress or " preliminary parliament " for the discussion of the whole question of federal reform.

In 1815 the Sovereigns had reorganized Germany without consulting the people: now the people were to reorganize Germany without consulting the Sovereigns.

In the meantime the Federal Diet had been comporting itself in the political storm like a water-logged vessel, rolling helplessly at the mercy of wind and wave. On March 1st it had issued a proclamation containing soothing phrases about the desirability of national unity and its desire to mother the nation with tenderer care than heretofore, but perceiving that its opinions were held as of no account, it soon relapsed into inaction.[1]

Cordially welcomed by Senate and citizens, delegates to the number of 576, drawn from all parts of Germany, but chiefly from the South, attended the national congress at Frankfort on the last day of March, and held sessions for four days. It was regarded as a propitious sign that Prussia contributed one quarter of the total number of delegates, but as regrettable that only two came from Austria. The day before the congress met, the Federal Diet, judging where events were tending, had declared its willingness to convene a national assembly in its own name, reasoning that by so doing the Princes would be able to claim credit if good came of the plan.

Again, as at Heidelberg, the republican party made a determined attempt to capture the congress, but finding itself hopelessly outnumbered, it broke from the constitutional majority and expended its energy in fomenting revolution in Baden and elsewhere. The more impetuous reformers were in favour of proceeding at once with the drawing up of a constitution and the organization of a federal empire, without waiting for further instructions from the nation. Calmer counsels prevailed, however, and the congress confined its attention to arrangements for convening an elective, representative parliament possessed of an authoritative mandate. Having agreed that this body should be elected by universal and equal suffrage on the basis of one deputy to every 70,000 (later altered to 50,000) inhabitants, sketched a short charter of "fundamental rights of the nation," and appointed a committee of fifty (six places being reserved for

[1] Baron Stockmar, just appointed Prussian plenipotentiary to the Diet, wrote of it about this time (May 28, 1848): "From its constitution and from the way in which it is managed, the Diet has been since 1815 to the present day a miserable, despicable, and despised machine. All Governments used it only as the instrument of a false, dishonourable policy, alike ruinous to Princes and people, so that it is considered and treated at present as the true representative of falsehood, of baseness, and of the principle of destruction. . . . To belong to such a body is a real misery" (*Memoirs of Baron Stockmar,* vol. ii., p. 262).

Austria) to make the necessary arrangements for the election of a National Assembly, and in connection therewith—a crowning act of arrogance—to confer with, and if needful advise, the Federal Diet, the congress on April 4th closed its meetings and dispersed with cordial " Au revoirs ! " amid the same jubilation which had greeted its arrival in the imperial city.

Invited now to summon a national parliament, the Federal Diet accepted the task in the hope of re-establishing itself in public confidence, yet also fearful of the consequences of refusal ; it even adopted a resolution empowering this parliament to adopt a constitution for all Germany. The various Governments were left to devise their own electoral arrangements, with the result that the Assembly was chosen on different franchises. Some Governments entered into the movement with energy, and in Prussia particularly earnest endeavours were made to secure the return of men of moderate views, pliant, and sure to give prominence to Prussian interests. Before the Prussian deputies, many of whom were noblemen and Government officials, journeyed to Frankfort they were bidden to remember that they went there as Prussian subjects, and to act accordingly. Only in Austria was the project of a national parliament received with apathy and unconcern. There, too, the Government was now eager that the country should be well represented, but the nation as a whole was half-hearted, and Bohemia and the Slavonic territories in general flatly ignored the *congé d'élire*. The result was that Austria's direct voice in the assembly was far inferior to that of Prussia.

The German National Assembly so elected met at Frankfort, in the historical St. Paul's Church, on May 18th, four days before the Prussian National Diet held its first session in Berlin. Thus it was that while at that time the eyes of Berlin were turned to Frankfort, the eyes of Frankfort were turned to Berlin ; Frederick William IV, curious to know what the empire-makers on the Main would do, the Frankfort reformers wondering whether that monarch would try to take out of their hands the task of creating a new Germany.

The National Assembly was a representative and weighty gathering, for its 550 members included most of the political and many of the best-known intellectual leaders of Germany. Because representative, it was thoroughly mixed in composition ; there were among its members Ministers of State and other high officials, bishops and clergy, poets and journalists, professors and lawyers, landowners and merchants; monarchist rubbed shoulders with republican, constitutionalist with absolutist, Protestant with Ultramontane, Great German with Little German and Particularist. Among the best-known members were: of statesmen, the Austrian Anton von Schmerling (President of the Federal Diet), General von Radowitz (the confidant of Frederick William IV), H. W. von Gagern, and Georg von Vincke; the historians Dahlmann, J. G. Droysen, and Georg Waitz; the Munich theologian Ignaz Döllinger, Arndt, now a worn-out old man,[1] the poet Uhland, Jakob Grimm, Robert Blum, the Leipzig democratic leader, and not least famous "Father" Jahn, the patron of the gymnasium. Yet while thus every colour and shade of party feeling was represented, democracy was for a time supreme, jubilant in the celebration of its heyday. A contemporary writer records that the most reactionary of politicians thought it discreet to go about Frankfort wearing the republican emblem, the national cockade.

The National Assembly of Frankfort has often been called, in quite misplaced satire, a "professors' parliament." If the description itself is not altogether inexact, the unfavourable deductions commonly drawn from it are almost wholly so. The popular idea of the German professor, the object of so much banal caricature even in his own country, is that of a harmless theorist of the study, whose interests and speculations have no relation to actuality and the practical affairs of the world. Like most generalizations applied to classes and groups of men, this wholesale disparagement of German academic teachers is undeserved, and to no section of them is it less applicable than to the occupants of the chairs of history. Omit from the history of German constitutional reform and German unity the names of the much-maligned professors, and it will be found that most of the really eminent protagonists of these causes are ignored.

The unity movement, indeed, received a powerful impetus in the middle of the century from the brilliant band of historians which had risen up under the influence of the fathers of modern German historiography, Ranke and Dahlmann. Ranke, the cosmopolitan historian, like Goethe, the cosmopolitan man of letters, had not warmed to the idea of national unity, though, like

[1] A pathetic picture is drawn—evidently by a spectator—of this aged and persecuted hero of a hundred democratic fights, as he faced the Assembly at one of its early sittings, in the contemporary work *Die deutsche Revolution* (vol. i., p. 583), by Wilhelm Zimmermann, a member of the National Assembly, published in 1851.

the philosopher of Weimar, he had lived through the liberation struggle and had been an eyewitness of the great national awakening to which the struggle gave rise. All the more remarkable, therefore, was the fervour with which the most brilliant of his pupils threw themselves into the movement. Conspicuous among them were Waitz, Giesebrecht, and Sybel. By their writings and lectures as university teachers these and other men powerfully influenced the political thought of their generation, and helped to prepare the way for the practical work of the statesmen to whom was to fall, at a later date, the task of giving form and substance to the unitarian aspirations which more and more had become the common meeting-point of the German races. They differed greatly in constitutional theories, and in their views of ways and means, yet one assumption at least they had in common, that unity could be realized only under Prussian leadership, and that the day of Austria's supremacy in Germany was over. It was a small band of professors of history who in 1847 established the *Deutsche Zeitung* in the service of the twin causes of constitutional reform and national unity.

These men, together with the later leaders of the Prussian school of historians, like Droysen, Häusser, Duncker, Freytag, and above all Treitschke, rendered to the national movement a service of incalculable value. And if it should be objected that, by reason of their preoccupation with politics, much of their scientific work has suffered in temper and method of presentation, it may be said with truth, in partial exculpation, that many of the German historians of the middle period of last century became politicians against their will. To have kept out of the political current would have seemed to them treachery to the aspirations of their nation and to the spirit of the time.

Gagern was chosen President of the National Assembly, and he voiced the dominant sentiments in the words, "We are here to create a constitution for Germany, for the entire Empire, and our mandate and authority for this work lie in the sovereignty of the nation. Germany wishes to be one, ruled by the will of the people, with the co-operation of all its members. To make this co-operation possible for the Governments also is part of the task of this assembly."

Disregarding divisions upon questions secondary to the main issue, the delegates fell into two broad groups. The larger of these was made up of men of strong popular leanings, warmly attached to progressive constitutionalism, yet for the most part ardent monarchists. Its watchword was "Unity through liberty," for it saw no hope of permanence for an empire which was not broad-based upon the people's will. Convinced also that Germany was no longer large enough for Austria and Prussia, it sought union on the basis of Austria's exclusion and Prussian hegemony. Its great fear now was lest the national movement should be allowed to drift further; its great hope was to carry it to success on the new wave of enthusiasm. Unfortunately, this group was severely handicapped by the action of the republicans, who hung on its skirts, and at times seriously impeded its action. The other important group was that of the advocates of a Great Germany, i.e. a federated empire in which Austria should still have a place. In this group fell most of the Conservatives, Ultramontanes, and South Germans.

Gagern occupied a middle position; the federal union which he sought was one from which Austria was to be excluded yet not entirely cut off, for he hoped that she would attach herself to it in virtue of a supplementary treaty of alliance. From the first, therefore, it was his endeavour, by making use of moderate influences on all sides, to concentrate the thought and effort of the assembly on this practical aim. His great difficulty lay less in the violence than in the variety and above all the unpractical character of the sentiments which he had to rebut or to conciliate. Many of his own friends were more concerned to devise a perfect constitution than to ensure the national unity without which such a constitution would be useless, to define ideal rights than to place on a sound working basis the legislature which would have to make these rights a reality.

A committee of seventeen experts, appointed by the Governments on the invitation of the Federal Diet, and consisting for the most part of men of Liberal ideas, had in the meantime been busily engaged upon the revision of the constitution. Its spokesman was Dahlmann, and the draft scheme produced was substantially his work. In its original form it proposed a hereditary Emperor, Ministers accountable to Parliament, an upper house composed of reigning Princes and Imperial Councillors chosen by the federal Governments and legislatures, and a lower house elected by universal and equal suffrage. The federation was to include the whole of Prussia, but of the Austrian Empire only the Cisleithan territories—in other words, Hungary was to be left out. It was taken for granted that Austria would refuse to enter the federation on these terms, and that the imperial crown would in consequence fall to Prussia. The reception given to this scheme was nowhere flattering. The Diet rejected it as impracticable and unsuited to the existing situation. The Princes were particularly indignant that they should be expected to sit in the same chamber with commoners, and these their own subjects, and so numerous withal that they might at any time be outvoted. In the country opinion was not more favourable. For the Liberals the scheme was too Conservative, for the Conservatives it was too Liberal. Moreover, to the democrats everywhere the idea of Prussia, the home of reaction, giving to the federation a hereditary Emperor was intolerable. Out of Prussia this feeling was not even confined to the democrats. In Würtemberg, as has been said, Prussia was regarded as not belonging to " pure " Germany, but rather as an alien element, and its martial King openly declared that while he thought it no indignity to recognize a Habsburger as Emperor, he would " never subordinate himself to a Hohenzollern." So unpopular was the northern kingdom at the time, that Prince John of Saxony could say, " If the nine Electors of the old German Empire were restored, the Prince of Reuss-Greiz would have a better chance of being Emperor than the King of Prussia." [1]

There was little need for anxiety on Prussia's account, however, for Frederick William IV not only did not want the imperial crown for himself, but he had already promised Metternich that he would do everything in his power to secure it for Austria. Whatever the National Assembly might propose, his mind was perfectly clear upon three things: Austria was not to be put out of Germany; any union that might be formed must have the assent of all the Sovereigns; and there should be no parley with the pernicious catch-cry of the democratic party, the sovereignty of the people. At heart he still clung to the hope of returning to the past and seeing the ancient Empire restored in all its glory, with the Emperor of Austria as its head, and himself, a man fitter for a convocation of saints than bivouac or battlefield, as the Commander-in-Chief of its army. His " one most fervent wish," wrote Count Bülow, the Prussian

[1] Count Beust hazards the interesting speculation that if the wayward Bavarian King Ludwig had remained on the throne in 1848 " it is scarcely to be doubted that he, the German Prince *par excellence*, would have been chosen Emperor at Frankfort, and I am certain that he would not have refused the Imperial crown." He adds the qualification: " A transient but highly interesting period would thus have been added to the annals of the nineteenth century " (*Memoirs*, vol. i., p. 36).

Minister-President, to Count Bernstorff, then Prussia's ambassador in Vienna, " is to set the Roman imperial crown upon the head of the Emperor of Austria."

In a letter to Prince Albert of Coburg, the King drew a fantastic sketch of the new German Empire as he pictured it. At its head, assisted by a council of Princes and a representative assembly, was to be the Habsburger, bearing again the title of Roman Emperor ; but his position was to be honorary, for below him was to be a " German King," acting as the supreme executive head of the nation and at the same time as the Imperial Generalissimo. This King, who was thus to be inferior to the Emperor in office but superior to him in power, was to be elected at Frankfort, duly presented publicly to the people in the old Roman way, and consecrated with pomp by the Archbishop of Cologne if a Roman Catholic, or by a Protestant archbishop, to be created for the purpose, if a Protestant. The King communicated this alternative scheme to Dahlmann, who vainly tried to convince him of its futility.

As Dahlmann's draft constitution was unacceptable, the National Assembly appointed a committee of its own, Dahlmann being one of the thirty members, to draw up another. Meanwhile, the most urgent task was the creation of a Central Power or Executive, and a separate committee of fifteen was directed to confer upon this difficult question. Opinion wavered between a single person and a directory of three, one each for Austria, Prussia, and the minor States collectively. Gagern had originally been in favour of a triumvirate, but later he judged that the disturbed condition of so many of the German States at the time called for a strong personal executive. This view the Assembly accepted, and it was decided to appoint a provisional executive authority in the form of a Vicar of the Empire or Imperial Administrator (*Reichsverweser*).[1] This officer was to exercise the powers necessary to the safety and welfare of the federation, to have supreme command of the army, and to represent Germany in foreign affairs, including commercial relationships, but in all decisions relating to war and peace, and to treaties with foreign Powers, was to act in conjunction with the National Assembly. The Imperial Administrator was to nominate Ministers, responsible to the Assembly, and no order of his was to be valid unless countersigned by one of them.

[1] An office and title taken from the old Empire, in which the *Reichsverweser* or *Reichsvikarien* were the Princes who carried on the imperial business during the *interregnum* between the death of an Emperor and the election of his successor.

On June 29th the Assembly, by an overwhelming majority (436 against 84) elected to the executive office Archduke John of Austria, brother of the Emperor Francis, a man marked out by his statesmanlike qualities and popular sympathies. Then the incredible happened, for the Federal Diet promptly sent to the Imperial Administrator a message of greeting as "the chosen of the Governments." Arriving on July 11th at Frankfort, whose population received him with public honours, the Archduke, who in the meantime had privately assured the Governments of Prussia, Bavaria, and Saxony that he intended to work harmoniously with them, was formally installed in office. First he received his authority from the assembly of the people, and then he waited on the Diet of the Princes (July 12th), whose President solemnly transferred to him, as "the legitimate head of the provisional central authority," the rights and duties of that august body, ending the ceremony with the words, "With these declarations the Federal Diet regards its work as ended." Having thus apparently divested itself of authority, it might have seemed that all that remained for the Diet to do was to die, as it had failed to live, with dignity. Instead, it still clung for a time to a titular existence, awaiting developments.

The Archduke lost no time in surrounding himself with the due paraphernalia of state. He appointed a Ministry, with Prince Charles of Leiningen, step-brother of Queen Victoria, as President and Foreign Minister, Under-Secretaries of State, Councillors, and a small army of civil servants, for most of whom there was little or nothing to do except to receive their salaries; he ordered the levy of federal troops and nominated generals to command them; he sent envoys to a number of foreign Courts and in turn accredited their representatives—for the most part the old envoys to the Diet—to his own Court in Frankfort. Outwardly the vicegerency seemed, from the first moment of its creation, a stately and imposing institution; in effect it was little more than a make-believe. Difficulties arose at once over the exercise of executive authority. The Governments had readily given an intellectual assent to the creation of this office; but on reflection they were not equally ready to forgo their powers in consequence. Invited to make the vicegerency a reality, they now began to neutralize their former action by the simple expedient of ignoring it. Hence when the Governments were called upon to arrange parades in the garrisons on a given date, in honour of the Archduke as the supreme head of the army, they all with one consent made excuses. The least substantial of the Imperial Administrator's powers, though they were powers upon which all the rest ultimately depended, proved to be those relating to the army. "How many troops have you at your command?" he was asked one day. "I have only the Frankfort militia, and I cannot count with certainty on that," was his answer; and he spoke the literal truth.

While thus engaged in creating a new order of society at home, the philanthropists of Frankfort lent a sympathetic ear to the sorrows of countries not favoured, like their own, with the promise of immediate political unity. With all their emphasis of Germanism the citizen of the world came to the surface as they discussed the condition of Poland, of Italy, and of Schleswig-Holstein; and for each national problem they found a satisfactory remedy.

So far the National Assembly seemed to have reason for elation as it saw its plans succeeding beyond expectation. It had made sure of the desired federation, or so thought, and had given to it a provisional head, with a whole hierarchy of Ministers and bureaucrats. Much still remained to be done, however, and chiefly there had to be drawn up and enacted that charter of the people's fundamental rights—the inevitable *droits de l'homme*—which was intended to form so important a part of the constitution.

To this fascinating occupation it now devoted its attention. The task soon proved to be far more complicated than the reformers had imagined, for all sorts of rights and liberties were suddenly discovered to be inherent in the citizenship of the new Empire, and when once the catalogue had been opened it was found difficult to close it. Further, when rights had been proposed there were objections to be answered and amendments to be considered, and this required much time. The Conservatives would have been satisfied with a very short and select list, or even with none at all, but the Liberals and Democrats were for thoroughness. Before long the declaration of the rights of the German nation was found to have run to over a hundred articles, yet no one could say how many more were still to come; for having tasted of the fruits of the tree of liberty, the friends of the new charter were eager to remain at the feast. "What a joy," an enthusiastic deputy exclaimed at that time, "to be able at last to draw up the law for which for thirty long years we have so ardently and yet so vainly longed!" It was one thing to draw up a law, however, and another to make it a reality. The makers of the Frankfort constitution fondly dreamed that rights were created by writing them down on paper. Later, the "fundamental rights" of the German nation were, indeed, proclaimed as federal law by the Archduke, and were embodied in the new constitution, yet most of these rights have not even to-day, after nearly seventy years, materialized.

Yet all the time the Assembly forgot that precious time was rapidly passing unimproved. Prince Chlodwig Hohenlohe wrote with prophetic insight on August 31st: "It seems rather a bad look-out for national unity. The time when the iron was hot and unity could have been hammered out was wasted in idiotic, futile prattle, and the separate nationalities, Prussia in particular, are now so reinforced that we are further from unification than ever." The disposition of the Assembly to dissipate its strength upon unessential things contributed to its undoing, for while the deputies talked the national enthusiasm was fast evaporating. Within the Assembly itself the same fatal symptom set in. As the strength of the revolutionary movement had decreased, one of the strongest motives for cohesion became weakened. Doubts arose as to whether the power and authority of the Assembly had any reality apart from the deputies' faith in themselves. And that faith was waning. So the harvest passed and the summer ended, yet the national cause still hung in the balance.

Two events in particular now accelerated the demoralization which had already set in. The attempt of the National Assembly, early in September, to upset the Truce of Malmö, which had been concluded between Prussia and Denmark, then engaged in the first war over the Elbe duchies,[1] led to the resignation of the head of the Ministry, and Schmerling succeeding him, the accompanying redistribution of portfolios gave to the reaction a notable victory. A little later the popular cause was discredited by a brutal crime for which it was neither directly nor indirectly responsible. It was the misfortune rather than the fault of the Assembly that its proceedings had attracted to Frankfort from all parts a crowd of political adventurers and incendiaries, whose agitations and intrigues kept the city in turmoil. There were also occasional popular outbreaks, and these the Assembly showed no capacity to prevent or curb, greatly to the disgust of all friends of order. The climax was the murder, on September 18th, in the public street, of two delegates of the Right of high position,

[1] See Chapter IV, p. 167.

the Prussian General von Auerswald (mistaken, it was said, for General von Radowitz) and Prince Felix Lichnowsky. The crime was one of unmitigated barbarity, senseless and purposeless, and it only served to strengthen further the hands of the reaction.

On October 19th, five months after its first meeting, the National Assembly began to debate the constitution as finally drafted. It was divided in orderly form into seven parts, dealing consecutively with the Empire, its extent and parts ; the Imperial Executive, its rights and duties ; the Diet ; the head of the Empire ; the Imperial Court of Justice ; the fundamental rights of the German nation ; and constitutional guarantees, with the electoral law for the Diet.

The opening articles were a direct challenge to the Great Germany party, for they declared that the new Empire was to embrace the States comprised in the Germanic Federation, besides Schleswig, with the proviso, intended to meet the case of Austria, that if a German territory were united to a non-German under the same Sovereign, such a German territory should have its own constitution and be alone admitted into the federation and become subject to the imperial constitution and legislation. This meant the splitting of the Habsburg monarchy into two parts, a course to which Austria was known to be opposed. Her delegates and their allies warmly contested the proposal, and Gagern, by way of compromise, urged an amendment of which the effect would have been to exclude Austria from the federation, yet to associate her with it as part of a wider union. This alternative, of which much was to be heard in later years, was rejected and the original proposal approved by a large majority.

Other articles provided that the federated States were to continue politically independent, but were to cede much of their sovereign power to a central Government, consisting of the Emperor of Germany, an executive, and a Diet. The Government's jurisdiction was to comprise all foreign affairs, the army and navy, trade, customs, and communications, i.e. railways, waterways, post, etc.

The Emperor was to be not only a constitutional but a parliamentary Sovereign, governing through a Ministry responsible to the legislature, and only retaining as his special prerogatives the power to declare war, the supreme command of the army, and the right to represent the Empire in foreign relations. The legislature was to consist of an upper House of States, half of whose members were to be nominated by the Princes and the rest by the State Diets, and a popular chamber elected on manhood suffrage (twenty-four being the qualifying age), to which end the country was to be divided into single-member electoral districts, each with a population of 100,000. The two houses were to have equal legislative power, except that the sanctioning of the budget was to rest altogether with the people's representatives. In effect the Princes, as such, were to have as little weight in the national Diet as the people had hitherto had in the Diet at Frankfort.

While the Assembly was engaged upon this part of its task, unforeseen difficulties arose and threatened to spoil the work which had been so painfully accomplished. The Sovereigns and their Governments suddenly awoke to the importance of the measures which were maturing in St. Paul's Church under their very eyes. Acting under pressure, they had seemed to give a general assent to these proceedings; for had not their mouthpiece, the Diet, formally accepted the Imperial Administrator and made over to him its powers and duties? Now that danger of revolution was past, they began to view the question more critically, and to reconsider their attitude. There is no reason to suppose that the later action of the Princes, in revoking their assent to the preparation of a constitution, was merely the fulfilment of a dark design determined on from the beginning. It is questionable whether in their state of mind when that assent was given they were even able to think so clearly or so far. In accepting a proposal for the reorganization of Germany, they had yielded to panic and the compulsion of events; but having made the first surrender, it is probable that they would have been prepared to accept the consequences had that course seemed inevitable.

Directly, however, it became apparent that the National Assembly had ceased to be the faithful reflection of the national mind, that the popular movement was exhausting itself, and that enthusiasm for unity on the lines originally proposed had given place to growing apathy, they no longer held themselves bound by pledges given in totally different circumstances. If a democratic empire, called for by the fervent acclaim of a united nation, would have been a leap in the dark, much more adventurous seemed such an experiment in the now tempered state of public opinion. It was easy, therefore, for the Princes to persuade themselves that the best service that they were able to render to Germany in this critical situation was to save her from her friends, and that in renouncing their earlier attitude they were protecting the nation against unjustifiable risks. Well might the Prince Consort of England write at this time (December 17th): "I see symptoms in the German Sovereigns of an inclination to repeat all the old faults which have been within an ace of costing them their heads. *Rien oublier et rien apprendre* is the motto of many."

"The Assembly at Frankfort," wrote Bülow gleefully to Count Bernstorff on December 20th, "is beginning to feel its impotence; it is no longer a danger to us." Now, when it was certain that a reaction had already set in, the King of Prussia came forward and invited the Princes to take the federal movement again into their own hands. An empire was well enough, but the proposed constitution virtually took away from the Princes the power which they possessed in the existing Federation, and to such a usurpation he for one was not prepared to agree. Accordingly he suggested the formation of a college of the five German Kings, which, with the Imperial Administrator, should act as the Executive, and thus serve as a breakwater against the assumptions of the new Diet, governing Germany, yet without materially infringing the sovereignty of any of the federal territories.

None of the other States favoured this alternative, however, and least of all Austria, whose attitude was decisive. There a change of ruler as well as of Minister-President had taken place, for on accepting that office Prince Felix von Schwarzenberg had stipulated that the Crown, too, should make a new start, and the Emperor (since 1835 Ferdinand) had given place to his nephew Francis Joseph, the most gifted of the archdukes, then a youth of eighteen. Schwarzenberg, whose appointment took effect on November 22nd, was by calling both soldier and diplomat, and a man of strong and masterful character, as arrogant as Metternich, but ruling by sheer will-power where Metternich had ruled by craft, and he faithfully adhered to the policy of ascendancy.

One of his first acts after taking office was to demand that the whole of Austria, independent of race, should be admitted into the Bund, a sign that he did not even yet regard the existing status as hopeless. Invited now by the Prussian Government to state his position, he replied (December 13th) that Austria was not averse to the formation of a smaller union within the larger, but she must have a right to enter both as an undivided dominion. As for the Frankfort Parliament, he ridiculed it, with all its works, and said that the only constitution possible was one upon which Austria and Prussia should agree between themselves, and that the object of such a constitution must not be the creation of a federal State, but the reform of the existing union. A stronger Executive might be expedient, and he was prepared to accept in principle Frederick William IV's idea of a college of Kings, each of whom should represent a group of minor Sovereigns. A body composed, like the existing Diet, of delegates of the Princes would be indispensable, but a popular legislature was out of the question. Schwarzenberg advised that Bavaria should first be won for action on these lines, and thereafter the other Sovereigns one by one, hinting that any resistance by the minor States should be overcome by resolute measures. The reference to Bavaria had a special significance, for all the time the Bavarian Government was entreating Austria to remain in the federation as a counterpoise to Prussia.

In general this arrangement was acceptable to Frederick William IV, whose only clear conviction was that by hook or by crook every scheme based on the exclusion of Austria must be rejected. With that exception his notions on the subject of federal reform never ceased to be hazy and incoherent. "I admit at once," he wrote in a note of January 4, 1849, "that I do not feel myself in a position to form any definite picture of the Germany that is to be. My imagination has no lack of pictures and wishes, but they are not such as I have felt justified in recommending for consideration at the present time."

Far otherwise was it with Austria. Schwarzenberg at least knew what he wanted, though he was indifferent about the means for attaining his ends. Whatever the National Assembly might do, or the other States want to do, he was determined that the Bund should remain as the pledge of Austrian hegemony. On December 28th he addressed a note to the National Assembly, saying that Austria reserved the right of decision upon the question of joining the proposed new Federation and would recognize no imperial constitution which had not received the approval of the Princes, and first of all of the Emperor.

While the Princes and Governments were negotiating and plotting amongst themselves, the National Assembly continued its deliberations, and early in January it reached the critical question of the presidency of the new Federation. The choice lay between a hereditary Emperor, as favoured by the majority, and an electoral college of Princes, chosen for life or for a term of years—twelve, six, and three were all proposed. A week's dreary talk failed to produce either agreement or a decisive majority either way. Then it became known that the Prussian Government contemplated the issue to all the Governments of a circular note intended to pave the way for an understanding with the Frankfort Assembly. While it was still under consideration, Schwarzenberg, on January 19th, sent to Berlin a further statement of his opinions and demands. Briefly he proposed that the Frankfort constitution should be rejected and its authors ignored, and that the five Kings should prepare a constitution of their own, informing the Imperial Administrator of their intention. Lest resistance should be offered to this procedure, he suggested that a force of 40,000 Prussian, Bavarian, and Würtemberg troops should occupy the environs of Frankfort, as an earnest of what the National Assembly and its friends might expect if they did not quietly and expeditiously disperse. Austria was at the moment occupied in suppressing insurrections both in Italy and Hungary, but he magnanimously offered to contribute to the army of defence and defiance a thousand men.

Although forestalled by this manifesto, the Prussian Cabinet was not deterred from issuing its own circular, though the King's assent to it was obtained only with difficulty. In this (January 23rd) it urged upon the Governments, in contrast to the Austrian attitude, the importance of a good understanding with the National Assembly, and pointed out that if Austria refused to enter a reformed federation, as seemed likely, it would still be possible to maintain the Bund while the rest of the States formed a separate and more intimate union. Finally the note declared that the King of Prussia would not accept any position that might be offered to him by the National Assembly, except with the free acquiescence of the German Governments, for he and Prussia sought no privileged position.

To this circular Schwarzenberg replied (February 4th) that Austria was not disposed to be excluded from a close union with the other German States, and that the basis of such a union must not be inconsistent with the integrity of her entire territory; she would not agree to any arrangement which implied her exclusion from Germany. He therefore favoured a loose federation on the old lines, incorporating all the German States as before, with all their territories.

By the issue of the note of January 23rd Prussia seemed to have shaken herself free from the old weak dependence upon

Austria. The object of the note was to bring into line the Governments of the secondary and small States, to relieve them of any fear of Prussian domination, and to convince them that they might with perfect safety make common cause with her, and this object appeared to have been attained. Not only did the note turn the scale against Austria in the National Assembly, but when Prussia invited the Governments to appoint plenipotentiaries to confer with her upon the question of federal reform nearly all the smaller States responded, though the kingdoms kept aloof on the plea that they could not accept any change which would give Germany a monarchical head or exclude Austria. Conferences were duly held at which a draft constitution was discussed. One of the amendments introduced was specially obnoxious to Prussia—the proposal that there should be a federal parliament elected on manhood suffrage. Then Frederick William IV again changed his mind. The thought of parting company with Austria was painful to him ; he had no mind to be thrown entirely on the support of the smaller States ; and he cordially disliked the idea of being indebted to a democratic body like the National Assembly. He returned, therefore, to his old idea that Francis Joseph should be the Roman Emperor and he the Imperial Generalissimo.

On March 4th Austria received a long-delayed constitution, and it was given for the whole State in recognition of the unity of the Habsburg dominion. Schwarzenberg thereupon notified the Austrian representative at Frankfort that Austria must be admitted into the Federation as a whole, and that the constitution prepared by the National Assembly must be amended accordingly. His idea of German unity was a polyethnic empire of seventy millions, little more than half of them Germans, and the rest consisting of Magyars, Poles, Czechs, Croats, Slovenes, and Italians. The executive power was to be vested in a directory, in which Austria and Prussia should preside alternately, and the popular legislature upon which the Assembly had set its heart was to give place to a House of States consisting of seventy members, nominated by the Governments and Diets of the federal States. For the purpose of the directory Germany was to be divided into groups of States, each represented by a King. Schwarzenberg's object, or one of his objects, in producing this plan was obvious—he wished to degrade Prussia by elevating the secondary States : Prussia was henceforth to be one of five kingdoms to which Imperial Austria would condescend to assign so much of her power as she chose. Sincere or disingenuous, this was his final answer to the democratic movement of 1848. The Governments of Austria and Prussia were alike in hating this movement, but Austria hated as well the idea of giving place to Prussia in Germany, and Schwarzenberg's ultimatum was intended to silence both the National Assembly and Prussia simultaneously. So far as Austria herself was concerned, it meant the restoration of the *status quo ante* with little practical change.

That Schwarzenberg was wise in thus playing fast and loose with so true and attached a friend of Austria as Frederick William IV must be doubted. Had he seriously wished to come to an agreement with that ruler, he might even now have done so on terms which would have secured to Austria much of her old supremacy in Germany. The Prince Consort of England wrote with truth (August 1854): "*Prussia* would at any time rejoice in a difficulty for Austria. The *King* will always be ready to sacrifice even Prussian interests for Austria." One of the faults of Frederick William IV was the rare and noble fault of an excessive faith in his friends. It was a misfortune for the dealings between the two Powers at this time that while Austria trusted Prussia too little, Prussia trusted Austria too much; more worldly wisdom on both sides might have produced an amicable relationship which would have enabled them to work together, at least for some time longer.[1]

A strong sense of resentment was created in the National Assembly that Austria should have stepped in at the last moment with the deliberate design of wrecking the work upon which it had been labouring so long and so lovingly, and the immediate effects were a violent revulsion of feeling in favour of Prussia and the Prussian King and a determination to complete the constitution and choose the head of the new Empire without further delay. On March 27th the Assembly resolved by majorities of twenty-seven and four votes respectively, that the office should be held by a reigning German Prince and should be hereditary, and on the following day a proposal to offer it to Frederick William IV of Prussia received the support of 290 delegates, while 248, representing in the main Austria, Bavaria,

[1] Count Beust says of Schwarzenberg that "he had the greatest contempt for the human race, but he had not a profound knowledge of human nature, and this deficiency explains and excuses much that he did and much that he left undone" (*Memoirs*, vol. i., p. 91).

and the Ultramontane and democratic parties, abstained from voting. The duty of waiting upon the King was entrusted to a committee of thirty (representing all the States with the exception of Austria), together with the President of the Assembly, now Dr. Eduard Simson, for Gagern had become the head of the Imperial Ministry in December.

Archduke John, who had secretly hoped that the choice would fall on himself, wished to resign at once the thankless position of Imperial Administrator, but he was persuaded to remain in office and await the development of a situation which was more uncertain than ever. What would the King of Prussia do? The King of Bavaria had at once written to implore him not to accept the invitation. Frederick William replied that he would so deal with the situation as to convince the Princes that Prussia had never been deserving of their mistrust. He hinted, however, that it would be proper for him to take over provisionally the functions of the Imperial Administrator, whom he now perversely regarded as the agent of a revolutionary movement. The letter was a plain intimation that the offer of the imperial title had no fascination for the King, and that in any event he would never receive it as a gift from the nation. This was, in fact, the decision which he gave to the Frankfort deputation which waited on him at the Royal Castle in Berlin on April 3rd.[1]

"In the resolutions of the German National Assembly which you bring to me," he said, "I acknowledge the voice of the German people. This call gives me a claim the value of which I am sensible of. . . . But I should not be establishing Germany's unity if, in violation of sacred rights and my earlier explicit declarations, I adopted, without the free acquiescence of the crowned heads, the Princes, and the free cities of Germany, a decision which would have consequences so momentous for them and the German races ruled by them."

Probably the King never came to an important decision in matters of State with a clearer conscience. Many reasons spoke for acceptance, among them the facts that a decided majority of the National Assembly was favourable to a Prussian emperorship, that the new Diet of his own kingdom wanted it, and that

[1] The editor of the *Memoirs of Baron Stockmar* says that "only the evening previously the King had been willing to accept the crown offered to him on condition of the subsequent agreement of the German Princes and States, but during the night he had again changed his mind."

many of his nearest friends were pressing him to agree, on the ground that the chance might never occur again. One consideration only weighed seriously on the other side, and it was this which determined him—the fact that the offer came from men who had no right to make it. John the Baptist might baptize the Messiah in Jordan, but no vote of a popular assembly could confer the grace of God upon a Prussian Sovereign. He declined to accept the offer—for he did not explicitly reject it—" because the people alone cannot dispose of the crown and because the emperorship offered would have been little more than an ornamental sovereignty, a tool of parliament." " I can give no definite answer," he wrote to Bunsen later; " we accept or refuse only what can be offered : but they have absolutely nothing to offer. It is an affair which I must settle with my peers." To the same correspondent he spoke of a democratic crown, so created, as " a crown of shame " ; to the patriot Arndt, who now saw the dream of his life wrecked, he spoke of it as a symbol of slavery.

And yet Frederick William IV deserved not the opprobrium but the gratitude of Germany for the decision to which he came. The poet-politician Ludwig Uhland, to the last a member of the National Assembly, said that " no head could rule over Germany which was not well anointed with democratic oil." It was fortunate for Germany that the most unpractical of Prussia's rulers did not accept the imperial crown, either with or without that unction. For no man was less fitted to bear so great a responsibility. As the King of Prussia he had proved himself a failure, but, as the Emperor of Germany he would have been a disaster ; under his feeble rule every tendency towards a true and permanent national cohesion might have been weakened, the inter-State rivalries have multiplied, and the unity movement have been thrown back to the starting-point. With faithful self-revelation he said at this time to Beckerath, " I am not made of the stuff of which Frederick the Great was made : he would have been your man."

In declining to accept the offer of the National Assembly the King had promised to confer again with the Governments, in order to learn their wishes and to ascertain whether it would still be possible to agree upon the basis of a strong empire. Austria had already made up her mind on this question, for two days later, on April 5th, Schwarzenberg, who keenly resented the slight put upon Austria and her reigning house by the action of the Frankfort Assembly, recalled the Austrian delegates, determined to ignore the Assembly henceforth, and simultaneously let it be known that the Emperor would recognize no German Sovereign in the Federation above himself, nor allow any outside interference in Austrian affairs. Nevertheless, the faith of the empire-makers was not yet quenched, and on April 11th the Assembly reaffirmed its adhesion to the complete constitution. Most of the Governments, and of the Diets nearly all, had in the meantime formally accepted it. Only the kingdoms stood out, with one exception, Würtemberg, whose Sovereign accepted the vote of the Diet under protest. On April 21st the Prussian Lower House, on the motion of Karl von Rodbertus, voted recognition by a narrow majority, but the Government ignored the vote.

The Prussian Cabinet duly circularized the Governments, as had been intended. The King, they were told, would be willing to succeed Archduke John and to take the leadership of a federation of States to be formed by mature agreement, if an invitation so to do reached him from them : they were therefore asked to declare their will, leaving the question of a constitution to be decided later when the character of the federation had been determined. On Austria's behalf Schwarzenberg refused to consider such a proposal, and said that as the Emperor had urged the Archduke to remain in office there was no need for the King of Prussia to take his place. Not only would Austria decline to become part of a federal State, however, but she would insist on maintaining all her rights under existing treaties. Of the secondary States, Bavaria replied unfavourably, and the remainder were lukewarm, while nearly all the small States —twenty-eight in number—were willing to accept Prussian leadership. In the absence of frank acquiescence by the kingdoms, however, Frederick William IV did not proceed further with his proposal, and at the end of April he abruptly announced that he had definitely decided to decline the invitation.

This decision marked the beginning of the end of the National Assembly. The Austrians had already returned home, and of the German delegates many of the best known had likewise left Frankfort, convinced of the uselessness of further action, while others retained only a listless interest in the proceedings, looking on and awaiting developments ; daily the ranks of the constitutional party became thinner. " The German nation is about to give itself the freest of all constitutions, and no power on earth can prevent it," Beckerath had said when the Assembly was in the midst of the debates on the charter of national liberties. Nine months more had passed, and still the constitution had not taken shape, and its chances of doing so were daily growing weaker.[1]

Soon the Assembly itself was to end before the completion of its task. Receiving from the nation, in virtue of a mandate than which none more popular, more direct, or more explicit was known in German history, the commission to bring to a head the long-protracted movement for unity, by means of a constitution which should express the people's sovereign will, it had met fully convinced of its power and right to fulfil the great trust, never wavering in the faith that the days of reaction were over and that for the German nation a brighter future was about to open. The spirit of statesmanlike restraint which had in general ruled its proceedings had been overborne at times by violent recrimination and wild disorder, yet even in the moments of tense crisis, when its own fate and the fate of the cause committed to its care had seemed to hang in the balance, the saner elements had invariably conquered, the tempest had been calmed, and the voice of reason had again prevailed.

No member and no party had gained all they wished, yet all had had a hearing for even the most impossible theories and the most unworkable schemes. The result was a compromise which disappointed the hopes of the extremists on both sides. If, on the one hand, the revolutionary longings of those who fondly dreamed that the future of Germany lay with republicanism had not been realized, so, on the other hand, the designs of the reactionaries, who lamented that the best of German life would pass into oblivion with the Bund, had been frustrated.

[1] Referring in 1870 to the prospects of the unity movement in 1849, Bismarck, soon to be the first Chancellor of the German Empire, said: "At that time things looked well for a union of Germany under Prussia. The little Princes were mostly powerless and in despair. The Austrians had their hands full with Hungary and Italy. The Emperor Nicholas at that time would have made no protest. If before May 1849 we had been decided and had settled with the minor Princes, we might have had the South. . . . But time was lost with delays and half-measures, and the opportunity passed away" (Busch, *Bismarck in the Franco-German War*, vol. ii., pp. 41, 42). In his memoirs (*Gedanken und Erinnerungen*), published in England with the title *Bismarck, the Man and the Statesman*, he retracts this view, holding that "the conditions, both personal and material, in the Prussia of those days" were "not ripe for the assumption of the leadership of Germany in war and peace" (vol. i., p. 63). In quoting from this book hereafter I have used the English version, referring to it as *Reflections and Reminiscences*; for occasional alterations of the translated text I accept responsibility.

Yet at least the cause of unity and liberty seemed to have come to fruition, for a constitution had been framed in which a place was found not only for an Emperor but for the nation and a National Legislature,

Now, with the suddennesss of an apparition, the autocracy which was believed to have been destroyed gave signs of life, and the hand which had lain paralysed and helpless was again lifted to strike. The Diet was thought to have been superseded, its prerogatives destroyed, its paraphernalia committed in contumely to the rest of the lumber stored in the musty attics of the federal palace in Frankfort. Instead, it was discovered that it was the National Assembly that was to go, while the Bund, so long ridiculed and so often threatened, was once more to defeat the designs of its enemies.

The Moscow retreat of the national movement, which but a year ago had seemed so near its goal, now began. Already the National Assembly had lost its representative character, and the claim that it expressed the nation's mind had ceased to be any longer true. With the forfeit of its authority the Assembly was no longer feared by the Governments, and, worse still, it was no longer respected. " Everything is in order," was the cryptic answer given by the reactionary Minister Schmerling, when asked at this time how matters in the Assembly were faring. Everything truly was in order for the collapse of the constitutional movement as personified by the Frankfort Parliament. The voice of the people, which for a time had seemed to shake the seats of the mighty, ceased to alarm as soon as the Princes and Governments knew that behind it there was neither national power nor national will. One by one the parties had shed their more moderate members, the reactionaries leaving willingly the scene of their useless efforts, the ardent friends of unity withdrawing in dejected and chastened spirit. On May 4th, disheartened but still not dismayed, the Assembly invited the Governments to put in force the constitution, ordered elections to the Diet of the Empire to take place on July 15th, and fixed the Diet's first meeting for August 22nd; but its authority had ceased to carry weight, and the order was disregarded. A few days later the Prussian deputies were recalled, and the end of the month saw the withdrawal of all but the less influential of these. Great as was still their faith in the cause of unity, even Dahlmann, Gagern, Arndt, and Simson recognized that for the present no more could be done for it in Frankfort. At last only a rump, representing the extreme democrats, remained, its members wrathful at the turn which events had taken, yet still indisposed to bend the neck to the revived and hated emblem of autocracy, the Bund.

Unable to continue its sittings at Frankfort, this faithful remnant removed, at the end of May, to Stuttgart, the capital of a kingdom whose people had staunchly adhered to the democratic cause alike through dark days and bright. There the Assembly professed to reconstitute itself, and then with make-believe assurance it resumed its deliberations, even creating an Imperial Regency in place of the Administrator. But its doom was sealed. On June 18, 1849, a body of Würtemberg troops entered its meeting hall and bade it disperse. Thus the last flicker of life died out of the National Assembly amid circumstances of unexampled humiliation and irony. Called into existence to proclaim the principle of popular sovereignty, this first great inquest of the nation succumbed to the soldiery of the reaction, arrogant and vindictive in the consciousness of resuscitated power.

The bitter memories of the national disappointments and disillusionments of 1848 and 1849 have been erased by the political triumphs won twenty years later. Germany has now for nearly half a century enjoyed the unity which was denied to her at Frankfort, yet the fate of the National Assembly will stand out always in national history as a supreme tragedy of foiled hopes and aspirations, of faith and confidence shattered and destroyed at the very moment of apparent fruition. It is easy to make light of the dreams in which the constitution-makers of those days indulged. There was, indeed, a singular and almost frivolous *naïveté* in the credulity of many of those men, in their wonderful gift of self-deception, in their faculty for believing and seeing what they wished to believe and see. Yet one might well ask where the world would stand to-day if the friends of hopeless causes and impossible loyalties had not refused to recognize defeat, and made every rebuff a call to fight better. Behind all the impracticable idealism, all the pedantry, doctrinarianism, and wild theories that found expression in St. Paul's Church, there was that elevation of spirit and that force of conviction which have been the sword and panoply of all earnest combatants in the struggle for human progress in every age. The world in its superior way smiles at the extravagances of these men, yet in its best and truest moods it knows that, compared with the moon-raking and sky-scraping fancies of the impracticable enthusiast, its own exceeding wisdom is foolishness indeed. The German who, looking back to that distant time, lacks the sense of its greatness and dignity, and can recall without emotion the large-spirited heroism of the foiled and broken deputies of Frankfort, men for the most part unnamed and unknown, who in making a constitution were also trying to make a nation, confesses insensibility to one of the most moving passages in his country's history.

And, after all, the success denied in 1848 and 1849 was only deferred. The National Assembly seemed to have failed completely and ignominiously, yet it had in truth kindled in the German nation a fire which was not again to be put out. If the so-called " failures " of political life—for such are almost always the pathmakers of progress—were able to return to the scenes of their unrequited toil, great would be the surprise of the democrats of Frankfort to see how far the constitution of the German Empire of to-day had been modelled upon their own untimely efforts. These merely anticipated many of the most important achievements of 1866 and 1871—the ejection of Austria from Germany, the close federation of all the remaining States, the hereditary emperorship vested in the house of Prussia, uniform imperial law and justice, manhood suffrage, a unified army, and the rest. There is truth in the verdict of a contemporary German historian, Hans Delbrück, that the " professors' Parliament of Frankfort " was more statesmanlike and saw more clearly the needs of Germany than the Sovereigns who destroyed its handiwork.[1]

The failure of the National Assembly and the rejection of its constitution left the question of federal reform even more unsettled than before, and the outlook was not improved when, in May, the flames of revolution, damped down for a time, burst forth anew. In parts of the South, in Saxony, Hanover, even in Prussia, dangerous tumults occurred, and in some places the troops sent to quell disorder sided with the insurgents. The rulers of Bavaria, Saxony, and Baden, unwilling to trust Prussia in the hour of peace, were quick to appeal for help when the security of their territories was threatened, and in the common cause of order Frederick William IV promptly responded to their call. The Prince of Prussia led the Prussian troops against the insurgents in Baden, where part of the soldiery had joined the rebels, and he both restored the Grand Duke's authority and reorganized his army. The revolutionary movements again

[1] *Bismarcks Erbe*, p. 12.

quelled, the further development of the German question for some time took the form of a diplomatic duel between the two major Powers, Prussia endeavouring with increasing urgency to help the reform movement forward, Austria endeavouring, with equal purpose and greater success, to obstruct every attempt at progress. Prussia was prolific of schemes ; if one failed to attract her fastidious rival, always another was soon ready. The secondary States likewise tried their hand at negotiation in turn, but their feeble efforts were quite subordinate to those of their powerful allies.

The boldest move made by Prussia was the formation of the Union, an agglomeration of the smaller States favourable to federation under her leadership. Grateful to Frederick William IV for the help of his soldiers in overcoming the revolution, the Kings of Saxony and Hanover joined him on May 26th in forming the " three Kings' alliance," and backed by this combination a new experimental constitution, which had been drawn up by General von Radowitz, was put forward for discussion. Just before this the Czar, fearing constitutionalism even more than German unity, had warned the King that he would regard any reconstruction of the Federation without Austrian co-operation as an infraction of the treaties of 1815. Austria, however, was still well able to look after herself, even had Prussia been disposed to ignore her ; having by this time, with the assistance of Russian troops, almost quelled the Hungarian revolution, she was now able to resume the old *rôle* of obstructionist in Germany. The Union scheme was, however, an honest endeavour to do justice to Austrian and Prussian claims equally, for while it proposed the formation of a German federation from which Austria was to be excluded, it was an essential part of the arangement—the idea will be remembered as Gagern's—that the Federation should enter into a perpetual alliance with Austria for mutual defence. This was the scheme of which Lord Palmerston spoke later as " a very good European arrangement."[1]

The draft constitution drawn up on this basis adopted certain features of the abandoned Frankfort constitution, but omitted just those provisions which to the Liberals were most important. There was to be a national parliament, but the proposed equal

[1] " We should have no objection," Lord Palmerston wrote to Lord Cowley on November 2, 1850, " to see Prussia take the first place ; on the contrary, a German union embracing all the smaller States, with Prussia as its head, and in alliance with Austria as a separate Power, would have been a very good European arrangement."

and universal franchise was to give place to a fanciful indirect franchise based upon that recently introduced in Prussia, with its income qualification and its grouping of the voters in three classes ; the parliament itself was no longer to have exclusive control over finance, but to share its power with a House of States nominated in moieties by the Governments and legislatures of the various States ; no law was to be valid without the Government's consent ; the Sovereigns were to be given a more authoritative position, for the hereditary Emperor was to be replaced by a College of Princes, with the King of Prussia as President, and as such exercising the executive power and also a veto on legislation ; and the fundamental rights of the nation as proclaimed at Frankfort were to be curtailed and left to be adopted by the federated States at discretion.

Such as it was, the Union scheme might have succeeded had Frederick William IV, taking advantage of the momentary revival of Prussia's prestige and the Princes' consciousness of indebtedness to her, pressed it vigorously at the beginning. Instead of seizing his opportunity, however, he hesitated and vacillated, and in the end sacrificed a golden chance which never returned. Nevertheless, a congress of Imperialists met at Gotha at the end of June, at the invitation of Gagern, Dahlmann, and others, and approved both the scheme and the immediate summoning of a National Diet to decide upon its adoption. By the end of August nearly all the small States had signified their adhesion. Austria, on the other hand, held aloof, and, owing to her hostile attitude, Bavaria and Würtemberg also refused to join, a decision which in the end led to the withdrawal of Saxony and Hanover. Once again Prussia found herself dependent upon the small States, many of which were all things by turn and nothing long.

The position of the Bund in the meantime was an ambiguous one. Putatively it was still in existence, because the federal scheme which was to have superseded it had broken down ; but so also was the Imperial Administrator. Archduke John, in spite of his disappointment at missing the purple, had continued to hold his office and discharge its duties, contending that he personified the old Federation until it should have been replaced by a new one. Now he was compelled to accept, on Schwarzenberg's proposal, an arrangement (leading to his resignation in December) by which Austria and Prussia were to take over until May 1, 1850, the power which had been transferred to him by the Diet a year before, the two Governments in the meantime to decide upon a new federal constitution. From Prussia's standpoint the importance of the agreement lay in the fact that it seemed to place the rival Powers for the first time in a position of equality within the Federation, yet to leave still open the question of forming a smaller union under Prussia's leadership. Bernstorff, the Prussian Minister in Vienna, appears to have negotiated the agreement to a large extent on his own authority, but Frederick William IV, only too well pleased by the thought that Austria had abandoned her dog-in-the-manger attitude, gave ready assent, and it was embodied in a convention of September 30th.

To Schwarzenberg, however, the convention was only a pretext, intended to quiet Prussia and to gain time for himself, for he still counted on the revival of the Bund. As there was no further move on the part of Austria, Frederick William, after months of waiting, convened a parliament of all Germany to consider and adopt his Union constitution, and it met at Erfurt on March 20, 1850. Bunsen wrote the month before (February 20th): "The Princes are wavering more or less, now that the hour of danger is past. Still, they are bound by their popular parliaments, finances, and necessities, and cannot shake these off, as many of them do their words and engagements." That was a too charitable judgment. The rulers of Saxony, Würtemberg, and Mecklenburg-Schwerin had already abolished the constitutional reforms which had been wrung from them under the menace of revolution, and even the King of Prussia, so eager to give the German nation some sort of political unity, was now whittling down the concessions which he had promised to his subjects two years before.

The Erfurt parliament faithfully reflected the changed situation. It was a very different National Assembly from that of Frankfort. Most of the States of the Bund were represented, but some of the exceptions were ominous—all the four secondary kingdoms and, of course, Austria. Among the deputies were no republicans and hardly any democrats ; some of the old champions of constitutionalism—among them Gagern, Vincke, and Simson—were there, but it was for the most part composed of pliant Government men, summoned to do what was required of them and prepared to obey orders ; two of the best-known members of the Prussian Court party, Otto von Bismarck and Ludwig von Gerlach, sat in the lower chamber. In no respect could such a gathering be regarded as representative of the nation. The constitution of May 26th was adopted by both houses with few modifications, whereupon the deputies were sent home (April 29th) with the intimation that Prussia would continue direct with the Governments all such further negotiations as might be necessary. No one who took part in the proceedings was more convinced than Radowitz, the author of the Union project, that he had been privy to a fraud on the nation.

A few days previously Schwarzenberg had played his trump card. If Prussia had on her side the great majority of the small States, the four kingdoms had returned to Austria. The moment, therefore, was propitious for a bold counterstroke. Accordingly, he determined to revive the Federation and the Diet, relying for support on the distrust of the States of any new adventure, their weariness of the agitations and intrigues which had so long kept the nation in a state of ferment, and the opposition of the South to Prussian leadership. On April 19th he issued to the Governments, except that of Berlin, an intimation that inasmuch as it had not been possible to agree with Prussia on the formation of a new central Government, it was desirable that the States should confer together, and Austria, therefore, as President of the Federation, took upon herself the duty of convening the Sovereigns to a congress at Frankfort. He added that those States which were not willing to attend would forfeit the right to vote, while being bound by any resolutions that might be adopted. Rejecting an offer of Prussia to join the rest of the States in conferring on the question of federal reform subject to the conditions that the Diet should not be revived and that nothing should be done to interfere with the Union, Austria duly summoned the plenipotentiaries to Frankfort for May 10th.

The dispute was now narrowed to a single definite issue, which could no longer be evaded or ignored. On the one hand, Austria was fighting for her old status and rights. She had ruled Germany for five centuries and was determined to rule in the future, but to that end the existing federal organization must as far as possible be maintained.

Prussia, on the other hand, was making a final, though still half-hearted, bid for the leadership of Germany, and since this claim was unrealizable in the existing Federation, she hoped to realize it through a new union to be created alongside of it. In no circumstances was Prussia prepared—so Frederick William IV had persuaded himself—to submit again to the domination of the old Diet, there to be once more reduced to the level of the smallest of the States. Hence, the most effective answer to Austria's challenge was to hasten the adoption of the Union constitution, and with this end in view the King invited the Princes who had given to it their assent to meet him in Berlin on May 8th. Although there had been secessions in the meantime, a majority of the earlier adherents responded, and while twelve approved the constitution outright, the rest either gave a partial assent or asked for time for further reflection. As the constitution could not be put in operation at once, the Union was prolonged until July 15th and a committee of Princes was appointed to carry on its business temporarily.

On the same day that the conference of Princes at Berlin ended without decisive result (May 16th), the plenipotentiaries summoned to Frankfort formally reconstituted the Diet, which began its deliberations under the presidency of Count Thun. The Governments of only eleven States took part, but these included all the minor kingdoms, and so supported Schwarzenberg felt sure of victory. Nevertheless, he was prepared to use his power moderately, and to offer Prussia important concessions if only she would abandon the Union constitution and approach the question of federal reform on Austrian lines ; he even offered to acknowledge the Union so long as it was confined to North Germany, and to make the reform of the Diet the subject of conferences at Vienna in which the partisans of both Powers should be allowed to take part, unpledged to any present plan. Prussia refused, the King wishing to keep faith with his Union allies, undeterred by the fact of several additional defections and the prospect of more. At this time there were ominous portents of more violent differences, and both at Vienna and Berlin the possibility of war was seriously discussed. As if such a test of his principles and resolution were not severe enough, Frederick William IV was further discouraged by the knowledge that Czar Nicholas I was altogether on Austria's side and viewed the Union project with marked hostility. Once more he wavered, and the foothold lost in so doing was never recovered.

Prussia's cup of humiliation had for some time been filling fast, but it was not yet full. Two ignominious surrenders remained to be made before the bitter draught was complete. These were the conventions of Warsaw and Olmütz. The first arose out of a rising in Hesse-Cassel early in 1850. Ever since its admission to the Federation, electoral Hesse, owing to the obstinacy of its rulers, had been a nuisance to its allies, and particularly to Prussia, its next-door neighbour. During the domination of

Napoleon the electorate was made part of the kingdom of Westphalia, and on the restoration of its independence in 1813 the Electors had vented their soreness upon their subjects. In January 1831 these succeeded in turning the tables upon the reigning Prince, from whom they wrested a fairly Liberal constitution providing for a single chamber. The constitution had been fortified by a good electoral law, and, improved by modifications made in 1848 and 1849, it had enabled Hesse to pass through the strain of the revolution peacefully. The self-willed Elector Frederick William I had always grudged his people the concessions made in 1831, though the relations between his Government and the Diet continued to be harmonious until 1850, by which time the rest of Germany had settled down from the late unrest, the peoples to count up their gains, the Princes to count up their losses. In February of that year the Elector made an unfortunate choice of Ministers in placing in power one Hassenpflug, a capable but morally and politically unprincipled man. After having been dismissed from the Elector's service in 1830, Hassenpflug had successively served the Prince of Hohenzollern, the King of Holland, and the King of Prussia, until he again appeared in Hesse, again to be ejected —this time by an indignant populace.

No sooner had Hassenpflug formed his Ministry than he decided to emasculate the Chamber for the wanton purpose of restoring the absolutist system which had been abolished nearly twenty years before. After overriding one provision of the constitution after another, he finally announced that the Elector intended to dissolve the Chamber altogether, and demanded a six months' vote of taxes before that was done. As no budget had been presented, the Chamber refused to depart from the usual constitutional forms, and in June it was dissolved with insult. From the election which followed, the despotic Minister hoped to obtain a more tractable house, but in this he was disappointed. While in the dissolved Chamber the Government had at least one supporter, in the new Chamber it was faced by unanimous opposition. Unable to obtain money by constitutional means, the Elector ordered the collection of taxes to proceed as usual, but the bureaucracy from top to bottom refused to obey him. A state of siege was illegally proclaimed throughout the country in September. Hesse at an early stage had joined the Union, though Hassenpflug had lost no time in making known his preference for the Bund as it was, or might be after Austrian revision.

Now in his extremity the Elector appealed to the Federal Diet for armed assistance, though he had before challenged its right to interfere in the internal affairs of his country.

There was as yet no violence in the electorate; the attitude of the population was simply one of passive resistance to outrageous acts of illegality; even the army sided with the civil population, and nearly the whole of the officers resigned their commissions. In the end the Elector and his Ministers deemed it discreet to leave the country.

Suspecting in the attitude of the people of Hesse a revival of revolutionary tendencies, the Federal Diet, in the name of order, promptly promised the Elector the assistance asked for, and duly ordered federal execution, whereupon a body of Austrian and Bavarian troops entered the electorate with a view to compelling submission. Judge Jeffreys courts were set up under the presidency of Count Rechberg, later the Austrian Foreign Minister, for the trial of recalcitrant State officials, and drastic punishment was awarded wholesale. The Diet went to the length of annulling the constitution of 1831 as contrary to federal law, and empowering the Elector to publish one of Hassenpflug's making, providing for two Chambers instead of one, the lower house eligible upon a narrow franchise.

In face of this provocative action Prussia could not remain inactive. Hesse was still nominally one of the States of the Union, which had guaranteed its constitution, but that fact alone did not, perhaps, justify intervention. Nor need it be concluded that the Prussian Government was greatly concerned about the relative merits of the rival constitutions. It was convinced, however, that constitutional disputes, in Hesse as at home, were mischievous, and that continued turmoil in the adjacent electorate would be dangerous for Prussia, now again happily tranquil. Fearing thus the effects of disorder upon his own kingdom, Frederick William IV had already called upon the Elector to return to the constitutional status of 1831 and settle down to peaceful government, and in self-protection he had covered the two military roads over which he had a right of passage across the electorate. Now he found that intervention had brought him to the brink of a war in which Prussia might have to face Austria and the two southern kingdoms single-handed.

When, several months before, in a conversation with Schwarzenberg in Vienna, Count Bernstorff, the Prussian envoy there, met the demand that Prussia should dissolve the Union with the answer that it could not be done with honour, Schwarzenberg had said: " Then you had better prepare for war ! " Thereupon the envoy had quietly answered: " We *are* prepared." It was not correct, however, whether Bernstorff knew it or not. The Prussian army still rested on the old *Landwehr* basis, but it had been neglected, the term of service had been reduced to two years, and economy had been carried to such extremes that there was not even a sufficiency of officers. Finally, war was costly, and the King had neither money nor, in the existing strained relationships with his Diet, the prospect of obtaining any for an adventure of the kind.

When, therefore, at Austria's request, the Czar convened a conference at Warsaw (October 15, 1850) to discuss German questions, Frederick William could not refuse to take part. The questions raised included, in addition to the dispute about Hesse, the German and Prussian relations to the Danish fiefs of Schleswig and Holstein (a question here passed over, since it will receive special treatment later), and federal reform. Count Brandenburg, now for a year the head of the Ministry, attended as the Prussian plenipotentiary. Russia and Austria demanded jointly that Prussia should accept the action of the Diet, evacuate Hesse at once, and leave the question of German unity alone for the present, since it created only trouble and ill-will. Unable to make such a surrender, Brandenburg returned home for instructions, while Austrian and Bavarian troops marched further into Hesse and a bloodless collision with the Prussians followed. Frederick William had no more heart for fighting Austria than Dogberry for arresting rogues, and though, like the Prince of Prussia, his brother, he professed to favour mobilization, he refused to vote for it, and left the responsibility to his Ministers. As a majority, persuaded by Brandenburg, opposed that extreme measure, the King with relief called a retreat and left Austria in virtual control of the electorate. No other result could have been expected, for the King, in taking leave of the troops which crossed the frontier, had addressed to the general in command the earnest admonition, " I hold you responsible by your head that no blood is shed ! "

A few days later Brandenburg died suddenly. Sybel accepts, but other historians reject, the story that his end was due to mortification at the humiliating episode in which he had been compelled to take so thankless a part and at the reproaches of the war party. He was succeeded as Minister-President and Foreign

Minister by Baron von Manteuffel, hitherto Minister of the Interior, who brought into the Cabinet, which he directed for eight years, a strong anti-Liberal bias. This surrender to Austria probably saved Germany from a premature civil war, but it cost Prussia heavily in reputation and prestige, and encouraged Schwarzenberg in the determination to carry humiliation still further.

The Warsaw convention was called a compromise, but it was one of those compromises in which the surrender is all on one side, for it amounted to a declaration on Prussia's part of her willingness to go back under the old yoke of the Bund, its Diet, and Austria. On November 15th the Prussian Government announced to its allies the formal suspension of the Union constitution, adding that it would be prepared to take up the question of the Union again as soon as a reformed constitution for all Germany had been agreed upon. To Prussia's faithful allies this capitulation seemed like calculated betrayal, and their disappointment was profound. The humiliation of Warsaw was consummated at the end of the month at Olmütz. There Prussia accepted the further terms of surrender just as her rival, behind whom was Russia, dictated them; there was no resistance and hardly a protest; Austria drew up the compact, and all that Prussia was allowed to do was to sign her name in acquiescence. The effect of the so-called Punctation of Olmütz, concluded on November 29th, was that the Germanic Federation was revived as if nothing had happened, and the menace to its future swept aside by mutual consent. Thus at one stroke the whole of the work of the past three years in the cause of German unity seemed to have been undone. It was as though the National Assembly and the Erfurt Parliament had never met and all the laborious negotiations between Prussia and the other Governments had never taken place. Without bearing any of the toil and stress of those years, Austria, by simply holding her hand until the favourable moment for intervention arrived, had effectually checkmated her rival's plans and brought the question of unity to a standstill.

Schwarzenberg had often said, "Our strength lies in waiting," and for once it seemed as though Austria had not waited too long. It was, indeed, part of the bargain that the question of federal reform should be reopened without delay, but it was to be reopened by Austria in her own way. Prussia for all her pains had achieved nothing save chagrin and humiliation, while she had lost much—influence, prestige, and, above all, the respect of the States whose support she had first won and then cast aside. All the King's concessions had ended in failure, and now, as a crowning ignominy, he had been made the laughing-stock of Europe. If Schwarzenberg's policy was correctly expressed in the words, "D'abord avilir, puis démolir la Prusse," one-half of it had already been made good.

Not the least ignominious part of the one-sided bargain was the King's recall of Bernstorff, his ambassador at Vienna, whose courageous attitude had made him inconvenient to Schwarzenberg. Count Usedom, the Prussian ambassador in Florence, told Prince Hohenlohe many years later (December, 1866), by way of illustrating "how men could change their opinions," that "it was Bismarck who drove Manteuffel to Olmütz," and his explanation of the surrender was that "at that time Bismarck looked upon the Austrian alliance as the sole means of salvation." There was a more convincing reason for Bismarck's attitude, however, and it was the knowledge that Prussia was not in a position to go to war. Many years later he told the Imperial Diet that the Minister of War assured him at the time that Prussia's army was so inferior that it could not have prevented the Austrians from occupying Berlin.[1] It was under the influence of the events at Olmütz—galling to all friends of German unity—that Prince Albert wrote to his brother, Duke Ernest of Saxe-Coburg (January 18, 1851): "Emperor Nicholas is at present complete master of Europe. Austria is only an instrument, Prussia a dupe, France a nonentity, whilst England, whose affairs are conducted by a statesman (Lord Palmerston) devoid of public morality, is less than nothing."

Prussia's relations with the secondary States also were now worse than before. These States saw Austria, which was to have been put out of Germany, confirmed in the old position of primacy and Prussia again restored to the *rôle* of make-weight. They had not played a fair game, but the result was quite to their liking. In truth there had been little straightforwardness about any of the Princes and Governments on one side or the other.

[1] Speech of January 24, 1882. See also his *Reflections and Reminiscences*, vol. i., pp. 68, 72, 75, and 77. Nevertheless, Bismarck never forgot Russia's share in the transaction. Speaking on one occasion of Russia's services to Prussia during the reign of Frederick William III, he said: "The balance (*Saldo*) which stood in Russia's favour in the Prussian account was exhausted by the friendship—I might almost say the servility—of Prussia during the entire reign of Nicholas I, and at Olmütz I can assure you it was liquidated."

Schwarzenberg's actions had been marked by so much duplicity that Bernstorff, to whom fell most of the personal negotiations with him, never knew when to believe him. Frederick William IV himself, though straightforward in his dealings with Austria, even in spite of his weakness and vacillation, had played fast and loose with the National Assembly and the popular cause, just as the tactics of the moment seemed to require. If he had alienated the strong Liberal sentiment in the country and yet had failed to win for his plans the Governments whose support was essential, his own instability and want of conviction were chiefly to blame. At that time even upright men, which few of the leading actors in the political drama were, deemed crooked means to be justified by the impossibility of attaining their ends by straight ones. The purist Count Bernstorff had indulged in a little intrigue on his own account. While the King still held sturdily to the Union, Bernstorff promised Schwarzenberg, in a private letter (June 19, 1850), that if he would abstain from any further action with regard to the old Diet at Frankfort "he for his part would do everything in his power to prevent any further progress of the Union in Berlin."

The curtain was about to fall upon this tragi-comedy of political intrigue, and it was easy to see what the *dénouement* would be. In return for Prussia's surrender Austria had agreed to the immediate holding of conferences of Ministers to consider what (if anything) should be done to reform the existing Bund, but without giving any definite pledge of action, and these conferences began in Dresden on December 23rd. Schwarzenberg was the president, and he had a capable colleague in Count von Buol-Schauenstein, while the Prussian plenipotentiaries were Manteuffel, the head of the Ministry, and Count von Alvensleben-Erxleben. Austria proposed that the functions of the Diet should be divided, the full body to deal with legislation, and a college or directory to act as the executive. This college was to consist of seven plenipotentiaries with nine votes—two each for Austria and Prussia, one each for the other four kingdoms, and one for Baden, Holstein, Luxemburg, and the two Hesses together: the rest of the States were to have no representation, even in mediatized form in groups. Against this proposal the small States warmly protested, and Prussia taking their side, not only because most of them were her allies of the Union, but because such an arrangement would have assured to Austria a permanent majority, two members were added to represent these States. Some of the Governments still pressed for a parliament nominated by the Diets of the States, but the two major Powers combined to defeat the idea. On the other hand, Austria refused to accept Prussia's claim to an equal voice in the presidency. Finding at length that his scheme met with more criticism than support, Schwarzenberg abandoned it.

Then Frederick William IV surpassed his past record for incalculable diplomacy and weak manœuvring by inviting Austria to enter into an alliance, carrying a reciprocal guarantee of the territorial integrity of both of the allies. The proposal came to nothing, but it paved the way for Prussia's capitulation on the reform question. In April 1851 the King agreed, at Austria's invitation, to enter the Federation again, virtually without conditions, and to call on his Union allies to do the same.

Thus after years of incessant wrangling the rivals for hegemony in Germany appeared to be left where they were before. Yet such was not quite the case. It was true that for the present the Federation was to remain and Austria in it, but the Union movement, though apparently frustrated, held the secret of Germany's future reorganization: it was a sign that the days of a Great Germany were numbered.

Having settled the political question between them, at least provisionally, Austria at this time endeavoured to challenge the economic predominance which Prussia had gradually been asserting in Germany by the help of the Customs Union. By the prospective admission to the Union of Hanover and Oldenburg respectively—to take effect only after the renewal of the Union, which was nearly due—in virtue of treaties concluded in 1851 and 1854, only the Mecklenburgs and the Free Cities, besides Austria herself, remained outside. Austria had watched this movement with growing suspicion, recognizing that the economic unity of Germany under Prussian leadership could hardly fail to help forward political unity under the same leadership. As in so many other things, however, the statesmanship of Vienna had allowed the evil to go too far before proposing a remedy. The Customs Union had become firmly rooted in the commercial life of the nation, and the belated efforts which it now made to wrest from Prussia an advantage which was due to its own supineness and neglect never had the slightest chance of success. The existing Customs Union treaties would expire at the end of 1853, and negotiations for their renewal were to open in Berlin in April 1852. Hoping to give to them an entirely different turn, Austria invited all the States, with the exception of Prussia, to confer with her in advance, and a conference was accordingly held in Vienna in January. Much sympathy was shown to the Austrian desire to be admitted to full partnership in the Union, but the necessity which would have arisen for revising its basis in a more protectionist sense was at once seen to be an insuperable difficulty. Nevertheless, the idea of a separate union, consisting of Austria, three of the secondary and several of the minor States, was seriously considered as an alternative to Austria's inclusion in the existing *Zollverein*, though no formal agreement resulted. In the event the Customs Union was renewed on the old basis for twelve years (April 4, 1853), but was supplemented by a separate customs and commercial treaty with Austria, providing for a reciprocal reduction of certain duties, arranged just before (February 19) by Prussia and subsequently accepted by all her allies. This treaty, which was concluded for twelve years, contained a rash speculation upon the future in the form of a provision that within that period negotiations should be opened with a view to the admission of Austria into the general Union.

The revolutionary movement exhausted and the question of federal reform cleared out of the way, the Princes were now able to set up house again in Frankfort, hoping that the new lease of life granted to the Federation and its Diet would not be disturbed for a long time. So the old routine was restored, the old mummery resumed, and the Diet went its way as before. One of the first acts of the two reconciled allies was to make war against the democratic ideas which had been at the root of the trouble. Had there been no Liberal awakening, there would have been no German question to solve. To the short-sighted statesmen of the time it seemed, therefore, that the secret of tranquillity was now to sit on the safety-valve. To undo "the shame of the revolution" became for the King of Prussia an absorbing purpose, to be prosecuted with fanatical ardour as far and as long as seemed safe. He had given to Prussia a constitution, yet had he dared he would now have abolished it by a *coup d'état*. "The King," Bunsen wrote, "had resolved to direct all politics by himself alone; he would have a dictatorship by the side of the constitution, and yet be considered a liberal constitutional Sovereign, whereas he considered the liberal constitutional system to be one of deceit and falsehood."[1] Saner minds and stronger wills than his own stayed his hand, but though

[1] Evidence to the same effect is contained in the *Letters of Alexander von Humboldt to Varnhagen von Ense.*

Bunsen appealed to him on the sanctity of the royal oath, it was no scruples on that score that deterred him. What he did was to thwart the even course of constitutional life, by refusing to pass laws, as required by the constitution, giving effect to rights there laid down, by exercising his veto whenever possible to the prejudice of Liberal measures, and by giving to laws and ordinances actually issued a narrow and perverted interpretation. Finally, at death he left behind him a document in which he charged his successors one by one to disown the constitution which he himself had not ventured to repeal.

The Austrian Government carried out the counter-revolution by measures which, if more violent, were at least more straightforward. On the last day of 1851 the constitution granted in March 1849 was arbitrarily repealed, the legislature dissolved, absolutism revived, and the spirit and system of Metternich re-enthroned. The revived Federal Diet bravely seconded the efforts made by the rulers of the larger States to hurl back the democratic advance, and with such success that for Germany the succeeding decade was a period of unbroken political reaction. One of the Diet's first acts (August 23, 1851) had been to annul the fundamental rights affirmed by the Frankfort Constitution and to call for their repeal or revision in those States whose Governments had adopted them.

Again, as in the persecution of the demagogues thirty years before, it was in Prussia that the policy of reprisals took the most ignoble forms. Hundreds of patriotic men, who had given their best strength of heart and intellect to the service of their country, were compelled to seek the hospitality of more tolerant lands. It was said of France at the time of the revolutions of 1830 and 1848 that "her ideas of liberty became an article of export." In Germany it was not liberty but the men who loved liberty and sought it that were exported in those days, but for them exportation meant flight from the gaoler and banishment for years or for life. Theodor Mommsen, Ludwig Uhland, Fritz Reuter, Julius Froebel, Georg Herwegh, Heinrich Heine, Gottfried Kinkel, Arnold Ruge, and Richard Wagner were among the intellectuals for whom at that time their country had no longer a home. Of politicians who shared the same fate there were Karl Marx, Ludwig Bamberger, Wilhelm Liebknecht, Johannes Miquel, Karl Schurz, and, not the least noteworthy, Lothar Bucher and Moritz Busch, later to become the agents and confidants of the arch-reactionary Otto von Bismarck.

A generation later the fact that a man had been a revolutionary of 'forty-eight was to be a seal of distinction, but at the time fidelity to democratic ideals brought neither honour nor joy. Most of the better-known exiles, who had careers to return to when the time of persecution was overpast, found temporary refuge in England or Switzerland, but the majority of the less known and the unknown crossed the Atlantic and made in the United States a permanent and congenial home. German emigration to America heretofore had for the most part been the emigration of peasants and labourers, broken by poverty or harassed by intolerable feudal customs. With the discovery of this new and kinder fatherland across the seas, where to the wondering exile life seemed to be freedom and freedom life, new types of citizens, higher in social and intellectual status, joined the exodus in ever-increasing numbers, carrying with them education and skill, wealth and enterprise, and above all new hopes and the inspiring sentiment of gratitude of men to whom were offered, as an uncovenanted right, a larger outlook and a consciousness of security and fair-play which had been refused to them by the land of their birth.

CHAPTER III

(1851–1861)

BISMARCK—THE FIRST PHASE

THE history of the Bund and its Diet for the remaining years of their existence is in the main the history of a more concentrated struggle for leadership in Germany between the two States whose rivalry had been suspended for a brief breathing-space at Olmütz, Prussia renewing her claims as before, Austria tenaciously resisting any change that would diminish her power, not perceiving that by her refusal to concede a little she was risking the loss of all, nor conscious as yet that the superiority of which she boasted was no longer a reality but a phantom. That harmony and understanding would be restored between the rivals already seemed hopeless. They were like members of a family who could be good friends in other people's houses, only not at home. For while their interests as European Powers, if not always identical, were at least as a rule reconcilable, their interests as German States had become permanently antagonistic. They could not both be in the first place, and each of them knew that it was in the other's way.[1]

In his memoirs of that time Count Beust, who entered the Austrian State service too late to influence the course of events, for the catastrophe of 1866 had already occurred, professes to regard the Olmütz agreement as a blunder on Austria's part, and criticizes Schwarzenberg for neglecting to require from Prussia guarantees that the Radowitz Union project should not be revived. He contends that the Austrian Minister failed to appreciate the gravity of the issue involved, viz. whether Austria should continue a member of the Federation, and holds that this question should have been decided when she was still at the height

[1] Cf. Friedjung, *Der Kampf um die Vorherrschaft in Deutschland*, vol. i., p. 35.

of her strength.[1] All such argument ignores the really vital point, which was that the fundamental issue between Austria and Prussia was not one of federal reform or any constitutional theories, but of power. Guarantees, even if they could have been obtained, would have had value only so long as Austria had been able to enforce observance of them. Austria was still the head of the Federation and in full possession of her old privileged position. Whether that position was to remain unchallenged, however, depended not upon treaties and paper formulas, but upon proof of superior strength; and it was inevitable that, directly such proof was wanting, the leadership of Germany would pass out of her grasp and her ejection from the Federation follow.

There were already outsiders who clearly recognized whither events were tending, and who suspected that Prussia was stronger than the resolution of Frederick William IV and Austria weaker than the will of Schwarzenberg. Louis Napoleon suspected it in France, as did Prince Albert and Lord Palmerston, with greater certainty, in England. Visiting Germany in 1844, Lord Palmerston formed the opinion that Prussia even then had the nation's future in her hand. " One cannot visit the country," he wrote from Dresden on October 13th, " without being struck with the great intellectual activity which shows itself in all classes. . . . In short, Prussia is going to lead in German civilization, and as Austria has gone to sleep and will be long before she wakes, Prussia has a fine career open to her for many years to come." He even thought, five years later, that a blunder was committed when Frederick William IV, by refusing the imperial crown, delayed longer the inevitable hegemony of the northern kingdom. It is one of the contradictions of Palmerston's career that he subsequently failed, on more than one critical occasion, to reckon with Prussia according to his early and just valuation.

Not only did the two rivals fight each other within the Diet of the Federation, but they continued to force the rest of the States into partisanship. Austria, being in possession of the presidency, had on her side the advantage of treaty right and the sanction of tradition. Upon most questions she could count upon a majority, for not only did the secondary States as a rule work with her, but some of the smaller States seceded from Prussia and went over to the opposite camp. For a time, therefore, Olmütz seemed to make Austria's position in Germany

[1] *Memoirs*, vol. i., p. 101.

stronger than before. Where Prussia had a vital interest in breaking down or neutralizing her preponderating influence in the Diet it could only be done by skilful manœuvring or hard bargaining.

A change came in the relations of the two Powers when there appeared in the Diet in 1851, first as understudy to the Prussian envoy, Herr von Rochow (May 11th), then as plenipotentiary (July 15th), Otto von Bismarck. In him Prussia may be said to have recovered her lost will. A deputy in the Prussian United Diet of 1847, in the Prussian Diet of 1849, and in the German Parliament of Erfurt in 1850, and a King's man by descent and predilection, Bismarck very early seemed to be marked out for distinction in public life. In his own circles he was already spoken of as one of the coming men of the political world. He had first drawn upon himself the King's favourable notice in 1847 by his ultra-royalist utterances as a member of the United Diet. Since then his opinion had been held in high regard both by his Sovereign and the Government, and during the events which preceded Olmütz he had been called into counsel in Berlin. His knowledge of human nature, his geniality (when occasion required it), native shrewdness, and mother-wit, and above all his dominating will, born on the fertile soil of the feudal Mark of Brandenburg, singularly fitted him to be the representative at the Federal Diet of a Government which for the present had no hope of asserting its rightful place and gaining its ends save by judicious diplomacy and careful handling of men.

Only the Liberals saw his emergence from comparative obscurity with apprehension. His short career as a parliamentary deputy had justly given him the reputation of a typical reactionary, uncompromising in his attachment to the principle of monarchy by the grace of God and hostile to any concession to the idea of popular sovereignty. A man who could publicly confess that for him "Prussia's honour meant her abstinence from any shameful union with democracy" was not likely to enjoy the confidence of a party which had just tried conclusions with autocracy and had failed in the encounter.

In the Federal Palace and the social centres of Frankfort he had learned all there was to know about the tricks and stratagems, the subtleties and sophistries, the backbiting, eavesdropping, and intrigue which made up the stock-in-trade of the average German diplomat, and the result was that his opinion of the morality of the Diet was no higher than his opinion of its intellectual capacity. According to his later confessions he lived while at Frankfort in an atmosphere of mendacity. To his Austrian colleagues he was wont to say, " It is all the same to me whether you are speaking or the wind is whistling in the chimney-pots, for I do not believe a single word you say." What these colleagues said to him in return is not known, but they thought him bumptious, arrogant and overbearing, and herein did him no injustice. Certainly the members of the Frankfort Diet were not a happy or a harmonious circle.

" Intercourse here," Bismarck wrote from the federal city to his wife on May 18, 1851, " is at bottom nothing more than mutually distasteful espionage. All that people torment themselves about are trivialities, and these diplomats, with their pompous pettinesses, are already more ridiculous to me than the deputies of the (Prussian) Second Chamber in the consciousness of their dignity. No one, even the most malicious doubter of a democrat, can believe how much *charlatanerie* and pomposity is concealed in this diplomacy." " Heine's well-known song, ' O Bund, du Hund, du bist nicht gesund,' " he wrote to the same correspondent, " will soon become by universal consent the national song of Germany." If, in later years, in his practice of statecraft in a wider arena, Bismarck failed at times to play fairly and to run straight, some part of the blame should be set down to his depressing and demoralizing experiences of the sinuous diplomacy which flourished at Frankfort in the middle of the century.

Bismarck may have regarded the capitulation of Olmütz as unavoidable, as circumstances then were, but to him, as to all Prussian patriots, it was none the less a humiliation which could not be allowed to blemish the national reputation permanently. The episode epitomized for him with poignant faithfulness the entire Austro-Prussian, the entire German, problem. It was the eternal problem of political life and relations everywhere, *Suum cuique.* Within the sphere of federal government Austria claimed everything : how was Prussia to gain her rightful share of influence ? To that problem he was to address himself.

Before his Frankfort days he had been a member of the Great Germany party, and he had hitherto favoured the retention of Austria in the Federation. Almost his last words as a parliamentary deputy had been a frank declaration of his unaltered acceptance of the idea that Austria was " a German Power which had often and gloriously wielded the German sword." Nevertheless, he had taken care to add that Prussia's honour required that "nothing should happen in Germany without her assent, and that whatever Prussia and Austria, after independent deliberation, regarded as reasonable and politically right should be carried through by them as Powers equally responsible for Germany's protection."

Now that the duty of representing Prussia's interests at the Diet fell to him, he was still determined to work hand in hand with Austria, if possible, though he was equally determined that such co-operation should be on the basis of parity and mutual concession. He saw that Prussia must, at all costs, be freed from Austria's influence and pressure, and doubtful even then whether emancipation would be won without a military struggle, he held that it was Prussia's best policy to husband her strength. Holding that standpoint, he was determined to support in every situation a national policy based on sheer egoism.

For a time large events in European politics overshadowed the federal question and kept both Prussia and Austria occupied in other directions. The first of these events was the Crimean War, regarding which Prussia occupied a position of neutrality and isolation—a position which, however justifiable from the standpoint of national expediency, was certainly far from glorious. It was not the dispute of the Latin and Greek Churches about the Holy Places, nor yet the interests of Turkey's Christian populations, that drew Great Britain into that long and fruitless struggle, but jealousy of Muscovite aggression in the East and a vague fear that unless Russia were checked betimes she would become a danger to Europe. Ten years before, Czar Nicholas I had been urgent in his desire to work hand in hand with Great Britain in the Oriental question. It was in 1844 that he first spoke, in conversation with Lord Aberdeen and Sir Robert Peel, of the "Sick Man." He was then willing to see Great Britain established in Egypt and Crete if only Constantinople could be left in Turkish hands until Russia's hour for occupying it should arrive.

It is probable that the number is few of those who believe in this day that the British nation would have allowed itself to be drawn into that struggle had it had a firmer hand—or any hand at all—upon its own affairs, or understood more clearly the character of the influences which were working towards war. One of these was the intrigue of the wayward and disloyal ambassador at Constantinople, Lord Stratford de Redcliffe, long "the voice of England in the East," who systematically disobeyed his instructions and encouraged Turkey to resist Russia's demands by unwarrantable pledges that British support would be forthcoming. Sir James Graham, in August, 1853, warned his colleague, Lord Clarendon, the Foreign Secretary, of the dangerous game which the ambassador was playing, and urged that the Government should be ready to supersede him "without loss of a day." Clarendon himself wrote to Lord John Russell in October that the ambassador had "never entered seriously into the views of the Government and had been making political capital for himself," and again in November that he was "bent on war." There was no secrecy whatever about Stratford's duplicity—everybody knew it—yet he was nevertheless allowed to remain at his post until the mischief had been done.

It may be true that Russia wanted war with Turkey, but Stratford had determined long before that she should have war with Turkey's friends as well, and that in Oriental policy British Ministers should go his way. Perhaps it was Lord Palmerston's way as well, for that statesman was widely believed to be behind him in the conspiracy. Count Vitzthum's opinion of Stratford is interesting as that of a fellow-diplomat: "Scarcely ever has an ambassador played such a *rôle* as Lord Stratford at that time, for he ruled not only in Constantinople but in London." On the other hand, France had sent as her representative to the Bosphorus the impetuous M. Lavalette, with the tacit commission that if events did not shape themselves for war he should give them the necessary assistance. Between them the two ambassadors had no difficulty in making trouble.

Louis Napoleon, too, played the game of diplomacy singularly well at England's expense. Cosmopolitan in education and training—for he had studied life and mankind in five countries besides his own, in England, America, Germany, Italy, and Switzerland—this enigmatical man had a positive genius for politics, and he would have made a reputation in that sphere even without the assistance of a distinguished kinship. A Bonaparte more than a Frenchman, the birthmark of the adventurer was upon him, and the spell of the Great Napoleon lured him from an early age into dangerous ways. He had taken part in two insurrections before he was thirty—in the Romagna in 1831 and at Strassburg in 1836. Transported to America for complicity in the second of these, he made a third attempt at a rising in 1840, when he landed at Boulogne, and for punishment was compelled to sojourn for six years, a prisoner, in the "land of Ham." Escaping to London, he remained there until he was able to return to France as a free man in the year of revolutions, 1848. Since his invasion of the sphere of high politics his rise to fame had been uncommonly rapid. Returned a member of the National Assembly in June 1848, he was elected President of the Republic in the following December; three years later, again in December, after a daring *coup d'état*, which gave him a more pliant legislature, he obtained re-election for ten years by an overwhelming vote; and after a further interval of a year, once more in December, the Prince-President was proclaimed hereditary Emperor as Napoleon III (December 2, 1852).

The *coup d'état* of Paris of 1851 was followed by a *coup d'état* in London, for without seeking the authority either of his Sovereign or his colleagues, because knowing that it would be refused, the Foreign Secretary, the wilful, rash, intemperate, great-hearted Palmerston, promptly acknowledged Napoleon's new status, an act of indiscretion for which he was required to resign office. As a rule, the full significance of acts of national policy is seen only in later years. It is certain that England's ready endorsement of Louis Napoleon's *coup d'état* strengthened the ties of friendship between her and France and paved the way for the conclusion of the alliance which made the two countries comrades in arms in the Crimean War, but it is also arguable that a less cordial recognition of the Emperor might have made that war impossible, since France could not or would not have waged it alone.

Never before had a British statesman been questioned by his Sovereign upon maxims of statecraft as was Lord Granville, the succeeding Minister, by Queen Victoria, who, alarmed by Lord Palmerston's escapade, urgently wished to know what the foreign policy of her Government really was and by what principles it was guided. "The Queen, considering times to have now changed, thinks that there is no reason why we should any longer confine ourselves to mere abstract principles, such as non-intervention in the internal affairs of other countries, moral support to liberal institutions, protection to British subjects, etc., etc." To this challenge, of which the real authorship could not have been uncertain, Lord Granville gave the reply, at that time so truly and pathetically British, that "it is not the policy of this country to make engagements except in view of the circumstances of the moment."

Nevertheless, it was not long before the British Cabinet was blindly abandoning itself to Napoleon's leading, and the pace quickened when, within a year, Palmerston was recalled to office as Home Secretary in Lord Aberdeen's ill-fated Ministry (December 1852), in which Lord John Russell and Lord Clarendon were successively Foreign Secretary. Trading astutely on the nation's fear of Russian aggression in the East, and its superstitious concern for the integrity of the Turkish Empire in Europe, Napoleon gradually drew England into the orbit of French policy, and henceforth their course was identical, and it made directly for war. Foreign distractions were at that time, if not a necessity, at least a convenience to the new Emperor. He had to cover up the recent *coup d'état*; the thirst for prestige was already upon him; and he welcomed an opportunity for trying the spirit and efficiency of his army. He had declared at Bordeaux (October 9, 1852): "Certain persons say the Empire is only war. But I say the Empire is peace (*l'empire c'est la paix*), for France wishes it." He understood the volatile emotions of his countrymen too well, however, to be in any doubt that their love of tranquillity was at the time a pose, and that a successful war would be more popular than a humdrum peace.

The Crimean campaign was both designed and decided on by Napoleon; England came in because for safety's sake he needed an ally. Lord Aberdeen, as the leader of the "moral influence" party in his Cabinet, earnestly strove to curb the warlike proclivities of Palmerston and Russell, but in the end he, too, succumbed to the dominating influences. It was literally true, as Aberdeen and Clarendon both said, that England "drifted" into that great blunder; never was war more lightly trifled with; never were the objects of a war less carefully considered, its chances less carefully weighed, or its prosecution less carefully planned. Later, Aberdeen wrote (1857) that the war, though "most unwise and unnecessary," was "strictly justifiable in itself," yet he confessed, "It is possible that by a little more energy and vigour . . . in Downing Street it might have been prevented"; and to the last that tragedy of errors lay heavily upon his sensitive conscience. An enterprise entered upon with such an absence of reflection and honest conviction could not have gone well. Nevertheless, the nation unquestionably welcomed the war, at first apathetically, but enthusiastically when once its patriotic and militant instincts had been roused; for forty years of peace had dulled its perception of the horrors of the battlefield, and made it ready to endorse this method of settling a dispute over issues which it never understood.

Russian troops had crossed the Pruth into Moldavia in July 1853, and as her demand for their withdrawal was disregarded, Turkey declared war upon the aggressor on October 5th. Hostilities broke out at once between these Powers, but it was not until the following March that France and Great Britain actively took the Turkish side. Foreseeing where events were tending, Prussia and Austria concluded a convention (April 20, 1854) by which they agreed to stand aside as onlookers but to put armies in the field if their own interests required it. Soon it became clear that this Laodicean attitude pleased neither side, and both from the East and the West came the demand that the two Powers should declare themselves either cold or hot. The Court and Government in Berlin were divided upon the question of Prussia's obligation and interest in the matter, though the overwhelming weight of influence was on the side of neutrality. That was hardly in accordance with the expectation of the Czar, who, when asked in 1853 by the British Ambassador in St. Petersburg what Prussia would do were he to go to war, replied at once that she " would approve as a matter of course." Accustomed as he had been to give to Prussia her marching orders, as he had so lately done at Olmütz, it seemed inconceivable that his vassal would fail him in the critical moment. Both before the outbreak of the war and later the Czar made strenuous efforts to attract to his side both Prussia and Austria, basing his claim to the latter's reciprocal help upon the great service which he had rendered to the Emperor in the suppression of the Hungarian revolution, but it was in vain. How far the two German Great Powers might have restrained their old ally had they been seriously disposed to do so, is a question which has been much discussed. It is at least probable—and there are German writers who accept the view—that if at the outset they had resolutely discouraged the Czar from embarking upon a course of action in which they were not prepared to support him, he would have drawn back and peace might have been preserved.

Frederick William IV, in particular, has been severely judged for a neutrality which was throughout so much more benevolent to Russia than to the Western Powers. His position, however, was one of great difficulty. He had to choose between three conflicting sentiments—loyalty to his brother-in-law the Czar and the dynastic tie between the two countries ; loyalty to and a desire to co-operate with Austria, the head of the Germanic family, whose union with the Western Powers was probable ;

and a weaker though still real sympathy for England as a Protestant Power, whose Sovereign he sincerely revered. Of these contending influences the most powerful was that which drew him towards Russia, and recalling the injunction contained in his father's will, "Do not neglect to promote unity between the European Powers; above all, may Prussia, Russia, and Austria never separate from each other," this was the influence which prevailed.[1] Even had it been insufficient, two other considerations would have made it impossible for him to join the allies; one was his strong prejudice against Napoleon as the representative of a revolutionary order of ideas, and the other his repugnance to the idea of Christians fighting Christians with the aid and in support of a Mohammedan Power. Secretly also he entertained the hope that it might be his privilege to come upon the scene at the proper time as a mediator—a part more consonant with his feelings as a Christian King than that of a combatant.

Prussia had certainly no obvious interest in adopting an attitude of active antagonism against Russia, the extension of whose influence in the East she had not even Austria's reasons for fearing, and the expectation that she would as a matter of course fall into line with the Western Powers had no other justification than the accepted tradition that Prussia had no right to have a policy of her own in European affairs. On the other hand, what was open to justifiable reproach in her action at that time was the fact that while professing neutrality Prussia in effect rendered to Russia every service in her power. While making fair speeches to the allies, the King was all the time assuring the Czar of his unchanging fidelity. The younger Niebuhr, his private secretary, wrote with scholarly pedantry: "I cannot indeed reproach our policy with lack of outward truth, but I do charge it with insincerity towards ourselves" (August 22, 1854). The fact was that, however much might have been said for an attitude of strict and impartial passivity, the double policy actually followed lacked truth both in the inward and outward parts.

Political parties were divided on the subject. The Liberals

[1] Baron Stockmar wrote in March 1854: "Prussia—unfortunate country! The King is under Russian sway, partly from fear of Russia, partly from a senseless sentimental feeling for its Emperor, as representative of the Holy Alliance. . . . The Court party is, partly from habit, partly from self-interest, similarly devoted to Russia; it adores the Emperor as the champion of reaction, and sees in his weakening its own fall."

in general welcomed the hope of seeing a blow struck at Russia, as the stronghold of reaction, wished Prussia to assist in a proceeding so desirable, and were distressed beyond measure when it became clear that their country was not to be the active ally of Western progress, but its surreptitious antagonist. To the Conservatives, on the other hand, the Czar appealed as the only sure bulwark on the Continent against revolution and because his Government was still what they wished that of Prussia to become again, an unmitigated autocracy, and their sympathies were, therefore, altogether on Russia's side. Both of these parties had powerful allies in the Press, the pro-Russian case being advocated, as of old, by the *Kreuzzeitung* and the anti-Russian case by the *Preussisches Wochenblatt*, a journal which came into prominence about this time as the organ of the Bethmann-Hollweg, Goltz, and Pourtalès group.

Many of the extremer feudalists openly advocated a defensive alliance with the Czar in opposition to the Western Powers, obnoxious because of their Liberal institutions, even more than to Turkey. The most prominent member of this party opposed any such heroic display of principle. This was Herr von Bismarck, Prussia's envoy at Frankfort, whose influence both in the Federal Diet and in Berlin was exerted in favour of a policy of strict neutrality. The immediate interests involved in the war were no concern of his ; all he cared for was how Prussia might benefit by the coming confusion and the later readjustments. An opportunist standpoint, neither strong nor ingenuous, was avowed in the advice which he gave to Manteuffel during the war : " We should make it doubtful as to our joining Russia or the Western Powers, and this would increase our influence on the course of events." All the time he was determined to do his best to prevent Prussia from taking sides either actively or passively against the Czar. Already he was considering the help which Prussia might need in coming years in the solution of her own national problems, and viewing the question from this standpoint he was convinced that the friendship of Russia was for Prussia essential. Comparing the advantages offered as allies by Russia, France, and Austria, he wrote : " We must look abroad for allies, and among the European Powers Russia is to be had on the cheapest terms ; she wishes only to grow in the East, the two others wish to grow at our expense." Throughout the negotiations Bismarck was constantly being called to Berlin by the King, in order to advise Manteuffel and keep him in the path of unwavering neutrality whenever he showed a disposition to deviate towards the Western Powers.[1]

The war did not prosper as the allies had hoped, for the task before them proved for a long time greater than their powers. As time went by, and no decisive result was reached, the pressure of the Western Powers upon Russia's neighbours increased. Every argument and inducement they could think of was used to persuade Austria and Prussia to abandon their attitude of embarrassing neutrality for one of active co-operation, with a view to the speedy end of the conflict, but without effect.

Amongst the King's advisers [2] one man at least was altogether convinced that his country was not doing its duty in thus standing aside. This was the Prince of Prussia, whose letters to Count Bernstorff on the Crimean War are in tone, temper, and manly spirit among the most statesmanlike documents he ever penned. He had no wish to see Russia unduly weakened, but he regarded her pretensions as a menace to the rest of Europe, and was wishful that she should be required to recognize that there were limits beyond which she could not be allowed to go. In a letter of August 1, 1854, he protested against "the dishonest and uncertain course we have adopted, which is the reason why I must give up taking any further part in affairs." "There can be nothing more difficult," he wrote later, "than to have to defend a policy which offers so few points capable of being defended." He was troubled by apprehensions as to how Prussia would stand after the war. "Our position will be most awkward," he wrote, "since we want to remain merely spectators of the drama, and if we succeed in this who will inquire about the spectators when the play is over? It is only the actors who are concerned in the success of the piece." To make the family division more complete, while the Queen was just as devoted to Russia as was her

[1] For evidence on the point see Bismarck's speeches in the Imperial Diet on February 19, 1878, and February 6, 1888; also his *Reflections and Reminiscences*, where he speaks of "one of the crises in which the King had summoned me to Berlin to aid him against Manteuffel" (vol. i., p. 123); and again, "the King frequently sent for me to frighten the Minister when he would not agree with him" (*ibid.*, p. 139).

[2] To these Moltke, the later Field-Marshal and famous strategist, could not yet be counted, but he wrote on January 25, 1854: "It seems to me that the German Powers are playing a pitiable *rôle*. Obviously any further increase of Russia's power is more dangerous to them than to others, yet they are leaving the Western Powers to pull the chestnuts out of the fire. That will never be forgiven us, and our prestige in Europe will not thereby be increased" (*Briefe des General-Feldmarschalls Grafen Helmuth von Moltke*, vol. i., p. 153).

husband, and far less discriminating in her manner of showing it, the wife of the Prince of Prussia was warmly attached to the cause of the Western Powers.

Manteuffel in theory agreed with the Prince, but if his spirit was often willing, his flesh was always weak. He pronounced the strongest possible judgment upon the equivocal policy for which he was responsible when he admitted in a despatch to Count Bernstorff that if Prussia followed consistency or conviction she would take the side of the allies. " Prussia," he said, " though by no means always sharing the views of the Western Powers, and therefore not disposed to acquiesce in the demands arising therefrom, where she does not esteem such demands to be consonant with her own interests, is yet far from denying that fundamentally she is in agreement with the Western Powers." Manteuffel's maxim was " Cold blood and not too much action." " I cannot understand," he wrote on May 27, 1854, " the shortsightedness of many people who are eternally urging resolution. This resolution would mean nothing else than the surrender of the Prussian standpoint and self-sacrifice for one of the two parties." Yet all the time neutral Prussia was freely exporting arms to Russia, insomuch that France threatened a blockade of the Baltic ports, and in the middle of the war a Russian loan was floated in Berlin.

Both in England and France the feeling against Prussia was a bitter one, for the two nations felt keenly that Prussia was not playing fairly. In February, 1855, Lord John Russell went to Berlin in the hope of moving the King by earnest expostulation, but convincing himself on his arrival there that an interview would be futile, he did not seek it, and returned home without presenting his credentials. So far did the King's bias for Russia carry him that he dismissed Bunsen, Bonin, and other advisers who had made themselves objectionable to St. Petersburg. Even when Austria at last (December, 1854) joined the allies, Prussia continued to stand out and to neutralize their efforts. Invited on December 16th by the three Powers jointly to throw in her lot with them, there seemed for a moment a chance that this step would be taken, but as soon as Manteuffel professed to be willing the King again refused, and showed greater alacrity in assuring the Czar that he had resisted temptation than in communicating his decision to the other Powers. Manteuffel's defence was that if Prussia had joined it would have been as a " mere appendix to Austria." Lord Clarendon told Count

Bernstorff that his country had in fact become " a Russian province," adding bluntly that the policy followed by his Government was " neither European nor German nor yet Prussian." By this time Piedmont had joined the allies with a small force (January, 1855), less from interest in the questions in dispute than from a desire to win her spurs in a European struggle and to establish claims to reciprocal service in the cause of Italian unity.

The Czar's death on March 2, 1855, was the occasion of further efforts to accelerate the lagging steps of peace ; yet still the war dragged on, and it was only on the fall of Sebastopol in September, after a siege of 350 days, that the worn-out combatants agreed to cease hostilities.

Prussia by her equivocal methods had earned another Olmütz, and the allied Powers did not spare her humiliation. " If when a peace is arrived at," the Prince Consort of England wrote in March, 1854, " to which Prussia has in no way contributed, but in the way of which she, on the contrary, acted as a stumbling-block, she should then set up claims, she will he astounded at the manner in which they will be received." Prussia did set up claims, and the effect was that which had been predicted. When a conference to consider conditions of peace had been agreed upon and the Berlin Government claimed to be admitted as of right, the claim was promptly refused. The Prince of Prussia at least was conscious that the rebuff was well merited, though it deeply hurt his pride. " How can we possibly be trusted ? " he wrote : " we are already paying for our shifty behaviour." When Count Bernstorff protested to Lord Palmerston, who early in 1855 had formed his first Ministry, that England would yet be glad to welcome Prussia as an ally, Palmerston answered surlily : " Prussia never wants to approach England unless she needs help, so that we are perfectly well able to do without her." After Austria had withdrawn opposition to Prussia's admission, France and England still resisted, and though, in the end, she was allowed to be represented, it was only on the King's urgent entreaty and by sufferance. " More than this," wrote the Prince of Prussia, " we could not properly expect nor demand, since we never had the courage to agree to the conditions which the enemy had accepted. So that although we at last desisted from our course of not very immaculate policy, we have still come off with a black eye." The humiliation rankled in Bismarck's mind for long years. He was for playing a Coriolanus part, and keeping away from the conference—for renouncing a favour of which the acceptance meant certain loss of dignity.[1]

The terms of peace were embodied in the Treaty of Paris of March 30, 1856. The stipulations included the integrity of the Ottoman Empire, the neutralization of the Black Sea and its opening to commerce, the prohibition of ships of war within that water and of Russian or Turkish arsenals upon its shores, and the retention by the Danubian Principalities of existing rights under Turkey, under the guarantee of the Powers. On the other hand, the Sultan renewed his unsubstantial promises—no guarantees were offered—of better government for his Christian subjects. Count Beust relates that on returning from Paris the French ambassador to Vienna, Baron Bourqueney, summed up the treaty in the words, " Quand vous lisez ce traité vous vous demandez, quel est le vaincu, quel est le vainqueur ? " Events were to prove that it accomplished little and settled nothing. Lord Palmerston gave the Black Sea clauses in particular a life of fourteen years at the most, and therein he prophesied truly. Both Great Britain and France renounced territorial claims—the latter unwillingly—and when the Government of Piedmont rashly advanced them, it was bidden to be content with a purely moral reward.[2]

Great Britain and France were equally glad to be out of a struggle which brought them no glory, asserted no high principle, and achieved no lasting purpose of good, but their blunders and misfortunes did not mitigate the egoism of the part played by Prussia, whose abstention was dictated not by moral scruples, or any fine balancing of right and wrong, but by a calculated expediency. What Bismarck thought privately of his countrymen, whom he had done his best to compromise, appears from a letter written by him in the following year to Ludwig von Gerlach (May 2, 1857), in which he said : " We are the best-natured and least dangerous of politicians, yet in reality no one trusts us ; we are regarded as uncertain as allies and harmless as enemies."

On the whole Great Britain lost most by the war. Soon

[1] Recalling this episode in a speech in the Imperial Diet on February 6, 1888, Bismarck said that it was for Prussia " a sort of Canossa. . . . We were under no necessity to pretend to be a greater Power than we were and to sign the treaties of that time. But we ' ante-chambered,' and in the end were allowed to sign. That will never happen to us again."

[2] When Cavour pressed for a territorial reward, Lord Clarendon replied that the Italians " must be satisfied with the glory they had acquired and the high honour their conduct had conferred upon them " (Greville's *Journal of the Reign of Queen Victoria from* 1852 *to* 1860, vol. i., p. 301).

France cruelly jilted her. The Emperor had found unattractive an alliance which had bound him not to seek territorial advantages, and he resented his emergence from the exhausting struggle without material gain. Fearing that Great Britain would continue to place a brake upon his ambitions, he gave a ready response to Russia's advances, and soon his late enemy stood nearer to him than his late ally. In September, 1857, the Czar Alexander II and Napoleon met at Stuttgart as friends. For Great Britain, however, the war produced a crop of further troubles with Russia, the end of which came only half a century later. Only Turkey remained her friend, and Turkey's attachment was never other than an embarrassment, for it carried with it grave responsibilities and perplexities.

Having during the Crimean War asserted independence of Austria by refusing to be drawn into the alliance with her against Russia, Prussia now became bolder and in the Italian campaign of 1859 allowed her rival to experience the distress of complete isolation. No Power ever went to war hampered by a larger moral handicap of European antipathy than Austria when on April 27, 1859, her troops crossed the Ticino and entered the dominions of the King of Sardinia. Just a month before, Lord Derby, the British Prime Minister, had hazarded the opinion that "the prospects of peace have never been so bright as to-day," words anticipatory of a similar and still more unfortunate prophecy made by the British Foreign Office in 1870. War had been brewing for many months, and all the rest of the world was expecting it. Austria's act was a formal declaration of hostility against the Italian unity movement, and it drew upon her the opprobrium of all friends of nationalism and liberty. Lord Palmerston, the friend of "struggling nationalities," faithfully reflected English sentiment towards Austria in words written to Lord Granville on January 30th. "As for myself," he said, "I am very Austrian north of the Alps, but very anti-Austrian south of the Alps. The Austrians have no business in Italy, and they are a public nuisance there. They govern their own provinces ill, and are the props and encouragers of bad government in all the other States of the Peninsula except in Piedmont, where fortunately they have no influence." Austria, however, held her Italian territories in virtue of the Treaty of Vienna of 1815, under which she regained the provinces which for a time had been lost to France, and being a party to that treaty, England was bound to neutrality.

Louis Napoleon had no such scruple. He had made the cause of Italian unity his own and had left Austria in no doubt that any attack upon the King of Sardinia would be regarded as a declaration of war against himself. Already in foreign politics Napoleon had begun to play with certain master phrases, like "nationality," "equilibrium," and the policy of "compensations." His devotion to the cause of nationality was sincere and sometimes unselfish. It showed that he shared to the full the Frenchman's enthusiasm for great ideas, and it also seemed to place him in the direct line of his illustrious ancestor, who built new kingdoms upon the ruins of old empires. In espousing the Italian question, however, Napoleon had two ends to serve—Italy's and his own. Meeting Cavour at Plombières by arrangement on July 20, 1858, he agreed with him upon a plan of which the ostensible object was the emancipation of Lombardy from the Austrian lords of misrule, though it was a condition that France was to acquire Nice and Savoy as the price of her services. A third but essential part of the agreement was the marriage of Prince Napoleon with Princess Clothilde, daughter of Victor Emmanuel. The meeting had to the last been veiled with the secrecy that befitted its purpose. The French Foreign Minister himself was unaware of it, for in the midst of the interview there arrived a telegram from Walewski informing the Emperor that "Cavour was at Plombières."[1] The Chancelleries of Europe only learned at a later date exactly what was arranged at that time, but already suspicion of Napoleon's territorial greed was creating widespread uneasiness. These suspicions the Emperor himself did little to allay, in spite of his reiterated intention to "respect treaties." "I have no ambitious views like the first Emperor," he told Lord Cowley at that time, "but if other countries gain anything France must gain something also."

On January 1, 1859, at his New Year reception of the Diplomatic Corps, Napoleon said to the Austrian ambassador, Baron Hübner, that "although the relations between the two Empires were not such as he could desire, he begged to assure the Emperor

[1] Related by M. de Mazade in his book *Le Comte de Cavour*. Napoleon faithfully adhered to the maxim of his greater relative, who "never gave full confidence to any one." He told the Prince Consort of England on the latter's visit to him at Boulogne in September, 1854, that "he did not allow his Ministers to meet or discuss matters together—that they transacted their business solely with him. He rarely told the one what he had settled with the other" (Martin's *Life of the Prince Consort,* vol. iii., p. 110). A curious illustration of Napoleon's secretiveness towards his Ministers is related by Greville in his *Journal of the Reign of Queen Victoria from* 1852 *to* 1860, vol. i., p. 311.

of Austria that his personal feelings towards his Majesty remained unaltered." Europe mentally reversed the order of the phrases, in order to give them their due significance, and awaited the sequel with anxiety. Victor Emmanuel promptly responded to his partner's lead. In opening the Piedmont Chamber a few days later he said: "Our horizon is not clear . . . for while we would respect treaties we cannot remain insensible to the cry of anguish which reaches us from so many parts of Italy." Everywhere the words were interpreted as giving substance to Napoleon's vague suggestions of coming disturbance. Good advice was freely offered to all the three rulers concerned by disinterested friends, and had it been heeded peace might have been preserved. The Prince (now Prince Regent) of Prussia guardedly but pointedly urged both Austria and France to refrain from provocative action in any direction, and above all not to interfere with existing treaties. The same pacific influence was offered by Great Britain. While Queen Victoria and the Prince Consort used all their powers of persuasion upon Napoleon, the Government sought to restrain Austria.

On January 12th Lord Malmesbury, the Foreign Secretary, addressed through Lord Augustus Loftus, the British ambassador in Vienna, a grave warning to the Austrian Government imploring it to cultivate good relations with France, to co-operate heartily in the carrying out of the necessary reforms in the Central Italian States, and generally to abstain from any interference of an aggressive character in Italian affairs. The arrogant and self-willed Count Buol-Schauenstein had become President of the Council and Foreign Secretary on Schwarzenberg's death (April 5, 1852), and with true Austrian reluctance to face facts, he ignored the warning. "I know of no Italian question," he told the ambassador. "I can understand a Danish or a Swedish, but I recognize no Italian question." He also refused to negotiate for the removal of Austrian troops from the Roman States, remarking: "We entered those States without any previous arrangement with France, and we can leave them in like manner." Buol forgot that intruders who, though they may have entered by the door, neglect to withdraw betimes, have often to make a violent exit by the window. Urged by Loftus to give at least the assurance that Austria would not move a soldier across the Italian frontier without previous agreement with France, he flatly declined to do so. A special mission to Vienna, undertaken at his Government's request by Lord Cowley, then British ambassador in Paris, failed to produce the hoped-for conciliatory effect.

Towards the end of March the proposal of a European congress was made by Russia with Napoleon's acquiescence, and the prospects of peace seemed for a moment to become brighter when the British and French Governments agreed to press upon Austria and Sardinia a scheme of disarmament. Sorely against his will Cavour accepted the proposal, albeit hoping that Austria would reject it. For Cavour wanted war, convinced that the hour had come for striking the blow that was to win for his country independence. He was also prepared to pay the full price of so great a victory: for he did not want national liberty as a gift. Just before war broke out he wrote to the Italian General La Marmora: "In order that the war may reach a fortunate issue we must prepare for greater efforts. Woe to us if we triumph solely by the aid of France." Austria's refusal of a congress except on her own terms made it certain that Cavour's wish would be gratified.

On April 19th Count Buol peremptorily called upon the King of Sardinia to disarm, and threatened that failing compliance within three days Austrian troops would enter his territory. Knowing that France was behind him, the King refused, and the threat was duly carried out. Now Napoleon was as good as his word. Receiving Austria's invasion of Piedmont as a direct challenge, he responded to it with masterly promptness. Despatching one force of 40,000 men by sea, he hurried a second across the Alps to the help of Victor Emmanuel's menaced army, and it entered Piedmont at the end of April. On May 3rd Napoleon formally declared war on Austria. A succession of small engagements culminated in the decisive French victory of Magenta (June 4th), followed closely by that of Solferino (June 24th), and within a month Austria found herself hopelessly outclassed and beaten.

The Emperor Francis Joseph had already urgently sought help from Prussia, and sought it as a right even more than a favour. His idea was that a German army should occupy Napoleon on the Rhine, leaving Austria to settle with Sardinia alone, as she had done to such purpose at Novara ten years before. His invitation had been supported by the Governments of most of the secondary States, which regarded Prussia as bound in duty to lead them in a concerted expedition for the relief of their hard-pressed ally. Only Prussia had held back, the

Prince Regent imposing the condition that he should have command of the whole of the German federal forces, while the Emperor was willing to concede to him only a joint command. So much time was lost over negotiations that by the time Prussia seemed willing to move Napoleon had completed the work of conquest, and it was too late for help to be of use.

Disgusted at what he regarded as Prussia's treachery, fearing also that worse defeat than he had already sustained might permanently compromise Austria's position in Germany and correspondingly increase the prestige of Prussia, Francis Joseph hastily concluded the Peace of Villafranca (July 11th), by which he ceded the greater part of Lombardy to Napoleon for retrocession to Sardinia, but retained Venetia subject to the condition that it became part of a Confederation of Italian States, of which the Pope was to be the honorary President. The dispossessed rulers of Parma, Modena, and Tuscany were to have been restored to their thrones, but in face of the strong national spirit prevailing this proved impossible, and these territories were shortly afterwards incorporated in Sardinia.[1]

The unity party in Italy had counted on a war to a finish, and the war was to have seen the extrusion of Austria from the peninsula. At the time, therefore, the Peace of Villafranca created great disappointment. Cavour condemned it bitterly, and resigned rather than be a party to it.[2] Napoleon had declared his intention to "free Italy from the Alps to the Adriatic." After Magenta he had still addressed to the Italians from Milan the seductive words, "Animated by the sacred fire of patriotism, be soldiers to-day, for to-morrow you will be citizens of a great country." Even now, in a proclamation to his army, he spoke of Italy as "henceforth the mistress of her own destinies." Italian patriots, however, only saw that Napoleon had alone determined the conditions of peace and that these conditions left their country still far from unification or freedom. The likelihood is that the Emperor never once wished Italy to be completely unified. His idea was that she should be divided into a northern and a southern kingdom, with a papal enclave between, as a sort of buffer State. The Peace of Villafranca was duly confirmed at Zurich in

[1] "The disposal of the Tuscans and Modenese," Lord John Russell wrote in September, "as if they were so many firkins of butter is somewhat too profligate."

[2] Before many months Cavour recalled his condemnations. "The military and political campaign following that treaty," he wrote to Prince Napoleon, "has done more for Italy than the military campaign which preceded it. . . . Blessed be the Peace of Villafranca!"

November. In the midst of the war, of which one result was that Italy ceased to be, in Metternich's words, " une expression géographique," that aged statesman passed out of a world with whose political ideas he had no longer anything in common (June 11th), and knowing that even his own Neapolitan dukedom had become an anachronism.

The chagrin of the Italian people was increased when in due time Napoleon sent in his bill, the charge being the cession of Nice and Savoy, according to the agreement of Plombières. Not Italy only but all Europe condemned this transaction as an outrage upon political morality and public law. In claiming these territories, Napoleon, indeed, spoke speciously of the " natural " and " historical " frontiers of France, but the world at large regarded his act in its true light, as one of spoliation. Cavour was never proud of the bargain which he had struck at Plombières, and he gave to it the proper label when he said to Baron de Talleyrand, as the latter signed the formal treaty of cession on Napoleon's behalf, " Et maintenant vous voilà nos complices ! " For the sake of appearances the Emperor submitted the question of the future overlordship of the acquired territories to a *plébiscite*. France was then in virtual possession, however, and the manufacture of public opinion was not difficult, so that the overwhelming vote of approval which she received had no great moral value. The historian Freeman stated the truth of this transaction fairly when he said that for half a day's work Napoleon had taken two days' pay.

The episode of Savoy and Nice showed Napoleon to the world in his true colours as a conspirator against the territorial settlement of the Continent as confirmed by the Congress of Vienna. He had not long been Emperor before he had sprung upon Europe all sorts of disquieting schemes of annexation. M. Guizot wrote of him to Lord Aberdeen on December 21, 1851 : " Comme la situation deviendra difficile, comme il a l'esprit chimérique et rêveur, il se pourrait bien qu'un jour, pour échapper à ses embarras intérieurs, il rêvât et cherchât quelque remaniement territorial qui relevât sa popularité. Peut-être même rêve-t-il déjà." He had, indeed, even then set his imagination to work, for he was a born intriguer, and so long as he had to do with intellects of the second rank he invariably intrigued with success.[1] In 1852 he suggested to Schwarzenberg

[1] Lord Malmesbury records in his Diary a conversation with Louis Napoleon on March 30, 1849, in which the then Prince-President spoke of "the absolute

a bold project of partition generously devised so as to give each of the Continental Great Powers something. Austria was to have Moldavia and Wallachia, Prussia Hanover and Oldenburg, Russia Constantinople, and France the Rhine frontier and Belgium. His ingenuity in disposing of other nations' territory was similarly exercised in relation to Africa ; for five years later, when at Osborne (August, 1857), he suggested to the Prince Consort of England that Morocco should go to Spain, a part of Tripoli to Sardinia, Egypt to England, and a part of Syria to Austria. His idea was that the Mediterranean should become, not a French lake as his uncle had planned, but a European, the whole of the African littoral passing into the possession of the appropriate Continental Powers ; only Germany was not at that time to have a share.

These wholesale proposals were of a speculative character, however, and perhaps intended only to afford the pretext for his really serious design, which was the recovery of the eastern frontier of France as it was prior to the second Peace of Paris of November 20, 1815. Napoleon's hope of regaining the Rhenish territories then restored to Germany increased with the conclusion of the alliance with Great Britain at the time of the Crimean War. Upon that alliance he built many schemes which were fated not to be realized. In sundry conversations with Lord Clarendon, the British Foreign Secretary, during the war, and particularly in 1856, he had asked if Great Britain would acquiesce in the holding of a European Congress " pour remanier les traités et la carte de l'Europe," which meant for France the pushing forward of her frontier eastwards. Clarendon did his utmost to dissuade him from entertaining any such illusory idea, but on each occasion with only momentary success. To the Prince Consort in August of the following year he spoke of his wish to see the treaties of 1815 revised : " they were bad," he said, " they had been frequently infringed, and they remained as a memorial of the union of Europe against France." He then advanced a claim to the Palatinate, the fortress of Landau, Saarbrücken, and Saarlouis. Warned by the Prince that he was venturing upon treacherous ground, he refrained from further pressing his views, yet without relinquishing the hope of their fulfilment, though convinced that for support he

necessity of modifying the treaties of 1815," hinted that "France and England together could remodel everything," and assured him that France would not be jealous if England gained more power in Egypt (*Memoirs of an ex-Minister*, 1885 edition, p. 180).

must look elsewhere. Already he had made overtures in another quarter—Prussia.

In the seizure of Savoy and Nice the Emperor's designs against his neighbours' landmarks took for the first time practical shape. No European statesman had been on more confidential terms with Napoleon, or had done him better service, than Lord Palmerston, but even his faith and patience were now exhausted. It was Palmerston's indignant protests and not John Bright's "Perish Savoy!" speech which voiced the true mind of England over the affair. "The Emperor's mind," he wrote to Lord Cowley in April, 1860, "seems as full of schemes as a warren is full of rabbits, and like rabbits his schemes go to ground for the moment to avoid notice or antagonism." When in the previous month the French special envoy to London, Count Flahault, on the eve of his departure for Paris, asked what message he might take back to Napoleon, Palmerston bluntly told him that he suspected his master of playing a double game and that if he wanted war with England he could have it, adding the assurance that the result would not be to his liking. "France," he wrote later in the same year (November 2nd), "is an essential element in the balance of power in Europe and, I may say, in the world. All that we want is that France should be content with what she is, and should not take up the schemes and policy of the first Napoleon, which many things of late lead us to think she has an inclination to do." The unrest caused by Napoleon's territorial manœuvring became at last so great that in the summer of 1860 Lord John Russell on behalf of Great Britain concluded a formal agreement with the Prussian and Austrian Governments, whereby each of the three Powers pledged itself to make known to the others any proposal affecting the existing equilibrium of Europe which came to its knowledge.

Prussia's part in the Italian war has never ceased to afford material for controversy. What was the real explanation of her failure to intervene in Austria's behalf? Two theories have been advanced, and both of them will always have adherents. One is that Prussia's abstention was deliberate, and was a retaliatory measure intended to avenge long years of insult and humiliation, to pay back old scores, compel Austria to experience the mortification of isolation, and so bring home to her the value and advisability of Prussia's friendship. According to this view, Prussia wanted Austria to be beaten, and purposely delayed action until help was too late. Bismarck was amongst those of the King's advisers who were in favour of desertion pure and simple. He had no desire to see Prussia's resources pledged to the support of Austrian interests abroad, knowing that the time was soon coming when all her strength would be needed for a contest with the traditional adversary at home. "Austria," he wrote in 1854, "can demand actual military assistance only when Germany is threatened with war which has not been provoked by wilful aggression on the part of Austria herself. Neither our duty nor our interest goes beyond this. If we are to go further, Austria must name a definite joint aim, and state exactly what she proposes."

In return for assistance against France, however, Austria offered to Prussia nothing at all save a fair prospect of disaster. Bismarck was at that time ambassador at St. Petersburg, and there Gortchakoff told him that if Prussia took sides against France, Russia would enter the field against both of the Germanic Powers. For that reason, if for no other, Bismarck advocated a policy of abstention, convinced that directly Prussia interfered on Austria's side she would be betrayed. "From the moment that we took the war upon ourselves," he wrote to his wife in one of the few domestic letters in which he touched on politics (June 28, 1859), "I should less fear France than Austria." "With the first shot fired by us on the Rhine," he wrote four days later, "there would be an end to the Austro-Italian war, and instead a war with Russia and France would take the stage, a war in which Austria, as soon as we had taken the burden from her shoulders, would give us just as much or as little help as might be compatible with her own interests." [1] It was widely believed in Berlin that directly signs appeared of a determination to intervene Napoleon intended to transfer the theatre of war from Italy to Germany.

The other view is that the Prince Regent honestly intended to go to the assistance of his federal ally, but in his own time, as determined by the facts of the military situation as he knew them. The Prince himself said later that it was his policy "to allow the French to be fairly engaged in Italy, so that at the moment when Germany declared war upon France we should only find in the latter country a comparatively small

[1] Moltke shared this view. He wrote to his brother in July, 1859: "Had Austria wanted us as allies, she could have had us long ago. But she wanted us as vassals, without conditions, without reciprocity, without any security that she would not conclude peace on the day that we declared war" (*Briefe des General-Feldmarschalls Grafen Helmuth von Moltke,* vol. i., p. 164).

portion of its armies, and that thus our game would be made easier." There seems to be no justification for doubting the Prince's good faith; his straightforwardness on the Crimean War question entitles him to credence.[1]

Not only so, but Napoleon firmly believed that Prussia was bent on attacking him, and also feared that if Prussia came in on Austria's side Russia would refuse to help him. His explanation of the sudden peace, that the war threatened to become a larger undertaking than was proportionate to the French interests involved, was no doubt, from his standpoint, sufficient and convincing. Replying to the Senators and deputies who welcomed him back at St. Cloud, he said: "When the destinies of my country seemed in peril I made peace." Not for the first time in his career, therefore, he acted the part of a wise opportunist. The best of his troops were locked up in Italy, and it would have been difficult, if not impossible, to oppose a German army on the Rhine with an equal force. At the beginning of July, indeed, apprehensive that Prussia might enter the struggle, he invited the British Government to intervene as mediator and suggested an armistice on terms which would have saved the face of France. Lord Palmerston was unwilling to pull chestnuts out of the fire for Napoleon, and the combatants were left to do their own bargaining. Finally, it is probable that the toll of life entailed by the victory of Solferino had frightened Napoleon, whose nerves had not been schooled by the severe discipline of the battlefield.

The Italian war, while it may have led Prussia to overestimate the military strength of France, had for her the inestimable advantage that it compelled Austria to reveal to the world for the first time her inherent weakness. Henceforth, although she continued to be an obstacle to the settlement of the German question, she ceased to be a source of terror. The effect of Prussia's attitude was further to embitter the relations between the two Powers. After the conclusion of peace the Emperor of Austria complained bitterly that he had been compelled to accept humiliating conditions because "his natural friends, upon whom he had counted, had not given to him the assistance which he had expected," and in a later manifesto issued from Schönbrunn he still spoke harshly of Prussia's desertion of him.

[1] In a letter to Duke Ernest of Saxe-Coburg-Gotha the Prince Regent wrote from Baden in September, 1859: "You are right in attributing Prussia's present isolation to her attitude in recent events"; but he proceeded to defend his country from the charge of an intended desertion of Austria and to blame the too hurried conclusion of peace.

Nevertheless, the ill-humour soon passed away, and through the mediation of the King of Bavaria a meeting of the Emperor and Prince Regent was arranged at Teplitz in the year following the war (July, 1860).

Political events at home had in the meantime taken a new direction. A well-defined era in the life both of Prussia and Germany closed, and a new chapter in the history of national unity opened, when in the autumn of 1858 Frederick William IV, smitten by insanity, was compelled to institute a regency in favour of his brother the Prince of Prussia, afterwards William I. Nearly a year before the Prince had been made quasi-Regent with the title of "deputy," for the reactionary Manteuffel Ministry would not trust him further. Now, the need having become greater, he insisted upon a full regency, and he had his way, the disabled Sovereign living in restraint at Sans-Souci until his death on January 2, 1861.

It cannot be said that the King's disappearance was a misfortune for his country, for as a statesman he had been a failure. He never spared himself for his people's sake, but his nervous activity was tragically poor in fruitful results, and where his zeal was greatest its objects were usually the most impracticable and the least to be desired. No Sovereign had a kinglier spirit, but none a less kingly understanding; he could bear the trappings of kingship with perfect dignity, but its responsibilities were altogether beyond his powers. The impression left by a study of his character and public acts is that of a man of unpractical and irresolute character, suited as few others to adorn private life in spheres in which graces count for more than utilitarian gifts, but utterly unfitted to rule men or direct affairs. Many people have ideas, but only the few have good ones; and Frederick William IV was only too often to be counted to the majority. Always well-meaning and benevolent, his wish to do the right thing was constantly neutralized by his instinct for choosing the wrong.

His idiosyncrasies and extravagances might have been kept in check had he had around him advisers strong enough to override his emotional judgments, but these, partly through his own fault and altogether to his misfortune, were lacking, and a disposition to listen to many counsels was not supplemented by any assurance that he would end by following the wisest.[1] A

[1] Bismarck writes of him: "He never at any time had superior advisers who could direct him and his business. He reserved the right to choose from the

bad strong ruler is almost less dangerous to a State than a weak good one. A full-blooded and less high-principled Hohenzollern of the type of Albrecht Achilles was far more useful to the commonwealth than this virtuous, dreamy, star-gazing mystic, nursing in his crazy brain impossible schemes and pursuing fantastic will-of-the-wisps in the pathetic belief that they were marvels of statesmanship.[1] Whatever his limitations, however, and they were many, the fact remains that his was a noble character—as noble in its larger faults as in its virtues.

The Prince of Prussia was at this time sixty-two years old, yet he had come little before the public gaze since the revolutionary days of 1848, when his supposed hostility to the constitutional movement made him very unpopular and led to his withdrawal for a time to England. Earlier still, he was believed to have conspired against Hardenberg when that Minister still honestly wished to give Prussia a constitution, and to have hardened the will of his father Frederick William III whenever there had been signs of a disposition to yield to popular demands. Yet these political indiscretions of his youth, if indeed he was guilty of them, had left no ill-will in the national mind. His training had been that of arms rather than of statecraft; he had been in the army for nearly fifty years, and he was a soldier with heart and soul. Yet in recent years he had repeatedly given evidence of ripe political judgment and a clear grasp of foreign questions. He had long been in conflict with his brother's weak and devious political manœuvring. He had openly quarrelled with him over Olmütz, and he had not concealed his disgust at the humiliating part which Prussia had been compelled to play in the Crimean War. Now as Regent he appeared to favour moderate Liberalism, and therein again he contrasted strongly with his brother's marked leanings towards reactionary measures.

His private character also was above reproach, and already he had given many proofs of that instinct of fidelity to duty which led him, during the many years of sovereignty that awaited

counsels given to him not only by each individual Minister but also with far greater frequency by more or less clever *aides-de-camp*, privy councillors, scholars, dishonest place-seekers, honest visionaries and courtiers, and often decision was long delayed" (*Reflections and Reminiscences*, vol. i., p. 305).

[1] Sir Stratford Canning, who visited the King during the revolutionary days of April, 1848, wrote at the time: "Never was there a more good-hearted man than he who wears the Prussian crown, with more talent and knowledge than fall to the lot of many gifted men; but alas, that which gives weight to the sceptre and dignity to the robe, and political authority sufficient to the language of royalty, is not in proportion" (*Life of Stratford Canning*, vol. ii., p. 170).

him, to subordinate personal interests of every kind to the public good. It was recalled to his praise how as a youth, yielding to the stern code of his dynasty, he had made the hardest sacrifice of personal inclinations within human power by sacrificing love to duty. It was when for reasons of State he broke off a warm attachment to the beautiful and gifted Princess Elisa Radziwill, and espoused the daughter of a reigning Prince (Princess Augusta of Weimar), in deference to the will of calculating Ministers and cold-blooded jurisconsults.

The new Regent did not lack for advisers in his early days, though later one only was to suffice. Soon after his appointment the King of Saxony waited upon him and told him frankly that all the German Princes were apprehensive that Prussia wanted to absorb their territories. The Prince vigorously repudiated the idea, but his visitor was not reassured when, pointing to the position of Hanover upon the map of Germany, he proceeded to declare that in no circumstances would he tolerate the growth of a strong State in the middle of his Prussian provinces.

The liberal-minded Duke Ernest of Coburg did his best at that time to win him, and Prussia under his guidance, for progressive ways. As " a German prince and a plain German citizen," he addressed to the new ruler a statesmanlike appeal in which he urged him to throw over the feudal reactionaries, and unite the progressive political, military, and intellectual forces of the nation in a moderate party, so increasing the influence of Prussia and enabling it to make " a moral conquest " of Germany. " Prussia stands at the parting of the ways," he said ; " what if Prussia should hold back and the feudal party should again acquire governmental influence ? " He warned the Regent that if the hopes of the middle party were disappointed there was a certain prospect of its dissolution, with the result that the right wing would strengthen the party of reaction and the left make common cause with the subversive elements in society, leaving a weak and ineffective remnant incapable of exerting any active influence on public affairs. By setting herself at the head of the progressive forces, he said, Prussia might assert for herself an honourable " moral ascendancy " in Germany, but failing such an ascendancy she would be able to count only on " military and diplomatic conquests," and that at the cost of great moral and material sacrifice. Few more remarkable political prophecies are on record.

The regency began well, and once more there seemed the

promise of spring-time in Germany. The Regent's first act of government was to dismiss the Manteuffel Ministry, whose conduct in the Olmütz affair and later during the Crimean War he had neither forgotten nor forgiven. Invited to resign, Manteuffel demurred, out of a misplaced concern for the welfare of the country, whereupon the Regent put in his place Prince Karl Anton von Hohenzollern, a man of Liberal leanings, who gathered round him a Cabinet of congenial colleagues, which went down to history as the "Ministry of the New Era." Of the old men, von der Heydt (Finance) and Simons remained, while the new men included Schleinitz (Foreign Affairs), Bonin (War), Schwerin (Interior), Pückler, Patow, Auerswald, Flotwell, and Bethmann-Hollweg—for the most part Old Liberals. Lively hopes were excited in progressive circles by the Prince's first official address to the new Ministry. "Prussia," he said, appropriating the words of the Duke of Coburg, "must make moral conquests in Germany by adopting wise legislation, by cultivating all the moral elements in the nation, and by utilizing the influences which make for unity, like the Customs Union. The world must know that Prussia is everywhere prepared to protect the right." The words were vague, but the sentiment was excellent; Parliament was pleased; the Liberals believed that a turn in political events was at hand; and the nation at large brought to the Regent an almost unquestioning confidence. This was seen in the general elections which immediately followed. As the reactionaries had been put out of office, there was no electoral manœuvring, and the nation was able to make a free and unfettered use of its rights. The result was the return in January of an overwhelmingly Liberal Lower House. In many constituencies the Liberals refrained from putting forward candidates of their own, and accepted the Ministerial nominees as Liberal enough. To the joy of the nation at large, a genuinely progressive spirit appeared to assert itself in administration; greater liberty was allowed to the Press, and the law of association was relaxed.

There was no immediate visible change in the Government's foreign policy. Like the displaced King, the Regent was warmly attached to the Austrian reigning house, yet without any trace of his fantastic conception of the Empire and Emperor as sacrosanct institutions. Certainly he was not disposed to allow Prussia to be ignored, and he was not a man upon whom a Schwarzenberg would have tried to impose a second Olmütz.

It cannot be said that upon the question of national unity

he held very decided opinions at that time. He was convinced that Prussia was "destined to be the head of Germany," but that destiny he was not anxious to accelerate. He was sure that German unity was not intended to come by a Frankfort Parliament or be thrown up like sea-wrack by some wave of constitutional reform. "He who would rule Germany must first conquer it," he wrote in 1849, and because Prussia had failed ignominiously in her encounter with Austria in the Hessian constitutional conflict of 1850, he believed that the question of Prussian hegemony had been put back indefinitely. "There was a general feeling," he wrote in 1851, in reference to this episode, "that the moment had come for Prussia to assert the position which history designed for her. But it was not to be. I see no immediate prospect of it; it must have been premature, and I believe that *we* shall not see Prussia take the position we wish for her."

Circumstances had changed for Prussia since then, for a Bismarck had come into the foreground of her political life, and with him a new impulse had been given to her statecraft, yet unity seemed no nearer. Visiting Prussia for the coronation at Königsberg on October 18, 1861, Lord Clarendon wrote home to Earl Russell: "The King of Prussia has before him one of the most glorious enterprises monarch ever undertook. If he had a little more of his ancestor Frederick (the Great) and less of his brother Frederick William, he would be at the head of Germany in two years." But the new King was in no hurry to be at the head of Germany. Accepting Prussian hegemony as inevitable and right, he yet looked forward to it without any lively satisfaction. So late as January, 1863, he wrote to the British ambassador to Berlin, Sir Andrew Buchanan, that he had no "expectation of living to see the consolidation of Germany, but he hoped that his son or grandson would do so." To the last year of his life he remained in spirit and sympathy far more a Prussian than a German Sovereign.

In the second year of the regency he made the acquaintance of Louis Napoleon at the Emperor's urgent request. Napoleon wanted Prussia as an ally, and had already frankly avowed it to Bismarck when that rising diplomatist was despatched to Paris in March, 1857, in order to sound the Emperor as to his willingness to allow the King's troops, in case of need, to pass through French territory on their way to the Swiss province of Prussia. That suggestion had not been received in an unfriendly spirit, though in the event it had not been pressed, owing to the peaceful adjustment of the Neuchâtel dispute. Two years before this Bismarck had casually met Napoleon, who had assured him in general phrases of his good feelings towards Prussia, and of his wish for intimate relations with her.

Now the two men, thrown into closer contact, formally took each other's measure. Of Bismarck the Emperor said: "Ce n'est pas un homme sérieux," and lived to regret his want of insight. "People exaggerate his intellect, but underrate his heart," was Bismarck's truer verdict upon the restless schemer, who, as we have seen, was already hatching plots for the aggrandizement of France at the expense of her neighbours, and the discovery of the sources of Napoleon's weakness and strength furnished him with a cue which helped him to many successes and saved him from many mistakes in his later dealings with the Emperor. In sundry conversations Napoleon discussed with the Prussian envoy the probable effects of the cession to France of German territory on the left bank of the Rhine, disclaiming indeed, any large expectations of the kind, yet suggesting that "une petite rectification des frontières" might at some date be desirable and prove feasible, and for the rest letting it be understood that if he needed more space he would look to the Italian possessions of Austria. In order that Prussia should have an interest in any territorial arrangements in France's favour he suggested that she might find compensation in the annexation of Hanover and the Elbe Duchies, the occupation of which would enable her to become a strong maritime Power, and to assist in destroying Great Britain's oppressive mastery of the sea.

These overtures were purely informal, and were made more or less speculatively, *pour tâter le terrain*, yet behind them was a serious desire to co-operate with Prussia to mutual advantage. "Why should we not be friends ?" he asked. "Let us forget the past. Statesmen must occupy themselves with the future." Perhaps because there was more intellect than heart in this sentiment, Bismarck professed to be attracted by it, and he repeatedly came back to the idea of a Franco-Prussian *entente* as an alternative, or a complement, to one with Russia. He had no wish at that time for a formal alliance with France, but he was determined to live on good terms with her, not for friendship's sake, but in order to convince other countries that Prussia counted amongst the forces of Europe, and that she did not stand alone. He was even eager to see the King and the Emperor on visiting terms, and was then doing his best to dispel the disfavour from which Napoleon, as the crowned representative of a revolutionary democracy, suffered in Ministerial and still more in Court circles in Berlin.

Perhaps at a formal alliance he would not have stopped short had it been certain that Prussia's interests would have been served by it. In a long correspondence on the subject with his friend General Ludwig von Gerlach at that time he scoffed when that unbending royalist professed horror at the thought of such a compact between legitimacy and revolution. For who, then, he asked, were legitimate; how far back must the clean record go? Were not half the Sovereigns of Europe—of Spain, Portugal, Belgium, Holland, Greece, Sweden, England—of revolutionary origin; were not three of the Kings of Germany created by the uncle of this same Napoleon? Confessing his frankly opportunist standpoint, he wrote (May 2, 1857): "France counts for me, without regard to the person at her head for the time being, merely as a piece, though a necessary one, in the game of political chess—a game in which I am called upon to serve only my own King and my own country. In the foreign service of my country I cannot reconcile with my sense of duty, either in myself or others, sympathies and antipathies with regard to foreign Powers and persons." [1]

The Prince Regent did not welcome the meeting with the Emperor, but he could not politely evade it. In order, however, to banish possible suspicion from the minds of the German Princes, he invited the four Kings, the Grand Dukes of Baden and Hesse, and several of the Dukes to be present. The meeting took place at Baden-Baden on June 16, 1860. After Napoleon had conferred with the minor Sovereigns, he met the Prince of Prussia alone. It was an embarrassing interview, marked by eagerness on one side and diffidence on the other. Describing it later, Napoleon said that the Prince Regent's attitude towards him was that of "une jeune fille pudique qui craint les propos d'un vert galant et qui évite de se trouver longtemps avec lui," and this was, in fact, just the position. Napoleon assured the Regent that he had sought the interview for the purpose of assuring him that his sentiments towards Prussia and Germany were entirely friendly. Nevertheless, he suggested the cession to France of German territory, promising that if the Regent would further it he would approve of a suitable addition to Prussia in return. The Regent, as he told Bismarck later, neither assented

[1] Quoted in *Reflections and Reminiscences*, vol. i., p. 171.

nor refused, and probably allowed Napoleon to think that he had an open mind on the subject, though the matter was not pursued further at the time.

Before the federal Princes departed from Baden the Prince Regent made an earnest attempt to convince them of Prussia's loyalty, and to remove apprehension. He assured them (June 18th) that it was his wish and hope to arrive at an understanding with Austria, and added: "I consider it to be the first task of the German as of the European policy of Prussia to safeguard not only the territorial integrity of the common fatherland but that also of the individual Sovereigns." The assurance does not appear to have carried conviction to every mind. In a conversation with the Prince on the following day, the King of Bavaria, who had least to fear from Prussia, voiced the existing incertitude, and to his direct questions received equally candid answers. The Regent warmly defended himself against suspicions of reactionary intentions. "Having found a constitution in existence," he said, "I consider it my duty to conform to it and not to falsify it with unnatural interpretations." Questioned as to his opinion of the chances of the States again working together, he said: "Austria must cease to treat Prussia as a *parvenu*, and must recognize her as a Great Power and an equal."

From Baden the assembled Princes took away a clearer conviction than before that there was no longer a puppet on the throne of Prussia and that the Regent was a force to be reckoned with. Napoleon had said in his conversation with the Regent: "L'Autriche est bien malade." The dictum of the great man was buzzed amongst the Sovereigns and their Ministers, and it created alarm. Some of the secondary States began to fear for their fate if Austria, after all, were to prove a broken reed. At that time Bavaria in particular still looked as before to Vienna, while Würtemberg had renewed her old attachment to France and the Napoleonic line: only Baden of the larger States was genuinely friendly to Prussia.

It was in the month following the Baden colloquies that the Regent met the Austrian Emperor at Teplitz (July 25th). Francis Joseph had also called to his side a new adviser. Count Rechberg-Rothenlöwen had succeeded Count Buol as Foreign Minister (May, 1859), and the appointment seemed a good omen. Rechberg had hitherto been President of the Diet at Frankfort, where he and Bismarck had been on excellent terms. A grateful and faithful disciple of Metternich, of whose autocratic spirit a portion had fallen to him, he had a reputation for impetuosity but also for unvarying fairness. While convinced of Austria's unassailable strength, and determined to repel any challenge of her position in Germany, he was not merely averse to a breach with Prussia, but heartily wished for the continuance of the existing dualism, though on the old basis. Rechberg remained in office when in the following year (December, 1860) Schmerling became head of the Cabinet.

The Teplitz meeting was marked by warm protestations of friendship on both sides, but as soon as conversation entered political channels agreement was less reserved. The Prince Regent had carefully thought out a scheme of concessions and counter-concessions, Prussia offering to Austria an alliance under which her existing possessions, including Venetia, were to be guaranteed, while in return the presidency of the Federation was to be exercised by the two States alternately, and in future wars Prussia was to command the armies of the North and Austria only those of the South. Proposals to this effect were made, but while the Emperor welcomed the idea of an alliance he was in no mind to renounce any of his prerogatives as head of the Federation, and upon the general question of federal reform no advance was made. The Regent wrote to Prince Albert, with whom he carried on at this time a busy exchange of views, that the meeting led to no written or even verbal engagement of any kind, but only to "a thorough discussion and communication of ideas." It was clear, however, that in all he said the Emperor had assumed that Austria was still undisputed mistress in Germany and intended so to remain.

Before a year had passed Napoleon's visit was returned at Compiègne (October, 1861). "Diplomacy is listening attentively," Prince Albert wrote just before the meeting took place. It listened, but heard nothing, for there was nothing to hear. More than before Napoleon tried to draw near to the Prussian ruler—the Regent had become King in January—but he met with no encouragement. Yet no unpleasant or inopportune questions appear to have been raised, and the King, who went to France with uneasy forebodings, returned home with relief.

German unity had a warm friend in England at this time in the Prince Consort, who watched the slow progress of events with the deep concern of a German Prince of strong Liberal sentiments who united to enthusiasm for the national cause a firm conviction that Prussia was its only hope. He saw, however, that in order to justify herself to Germany it was necessary that Prussia should identify herself with the wider nationalism, sink her own interests in those of the whole nation, pursue a bold and consistent German, and no longer a merely Prussian, policy, and above all give proof of belief in Liberal principles and of a determination to apply them.

For like his brother, Duke Ernest of Coburg, he believed in the old democratic principle of "Unity through liberty." "It is not," he wrote, "a Cavour that Germany needs, but a Stein." In a letter dated March 12, 1861, the Prince appealed to the King, with a confidence which may have been exaggerated, consciously or unconsciously, by his desire to influence him at a turning-point in national history, to take occasion by the hand, and lead Germany into the land of promise. "My hope," he wrote, "like that of most German patriots, rests upon Prussia—rests upon you. It rests upon Prussia, which has only to manipulate her constitution skilfully in order to find within herself all the means of satisfying the requirements of the time—of serving as a model for the other countries of Germany—and of ingratiating the sympathies of those countries in such a way that they must desire the direct connection with the Prussian system. It rests upon you because you have succeeded to the throne without being entangled or fettered by the miserable policy of reaction, to which, indeed, you were often yourself a victim, and because your known loyalty of character makes you regarded by the Germans as the type of their oldest saying, 'Ein Wort ein Mann!' ('What he says he means'). . . . Let no one succeed in shaking your confidence in your own people and in the German nation!"

"Prussia," he wrote two months later, "must first be morally master in Germany before she can lift up her head in Europe, and this she will become not by sudden resolutions, not by wild, impulsive yearnings, not by urging claims diplomatically, but by a slow, well-thought-out, persistent, courageous, truly German, thoroughly Liberal policy—a policy which meets the requirements of the age and of the German nation, and makes it impossible for the individual Governments to act otherwise than in the same spirit with it and upon the same principles."

The words deserve to be recalled not merely because of the insight, the clearness and sanity of judgment to which they bear witness, but as marking the antithesis of the policy which was soon afterwards adopted in Prussia, and so gave direction to the entire course of Germany's later political development.

CHAPTER IV

(1858–1863)

THE PRUSSIAN CONSTITUTIONAL CONFLICT

WHILE the federal controversy still dragged on, there occurred in Prussia a constitutional struggle which for a time threw a shadow upon other domestic questions. Long before he became Regent the Prince of Prussia, a soldier by instinct and training, had been impressed by the need for a stronger and more efficient army and for a reform of the existing military organization. With true insight he had recognized that in the altered conditions of military science and *technique* the day of the old militia was over, and that Prussia's position would be strengthened and her capacity to meet future tasks be assured, only to the extent that she had at command a sufficient force of highly trained and highly disciplined men. He had seen with increasing anxiety the growing military strength of France, Russia, and even of Austria, and he feared that in the event of a clash with either of these Powers before Prussia had had time to adjust her military system to the altered situation the result might be disastrous. The memories of Olmütz and all the other humiliations which there found their climax were a constant warning that Prussia would never be able to assert her rightful position in Germany and Europe until she could depend altogether upon her own strong arm. Military defects which had come to his knowledge when engaged, as Prince of Prussia, in quelling the Baden insurrection of 1849 and the slowness of the mobilization of his forces in 1859, when Austria was eagerly waiting for Prussian help, had also convinced him that radical reforms in organization were necessary if the army was to become an absolutely reliable weapon in serious warfare.

His first act as Regent, therefore, had been to replace the stagnant Ministry of Manteuffel, which had neglected the army, by a Cabinet of more progressive men. In his first address to the new Ministry he had hinted at an early scheme of army reform. "The army which created Prussia's greatness," he said, "was reformed at the time of the War of Liberation, but forty years' experience has shown the need of great changes. For these not only quiet political conditions but much money is necessary, for it would be a political blunder, which would entail a severe retribution, were we to be satisfied with a cheap military administration, which failed to meet expectations at the critical moment. Prussia's army must be strong and imposing, in order that it may be able, if necessary, to throw a heavy political weight into the scale."

The Prussian army at that time was still organized on the *Landwehr* basis introduced by Scharnhorst early in the century. The collapse of Prussia under Napoleon's onslaught had proved the insufficiency of the standing army and its Frederician traditions. After the defeat of Jena the nation rose *en masse* at the King's call, and it was this national army which retrieved Prussia's fortunes and turned humiliation into victory. The unity of the army with the nation, in spirit as well as person, was no mere phrase in those days: then as never before or since the army represented the organized national spirit and will. At a public dinner in Berlin in 1814, Blücher could propose a toast "To the happy union of the military and the civilian class by means of the *Landwehr*."

During the War of Liberation the manhood of the nation had been under arms, and the principle of universal military service was confirmed by a law of September 3, 1814. Nominally the period of service with the colours was three years, reducible to one year in the case of those who attained a certain educational standard and maintained themselves while serving, though in fact two years with the colours had become the general practice with the whole of the rank and file. Two years in the reserve of the line followed, after which came seven years in the first ban, followed by an equal term in the second ban, of the *Landwehr*. In war-time the line regiments and the first ban of the *Landwehr* were mobilized for field service and the second ban was available for manning the garrisons and fortresses. Substantially this was the arrangement which had continued since. The changes now proposed related mainly to the annual levy of recruits and to the position of the *Landwehr* in the army system. When the existing basis of the army's organization was laid down in 1820, 40,000 men were called up yearly on a population of eleven millions. In 1859 the levy continued about the same, though the number actually liable to be called up, on a population of eighteen millions, was 63,000. As the first ban of the *Landwehr* consisted of men between the ages of 25 and 32 years, it was found that on mobilization more than half of the field army consisted of heads of households, while a large part of the unmarried men of military age remained at home.

The measures upon which the Regent had set his mind were intended to apply upon broader and most efficient principles the constitutional obligation of military service, by increasing the annual levy to 63,000, enabling him to create forty-nine new regiments—thirty-nine of infantry and ten of cavalry, by making three instead of two years' service with the colours the fixed rule, by reducing to a minimum the excessive exemptions, by increasing to four years the period of service with the first reserve and curtailing that with the *Landwehr*, and, finally, by improving the entire system of training in the case both of officers and men. A larger part of the young manhood of the nation was thus to be brought under arms, and more of the older men were to be passed into the last reserve. Thus he aimed at creating a larger, a more vigorous, and a more efficient force. Hitherto the field army had numbered about 200,000 and the reserves 400,000; now the former was to number 371,000 and the latter 289,000, a change implying no great difference in numbers, but a vast difference in effective fighting strength. The annual cost of the reorganization scheme was estimated at nine and a half million thalers, or nearly a million and a half pounds sterling.

In deciding to introduce these reforms the Regent had the energetic support of General Edwin von Manteuffel, chief of the Military Cabinet, General Hellmuth von Moltke, since 1858 head of the General Staff and a man in whom, as a strategist and organizer, he had already begun to place great confidence; and above all, of General Albrecht Theodor von Roon, who had suggested the main principles in a memorandum written just before the regency took effect. At the last moment Bonin, the Minister of War, became convinced that the proposals as they stood had no chance of success, and with the idea of making the scheme more acceptable, he recommended that the war strength of the battalions should be reduced by one-quarter, that part of the men should be released from service in the winter, and that the older men of the *Landwehr* should be exempted from liability to yearly training. The Regent rejected these recommendations point-blank, whereupon (December 5, 1859) Bonin, drawing a right conclusion from his rebuff, resigned and made place for Roon.

In the speech from the throne with which the Diet was opened on January 12, 1860, the Regent announced the intended introduction of an army reform bill, and in view of the wide-spread controversy, endeavoured to allay alarm as to its objects. "Recent decades," he said, "have revealed the nation's readiness for sacrifice and its martial spirit, but they have also brought to light grave defects in the military system, and the removal of these is my duty and my right. It is not my intention to break with the traditions of a great era; the Prussian army will remain in the future what it was in the past—the nation in arms. Give, then, to the proposals, which have been maturely weighed, and which pay equal regard to civil and military interests, your unprejudiced examination and your assent. Such assent will in every direction give evidence of the country's confidence in my honest intentions. No measure of equal importance for the protection, greatness, and power of the fatherland has been laid before the national legislature."

On February 10th the bill was introduced, together with a bill for abolishing the exemption of the knights' fees from the land tax, by which measure a large part of the cost was to be met. At that time the Lower House of the Diet was as strongly Liberal in constitution as the Upper House was Conservative, yet it had hitherto been friendly and even compliant to the Government, and had assented, albeit grudgingly, to certain military changes of a minor order. Now it was thought to be high time to make a firm stand. Manteuffel said at the time, "If the Liberals are wise now, they are sure of remaining in power for many years." Whether or not it would have been prudent to accept the military reforms at once, before they became involved in a dispute over constitutional rights and doctrines, may be an open question. It is certain that its attitude during the subsequent "conflict" committed Prussian Liberalism to a weary sojourn in the wilderness, which at the end of forty years was still unfinished.

In the country at large the scheme was not received with favour. The principal objections were directed against the proposal to dethrone the *Landwehr* from the important position which it had hitherto held, a feature of the scheme regarding which even military opinion was acutely divided. There was also a strong party which believed that two years' service with the colours was sufficient under modern conditions, and that the Government should be willing to concede that point if given its way in other matters. The industrial and commercial classes in particular objected that the longer term of service would prove a serious handicap to Prussia's further economical development, which had of late years made marked progress. The economists deplored the increase of the army estimates, regarding as inordinate the addition of a million and a half pounds to the relatively small budget which satisfied the national demands of that day. Finally, Liberal and democratic politicians disliked the scheme from a fear that with the increase of the military power of the Crown the forces of reaction would be strengthened.

The army reform bill was duly referred to Committee, and from the first it was apparent that there was no hope of its acceptance by the Diet. Major-General Stavenhagen, a retired officer, Liberal in politics but conservative in military notions, proposed amendments calling for the retention of the *Landwehr* as part of the line and the reduction of the term of service for the infantry to two years, changes which would have meant either a saving of money or an increase in the number of trained men, and these amendments were carried by large majorities in spite of Ministerial protest. The Government, foreseeing that the Lower House would uphold the vote of the Committee, now looked around for a way of carrying its scheme without the necessity of obtaining parliamentary sanction, thus evading the risk of negative votes. Was a new law necessary at all ? The essential principles of army organization were laid down in the law of 1814. At the time that law was passed the King was absolute, but though a constitution had been granted in the meantime, it did not alter the King's unlimited control over military administration. It followed, so the Government's legal advisers contended, that every vital part of the scheme of reform might be carried out without new legislation. The raising of the necessary money did, indeed, create a difficulty, but perhaps the Diet would be willing to recognize accomplished facts and pay the bill when tendered.

Accordingly, the Government separated the administrative from the financial side of the scheme, and in May invited the Diet to vote nine million thalers for the adoption of such measures, conducive to greater military efficiency, as might be practicable in virtue of laws already in force. The Minister of Finance spoke of the vote as provisional, and let it be understood that in granting it the Diet would not be prejudging the complete scheme as presented before. In this belief the Lower House agreed to vote, for one year only, the sum asked for. The Upper Chamber, less responsible in composition and uncompromisingly Ministerial in sentiment, set every consideration of prudence at defiance, and incontinently plunged with blundering tread into the dangerous quicksands of constitutional conflict, dragging the Government after it. It objected to any reduction of the original estimates, urged the Minister of War not to modify his proposals, and affirmed its willingness to vote whatever sum of money might be needed. Fortified by this encouragement, and disregarding the fact that the grant sanctioned by the Lower House was limited to a single year, the Government proceeded to put into effect the full scheme, and accordingly the new regiments were embodied and the new officers received their commissions.

On the death of Frederick William IV on January 2, 1861, the Regent succeeded him as William I, and the first Diet of the new reign met on January 14th. In his speech from the throne the King reminded the Diet that if great expectations were built on Prussia's foreign policy, it must be prepared to make the sacrifices necessary to the due strengthening of the army. A violent quarrel between the Government and the Lower Chamber began at once. Even now the Chamber did not object to the new regiments, and it voted an addition to the army estimates for another year, but it demanded a reduction of the term of service and the retention of the *Landwehr* on its old basis, and above all it insisted that the Government must embody all its proposals in the budget and accept the decision of the Diet upon them as a whole.

Strong feeling was excited in the country, and, recalling the late hard struggle for constitutional liberties, the nation threw itself into renewed vehement controversy. A suggestion of the changed temper of public opinion was shown by two by-elections which took place in the autumn, for in them constituencies which in 1858 had rejected democratic candidates now returned staunch leaders of the popular cause—Benedict Waldeck and Hermann Schulze-Delitsch, the former a well-known member of the Frankfort Parliament. Everywhere the democrats joined hands as in the political conflicts of ten and twelve years before, and the result was the formation of a new party which was intended not only to voice the opposition to the Government's scheme but to do battle with autocracy in every form. This was the party of *Fortschritt* or Progress, among whose earlier leaders were, besides Waldeck and Schulze, Theodor Mommsen and Franz Duncker, the historians, Rudolf Virchow, the bacteriologist, Johann Jacoby, Hans Victor von Unruh, and Max von Forckenbeck. By combining opposition to the army scheme, of which it honestly doubted the necessity, with the advocacy of the deferred political aspirations of the middle and working classes, the Progressist party sprang at once into favour with the nation, which was ready and waiting for a strong democratic lead.

It seemed that the new King was about to expose himself to a distrust and resentment almost as deep and widespread as had been aroused in the revolutionary days of March, 1848, and the unpopularity which he incurred in his own monarchy became magnified in the eyes of the other German peoples. At this conjuncture an event occurred which called the nation back to the impersonal aspects of the dispute. Thrice during his reign William I narrowly escaped the hand of the assassin, and on each occasion the crime synchronized with legislative measures which roused strong public prejudice and passion. The first attempt on his life was made at the outset of the constitutional conflict by a fanatical student of Leipzig named Becker, who waylaid him at Baden-Baden (July 14, 1861), and fired two shots at him, without serious effects. His escape evoked a warm outburst of loyalty, which showed that the nation's unflinching defence of its constitutional rights, as it understood them, implied no hostility to the ruler. New elections in December added to the Government's discomfiture, however, for they showed the broad mass of the people to be solidly behind the constitutional party. Although the King had directed the Cabinet to use all possible influence, short of intimidation, to secure the return of a more pliant Lower House, the Conservatives were reduced to an impotent body of twenty-four.

No sooner did the Lower House meet (January 14, 1862) than the struggle entered a new and more definite phase. The irreconcilable democrats had overborne the moderate Liberals, who would have preferred concession and compromise to conflict, and now they abandoned defensive for offensive tactics. Refusing to accept the army estimates as presented, on the ground that the classification of expenditure was too summary, they proposed a resolution calling upon the Government to give full details, instead of asking the Diet to vote money in the dark, yet also, as before, demanding the reduction of the period of service to two years. This challenge the Government interpreted as an attempt to invade one of the most important of the Crown's prerogatives, its sole right to determine army administration and to direct the executive. The resolution was carried, though not by a large majority, and the Government answered by dissolving the Diet (March 11th). Both sides now knew that they were committed to a war to the knife.

In the meantime the Cabinet, though still united as to the necessity of the military proposals, had become divided as to the method of realizing them. Before the elections took place the three Conservative Ministers, von der Heydt, Roon, and Bernstorff, presented a memorial to the King urging that the Government should "utilize all legal means at their disposal to exercise a legitimate influence" on the result, such as the issue of instructions to the Chief Presidents, District Presidents, and Landrats regarding the candidates whom they were to support. They wanted "a Liberal administration on Conservative lines," and urged that the army reorganization scheme should still be adhered to, but with a reduction of the estimates, if that were possible.

The Liberal Ministers issued a counter-memorandum, endorsing likewise the reorganization of the army, with retrenchment in the military estimates, but recommending the presentation of the budget in detail. The King adopted the programme of the Conservative section of the Cabinet and also accepted the proposal to influence the elections subject to the stipulation "without applying any measure of intimidation." The result was that the more Liberal Ministers, Auerswald, Schwerin, Patow, Bernuth (who had succeeded Simons), and Pückler, resigned, and men in fuller sympathy with the military scheme—Itzenplitz, Lippe, Holzbrink, Mühler, Jagow, and Prince Adolf von Hohenlohe-Ingelfingen, took their places, the last-named succeeding as head of the Cabinet. Nevertheless, the elections in May resulted in the return of a Lower House more hostile to Government than before. The parties of the majority numbered 285, and opposed to them was a fragile coalition of 67; in a House of more than 352 members there were now only twelve Conservatives. In the hope of conciliating the more moderate section of the Opposition, the Government agreed to specialize the budget, as had been demanded. This concession, however, did not satisfy the majority, who claimed that the whole scheme must be submitted to the unconditional decision of the Chamber. As the Government refused to surrender, the House declared the organization proposals to be unconstitutional, and by a vote of 273 against 62 struck out of the budget all the votes required on their behalf, disregarding the warning of the Finance Minister that by so doing it might " bring about a condition in which something might happen that was not expressly provided for by the constitution "—a veiled threat of which the meaning was unmistakable.

Nevertheless, the Ministry as a whole appears to have had no idea at this time of defying or even contesting the budget right of the Diet. Early in September eight members, including Roon and Bernstorff, warned the King that this decision should be accepted and the Diet be again dissolved, " because the Ministry would be violating the constitution if it usurped the right to spend the country's money against the expressed vote of its representatives and without a legalized budget." Already, however, the King had decided to govern without a budget if he could not have his way with one, and on learning that this was his intention, Bernstorff resigned, and obtained leave to return to the London embassy, heartily glad to be out of the quarrel. At the King's invitation four other dissentient Ministers, all moderate Conservatives, also resigned.

In the struggle which followed, the King, the Government, and the Upper House, almost solidly Conservative, were ranged on one side, challenging a literal interpretation of an ambiguous constitutional doctrine, barely twelve years old; while on the other side was the popular assembly, strong in unity and resolution and in the consciousness that behind it was the overwhelming voice of the nation.

A deadlock having again been reached, the sittings of the Diet were adjourned. Convinced now that if headway was to be made against an opposition which hitherto had proved intractable stronger measures would be needed, and that for stronger measures he must look to stronger men, the King now turned to the rising hope of Prussian diplomacy, Herr von Bismarck. Barely four months before this (May 22nd), Bismarck had been translated from the St. Petersburg embassy to that of Paris, where he had since been chafing under a feeling of uselessness and neglect.

The decision to call the notorious Brandenburg Junker was

taken on the urgent advice of Roon,[1] who had returned to the idea again and again, yet the King had serious misgivings. Bismarck had many friends at Court, who knew and appreciated his strength and firmness, but, like all strong men, he had enemies amongst the weaklings. In the country he was unpopular by reason of his political opinions, which savoured too strongly of feudalism for a constitutional age, and it was apprehension on this account that for a time prejudiced the King against him, for almost it seemed that by summoning to his assistance so pronounced a reactionary he would needlessly add to his difficulties.[2]

Bismarck kissed hands as a Minister on September 23rd, but it was only on October 8th—called by Duke Ernest of Coburg "a day of good-fortune in German history"—that he was formally appointed Minister President and Foreign Minister. At this juncture there was a moment when the King for the first time seriously wavered and was on the point of yielding. Bismarck has related how desperate the situation had become when the King summoned him to his palace at Potsdam in order to take office. The outlook seemed hopeless; perplexity and despondency reigned; the King, in despair, had written out his abdication, and the document lay on the table before him. If Bismarck, he said, would agree to take office, he would give place to the Crown Prince. The faithful Brandenburger reversed the offer, and agreed to take office only if the King abandoned the idea of fleeing from duty; and on that condition the compact was sealed.

The new Minister's first parliamentary act was to withdraw the budget for 1863. He was ready for peace on the King's terms, but if the Lower House did not want such a peace he was equally ready for war. The Chamber should, however, have another chance of returning to reason. Accordingly, he first tried persuasion. Speaking in the Budget Committee on September 30th, he said:

"The conflict was being taken too tragically and too tragically

[1] "I shall speak to his Majesty on the seventh [September]," Roon wrote to Bismarck on August 31st, "at a very confidential audience which he has promised me on that day." On September 18th he was so far sure that his friend's time had come that he telegraphed to him in Paris, "Periculum in mora. Dépêchez-vous."

[2] Speaking as a contemporary, Beust says of Bismarck at the beginning of the 'sixties that "the great and small States all took him for a restless spirit, possibly dangerous, but unlikely to remain long in power. . . . By the general public, with the exception of the ultra-Conservatives, he was not only underrated but thoroughly detested" (*Memoirs*, vol. i., p. 221).

described by the Press. The Government sought no struggle, and if the crisis could be adjusted with honour it would gladly help. Excess of individual independence made it difficult to rule with a constitution in Prussia; in France it was different, for there individual independence was lacking. A constitutional crisis was no shame but an honour. Perhaps they in Prussia were too educated, too critical to bear a constitution."

All that was meant to be complimentary, but it was not convincing. What followed was alarming. "Germany," he added, "did not look to Prussia's Liberalism but to her power. Prussia must concentrate her power until the favourable moment —which several times already had been allowed to pass—for her frontiers were unfavourable to a healthy body politic." Then followed a passage which from that time forward was accepted as a crystallization of Bismarck's conception of statecraft:

"The great questions of the time will be decided not by speeches and resolutions of majorities [1]—that was the mistake of 1848 and 1849—but by blood and iron."

The words threw the political world into perturbation, and the orator soon found that he had overturned a hornets' nest. Even the King was seriously alarmed and expostulated, nor was he reassured by his Minister's attempt to explain away the vigorous metaphor.[2] And yet in fairness to Bismarck it should be remembered that the famous "blood and iron" sentence is usually quoted in detachment, as though it had been flung at his opponents as a defiant ultimatum. It was really part of a speech which was intended to be persuasive and conciliatory, and to afford the Lower House an opportunity of reconsidering a critical situation. "This olive branch," he had ended sentimentally, "I plucked at Avignon,[3] in order to offer it as an emblem

[1] The words are usually interpreted as referring to Prussian parliamentary majorities, as they were then asserting themselves, and thus as a deliberate disparagement of constitutional life. It seems probable that Bismarck had also in mind the Diet in Frankfort and the rule of decision by majority which governed most of its business, and made it possible for Prussia to be outvoted by any chance combination which Austria might succeed in organizing against her. "The thousand-year-old history of German dualism," he once wrote to Manteuffel, in the same sense, "cannot be abolished by the mechanism of majority-voting." Bismarck's word for this policy of "out-voting" was "Majorisirung."

[2] In a speech made in the Imperial Diet on January 28, 1886, Bismarck gave an explanation of the famous phrase more ingenious than convincing. What he meant, he said, was: "Put the strongest possible military power, in other words as much blood and iron (i.e. men and munitions), as you can into the hands of the King of Prussia, then he will be able to carry out the policy you wish." He repeats this explanation in his *Reflections and Reminiscences* (vol. i., p. 310).

[3] Bismarck had visited Avignon on his way back to Paris from Biarritz. He

of peace to the popular party, but I see that it is premature." For the rest, the "blood and iron" speech was notable for other sentiments and other examples of robust utterance which plainly indicated that Prussian political life was unlikely henceforth to suffer from monotony.

However sincere his appeal for accommodation may have been, the Liberal majority had gone too far for retreat. Several years before (1858) Bismarck had criticized the self-same Diet because of its tameness and subserviency. "The disease to which our parliamentary life has succumbed," he then said, "is, besides the incapacity of the individual, the servility of the Lower House; the majority has no independent convictions; it is the tool of Ministerial omnipotence." The Lower House had cast off that disease; and in an influx of new vigour it was about to show Bismarck more independence than he had bargained for. His opponents believed, and believed rightly, that if an infraction of the constitution were to be lightly tolerated at one point, the whole parliamentary system was a farce and Prussia might as well be put back to the days of 1848. They felt also that the cause of German unity was involved. One reason why Prussia's advocacy of this cause had never enlisted the hearty attachment of the more liberal States was her political stagnation, which gave rise to the apprehension that Prussian leadership would be leadership backward. Another victory for reaction in Prussia would confirm that view, and further thwart the aspirations of the German nation. Nor, finally, was there anything in the past of the new Minister to justify confidence that the causes dear to the popular party would be safe in his keeping. They saw in him only the representative of a feudal aristocracy which had for generations maintained a greedy grasp upon political power and class privilege, the uncompromising champion of monarchy by the grace of God, the resolute anti-parliamentarian, who was prepared to fight to the utmost any extension of the concessions made to democracy by Frederick William IV. Suspicions of such a man were not to be allayed by flattering phrases and sentimental talk about olive-branches.

Bismarck's overtures were, therefore, rejected. In its sittings of October 6th and 7th the Lower House discussed a resolution of the Budget Committee calling upon the Government to submit to its decision as speedily as possible the estimates for 1863,

wrote to his wife thence on September 14th: "All around are olives, mulberries, figs, and red grapes."

and declaring as unconstitutional any expenditure which had been expressly rejected by a resolution of the House; and in spite of the Minister's protest that the adoption of this resolution would imply the refusal of compromise, it was approved by 251 votes against 36. On the other hand, the Upper House voted for the estimates in the form proposed by the Government, whereupon the people's chamber declared its action to be unconstitutional and therefore "null and void."

A deadlock had now occurred, and though Bismarck tried to divide the constitutional party, even offering seats in the Cabinet to one or two of the Old Liberals, he failed. Now in earnest he sharpened his knife; the knot which could not be unravelled must be cut. On October 13th, five days after his formal appointment as Minister-President and Foreign Secretary, the Diet was prorogued, with the declaration that as it had refused to vote the needed supplies it was the regrettable duty of the Government to carry on the business of the country without the formalities provided by the constitution. Nevertheless, he entertained the confident hope that sanction would be given later to such measures as might be adopted for that purpose. Before the Diet met again in January (1863) the Cabinet had been reconstituted, with Roon still at the Ministry of War, but with two new men, Baron von Bodelschwingh and Count F. A. zu Eulenburg, holding the portfolios of Finance and the Interior respectively. Once more the majority in the Lower Chamber struck from the budget the costs of the army reorganization scheme, and when the Upper House refused to adopt the budget as amended, and restored it to its original form, the constitutionalists below, as before, declared the proceeding invalid. Bismarck, not without a fierce joy, took up the gauntlet thus thrown down. The dispute dragged on without result until May 27th, when the Diet was again prorogued.

Petitioned by the Lower House in that month to remove the Ministry, since it was no longer able to work with it harmoniously, and to abandon the system for which it stood, the King replied defiantly. "My Ministers possess my confidence," he said; "their official actions have been done with my sanction, and I am grateful to them that they are so earnest in opposing the constitutional endeavours of the House of Deputies to extend its power." In announcing the close of the session, Bismarck regretted that the Lower House had refused its co-operation in the work of the Government, and added that steps would be taken to give effect to the measures necessary to the country's welfare, and he again expressed confidence that the Diet would in the end approve whatever action might be taken. The declaration was the prelude to a *coup d'état* not unworthy of the Elector of Hesse, for the Government proceeded to govern without a budget.

Nevertheless, not all the Conservatives viewed with approval, or even with indifference, the dangerous ways which the King and his Ministers were treading. Bernstorff and those of his colleagues who thought with him had resigned rather than identify themselves with wrong-doing and play tricks with their consciences. Even so sturdy a royalist as Lieutenant-Colonel Vincke wrote to the King on New Year's Day of 1863: "The people are loyal to your Majesty, but tenacious also of the right which article 99 of the constitution [relating to the budget] unequivocally guarantees to them. May God in His grace avert the unhappy consequences of a great misunderstanding!"

At the beginning of June fresh fuel was added to the flames by the issue of a drastic Ordinance, faithful to the tradition of the Carlsbad Decrees, restricting the Press. The measure was not only held to be contrary to the constitution, but it was made more offensive to the nation by being issued while the Diet was not sitting. The position of the Government was not improved when it became known that the Crown Prince Frederick, whose natural openness of mind had increasingly disposed him to Liberal ideas since his marriage with the Princess Royal of England in 1858, was warmly opposed to the Ordinance. Visiting East Prussia at the time, he was able to judge for himself, by the coolness shown to him as the King's representative, how deep was the resentment felt by the middle classes, then the backbone of the Liberal party, and at Danzig he took the unusual step of publicly criticizing the Ordinance, declaring that it had been issued without his knowledge and that he took no responsibility for it. The incident led to a warm exchange of letters between father and son, the result of which was that the Crown Prince had to promise not to interfere again in public controversy.

What the Crown Prince could not say publicly, however, he could still write, and in a letter to Bismarck (June 30th) he bitterly reproached him for "having found no other means of coming to an understanding with public opinion than by imposing silence on it. . . . And what results do you anticipate from this policy? The pacification of agitated feelings and the restoration of peace?

Do you imagine that you can pacify agitated feelings by means of fresh violations of the sense of justice? You expect to be more successful in the new elections. To me, however, it appears to be contrary to human nature to hope for a change of opinions when these are constantly being aroused and irritated by the procedure of the Government. I regard those who lead the King, my father, on such a path," he added, "as the most dangerous advisers for Crown and fatherland." For two years the Crown Prince absented himself from all sittings of the Cabinet by way of protest against the course of lawlessness upon which Bismarck had entered. Queen Augusta and the Queen Dowager, the widow of Frederick William IV, were equally opposed to the despotic Minister.

Seriously disconcerted by the widespread disaffection which was caused by this subtle attempt to stifle public opinion, Bismarck deemed it prudent to bow before the storm. When the Press Ordinance was laid before the Diet, the Upper House promptly approved it, but the Lower House condemned it by a large majority, and the Government, fearing to increase the area and deepen the spirit of strife, silently repealed it later in the year.

In September the Diet was again dissolved. "I had no heart for it," Bismarck wrote to his wife at the time, "but there was nothing else to do, though God knows what is the good of it. Now the electoral swindle begins." And "swindle" it was. The Government tried to handicap the Press; it removed or cashiered judges and other State officials who had voted with the Opposition in the Diet, and by the help of a pliant bureaucracy resorted to all the devices for corrupting public opinion and silencing resistance which in those days formed part of the recognized system of government. The whole duty of citizenship under the existing system of crypto-absolutism was clearly defined in a reply addressed by the King to a Parish Council in a remote part of the kingdom whose members had asked how they were expected to vote in the election. "An attitude hostile to my Government," he told them, "is incompatible with fidelity to my person, for my Ministers have been called to their offices in virtue of my confidence and have to support me in the discharge of my great and serious duties." It was all to no purpose; in the new Lower House there was a larger Opposition than before, the Progressists and democrats alone numbering 143. The Diet was, however, a formality in those days. For nearly four years the King and his Cabinet carried on the financial business of the country without its co-operation. The Diet met, discussed, criticized, and legislated, but it was not allowed to exercise itself over money bills.

It is only possible to be just to the disputants in this historical struggle if their different points of view are kept in mind. Looking back upon it the German politician of to-day, lacking the intense earnestness which made the greatness of the heroic age to which the struggle fell, is apt to judge it as merely an academic controversy over barren theories, carried, owing to sheer obstinacy on both sides, to the point of irrational exasperation. From first to last, of course, the struggle was fought over constitutional theories, but these theories were unmistakable realities to their adherents. The tragedy of the episode lay in the fact that the combatants were all the time disputing about different things; the Liberals arguing on the principles of constitutionalism in general, while the Government vainly endeavoured to bring them back to the fact that the point at issue was the interpretation of the constitution of Prussia only, a State in which democratic and parliamentary government had never existed. It was a fundamental error of the popular party that, following too readily the guidance of the jurisconsult Gneist, whose mind was saturated with English constitutional law, it ever kept in mind English conditions, and argued from English constitutional principles and premises, forgetting that these principles and premises did not rightly apply. The secret of the trouble, therefore, was less that the disputants were viewing a controversial question from different standpoints, and therefore in different aspects, than that they were contending for different constitutional theories, so that, lacking a common ground of argument, agreement was impossible.

For the constitution of Prussia did not then, and does not to-day, give to the popular assembly absolute control over finance. Under it a budget or a money bill requires the assent of the Crown and the Upper Chamber just as necessarily as that of the Lower House, whose legislative competence is no larger than that of either of the other two factors.[1] The claim of the Lower House to omnipotence in finance, in virtue of its *liberum veto*, was there-

[1] Article 99 of the Prussian constitution provides that "All revenues and expenditure of the State must be estimated in advance for every year and be included in the budget, which latter shall be fixed yearly by a law," to which all the three legislative factors, i.e. the Crown and the two Chambers, must assent. Similarly, taxes and revenues once voted can only be revoked by a law: if not so revoked, they continue in force from year to year.

fore denied by the very law to which appeal was made, and when his opponents threw at him their English-made theories and precedents Bismarck answered with perfect justification, "In Prussia only that is constitutional which rests on the Prussian constitution," and the very basis of that constitution was the equal power of the Crown, the first and the second Chamber in legislation. "Alter this equality to the prejudice of the Crown," he said with complete truth, "withdraw from this general rule the legislation relative to taxation, its collection and expenditure, and you destroy the independence of the Crown in favour of majorities." When they attacked him as a reactionary and compared him to Strafford, he replied that every such reproach was in effect aimed at the person of the King, whose servant he was and whose will he was executing; and that inasmuch as upon this question the King had exactly as much legislative power as either chamber of the Diet—in effect twice as much as the Lower Chamber, since the Upper House was altogether on his side—the deputies were really the unconstitutional party, for they were endeavouring to read into the constitution a claim which was neither written nor implied therein.

It was in vain that Gneist charged Bismarck with raising again the banner of absolutism, assured him that "the country would not rest until it had been thrown down," and vehemently declared that the budget which, though not approved, was to be enforced, "bore the mark of Cain upon its face." The Minister rejoined with unruffled temper: "Whatever rights the constitution accords to you shall be conceded without curtailment, but whatever you demand beyond that we shall refuse."

Perhaps the theory of the Government was hardly less one-sided. It was that, while the Diet had a perfect right to approve expenditure, it was not justified in refusing its approval. Such a claim meant, in effect, that it was the Government's right to ask for money and the Diet's duty to give it. That claim, too, was arbitrary and was unsupported by the letter of the constitution, yet it was held to be a logical deduction from the omission of the constitution to provide for the situation which would arise when a budget could not become law because the three legislative factors were unable to agree upon it. Bismarck himself had foreseen and had tried to forestall this *impasse* when the constitution was being drafted, and now it had arrived. In countries under party government such a situation merely caused the inconvenience of a change of Ministry; in Prussia, where the

Government remained in spite of parliamentary opposition and votes of no-confidence, the result was a deadlock.[1]

What, then, was the reasonable solution of the difficulty? The question was one of greater importance for the popular party than for the royalists, whose leaders were either fighting, like Bismarck, for the prerogatives of the Crown, or, like Roon and Moltke, for the efficiency of the army, and in either case cared little or nothing for the rights of parliament. Bismarck advised compromise in a speech memorable because it contained the germ of the doctrine, attributed to him ever afterwards, against his protests, that questions of right are questions of might. "If compromise," he said (January, 1863), "fails owing to one of the parties concerned seeking to carry out its own views with doctrinaire finality, compromise gives place to conflicts, and—since the life of the State cannot stand still—these conflicts become questions of power. Whoever has power at command will go forward in his own way."[2]

For the democrats compromise upon a principle so sacred as that for which they were contending would have seemed treachery against conviction and honour, and the fight continued. It is not necessary to follow the future course of the struggle, for it developed no new aspects. The relationships between Governments and Opposition parties are seldom for a long time cordial in German parliaments, whose organization, business, and procedure remind the deputies at every turn that their function is the nominal one of discussing—if they are so disposed—and passing Cabinet measures. During these four years of budgetless administration the Lower Chamber showed greater boldness in challenging this theory of legislation than it had shown in the early days of constitutional government, when Crown and parliament were settling down into their working

[1] In a letter to Lieutenant-Colonel von Vincke (January 2, 1863), in reply to his protest, quoted above, the King stated the position in the words: "The House of Deputies has exercised its right and reduced the budget. The House of Lords has exercised its right and rejected the reduced budget *en bloc*. What does the constitution prescribe in such a case? Nothing! Where, as shown above, the House of Deputies has used its right to the undoing both of the army and the country, I must supplement that 'nothing,' and as a good *paterfamilias* carry on the household and account for my actions later. Who, then, has made article 99 nugatory? Certainly not I." (Quoted in Bismarck's *Reflections and Reminiscences*, vol. i., p. 333.)

[2] Challenged thereupon by Count von Schwerin with having in these words enunciated the doctrine that "might goes before right," Bismarck warmly repudiated the deduction.

relationships ; and it might appear to have exhausted itself in the effort, for there has never been a prolonged repetition of the same independence since. Of the principal combatants on the Ministerial side probably Bismarck and his colleagues Roon and Moltke derived most satisfaction from the conflict. To the King it was a source of distress and anxiety. Bismarck often related in after years that he had periodical fits of nervousness during the struggle and that he was throughout haunted by the thought of Charles I's untimely end. That the King, who was no coward, was really as apprehensive as this over a dispute which never transgressed polemical channels may well be doubted ; and in particular the picture which he is said to have drawn of himself suspended from one gibbet and his Minister from another may fairly be ascribed to a sense of humour, of which he was by no means devoid.[1]

Bismarck's appointment to office was an indication that other questions besides that of army reorganization would now be advanced beyond the dead points, though the struggle over army reform was none the less a preliminary step. The greatest of these questions was that of national unity. He had left Frankfort in 1859 carrying with him the mournful reflection that Austria still ruled matters there with a high hand, and that there was no immediate hope of dethroning her.

"After eight years of official experience at Frankfort," he wrote to the Minister Schleinitz on May 12, 1859, "I have taken away the conviction that the federal arrangements form for Prussia an oppressive, in critical times a mortally dangerous, fetter, without affording us the equivalent which Austria, with a quite disproportionately large degree of free action, derives from them. The German Great Powers are not measured with the same standard by the Princes and Governments of the smaller States ; their interpretation of the purposes and laws of the Bund is modified according to the requirements of Austrian policy. . . . We have always to face the same compact majority, the same claim to Prussian submission."

He was convinced, therefore, that until Prussia broke down this assumption of superiority she would never acquire the

[1] "'I can perfectly well see where all this will end. Over there, in front of the Opera House, under my windows, they will cut off your head. and mine a little while afterwards.' . . . When he was silent I answered with the short remark, 'Et après, Sire ?' 'Après, indeed ! Then we shall be dead,' answered the King" (Bismarck's *Reflections and Reminiscences*, vol. i., pp. 311–12).

consideration, respect, and influence to which she was entitled, and that it might be wise policy so to act that the Diet might put itself in a wrong and untenable position, so precipitating changes.

"I think," he said, "that we should readily take up the gauntlet and regard it not as a misfortune but as an acceleration of the crisis, essential to improvement, if a majority at Frankfort were to adopt a resolution to which we might be able to object as going beyond the competence of the Diet, as an arbitrary alteration of the purpose of the Bund, and an infraction of federal treaties."

The closing words are specially significant, for they illustrate one of the subtlest methods of Bismarck's diplomacy, resorted to again and again in his relations with Austria and France—his habit of endeavouring so to influence the course of events as to bring about the crisis which he desired, while putting his opponents in the wrong.

Bismarck has often been represented as having taken office with a clear and definite programme for the settlement of the German problem, complete in every detail, and legends of his preternatural foresight have been evolved by pious scribes and credulous admirers. Justice can be done to his reputation without crediting him with powers which he did not possess. That he clearly foresaw the exact course which events in Germany would take must be doubted. "It is a misunderstanding of the essence of politics," he said on one occasion, "to suppose that a statesman can draw up a far-going plan and lay down as in a law what he intends to do in one, two, or three years," and no man was more conscious than he that successful politics must largely be a matter of opportunism. It is true that he had written to Manteuffel in July, 1857: "I am convinced that at no distant time we shall have to fight Austria for our existence and that we cannot avoid such a struggle." But in that belief he did not stand alone; most people believed the same thing; the idea of a coming conflict was in the air.[1] As to what was to follow we have the words which he wrote to his wife from Frankfort several years before: "We all act as though we believed of each other

[1] In the year following his appointment as Minister he wrote to Count Goltz, his successor in the Paris embassy, in reference to the Austrian question: "I am in nowise frightened of war. . . . You will perhaps be convinced very soon that war is also part of my programme" (December 24, 1863).

that we are full of thoughts and plans, if only we would express them ; and all the time we none of us know a hair's breadth more what will become of Germany."

Most people looked for the reorganization of Germany, and many people had long ago formed definite ideas as to the form of union which they wished to see introduced, but no man dared as yet to predict the development of events with confidence. The Bund might simply be rehabilitated ; or Germany might be coalesced into a federal State from which Austria was excluded ; or there might in the future be two unions, one of North and another of South Germany ; or the States of the North might go their own way under Prussian leadership and leave those of the South to bargain or not with Austria as they pleased. In the abstract any one of these alternatives might still have seemed a possible solution. The one clear conviction which had been brought home to Bismarck by his Frankfort life was that Austria's arrogant claim to superiority must be challenged and shattered. Until that end had been attained all the talk of a new Germany would continue to be as fruitless as hitherto.[1]

Lamenting that Prussia had not seized the opportunity offered by the Italian war of taking the lead in Germany, Helmuth von Moltke, a man destined to be Bismarck's intimate colleague for nearly a generation, wrote three years before (July, 1859) in one of a series of political letters to his brother marked by great insight and prescience : " A bold resolution can only be taken by *one* man. A Frederick the Great is wanted who will take advice nowhere, but rely entirely upon himself." In Bismarck the man needed by Germany had been found. Nevertheless, it is clear that he was persuaded at this time that the sundered States were not yet ready for unity, and he was not the man to pluck fruit before it was ripe. He wrote to Schleinitz in May, 1859 : " I would like to see the word ' German ' replace ' Prussian ' on our banner only when we are more closely and more opportunely bound to our countrymen than has hitherto been the case." Again : " I see in the existing federal relationship an infirmity of Prussia which sooner or later we shall have to heal *ferro et igni*,[2] unless we undergo a cure for it betimes. Even if to-day the Bund were merely dissolved, without anything

[1] See Note on pp. 158–161.

[2] " It is *ferro et igni*," he had said seven years before, " which will have to settle the quarrel opened since the time of Frederick and Maria Theresa for domination in Germany."

being put in its place, I believe that on the basis of such a negative achievement better and more natural relationships would be established between Prussia and her German neighbours than heretofore."

That a man so clear-sighted and of character so resolute had taken up the German question, however, was a sign that the question could no longer stand still and that a turning-point in German history had come. Of one thing he was convinced—that the question would never be settled by argument or any of the exalted methods of the patriots whose watchword was "Unity through liberty." That policy had been tried by the peoples for half a century, and had failed because the majority of the Princes would not have unity in that way or, if left to themselves, in any other. Still, two generations after the dissolution of the old Empire, Germany continued sundered and broken, and the rulers preferred it so, because in the separation of the multifarious sovereignties seemed to lie the surest security for their political independence. Isolation with weakness was more attractive to them than unity with strength. It was a short-sighted blunder for which several of the Sovereigns were before long destined to pay with their very existence: the States which later were merged in Prussia were the sacrifice made by a particularism which refused to look beyond the conditions and interests of the moment.

In one respect the position had changed since 1859. Magenta and Solferino had shaken the old faith in Austria's military strength and revealed the despotic Habsburg State to be but an imposing image resting on feet that were part of iron but most of clay. Now amongst Austria's allies there were few that doubted that the true centre of the German political system was no longer the South but the North, though not every one had the courage or the candour to admit that the North meant Prussia. Yet still the struggle for leadership continued, Austria persisting in the belief that she had both right and might on her side, Prussia equally sure of her might, and by that title claiming right as well. More and more the dualism was becoming a dualism in name only, since though there were still two minds there was only one strong will.

The unity movement had received a new impetus after 1859 owing to the triumph of the national cause in Italy and to the vigorous agitation begun in that year by the National Association (*Nationalverein*). This organization owed its origin mainly to a little band of Liberals, first amongst whom was Rudolf von Bennigsen, a Hanover statesman of marked ability and high character, and it was intended to serve as a meeting-point for all the efforts favourable to the creation of a German federal State under Prussian leadership. Formed at Eisenach, it wished to make Frankfort its headquarters, but the Senate of that city, fearing to incur the displeasure of the Federal Diet, drove it away, whereupon it was welcomed in Gotha by the Liberal-minded ruler of the duchy. The Association represented Little Germany aspirations, and at Austria's request some of the Governments friendly to the existing federal basis suppressed its branches, with their agitation, in their territories. Nevertheless, the Association prospered greatly and did an important work. Under its influence a host of propagandist organizations of all kinds —political, municipal, musical, gymnastic, commercial—were established; and through their instrumentality the agitation of the earlier *Burschenschaften* and the Jahn societies was repeated in a spirit of equal if soberer earnestness. Urgent resolutions in favour of unity were passed by some of the parliaments of Central and South Germany; local congresses and conferences were held in sympathy with the same object; once more the nation's unchanging faith that destiny was welding it into one was attested in the eyes of rulers, of whom some were hostile, many apathetic, few friendly to the great cause.

The King of Prussia himself seemed to catch some of the fervour of the time, for meeting the Grand Duke of Baden and his Minister-President at Ostend in the summer of 1861, he listened with favour to their proposal of a strong central government, of which Prussia should be the head, co-operating with a parliament of the nation. The scheme outlined was not novel, for it repeated the main features of the untimely constitution which had been adopted by the "three Kings' alliance"; what was novel and welcome was William I's apparent acceptance of it.

At the same time he was as hostile to an open breach with Austria as his brother, the late King, had ever been. The year before, Bismarck, at a conference to which he had been called together with the Ministers Schleinitz and Auerswald, had urged that, while Prussia might still be able to accomplish her German mission in agreement with Austria, it could only be after "the conviction had gained ground in Vienna that in the opposite case we should shrink from neither rupture nor war." Thereupon Schleinitz had spoken in favour of putting good relations with

Vienna first and of maintaining them at all costs, and this view the then Regent appeared to endorse.[1]

Meanwhile, a still more ambitious scheme was receiving consideration in Vienna. Its author was Julius Fröbel, an ex-revolutionary of the 1848 days, who had shed his hot humours in exile, and had been taken into his service by Schmerling, now head of the Emperor's Ministry, as an agitator for the Great Germany solution of the federal question. This scheme was first submitted to the Austrian plenipotentiary to the Federal Diet in June, 1861, and through him came to the knowledge of the Ministry and the Emperor. Fröbel proposed an empire to be co-extensive with the existing Bund, the office of emperor to be hereditary in the Austrian house. There was to be a central Diet of two Houses, meeting at Frankfort, one the House of Princes, composed of reigning Sovereigns or Royal Princes, of which the King of Prussia was to be the president, Austria being represented therein by an Archduke, and the other a national assembly, composed of nominees of the State legislatures. There was a certain *naïveté* about the cautious and clandestine measures that were to be adopted for preventing the premature disclosure of this project. The constitution was to be drawn up and all the necessary preparatory arrangements were to be made in secrecy, and the completed work was to be sprung upon a wondering world upon a given day.

The plan failed to make a favourable impression upon the Emperor and his advisers, though more might have been heard of it but for the fact that about the time Count Beust, the Saxon Minister, was pushing a scheme of his own, for which he had a parent's fond admiration. This scheme would have continued the Federation, with a central administration located at Frankfort, but proposed, as an alternative to a standing Federal Diet, conferences of Ministers of all the States to be held twice a year, at Ratisbon under Austrian and at Hamburg under Prussian presidency, together with an assembly of delegates of the German legislatures, to be convened whenever the Governments thought necessary, and a Federal Tribunal for the decision of constitutional disputes. This scheme of a travelling exhibition of federal impotence, though ingenious, pleased no one altogether. The King of Würtemberg spoke of it as being "as impractical as it is dangerous," while the verdict upon it of the Baden Minister, Baron von Roggenbach, a warm advocate of Prussian hegemony,

[1] *Reflections and Reminiscences*, vol. i., p. 258.

was, "This is offering the German nation not bread but a stone." Austria refused to consider it, since it seemed to countenance the old heresy of parity between the rival Powers, though Beust was in reality far more concerned to give greater prominence to the secondary and minor States, so creating a counterpoise to their powerful allies.

When invited to express an opinion, Prussia replied that she was agreeable to the retention of the Federation (December 20, 1861), but with restricted powers, and subject to the condition that those States which wished to form a closer union within the Federation should be free to do so. Virtually this proposal was a revival of the Union project, and having believed this to be dead and buried, the Emperor resented it, as a renewed invitation to efface Austria from the map of Germany; and he induced all the secondary States to join him in an identical protest (February 2, 1862). As a counter-move he also persuaded these States to join Austria in proposing in the Diet the institution of a federal directory with an assembly of delegates, a proposal which, when introduced, Prussia successfully opposed on the ground that if a representative assembly was to be created at all it must proceed directly from the nation.

Shortly after he became Prussian Minister-President, Bismarck, in the hope of clearing the air, invited the Austrian ambassador, Count Karolyi, to a frank exchange of views (December, 1862), the result of which he published in a circular despatch (January 24, 1863). He told Karolyi that the relations between the two States could not continue as they were, but must become either better or worse, and while he sincerely hoped the former, he was bound to anticipate the latter in view of Austria's attitude. What was to be the end? When the Count suggested that in the event of Austria being attacked by France Prussia would assuredly be found fighting on her side, Bismarck replied that that was an unjustifiable assumption, of which it would be wise to rid himself. Given the continuance of the existing tension, the probability was that if the situation of 1859 were repeated Prussia would ally herself with one of Austria's enemies. He added that Prussia would be guided entirely by Austria's policy towards her; if that policy became one of friendship, Prussia would reciprocate it, but if Austria persisted in her dog-in-the-manger attitude and continued to plot against Prussia in the other States, she would have to accept the consequences. When the Count protested that Austria could not agree to surrender her traditional place in Germany, Bismarck suggested that the centre of Austria's rightful influence was not Vienna but Budapest, an idea for which he had often tried, while Prussian ambassador in Paris, to win a favourable hearing from his Austrian colleague.[1]

Count Vitzthum, in a letter of the time, speaks of the conversation as causing "grave anxiety." It may be regarded, indeed, as Bismarck's first formal warning, uttered with an authority which had long ceased to give urgency to the words of Prussian statesmen, that for Prussia and Austria the parting of the ways had come. For the moment the effect in Vienna seemed to be moderating and salutary. The Court and the Government were shocked at such plain speaking, but Count Rechberg assured the Prussian ambassador that Austria was as desirous of amicable relationships as Prussia, and that he looked forward hopefully to cordial co-operation in the congenial task of stemming revolutionary movements.

At this time the Emperor's advisers appear to have come to the conclusion that if Austria was to take the initiative on the German question she must do so at once. The moment seemed singularly opportune for a decisive attempt to isolate Prussia and win the rest of the States in a body for the Great Germany idea. Prussia was in the throes of the constitutional conflict; her Government was in bad repute throughout Germany; in the South in particular the memory of the betrayal of 1859 rankled; of the secondary States only one, Baden, and of the small States few were truly friendly to her; and it was doubtful whether the German nation, in its existing mood, would be disposed to listen to protests or proposals emanating from Berlin. If there was ever to be federal reform on Austria's lines, now was the time for it. Accordingly, the Emperor convened a congress of the Princes for the purpose of considering the reconstitution of the Federation.[2] The congress met at Frankfort

[1] The idea of Budapest becoming the capital of the Austrian dominion and the Austrian centre of gravity did not originate with Bismarck. Talleyrand after 1805 proposed to Napoleon that Austria should be moved on towards the East and be compensated for her losses on the Danube by the acquisition of Serbia, Wallachia, and Bulgaria, and the proposal is said to have reached the Court of Vienna. The German publicist Friedrich von Gentz wrote in 1806: "Vienna must cease to be the seat of government, which must be removed to the centre of Hungary, and this country be given a new constitution. With Hungary, Bohemia, Galicia, and whatever else remained of Germany it would still be able to face the world." In the middle of the century, when the unity question became acute, German political writers revived the idea.

[2] The Mayors of the four Free Cities were also invited and attended.

(August 17, 1863), and all the Princes were present save one—the King of Prussia. The Emperor had visited him at Gastein at the beginning of the month and urged him to take part. Left to himself, he would probably have been willing, but Bismarck was with him and dissuaded him on the twofold ground that it was Austria's design to strengthen the federal tie on the existing impossible basis and that a congress of the rulers could in any case only tend to practical results if preceded by a conference of their Ministers.

The congress was opened with great state, Francis Joseph presiding, yet the proceedings had not gone far before every one realized their unreality in the absence of the principal figure. A majestic play had been brilliantly staged, but when the curtain rose upon the first scene the leading actor was missing. In the awkward situation King John of Saxony volunteered both to write a letter of invitation to the absent monarch and to be its bearer, the congress thereupon adjourning until the royal courier should return. The invitation found the King, now at Baden-Baden, in two minds, but there could be no doubt which would prevail, for Bismarck was still with him keeping watch and ward over his wavering will. All the instincts of courtesy urged him to go. "Invited by thirty Princes, with a King as courier—how can I refuse?" he asked. Bismarck thought only of policy, and replied that if the King went to Frankfort, he, his Minister-President, would return to the home of his fathers and stop there. The invitation was, therefore, again declined.

Nevertheless, the congress continued its work, and after ten sittings duly adopted a draft constitution. Under this Austria was to retain her position at the head of the Federation, a condition declared by the Emperor to be indispensable; the Diet was to be continued; a directory of Princes was to be created for executive purposes, Austria, Prussia, and Bavaria having each one vote; and there was to be a deliberative assembly of delegates appointed by the State legislatures. Such a constitution was a mockery of the national expectations; it showed, as the Austrian historian Friedjung frankly says, "how little Austria had to offer to the German nation."[1] For Austria, however, the only thing that really mattered was that she should continue to dominate the Federation, and under the Emperor's scheme that was certain. The draft was adopted by a substantial majority,

[1] *Der Kampf um die Vorherrschaft in Deutschland*, vol. i., p. 59.

though not a few of those who approved it did so with avowed or hidden reservations. All the four Kings voted for it, but the Grand Dukes of Baden, Saxe-Weimar, Oldenburg, and Mecklenburg-Schwerin opposed it. The draft was sent to the King of Prussia with a second collective letter commending it to his acceptance. In closing the congress on September 1st the Emperor, whose conduct of its proceedings had won general praise, held out to his allies the hope of a second congress at an early date, in which their labours would be brought to completion. It was unpropitious, however, that a national conference, hastily convened at Frankfort under Liberal auspices, pronounced strongly against the scheme.

The King of Prussia had referred the draft constitution to his Ministry of State, and on September 15th this body reported on it adversely and proposed an alternative basis of reform. By this Prussia was to have equal rights with Austria in the direction of the affairs of the Federation, the presidency to be held by them in turn; the two States were to have a right of veto upon any federal declaration of war which was not in defence of federal territory; and the idea of an assembly of delegates was to give place to a national parliament, proceeding from direct election, in which the whole of the States should be represented in the ratio of population. The King, on September 23rd, communicated the substance of this report in his reply to the letter from the Congress Princes, informing them that he could only assent to the extension of the competency of the Federation and of its central authority on condition that reform followed these lines. That his Minister-President had been genuinely converted to the idea of a democratic legislature may be doubted. Had Austria made the proposal, he might have been the first to condemn it; but knowing that it was a concession to the nation which it was beyond Austria's power to offer, and seeing in it a hope of winning popular sentiment to Prussia's side, he adopted for expediency's sake a measure which went counter to some of his strongest prejudices.

The federal reform question had again entered a critical phase, and for the moment it seemed as though no further progress could be made unless one of the two rivals gave way. Now, however, the situation was suddenly changed by events which directed the energies of both into an entirely different channel, yet one which was to carry the federal controversy by devious ways to the predestined goal. These events centred in the dispute over the Elbe duchies, a subject too large for further reference here.

In the meantime there had been interludes in domestic affairs. One of these occurred in the spring of 1862 in the form of another quarrel with the Elector of Hesse, the same who had given so much trouble in 1850, and this time matters were settled in Prussia's way. In May that erratic ruler, recovering from the shock of his expulsion twelve years before, decided that the time had come for again suspending the constitution. Disorder threatening in consequence, the King of Prussia wrote a letter of expostulation to his wilful neighbour and in order to increase its urgency sent it by the hand of a General. The Elector did not recognize the right of Prussia to interfere; if he had suspended an entire constitution, William I had suspended a part, and he refused to receive the King's messenger, haughtily throwing the letter on the table. Count Bernstorff, the Foreign Secretary, asked Bismarck's opinion of the political significance of this insult. "The fact of the Elector throwing a letter on the table," was the laconic reply, "is not a good *casus belli*, but if you wish for war only appoint me your Under-Secretary and I will promise to bring about civil war within a month." Bernstoff is said to have "drawn back horrified."

Nevertheless, the Government, perhaps amused rather than dismayed by the grave warning of Lord Augustus Loftus, the British ambassador, that he should "let the Hessian question alone, since it was a European question," promptly demanded the dismissal of the Ministers who had given the Elector such bad advice, and on a refusal broke off diplomatic relationships with the Hessian Court. The question was raised in the Federal Diet, which accepted the joint proposal of Prussia and Austria that the Elector should be called upon to restore the constitution of 1831 on pain of federal execution. Before a month had passed the Elector had capitulated and called into office a Liberal Cabinet. No sooner did the Estates meet again at the end of October, however, than the frivolous ruler sent them home and once more dismissed his advisers. Bismarck was now in power, and he judged that the time had come for speaking plainly. In a vigorous note of November 24th he threatened that unless a condition of order and tranquillity were at once and permanently restored, the Prussian Government would set the Diet in operation and the Elector would have to take the consequences. "The Prussian Government, in its own interest," he wrote, "cannot tolerate the existence in the midst of its provinces and of Germany of a hotbed of renewed excitement and disquiet." Frightened by this unaccustomed language and of the contingency to which it pointed, the Elector revoked the dismissal of his Ministry, called the Estates together again, and the constitutional crisis ended.

Prussia emerged from the episode triumphant in every way; she had brought the obstinate Elector to his knees, carried Austria with her, and had forced her will on the Federal Diet. The humiliation of Olmütz was in a fair way of being effaced.

"The State," Bismarck once wrote, "cannot stand still." Least of all can this be the case in relation to foreign affairs. It was soon seen that under the new guidance Prussia's foreign policy was to be marked by an independence and force which had for a long time been lacking. In March, 1861, Victor Emmanuel had been declared King of Italy by the first national parliament. The new kingdom was recognized by Great Britain in the same month; by France in June; by Prussia only in July of the following year, yet even then to the deep disgust of the legitimist Conservatives and of the Roman Catholics. Although Bismarck was not yet a Minister, no important act of foreign policy was adopted without his advice, and his influence was altogether on the side of Italian unity. His thoughts were of Prussia's rather than of Italy's advantage, though the idea of Austria continuing to lord it in Italy was to him as unnatural as her domination in Germany. To the Foreign Secretary Bernstorff he wrote of Italy at the time: "When once she stands on her own feet I cannot think of a more welcome creation for Prussian policy. It is my conviction that if Italy did not arise of herself we should have to invent her."

All this time the political relations of Prussia and France continued uncertain, the Emperor still cherishing the idea of an alliance, the King neither accepting nor positively rejecting it, though never for a moment regarding it with favour. Nevertheless, overtures from France were reciprocated all the more readily in another direction, where political obligations were not directly involved. Following the conclusion of the Cobden commercial treaty with England of January 23, 1860, Napoleon, hardly foreseeing the importance of his act, proposed to Prussia in the following year the conclusion of a similar treaty on the basis of most-favoured-nation treatment. That meant for Prussia that she would need either to secede from the Customs Union or to carry the other German States with her into the new agreement when the treaty underlying the Union came to be renewed as from the end of 1865. Confident that the community of economic interest which had brought the Union into existence would require its continuance, he did not doubt that the latter alternative would prove feasible, though he was prepared for opposition in the first instance.

A more difficult question was the relation to the proposed agreement of Austria, whose convention with the Customs Union secured to her special advantages, which might be forfeited if Prussia carried her point. Count Rechberg, the Austrian Foreign Secretary, offered to the French treaty proposals resolute resistance, declaring them to be incompatible with both the spirit and the letter of the treaty of 1853, one of whose provisions, as has been shown, contemplated the admission of Austria to the Customs Union at a later date, so unifying the entire area of the Federation for customs purposes.

Many of the States of the Union likewise received the proposed arrangement with France with distrust and hostility, and asked that they might be called into the negotiations before Prussia came to a final decision. Their request was refused in circumstances which increased the prevailing dissatisfaction. In April, 1862, the draft of the treaty had been communicated to all the Governments and their prompt acceptance invited. Influenced doubtless by the apparent success with which Austria was organizing opposition, Prussia nevertheless signed the treaty (August 2nd), without waiting for the replies of her allies, who in consequence were placed in the position of having either to make a humiliating surrender or to withdraw from the Union.

Of the secondary States, Hanover, Bavaria, and Würtemberg all protested their unwillingness to accept the treaty thus concluded over their heads. Saxony proved more compliant; Count Beust's Ministry was still equally hostile, but it was compelled to set material interests against political, and as an industrial and free trade country Saxony stood to gain by any concessions which might be made by the Union to France in return for lower tariffs there. In Prussia both Chambers of the Diet voted approval of the treaty and its acceptance as part of the basis of the new Customs Union, though disagreement with the army organization scheme and a premonition of worse trouble to come had already changed the general attitude of the popular parties towards the Government from one of deference to one of suspicion.

Negotiations for the renewal of the Customs Union were duly

opened in 1863. In the meantime Bismarck had become the Prussian Minister-President, and he was a hard as well as a shrewd bargainer. Already he had denounced the old treaties (December, 1862), giving Prussia's allies to understand that the choice before them was the acceptance of the agreement with France as it stood or the dissolution of the Union—a far more serious matter for them than for Prussia. For a long time no progress was made. Most of the larger States continued to protest, and Austria was behind them with encouragement and counter-offers. So remote did agreement appear to be in the summer of 1864 that Prussia then concluded a new provisional treaty of union with Saxony, Hanover, Hesse-Cassel, and some of the smaller States, while for a time there seemed a likelihood that Austria might succeed in forming a rival union, embracing Bavaria, Würtemberg, Nassau, and Darmstadt. Recognizing at last the futility of resistance, and being assured of Prussia's willingness to conclude a new treaty with Austria outside the Union on equitable terms, the hostile Governments capitulated. Before the end of the year the renewal of the Customs Union was assured, and all that remained was to agree with France upon certain modifications of the treaty of August, 1862, which were necessary in order to meet Austria's reasonable expectations. With the conclusion of the general treaty of May 16, 1865, Austria was again and permanently excluded from the Customs Union of the German peoples, while Prussia's economic predominance in Germany was not merely confirmed but strengthened.

Rechberg had attached the greatest importance to the retention in the revised treaty between Austria and the Union of the article providing that negotiations for the admission of Austria to full membership should be opened before the treaty expired twelve years later. Bismarck, wishful to oblige so excellent a colleague, whose position he knew to be far from secure, had favoured that concession, which he regarded as without importance, since he was convinced that the special economic and social conditions of Austria would in any event make her inclusion impossible. A majority of his colleagues were against him, however, and in his absence, when the question came up for settlement in the Cabinet (October, 1864)—he was at Biarritz, seeking health—they succeeded in persuading the King and in carrying their point.

Early in the year 1863 there was offered to Bismarck an opportunity of serving Russia in a critical situation and simultaneously of putting to the test the quality and strength of the apparent friendship between that Power and France, and this opportunity he was prompt to use. Undeterred by the terrible reprisals which followed the revolution of 1861, the Poles again broke into insurrection in Warsaw in January, 1863. With the avowed object of preventing the spread of the movement to East Prussia, yet more for the purpose of doing Russia a good turn, Bismarck persuaded the King to conclude with Czar Alexander II a military convention (February 8th) under which the two Governments were to make common cause against rebellion amongst their Polish populations. In the event of a rising the troops of both the countries were to occupy the frontier districts and to be allowed to cross over into neighbouring territory. Prussia did, in fact, mass a large force upon the Russian frontier, and General von Alvensleben, who negotiated the treaty in St. Petersburg, was instructed to inform the Czar that it was at his service if needed. Prince Gortchakoff was then the Russian Chancellor and at the height of his power. Bismarck was glad to work together with so great a man, and he had a further inducement so to do in the conviction, which he had already confessed to Bernstorff (November, 1861), that the existing feeling of good-will between the two countries was purely dynastic and that the nations themselves were going more and more apart.

As soon as the Polish convention came to the knowledge of the other Great Powers, it roused a storm of indignation, in which the democratic party both in Prussia and Germany generally fully shared. Bismarck himself appears to have thought at the time that he had done a dangerous thing, for on February 20th he wrote with relief to the King that "seeing how matters seem to be shaping themselves in Poland . . . we shall hardly be called upon for active co-operation there, and the convention thus gives us the advantage of having secured cheaply for the future the gratitude of Czar Alexander and Russian sympathy." [1] Napoleon was quick to voice the displeasure of Western Europe. True to his enthusiasm for the cause of nationalism, he had taken the Polish question warmly to heart. When meeting the Czar at Stuttgart in 1857 he had told him that only one shadow fell on the amicable relations between their two countries, the woes of Poland, and that the more the Czar could do to alleviate the

[1] In his studiously apologetic references to the Polish treaty in his *Reflections and Reminiscences* (vol. i., p. 342) Bismarck speaks of it as having "a diplomatic rather than a military significance," which in the event proved to be the case.

condition of his Polish subjects the more surely he would be able to count on the friendship of the French nation. Now he declared that such a convention made the Polish question no longer a local but a European concern, and he invited the Cabinets of London and Vienna to join him in an identical note of protest to Prussia. The British Cabinet, while condemning the convention, was unwilling to take so serious a step. Lord Palmerston had ceased to trust Napoleon, and it was his opinion that the proposal of intervention was merely a trap; he suspected, indeed, that the Emperor was determined beforehand that the note of protest should be one which Prussia would be compelled to reject and that he would make its rejection a pretext for occupying the Rhenish provinces. On the other hand, Earl Russell, the Foreign Secretary, believed that Bismarck was not the tempter, but the tempted, and that Napoleon's remonstrances should be addressed to St. Petersburg. As Austria also declined to take action, the proposal fell to the ground. In the meantime Bismarck had assured the British ambassador in Berlin that the convention was without practical importance and "a dead letter," and that there was no likelihood whatever of its provisions being put into operation; in the event it was not ratified.

Matters became graver when from April forward the same Powers, jointly and severally, made urgent representations to the Czar's Government on behalf of the Poles, basing their action on the fact that they were parties to the treaty of 1815, which revised the frontiers of Russia's Polish dominions. France emphasized the need for a condition of permanence, which could only be created by the application of humane and benevolent measures; Austria wanted peace in the interest of the tranquillity and security of her own Polish province, Galicia; Great Britain felt strongly on the subject of fidelity to treaties. Earl Russell went to the length of proposing an elaborate programme of reforms—a political amnesty, representative government, a Polish administration, liberty of conscience, the use of the national language, and the like: in short, just such a programme as might, *mutatis mutandis*, have befitted Ireland at that time had British statesmen been as conscious of the urgency of ameliorative measures in near as in distant centres of misrule and discontent. Gortchakoff treated lightly this well-meant advice as a species of dictation, and when a little later the British ambassador showed him another eloquent despatch, in which Russell hazarded the opinion that Russia had forfeited her title to Poland because of her neglect to fulfil her promises to its inhabitants, he refused to accept it until this sentence had been omitted.

To all these representations Russia replied that she did not recognize any outside right of interference, while the Czar urged the King of Prussia to do his utmost to detach his Vienna friend from the Western Powers. That the Czar was prepared if necessary for another trial of strength appears from his invitation to King William that he would state his position. " How do you interpret the duties and interests of Germany in this situation ? " he asked on June 1st. " If it comes to a rupture, what will be your action ? What do you expect from Germany ? What do you expect from Austria ? I know that I can rely on you, as you can on me."

Notwithstanding that Russia still refused to accept remonstrances, and in September declared that the matter was closed, Napoleon fell back upon the idea of a European conference. The idea of a conference had upon Napoleon all the soothing influence of the " comfortable word Mesopotamia." Conferences were his unfailing cure for Continental discords and disputes, and his belief in them was never shaken. His confidence in this specific was subject to one qualification only : the medicine must be administered by himself. Unless France, therefore, convened the conference, the Governments which conferred would labour in vain. Accordingly he made a proposal to this effect in November. But the conference was to consider other questions besides the condition of Poland. " The political edifice of Europe," Napoleon wrote, " reposes on the Treaties of Vienna, yet it is crumbling away on all sides." " It is impossible not to admit," he said, "that on almost all points the treaties are destroyed, modified, disregarded or menaced. Hence there are duties without rule, rights without title, pretensions without restraint." It was a daring claim to be made by the man who had seized Savoy and coveted the Rhine provinces. Great Britain once more proved the spoke in the wheel. Lord Palmerston saw danger ahead. Napoleon wanted an adjustment of his eastern frontiers, but he was not the only ruler who hankered after new territory at the expense of some one else. Fearing that the inevitable clash of interests which a European conference would create might lead to a general Continental war, Palmerston declined to allow his country to take part. Earl Russell made the mistake of giving his Government's reasons for abstention and even arguing them. He objected to a roving inquiry " without fixed objects ranging over the map of Europe and exciting hopes and expectations which they might find themselves unable either to gratify or to quiet." The consequence was that while all the other Powers except Prussia were equally opposed to a conference, Great Britain alone bore the reproach for its rejection. By thus wrecking the project she wounded Napoleon in a specially sensitive place.

The well-intended action of the Powers did the Poles neither good nor harm. The most substantial result of the episode was that it drew Russia and Prussia nearer together and prepared the way for their later co-operation in other directions. Bismarck does not appear to have taken England's action unkindly, for meeting Lord Granville, then Foreign Secretary, a little later, he assured him of his "general wish that England and Prussia should be good friends."

Nevertheless, the episode threw light upon Bismarck's attitude towards the problem of Polish nationality, later to become a capital question of Prussian politics. His opinion of the problem at this time may be noted here for future reference. "Every success for the Polish national movement," he wrote to Count Bernstorff in 1861, "is a defeat for Prussia, and we cannot fight against this element by simple justice, but only according to the rules of war. The Polish question cannot be judged with impartiality, but only with hostility."

Bismarck's Visit to London in June, 1862.

Careful consideration of all available data has forced me to the conclusion that the utterance attributed to Bismarck in the often-told story of the dinner given by Baron Brunnow, the Russian ambassador in London, to the Grand Duke of Saxe-Weimar in June, 1862, must be discounted severely, and for that reason I hesitate to refer to it in the text. Count Vitzthum von Eckstädt, the Saxon envoy in London, first gave currency to the story in his Memoirs, *St. Petersburg and London*, and it is to the effect that at this gathering Bismarck (making a purely unofficial visit to London from Paris at the end of June) met Disraeli, to whom he spoke "somewhat" (*ungefähr*)—an important qualification, invariably ignored by the later retailers of the conversation—as follows:

"I shall soon be compelled to take over the direction of the Prussian Ministry. My first care will be to reorganize the army, with or without the help of the Diet. The King has rightly undertaken this task, but he cannot carry it through with his present advisers. When the army has been brought to a condition in which it will command respect, I shall seize the first pretext for declaring war on Austria, dissolving the Germanic Federation, subduing the secondary and small States, and giving Germany national unity under Prussia's leadership. I have come here to say this to her Majesty's Ministers."

Vitzthum relates that this utterance was repeated to him by Disraeli himself. It is noteworthy, however, that Disraeli has left no record of it, and though his biographer, Mr. Buckle, quotes it, he does it on Vitzthum's authority. That Bismarck does not record this special incident of his London visit, or give any indication of the words attributed to him, may not in the circumstances be peculiar. There is, it seems to me, strong internal evidence that Bismarck cannot have spoken exactly as Vitzthum represents. It would not have been accurate, even had it been judicious, to say at that time that he was about to become Minister-President of Prussia. The fact is that his future was altogether obscure. In the preceding January he had written to his sister from St. Petersburg: "I should be ungrateful both to God and man if I said that I was not happy here and wanted a change: I am more frightened of (entering) the Ministry than of a cold bath. I would rather take any vacant (diplomatic) post or return to Frankfort, or even Berne, where I felt very comfortable." Just before the London visit he had, in fact, received the Paris embassy, and while he no doubt regarded the appointment as a stepping-stone to the Cabinet, he was apparently still not wishful to be called up higher for a time; the outlook at the time was far from certain. On reaching Paris he writes on June 2nd to Roon, who was eager to see him in the Ministry, preferably at the head: "I still flatter myself with the hope that I shall seem less indispensable to his Majesty when I have been out of his sight for a while, and that some hitherto unrecognized statesman will be found to supplant me, so that I may ripen a little more here." Even on July 15th he writes to the same correspondent that he has heard that "the King is doubtful whether I can be of any use in the present session, and whether my appointment, if it takes place at all, ought not to be postponed till the winter. . . . If I am asked for my opinion, I shall give it in favour of keeping in the background a few months longer."

The day before he had written to his wife likewise that the King could not decide whether to ask him to be Minister-President or not —and, indeed, when later he made the appointment, he did it, as we have seen, with misgiving—so that he was preparing to remain in Paris until the winter.

In the meantime, "in the lack of any kind of political task or business," as he writes in *Reflections and Reminiscences* (vol. i., p. 281), he makes this visit to England, and afterwards starts for "a longish tour in the South of France," where he "forgets all about politics and reads no newspapers." In August he is making holiday plans for the following year on the assumption that he would still be in France. Even when in September he is called to Berlin to see the King he goes with the intention of asking that he may be allowed to settle down in Paris, though in the event he is offered and accepts office with the provisional presidency of the Ministry until Hohenzollern should retire, when he was to succeed him and take also the portfolio of Foreign Affairs.

The facts known, therefore, do not suggest that Bismarck's position in June could have justified him in announcing beforehand a Ministerial programme so ambitious and sensational as the one credited to him by Vitzthum. Moreover, as to the programme itself, Bismarck was never a boaster, and the words ascribed to him are not in his manner. Finally, even had he gone to London with the object of divulging his purposes to the Government there, it is not likely that he would have first unbosomed himself to the leader of the Opposition, whom he had never met before. If he communicated such intentions to any of the Queen's Ministers, it would be to the head of the Government (Lord Palmerston) or the Foreign Secretary (Lord Russell), and it is significant that neither of them has left any record of his having done so.

It is quite possible that, in the course of this unofficial voyage of discovery, Bismarck may have discussed with Disraeli and others some or all of the measures enumerated by Vitzthum, and even have appeared to advocate them. But to have represented them, to a Government so friendly to Austria as the British Government then was, as the basis of a coming Ministerial programme, would have been an act of arrogance and indiscretion quite unworthy of so skilful a diplomat.

It is also justifiable to recall how in a letter written to Count Beust on October 10th, just after his appointment to office, Bismarck said:

"Considering your knowledge of men and affairs, I need not assure you that I stand quite aloof from all the adventurous plans that have been attributed to me by political novices and by opponents in the Press. The untruthful, distorted and disconnected reports of supposed sayings of mine, by which people have endeavoured to bring my judgment into discredit, must have been appreciated by you with a full knowledge of the facts. I do not feel called upon to force Prussia into the channels of Sardinian policy, and if any one in my position had any such feeling he would have no basis upon which he could reduce his theory to practice. . . . As to internal affairs, my most urgent duty is to preserve and strengthen the power of the Crown against the increasing influence of the representative Chamber and the parliamentary officials. I consider that this task can be accomplished without departing from the positive injunctions of the constitution. I shall endeavour to spare as much as possible the feelings of sticklers for constitutional forms, and to return as soon as possible to constitutional forms, always bearing in mind, however, that our constitutional oath places 'fidelity to the King' first."

Bismarck had no severer critic in later years than Beust, yet Beust affirms that this utterance "must not be regarded as wanting in sincerity."[1] In fine, while accepting it as perfectly credible that Bismarck may, in the way of speculation, have mentioned in conversation some or all of the measures enumerated by the Saxon envoy, I regard as questionable the story that he avowed these measures as representing the deliberate programme of a Government which had not been formed and did not at the moment appear imminent, and as still more doubtful the idea that he intended to communicate them to a Cabinet to which he was not accredited and whose cool attitude towards Prussia was well known to him.

[1] *Memoirs,* English translation, vol. i., pp. 206–7.

CHAPTER V

(1846–1865)

THE ELBE DUCHIES AND THE DANISH WAR

IN the memories of Prussians of to-day the Danish war of 1864 lives chiefly owing to the fact that it renewed a military reputation which had become tarnished, and added to their country the flourishing double province of Schleswig-Holstein. For Germany at large the most important political effect of the war was the fact that it directly brought on another, of which the purpose and result was the ejection of Austria from the Germanic household.

How far the Danish war may be justly regarded as a war of necessity, as an event which, in Bismarck's favourite phrase, lay "in the nature of things," may at one time have been a disputable question, but it is such no longer. Writing long after the leading figure in this episode passed away, leaving behind him not a few ungarnished disclosures of the aims and motives which influenced his public life, it is possible to give to the question a positive answer. Bismarck wanted the war, intended and schemed it, from the beginning. For this statement we have his own testimony. He has left it on record that from early days he coveted for Prussia the territories which divided her from the Danish monarchy proper, and that his chief reason for so doing was the knowledge that without the double seaboard which they offered Prusso-Germany could never hope to become a maritime Power. Even if, he said, three wars had been necessary, as in the case of Prussia's conquest of Silesia, he would have fought them for the sake of such a prize. "The diplomatic campaign of which I am proudest was that over Schleswig-Holstein," he said on one occasion; and when asked if he wanted the duchies from the first, he answered, "Yes, certainly, immediately after the death of the King of Denmark" (in 1863), adding that although he knew that to carry his will would mean a determined struggle with the King, he never once despaired of success. Evidence to the same effect from the same source might be multiplied.[1]

The dispute over the duchies was, and still is, full of difficulties: it involved questions of succession, claims of agnates and cognates, sovereign rights and fief rights; it was complicated by disputatious treaties and equivocal agreements; it involved issues which brought into operation the German federal laws; and it became the subject of repeated conferences between the European States, of which four at least—Denmark, Austria, Prussia, and Russia—were directly concerned. Ponderous disquisitions have been written upon the episode since it became a closed chapter of history, yet even now it presents a legal labyrinth unique of its kind. It was of this dispute that Lord Palmerston said in 1863 that only three men had ever understood its clue—one was the Prince Consort, and he was dead; the second was a Danish Minister, who had gone mad over it; and he himself was the third, and he had forgotten it.

For present purposes, since the question now possesses only historical interest, it will be sufficient to follow the threads of the story from the eve of the final developments.

There had been quarrelling over Schleswig and Holstein for centuries, but it had been confined to Denmark and the duchies. It was only when the dispute became part of the problem of German unity, and Austria and Prussia were drawn in, first as allies and then as antagonists, that the decisive stage was reached when a settlement became inevitable. Schleswig and Holstein, bound to each other by essential community of race, language, and institutions, were also bound by personal union to the Danish Crown; the Danish rulers were kings in Denmark and dukes in the duchies. Holstein was altogether German in population, and from the time of Charlemagne it had formed part of the Holy Roman Empire; while of the population of Schleswig a portion, living in the extreme north, was pure Danish. The duchies had immemorially enjoyed a wide measure of self-government, and successive Sovereigns had guaranteed to them this autonomy, and the many local rights and immunities attached to it. They had their own constitutions, Diets, administrations, and judicial systems, and their inhabitants enjoyed identical civil rights. The duchies valued their union almost as much as their political independence; the motto of the hardy peoples

[1] Cf. *Reflections and Reminiscences*, vol. ii., pp. 10, 11.

of this sea-girt region was " For ever undivided," and the Danish Kings in their coronation oath swore to preserve unruptured the ancient bond.

With the dissolution of the Empire the connection of Holstein with Germany temporarily ceased, and though together with the small duchy of Lauenburg it entered the Germanic Federation created by the Congress of Vienna in 1815, it did so mediately in the person of the King of Denmark, whose title to sovereignty was still unquestioned.

Throughout the first half of the century successive Danish Kings sought, first by mild and later by stronger measures, to make the union between their kingdom and the duchies more definite and intimate. In their resolve to complete the unity of the Danish dominion the Kings had behind them a strong national movement represented by the " Eider Danes," who wished, by extending the limits of the monarchy to the river Eider, dividing South Schleswig from Holstein, to cut off German influence. And just as in Germany the democrats of that time sought to obtain national unity by the creation of constitutional government on popular principles, so the Danish democrats held out to the people of Schleswig the promise of popular government as the price of unity. On July 8, 1846, in an " open letter," Christian VIII, as Duke of Schleswig-Holstein, proposed a complete territorial and constitutional union between Denmark and Schleswig, and the subjection of both duchies to the Danish Crown law. For the latter measure there was a strong reason. The Danish Crown might descend in the female line, but agnatic succession applied in the duchies. The male line of the Danish royal house, however, was about to become extinct, and unless the duchies were joined to the kingdom they would pass to one of three collateral families, that of Augustenburg. Against the proposed changes not only the heads of the families whose claims were thus threatened, the Dukes of Augustenburg and Glücksburg and the Grand Duke of Oldenburg, but also the Estates of both duchies, promptly protested.

Towards the end of 1847 the King approved a new constitution, framed on Liberal principles, which was intended to give effect to these changes, but he died before it could receive his signature (January 20, 1848). One of the first public acts of his successor, Frederick VII, was to sign and promulgate this document.

The spirit of revolution was abroad at the time, and in few

European countries were the peoples in a mood to parley with despots. Accordingly, the population of Schleswig, incensed at this infraction of its ancient liberties, rose in insurrection, and was at once joined by Holstein. With a view to the better assertion of their independence, the Germans of the northern duchy also called for its admission into the Germanic Federation alongside the sister territory. Throughout Germany there was a responsive outcry. Thousands of armed volunteers crossed over into Schleswig in order to assist the national rising and repel the inroad of Danish troops from the north, while the King of Bavaria sent officers to help in organizing and directing the rebellion. All political parties alike, whether Conservative, Liberal, or democratic, each from its own standpoint, as the special guardian of legitimism or constitutionalism or the principle of popular sovereignty, condemned the action of the Danish King as high-handed and indefensible.

As the Duke of Schleswig was also ruler in the sister duchy, and as this duchy was a member of the Germanic Federation, the Diet was compelled to move, and accordingly in April it commissioned Prussia to assert the federal authority in Holstein. The Duke of Augustenburg, Christian August, had already invoked the help of the King of Prussia, who had formally signified his recognition of the union and independence of the duchies, as well as of the agnatic principle—which meant the acknowledgment of the Duke's claim to the succession—and sent troops to the frontier, calling upon other North German States to co-operate. Denmark, on the other hand, had appealed for help to Russia. For the present, however, the Czar, though jealous of the duchies becoming a German State, owing to their value for maritime purposes, was indisposed to interfere, and counselled a policy of procrastination. In the meantime a rival Government had been formed in the duchies, with its seat at Rendsburg, on the Schleswig-Holstein frontier, and with it both the Duke of Augustenburg and his brother, Prince Frederick, openly associated themselves.

It is doubtful whether the King of Prussia believed that serious warfare would result from his action. He was on good terms with the Danish King, and had already endeavoured by admonitory letters to convince him of the error of his ways. Even now he was of opinion that all that was necessary to a peaceful solution was a show of force, and therein he entirely misread the Danish spirit. Nevertheless, time might still have been gained for peaceful negotiations had not the Danish army, massed near Flensburg, fallen on the troops raised by the duchies, and forced them back to the Eider. Thereupon the Prussian force, under General Wrangel, crossed the frontier river and drove the Danes out of Schleswig. In this military operation Austria had so far taken no part. Though holding the presidency of the Federation, she had sent no troops to Schleswig, being unwilling to prejudice and imperil her relations as a European Power by joining in a dispute in which she had as yet no direct concern, but, on the contrary, well satisfied that Prussia, having precipitately involved herself in difficulties, should continue to bear the odium of interference.

For European opinion on the whole was hostile to Prussia. The declaration of Frederick William IV that the duchies could descend only in the male line, with the implied suggestion of the impending division of the Danish monarchy, had created great uneasiness in the Courts and Chancelleries friendly to Denmark and her dynasty, and the suspicion was entertained—unjustifiably at the time—that Prussia protested against Danish annexation only because she contemplated annexation herself. The retention of Denmark and the duchies as an undivided sovereignty was regarded as the interest of all the Great Powers. England's traditional sympathies made her unwilling to see Denmark weakened; Russia, as representing the Oldenburg line, had dynastic interests in the kingdom which were opposed to the interests of Prussia; even Prussia had to reckon with the probability that Denmark, if convinced that her existence was seriously threatened, would look to an alliance with Sweden; while Austrian statecraft, though seldom prescient, must have been alive to the possibility that the detachment of the duchies from Denmark would bring them more directly within the Prussian sphere of influence.

By the summer isolation had become uncomfortable for Prussia. Denmark, though unable to withstand her enemy on land, was more than a match for him on sea, and the blockade by Danish vessels of the North Sea coast, with the consequent serious injury inflicted upon Prussian maritime trade, was proving very effective. Moreover, Frederick William IV's conscience was troubling him. Whatever may be said of the King as a statesman, he had hitherto shown a profound respect, and even veneration, for the principle of legitimism, and his hostility to revolutionary movements was not merely sincere but vehement. Distressed by the thought that he was warring against a lawful ruler and aiding and abetting an insurrectionary cause, his resolution began to waver, and when England and Russia offered mediation, the offer was accepted. With the Englishman's instinct for rough-and-ready solutions, Lord Palmerston, recognizing that the question of nationality was at the root of the trouble, proposed that the northern part of Schleswig, being Danish, should be joined to Denmark for good and all, and that the rest of the duchy, being essentially German, should be joined with Holstein to the Bund, while continuing still in personal union with Denmark. Prussia might have agreed to a solution on these lines had not objection been raised in other quarters. The provisional Government which had been set up in the duchies had in March proposed the same solution, but now it did its best to thwart it, and Denmark also disagreed.

To make matters worse, Sweden came to her neighbour's help, and Russia warned Frederick William IV that the occupation of Jutland, which had been overrun by Wrangel's troops, was a bar to peaceful negotiations. The King therefore ordered Wrangel to withdraw, much to the disgust of that despotic soldier and of Prussian opinion. The negotiations were now resumed, and the provisional basis of a truce was duly arranged. One of these conditions was that pending a final settlement the troops of both of the belligerents should evacuate the duchies, but that a small federal force might remain in the south of Holstein. With this condition Wrangel refused to comply, and as Frederick William IV feared to supersede him, hostilities again broke out. After a further period of wearisome negotiations, which threatened repeatedly to break down owing to obstinacy on both sides, a seven months' armistice was concluded (August 26, 1848), at Malmö, on conditions which more than half recognized the Danish claims, for it approved the separation of Schleswig from Holstein. The Danish Government had for a long time been illiberal in its treatment of the German population of Schleswig, and the intolerant restrictions upon the right of public worship and the use of the German language had, in particular, created great bitterness. It was part of the bargain now concluded that all such restrictions should be removed.

For the rebuff which was inflicted upon the German national cause by the Treaty of Malmö, Frederick William IV was held to be guilty, and he lost still further in popularity. The National Assembly, still in futile session in Frankfort, was indignant at what seemed to be an act of betrayal, and called for the renunciation of the treaty, a decision which, though soon afterwards reversed, led to the resignation of the Ministry. It was significant that the friends of peace at that time were the Conservative monarchists, and that the belligerents were the extreme democrats. For the popular parties no measures against Denmark were too strong, and they called for the proclamation of a united federal war against the offending kingdom.

In the spring of 1849 hostilities broke out afresh and continued with varying fortunes for several months. On July 10th, at Berlin, a further armistice was arranged, and with it were concluded preliminaries of peace, under which the Prussian troops evacuated Schleswig. That duchy was now placed provisionally under three commissioners, representing Denmark, Prussia, and England respectively, while Holstein received two Stadholders. Another year passed, however, before a definitive peace was concluded between the combatants with the help of the Powers (July 2, 1850). By it Prussia withdrew from the struggle and practically recognized the *status quo ante*. Such an issue of the war was regarded at home as a weak surrender, and for it Frederick William IV was never forgiven. He was, however, the victim of superior force, for all the Powers were against him, Russia most of all, and he was heartily glad to be out of the complication. Desultory fighting continued for a time between Denmark and the duchies, but there was no longer any doubt as to the outcome.

It was in part the urgency of a settlement of this dispute, which kept the Powers in a state of alarm, that led the Czar to offer his services as mediator, or more truly as adjudicator, at the conferences held at Warsaw and Olmütz in October and November, 1850. Nicholas I cared less for the rights and wrongs of the dispute than for the quelling of the revolutionary movement in the duchies and the preservation of the peace of Europe, and when Austria and Prussia showed reluctance to agree he laid down the law in no uncertain terms. Neither Prussia nor Germany, he said, had any business to interfere in Schleswig at all, and as for Holstein, he threatened that unless the Bund would at once undertake to restore tranquillity there he would do it himself. By the Punctation of Olmütz (November 29th) it was agreed that the Holstein question should be referred to the Federal Diet for settlement, and that Austria and Prussia should at an early date send commissioners to the duchy with a view to a general pacification.

Shortly before this the first Protocol of London (August 2, 1850) was signed by Russia, Great Britain, France, Sweden, and Austria, which thereby recognized the integrity of the Danish kingdom, while reserving a pronouncement upon the question of succession. Already the Danish King had issued a manifesto in which he formally declared that Schleswig should not be incorporated in the monarchy. The call for the cessation of hostilities was now urgent in Germany, and early in the following year a force of Austrians, commissioned by the Diet, suppressed the rising in the duchies. Finally, the question of succession was decided by the Treaty of London (May 8, 1852), which, after affirming the integrity of the entire Danish monarchy, declared that in the event of the male line of the Danish royal house dying out the crown should fall, both in Denmark and the duchies, to Prince Christian of Schleswig-Holstein-Sonderburg-Glücksburg and his heirs. It was expressly stated that the reciprocal rights and obligations of the King of Denmark and of the Germanic Federation relating to the duchies of Holstein and Lauenburg, together with the rights and obligations established by the Federal Act of 1815 and by the existing Federal Law, were not affected by the treaty.

In the meantime the King of Denmark had repeated his pledge not to incorporate Schleswig, as well as the old promises to remedy the grievances of his subjects in the duchies, undertakings held later both by Prussia and Austria to be so important that the Treaty of London stood or fell with their faithful observance. This treaty was accepted and signed by Great Britain, France, Prussia, Austria, Russia, Sweden, and Denmark, but not by the Germanic Federation, which did not take part in the London conference. " The poor Schleswigers have to pay for everything," was the comment of Prince Albert on this settlement. Now the Duke of Augustenburg was induced to renounce, both for himself and his family, all claim to the succession, in consideration of compensation over and above the value of his properties in Schleswig which had been confiscated by the Danish Government, a settlement which gave him the sum of between three and four hundred thousand pounds.[1]

[1] " We promise for us and our family," ran the renunciation, " on our princely word and honour, not in any way to counteract the resolutions which His Majesty (the King of Denmark) may have taken, or in the future might take, in reference to the arrangement of the succession to all the lands now united under His Majesty's sceptre." His son, the later claimant, accepted the price of renunciation, and did not openly protest against his father's act until seven years had passed.

In accepting this settlement Prussia stultified her past action and acknowledged as legitimate claims which she had contested in a long and arduous war. It is probable that the King's compliant attitude was connected with a decision which the Powers meeting in London at that time had given in his favour in another territorial dispute. This was the question of Neuchâtel. This little principality had come to the Electors of Brandenburg at the end of the seventeenth century, and after changing hands at the will of Napoleon it returned to Prussia in 1815. In the revolutionary movement of 1848 the people of Neuchâtel threw off Prussian sovereignty and established a republic. The London agreement of 1852 (May 24th) reasserted Prussian rule, though only nominally and, as it proved, temporarily. The ultimate settlement of the question may be anticipated here. For four years the Royalist and Radical parties in the principality held each other in check, until in 1856 a republic was again proclaimed. In March of the following year a congress of ambassadors met in Paris to determine the future of the restless population, and by a treaty concluded in May the King of Prussia renounced all rights in the principality and agreed to its incorporation as an independent republic in the Swiss Confederation, which paid him a million francs as compensation. For Prussia the loss of Neuchâtel was no misfortune. An isolated enclave within the frontiers of Switzerland, with France to the west, it was like a house to which the owner has no right of way. The nation in general, therefore, regarded its abandonment—as it had before regarded its possession—with complete unconcern.

Prussia's withdrawal on the duchy question contributed towards another notable episode which fell to the year 1852, yet of which the full significance was realized only in later years. This was the sale of the federal navy which had been industriously created by the National Assembly of 1848 and the States of the Union, partly by votes of public money and partly by collections. Transferred later to the revived Diet of the Federation, it had been neglected, like so much else in the care of that soulless and irresponsible body. Now deeming it superfluous, the Diet, to the disgust of all patriotic Germans, ordered it to be sold by private treaty, and the transaction was completed by Hannibal Fischer, a former Federal Minister of Marine.

It has seemed desirable to indicate in broad outlines the development of the Schleswig-Holstein dispute in the middle of the century, in order to make clear the Prussian position and contention at that time. The dispute was then regarded as essentially one between Denmark and the duchies, and the action taken by Prussia, both independently and in conjunction with Austria, contemplated an adjustment from that standpoint only. Had Denmark been willing unequivocally to respect the treasured political union and autonomy of the feudatory territories, it is possible that there would have been no later trouble. The position created in 1852 was virtually the *status quo ante bellum.* The Treaty of London certainly gave no countenance to any pretension, however contingent, on the part of Prussia to scot or lot in the territories, nor, in spite of the speculations which were indulged in by an aggressive section of public opinion, did the King or official Prussia in general as yet advance any such claim. True to his own words, the King had stood forth as the champion of three principles—the autonomy of the duchies, their continued union, and succession in the male line, with the consequent endorsement of the Duke of Augustenburg's claim. That is the essential fact to be remembered in following the subsequent course of events.

Eleven years passed before the dispute again entered an acute phase (1863), and though it now took at once a new development, the contestants were the same. Bismarck had come upon the scene, however, and a clue to his action throughout the final stages of the dispute may be found in words which he wrote on December 22, 1862, shortly after he became Prussian Minister-President: "It is certain that the Danish question can be settled in a way desirable for us only by war. An occasion for war can be found at any moment that our relation to the Great Powers is favourable for waging it." At the end of March, 1863, Frederick VII of Denmark issued a patent formally annexing Schleswig, while leaving to Holstein its old autonomy. He appeared to have chosen the time well. Prussia, as we have seen, was in the throes of the constitutional struggle. The relations between the Government and the Diet were hopelessly strained. With a bitter political quarrel in progress at home, therefore, it seemed unlikely that Bismarck would welcome adventures abroad. Nevertheless, the Prussian Government promptly invited Austria to join in a formal protest, to be followed, in the event of its failure, by armed intervention. The fact that Prussia had taken the initiative was one of significance for the new relations of the two major Powers. Hitherto it had been Prussia which in German affairs had co-operated with Austria; now the order was reversed.

Apathetic on the question twelve years before, Austria now needed no persuasion. Still she had no direct interest in the duchies, which for her had no material value, yet it was obvious that for Prussia they would be of great importance, in giving her a larger seaboard and command of the neck of land dividing the North and Baltic Seas, already marked out for a canal. Above all, remembering the keen interest of all the German States in the Schleswig-Holstein question, as shown in 1848-1852, Austria was apprehensive that by remaining aloof she would be abrogating her claim to the leadership of Germany in favour of her ambitious rival.

The Lower House of the Prussian Diet did not allow Bismarck's proposal of intervention to pass without protest. On April 17th it declared by resolution that "the Prussian Government, owing to its isolation, was not in a position to wage war against Denmark, and were it proposed the House would resist any such measure, since it was bound to fail." Bismarck's reply was one of defiance. "I can assure you and foreign countries," he said, "that if we (the Government) think it necessary to wage war we shall do so with or without your consent."

As the first protest proved unavailing, the two allied Governments induced the Federal Diet in July to demand of Denmark the annulment of the patent and the restoration of the union of the duchies, failing which the allies would occupy Holstein. Lord Palmerston had declared in the House of Commons (July 23rd) that if the independence and rights of Denmark were violently attacked "those who make the attempt would find in the result that it would not be Denmark alone with which they would have to deal." It was an unfortunate speech, for although Lord Palmerston no doubt had in mind the contingency of French and Russian as well as British action, his words were justifiably regarded as a moral pledge that his own country, at any rate, would not remain neutral. Thus encouraged, the Danish King refused compliance, and the matter dragged on until September, when he laid before his parliament a new constitution formally uniting Schleswig to the monarchy.

In the meantime endeavours, not all of a discreet kind, were being made by disinterested Powers to avert disaster. Protesting in a circular despatch of September 3rd against the threatened occupation of Holstein by federal troops as an infraction of the laws of the Bund, the Danish Ministry added the significant words, "We have every reason to believe that we shall not be dependent on our own resources in a struggle in which not only the fate of Denmark but the holiest interests of the entire North are concerned." It was not difficult to surmise the origin of this inspired menace when, in a note of September 29th, the British Government reminded the Federal Diet that "Her Majesty is by the Treaty of London of May 8, 1852, pledged to recognize the integrity and independence of Denmark," and accordingly declared that it would "not recognize the military occupation of Holstein as a legitimate use of the power of the Germanic Federation." Nevertheless, the British invitation that the Diet should accept the mediation of the Powers was declined on the ground that an act of execution in Holstein was a purely internal affair of Germany, and that the Federation had not been a party to the Treaty of London.

It is questionable whether the British Government had any idea of the strength of the will which it had ventured to challenge, or of the fact that the Prussia with which it had had to do since the regency was not the compliant Prussia of old—Austria's tool and Europe's scorn. There were British Ministers and diplomats who had not even yet succeeded in mastering the Prussian Minister-President's name and rank, and who, either from indolence or affectation, called him alternately "Monsieur de Bismarck" and "Count." Lord Palmerston, accustomed to lay down the law upon all questions of Continental politics in which he took a hand, hardly gave a thought to the audacious chanticleer who was challenging his own roost. He was now eighty years old, and with the obstinacy of despotic age, refused to believe that the Prussia which he had known for half a century was capable of producing a strong statesman. He therefore persisted in applying to Bismarck the measure which he had applied to his weak predecessors, with the result that in the ensuing battle of wits and wills he was beaten at his own game.

Like the Government, the nation warmly sympathized with Denmark—all the more since a beautiful daughter of the Danish royal house had just before (March, 1863) become Princess of Wales—with just as much or as little understanding of the questions at issue as English public opinion in general shows upon foreign politics at any time. The Queen stood almost alone in taking the Prussian side of the dispute, believing that Prussia was fighting for the independence of the duchies, a cause to which she was warmly attached. The three points which she urgently impressed upon her Foreign Secretary, Lord Granville, were "not to let this country be dragged into a useless war, not to agree to a settlement which could not be durable, and not to let a Sovereign be imposed upon the duchies against their will and wish." Perhaps the Queen's known German leanings made the sympathies of the Government and nation more Danish than they might otherwise have been. In any event the consequence of official sympathy so generous and emphatic was to encourage Denmark to indulge expectations of assistance which never had a chance of fulfilment.

For the rest, Denmark was not free from reproach. She had hitherto ignored her pledges, given repeatedly since 1848, to respect the independent life of the duchies, to afford to their populations equal rights, and to allow to the Germans of Schleswig the free use of their language and the free exercise of their religion. By administrative measures and much petty chicanery in their execution, and by flooding the duchies with Danish officials, a systematic attempt had been made to eradicate German influence. Even when urged by so partial a friend as the British Foreign Secretary, Lord Russell, to do its utmost to satisfy the legitimate expectations of the German Powers, and above all to abandon any attempt to incorporate Schleswig in the Danish monarchy, the Danish Government remained obstinate. At a later stage of the dispute, Russell argued with the Berlin Cabinet that while Denmark's undertakings in regard to Schleswig and Holstein might have induced Prussia and Austria to enter the treaty of 1852, her failure to discharge these undertakings did not invalidate the treaty or justify the two Powers in wishing to evade it. *Prima facie*, that seemed a reasonable contention, though at least there was something to be said on the other side.

On November 15th the King who had thrown this apple of discord into the midst of the European Powers died, and with his death the male line of his dynasty became extinct. The dispute over the duchies now took a new aspect; to the question of constitutional rights was added the still more thorny question of succession. Prince Christian of Glücksburg was duly proclaimed King of the Danish monarchy, inclusive of the duchies, as Christian IX. Although this was in accordance with the provisions of the Treaty of London, his succession in the duchies was at once disputed by Prince Frederick of Augustenburg (in whose favour his father to this end renounced all claims—the claims of which he had been bought out in 1852), who, as "the first-born prince of the next line of the Oldenburg house," issued a proclamation saying that as Duke Frederick VIII he " entered upon the government of the duchies, and therewith all rights and duties " belonging thereto.

Of the German Sovereigns, Duke Ernest of Saxe-Coburg-Gotha was the first to recognize the new claimant, and it was at his capital, Coburg, that Prince Frederick provisionally established himself and formed a Ministry. The rulers of other States, among them Bavaria, Saxony and Hesse, similarly took his side, and German public opinion was almost wholly in his favour. The National Association promptly began an active agitation on his behalf, and a national congress, meeting at Frankfort, declared for him. The duchies themselves likewise supported the Prince. Popular meetings were held, organizations were formed for his support, and collections of money were made for the purpose of defending the rights of the duchies against Denmark. A large part of the officers of Holstein refused to take the oath to the Danish King, and, meeting at Kiel, together with the knights of the duchies, adopted for presentation to the Federal Diet a petition affirming the rights of Duke Frederick and calling upon that body to protect them. To add to the general unsettlement, it was now that Napoleon judged the time opportune for declaring (November 5th) that he no longer regarded the treaties of 1815 as binding and for proposing a conference of the Powers for the purpose of setting the entire European house in order. Bismarck, on Prussia's behalf, accepted the proposal, not because he wanted a conference, but because he wanted Napoleon's favour. Great Britain refused to take part, and as the rest of the Powers hung back, Austria in particular fearing the reopening of the Italian question, the idea had to be abandoned.

King Christian had meanwhile declared Schleswig a part of Denmark, and Russia, France, and England seemed disposed to support him. Everything now depended upon the action taken by the two leading States of Germany. Austria was a strong partisan of the Prince of Augustenburg. It was obviously to her interest that the duchies, if they were no longer to be attached to Denmark, should in no circumstances pass to Prussia, and the surest way of preventing this was to take a leading part in the adjustment of the dispute. The King of Prussia, for his part, was quite ready to co-operate with Austria, convinced that such joint action would prevent the question of the duchies from becoming a German concern, in which all the States might claim to be consulted, and would be likely to conciliate European opinion.

On October 1st the Frankfort Diet had threatened federal execution against the royal and ducal ruler of Schleswig-Holstein in the event of his refusal within three weeks to restore the constitutional *status quo*, and as its warning was disregarded, it proceeded on December 7th to give effect to this *ultima ratio* against refractory members of the Federation. Accordingly, a body of Saxon and Hanoverian troops, 12,000 in number, occupied Holstein, while an Austrian and Prussian force held itself in readiness on the German frontier. No immediate hostilities took place, for the Danes withdrew their army into Schleswig, whereupon the Prince of Augustenburg appeared in Kiel and set up what his patron and relative the Duke of Coburg called a " sort of Government," two at least of whose members were lent by that ruler.

Prussia and Austria now endeavoured to persuade the Diet to interfere similarly on the question of Schleswig. On its refusal on the ground of non-competence (January 14, 1864), the allies declared that they would take action on their own account, justifying this attitude by their special position as derived from the treaties of 1850 and 1852 and the rights which they had defended against Danish aggression. Before this (December 24th) the British Government had demanded that the federal troops should confine their action to Holstein, intimating that any extension of operations to Schleswig would make difficult the continued neutrality of Great Britain, and had made formal proposals to the Powers for a conference, to be held either in Paris or London.

Once more the European Governments had to reconcile themselves to the fact that a new spirit directed affairs in Berlin and that Prussia was no longer the Prussia of 1852. Besides, the dispute had gone too far for conferences. Bismarck would not listen to the idea unless Denmark agreed first to restore the *status quo* by annulling the constitution of November 18, 1863, and when this condition was rejected he was not sorry. He had Austria on his side, and he was confident of attaining his end by her co-operation. "In 1849," he said, "Prussia stood alone against four Great Powers. Now there are two against three—that is a better hand." The French Emperor, still sore that his own proposal of a conference had come to nought, was likewise lukewarm, on the ground that to interfere in a sense unfriendly to Germany would show antagonism to the cause of nationality. Later he told Lord Clarendon that if he did intervene he would be prepared to back up his arguments by force and that the price would be the liberation of Venetia and perhaps "something on the Rhine."

At a Council of State held shortly after the death of the Danish Sovereign, Bismarck reminded the King that each of his immediate predecessors, as far back as the Great Elector, had made an addition to Prussian territory, and suggested that his opportunity for doing likewise had now come. "While I spoke," he has written, "the Crown Prince lifted his hands to heaven as though he doubted my sanity; my colleagues kept silence."[1] Nevertheless, never were wild words more soberly spoken. There can be little doubt that even then his plans for the future were definitely formed. In their subsequent joint action Austria and Prussia seemed to have buried the hatchet, yet if they worked harmoniously their motives and ends were alike different.

Rechberg, the Austrian Foreign Secretary, had no other idea in view than the restoration to the duchies of their rights and their settlement under Augustenburg, and, these objects accomplished, he expected that the question would be closed and the allies leave the country. To Bismarck Austrian co-operation was welcome for its own sake, since it placed the two Powers for the first time in a position of parity in German affairs; but already his true objective was to bring Denmark, by hook or crook, to blows, with a view to wresting from her the duchies which were recognized to be hers by the treaty of 1852.

Of this treaty he had said in the Prussian Lower Chamber just before (December 1, 1863): "The signing of the treaty may be a matter for regret, but as it has been signed, honour and wisdom both require that no doubt should be entertained of our faithful regard for treaty obligations." Nevertheless, he took care to add that Denmark must be held bound by the same considerations, and that if her King failed to fulfil his duties under one agreement he could not expect to retain his rights under another. The ulterior and secret purpose of his policy even at this time was avowed only at a later date. Speaking in the same Chamber on December 20, 1866, he confessed that while the personal union of the duchies with Denmark would have been preferable to their formal incorporation in that kingdom, and an independent principality better than personal union, he had always regarded annexation to Prussia as the best solution of all and the one to be aimed at. "Only the event," he then said, "could show which of these solutions would be attainable. Had

[1] *Reflections and Recollections*, vol. ii., p. 10.

personal union been the maximum attainable, I should not have been justified in Germany's interest, in the then condition of affairs, in rejecting such *a payment on account*."

Difficulties arose with the Prussian Diet immediately it was asked to vote money for military measures. The Lower House was willing that Prussia should fight to win the duchies for the Prince of Augustenburg, but so little did it as yet divine Bismarck's intentions that it was fully persuaded that he was working for their retention under Danish rule. Accordingly, it flatly refused a vote, and with a new-born passion for the rights of Sovereigns, the democratic party, whose motto hitherto had been "not crowns and thrones but men," proposed a resolution declaring that "the honour and interest of Germany" required that all German States should protect the rights of the duchies, should acknowledge the Prince of Augustenburg as the reigning Duke, and should afford him effective support in the assertion of his rights. The resolution was adopted (December 2, 1863) by a large majority after a debate, in which the historian Heinrich von Sybel, afterwards the loyal apologist of Bismarck's statecraft, had declared that "the people of Schleswig-Holstein do not want to be Prussian. Let me say that with the fullest knowledge of the facts."

A fortnight later the Diet emphasized this attitude by presenting an address to the Crown affirming its conviction that any money placed at the disposal of the existing Government would not be employed to the best interests of Prussia or Germany, and calling upon the King to withdraw from the Treaty of London, to acknowledge the Prince of Augustenburg forthwith as the rightful Duke of Schleswig and Holstein, and to take steps in the Federal Diet to enforce his rights by practical measures. It would appear that the King himself at this stage of the dispute sympathized with this view. Not only had he on December 1st bidden his Minister, when speaking in the Diet, not to oppose the idea of an independent Holstein, since he was not himself averse to it, but while he received the Chamber's address with a refusal and a reminder that the direction of foreign affairs was his concern, he wrote to Bismarck (December 17th): "The worst is that it (the Chamber) wishes what I also wish in my heart yet cannot say frankly to the House."

Bismarck, quick to seize an advantage, saw in the Diet's attitude another attempt to usurp rights which were not conceded to it by the constitution. If the claim of the Diet to exclusive control of finance was unwarranted, much more this new pretension to control the Executive in relation to questions of peace and war, for here it had not even a participatory voice. "It is a question," said Bismarck on January 22nd in the Lower House, "of a struggle between the house of Hohenzollern and the House of Deputies for the rule of Prussia. According to the constitution, the rights over peace and war, the right to choose his Ministers, and the entire executive power belong to the King. You, on the other hand, claim that in foreign affairs the King shall follow not his own intentions but yours, and that even in the choice of the measures necessary to protect the rights and the honour of the country he shall adopt your ideas ; in plain language, you wish to make the right of the Crown in regard to questions of peace and war dependent upon your vote. . . . You claim that the King shall at your bidding wage a war of conquest in order to win Schleswig for the Duke of Augustenburg."

It was a curious situation—the democratic Chamber inciting a militarist Government to undertake against its will a war of aggression for objects which were not directly Prussian. For so the Liberals at that time interpreted Bismarck's plans. Unable to squeeze money out of the Diet, the Government obtained it by renewing railway concessions.

The allied armies, the Prussian under Prince Frederick Charles and the Austrian under General von Gablenz, with Wrangel as commander-in-chief, entered Holstein on January 21st and Schleswig on February 1st, and war began in earnest. The Danes promptly appealed for help to France, Russia, Great Britain, and Sweden, but none was forthcoming. In the circumstances the campaign, though vigorous, was short ; the decisive blow was given by the battle and capture of the forts of Düppel (April 18th), a gallant feat performed by the Prussians without the help of their allies. Denmark fought resolutely and bravely, but she had to contend against unequal odds, for Prussia and Austria between them had at disposal about 60,000 men wherewith to meet a force one-third smaller ; and, moreover, the Prussians were armed with the deadly Dreyse needle-gun.

Before this time the Crown Prince had begun to suspect that his father's Minister was playing a dark game. For him the question was not so much a Prussian as a German question. He sympathized heartily with the wish of the duchies for an independent political existence apart from Denmark, and favoured the claim of the Prince of Augustenburg. Through him the

Prince in February, and again in April, made proposals pledging himself to be all but a vassal of Prussia if only the King would help him to the disputed throne : he would enter into a military and naval convention under which his troops would be subject to the King's supreme command, would join the Customs Union, give to Prussia a naval station in Holstein, and allow her to garrison Rendsburg and to build the long-contemplated North-Baltic Sea Canal. Pressed to regard favourably these proposals, Bismarck took refuge in the plea that Prussia must " act according to circumstances." The reservation seemed to justify the Crown Prince's worst suspicions. In a letter of April 17th he imputed to Bismarck " secret ideas of a Prussian policy of expansion," and added : " I will only state briefly that my opinion is that the prosecution of them would entirely falsify our whole German policy, and would probably place us in an unenviable position before Europe. It would not be the first time that Prussia had tried to be better than everybody else, only finally to fall between two stools."

Already, indeed, Bismarck had sounded Louis Napoleon as to the conditions upon which he would be prepared to support Prussia in the annexation of the duchies, though the King had not been won over to the idea, and viewed with grave apprehension the risks involved. " The plan," he wrote to his Minister on April 16th, " will create a general coalition against us, since it will drive the secondary States into the Austrian camp, for in this policy of annexation they will see their nightmare for fifty years realized for the first time, and will regard it as an earnest of their own fate. Austria, Germany, England, and Russia would be sure to be against us, and we should be alone, bound only to the hereditary enemy and its inscrutable leader. That is more than dangerous."

Peace negotiations were opened at a conference which met in London at the end of April, under the presidency of Lord Russell, the belligerents assenting to an armistice for a month, dating from May 12th. Prussia and Austria had agreed to take part without binding themselves in any way, and one of their first acts was to give formal notice of withdrawal from the Treaty of 1852. That done, they joined in the proposal that the duchies should henceforth form a separate State, independent of Denmark, under the sovereignty of the hereditary Prince of Augustenburg.[1]

[1] The allies made this joint declaration on May 28th. On the previous day the King of Prussia had written to Bismarck : " We did not decide yesterday how

The Danish delegates refused the unconditional cession of both duchies, but were willing to accept the reasonable compromise, proposed by Great Britain, that Denmark should retain the northern part of Schleswig, with the river Schley as the boundary. Austria and Prussia in turn rejected this alternative, but were prepared to submit the frontier question to friendly mediation. Denmark refused to make any further concession, however, and particularly rejected the proposal of the French plenipotentiary, of which the author was Napoleon himself, that the inhabitants of North Schleswig should decide upon their future nationality by *plébiscite*. The result of the deadlock was that the conference separated in June without accomplishing any practical result. Lord Clarendon summarized the position in a remark made to the Prussian plenipotentiaries : "You entered the conference as masters of the situation and you have left it as masters of the situation." Nevertheless, he believed that Prussia's success was diplomatic only, and would not last.

Relying still upon the sympathy of friendly States, which hitherto had failed to materialize, the Danes again took up arms (June 26th). It was only a flash in the pan, however, for three days later they were decisively beaten at Alsen (June 29th), and their capitulation was now unconditional. A truce was signed on August 1st, and was followed on October 30th by the Peace of Vienna, under which the King of Denmark formally ceded the three duchies of Schleswig, Holstein, and Lauenburg to Austria and Prussia without condition, binding himself to acknowledge whatever disposition of these territories the allies might decide upon. "I rejoice sincerely," the Prussian Crown Prince wrote to Bismarck a little later (November 18th), "that peace is at last ratified, and that the duchies, emancipated for ever, will henceforth form an independent part of the Germanic Federation. May the most legitimate of the claimants now be instituted in his legal inheritance as Duke, and the affair be thus brought to a worthy conclusion ! " It was still, however, Bismarck's intention to "act according to circumstances." It was not without a calculated design that he had with Austria's acquiescence resolutely opposed the wish of the secondary States that the Federation and its Diet should be allowed to take part in the settlement.

The part played by Great Britain throughout the Danish war

Bernstorff (the Prussian ambassador in London) should be instructed as regards the Hereditary Prince of Augustenburg. It appears to me that we must mention him *franchement*, in order not to be behind Austria and the others."

—resolute in words, indomitable in despatches, but halting and timorous in deeds—was not one that could be recalled by her in later years with special pride. Not only did the British Government follow a policy of captious meddlesomeness, but it meddled without any serious intention of supporting its brave diplomatic protestations by any measure of force. Lord Russell's right hand had done valiantly, but its weapon had not been the sword of Gideon but the pen of the ready writer. Having done her best to encourage Denmark to stand firm, no sooner did it become evident that a war over the duchies could not be fought with paper bullets than Great Britain withdrew into the background and allowed the little country to carry on the struggle alone and succumb in the effort. As late as June 17th, Russell declared in the House of Lords: "Her Majesty's fleet is ready for any service which it may be called on to render." [1] The vain boast meant nothing and achieved nothing; the roaring on this occasion was not that of the British lion but of Snug the joiner. Not without justification did Lord Derby accuse Russell at the time with having followed a policy of "meddle and muddle." Yet the blame was not wholly or primarily that of the British Foreign Secretary. An even larger share fell to the impetuosity of the Prime Minister, Lord Palmerston, and to his refusal to accommodate himself to an entirely new situation in European affairs. Criticizing in the House of Commons in 1850 Palmerston's propensity for interfering in the concerns of other nations, Sir Robert Peel had bidden him "beware that the time does not arrive when, frightened by your own interference, you withdraw your countenance from those whom you have excited, and leave upon their mind the bitter recollection that you have betrayed them." That was the exact position in 1864.

Contrary to tradition, the Tories of that day, aided by the Manchester Liberals, showed themselves better friends of Germany and the German cause than the Liberals. Disraeli, of whom Count Vitzthum, the Saxon envoy, was a busy though not altogether successful prompter in German affairs, had opposed the Foreign Secretary's blundering policy at every step, and on July 4th he

[1] Count Beust, in his *Memoirs* (English translation, vol. i., p. 242), relates a conversation with Bismarck at Gastein in 1865, in which that statesman claimed that he had "taken precautions" to make sure that the Danes would fight. "I made the Cabinet of Copenhagen believe," he said, "that England had threatened us with active intervention if hostilities should be opened, although, as a matter of fact, England did nothing of the kind." Whatever Bismarck may have done, the fact remains that British diplomacy made such a ruse superfluous.

scored a legitimate if not a virtuous triumph when he won a large part of the House of Commons—295 votes against 313—for his vote of censure on the Government for having "failed to maintain their avowed policy of upholding the independence and integrity of Denmark, lowered the just influence of this country in the councils of Europe, and thereby diminished the securities for peace." The Government saved itself from defeat, though only as by fire, for taunts of weakness and cowardice showered upon Ministers from both sides of the House. It was only Palmerston's personal popularity and his still overshadowing prestige that prevented the rout of Liberalism at that time. Nevertheless, the soberer judgment of the nation was not that England should have gone to war, but that she should have minded her own business.

At the conclusion of the Danish war the Prussian Government sought to bring the constitutional conflict to a close by acknowledging the budget rights of the Diet to the full, and seeking sanction for the expenditure which had been incurred irregularly. All Bismarck asked in return was that the army reorganization scheme should be completed and that the House of Deputies should vote the money necessary for that purpose. A large section of the House was eager for peace on these terms, but the majority were not satisfied with an offer of repentance on conditions, and in proof of good faith demanded the abandonment of certain features of the army scheme to which they had never assented. As the King would not accept indemnity on these terms, the "conflict"—which was now in truth a conflict only in name—continued.

After the Peace of Vienna, Denmark disappeared from the drama of the Elbe duchies, and the stage was henceforth monopolized by two principal actors. The allies having wrested the territories from their vanquished opponent as a legitimate prize of victory, the question of their disposal now arose. However obscure his actions may hitherto have been, there was no longer any doubt as to the reason for Bismarck's refusal to fight the battle of the duchies in the name and for the sake of the Prince of Augustenburg. To have done so would have been to call in question the title of the King of Denmark, and that was no part of his deeply-laid calculations. Hitherto he had justified the Danish title by the declaration of the Treaty of London. His true reason for insisting on it, in opposition to the whole tenour of Prussian diplomacy under Frederick William IV, now became plain ; for if the King of Denmark had no claim to the duchies he was obviously unable to give them away. If Prussia was to be able to establish a justifiable claim to the reversion of one or both of these territories, the title-deeds must come from the hands of the legitimate owner, and the owner, by the assent of the European Powers, was King Christian. Would the headstrong House of Deputies now confess its blundering obstinacy in urging him, with gibe and threat, to waste Prussian life and treasure in thrashing Denmark for the sake of the Augustenburg ? Would it still demand that the duchies, lawfully transferred by sign and seal into the hands of Prussia and Austria, should be constituted an independent State under a new Sovereign—a new ally for Austria in the Diet, and a new centre of particularism and intrigue to be added to the thirty which existed already, every one of them a practical argument against unity ? He might not have been sure as yet that it would be possible to secure the duchies for Prussia, but he was determined to make the attempt.

In pursuing this design Bismarck had against him, as he said later, " not only the Austrians, the English, the Liberal and non-Liberal small States, the Opposition in the Prussian Diet, influential people at Court, and a majority of the newspapers," but the entire royal family—the King, the Queen, and the Crown Prince and Princess—all of whom, while sharing his view of the necessity of protecting the liberties of the duchies, were agreed in seeking for Prussia no immediate advantage, believing that the frank renunciation of political interest would be amply compensated for by gain in moral influence. For Bismarck, however, moral and material values were incompatibles and subject to different equations, and he never set one against the other. When, on August 22nd, the Prussian and Austrian rulers, with their Foreign Ministers, discussed the question at Schönbrunn, he had listened with dismay to the King's frank confession that " he had no right to the duchies and therefore could make no claim to them." On that occasion he had endeavoured to persuade the Emperor to withdraw from the affair altogether and leave Prussia in possession, assuring him that if Lombardy had been the stake, Prussia would have been equally accommodating, but no agreement was reached.

So well did Bismarck keep his secret, that up to this point some of his nearest official associates had not divined his ultimate aim. Roon, the Minister of War, was in the dark, and Bernstorff, the ambassador in London, had gone through the London conference without a suspicion that annexation was contemplated. "The less the Government gives the impression of wishing to obtain territory," Bernstorff wrote home in May, "the stronger will be the position of Prussia abroad and in Germany. . . . The frank explanation that Prussia merely desires to secure the complete independence of that German territory, and its indissoluble union with Germany (' under the sceptre of some German prince ') must make a tremendous impression in Europe." [1]

Clear in his own mind what the ultimate fate of the duchies should be, Bismarck had now so to influence the development of events as to make the desirable become inevitable and so attain his goal. The more the suspicion that Bismarck was working for annexation seemed to be justified, the more Rechberg identified himself with the Prince of Augustenburg and urged upon Prussia his recognition as an independent ruler, with a view to the termination of the *condominium*. To this pressure Bismarck replied, with aggravating *sang-froid*, that there was no hurry, knowing that Prussia had everything to gain by delay, and that the longer he could defer a settlement the more likely was it to be one on Prussia's terms. For Austria the duchies were a shoe that pinched, and she anxiously sought relief. Owing to their situation there could be no question of her retention of either of them, and even had not distance been an objection the nationality and religion of the inhabitants would have offered an insuperable objection. Accordingly, Austria tried to sell out her interest in the duchies, and therein played the first bad move in a game of wits in which she hardly once showed to advantage. If Prussia were given a free hand in the duchies, would the King cede a slice of Silesia in return, or even guarantee to Austria the retention of her remaining Italian possessions ? Bismarck declined, knowing that as Austria would have to abandon the duchies sooner or later, whether she wished or not, any such chaffering was unnecessary.

A change of Ministers took place at Vienna about this time, without, however, entailing a change of policy. The failure of Count Rechberg to secure the retention in the revised commercial treaty between Austria and the Customs Union of the article stipulating that negotiations for the admission of Austria into the Union should be opened at a later date had created great

[1] Count Vitzthum, who could not be accused of undue leanings towards Prussia, wrote in the London *Times* in December 1863 : "The Germans do not want to make any conquest : that (idea) is all sheer nonsense,"

disappointment, and accentuated the incompatibility between him and Schmerling. The result was that both Ministers resigned simultaneously, with a view to the Emperor choosing between them, and Rechberg was allowed to go (October 27, 1864). The strong anti-Prussian party welcomed Rechberg's fall, and regarded it, albeit prematurely, as an intimation to Prussia that Austria's past policy of conciliation on the duchy question was to be abandoned. Rechberg's unconcealed desire to work harmoniously with Prussia on all questions had made him many enemies at home, who viewed each of his attempts in that direction as a needless concession and a sign of weakness. It was not his fault that the rivals had, nevertheless, drifted more and more apart.[1] Bismarck, who as a rule judged his contemporaries severely, speaks of this opponent as "an irascible though honourable man."

On the advice of the outgoing Minister, Count von Mensdorff-Pouilly was appointed his successor. Mensdorff, then Governor of Galicia, stood high in the Emperor's favour, though the choice of him may have been determined in part by the fact that he had acted as the Austrian commissioner in Holstein during the settlement following the Danish war of 1848, and had thus acquired a special knowledge of the local bearings of a complicated problem. Contrary to the hopes of the reactionary party, the new Foreign Minister showed every disposition to emulate the spirit of his predecessor. Mensdorff was a man of fine feeling and dignified character, sincere and straightforward in all his public actions, but perhaps fitter for the diplomacy of half a century later than that of his day and of the man with whom he had to deal.

Like Rechberg, he was determined not to allow Prussia an entirely free hand in the duchies; like him, he wished to see the Prince of Augustenburg seated on the vacant throne. He was even more outspoken than Rechberg in identifying Austria with the Prince's candidature. Nevertheless, he confidently hoped for an amicable settlement of the dispute. As he wrote to his relative the Duke of Coburg later in the year, it was his intention

[1] Friedjung holds that, in spite of his conciliatory policy, Rechberg came on the scene too late to succeed in preventing a violent rupture. "Had Rechberg," he writes, "entered upon office a few years earlier, say at the time of the Crimean War, he might have been able to draw closer the alliance with Prussia; in his day, however, the division between the two Powers had already become incurable. In trying to combat this disease he was its first victim" (*Der Kampf um die Vorherrschaft in Deutschland*, vol. i., p. 103).

"to do all he could to prevent the German rent from widening." Not only so, but for a time he was strong enough, with the Emperor's support, to hold in check the forces which were deliberately working against a policy of conciliation. Of these forces the most powerful spokesman was Baron von Biegeleben, a Hesse-Darmstadter who, like the Saxon Beust at a later date, entered the service of Austria carrying with him a more than Austrian antipathy against Prussia, a qualification the more dangerous inasmuch as he exercised considerable influence upon the German policy of the Foreign Office.

Mensdorff signalized his entrance into office by a powerful appeal to the good-will of Prussia. In a series of despatches of November 12th, he reaffirmed the "attachment of the Austrian to the Prussian reigning house," and on the Emperor's behalf begged the King, in the interest of peace and the preservation of the old alliance, to emulate him in "the virtue of renunciation." Discussing the several possibilities of settling the dispute, he rejected first the idea of annexation by Prussia as a probable cause of offence to all Germany, whose interest in the duchies would be rudely ignored and overridden by such a measure. Not more acceptable was the idea of the duchies becoming dependent and parasitic, for the federal law recognized only independence and equality between the allies. The only satisfactory solution remaining was to convert the duchies into a sovereign federal State with the full rights of one. If, however, the duchies were not to be divided, the question arose, Under whose rule should their independence be established? The choice, it was pointed out, lay between the Prince of Augustenburg and the Grand Duke of Oldenburg, and of these possible regents Austria regarded the former as having the stronger title. The Emperor's Government, therefore, proposed that they should both give an earnest of pacific intentions by installing the hereditary Prince Frederick in complete possession of the duchies without delay.

While this was the view officially put before the Prussian Cabinet, the Austrian Minister in Berlin, Count Karolyi, was authorized to make an alternative proposal. It was the old idea of territorial compensation; although Austria heartily disliked the prospect of a Prussian annexation of the duchies, she would agree provided she received an equivalent elsewhere, which meant in Silesia.

Neither proposal made any impression on Bismarck. The appeal to "the virtue of renunciation" in particular did not attract him, and he refused to recognize any rights of succession, whether on the part of the Prince of Augustenburg or the Grand Duke of Oldenburg. From the first he had consistently taken his stand on the Treaty of London, which affirmed the title of the King of Denmark. But the King having, as rightful ruler, formally surrendered the duchies, the title by which they were now held could not be open to question. He even hinted that if Austria pressed the claims of her favourite too far a claim might be advanced on behalf of the house of Brandenburg, in virtue of ancient dynastic ties.

In the meantime the German population of the duchies was beginning to reconcile itself to the evident fact that the question of its future government, for which it had struggled with Denmark in two wars, was to be decided over its head. The noble families (*Ritterschaft*) were on the whole in favour of annexation to Prussia; people with a material stake in the country were already asking themselves whether Augustenburg rule or Hohenzollern rule would be the cheaper, and what there was to choose between them; and amongst the masses in general, conscious of their helplessness, a spirit of apathy was spreading. When the year 1865 opened, the Prince of Augustenburg knew that he had lost the game; his "Government of a sort" at Kiel still continued in name, though preparations were quietly being made for winding up its affairs, and official documents were being removed to secret places.[1] Privy Councillor Samwer, the Prince's adviser and propagandist-in-chief, who had been lent for that purpose by the Duke of Coburg, wrote to Gotha in December that annexation seemed inevitable, and that if Prussia was bent upon it nothing could be done to prevent it: his only hope was that the King was opposed to it. Napoleon himself was now believed to favour this measure, subject only to ratification by a vote of the population.

For month after month the two Governments continued to engage in barren negotiations. Occasionally they seemed to draw near to an understanding, but always some new qualification was imposed by one side or some new concession demanded by the other, just in time to prevent agreement. Early in the year Bismarck had asked the military and naval authorities to say what were the minimum demands which Prussia should put forward in the event of the idea of annexation being abandoned as impracticable. The answer was that Prussia must have supreme

[1] Duke Ernest II of Saxe-Coburg-Gotha (*Aus meinem Leben und aus meiner Zeit*, vol. iii., p. 472).

control of the army and navy of the duchies, both in regard to organization and administration, and must have full possession of Kiel, Friedrichsort, and Sonderburg-Düppel, as well as the right to garrison Rendsburg. To these claims the Minister of Commerce added the demand that Prussia should be free to build and work the long-projected North-Baltic Sea Canal and to fortify each entrance; that Schleswig and Holstein should join the German Customs Union; and that their customs, post and telegraph systems should be assimilated to those of Prussia and the administration of these be exercised by that State. It might seem as though for a moment Bismarck was willing to give up the duchies on these conditions, and at least he notified Austria to that effect. No sooner had word been sent, however, than he recanted, advancing supplementary demands the effect of which was to make the offer nugatory and to Austria unacceptable. Now it was stipulated that the entire military law of Prussia should be introduced into the duchies, that the soldiers and sailors should be called up by Prussian officials, should take the oath of obedience to the King of Prussia, and should even be liable to serve in Prussian garrisons.

This was the "February programme" (February 22, 1865), which may be regarded as the only serious Prussian offer of compromise. It was evident, however, that if the duchies were to be held subject to these conditions Prussia's essential object would have been secured; their independence would have been destroyed; and every vestige of sovereign right having disappeared, they would have become in effect vassal provinces of Prussia. In Vienna every one, from the Emperor downward, regarded the Prussian demands as unconscionable. The overbearing Biegeleben expressed the general sentiment of the Foreign Office in the words "I would rather grow potatoes than be a ruling Prince under such conditions." In its reply of March 5th the Austrian Government intimated its willingness to assign to Prussia advantages proportionate to the sacrifices which she had made; she might have Kiel and build the desired canal, garrison Rendsburg as a federal fortress, and require the duchies to join the Customs Union; but, objecting that the further demands would have the effect of making the new Sovereign a mere puppet and the duchies an appanage of their powerful neighbour, it rejected them, and made the counter-proposal that the independence of the duchies should be re-established.

While professing to seek a peaceful solution of the difficulty, Bismarck was nevertheless busily preparing for the more probable eventuality of war. He was again sounding Napoleon, through the Prussian envoy in Paris, Count von der Goltz, and through the French ambassador in Berlin, Count Benedetti, as to his attitude in the event of Prussia and Austria coming into collision. He was less wishful than before for a formal alliance with France, but he still regarded the Emperor's good-will as for the time a valuable asset. His idea was to play off France against Austria, using the friendship of the one as a means of obtaining better terms from the other. Great, therefore, was his relief when he was assured that Napoleon seemed to approve of the idea of Prussia's annexation of the duchies.

How deliberate Bismarck was in the double game which he was playing appears from a letter written to Count von der Goltz about this time (February 20, 1865). "I do not regard the Austrian alliance as used up," he said, "and I believe that we can do better business by keeping Vienna in suspense between hope of our assistance and fear of our going over to Austria's enemy (France) than by compelling Austria needlessly to prepare for an irrevocable breach with us. It appears to me more politic to continue the existing wedlock in spite of little jars, and if divorce should really be necessary, to accept the facts just as we may find them, than to break the tie in face of all the disadvantages of indubitable perfidy without the certainty of experiencing later better conditions as a result of a new union."

That he nevertheless then believed the issue of the dispute to be near is shown by the following words in the same letter:

"His Majesty's policy has a strong support, firstly, in the fact that, thanks to circumstances, we are in possession of the duchies in a larger measure than Austria, and in virtue of such possession are creating ever-increasing securities for its continuance; and secondly, in our determination not to leave the country unless we are satisfied or are driven out by force. No Power would lightly enter upon war of attack for the purpose of ejecting us. We know definitely what we want—annexation, if it is to be had without war, or if other causes bring about war before the decision to annex is taken; but in any event a relationship (to the duchies) which will place in our hands the fortresses and naval harbour and the disposal of the armed forces and other rights in the duchies. To go to war with European Great Powers for the difference between these two solutions (that is, unconditional annexation or such a condition of dependence as would give to Prussia the substance of possession) does not appear to me a step proportionate to the value of the object to be attained. Rather, however, than reduce our claims below those advanced in the second solution, we would draw the sword, sure of the complete sympathy of the country."

For the confidence of the closing words there seemed to be justification. By this time the opposition to annexation had almost died down in Prussia. Even the Liberals had begun to repent and forget the chivalrous indignation with which they had received the Minister-President's first open confession that the duchies had not been seized as a prize of war for the ulterior purpose of creating a new German princeling.

As yet no suspicion existed in Vienna that the dispute was not capable of a pacific adjustment. " The affair will not be settled without irritation on Prussia's part," Mensdorff wrote to the Duke of Coburg on March 27th, " but we have by no means blocked the way, and we count on the same attitude in Berlin as soon as quiet deliberation regains the upper hand." Austria in the meantime had succeeded in winning for her solution of the difficulty the States usually hostile to her rival, and on March 19th Bavaria, Saxony, and grand-ducal Hesse, with her concurrence, gave notice in the Diet of a resolution recommending the provisional recognition of the Prince of Augustenburg's claim to the succession. Prussia answered this challenge by removing the naval station of Danzig to Kiel (March 24th), in sign that, whatever the Diet might do or not do, she had no intention of leaving. The resolution of the secondary States was duly carried on April 6th, after Austria had declared her readiness to abandon her rights in the duchies provided Prussia would do the same. Prussia refused, and emphasized her attitude by pushing forward with the naval works at Kiel, while Roon, the Minister for War, declared in the Lower House of the Diet, in introducing a Navy Bill, that Prussia would never relinquish that port. When Austria protested against Prussia's action, Bismarck replied maliciously that if, owing to geographical reasons, she was unable to use Kiel for naval purposes, it was inconsiderate to grudge Prussia the opportunity.

On May 29th the dispute, now become critical, was submitted to a Council of State held in Berlin under the presidency of the King. Bismarck put forward three possible solutions. The first was that Prussia should be content with the programme of February 22nd, which he believed might be obtained by peaceable means, subject to the abandonment of the demand that the troops of the duchies should be embodied in the King's army and take the oath to him. The second solution was the annexation of both duchies subject to compensation to Austria, though he pointed out that this solution was blocked by the difficulty that Austria would insist on compensation in territory, and Prussia had no territory to offer. The third solution was to annex outright without compensation at all, a step which meant war. His view was that while war with Austria was inevitable sooner or later, it was not to be recommended at that moment. Of the other Ministers, some, and notably Bodelschwingh, were for peaceable, but most were for forcible, action. The only voice which was raised emphatically against war was that of the Crown Prince, who warned the Ministry against the danger of annexation and of a war which would be sheer fratricide, and favoured the recognition of the Prince of Augustenburg, subject to his acceptance of the February conditions. Perplexed by this diversity of counsels, the King was unable to make up his mind. Fidelity to the Austrian alliance and personal attachment to the Emperor disposed him against war, and apart from these scruples there was the risk of failure to be reckoned with. Turning to Moltke, he asked, What did the army think ? Moltke counselled annexation, adding that even if it led to war the reward would be worth the price.[1] The answer was not the one which the King hoped to receive ; he remained still unconvinced, and the Council broke up without any decision being arrived at.

On June 24th Austria took a further step forward on the path of conciliation. Now she would be willing to concede to Prussia a naval port (i.e. Kiel), and the occupation of a federal fortress, provided that if Prussia garrisoned Rendsburg, in Schleswig, Austria should garrison Rastatt, in Baden, and that if Prussia sought territory beyond Kiel harbour, Austria should receive as compensation either the little State of Hohenzollern or certain frontier districts of Silesia. The military organization of the duchies was to be left an open question for the Federal Diet to decide, while Prussia was to be allowed to arrange with the new ruler such matters as the building of the Kiel Canal and the

[1] That the idea of war now prevailed in Prussian military circles is shown by a letter written by Moltke to a brother on June 24, 1865, in which he says : "So much is clear to me that from internal and external considerations Prussia cannot give up possession (of the duchies). . . . There are only two alternatives, to compensate the *condominus* or declare war on him, *or cause war to be declared.* The first is only possible by the cession of Prussian territory (i.e. Silesia), and this idea has hitherto been resolutely rejected by the King ; the second is therefore not impossible, though the consequences would be quite incalculable."

commercial relationships of the duchies with the rest of Germany. Influenced by the King's evident unwillingness to be pushed to extremes, Bismarck seemed for a time to regard these proposals as a fair attempt to meet him at least half-way, and on July 3rd he went so far as to say that the only outstanding question was the choice of the new Regent; if Austria would accept the Grand Duke of Oldenburg, matters might be arranged. Upon the question of succession, however, Austria was not prepared to give way.

About this time Bismarck's opposition to the Augustenburg claims received support in an opinion pronounced by the Prussian Crown Syndicate, to which he had referred the legal aspects of the succession question in the preceding December. A learned and weighty body, consisting of chosen judges and jurists, high administrative officials and professors, the Syndicate was yet a tribunal which, owing to its composition and purpose, was hardly likely to be coldly impartial on such a subject, since it was a Prussian institution and existed in order to advise on questions affecting the interests of the Prussian Crown. The president, the jurist August Wilhelm Heffter, came to the conclusion that the claims of Brandenburg were posterior to those of the house of Oldenburg. It was more to the point that a majority of his colleagues advised that King Christian IX of Denmark was the lawful heir and successor to the three duchies, yet inasmuch as he had by the peace of October 30, 1864, surrendered his rights to the Prussian and Austrian crowns the allies were under no obligation to consider any other claims. In order to emphasize the latter point, they pronounced unreservedly against the pretensions of the Prince of Augustenburg. Nevertheless, the effect of this timely judgment was weakened by the fact that the legal faculties of sixteen German universities had already acknowledged the Prince's claims to be valid.

Meanwhile, Prussia was quietly preparing for war. Asked to state the country's military resources, Roon assured Bismarck on July 9th that he could if necessary put 250,000 into Bohemia and leave 40,000 to operate in West Germany, besides 200,000 reserves for the manning of the fortresses and all other purposes. He added that the munition factories were working day and night and that the army would be ready the moment it was called upon.

The situation was not improved by the persistent agitation which was being carried on in Holstein by the Prince of Augustenburg and his friends with Austrian connivance. The agitation was regarded not only as an insult to Prussia but as a personal affront to the King, since the Prince was a Prussian subject and a military officer. Accordingly, the King wrote on June 3rd to the Emperor begging him to order the Prince's expulsion from the duchy. Before the reply came, Bismarck, meeting the French ambassador to Austria, the Duc de Gramont, at Carlsbad, authorized him on his return to Vienna to tell the Foreign Minister there that while Prussia did not want war it would assuredly ensue unless Austria at once altered her attitude on the Schleswig-Holstein question. On July 21st an ultimatum was sent to Vienna in which Prussia notified her refusal to negotiate further regarding the future of the duchies until the Augustenburg agitation had been suppressed ; when this had been done she would be willing to consider the recognition of the Grand Duke of Oldenburg, subject to the February conditions. If, however, Austria refused to help to restore tranquillity in the duchies, Prussia would do it alone.

While the issue of peace and war thus hung in the balance, a proposal of compromise, originating with the Austrian envoy to Bavaria, Count Blome, appeared for a moment to clear the air. It was the application to the duchies of the principle of " spheres of interest " which was to play so important a part in later international diplomacy. Prussia was to have Schleswig and Austria Holstein. Although honestly preferring an independent State under the Prince of Augustenburg, the Emperor agreed to the submission of the proposal to the King of Prussia as an alternative solution. Blome accordingly waited on the King at Gastein (July 26th), and, to his delight, the idea of partition was favourably received. Even Bismarck admitted that it might be acceptable provided only that in addition to the full possession of Schleswig Prussia acquired the special rights which she had already claimed. On August 7th the Emperor himself wrote to the King formally endorsing the plan. True, the prospect of solving the succession dispute in so sordid a fashion troubled his conscience, for throughout all the negotiations he had insisted upon "the virtue of renunciation," but he reflected: "What misfortune we should create and what offence we should give to the world if we two, the son of Frederick William III and the grandson of the Emperor Francis, were to turn from being friends and allies into enemies!"

While the Sovereigns were thus exchanging conciliatory letters, Bismarck had not ceased to mature his own plans. It is certain that at this time he was counting definitely on war, and devising means for bringing it about decently. On August 1st he wrote to the King words which show plainly the lines upon which he was working. "I am dominated," he said, "by the impression that your Majesty would enter on a war with Austria with other feelings and in a freer spirit if the necessity thereto arises out of the nature of things and out of monarchical duties." To Count Usedom, the Prussian ambassador to the Italian Court, who had been charged with the mission of sounding the King of Italy as to his readiness to co-operate against his country's traditional enemy, he wrote on the same day: "Austria's surrender is not yet impossible. We cannot yet bind ourselves to provoke a rupture and to bring about war. Our reflections on the subject, however, will be greatly influenced by the answer to the question, What shall we be able to expect from Italy if it comes to war?"

"A very simple sentence says everything," writes Sybel, referring to this episode: "the more reserved Italy was, the more would Prussia be disposed to conclude an indifferent agreement with Austria; the readier and more decided Italy showed herself, the firmer and more warlike would be Prussia's attitude towards Austria."[1] It was the old device of setting one State against another. How Bismarck made use of Italy will be seen by the sequel.

In the meantime, Count Blome's compromise was still open. In the definitive form in which it was reduced to a draft agreement, and after revision by Bismarck was placed before the King of Prussia, it stipulated that the rights secured to the two Powers by the Treaty of Vienna should be exercised in respect of Holstein by Austria and in respect of Schleswig by Prussia, but Prussia, in addition, having borne the heavier burden of the war, was also to be entitled to build and work the Kiel Canal, and to have two military routes and two telegraph lines through Holstein, while both duchies were to join the Customs Union. Kiel was to be a federal naval port and Rendsburg a federal fortress, but both were to be under Prussian command. Finally, Austria was to sell her rights in Lauenburg to Prussia for two and a half million Danish thalers, and to undertake not to cede Holstein to a third person until he had pledged himself to comply with the foregoing conditions. To all these stipulations Austria agreed, and they were formally embodied in the convention of Gastein, which was completed on August 14th, and ratified by the two Sovereigns

[1] *Die Begründung des deutschen Reiches*, vol. iv., pp. 181, 182.

at Salzburg six days later. The convention was to take effect on September 15th, when all Austrian troops were to be withdrawn into Holstein and all Prussian troops (with the exception of those stationed at Kiel and Rendsburg) into Schleswig. It was an essential part of the agreement that, while still retaining a sort of co-proprietorship of the two duchies, the two Powers were to divide their government, Schleswig being occupied and administered by Prussia and Holstein by Austria.

It was after the conclusion of the convention of Gastein that Herr von Bismarck was raised to the rank of Count.

CHAPTER VI

(1865–1866)

THE EXTRUSION OF AUSTRIA

In the lives of nations, as of individuals, there are climacterical periods, times of crisis, of fateful endings and new beginnings. For Germany such periods were marked by the year 843, when by the Treaty of Verdun the Carlovingian empire was divided into three parts; the year 1250, when with the death of Frederick II the glory of the Hohenstaufens entered eclipse; and the year 1648, when the Peace of Westphalia asserted the independence of the territorial Sovereigns, and so prepared the way for the ultimate paralysis of the imperial power. The year 1866, in which Austria and Prussia fought out the struggle for supremacy which had long been inevitable, similarly marked a turning-point in German history.

The arrangement confirmed by the convention of Gastein was an unnatural and impracticable one; all it did was to enable the contracting Powers to defer for a short time the disagreeable duty of looking facts clearly in the face. Ostensibly intended to repair a broken friendship, it did no more than, in Bismarck's words, "plaster over the cracks." As so often happens in international disputes submitted to the arbitrament of force, the political problem created by the war of 1864 proved more difficult than the military problem had been. It soon became evident that the convention pleased no one. The duchies themselves were incensed at an arrangement which repeated in another form the very offence for committing which Denmark had paid so severe a penalty. The Holstein Estates at once appealed to the Federal Diet for help, but inasmuch as the Powers in possession had made peace, there was no longer hope of relief in that quarter.[1]

[1] Three years later (1868) Moltke wrote: "In Holstein I have never heard a word of gratitude that the country has been emancipated from Danish rule,

In Germany the convention made the States unfriendly to Prussia still more hostile. The idea of destroying the ancient independence and union of the duchies, and of bartering their populations like chattels, aroused deep indignation, and a national congress of protest was at once convened at Frankfort, still, as ever, the chosen home of lost causes and impossible loyalties. This irate body went so far as to declare it to be a public duty to refuse to pay taxes to any Government which was identified with the Austro-Prussian policy of violence. The Cabinet of Berlin addressed to the Senate of the Free City a stern demand that it should suppress such incitements to disorder, and a milder expostulation was also sent from Vienna. With a courage more honourable than discreet, the Senate promptly refused to take orders from either quarter, an assertion of independence for which the burgesses paid dearly at a later date. The Governments and peoples of the secondary States were particularly angry with Austria. From Prussia they expected nothing better, but Austria they had trusted, and now they felt that their confidence had been betrayed.

If feeling was strong in Germany, it was hardly less strong abroad. In a circular despatch (September 14th) issued to the British diplomatic representatives abroad Lord Russell declared: "Violence and conquest are the bases upon which alone the partitioning Powers found their agreement. Her Majesty's Government deeply lament the disregard thus shown to the principles of public right and the legitimate claims of a people to be heard as to the disposal of their own destiny." It was a virtuous and proper sentiment, honestly entertained, but, like much earlier moralizing in the same quarter, it did not cost much. The British nation divided its indignation between Bismarck, who had duped Europe, and its own Government, which had left Denmark in the lurch.

No one was more indignant, or indignant with greater cause, at the course which events had taken than the Queen, now that her generous defence of Prussia, which had been intended to safeguard the independence of the duchies, proved simply to have played into Bismarck's hands and helped to further his schemes of aggrandizement. She, however, had already passed judgment upon that statesman when it became clear, a year before, that the duchies were to be betrayed. "It is quite right," she

though beforetimes it was not possible to picture it black and tyrannical enough."

said in a message to her Foreign Secretary (August 25, 1864), "that . . . Prussia should at least be made aware of what she (the Queen) and her Government, and every honest man in Europe, must think of the gross and unblushing violation of every assurance and pledge that she has given which Prussia has been guilty of."

Equally or more bitter was public opinion in France. Paris was aflame at the violence offered to the sacred cause of nationality, which had been the foremost object of French foreign policy under Louis Napoleon. On August 29th, Drouyn de Lhuys, the Foreign Minister, issued a warmly-worded circular to the French embassies condemning the convention as a triumph of force over right and an outrage upon the public conscience of Europe. Although Napoleon, in conversation with the Prussian envoy, condemned this document and professed to disown responsibility for its authorship and publication, it nevertheless faithfully expressed his mind. Bismarck received the affront quietly; for the present he had no intention of quarrelling with the Emperor.

Nor was the convention commended by the spirit in which Prussia at once began the administration of Schleswig. The Government appointed as governor General von Manteuffel, a capable soldier, who understood military discipline but not human nature. Not only did he, in the exercise of an indisputable right, clear out every trace of the Augustenburg agitation in the duchy, superseding all officials, high and low, who were suspected of heresy, and requiring the entire bureaucracy to take the oath of fidelity to the Prussian King, but his treatment of the population in general was austere and unconciliatory. "Let the people first learn obedience," said the new Governor, "and then they will soon learn to love us"—words of fatal import for the later treatment of the Danes of the duchy. The ways of this old martinet were even too harsh for the Government at home, and soon mild expostulations had to be sent from Berlin. Manteuffel also did great mischief by prematurely blurting out with soldierly bluntness his Government's intention to annex the duchy, and declaring that "every seven feet of Schleswig land which the Danes wanted back would first have to be covered by his body"—a brave resolution which, after Düppel and Alsen, there was little probability of ever putting to the test. Very different was the treatment of the Holsteiners by Austria, whose Governor, Field-Marshal von

Gablenz, promised in an early proclamation to respect their institutions, and in all his utterances and dealings avoided the spirit of ascendancy and conquest. The rival "sort of Government" at Kiel had degenerated into a mere centre of agitation for the Duke of Augustenburg, and this agitation Gablenz, acting on instructions, made no attempt to discourage. For a time, indeed, the hopes of the pretender revived.

Soon it became plain that the Gastein convention was merely intended to serve for Prussia as a starting-point for new negotiations for the settlement of the dispute. Hitherto the withdrawal of the allies from the duchies and the setting up of a new Sovereign had been, or had appeared to be, at least a possible solution, even from Prussia's standpoint. The negotiations on those lines were now a closed chapter. Bismarck had not acquired a half-interest in the duchies for the mere pleasure of entering into partnership with Austria, still less for the sake of admitting a third person into the firm; such was not his idea of putting Prussia's money to usury. He intended that Prussia should remain in Schleswig; the only uncertain question was how long Austria should be allowed to remain in Holstein. In pursuing his plans, however, he was still beset by hostility everywhere.

The convention had not been signed many months before the quarrel broke out anew in diplomatic discussions, marked on Prussia's side by great vigour and ingenuity, on Austria's by less skill but equal persistence. Now and then it almost seemed that the disputants were about to come to terms, but momentary approaches were invariably succeeded by fresh disagreements; always for one side or the other some condition was unacceptable or some concession inadequate. As time passed and the breach widened, Austria saw with growing clearness that Bismarck's real aim was annexation outright *à tout prix*, and annexation not of one of the duchies only but, sooner or later, of both.

In the meantime Bismarck was quietly preparing for the eventuality of war. His first concern was to know whether Prussia would be able to count on Napoleon's neutrality. The reports from Goltz had of late been encouraging, but upon so critical an issue he was not satisfied with the assurances of another. He proposed, therefore, that he should visit Biarritz, where the Emperor was expected in October. The King, still smarting under the August circular, was at first opposed to the meeting as suggesting a cordiality which he did not feel, but in the end he allowed his Minister to go on condition that he talked little and made no promises.

First calling at Paris, where he had satisfactory conversations with Rouher, the head of the Government, and Drouyn de Lhuys, Bismarck was in Biarritz at the beginning of October and remained there till the end of the month. Frequent conversations with the Emperor convinced him that he was well disposed to Prussia, and might be counted on with certainty to observe towards her a benevolent neutrality in the event of a war with Austria. Napoleon put forward territorial claims in return, but Bismarck succeeded in satisfying him without giving any definite pledge of assent.

The interview also determined at least one phase of the succession dispute. The Prince of Augustenburg told Prince Hohenlohe later that from it dated Bismarck's refusal to favour his claims further in any way. Previously he had appeared to be in entire agreement with him: "after his return he tried every possible subterfuge and evasion. . . . He (the Prince) was ready to make every possible concession, but Bismarck wanted annexation."

On November 5th the question again came before the Federal Diet in the form of a renewed proposal by Bavaria, Saxony, and Hesse-Darmstadt, that the allies should be requested to convene as soon as possible a representative assembly of Holstein, which should co-operate in the settlement of the question of succession, and to use their influence to bring about the admission of Schleswig to the Federation. After Austria and Prussia had succeeded in delaying decision upon this proposal, they secured its reference to a committee (November 18th).

All the time the Augustenburg agitation in Holstein continued with unabated vigour. Demonstrations were held in many parts of the duchy; deputations were received by the Prince, who in reply made stimulating speeches which, while not welcome to Austria, were as wormwood and gall to Prussia. Against these proceedings Bismarck protested to Vienna in letters which recalled the fact that although the Gastein convention had assigned to each State a special sphere of influence, their joint sovereignty remained unaffected, so that both were equally interested in everything that happened in either of the duchies. Austria declined to take action against the Prince or his friends, not recognizing the need for interference so long as their agitation did not transgress constitutional forms. In November she also rejected another proposal that she should cede to Prussia her interest in Holstein, as she had ceded that in Lauenburg, for a money payment.

So it continued to the end of 1865, at which time no progress had been made towards an understanding; rather, every indication pointed to growing estrangement and ultimate rupture. The new year brought fresh causes of alarm: there were more Augustenburg demonstrations, leading to renewed protests to Vienna, as futile as before. By way of compensation, however, the Schleswig-Holstein nobility on January 23rd addressed to Bismarck a petition urging the annexation of the two duchies to Prussia.

Three days later the Minister addressed to the Austrian Government a strong remonstrance, complaining of the open encouragement given in Holstein to revolutionary agitation objectionable to Prussia and dangerous to the monarchical principle, and asking for a plain answer, yea or nay, to the question whether Austria was willing to suppress them, so making a definite choice between the Prince of Augustenburg and Prussia. "A negative or evasive reply to our request," the letter continued, "would convince us that the Imperial Government does not desire permanently to go hand in hand with us, but that the tendencies hostile to Prussia—a traditional antagonism which we believed had been overcome—are stronger than the sentiment of cohesion and of common interest." He added that failing a satisfactory reply, followed by appropriate action, Prussia would reserve full freedom to adapt her policy to her own interests.

On February 7th Mensdorff returned the nonchalant challenge that what Austria did or allowed to be done in Holstein was a matter only for herself and her Governor, and that she conceded Prussia's right to exercise the same liberty in Schleswig. He added that far from pursuing a policy hostile to Prussia or Germany, Austria had gravely prejudiced her position with her old friends, the secondary States, owing to her fidelity to the Prussian alliance. Bismarck's reply to this challenge was the verbal intimation to Karolyi that Prussia's relations with Austria no longer partook of the late intimate character, but were those which existed before the outbreak of the Danish war—neither better nor worse than her relations with any other State.

That was all he could say as a diplomat, but his true opinion of the situation was very different. Convinced that it was hopeless either to lead or drive Austria, conscious that he had gone too far to be able to draw back, and recognizing clearly that he had brought Prussia face to face with the alternatives of another Olmütz or war, Bismarck now determined that his future action should so be diverted as to favour war, and if need be provoke it. The French ambassador in Berlin at that time, Count Benedetti, records how early in 1866 a diplomat told Bismarck: "Austria does not want war, and will be careful not to give you a pretext for it." To this the Minister is said to have replied: "I have a whole bagful of pretexts and even of plausible reasons. When the time comes war will break out without surprising any one." Reporting to his Government a conversation with him on the subject on February 11th, Benedetti attributes to Bismarck the words, "We shall go quickly, and perhaps we shall go far."

A fateful Council of Ministers was held in Berlin on February 28th. The King presided, and with him were, besides the Ministers, the Crown Prince, Count von der Goltz, the Prussian ambassador to France, and three generals. The King had now been persuaded, and in opening the proceedings he declared that the nation wished for the annexation of the duchies, so that withdrawal would now be a sign of weakness. "We do not want war," he said, "but we must go forward on our way without shrinking from it." Bismarck spoke openly, and even vehemently, for war: it was sure to come one day, he said, and it would be more advantageous for Prussia that it should be now rather than later. With the single exception of Bodelschwingh, all the other Ministers reiterated or endorsed his words, and the generals added their yea and amen; while Goltz gave the assurance that Napoleon's neutrality might be counted on. Now, as before, it was the Crown Prince who championed the unpopular side. Almost alone amongst the King's intimate associates and advisers he had throughout the controversies and frictions of the preceding two years retained a proper sense of the gravity of an armed conflict between the two peoples, and had reprobated it as fratricide and a crime against German nationality. Once more this courageous counsellor, the youngest and wisest of them all, raised his voice in earnest protest. It was in vain. Having won over the King, Bismarck knew that no one else mattered. The decision was therefore for war. It was understood that there was not to be a formal declaration of hostilities at once, but war was to be the end towards which future action should tend. The King closed the Council with the assurance that for Prussia the war would be a just war, since he had "asked God to show him the right way."

War having now been deliberately decided on, Bismarck was determined that it should not merely settle the dispute over the duchies, but should leave no outstanding question between Prussia and Austria undecided, so that at the end each should begin with a clean slate. For him the Schleswig-Holstein question was only one phase of the German question; more truly, it was the German question in miniature, and in the smaller as in the larger problem the essential issue was the same—the impossibility of a system of dualism, when of the rival Powers one merely claimed superiority while the other possessed it. For him the principal object of the war was to be the scission of the union which perpetuated this unnatural relationship and the ejection of Austria from a political fellowship in which she had no longer a rightful place.

In a grave despatch to the envoys to foreign Powers he referred pointedly to the necessity for facing the question of federal reform, laying stress upon the inadequacy of the existing military system, and urging that Prussia's interests were in a special manner identical with those of Germany, since the safety of the one was absolutely dependent upon the safety of the other.

From the beginning of March both of the Powers were making preparations for the apparently inevitable encounter—Austria even more openly than her rival, though not with equal seriousness. For while Mensdorff was just as opposed to war as ever, and may have regarded it as still avoidable, the pressure of the military party was becoming too strong for him. Few people doubted in Vienna at that time that Prussia was laying a trap into which she herself would fall.

Simultaneously with military preparations, Bismarck was also making political preparations—alliances where they were expedient and friendly agreements where they were not—and here Austria showed a singular lack of foresight.

Russia had already assured Prussia of an attitude of benevolent neutrality in consideration of friendly influence in Oriental questions at a later date. An understanding had been reached with France at Biarritz, but now it was necessary to make some more explicit statement on the compensation question. As soon as he returned to Paris from the War Council, Count

Goltz waited upon the Emperor in order to make sure once more of his neutrality and good-will. He told him frankly (March 5th) that the Schleswig-Holstein question had now been merged in the question of German unity, and that it was Prussia's aim, after having beaten Austria and acquired the duchies, to create a confederation of the North German States under her own leadership, with a constitution based on that proposed in 1849 for all Germany. What was Napoleon's attitude in this matter? Napoleon agreed to this large programme, but asked for compensations in case Prussia should add other territories than the duchies. Goltz favoured the idea, and several possible acquisitions were discussed—French Switzerland, South Belgium, Luxemburg, and portions of the Rhenish territories of Prussia and Bavaria. The conversation ended without definite proposals on either side, but Napoleon had received such encouragement that he was satisfied, and closed the interview with the assurance that "it would not be difficult to agree at the right time."

In reporting the incident to his Government, Goltz wrote: "I regard it as a gain that by postponing negotiations the Emperor has spared us the necessity of offending him by refusing his wishes." It is true that Goltz had not assented, but he had not dissented; he had even left upon Napoleon's mind the very definite impression that Prussia would be willing to cede to him German territory as the price of his neutrality. When, a little later, Napoleon returned to the question and asked outright for territory on the left bank of the Rhine, Bismarck instructed Goltz that, although the demand was one impossible to fulfil, "in view of the congress (then proposed by Napoleon), it is not advisable to refuse to negotiate upon it," while in June he told Benedetti in Berlin that the King was of opinion that if France had to have compensation it should be in the form of French-speaking districts, and "perhaps he might be able to persuade him to agree to the cession of Trèves, to which Napoleon might add Luxemburg." Once more nothing more definite was decided, as was Bismarck's intention. Nevertheless, Napoleon appears to have been satisfied with the assurances given to him; and it is probable that their very vagueness, far from detracting from their value, convinced him the more of Bismarck's good faith.

Having made reasonably sure of France, Bismarck next approached Italy. Here something more than a good understanding was desirable, and he was anxious for a military alliance. If Italy could be induced to fight on Prussia's side, two objects would be achieved—on the one hand, the French *entente* would be strengthened, and on the other hand, Austria would be compelled to divide her forces. It had not been without a deliberate purpose on Bismarck's part that a high Prussian order had been conferred upon Victor Emmanuel at the beginning of the year.

It was the folly as well as the misfortune of Austrian diplomacy at this time that it took far too lightly a situation which was pregnant with possibilities of disaster. Mensdorff had taken office as Foreign Secretary with the honest desire to accommodate and conciliate Prussia on the federal question, if that were possible. His efforts, however, failed to count on the support of an undivided Cabinet, for while Esterhazy was with him in the desire to find a basis of compromise and avoid a rupture at all costs, the section represented by the Minister-President, Belcredi, and Biegeleben believed that the only policy worthy of the Hofburg was one of arrogant defiance. If in the Schleswig-Holstein dispute Mensdorff was handicapped by the same division of counsels, it is also clear that he failed to recognize either the gravity of the issues at stake or the fatalism which seemed to be dogging his steps. As late as March, 1866, he wrote to Duke Ernest of Saxe-Coburg-Gotha with a lightheartedness which in the circumstances of the moment seemed to border on levity: " I have not invented the stupid Schleswig-Holstein question, and must unluckily swallow down the sins of past years. Whether or not we shall escape from this most tedious of all tedious affairs without a collision I cannot as yet say." When these words were written Bismarck had prepared Louis Napoleon for the collision as inevitable, and had made sure of his neutrality, and the negotiations with Victor Emmanuel had been opened.

It was solely due to Austria's short-sightedness that these negotiations succeeded or were even possible. " Austria arrives always too late," said Prince Napoleon, referring to this incident. Austrian procrastination, in fact, was throughout the great tragedy of the war of 1866. It might have been possible for the Emperor to have made sure of Italy's neutrality before Bismarck set his wits to work, had he only shown moderate foresight. In the previous autumn Victor Emmanuel, through his Prime Minister, La Marmora, had already attempted to come to an arrangement with him on the basis of the cession of Venetia in return for a payment of a thousand million lire; that done, he was prepared to conclude a commercial treaty with Austria and in certain eventualities even to assist her in war. The offer was rejected with that psychical blindness which has so often characterized Austrian statecraft in times of national crisis. Then Bismarck came upon the scene, and proposed a treaty of alliance under which Italy should help Prussia, and in the event of the war being successful receive Venetia as a reward. "Instead of buying Venetia with money which would enable Austria to reconquer both that province and Lombardy," he said, "it would be safer to invest the money in a war as Prussia's ally," and the argument at once went home.

Various forms of treaty were proposed and discussed—a defensive and offensive treaty of indefinite duration, a treaty to come into force only on the declaration of war, and a treaty for a limited term. Victor Emmanuel chose the last, and on April 8th a treaty of alliance, to last three months, was concluded on his behalf by General Govone in Berlin. By it Italy undertook to declare war upon Austria directly Prussia took the initiative, and neither side was to conclude peace or an armistice without the other's consent until Italy had secured Venetia and Prussia territory in Austria with an equivalent population. It was thus left to Prussia to decide when war should begin and, in effect, when it should end. If within three months war had not broken out, Italy was to regain full freedom of action. The treaty was perhaps as notable for its omissions as for what it contained: seeing that if Italy were attacked by Austria, Prussia was to be under no obligation to help her by action either on Italian territory or in Germany. While thus imposing upon Italy duties, it conferred upon her no rights.

In this document war was justified on the high ground of federal reform. The second article set forth that Prussia was to call in the aid of her ally "if the negotiations which his Majesty the King of Prussia has opened with the other German Governments, with a view to a reform of the federal constitution, conformable to the needs of the German nation, should fail, and his Majesty in consequence had to resort to arms, in order to give effect to his proposals."

In his attempts to win over the larger German States Bismarck was less successful. He tried to detach Bavaria from Austria by the offer of a reform of the Federation which would have given her the leadership and military command of the Southern States. Bavaria, however, had no great fault to find with the Bund as it was. It was for most of the States a comfortable arrangement under which they enjoyed equal rank, and were subject to little interference, while the presence of two powerful rivals in the union, so far from being objectionable, had the great advantage that it gave to the rest a feeling of security which they might not otherwise have enjoyed. The attitude of Bavaria was shared by the other secondary States. Throughout Germany Bismarck's action on the Schleswig-Holstein question had, in fact, created against Prussia a deep feeling of distrust and resentment. The minor States in particular feared to be Prussianized themselves, and with the fate of the duchies and the evidence of Bismarck's high-handed ways at home before their eyes, they were disposed to prefer the Bund with its freedom to a reorganized Germany under such a hard taskmaster. Even in Prussia public opinion was as yet far from endorsing the policy which was leading straight to war. "For the last month," wrote Field-Marshal von Blumenthal in his Diary on May 4th, "everybody has been crying out against Count Bismarck, saying that he is arrogant and wants war at any price." There were responsible newspapers, never open to the accusation of demagogic leanings, like the *Cologne Gazette,* which did not hesitate to say that Austria was in the right and Prussia in the wrong. Almost generally at that time Prussia was regarded as a wilful disturber of the peace and a nuisance to her neighbours and federal allies.

Meanwhile, in the duchies Bismarck resorted to measures of open provocation, devised for no other object than to make co-operation impossible for Austria, and to cast upon her affronts that might tempt her into acts of retaliation. On March 11th he caused an ordinance to be issued forbidding, on pain of imprisonment with hard labour, any attempt forcibly to set up in either duchy an authority opposed to the rights of the condominate Sovereigns. The threat, which was aimed at the Augustenburg advocates, and was obviously intended to humiliate Austria in their eyes, caused Mensdorff to invite the Prussian Government five days later to state plainly whether it sought to destroy the Gastein convention and the Germanic Federation together.

Bismarck's treatment of the challenge was characteristic of the man. While telling the Austrian ambassador that his answer to Mensdorff's question was a categorical "No," he added immediately: "If my intentions were different, do you really think I should have answered otherwise?"

Both sides were now actively mobilizing, and the secondary States were likewise preparing to take sides. Vienna was feverish and defiant, eager that the Prussian upstart should at last be humbled and taught a lesson, though far more convinced of the desirability of this correction than troubled about the possibility of administering it. Nevertheless, in the middle of April Mensdorff proposed a reciprocal cessation of warlike measures, and, still working for peace more than for war, the King of Prussia met these overtures in a conciliatory spirit, to the great disappointment of his Minister, who saw his plans threatened. At the last moment, however, the demobilization proposals broke down, since Austria was unable to expose herself in the South, where Italy was busily preparing for an attack. All this time Bismarck and Moltke were working closely together in the interest of a speedy appeal to arms. In a report of April 14th to the King, who was anxious as to the attitude of the secondary States, Moltke took a sanguine view of Prussia's chances, and ended with the words, "Only when we have once mobilized we must not fear the reproach of aggression. All delay decidedly worsens our position." A week later (April 22nd) Bismarck warned the King of the risk which would be incurred if peace were now "patched up and Austria allowed to choose a time for war less favourable to Prussia."

Already he had prepared the federal Sovereigns and Governments for a decisive turn of events when (April 9th) he placed before the Diet, through the Prussian delegate, Herr von Savigny, a proposal of federal reform on democratic lines, which had fallen like a bombshell upon the assembly.

Before the month closed Mensdorff made a last attempt to win Prussia over to a compromise. In a statesmanlike despatch to Karolyi (April 26th), free from the warmth which on both sides had crept into recent discussions, he renewed the old offer of special concessions in the duchies, and invited Prussia, subject to these, to accept as ruler such a claimant as the Federal Diet might judge to have the strongest right to the succession in Holstein. He intimated that if Prussia rejected this proposal Austria would refer the entire question to the Diet and the Holstein Estates. Bismarck's reply was a refusal and a denial of the right of the Diet to any voice in the matter.

From the beginning of May not only Austria and Prussia but all Germany was arming with vigour and haste. The Ministers of Bavaria, Würtemberg, Baden, Saxony, Darmstadt, Nassau, and several of the Thuringian States had of late been in frequent conference, and their discussions were carried on in a spirit more than ever hostile to the northern kingdom. There was no doubt as to which side the secondary States would take. To allow Austria to be beaten, or even weakened, would in their opinion give to Prussia a prestige which would make her unbearable as a neighbour and undesirable as an ally. The Würtemberg *State Gazette* expressed the general feeling when it declared on May 9th that " a direct or indirect domination of Prussia would be a far worse national calamity than conquest by France." So all the South German States felt and believed. Even in Prussia earnest voices of warning were raised by men of weight who believed that their country was in the wrong. In a letter written in tears, Bismarck's colleague in the Ministry, Bodelschwingh, begged him to keep the peace. " I entreat and implore you most earnestly," he wrote, " impute to Austria, with her equal rights in Schleswig-Holstein, only what is fair and not offensive to her honour; endeavour to secure us an honourable peace; and then solve the German question in such a manner that both Prussia and Austria will gain internal strength." To Roon, the Minister of War, his friend Ludwig von Gerlach appealed with equal urgency, begging him " by all that to you and me is holy " to do his utmost to prevent war, and so "keep unstained the conscience of the aged King and the nation."

Bodelschwingh seemed fated to be Bismarck's opponent on critical issues. He had resisted him in 1864 over the question of Austria's relation to the Customs Union. He had earned a black mark when at the Council of Ministers in February he opposed the idea of war, supporting his attitude by making difficulties when votes for military preparations were demanded. At another Council on May 14th he repeated that offence, and thereby sealed his doom. The King was in favour of forgetting the incident, and so wrote to his Minister-President, and when Bodelschwingh offered to tender his resignation chivalrously asked him to remain in office. That was not Bismarck's way. Before the end of the month he reported to his master that " Herr von Bodelschwingh, on the plea of nervous strain, has repeatedly asked to be allowed to resign, and I believe that it would be neither possible nor advantageous to move him to remain." The resignation took effect at once, and Herr von der Heydt took the vacant portfolio.[1]

Saxony was the first of the secondary States to prepare for war. There the traditional antagonism against Prussia was revived; the Saxons had never forgiven the laceration of their kingdom in 1815, when Frederick William III had carved for himself a new province out of one of its most fertile regions, and the old rankling hatred burst forth with fresh vigour. Now there seemed a chance of regaining the lost territory with interest. Hanover, spurred by a similar hope of aggrandizement, was hardly less eager for the fray; its share of the spoil was to be in the direction of Holstein and Westphalia. Bavaria and Würtemberg, too, had expectations—the one was to have part of the Rhineland, and the other the little State of Hohenzollern. Finally, Austria counted on Silesia. Almost it might seem that Prussia had been dismembered in advance. Austria and her allies never doubted for a moment that they would prove too strong for Prussia. They had nominally a large numerical superiority in men, and had they been willing to act together from the first, instead of dividing their forces, the result might have justified their confidence.

The Prussian nation, or even any large section of it, cannot be said to have wanted war, and the army itself had no strong desire for it; by both, indeed, France was regarded as the natural enemy of Germany, and in any case an enemy more dangerous than Austria.[2] The politicians and intellectuals were conscious that Austria had far too long played a domineering part and that the threatened struggle was with the one great obstacle to national unity, but this feeling did not extend to the masses of the people. Least of all was this the case in the Roman Catholic districts. In the Rhineland and Silesia there were priests, and even prelates, who openly condemned the imminent conflict, and on May 28th the Archbishop of Cologne (Melchers)

[1] Bismarck, who never forgave an affront, resented so deeply Bodelschwingh's opposition that in later years he brought about his virtual outlawry from political life.

[2] Many years later Moltke, who planned the ensuing campaign, wrote: "The war of 1866 was entered on not as a defensive measure, to meet a threat against the existence of Prussia, nor in obedience to public opinion and the voice of the people; it was a struggle long foreseen and calmly prepared for, recognized as a necessity by the (Prussian) Cabinet, not for territorial aggrandizement or material advantage, but for an ideal end—the establishment of power" (*The Franco-German War of* 1870–1871, Appendix, p. 417).

warned the King of the risks he was running and of the stubborn unwillingness of the reservists to join the colours.

In particular the democratic parties were still far too embittered against the Government, because of its unconstitutional treatment of the Diet, to be enthusiastic over any enterprise proposed by Bismarck. Already, in time of peace, he had shown his contempt for parliamentary institutions; if that could be done in the green tree, what would be done in the dry? From the standpoint of popular rights the prospect of military success was almost more alarming than that of failure, for success would inevitably confirm the Government in its attitude and probably doom the Diet to an indefinite future of impotence. Patriotism and political principle were thus in conflict. The choice which had to be made was a hard one, and the Liberals are not to be blamed if they chose the way that exposed them at a later date to much misrepresentation and undeserved obliquy.

The majority in the Lower House did its best to discourage the idea of armed action, and emphasized its conviction by once more refusing supplies. Therein it was at once supported by a large body of public opinion. Peace demonstrations were held in many parts of the country and petitions were freely addressed to the King by municipal and other representative bodies begging him not to unsheath the sword. When the Diet refused to vote money for the war, the Government issued Treasury bills to the amount necessary. It was about this time (May 7th) that Bismarck received his first baptism of fire in the form of a bullet aimed at him in Berlin by a crazy fellow named Cohen or Blind; he was injured, but not seriously.

At the beginning of May, while there yet seemed a faint chance of staving off hostilities, Louis Napoleon had again proposed his favourite specific of a congress of the Powers. It was his idea, however, that the congress should discuss other questions besides the Schleswig-Holstein dispute—for example, the question of Italy, the future organization of Germany, and perhaps incidentally the rectification of the French frontiers as determined fifty years before. In a speech made at Auxerre (May 6th), following a vehement attack upon Prussia in the *Corps Législatif* by M. Thiers, Napoleon said frankly that he "detested those treaties of 1815, which it is sought to-day to make the sole basis of our foreign policy." The congress was, in fact, to take a general survey of European politics, and to some extent recast the map of the Continent. Great Britain and Russia were favourable to the proposal, Lord Clarendon holding that if the Germanic Federation was going to be dissolved the Powers which had helped to create it ought not to be kept in darkness regarding the arrangements intended to replace it. Of the two disputants, Prussia gave a conditional acceptance to the invitation sent by France, England, and Russia at the end of May, while Austria imposed the stipulation that no proposal which would have the effect of giving an increase of territory to any of the participating Powers—the probable demand for the cession of Venetia to Italy, even more than the question of the Elbe duchies, was in the mind of Count Mensdorff—should be discussed. This condition was regarded as tantamount to a refusal, and the idea of a congress was abandoned.

"There are moments in history which never return," said Bismarck on one occasion. Such was the moment in which it was open to Austria to submit her cause to the adjudication of the Powers in 1866. Regarded in the light of later events, her refusal was undoubtedly a mistake, for it deprived her of the opportunity of setting herself right with Europe and of compelling Prussia to bare her motives to the full light of day. Even granting that Austria might have been pressed to cede Venetia, it was a renunciation for which, as events were soon to show, she was in effect already prepared, while, on the other hand, it is at least probable that the settlement of the Schleswig-Holstein question might not have left her empty-handed. Nevertheless, Bismarck's pretence that Austria's action in refusing the congress brought on the war was absurd; all that could be fairly maintained was that it made war from Prussia's standpoint less inexcusable. For if Austria had been bent on fighting at all hazards, it could only have been to her interest to have gained the respite which a congress would have offered her, with a view to using this for completing her military preparations, a paramount consideration in view of their backwardness.

While the congress proposal was still under discussion an attempt was made on new lines to bridge the widening gulf between the rival Powers. It originated with Baron Anton von Gablenz, brother of the Austrian General, who had for a long time lived in Prussia. His idea of federal reform was that Germany should be divided into northern and southern spheres of influence, under the military leadership of Prussia and Austria respectively, the other States being won for the arrangement by the promise of a central parliament, but to be compelled to assent, if needful, on pain of military occupation. The duchies were to become an independent State, under a Hohenzollern Prince, subject to the sale of Kiel harbour to Prussia and the repayment by the duchies to Austria of part of her costs in the recent war. The scheme was first submitted to Mensdorff, who was so pleased with it, or at least with the prospect of a pacific settlement which it seemed to offer, that he authorized Gablenz to sound Bismarck, who likewise was favourably impressed. The ensuing negotiations for a time seemed to run smoothly. It was to be part of the agreement that the proposed federal unions of the North and South should enter into an alliance, and that all Germany should guarantee the integrity of Austria's Italian dominion. Any difficulty which might arise with Bavaria was to be adjusted by the concession to her of a special position in the Southern federation.

It is nevertheless difficult to believe that in lending to this scheme an apparently indulgent ear Bismarck had any other idea in mind than the hope of dulling Austria's apprehensions and gaining time for more complete preparations for war. While the scheme was still under consideration, Duke Ernest of Coburg visited the King in Berlin (May 24th), and he relates that he found him, to his surprise, " by no means disposed to doubt that peace would be maintained." Conversing with Bismarck on the following day, however, he was assured that war must be definitely expected.[1]

On the other hand, the King of Prussia clearly approached the compromise in good faith, and was possibly prepared to accept it as the basis of a friendly settlement. Not so the Emperor, who declined to entertain the proposals on the ground that they came too late, though he may also have doubted the genuineness of this sudden change of front by a Minister who had hitherto shown so little disposition to be accommodating.

On the same day that Austria rejected the suggestion of a congress she transferred to the Federal Diet the question of the duchies as one which should no longer be left to the futile wrangling of the two German Great Powers, and instructed the Governor of Holstein to convene the assembly of Estates for the purpose of obtaining an expression of their views as to the future. The breach was now complete, for inasmuch as Austria

[1] *Aus meinem Leben und aus meiner Zeit,* vol. iii., pp. 514, 515.

had the secondary States on her side, the Diet was sure to decide in her favour.

Now had come the time for Bismarck to make his boldest cast of the dice. It was the proposal of a national parliament to be elected upon a democratic franchise. For it was a gamble pure and simple—a gamble for popularity, a speculation in a nation's political aspirations, aspirations which he had never shared in the past and did not share now. "Looking to the necessity," he wrote later, "in a fight against an overwhelming foreign Power, of being able in extreme need to use even revolutionary means, I had had no hesitation whatever in throwing into the frying-pan by means of the circular despatch of June 10, 1866, the most powerful ingredient known at the time to liberty-mongers, namely universal suffrage, so as to frighten off foreign monarchies from trying to put a finger into our national omelette." [1]

Bismarck had foreshadowed this move so long ago as January 13th in a letter to Count Usedom. "The German question rests for the time," he then wrote. "Should there be a further development in Austria's relationship to the secondary States in a spirit aggressive to Prussia, events might easily take a turn which would involve the existence of the Bund. In that case it is not improbable that Prussia might take a resolute initiative on the German question." Already (April 9th), as has been stated, the Prussian envoy to the Diet had thrown out vague suggestions of federal reform, and had by resolution invited the Governments to confer upon the necessary arrangements. The Diet had not appeared to take the matter seriously, and it was certainly in no mind to accept Prussia's leadership in a departure so unexpected. It had, in fact, referred the Prussian resolution to Committee with little concern one way or the other, even Austria offering no opposition. In Prussia the proposal was received by the Liberals with incredulity mixed with amusement, and a well-known humorous journal of the

[1] It has been suggested that in deciding to appeal to the German nation on the principles of the National Assembly of 1848, Bismarck was influenced by the ex-republican Lothar Bucher, who had already entered his service and into a relationship of great intimacy with him. It is equally probable that Bucher's friend Ferdinand Lassalle, who had several times met Bismarck in friendly discourse, had also sown the seeds of democratic reform in his mind. Two years before this (March 12, 1864) Lassalle had publicly predicted that within twelve months Bismarck would have "played the *rôle* of a Sir Robert Peel and given Germany a universal and direct suffrage."

day wrote that if Bismarck intended to become its competitor it would at once abandon the field to him.

No constitution had been drafted at the time, and perhaps Bismarck had at the best only a shadowy idea of what he thought might successfully bait the popular fancy. Urged to give some definite indication of his intentions to the Governments, which were unwilling to pledge themselves to abstractions, he agreed with Savigny upon certain broad principles, and authorized him to communicate them to his colleagues in Frankfort. The proposal was that a parliament should be elected by manhood suffrage, on the basis of one deputy for every 100,000 of the population. The existing powers of the Diet were to be extended, yet without any sensible restriction of the independence of the States, but there was no suggestion of a federal Sovereign. This outline, as notified to the Committee of the Diet on May 11th, was thought to be so moderate that the secondary States were not prepared to vote against it, and the sitting was adjourned so that they might obtain instructions. Only the Austrian representative protested.

While Prussia was thus plying the Diet with proposals of constitutional reform, Austria persisted in her endeavours to transfer the venue of the duchy dispute itself from Berlin and Vienna to Frankfort, and in the summoning of the Holstein Estates. In an identical note to the Powers she also disclaimed any desire for territory. If Austria's proceedings in Holstein at this moment were irregular, they were not nearly so irregular as Prussia's attitude had been for two years, yet with his genius for seizing hold of the weak points of an adversary's case and turning his mistakes to advantage, Bismarck professed a virtuous indignation, and succeeded in communicating it to the King. "The King is so constituted," he once said, "that if one wishes to determine him to assert a right it is first necessary to convince him that it is being challenged." This trait in his Sovereign's essentially candid and straightforward character he was able again to use with perfect success. We find the King writing to the Archbishop of Cologne at this time with unusual asperity: "In the Diet, Austria has one-sidedly and without the prior knowledge of Prussia torn in pieces the Treaty of Gastein, and contrary to that treaty has submitted to that body the question of the duchies, which should have been settled between us. So have succeeded one after another on

Austria's part, without cessation, perfidy, lying, and breach of treaty engagements."

In a note of June 3rd the Prussian Government protested against Austria's action as a breach of the Gastein convention, and pointed out that its result was that both Powers reverted to their original position under the Treaty of Vienna. Coming from a Power which had already violated both agreements, either in letter or spirit, in so many ways, which had systematically usurped the rights vested in Austria and Prussia jointly, had issued penal ordinances intended to suppress throughout both duchies any opinions on the question at issue contrary to its own, had itself agreed to refer the whole question to a European Congress, and, to crown all, had cancelled its old obligations and reclaimed complete liberty of action, this protest came with a very bad grace and with little force.

In the Diet, Prussia opposed the Austrian proposal on the ground that the Bund had nothing to do with Schleswig and that as regards Holstein its competence did not extend to the question of succession. Finally, in a note to the embassies abroad, Bismarck represented Prussia as the innocent victim of designing malice. "All our information points to the determination of Austria to make war on Prussia," he wrote. "The Austrian Government wants war at any price, partly because it counts on success, partly with a view to evade internal difficulties, and even with the avowed intention of retrieving its finance by contributions from Prussia or by an honourable bankruptcy."

The view held in Germany generally was less flattering to Bismarck and Prussia. It was faithfully reflected in a solemn letter of warning addressed to the former on June 11th by the Bavarian Minister-President, Baron von der Pfordten, an impressive document of State which it is impossible even now to read unmoved. Just two days before, in a letter written to Duke Ernest of Coburg, Bismarck had spoken of Pfordten as "one of the most honourable and most unprejudiced supporters of German interests," and this is what this high-minded statesman thought.

"The decision upon peace and war is imminent," wrote Pfordten. "It is my firm conviction that it rests in your hands, since it depends on the course taken by Prussia in relation to the duchies. If you want annexation at any price, war is inevitable. If Prussia decides to renounce annexation, war is impossible. If Austria began war for any other reason, she would certainly be isolated; but if war is brought about by the duchies, I for one believe that Prussia will be isolated. God is my witness that I am influenced neither by antipathy against Prussia nor sympathy with Austria. As a German I adjure you, take counsel again with your soul before the fateful word is spoken whose consequences will be incalculable."

Undeterred by Prussia's protests, Austria on June 5th invited the Holstein Estates to meet at Itzehoe six days later. Acting on instructions received from Berlin, the Prussian Governor of Schleswig, General Manteuffel, promptly served on his colleague Gablenz a notification, which had already been sent to Vienna, to the effect that inasmuch as Austria had appealed to the Diet, the Gastein convention no longer applied, and Prussia was at liberty to exercise complete co-jurisdiction in both duchies. Accordingly, Manteuffel had been authorized "in all peace" to set up garrisons in Holstein the next day, as Austria was at liberty to do in Schleswig. As for the convocation of the Estates, the King of Prussia's sanction was necessary to this step, and until it had been given the summons must be cancelled. Gablenz protested against this wanton insult, and declined to revoke the summons, which was just what Manteuffel hoped would happen. The Austrian Government had instructed Gablenz, isolated as he was and beyond reach of speedy relief, not to engage the Prussians with his small force, however provoked. He accordingly evacuated Rendsburg and removed the seat of government to Altona, whereupon Manteuffel issued a proclamation (June 10th) announcing that he felt "obliged to take over the government of Holstein," and coolly declaring that the Austrian Governor was superseded. Impotent to retaliate for this outrage, Gablenz withdrew his troops through Hanover, Hesse, and Bavaria to Bohemia, taking the Prince of Augustenburg with him, and left Prussia in possession of both duchies.

Matters reached a climax when on June 11th the Austrian plenipotentiary informed the Diet that Prussia had violently occupied Holstein in contravention of the Gastein treaty, and in consequence proposed the mobilization of the federal army (with the exception of the Prussian contingent) against the disturber of the peace. Inasmuch as the Federation was not concerned in the Treaty of Gastein, the resolution, as it stood, was out of order. Prussia protested accordingly, and promptly issued the warning that every vote for the resolution would be regarded as in effect a vote for war against her. In spite of this attempt to stifle the freedom of the Diet and to browbeat her federal allies, the division was fixed for the 14th. In the meantime Austria had broken off diplomatic relations with the Court of Berlin, and when the Diet again met a state of war already existed.

The resolution had been amended, on the proposal of Bavaria, by the omission of the reference to the Treaty of Gastein, yet, though changed in form, it was the same in substance and purpose, and Prussia offered to it a strongly worded protest. On a division being taken nine curial votes were given in favour of and six against the resolution. With Austria voted the four kingdoms of Bavaria, Saxony, Würtemberg, and Hanover, also electoral Hesse, grand-ducal Hesse-Nassau, and the sixteenth *curia* (comprising eight small States, including Frankfort), a total of nine votes. Six votes were recorded against the resolution —Mecklenburg, Luxemburg, Baden, and the *curiæ* comprising Saxe-Weimar and the Thuringian duchies (except Meiningen), Oldenburg, Anhalt, and Schwarzburg, and the Free Cities (except Frankfort). Prussia did not take part in the division. Her representative had already protested against the entire proceedings as a violation of the federal constitution, and he now, in the name of his Government, declared the Federation dissolved, at the same time notifying Prussia's intention to restore it on a new and broader basis. The Prussian scheme of federal reform, of which the essential features were the ejection of Austria from Germany and the institution of a national legislature, popularly elected, was already in the hands of the various Governments, to which it had been communicated on June 10th.[1]

To Prussia's drastic challenge the President of the Diet, Baron Kübeck, rejoined that inasmuch as the Federation, by

[1] The document was described as "Outlines of a new union corresponding to the conditions of the time." Bismarck affords the curious student an instructive peep into his political workshop in a letter written on June 11, 1866, to the historian Heinrich von Treitschke, accompanying a copy of the draft proposals, of which he spoke as "a mere skeleton, to serve as a basis for our deliberations." He added that it was to be published to the nation simultaneously with the outbreak of hostilities, and he invited Treitschke to draw up a manifesto to accompany it. "You know and feel," he wrote, "the deeper currents of the German mind, to which in such grave moments it is necessary to appeal, and therefore would be able to find the right response and speak with the warm language necessary to evoke it. Afterwards it would be desirable, with as little delay as possible, to elucidate the manifesto in pamphlets and newspaper articles in order to assure the right effect."

its constitution, was a permanent and indissoluble union of the German States, Prussia could not secede at will, still less claim to dissolve it. Such a declaration, however true it might be in law, no longer carried weight in fact ; for Bismarck the time had come for making good his prediction that the question of German unity would be settled not by speeches and resolutions of Diet majorities, but by force.

If anything could have persuaded the statesmen of Vienna of the danger which awaited Austria, it was the fact that though the ground was now being cleared for action, she was without allies out of Germany. The traditional foreign policy of Austria was one of alliances, and until the middle of the century that policy had stood her in good stead. Her refusal to stand by Russia in the Crimean War marked the end of the Holy Alliance, with the result that in the Italian war of 1859 she found herself without friends. Rechberg told the historian Friedjung that it had been his constant aim to find his way back to the abandoned policy of Kaunitz, Metternich, and Schwarzenberg, and to extricate Austria from the position of isolation into which she had fallen under Buol's influence. It was because the friendship of Russia was still impossible, owing to the hostility of Gortchakoff, and that of France unreliable, that he had endeavoured to work amicably with Prussia. His hopes had been disappointed, and now in the most critical moment in her history Austria found herself dependent upon the questionable support of several of the German States and the far from disinterested good-will of Louis Napoleon.

At the eleventh hour that astute diplomatist conceived the idea of negotiating a secret treaty with Austria which should at once secure compensations for France in certain eventualities and advance the cause of Italian unity another stage. The Duc de Gramont was sent to Vienna to conclude this treaty, and the details were arranged without difficulty during the four days June 9th to 12th. It provided that in the event of war between Austria and Prussia France should undertake to preserve towards Austria absolute neutrality, and to endeavour to keep Italy quiet. If the fortunes of war were favourable to her, Austria undertook not to change the *status quo ante bellum* in Germany except in agreement with France ; if unfavourable, she was still to come to an understanding with France before assenting to any territorial changes which might disturb the European equilibrium ; but in either event Austria was to cede

Venetia to France for retrocession to Italy immediately on the conclusion of peace.

Émile Ollivier is of opinion that Austria attached so much importance to this treaty that without it she would have tried to come to terms with Prussia. Yet it assured to Austria no new advantage, for Napoleon had already pledged his neutrality to Prussia, who, in virtue of the security thus offered against French attack, was able to leave her western frontiers unprotected and thus to hurl her entire army against the enemy. The only part of the treaty which, if realizable, would have been of value was Napoleon's undertaking to use influence with Italy in Austria's favour. This undertaking, however, was an empty pretence, since Italy had formed an alliance with Prussia not only with Napoleon's knowledge but with his good-will, and probably on his advice. Count Beust, who several months later became Austrian Foreign Minister, called the treaty the most incredible document which he had ever read, and indeed its humiliating terms appear to be comprehensible only on the assumption that the Austrian Government, when agreeing to them, was in the desperate mood in which men are incapable of drawing a fair balance between gain and loss.

In the tourney of diplomacy produced by the Austro-Prussian quarrel straightforwardness was often at a discount, but for versatility the part played by Louis Napoleon carried the palm. On the strength of this treaty he issued on June 11th a pompous manifesto, in the form of a letter to his Foreign Secretary, Drouyn de Lhuys, in which he deplored the failure of his congress scheme, yet confidently asserted that the moral power of France would enable her, without drawing the sword, to safeguard the two interests vital to her—the maintenance of the European equilibrium and the protection of the work which France had achieved in Italy. He added, with sublime courage, that in preserving an attitude of vigilant neutrality France would be strong in the consciousness of her disinterestedness.

The manifesto created a bad impression in Prussia, where it was regarded as a sign that France, though keeping out of the struggle, was determined to have a hand in shaping its results. For the King and Bismarck, however, it was sufficient for the present that Napoleon could be counted on to play the part of a benevolent neutral. In setting off for the war the King, "with tears in his eyes," said to Benedetti: "We are in the Emperor's hands: we count on his loyalty"; and his Minister added: "Our confidence in him is so great that we are not leaving a soldier on the left bank of the Rhine." In a proclamation to his people the King appealed to the patriotic spirit of 1813, and asked: "Who will take from us an inch of territory if we are firmly resolved to maintain the acquisitions of our fathers?" He added: "I have done everything to save Prussia the cost and the sacrifices of a war. My people know it, and God, who knows all hearts, knows it also." For the King the claim was sincere; he, at any rate, had done what was in his power to keep the peace. The more important question was, Had Bismarck?[1]

Conscious of the handicap with which his Government would make war abroad unless it succeeded in restoring political peace at home, Bismarck at the last moment sounded the leaders of the constitutional party in the Prussian Diet as to their willingness to come to terms. The answer was not encouraging: he was assured there could be no agreement and no supplies for the war until he sought an indemnity for the unconstitutional acts of the last four years. More money was obtained by prolonging the concessions of two railway companies, and the Diet was dissolved on May 9th, in the hope that a more tractable—Bismarck said a "more national"—Lower House would be the result. The elections did not take place, however, until July 4th, and the new Diet did not meet until the war was over.

It is characteristic of Bismarck's foresight that at this time he was already looking round in search of men able and willing to help him in the constructive work which would follow the war, and of his insight that it was not to his old party but to the Liberals that he turned. Amongst the men whom he approached was Herr von Bennigsen, the Hanoverian statesman. He even offered him the governorship of his native country as soon as Prussia should have occupied it, and was disappointed when the offer was vigorously refused.

Officially the war may be said to have begun on June 14th. Prussia made no formal declaration of hostilities against the German States opposed to her, however, for Bismarck had laid down the convenient formula that those States which were not

[1] Friedjung, writing from the Austrian standpoint, yet with exemplary discrimination and candour, says that Bismarck brought on the war by deliberately "injuring the interests and still more wounding the feelings of Austria so deeply" that in sheer bitterness she appealed to the sword, and this judgment may be accepted as true, yet not as exhausting the truth (*Der Kampf um die Vorherrschaft in Deutschland*, vol. ii., p. 554).

for were against her, and he acted accordingly. Nevertheless, before resorting to extremes the Prussian Government determined to make a final attempt to divide Austria's allies and to induce all the North German States to keep out of the conflict. The King of Prussia had a personal interest in the attitude of Saxony, Hanover, and electoral Hesse, because of kinship with their Sovereigns. Accordingly, on June 15th he invited these Sovereigns to enter into a treaty with him, binding them to reduce their armies at once to a peace footing, to observe an unarmed neutrality, and also to assent to the Prussian proposals for the reform of the federal constitution. In return Prussia was to guarantee the security and independence of their territories. All three declined his overture, whereupon Prussian troops crossed their frontiers. The defection of King John of Saxony in particular grieved him sorely, for he had for him a genuine affection. In a few days Prussia had occupied all three States, taken control of their resources, and either driven out, disarmed, or interned their troops. The invasion of Saxony was so rapid that King John withdrew at once with his army into Bohemia, there to join the Austrians. The blind King of Hanover eagerly entered the fray, but the stand made by his forces, if gallant, was short. The only pitched battle fought during the campaign on German soil was that at Langensalza between the Prussians and Hanoverians. Although in this engagement the Hanoverians repulsed the enemy, they were immediately afterwards surrounded and forced to capitulate (June 29th), with the result that the entire army was disbanded, sent home, and put on parole for the duration of the war. The power of the larger States of the North having been broken, the Prussian Government called upon the smaller States to cut themselves adrift from Austria and the Diet, and place their forces at Prussia's disposal, and most of them promptly obeyed.

All the States of the South, true to their votes in the Diet, were ranged against Prussia. Bavaria could not have entered the war except as the ally of Austria. Her leading Minister, von der Pfordten, did not altogether trust Austria, and he was almost alone amongst his countrymen in holding the conviction that she was about to enter upon a task far beyond her power, but strong traditional ties united these two neighbouring States, and the Bavarian King and Court were ardently attached to the Emperor and the policy followed by Vienna. On the other hand, the people of Bavaria in general, while they were as warmly disposed to Austria as they were antagonistic to Prussia, entered the struggle half-heartedly, not pleased that this attitude should have to take the form of armed co-operation, and wondering whether their quixotic attachment to the cause of the Prince of Augustenburg was not proving dear at the price. As soon as the war began to go badly and the defects of the Bavarian military administration showed themselves, the complaint that the Government had not remained neutral became loud and vehement. Würtemberg and Hesse-Darmstadt responded with greater alacrity to Austria's call. The Grand Duke of Baden, on the other hand, would have joined his Prussian relative had he been able, but his people were against him, and he was compelled to swim with the stream.

In Prussia there had occurred in the meantime one of those sudden transformations of public feeling which have been repeated so often since in German history. Up to the very hour when the tocsin of war rang out the nation had been hopelessly divided on the constitutional question, insomuch that patriotism had almost become identified with hostility to the Government. Now, in the time of danger, the spirit of controversy was allayed by the magic of a powerful national appeal. It was recognized that Prussia stood before one of the great decisive events of her history, and all the protracted feud over Schleswig-Holstein, all the wearisome squabbles about succession, *condominium*, and treaty rights, all the diplomatic subtleties and duplicities of the past two years, were forgotten in face of the larger issue which now occupied the foreground. However inadequate the justification of the war, it was seen that the question which it was about to decide was not merely the fate of the duchies, but the future of Germany and her peoples. Was Old Germany, dominated by Austria, to continue, or was a place to be found in Europe henceforth for a New Germany, in which Prussia would be supreme ?

Outside Prussia also there were, even among moderate people, altogether out of sympathy with Prussia's aggressive spirit and fully conscious of the enormity of a fratricidal struggle, many who regarded the war as the inevitable climax of the long-drawn-out controversy, and looked to it for the healing of the sundered German races. Still more consciously was the war regarded and welcomed in Italy as part of a historical struggle for national liberation and unity.

The harrying of the Saxon, Hanoverian, and Hessian armies

was a mere incident in the war, yet it gave the cue to the more serious hostilities which followed. Austria had appealed to the Diet to exercise federal execution against Prussia, and it had agreed. It soon became evident that she had undertaken a task far beyond her power. When the die had been cast there was much misgiving in Austrian military circles. The younger officers were eager for fight, but among the older men were many who gravely doubted whether this confidence was justified. Their apprehensions were fully realized. Too late unsuspected defects in the army and its organization came to light. The training, discipline, and *moral* of the men proved very unequal; there was a great lack of non-commissioned officers; and the commissariat arrangements were faulty. To magnify these disadvantages, the superior officers themselves were in general deficient in training, and in this respect altogether inferior to those of the Prussian army. Further, while the Austrian artillery was superior to that of Prussia, the Prussian infantry had again the great advantage of the new needle-gun, which had done so much destruction in the Danish war, for the Austrian military administration, ignoring the lessons of that war, had obstinately clung to an obsolete percussion gun. Finally, the force which it was found possible to put in the field fell far below the official estimates. The credulity of the Viennese upon this point was boundless, for they exaggerated the strength of the Austrian army just as the Parisians exaggerated that of the French army four years later. It was gravely stated that a million men would turn out under arms against barely half that number of Prussians.[1] The contemptuous attacks of some of the Vienna journals upon the Prussian nation and its political servility had likewise a singular counterpart in the arrogant attitude of the Paris Press towards the same people on the eve of the war of 1870.

Now also Austria had to pay the penalty of her resistance to every attempt made by Prussia to win the Diet's assent to the efficient reorganization of the federal army. To a large extent this army existed only on paper. All the States were liable to supply contingents proportionate to population, but as the need for their use was rare and uncertain, most of them failed to maintain the force expected, trusting to the protection

[1] Friedjung writes freely of the unpreparedness of the Austrian military administration and higher command in Books V and VII of his *Kampf um die Vorherrschaft in Deutschland*, vol. i., pp. 166–75 and 233–63.

offered by the larger States, and particularly by Austria and Prussia. The result in the hour of need was disastrous. Austria should have been able to count on the help of over 200,000 South Germans and 100,000 North Germans, of whom it was hoped that a large part would be immediately available for service in Bohemia. The actual force supplied did not reach half this strength. Bavaria's army on a war footing was supposed to be 72,000 strong, with reserves of over 100,000, for the most part of uncertain quality. She did not, in fact, furnish her prescribed contingent, for while the seventh federal army corps, for which she was responsible, should have numbered 53,400, its actual strength was only 45,000. What was lacking in numbers, however, was made up in variety; the eighth (South German) army corps numbered 35,000 instead of 47,000, but it had five commanders-in-chief, five different sets of service regulations, five kinds of signals, and guns of five different systems. The one army corps from North Germany was furnished by Saxony, Hanover, and electoral Hesse, but mainly by Saxony, whose military administration had been kept at a higher level of efficiency.

Worse still, instead of disposing their forces where they could be used to the best advantage, the various States, with true particularist jealousy, thought only of defending their own hearthstones against Prussian attack, forgetting that Prussia's success in Austria would mean their defeat in Germany. Concerned, as always, first for her own interests, Bavaria in joining Austria had taken care to stipulate that the primary object of her mobilization should be the safety of her own frontiers. She had even secured a pledge that if as a result of the struggle she lost territory she should be compensated elsewhere: the uneasy suspicion was abroad that, be the result victory or defeat, she hoped to secure part of Baden. Bavaria, in fact, hoped to go to war without fighting and without taking any risks. Thus the strongest of the allied States, which should have set an example to the rest, showed the greatest inertia. When the Saxons wanted to join the Bavarians on Bavarian soil they were bidden to keep away, and when the Austrian commander-in-chief called on the Bavarian general to join forces with his own in Bohemia he met with a flat refusal. Not a Bavarian soldier left the kingdom; from first to last Bavaria gave to her ally no useful help whatever. Saxony, on the other hand, did her duty promptly and loyally.

Still more was Austria weakened owing to the necessity of

giving battle simultaneously in two parts of the Empire, in the North against Prussia and in the South against Italy. A force of 74,000, forming the army of the South, was locked up in Venetia, under Archduke Albrecht ; deducting this force and the still larger force needed for the garrisons and otherwise for home defence, and disregarding the allied contingents left in Germany, and there for practical purposes isolated and impotent, the Austrian force available to attack Prussia or meet Prussian attack, as the case might be, was about a quarter of a million, to which were to be added 30,000 Saxons.

To complete the conditions of failure the preparation and execution of Austria's plan of campaign were placed in the hands of a man whose will was paralysed by distrust of himself. This was the gallant but ill-fated Field-Marshal Benedek, who was at the head of the main army of the North. Complete confidence was felt in Benedek both by the Emperor and the entire Austrian army ; only he himself failed to share it. Averse to taking command, he had tried to escape the responsibility, and when he obeyed it was only from the worthy motives of duty and patriotism.[1] He had wished to take command in Italy, where he knew his ground, and had guaranteed the Emperor success there. Had he and the Archduke changed places, the campaign might have resulted differently.

In organization, efficiency, generalship and spirit the Prussian army was all that the Austrian army was not, and its effective strength fell little if at all short of the estimate. The mobilization brought together a force of 355,000 effectives, and after all deductions for garrison and other home service, including a force sufficient to co-operate with Prussia's federal allies in coping with the hostile German States, there remained an expeditionary army of over a quarter of a million men, all highly disciplined, well armed, and well cared for. Moltke was the Prussian battle-thinker, and the three armies into which he divided his forces were commanded by Prince Frederick Charles (first army), the Crown Prince (second army), and General Herwarth von Bittenfeld (third army, or army of the Elbe).

[1] Benedek appears to have anticipated disaster. In one of several pathetic letters which he addressed to his wife at the time he wrote (June 20th) : "If I return to you as a beaten general, show compassion and permit me to bear my misfortune in silence, as befits a man. I go tranquil and resolute to face my destiny. . . . I am master of my nerves, fully conscious of my energy and my iron will," he added. When a man thus tries to rally himself he confesses that he is already undone.

Prussia's military system and the unconstitutional reforms of the last four years were now to be put to a critical test, for which the Danish war had been merely a preparation. Alone of the German States at the time Prussia had adopted universal service; all the secondary States had a system of conscription, with right of substitution. Austria's army was weakened by its polyethnic composition; Hungary, indeed, still disaffected because of the repeal of her constitution, kept out of the struggle, yet an army of Germans, Czechs, Poles, Croats, and Italians made a doubtful conglomeration. The Prussian army, on the other hand, was substantially homogeneous, and it worked with the efficiency and smoothness of a skilfully devised piece of machinery. Its buoyant confidence of victory also made victory half assured.

The Bohemian campaign was in the main a succession of small encounters, fought from Austria's northern frontier onwards towards the plateau which spreads beyond the base of the Giant Mountains, culminating in a single decisive encounter. Only for a short time did the fortunes of battle oscillate, yet even so strongly favouring Prussian arms, for no serious resistance was offered to the invaders, whose three armies were able to cross the passes down to the plain and unite almost with the punctuality of a parade. Then defeat after defeat befell Austrian arms owing to want of coherent plan, wavering decisions, waste of time, during which the enemy was allowed to choose his own dispositions, and the demoralization following upon a growing recognition of marked inferiority. Benedek never attempted the offensive, but finally concentrated his forces in the neighbourhood of Königgrätz, a fortified town on the upper Elbe, there to await the climax which he knew could not be long delayed, yet still uncertain whether to risk his fortunes upon offensive or defensive action.

During the last few days of June the Austrians had lost in killed, wounded, and prisoners no fewer than 30,000 men, against an estimated Prussian loss of barely half the number. Discouraged by repeated reverses and anxious as to what the morrow might bring forth, Benedek, brave and gallant soldier though he was, failed in the critical moment. Fearing the issue of a decisive encounter, he penned on July 1st perhaps the most pathetic message ever addressed from the battlefield by a general to his Sovereign: "I urgently entreat your Majesty to conclude peace at any price. A catastrophe is inevitable." The reply sent from the Hofburg was that the conclusion of peace was impossible, but that if retreat was unavoidable he must execute it decently and in order. In the hope of releasing the army imprisoned in the South, however, the Emperor simultaneously telegraphed to Napoleon inviting him to mediate between him and Victor Emmanuel, hoping that if Italy could be induced to withdraw from the war the conditions in the North would become more equal. The price which he was prepared to pay was the cession of Venetia.

His army having been recruited by two days of rest and his own hopes having revived, Benedek prepared to meet his fate. On July 3rd was fought the battle of Königgrätz, called also by the name Sadowa, which ended in a decisive victory for the invaders. Almost the entire forces on both sides were engaged, and numerically, therefore, the conditions were not unequal. The battle began at seven in the morning and lasted until late in the afternoon. The Prussians from the first secured the offensive, though more than once during the desperate encounter their onslaughts were brought to a standstill, and the Austrians answered by strong counter-attacks. Both sides fought with equal bravery, and to the point of exhaustion, insomuch that the victors were in no mood to make the most of their success, so that the Austrians were able to retire to a position of safety under cover of their brilliant artillery. The battle ended with a headlong flight of the beaten Austrians back to the Elbe and the fortress of Königgrätz, under cover of a gallant and indomitable body of cavalry, which in the trying ordeal never for a moment lost its nerve.

Bismarck, watching from afar the Prussian cuirassier regiments as they rode back in orderly array from the battlefield, instead of following on the heels of the retreating enemy, wondered whether he was the spectator of actual warfare or only of manœuvres. The truth was that the victors were unaware of the completeness of their victory or the demoralization of the enemy. The battle over, Moltke was down with fever, and in his absence initiative was weakened, and his generals were satisfied to rest for the moment upon the laurels already gained. Yet the needle-gun had wrought dreadful havoc. The Austrian losses in killed and wounded were about 30,000, besides 13,000 prisoners, while the Saxons lost about 1,600. The Prussian losses in killed, wounded, and missing were between 13,000 and 14,000. Next day the retreat was continued to Olmütz. The Bohemian war was at an end.

The fourth Chancellor of the German Empire, Prince Bülow, writing nearly fifty years after the event, described the victory of Sadowa as "a triumph of discipline." It was that, but it was also a triumph of military organization. Military writers have adversely criticized Moltke's strategy during the war, and it is certain that the slackness of the Austrian higher command helped him on more than one critical occasion.[1] The Prussian military machine itself, however, proved singularly efficient: both in the quality of their officers and men and in their material equipment the invading armies had every advantage in their favour. Against an enemy so scientifically organized, the Austrian forces, gallantly though they fought, had no chance. Bismarck had said not long before, while the issue of war still hung in the balance: "Foreign Cabinets and nations underestimate us; but the world will see with astonishment what an assertion of power the despised Prussia is capable of." Already his words had come true.[2]

In one detail the Prussian military schemes miscarried, as they deserved to do. Prussian agents, directed by Count Usedom, did their best to tie Austria's hands by fomenting revolution in Hungary. A far-going plot was hatched, money was available in abundance, and it was proposed that Italian troops—a miscellaneous volunteer army which had gathered round Garibaldi—should move into Hungary to support the movement. It was neither a creditable nor a very ingenious piece of strategy; but that it failed was due to no saving of effort on Bismarck's part, but rather to the refusal of the Italian General La Marmora to be associated with warfare of the kind. Through Count Usedom, Bismarck had maintained communication with prominent Hungarian *émigrés*—Kossuth, Türr, Klapka, Czaki, and others—ever since he became Minister-President,

[1] See, for example, Bonnal, in his *Sadowa*.

[2] Lord Palmerston died on October 18, 1865, just too soon to witness the falsification of his low estimate of the Prussian army. He wrote to Earl Russell on December 26, 1863: "The Prussians are brave and make good soldiers, but all military men who have seen the Prussian army at its annual reviews of late years have unequivocally declared their opinion that the French would walk over it and get without difficulty to Berlin, so old-fashioned is it in organization and formation and manœuvre." Yet when these words were written the army reorganization scheme had practically been carried through. Less excusably, for he was a younger man, Mr. Disraeli said to Baron Brunnow on August 5, 1864: "Prussia is a country without any bottom, and in my opinion could not maintain a real war for six months" (*The Life of Benjamin Disraeli, Earl of Beaconsfield*, vol. iv., p. 348).

believing that when the inevitable struggle between the two German Powers came Hungary might be induced to play an important part in Prussia's favour.[1] Active propaganda had been carried on through them in the disaffected kingdom from the time that war became imminent, and Bismarck was sanguine as to the results. To Count Scherr-Thoss he said: " I do not ignore the value which Hungary's help may have for us. . . . If we conquer, however, Hungary will also be free." [2]

At an early stage of the war the efforts of Generals Klapka and Türr to recruit Hungarian and other insurgents against Austria seemed to promise success. Klapka, a revolutionary of 1848, was to raise a rebel corps in Hungary, and Türr, one of Garibaldi's army which landed in Sicily in May, 1860, was to operate on similar lines in Serbia and Roumania. The idea was Bismarck's, and it was a source of distress to honourable soldiers,[3] though the King, for once disowning his truer instincts, allowed himself to be overborne by political considerations. Klapka formed the nucleus of a revolutionary force by recruiting volunteers from amongst the Hungarian prisoners of war, and by attractive offers succeeded in raising a body of 2,000 men.

Kossuth, who knew the difference between honourable and dishonourable revolutions, called the Klapka adventure a " ridiculous fiasco." In effect it achieved no military purpose, while casting discredit upon its author and his instruments. Klapka's hope to incite his countrymen to insurrection failed lamentably: for though he crossed into Hungary, not a man rose to his call, and throughout the whole campaign the population of the disaffected kingdom remained tranquil. Soon desertion set in amongst Klapka's officers, and even more amongst the unsavoury rank and file, and when he heard in August that an Austrian force was in pursuit of him he hastily withdrew to the safety of Prussian cover, fearful of the doom that in

[1] Sybel, describing Usedom as a " distinguished (*vornehmer*) aristocrat," makes an unnecessary demand upon his readers' credulity when he says that the envoy, in cultivating " intimate relations " with these revolutionary leaders, did so " as a matter of course without the authority of his Government," forgetting that that is just what a " distinguished aristocrat " would not do (*Die Begründung des deutschen Reiches*, vol. v., p. 72).

[2] Friedjung, *Der Kampf um die Vorherrschaft in Deutschland*, vol. i., p. 52.

[3] Field-Marshal Count von Blumenthal wrote in his Diary under date August 9, 1866 : " The intended formation of a volunteer corps in Silesia and the formation of the Hungarian Legion were odious to me at the beginning of the campaign, and I am glad that I was able to have nothing to do with either " (*Tagebuch*).

war-time awaits traitors. The Hungarian Legion cost Prussia in money, from first to last, the trifle of a quarter of a million thalers, but the loss to her and Bismarck's reputation was more serious.[1] Austria deeply resented these attempts to tamper with the loyalty of the Hungarians as not playing the game. In marked contrast to them was the action of La Marmora, who, when the war broke out, despatched into Central Italy the legion of deserters from Hungarian regiments which had been formed in the Italian army since 1859.

To make Benedek's defeat more galling, Archduke Albrecht had on June 24th shattered the Italian army under La Marmora at Custozza, at the first meeting, and put it out of action. Nothing is easier than magnanimity in the presence of success, and Moltke was generous in his criticism of the generalship which lost the battle of Sadowa; it was chance, he said, that had turned the scales.[2] To Benedek, however, the praise of his victors brought no consolation. He wrote at once to the Emperor approving by anticipation any judgment and any punishment that might be passed upon his disastrous conduct of the campaign; whether it were trial by court martial, imprisonment, degradation in rank, or dismissal, he would accept the award without murmur. The ungenerous treatment which he received, nevertheless, put his stoical fortitude to a cruel test.[3]

Happily for Benedek's shattered troops, the Prussians did not press their advantage, though the way to Vienna lay open before them, and had they pushed forward they would have met with no serious resistance. Now it was that Napoleon called "Halt!" much to the disgust of William I and his Headquarters Staff.

On the morrow of Königgrätz the Austrian Emperor had repeated his invitation to Napoleon to mediate, and empowered him to settle all details relating to the cession of Venetia. It was a *rôle* which Napoleon had from the beginning hoped to fill, however the fortunes of war might go, and Prussia's success

[1] Bismarck lived to be ashamed of the episode. Three years later he told Prince Hohenlohe that he would "never have thought of letting loose the Hungarian revolution if France had not interposed."

[2] Moltke wrote on August 19, 1866: "The campaign was, it is true, accompanied by almost unexampled good fortune, since not a single enterprise failed" (*Moltke in seinen Briefen*, p. 198).

[3] Benedek died on April 27, 1881, at the age of seventy-seven, "no longer a field-marshal, but one of the best men whom the Austrian army had produced," as Friedjung chivalrously says (*Der Kampf um die Vorherrschaft in Deutschland*, vol. ii., p. 563).

had given him a new and powerful reason for intervention, for it was a reminder that a dangerous rival had appeared on the scene. Sadowa had suggested an alarming possibility—the possibility of Austria being reduced to the level of a third-rate State, with consequences menacing to France and the political equilibrium of Europe. In order that this danger might be averted Austria must be saved from undue pressure. There was no time to lose, for unless he moved quickly it seemed likely that the function of mediator, which it was now more important than ever that he should discharge, would be wrested from his grasp, and he would have to stand aside, ignored and humiliated, after all his pompous words.

On July 5th, therefore, with the concurrence of Mensdorff, the Emperor telegraphed to the King of Prussia and Victor Emmanuel his wish to mediate between them and their enemy, simultaneously publishing his decision in the *Moniteur*, together with the fact of the cession of Venetia to France in trust for Italy. To William I he appealed in the name of friendship and generosity. "I know too well," he said, "your Majesty's magnanimous sentiments and cordial confidence towards me not to believe that after having elevated so high the honour of your arms you would receive with satisfaction the efforts which I wish to make to assist in restoring to your States and to Europe the precious boon of peace." However prettily this was said, it was not true. For the King was not feeling in the least magnanimous or disposed to peace. Only on Bismarck's pressing advice did he accept the offer, influenced by the fear that if Napoleon's *protégé* were pressed too hard effective aid might reach him by way of the Rhine. Nevertheless, neither King nor Minister ever forgave Napoleon for interfering. Bismarck said to his secretaries Abeken and Keudell at the time: "I predict that in a few years Napoleon will regret having taken sides against us." [1]

Italy at first refused to cease hostilities, since she was bent on redeeming the defeat of Custozza, and so of gaining Venetia as a prize of war instead of as a gift, and only when Prussia had brought pressure to bear on the King, and Napoleon had threatened to send a French fleet to Venice, was the refusal withdrawn.

[1] In a speech made in the Imperial Diet on February 19, 1878, Bismarck said: "I know well what I thought then, and I have not forgotten to put it to the account of the Emperor Napoleon. I did not forget his intervention, and perhaps it would have been more advantageous for French interests if France had not then taken upon herself the office of pacificator."

The stipulation of the Prusso-Italian treaty of alliance, that neither of the allies should lay down arms independently of the other, had been ignored by Italy's ally. Italy had as little to do with the conclusion of the succeeding peace as she had in 1859, when Napoleon stopped the war with Austria at Villafranca.

An armistice was concluded and negotiations over terms of peace were opened at Nikolsburg, Mensdorff's castle in Moravia. There Bismarck had around him a devoted band of secretaries and assistants, each one in his way irreplaceable—Abeken, the scribe, and confidant of both King and Minister; Thile, the discreet Under-Secretary; Keudell, the David whose music could banish the chief's evil spirits; and Lothar Bucher, the handyman, whose mastery of languages fitted him for service in any part of the world. From Nikolsburg Abeken wrote: "History will praise us for our moderation in not being at Vienna at this time, and it is pleasing to God that we are not there." It was certainly pleasing to Napoleon, and it was also due to him, for the King, had he been allowed, would only too readily have led his troops into the imperial city. He had, as Bismarck said later, counted on a triumphal entry into Vienna, "in the Napoleonic style." Even Moltke, however, with all his bellicosity, had opposed this idea as absurd. Answering one of his staff who seemed impatient to enter the capital, he said: "And what would you do when you got there?"

The difficulty was to keep the demands of the generals within moderate limits, for patriotic passions had been superheated and political ambitions inordinately whetted by victory. There was a general disposition amongst these men to magnify recent successes and to think that they justified resort to the severest reprisals. Not satisfied with having brought Austria to her knees, they wanted to continue their blows until the victim lay broken in the dust. "All is well with us," Bismarck wrote to his wife on July 9th, "and if we are not extravagant in our demands and do not believe that we have conquered the world we shall get a peace worth having. But we are as quickly intoxicated as dejected, and it is my thankless task to pour water in the foaming wine and to make it clear that we are not the only people in Europe, but that there are our three neighbours to think of." This mood of exaltation had taken hold of the King, to his Minister's alarm. Of the King's land-hunger he once said: "After the Gastein convention and the occupation of Lauenburg, the first addition made to the kingdom under

King William, his frame of mind, so far as I could judge, underwent a psychological change ; he developed a taste for conquest." Incited now by the military party, the King seemed bent on gaining for Prussia the utmost possible advantage, and he frowned when Bismarck warned him against excessive demands.

Bismarck had sent Prince Reuss to Paris in order to convey his views at first hand to Napoleon, and to strengthen the counsels of Count Goltz, the ambassador there. It was to be the business of the two diplomats to reconcile the Emperor to Prussia's conditions, and to listen to, without endorsing, whatever he might have to say on the vexed question of compensations. Goltz had on his side the influence of Prince Napoleon, Rouher, and La Valette (Minister of the Interior), while there was against him the more active influence of Drouyn de Lhuys, Walewski, the Duc de Gramont, and the Empress, supported by the Senate, who were all bent on resisting to the last Prussian aggression in Germany. Goltz had been charged with maximum as well as minimum demands, the former to be bargained with, the latter to be pressed at all costs. Bismarck's irreducible terms comprised the extrusion of Austria from Germany, the federation of the North under Prussian leadership, the abandonment by Austria to Prussia of her rights in Schleswig and Holstein, and cessions of territory by Hanover, Saxony, and the other occupied States. With South Germany he wished for the present to have nothing to do, for he was as convinced as the King himself that the cause of national unity would make surer and speedier progress if as a beginning federation were confined to the North.

"If Napoleon," he had told Prince Reuss, "should not show himself agreeable to our propositions, and intend to oppose our plans, and thus drive us to extremes, you are to give him to understand that we are prepared to light up a conflagration in Germany. Napoleon will see that he is mistaken if he reckons upon the help of revolution in Germany."

From the first, however, the Emperor made no difficulties. More or less half-heartedly he produced several impossible counter-proposals, such as the creation of two federal parliaments, for the North and the South, the exclusion of Saxony from the Northern union, and even the cession to that kingdom of the Rhine Province, but these he readily abandoned. On the other hand, Goltz received sympathetically his proposal that the States of the South should form an independent international union, to be connected with the Northern federation " sur des bases qui seront reglées par une entente commune des États allemands."

The delicate negotiations were not advanced by the fact that Goltz's earliest instructions were from time to time modified in accordance with the changing situation at the seat of war. Writing to Count Bernstorff from Paris, the ambassador told how the first conditions of peace, as communicated to him by Bismarck, were again and again " reversed by later telegrams, announcing a growing appetite at every halting-place." Before long the King was demanding that Austria should cede the remnant of Silesia and part of Bohemia, while of the German States which had fought on her side some were to be annexed outright and the others, including Bavaria and Saxony, were to make a large surrender of territory.[1] He talked, indeed, of asserting for Prussia " supremacy over all Germany." Moltke played up to this spirit of aggression, and was even prepared to begin a war against France at once if Napoleon carried provocation too far.

Never did Bismarck exert his despotic will to wiser purpose than when he insisted upon the paramount duty of moderation, an attitude in which he was warmly supported by the Crown Prince. On leaving the battlefield he had said to the King: " The dispute with Austria is decided; now we have to win back the old friendship." That was motive sufficient, but another consideration, equally strong, was the danger of embroiling France and alienating European opinion, never too friendly to Prussian aspirations.

On the whole Bismarck had little reason to complain of Napoleon's attitude to the proposed peace conditions. Only one serious obstacle held back agreement, and that was the satisfaction of the French claims for compensation. The Emperor had acted the part of an industrious middleman, and every labourer was worthy of his hire; what might he expect in return? Here Goltz was without a brief: all he could do was to receive the proffered suggestions sympathetically and duly report them to his chief. In the absence of a more definite result, therefore, Benedetti was instructed to visit the Prussian

[1] Bismarck told M. Thiers in November, 1870, that after Sadowa the King " would have destroyed Austria," but that he warned him that " it was too soon for that: we should not have been able to fill the empty space from Prague to Constantinople " (Thiers, *Notes et Souvenirs*, p. 91).

headquarters in Bohemia. Accordingly, in the middle of July the ambassador appeared at Nikolsburg, bearing a despatch in which Drouyn de Lhuys, while professing unwillingness to complicate matters at that late stage, gave him to understand that Napoleon could only assent to the proposed annexations if France, too, received a consideration, and he suggested a slice of territory on the left bank of the Rhine.

In his story of this episode Benedetti tries to make it appear that his arrival at the Prussian headquarters was welcome and that his overtures were opportune. It is evident from Bismarck's later utterances and from the contemporary reports of those around him, that the French ambassador was regarded as a bore, his presence as an untimely intrusion, and his proposals as embarrassing. Benedetti having appeared, however, all that Bismarck thought of was how to get rid of him, and on his side the object of the discussions, which lasted far into the first night and were continued next day and for many days, was rather to stave off than bring about any practical result. Benedetti remained at Nikolsburg about a fortnight, giving Bismarck no rest, and clamouring with increasing urgency for the settlement of Napoleon's little account, not indeed insisting that he must take the money away with him, but willing to accept a bill, to be honoured at a later date. The concession asked for was one which Bismarck, in spite of all his past disingenuous promises, was not, and never had been, either willing or able to make. For the present, therefore, it was to his interest to prolong Napoleon's uncertainty as long as possible, and find an excuse for deferring a definitive answer until Prussia, having disposed of her old enemy, should be free to negotiate on more advantageous terms. This he succeeded once more in doing, and Benedetti, to his mortification, went away with fresh promises, but with nothing else. It was one more masterly illustration of Bismarck's policy of "treating dilatorily" questions which were not ripe or opportune for settlement. The sequel will be told in a later chapter.

An event occurred on July 24th which decided Bismarck to complete the negotiations without delay. A telegram from the Prussian ambassador in St. Petersburg warned him that the Czar was anxious for a conference of the Powers, on the ground that as the questions which were being discussed at Nikolsburg involved the subversion of the European settlement of 1815, they should not be decided without regard to the neutral

States. Apprehensive of the result of procrastination, Bismarck urgently begged the King to be satisfied with the concessions he had already obtained from France and not to give Napoleon time to change his mind. "We cannot," he said, "rely on the other Great Powers supporting Prussia in greater demands, nor even in these." But the King was inordinately greedy. "It is a question," he said, "of getting as much money and territory as we can without risking everything." It had already been agreed that Prussia should annex, besides the Elbe duchies, the entire kingdom of Hanover, electoral Hesse, all but the northern part of Hesse-Darmstadt, and Nassau, with Frankfort. So liberally recompensed for a campaign which had really been little more than a *promenade militaire*, Bismarck declared that it would be for Prussia "a political blunder" to attempt to gain a few million thalers more from Austria or a few square miles more territory from her German allies. It was only the interposition of the Crown Prince that finally overbore intemperate demands. "Speak in the name of the future," said the King, turning to his son, when a critical council threatened to end in a deadlock.

The Crown Prince, who had led Germans against Germans against his will, declared for moderation and no further annexations, and the King capitulated, though still unwillingly.

Recording this episode, Sybel writes: "It will be difficult for posterity to judge otherwise than that such a relation between Monarch and Minister, such a combination of consciousness of victory and moderation, such a union of self-restraint and genius, has seldom appeared in history." [1] But it is necessary to add that the moderation, self-restraint, and perspicacity were altogether on Bismarck's side. Had the King had his way, he might have wrecked the peace, tempted France to form a new combination against Prussia, and lost everything by trying to grasp too much. The anti-Prussian party in Paris, incited by the Duc de Gramont, was, in fact, at this time urging Napoleon to make a military demonstration on the Rhine and assuring him that thus "without war, without a fight, without danger and without loss" he would be able to dictate terms, since "if Prussia holds Austria, Austria holds Prussia." Referring to this possibility in later years, Bismarck admitted (January 16, 1874) that even a small French force, united with the South German army, would at that critical juncture have "compelled

[1] *Die Begründung des deutschen Reiches*, vol. v., p. 298.

us to cover Berlin and abandon our successes in Austria." How much credit was due to the King for the generous terms offered to Austria is shown by the marginal comment which he added to a memorandum on the subject hastily drawn up by his anxious Minister. "Inasmuch," he wrote, "as my Minister-President has left me in the lurch, and I am not in a position to replace him, I have discussed the matter with my son, and as he shares the views of the Minister-President I find myself, to my sorrow, compelled, after the army's brilliant victory, to bite into this sour apple and to accept this shameful peace." Bismarck relates that the King wept with vexation at Nikolsburg when he was not allowed to continue the war.[1]

Bismarck was wont to claim in later years that his moderation in the treatment of Austria was due solely to a desire to make a new friend out of an old antagonist. That was to be the effect of his policy, but it was not its only or its principal cause. Prudential considerations played a decisive part. Several of these considerations have been mentioned, but there were others. He knew well that the appropriation of Austrian territory would have meant the addition to Prussia of a Slavic or at least of a Roman Catholic population, in either case an element of serious political danger. Not only so, but he was too far-sighted to ignore the fact that there was a point beyond which it would be dangerous to force humiliation upon the beaten foe. In calculating the weight of Austria's penalty, he had to reckon not only with Napoleon but with European opinion. He knew—no one better—that the Great Powers would not tolerate the extinction or even the undue weakening of the Austrian Empire, and that to attempt any changes which would disturb the existing equilibrium in favour of Prussia and the new Germany which was coming would be suicidal. So anxious was he as to the Czar's attitude in particular that at the beginning of August he despatched on a special mission to St. Petersburg General von Manteuffel, a favourite at the Russian Court, with instructions to reassure him of Prussia's determination to adhere to the line of moderation. To which let it be added that Francis Joseph was kept fully acquainted with the pressure which was being applied to Prussia in and from Paris, and that at one time in July it seemed likely that he would

[1] Friedjung writes: "It was no fault of his that several other of his royal and princely cousins on the small thrones of Germany had not to leave their countries" (*Der Kampf um die Vorherrschaft in Deutschland*, vol. i., p. 37).

abruptly refuse Bismarck's demands, break off the negotiations, and try his fortunes again in war. Finally, typhus and cholera had broken out in the victorious army, and the season was favourable to their spread.[1]

In the Preliminaries of Peace, as signed on July 26th and ratified two days later, Prussia offered and Austria accepted conditions substantially as Napoleon had approved them. The principal stipulations were that Austria should assent to the dissolution of the Germanic Federation and to exclusion from Germany as reorganized, renounce to Prussia her rights in Schleswig and Holstein, acknowledge the annexations which that State proposed to make in North Germany, and bear part of the costs of the war. The integrity of Austria was to be respected. There was much haggling over the indemnity question. Bismarck began by demanding a total sum of a hundred million thalers (£15,000,000), of which Austria was to pay one-half, reducible by fifteen millions to be required from Schleswig-Holstein as part of the war-bill of 1864, leaving a net penalty of thirty-five million thalers. In his draft, however, he had set down forty and not fifty millions as the gross sum to be expected from Austria, the difference being a margin upon which to bargain. Accordingly, when Austria protested he moderated his demand first to forty-five, then to forty, and finally to thirty-five millions, reducible to twenty millions by the payment due from Schleswig-Holstein. With creditable chivalry, Austria firmly opposed the annexation of any part of Saxony, the only one of the German States which had stood staunchly by her and the Federation, her plenipotentiary declaring in the Emperor's name that he would rather resort to arms again than sacrifice so faithful an ally. Bismarck thought such an attitude quixotic, but he respected it, and, rather than imperil peace, he agreed. On the other hand, he resolutely refused to assent to the proposal, also made by Austria, that Saxony should be excluded from the North German union of States.[2]

[1] When later the negotiations over the definitive treaty of peace lagged at Prague, Moltke wrote home (August 19th): "The diplomats have been negotiating at Prague for three weeks already—nearly as long as the campaign itself lasted. I fervently wish we could get our troops out of this war-, hunger-, and pestilence-ridden country."

[2] Beust claims to have prompted this demand for the purpose of bargaining, well knowing that it would be rejected, though he was not present when it was made; and he relates that when it was mentioned "Bismarck sprang up from his chair and threatened to break off negotiations," which is likely enough (*Memoirs*, vol. i., p. 325).

No other German State was mentioned in the treaty; all the rest of Prussia's enemies were left to bargain with the victor as best they might. Bavaria tried to come into the Nikolsburg agreement, but was repelled. "Do you know that I might make you a prisoner of war?" said Bismarck wrathfully to Baron von der Pfordten, when that Minister turned up one day, unsought and without a safe conduct, at the Prussian headquarters. The daring envoy beat a hasty retreat, and was seen no more. It would not appear, however, that Bismarck's brusque reception depressed him unduly, for the report which he conveyed to King Ludwig was such as to draw from him the prompt comment, "All is well, so now I can venture to recall Richard Wagner!"[1]

The preliminaries of Nikolsburg were confirmed in substantially the same form in the Peace of Prague, signed on August 23rd, the fourth article of which ran: "The Emperor of Austria acknowledges the dissolution of the Germanic Federation as hitherto existing, and gives his assent to a new organization of Germany, in which the Austrian Imperial State shall not participate. He also promises to recognize the closer federation which the King of Prussia intends to establish north of the Main, and agrees that the German States lying south of that line shall be free to enter together into a union whose national connection with the North German Confederation shall be a matter of later agreement between both sides, and which shall have an international and independent existence." Austria also ceded to Prussia all rights in respect of Schleswig and Holstein accruing to her in virtue of the Treaty of Vienna of October 30, 1864, subject to the condition that "the populations of the northern districts of Schleswig, if they of their free will advance the desire to be united to Denmark, shall be ceded to that State."

On the day that the Peace of Prague was signed the Federal Diet, which, though now reduced to a handful of members, had pretended to prolong its inglorious career at Augsburg, held its last sitting. The German peoples saw unmoved the end of the Bund and its once arrogant but now humbled executive; they had brought much ill and little good to the national life, and their extinction was at least a negative gain. A separate peace

[1] Prince Hohenlohe, then about to become a Bavarian Minister, writes in his Diary under date August 18, 1866: "The King is busy devising scenery for the opera 'William Tell,' and is having costumes made for himself, dressed in which he parades his room. Meantime, it is a question whether the kingdom is to lose the 30,000 inhabitants of Franconia and the 700,000 of the Palatinate."

was concluded between Austria and Italy, and the treaty embodying its terms was signed in Vienna on October 3rd. By it Venetia was ceded to the new kingdom.

Prussia was free to settle accounts with the hostile German States at leisure. Having but a poor opinion of the South Germans and their war preparations, Moltke's plan had been to concentrate all his strength upon their ally. "Therein," says the Prussian official history of the war, "lay the key of the whole position. A victory over the Austrian army would paralyse all the other enemies." This calculation was abundantly justified, for the opposition offered by the hostile German States was never serious, and while the Nikolsburg negotiations were in progress it flickered out ignominiously. A force of 45,000 Prussians, increased by contingents from Oldenburg, Mecklenburg, and other smaller States to 80,000, had been left behind to suppress Austria's South German allies if they ventured to show fight, which for the most part they were loath to do. Isolated skirmishes occurred throughout July, until, weary of being driven from pillar to post, the allies invoked the good offices of Napoleon and the Czar. Finally, an urgent appeal for peace was addressed to the King of Prussia, and it was granted on August 2nd.

The opponents of the war had predicted for it a duration of months or of years—Prince Hohenlohe feared that it would be "very long and very sanguinary," while Moritz Mohl, the Würtemberg publicist, believed that it would last for a generation—yet it was over in seven weeks.

On August 5th Bismarck invited the South German Governments to send plenipotentiaries to Berlin to discuss the conditions of peace, and all sent their Foreign Ministers; Bavaria was represented by Baron von der Pfordten, Würtemberg by Baron Varnbüler, Baden by Herr von Freydorf, and Hesse-Darmstadt by Herr von Dalwigk. All the States able to secure influence amongst the Powers had done so. Russia had spoken a good word for Würtemberg and Hesse; Austria and France had both pleaded for Saxony; the Prussian King himself was the protector of Baden, and had bidden his Minister deal gently with his son-in-law the Grand Duke; only Bavaria, in the time of its extremity, was without a friend.[1]

Bavaria wished for collective negotiations, but Bismarck refused the request point-blank, and treated first with Würtemberg

[1] *Memoirs of Prince Hohenlohe*, vol. i., p. 159.

and Baden. From Würtemberg, though it had been specially truculent when the war broke out, he required no cession of territory, but only the payment of eight million gulden (£670,000) by way of contribution to Prussia's war costs, together with the acceptance of the preliminaries of peace as concluded with Austria, in so far as they affected the South German States and their future relationships with each other, and the conclusion of customs and railway conventions with Prussia.

In the case of Baden the conditions were the same, except that the war-bill was only six million gulden (£500,000). The King of Prussia wished this amount to be reduced, on the ground that the Grand Duke had been compelled to go to war against his will by a rebellious and stiff-necked people. Bismarck drily reminded him that it was the people who would have to pay the bill, and the penalty stood.

The Preliminaries of Peace stipulated that the Southern States should be free to form a union of their own, but the Würtemberg and Baden plenipotentiaries pleaded that no attempt should be made to force their hands in the matter. Bismarck willingly agreed that they should be left to do as they pleased, since he had no desire to see the federation come into existence.

A further demand imposed upon Würtemberg and Baden, and later upon Bavaria and Hesse, seriously restricted the practical value of this option, for each of these States was required to enter into a defensive and offensive alliance with Prussia by the terms of which the signatories guaranteed to each other the integrity of their territories and undertook "in case of war" to pool their complete military strength for that purpose, the combined force to be under the command of the King of Prussia. A specific *casus fœderis* was neither defined nor mentioned in the treaties, which were concluded for an indefinite period, and for the present were to remain secret.

It was not intended that Bavaria and Hesse-Darmstadt should be let off so easily. With these States Bismarck negotiated together, inasmuch as territorial readjustments were contemplated in both cases. King William had in particular set his heart upon regaining the districts of Anspach and Bayreuth, which were transferred from Prussia to Bavaria in 1815, and Hesse was to have ceded a slice of territory to its neighbour by way of compensation. The Bavarian and Hessian Ministers bitterly protested against such harsh treatment, and entreated the French ambassador to urge Napoleon to intervene in order to save them from this humiliation. When the French Government accordingly made representations to Berlin on the subject, Bismarck relented. Calling Baron von der Pfordten to him, he first talked for some time as though contemplating no concession. Then, having sufficiently tormented his victim, he suddenly altered his tactics, and producing Napoleon's latest scheme of spoliation, proposing the annexation of the Palatinate,[1] he put it into Pfordten's hand. As soon as the bewildered Baron had recovered from the shock he was invited to say frankly which country he would trust in future—France or Prussia. The answer was not doubtful. The demand for territory—except for a small strip of land needed for the rectification of Prussia's frontier—having been withdrawn, the Bavarian Minister gladly entered into the military alliance and agreed to a war-bill of thirty million gulden (£2,500,000).

Hesse-Darmstadt, besides paying a contribution of three million gulden (£250,000), lost a large part of the province of Upper Hesse, the landgraviate of Hesse-Homburg (this being offered as a *solatium* to the cousin and successor of the dethroned Elector of Hesse-Cassel), and the fortress of Mayence. Further, it was stipulated that the remaining portion of the Grand Duchy north of the Main should enter the contemplated North German Confederation, the Grand Duke placing his troops under the command of the King of Prussia.

Annexations in North Germany were in Bismarck's mind when he proposed the reform of the federal constitution in June: there was to be a new union composed of fewer members. In a letter written to the Duke of Coburg he had compared Prussia with Rome, and, recalling how the ancient Empire had not been consolidated without "earning considerable odium by the rape of the Sabines," had said that the Germanic Rome of the future would be unable to avoid similar acts of violence, though he would "like to see them reduced to a minimum, leaving the rest to time."[2] The territories wholly added to Prussia, besides Schleswig-Holstein, were electoral Hesse, which had been a perpetual thorn in her side; Nassau, which likewise had been a quarrelsome neighbour, ostentatious in its devotion to Austria; Hanover, and the Free City of Frankfort.

The absorption of Frankfort was a foregone conclusion, and was the climax of a course of harsh and ungenerous treatment,

[1] See Chapter VIII., p. 296.

[2] Quoted in *Aus meinen Leben und aus meiner Zeit*, vol. iii., p. 528.

in which Bismarck's hand was plainly revealed. He had not forgotten how often the authorities and population of the Free City had been at pains to show that their sympathies were rather with the Southern than the Northern monarchy, and how in particular, when on the outbreak of war the troops of the rival States evacuated the garrison, the Austrians marched forth amid popular ovations, the Prussians in icy silence.

No sooner had the Prussians entered the city than they exacted bitter amends for its too ostentatious display of Austrian sympathies. General Falckenstein made an immediate war-levy of nearly half a million pounds upon the public treasury, and when General Manteuffel—the same who had ruled with a high hand in Schleswig—succeeded him, a further levy of over a million and a half pounds was demanded on conditions so impossible of fulfilment that the Mayor of the city, in despair, committed suicide. Unable to meet the exactions of its masters, the city sought the intervention of the Queen of Prussia, and at her solicitation the King ordered the moderation of the harsh tribute. Other vexatious demands were, however, imposed; the best of the private houses were converted into billets for the soldiers, who lived on the fat of the land, and the municipal officers were subjected to great indignity.

By the loss of his throne the blind King George V of Hanover paid the penalty not only of his own but of his predecessor's miscalculations. He had chosen to be on the wrong side in the late war, and his action in so doing had been the logical consequence of his earlier hostility to Prussia and his unwillingness to act as postilion on a national coach of which a Hohenzollern was to be the driver. Throughout the history of the Germanic Federation, however, Hanover had distinguished itself by attachment to Austria, and a constant and at times arrogant opposition to Prussia and the Prussian view of things. It was also Hanover's misfortune that it stood geographically in the way of a consolidated Prussian kingdom. Cutting deep into the heart of that kingdom the Guelphic lands had long been a Naboth's vineyard in the eyes of the Hohenzollerns. Sixty years before, by agreement with Napoleon, they had for a short time been in Prussian occupation, and William I had never concealed his desire to see them again part of his monarchy. Now that Hanover's fate had been committed to the fortunes of war he could at least plead that its ruler had brought disaster upon himself by neglecting a fair warning. In throwing down the boundary posts surrounding the Guelphic enclave, King William carried his sway to the Dutch frontier, and gave Prussia a wide front on the North Sea.

The Crown Prince of Hanover was offered the succession to the duchy of Brunswick, an appanage of the Crown, provided both father and son would agree to renounce all claim to the appropriated kingdom. As they refused, Brunswick, without losing its independence, was placed under a Prussian Regent.[1] The Czar had warmly interceded on behalf of Hanover's high-spirited ruler, but in vain. The King's reply (August 20th) seemed to confirm to the full the fears which had perpetually haunted the smaller States in all their relations with the northern kingdom.

"Believe me," he wrote, "nothing has more injured the monarchical principle in Germany than the existence of these small and impotent dynasties, which eke out their existence at the expense of the national interests, insufficiently discharge their sovereign duties, and compromise the reputation of the monarchical principle just in the same way that a large and poor nobility does that of the aristocracy. Public opinion is penetrated by the conviction that these small monarchies stand in natural and necessary opposition to the national interest."

Referring, in the same letter, to the Czar's fears as to where the promised national parliament might lead, he said: "I shall oppose revolution in Germany in the future as in the past, and shall no more subordinate myself to the exaggerated pretensions of a German Parliament than to those of the Prussian Diet."

Of his own relations to the Czar the King wrote: "Nothing is nearer to my heart than the strengthening of the tie which unites us. In none of my political combinations shall Russia's interests be injured; on the contrary, I shall esteem myself happy if I should be able in the future to find an opportunity of proving that I ever regard these interests as those of the oldest and most trusted ally of Prussia."

Of the dethroned rulers, the King of Hanover was the one who accepted his fate with least resignation. As he refused to come to terms on the dissolution of the kingdom his estate and privy fund were sequestered. Later in the year both England and Russia pressed the Prussian Government to devise some compromise. Bismarck proposed that in consideration of the King's

[1] An arrangement which continued until 1913, when the right of succession was restored to the lawful heir on his marriage with the Princess of Prussia.

renouncing the throne and repaying twenty-three million thalers (£3,450,000) of State money which he had sent to England, there should be paid to him an annuity of 700,000 thalers (£105,000) instead of his former civil list of 400,000 thalers (£60,000) derived from domains, and that this annuity should be secured on a capital of sixteen million thalers (£2,400,000), to be duly invested. He was also to retain a large private fortune invested abroad, and to be assigned certain castles and domains. As he still refused to renounce his rights as ruler, Bismarck did not press this condition, and the agreement was concluded without it and signed in September. As later, however, the King took part in dynastic agitations to the extent of financing a legion of Hanoverian and other soldiers pledged to the Guelph cause, the annuity was suspended. The Guelph Legion was maintained until 1870, when it was disbanded, each man receiving a payment of 400 francs wherewith to emigrate. The sequestered monies were officially known as the "fund for the combating of hostile Guelph endeavours against Prussia." Owing to the crooked use made of it—the bribery of newspapers, the payment of secret agents, and the maintenance of an elaborate system of espionage—it later became notorious in political life as the "Reptile fund." Adequate revenues upon which to support their establishment and dignity were also assigned to the other deposed rulers—to the Duke of Nassau £1,285,000 and to the Elector of Hesse £1,200,000, besides castles and estates.

The last of the treaties of peace to be concluded was that with Saxony (October 21st), which came out of the ordeal with the credit it deserved. Saxony agreed to join the alliance of the North German States, to reorganize its troops, which were to form an integral part of the new federal army and be under the chief command of the King of Prussia, and to pay ten million thalers (£1,500,000) towards Prussia's war costs; but it was allowed to retain its existing diplomatic representation, and the integrity of the kingdom remained intact. The Saxon Minister-President, Beust, whose attachment to Austria was passionate, had imported into his attitude to Prussia a bitterness of temper which the King did not share. His personal relations with Bismarck were also very strained, so that it was intimated to Dresden that the peace negotiations would fare better if he were kept out of them. Beust in consequence had tendered his resignation in August. In truth his position at home had been compromised from the first moment of his country's defeat, the grievance against him being, not that he had loved Saxony too little, but that he had loved Austria too well. Two months later (October 30th) he entered service under the Austrian Emperor, first as Foreign Minister. This change from the wings to the footlights of the stage was in every respect welcome to him, and his long-cherished desire to occupy in the larger sphere of European politics the prominent place for which he believed his talents qualified him was for a short time gratified. In the following February he succeeded Belcredi as head of the Ministry, and in June he was created a Count and received the title Chancellor of the Empire, a title previously held only by Kaunitz and Metternich.

The absorption by Prussia of four German States as the result of a war which most people, even at that day, regarded as having been forced upon her adversary, was not witnessed without compunction by the feudalist Conservatives, the party to which Bismarck himself had belonged. They saw in the annexations a wilful violation of the sacred principle of legitimism, and one of their number, the downright Gerlach, did not hesitate to remind Bismarck that the commandment "Thou shalt not steal!" was intended to apply just as much to the territories of Germany's Princes as to the chattels of her peasants. By the annexations (including Schleswig and Holstein) an addition of 1,306 German (or 27,758 English) square miles was made to the area of Prussia and an addition of four and a third millions to her population, which now numbered nearly twenty-four millions. More important than the expansion of Prussia, however, was the fact that in the throes of the conflict now ended the whole German nation was brought nearer to the final act of unity and consolidation.

Warfare was cheap in those days. Probably no war yielding to the conquering nation such substantial advantages was waged at so small a cost as the campaign of 1866. The total cost to Prussia of the operations in Bohemia and Germany was about fourteen million pounds, and of this sum two-thirds were paid back by the conquered States. Friedjung estimates the cost of the war to Austria at 215½ million gulden (about £18,000,000), against which she received thirty-five million gulden (about £2,500,000) from Italy as the share of the latter in the public debt of Venetia.[1]

One of the immediate results of the war was the conclusion

[1] *Der Kampf um die Vorherrschaft in Deutschland*, vol. ii., p. 549.

of the constitutional struggle which since 1862 had created discord and confusion in Prussian political life. The Diet had been re-elected on July 3rd, with results which showed that the old spirit of conflict was weakening ; a hundred Conservatives were returned where several years before there were barely a dozen, and the Progressists had decreased proportionately, though the moderate Liberals held the balance. The brilliant issue of the late campaign and the steps now being taken to form a North German Confederation were facts so large as to throw purely domestic questions into the background and make parliamentary frictions appear incongruous and trivial. The Government and the Diet both wanted peace, while the nation, elated by victory, was in no mood for quarrelling further over fine points of constitutional theory. Nor could it be doubted that this victory was in part a result of the very scheme of army reorganization which the constitutionalists had fought tooth and nail, not because they disapproved of army reform in itself, but because they differed from the Government as to the method of carrying it out.

Before the Diet reassembled there was a violent dispute in the Cabinet over the question whether or not it should seek an indemnity for its past unconstitutional methods of finance. While the war was still running its course Count Eulenburg, the Minister of the Interior, had drawn up a first draft of the speech to be read from the throne, and in it had proposed that "supplementary sanction" (*nachträgliche Gutheissung*) should be given to the irregular financial measures of the past four years. Eager to quieten the public mind and to prevent the recurrence of similar conflicts between the Crown and the Diet, he was even said to be willing to make the constitutional theory of Ministerial responsibility a reality.

The proposal to seek an indemnity in any form was, however, resisted by the other Conservative Ministers, and chiefly by Count Lippe, the Minister of Justice, on the plea that after the army reorganization had been justified by its success it was for the Diet and not the Government to give way.[1] Nevertheless,

[1] A Liberal historian, Heinrich von Sybel, who was himself a member of the Prussian Lower House, and had taken part in the constitutional struggle on the popular side, deems it a virtue in Bismarck that he did not use the victory over Austria for establishing a despotism at home. "In view of such a conjunction of political and military triumphs," he writes in his *History* (vol. v., p. 342), "how many of the great conquerors of ancient and modern times would have withstood the temptation to destroy completely the hostile empire abroad and

the majority authorized Herr von der Heydt, the Minister of Finance, to prepare an alternative draft explicitly mentioning the idea of indemnity instead of merely hinting at it.[1] Bismarck, with Roon, was at the war at the time, and so long as he was absent the King refused to consider either surrender or compromise. In the end Bismarck persuaded him, but only after a severe struggle and by making astute use of the argument that to ask the Diet for an indemnity would be to invite it to confess itself in the wrong, and that in granting it the Diet and not the Government would be capitulating.

The Diet was opened on August 5th, and an indemnity was accordingly solicited—" so settling the dispute for all time " —in terms that breathed neither menace nor arrogance. Very different in temper was the King's answer to the address of the Lower House in reply to the speech from the throne. Most of the constitutionalists were willing to grant the indemnity desired, assuming that it had been asked for in sign of repentance. To their surprise the King began by praising the reorganization of the army, without which the late victories would not have been won; then coming to the question in dispute, he declared that it had been his duty, in the absence of a budget law, to follow his own course, and that he would do the same thing again if a similar situation happened again, though he added immediately: " But, gentlemen, it will *not* happen again." The effect of this speech was that while the Upper House adopted the Indemnity Bill unanimously, the Lower House gave to it only a divided assent: there was a minority of 75 resolute dissentients against the 230 deputies in its favour.

In the majority were many Liberals who, like Twesten and Lasker, had hitherto refused any compromise on a question so vital to the maintenance of the rights of parliament, and to constitutional development. The minority was composed for the most part of men—prominent among them Jacoby, Waldeck, Schulze, and Virchow—far-sighted enough to perceive that the issue involved was far greater than the mere formal condonation of a Ministry which confessed that it had erred; that the question which was being decided was whether the constitutional movement should go forward or backward, whether the half-principles introduced in a constitution which was given in haste

subvert all constitutional restraints at home? But Bismarck was made of other stuff."

[1] Roon's *Denkwürdigkeiten*, vol. ii., pp. 309–11.

and repented ever afterwards should become petrified, and obstruct all further progress towards complete parliamentary government. In sealing that compact of accommodation and peace the Liberals who held the casting vote sealed the fate of their party and cause for over half a century. For it was true, as Bismarck had said, that the surrender was not the Government's but theirs. The Minister-President had put on the white sheet of penitence, but beneath it was still the cuirassier's uniform, emblematic of military domination present and to come. The Upper House voted the Indemnity Bill without demur, though the feudalists, with Kleist-Retzow as their spokesman, lamented the Government's weakness in proposing it.

The division in the Liberal ranks on this question had a permanent significance. The right wing of the *Fortschritt,* to the number of twenty-four, seceded and formed a new party with the name National Liberal, taking with it many able men who had fought long and resolutely for the popular cause, and whose attachment to progressive principles was still above suspicion. The best known of the seceders were Twesten, Bennigsen, Lasker, Forckenbeck, Unruh, Michaelis, and Hammacher. In the next Diet the new party formed a strong phalanx of a hundred.

Nor was the popular party the only one to be split over the indemnity question. The unconciliatory attitude of the extremer members of the Conservative party led likewise to a secession of which the outcome was the formation of the Free Conservative or Imperialist party. Honestly desirous at the time of exercising a liberalizing influence upon Conservative thought, this party soon found that it had undertaken a task beyond its powers, though it has ever since preserved an independent existence.

There were further discords when the Government recommended to the Diet for reward a list of generals who had distinguished themselves in the field. A majority of the Lower House, endorsing the action of the committee to which the proposal had been referred, wished to add Bismarck to the list, and this was done in spite of the protests of the no-indemnity party, which demanded that the name of Roon, the Minister of War, should also be omitted.

One drop of gall, but a large and bitter one, fell into the goblet of national joy a little later. Napoleon never remained long in the background. For him Sadowa had been a rude awakening, and instead of concealing his disappointment at Prussia's success, he proclaimed it by word and sign to all the world. Just when Germany and Austria were beginning to settle down to their new life he broke silence and exercised his rare faculty for saying the wrong thing. In a speech from the throne on February 14, 1867, he once more recalled his sudden intervention in the war and said: "I have not armed one soldier more, I have not called out a single regiment, and yet the voice of France has had influence enough to hold back the victors at the gates of Vienna. Our mediation between the combatants has led to an agreement which, while giving to Prussia the fruits of victory, has preserved the integrity of the Austrian territory with the exception of one province (Venetia), and by the cession of this province has consummated Italian independence."

Though true, this boastful claim was no longer new, and it would have been better had it been repressed, for it deeply mortified German pride without bringing comfort to the countries which were smarting under defeat.

CHAPTER VII

(1866–1867)

THE NORTH GERMAN CONFEDERATION

It was one of Bismarck's maxims of statecraft that questions which were either untoward or not ripe for action should be "treated dilatorily." That meant sometimes not treating them at all. On the other hand, no man had greater capacity for acting swiftly and decisively in emergencies, or was more conscious, in critical situations, of the importance of improving the opportunities and advantages of the moment. He had hurried to a conclusion the peace negotiations with Austria, on the principle of a settlement at any price, since delay meant danger. Now that the way was open for negotiation upon the question of federal reform he was equally resolved to lose no time, but to bind Prussia's willing and unwilling allies at once to the pledges of union which they had already given, lest they should spring upon him new difficulties.

Now for the first time he was face to face with the question of German unity in a practical form. It involved two separate problems. One related to the North German States, the form of the new union to be created, the organization of the necessary legislative and executive authorities, and the determination of their jurisdiction; the other and perhaps more difficult problem related to the future position of the States of the South, their relation to one another, to the union of the North, and to foreign Powers.

By the beginning of September (1866) the Sovereigns of most of the North German States had signified their willingness to enter the proposed Confederation and their acceptance of the convention which had been put forward as a basis of union. Backward States like the Mecklenburgs, which were still without constitutions and feared all innovations of the kind, hesitated, but the only really refractory members were the little duchy of Saxe-Meiningen, whose ruler had been deposed, and the still smaller principality of Reuss of the older line. The haughty attitude held towards Prussia by the Lady Disdain who ruled the destinies of the latter duodecimo State and the stubbornness with which she refused to bow to the victor's dictation deserved greater admiration than they received.

The majority of the States were incorporated in virtue of a treaty of August 18th: these were Prussia (including now, in addition to the old provinces, the kingdom of Hanover, electoral Hesse, the duchy of Nassau, the duchies of Schleswig and Holstein, the Free City of Frankfort, and the portions of Bavaria and the grand duchy of Hesse ceded to the monarchy), Saxe-Weimar, Oldenburg, Brunswick, Saxe-Altenburg, Saxe-Coburg-Gotha, Anhalt, Schwarzburg-Sondershausen, Schwarzburg-Rudolstadt, Waldeck, Reuss of the younger line, Schaumburg-Lippe, Lippe-Detmold, Lübeck, Bremen, and Hamburg. Mecklenburg-Schwerin and Mecklenburg-Strelitz joined in virtue of a treaty of alliance of August 21st, and later, by the treaties of peace concluded with them by Prussia, there were added the grand duchy of Hesse for its territory lying north of the Main, Saxe-Meiningen, Reuss of the older line, and Saxony, making a total of twenty-two.

The Governments were invited in November to send plenipotentiaries to confer upon a draft constitution to be duly laid before a constituent Diet, and they met in Berlin from December 15th until February 9th following. Sybel says that Bismarck dictated the main lines of the draft in the afternoon of December 13th to his secretary, Lothar Bucher, that Bucher and Rudolph Delbrück elaborated these notes during the night, and that on the following day the draft was approved by the King and a council of Ministers. Bismarck's feat in draughtsmanship, though notable, was hardly so unique as this.[1] Tentative drafts, made by different hands, were already lying about, and apart from these there was the laboriously wrought Frankfort constitution of 1848–9. From the material at his disposal Bismarck extracted

[1] It is hardly hypercritical to say that as a legal document and a literary production the German imperial constitution of to-day seriously suffers in form, phraseology, and clarity owing to the haste with which the original was drafted. Bismarck, in his *Reflections and Reminiscences* (vol. ii., pp. 296–7), calls attention to a curious instance of careless draughtsmanship in article 74, but more curious is the fact that the error in question was copied, undetected, from the constitution of the North German Confederation. Serious students of the constitution will be well advised to consult the original rather than translations.

the quintessence of its wisdom for what it was worth, yet it may fairly be said that the constitution as now drawn up for presentation to the federal Sovereigns was in substance no less his work than the Prussian Municipal Ordinance of 1808 was the work of Stein, who similarly and with great freedom used the labour of others.[1]

Reserving for a later chapter a fuller exposition of the federal constitution of Germany, in the form in which it was amended when the North and the South were merged in the completed Empire, it will be sufficient to indicate here merely its broad outlines. These followed the proposals made to the Frankfort Diet by Prussia on June 10th, though some features were directly borrowed from the charter upon which the Frankfort National Assembly had worked so industriously and lovingly. The union was to be called the "North German Confederation" (*Norddeutscher Bund*), and was to consist of twenty-two[2] States lying north of the river Main. The population of the federal territory was thirty millions, of whom twenty-five millions fell to Prussia alone. There was not to be an Emperor, as the Frankfort Parliament wanted, for an Emperor of a part of Germany was unthinkable, but instead a President, or, more accurately, a Presidency (*Präsidium*), vested in the King of Prussia, who cordially disliked the title as suggesting republican associations. While, however, the President of the old Bund had been a mere figurehead, a master of ceremonies, the head of the new Bund was to exercise far-going powers.

No great inroad was to be made upon the independent sovereignty of the federal States. Sybel claims it as a "supreme virtue" on Bismarck's part that Prussia did not impose on all the small States, of which her ruler had so poor an opinion, "an unlimited despotic will." It was, however, wisdom even more than virtue that dictated moderation. For Prussia it might have seemed a matter of indifference how large a devolution of State affairs was made in favour of the Confederation, for what she gave with one hand she was certain to receive back with the other. The States in general, however, were not ready for any far-going measures, and to have attempted them would have

[1] Another of Bismarck's secretaries, Moritz Busch, speaks of "the almost superhuman capacity of the Chancellor for work . . . sometimes creating and sometimes appropriating and sifting the work of others" (*Bismarck in the Franco-German War*, vol. i., p. 10).

[2] The final number, for the adhesion of several States—among them Saxony—being regulated by special treaties, came later.

been folly. Bismarck had promised that the sovereign rights of the States should not be unduly invaded, and he kept his word. Hamburg and Bremen even retained a free customs area. The Confederation was to take into its province foreign affairs and diplomacy, the questions of migration, citizenship and domicile, commerce, customs duties and taxation for federal purposes, weights, measures and coinage, with the issue of paper money, banking, patent law and the protection of intellectual property, consular representation, the railway system, merchant marine, inland navigation, the post and telegraph, penal and commercial law, judicial procedure, military and naval questions, and some other matters of common concern. Among the numerous questions left to the competence of the States as before were education, the relationships between State and Church, most departments of justice and the entire domain of civil law. The constitution had, as Bismarck said in his opening speech, "restricted itself to a due care for all the needs of a universal character, without allowing the federal authority to invade the autonomy of the several States beyond them."

It was natural that the new government should reflect, as faithfully as was practicable, the prevailing German monarchical system. In this system the Crown was not only an equal factor in legislation with the legislature, consisting as a rule of two Houses, but *motu proprio* it exercised full executive power, through Ministers directly responsible to it, and to it alone. Following this analogy, the federal legislature was likewise to consist of two bodies, the Federal Council (*Bundesrat*), composed of plenipotentiaries of the Sovereigns, and a representative assembly or Diet. The President of the Confederation was alone empowered to summon, adjourn, and prorogue the Diet, but the assent of the Federal Council was necessary to its dissolution. Every member of the Council was to have a right to appear in and address the Diet at any time, without being under obligation to attend if called upon. In legislation the Federal Council and the Diet were to possess equal power, the President having as such no legislative functions; while the executive authority was to be exercised by the President and the Federal Council. The President was to represent the Confederation in foreign relationships, to appoint embassies, conclude treaties (except that treaties relating to matters subject to federal legislation needed the assent of the Federal Council and the Diet), and to administer the army and navy and the postal and telegraphic services;

but in internal matters generally the executive power was vested in the Princes collectively as represented in the Federal Council.

The only Minister of State recognized by the constitution was the Federal Chancellor, who was to be nominated by the President, and was to be the *ex-officio* President of the Federal Council. It was his duty to countersign the orders of the President, and generally to direct the executive work of the Government. The concentration of so much power in the hands of a single Minister was not a mere whim of the Sovereigns and Governments, much less a device of Bismarck, designed to exaggerate his position and influence, but a result of the actual basis and conditions of federal organization. The Princes and States entered the Confederation as equals, none superior and none inferior to the rest. All accepted an equal restriction of their past independent sovereignty, and contributed this conceded right to the common stock, yet with the proviso that the new collective sovereignty, made up of so many parts, should be exercised by the collective will. With such exercise of authority the Cabinet system of Prussia or Bavaria, in which Ministers were for practical purposes autonomous in their various *ressorts*, was incompatible. In order that the Sovereigns might retain a real control over the central power which they had created, it was held to be necessary to exercise this power through a single executive officer, and this officer was the Federal Chancellor. There were, indeed, to be Committees of the Federal Council, formed for certain specified purposes, but they in nowise corresponded to the Ministries of the States.

The constitution of the Federal Council disappointed the minor States, which had hoped to see in it, in effect, a replica of the *Bundestag*. By following the old federal basis the result was that Prussia would have 17 votes (being the number of her former votes in the Plenum of the dissolved Diet, increased by those of the annexed States) and the rest of the States 25 together, so that with but little assistance she would be able to command a majority.[1] Of the old *liberum veto* not a trace remained.

The Diet was to be formed on the principle of one deputy to every 100,000 inhabitants, a ratio giving a total of 297 members, of whom 236 were to fall to Prussia. The mode of its election

[1] For the representation of the States in the Federal Council and the Diet see Chapter X., p. 384.

was to follow the Frankfort model, for it was to be chosen on a thoroughly democratic franchise—universal (i.e. manhood), equal, and direct. The acceptance by Bismarck of the principle of manhood suffrage has been the subject of endless controversy, and it is still sometimes regarded as one of the surprises of his career. There was really little mystery about his attitude. Of course, it went counter to every profession of his earlier years, but such a contradiction did not count with a man whose whole philosophy as a statesman was a protest against that shibboleth of the weaklings of political life, consistency. For him compromise was the only possible basis of constitutional life, and his concession of a democratic franchise merely attested the practical common sense of a wise man of affairs who was prepared to sacrifice his own preferences to the cause at stake. For he remembered that to have adopted any other principle of election would have been to ignore the entire trend of the national movement, every manifestation of which, in so far as it had emanated from the peoples as distinct from the Governments, had presupposed as the condition of unity a popular assembly elected by the nation's free and unfettered will. This was the argument by which he later justified his action to the constituent Diet. "We have in a certain sense," he said on March 28, 1867, "inherited universal suffrage as a legacy of the development of the German unity movement. We had it in the Imperial constitution as drafted in Frankfort; in 1863 we opposed it to the endeavours of Austria, and for my part I can only say that I know no better electoral law."

Further, Bismarck knew that he was building not merely for the present but for the future. In due time the Southern States, with their more liberal traditions, would come into the Confederation. But a parliament elected on oligarchic principles, though it might have been good enough for Prussia, would have been entirely unacceptable to peoples who had outgrown and overthrown oligarchy in their own States. Above all—and this perhaps was the motive which most influenced him—it was his desire to detach sympathy from Austria by persuading the nation that it could obtain under Prussian leadership concessions in the direction of a fuller constitutional life which it could never hope to receive from a State which had for half a century strenuously fought every endeavour to extend popular rights, and had been almost the last of the German States to accept the constitutional principle.

On this question, therefore, as on most others, Bismarck was influenced solely by considerations of expediency. Just as, though never a " parliament man," he nevertheless regarded a parliament as unavoidable, so, though he distrusted the principle of the popular franchise, he yet knew that no other franchise was practicable. He created a Diet and gave to it a democratic form because convinced that such a Diet and no other would enable him to meet the tasks which remained still to be discharged. His was the position of the man who marries for the sake, not of companionship but of convenience and good cookery, though in the event he obtained neither. From the beginning he neither loved nor honoured the Diet, and in later years it refused not seldom to render him obedience.

The draft constitution having been approved by the Governments, it was submitted to a Diet of the States, elected on February 12, 1867, on a popular suffrage. In the speech with which he opened this assembly at Berlin twelve days later, the King of Prussia emphasized the evils caused to Germany by past divisions and claimed that the Governments of the federated States had sought to achieve the maximum benefits of union with a minimum degree of disturbance to existing political arrangements. He added: " The regulation of the national relations of the North German Confederation with our fellow-countrymen south of the Main has been left open by the treaty of peace of last year (of Prague) as a matter for agreement. For the attainment of this mutual understanding our hand will be held out frankly and willingly to the countries of South Germany as soon as the North German Confederation shall have made sufficient progress in the establishment of its constitution to be in a position to conclude treaties."

As neither the Conservative nor the democratic groups had a majority, it fell to the National Liberals, a party of 79, who occupied a detached position, to hold the balance, and as they were ardent imperialists, they threw their influence in the Ministerial scale upon most important questions, and by so doing were able during the short life of the Diet to do work of great and lasting value. Dr. Simson, of Frankfort National Assembly fame, was elected President or Speaker, and one of the two Vice-Presidents was the National Liberal leader, Herr von Bennigsen.

The only business was the discussion and adoption of the draft constitution. The argumentative combats of the Frankfort Parliament hardly exceeded in vigour and vehemence the debates to which some of its articles gave rise. Again there came to light the old antagonism of political ideals which had been fought out upon so many fields since the beginning of the century by men whose intellectual outlook was too different to allow of reconciliation—at the one extreme the thorough-going democrats, at the other the feudalist Conservatives. The futility of the midsummer-night phantasies of 1848 had not discouraged the custodians of the popular cause, who strove for their principles with the old gallantry, and for their pains earned much opprobrium from opponents unable to enter into their world of ideas. They were still as stubborn and in many things as unpractical as ever, but the earnestness and honesty with which they contended for doctrines which to them represented everything worth caring for in public life were just as conspicuous as in the old Frankfort days.

To them the constitution was more than a set of regulations for the conduct of the new parliament; it was a declaration of faith which was to govern the nation's later political development, and they were determined that it should at least be worthy of its forerunner, the ill-fated constitution of 1849. Their ideal of unity through liberty had not been realized; now they dreamed of liberty through unity. Too old for illusions, they were still not too old for hopes, and their most ardent hope was that the constitution might prove a means of winning for Germany in time true popular government. Hence they sought to keep out of it anything that might hinder progress later.

The draft fell far behind their expectations, and very far behind their wishes. One of the principles vital to them was the supremacy of the Diet. But the constitution as drawn up failed entirely to meet this demand, for it gave the entire executive power to the President and Federal Council, who were to be as independent of the representative chamber as were the Sovereign and Ministry under the constitution of Prussia. The Radicals or Progressists, forming the extreme Left, wished to give to the Sovereigns merely a deliberative voice in legislation, exercised through a sort of council of delegates, the executive power being vested in the King of Prussia as President, and the Diet assigning to him Ministers subject to its own control. Bitter was their disappointment when it became clear that the popular franchise, upon which so much praise had been expended, was an empty and illusory concession, since the Diet itself was to have no control over the Government and its policy.

It is true that the National Liberals succeeded in obtaining theoretical expression of the principle of Ministerial responsibility, but the Government soon made it clear that this responsibility was only moral and not legal ; it simply implied that executive acts done by the head of the Government were by a legal fiction deemed to have been done by the Chancellor, who was to bear the brunt of public criticism. It did not mean that the Chancellor was to be subject, in any form whatever, to the control of the Diet, much less that he would be expected to stand or fall according as the Diet endorsed or disowned the measures for which he assumed official responsibility To every attempt to create a collective Ministry, to convert the Committees of the Federal Council into independent administrative departments, or in any way to divide the power and responsibility of the Federal Chancellor and bring him under the Diet, Bismarck offered resolute resistance, and he carried the majority with him, though narrowly.

The democratic view was forcibly urged by men like Twesten and Waldeck, who had grown old in political warfare. Strong as was their attachment to the cause of national unity, they declared that even that unity would be dearly bought if the price to be paid were the abandonment of principles dear to them as life itself and the frustration of all hope of seeing Germany take a place in the ranks of democratic States. To Waldeck the proposed Federal Council was so obnoxious—not least because it seemed to place his native Prussia at the mercy of the small States—that he was prepared at one time to reject the constitution bodily.

To Bismarck the democrats were well-meaning but utterly blind and mistaken *doctrinaires,* and his replies to their criticisms, though studiously conciliatory, were none the less uncompromising. Let them not, he entreated, imperil the new union by pressing abstract political principles too far ; the Confederation could only be created by the adoption of a policy of give-and-take all round ; the interests involved were so complex and far-reaching, that to increase difficulties needlessly would be to risk all they had been fighting for. Moreover, in political life nothing was final ; this was a time of transition, and some of the arrangements proposed might properly be regarded as temporary and experimental ; only let them not be put aside for others which, however perfect they might seem to be in theory, would not at present work in practice. " Let Germany only be lifted into the saddle," he had said, "and she will ride of herself." The homely simile carried greater conviction than all his arguments, and strengthened in their resistance to democratic innovations the static forces ever prone to tolerant contentment with outlived conditions.

Another question equally vital to the democrats was that of budget right. Here, again, the Frankfort demand of 1848–9 was urged—full parliamentary control over taxation and expenditure. With the recent constitutional struggle in mind, they wished to extend this control so as to bring military administration likewise under the effective power of the Diet. It was just the late conflict episode, however, that determined Bismarck not to parley with a party which sought to control the Executive and its policy in virtue of the power of the purse. Never, he said, would the federal Governments allow the fundamental basis of national security to depend on changing party majorities.

The constitutional provisions on this question were left in an unsatisfactory state. The broad principle was laid down that all estimates of revenue and expenditure must be duly embodied in a law, but inasmuch as the Federal Council was to have an equal voice in all legislation, that principle did not mean popular control. On the other hand, the Diet carried its demand for yearly budgets instead of triennial, as the Government wished. In connection with finance the National Liberals succeeded in passing an innocent-looking amendment, of which the full importance was to be realized only many years later; this amendment empowered the Government to levy taxes in general instead of merely "indirect taxes," as the draft constitution had proposed.

On the subject of the army and navy, which were both to be subject to federal legislation, the Government was equally firm in repelling innovations. The draft constitution had proposed that for the present the Prussian military laws should apply throughout the entire federal territory, and that the permanent regulation of the army should be left to a future law, subject to the stipulation that no alterations should be introduced in military administration without the consent of the King of Prussia as the federal commander-in-chief. The effect of these provisions was to make military service compulsory on Prussian conditions and to give to that State a dominating influence in military administration.

There was something to be said for this arrangement, unpalatable though it was to non-Prussians. The old federal army of Germany had proved a deception and a failure. All that Austria cared about in Germany was that she should be supreme therein ; to Germany's security against external enemies she was indifferent. With Austria's extrusion from Germany, however, the responsibility of national defence fell primarily upon Prussia, and this responsibility was not one to be taken lightly, for if Russia's friendship might fairly be counted on, that of France was quite uncertain.

Upon the principle of Prussian control, therefore, the Government would not hear of compromise. At Moltke's entreaty a majority of the House voted against a proposal to reduce the term of service with the colours from three to two years, but a concession had to be made upon the question of the peace strength of the army. The draft constitution proposed that for the first ten years the number should be equal to 1 per cent. of the population as enumerated in 1867, and the expenditure be fixed at 225 thalers or £33 15s. per man. In the course of long debates, in which men whose political reputations reached full maturity only in later years—Windthorst, Miquel, Gneist, and others—took a prominent part, the Radicals endeavoured to assert parliamentary control of the army to the extent of requiring the peace strength and expenditure to be fixed annually. In the end a compromise was adopted under which there was to be parliamentary control of expenditure but not of revenue—taxation once sanctioned continuing in force—while the peace strength and the cost were to be fixed at the Government's figures for four years, viz. until December 31, 1871, but thereafter to be regulated by a permanent law, instead of being variable from year to year.

The question of the duration of the Diet likewise gave rise to much discussion. The draft constitution proposed three years, but the Conservative sections of the House wished for five years, and the shorter term was adopted only by a narrow majority.[1]

One of the warmest disputes occurred over the question of payment of members. Bismarck was so entirely opposed to this principle that he had inserted in the draft constitution a direct prohibition of "either payment or remuneration." The disqualification was intended to counterbalance the universal suffrage : the vote was to be popularized but not, if it could be prevented, the composition of the Diet. In the end an amendment

[1] The quinquennial principle was introduced twenty-one years later (in 1888).

was passed, by a small majority, permitting such payment, though Bismarck declared that the Governments would in no circumstances give effect to it, and it had to be abandoned.[1]

So, too, the democrats thought that no constitution could be complete without a long catalogue of "fundamental rights," and recalling the many weeks of controversy expended upon the subject in Frankfort in 1848, they proposed that this omission should be made good. But Berlin was not Frankfort and 1867 was not 1848, and the proposal was summarily rejected on the plea that every State had now its own charter of political liberties and that generalization on so difficult a question was inexpedient.

But if the constitution was too Conservative for the democrats, it was too democratic for the Conservatives. A belated attempt was made by the feudalists to create some sort of upper house —the idea appears to have originated with Duke Ernest of Coburg—to keep the Diet in order. Conservative though he was, Bismarck resisted the idea of a brake of the kind, objecting that any senate which interposed between the Federal Council, representing the sovereignty of the States, and the popular assembly would either need to possess too much power or would be of no practical value. A proposal was made in the same quarter to extend the duration of the legislative period from three years, as it stood in the draft, to five years, but was defeated. Insidious attacks were also made upon the franchise, though with no greater success. To the Government's proposal that the franchise should be universal, direct, and equal, the majority parties had added secrecy, to the disgust of the Conservatives of all shades, who declared that the elector who dare not vote openly ought not to be allowed to vote at all. Attempts to introduce the householder franchise and the Prussian three-class indirect franchise

[1] Sybel writes (vi., p. 159): "Bismarck's hope to secure to the propertied and tax-paying classes in this way their legitimate influence in the Imperial Diet, in spite of the universal suffrage, rested on the idea that the actual receipt of money compensation would in future constitute for the deputies a forbidden form of bribery and entail the forfeiture of their seats, not indeed through judgment of the civil court but by the resolution of the Diet itself. Bismarck was deceived in these expectations. There have not been lacking deputies who have received remuneration, but the Diet has never shown any disposition to extend its disciplinary powers to the punishment of this breach of the constitution." These words were written before payment of members was legalized by an amendment of the constitution in 1906. It is to be noted, however, that although in 1867 Bismarck gave the assurance that the prohibition of payment would not apply to unofficial honoraria, legal proceedings were instituted in 1885 against deputies who were known to receive such honoraria, Bismarck's assurance being brushed aside by the courts as purely personal and of no legal value.

—than which Bismarck said no State had ever conceived a "more senseless or more miserable"—were likewise frustrated. A proposal to disqualify State officials from sitting in the Diet met with greater favour, and although it was in the end rejected, the condition was introduced that such officials might not have leave of absence in order to become members.

Bismarck never regarded the constitution of the North German Confederation, even after the revision which became necessary four years later, as quite satisfactory. It was a compromise between antagonistic interests, intended to reduce conflict to a minimum—between Empire and sovereign State, princely rights and parliamentary rights, new claims and old traditions—and like the best of compromises it struck but the roughest balance of justice. As finally adopted on April 16th, however, the great majority of the deputies were well satisfied with their handiwork. Nevertheless, in the final as in the earlier stages of the debate, it was to the moderation, largeness of mind, and clearness of outlook shown by the National Liberals and other deputies who, though not of that party, shared its spirit and temper, that the enactment of the constitution in a reasonable and workable form was due. The Progressists, logical to the last, ended by voting against the measure for the only reason that it did not give them all they wanted.

Now the consent of the parliaments of all the federated States had to be obtained. This procedure was a further concession to the democratic principle which Bismarck made with reluctance, yet, in the existing state of national sentiment, did not dare to oppose. The voting was in general little more than a formality. Some of the Diets were sorely tempted to do the work over again, convinced that they could do it better, but everywhere the Governments discouraged unnecessary interference, and in the end only one State—and that the smallest in the Confederation—refused to adopt the constitution. This was the principality of Waldeck. It was impossible, however, that the Confederation should be allowed to suffer shipwreck at the last moment, and the remedy for Waldeck's obstinacy was found by Prussia, which took over the entire administration of the little State. The constitution came into force on July 1st.

In the meantime acts of administrative folly had thrown a passing shadow over the domestic relations of the enlarged kingdom of Prussia. The two houses of the Diet had been prompt to accept the bill providing for the incorporation of the annexed territories. The populations of these territories also, on the whole, accepted their fate with better grace than might have been expected, and wise men would have left well alone. The constitution of Prussia was to come into operation on October 1, 1867, and until then the Government was given power to apply by rescript such special administrative measures as might be needed for the good government of the new provinces during a time of transition. Instead of reducing interference to a minimum, the Government brought home to the new-comers their new citizenship by the issue of all sorts of irritating orders and regulations superseding time-honoured institutions and customs. Unwarrantable changes were made in the judicial and financial systems of territories which had until lately been independent sovereign States; innovations—some progressive, others retrograde in spirit, but all subversive of established arrangements—were introduced in regard to delicate questions affecting personal liberty, like the right of migration and choice of occupation; and in many other ways the impression was created that a process of Prussianization was in store for the new provinces. The consequence was an outcry so vehement and widespread that the King himself intervened. In August, when visiting Ems for the first time as the ruler of Hesse-Nassau, the bruit of discontent reached his ears, and both there and also at Frankfort and Cassel, on his way home, he ascertained from deputations of local authorities where the hand of mischief had been at work. The result was the publication under his own name of a severe condemnation of the short-sighted conduct of his official representatives and a disavowal of their acts. The Minister of Finance, von der Heydt, offered in consequence to resign, but was induced to remain. One result of the King's intervention was that Frankfort was relieved of part of the heavy indemnity which had been imposed upon it, and another and more important was an entire change in the temper of Prussia's new citizens.

The election of the first North German Diet took place on August 31st, and the Diet met for practical work on September 10th. Bismarck had already been appointed Federal Chancellor and his Department duly constituted. This was the "Federal Chancellery Office," a board composed of councillors or heads of divisions subordinate in the first instance to a president, who, in turn, was directly responsible to the Chancellor himself. The first president was Rudolf Delbrück, a man of decidedly Liberal views.

It was significant of the political complexion of the first national parliament that the President (Dr. Simson) and Vice-Presidents were all men favoured by the Liberal or Liberal-Conservative parties. Throughout its early sessions, indeed, the Diet in general showed marked sympathy with progressive ideas. Never in German political history was so much done in so short a time for civil liberty. Hoary social abuses and time-honoured conventions were challenged with a freedom and light-heartedness which to the East Prussian Conservatives betokened coming catastrophe. As was the Diet, so was the Government. The feudalist-military party of Old Prussia, though good for pulling down, was useless for building up, and Bismarck ignored it, and accepted the willing help of the National Liberals, whose numbers had been increased by a contingent from the new Prussian provinces, and particularly Hanover. Thus it came about that a Minister whose past had been a consistent protest against Liberalism found himself, at the outset of his new career, dependent upon the co-operation of his old opponents.

The free spirit which reigned in the Diet at that time was shown in large as well as small things. Freedom of speech in Parliament was vigorously affirmed; obsolete restrictions were removed from marriage by the limitation of the arbitrary power of the mayors and the police; even the usurer was given more latitude by the abolition of the restrictions on the rate of interest, restrictions restored twenty-five years later. More important was the law giving the right of free migration, in virtue of which every subject of the Confederation was henceforth to be entitled to sojourn and settle, to acquire property, and to carry on trade and industry in any part of the federal territory. In sympathy with this provision the passport regulations were lightened and the irksome interference of the police with travellers was curbed. Already the system of a local registration of inhabitants—a police and not a statutory measure—was common in Germany, and not being regarded as an infraction of the liberty of the subject, it was not altered by the Liberal legislation of the day.

The law of free migration was the first step taken towards the emancipation of labour, and other measures to the same end quickly followed. It was the day of Lassalle's denunciations of the "iron law of wages" and of his scheme of national productive associations. Moreover, Socialism was already represented in the Diet by men destined to become famous later—August Bebel, Wilhelm Liebknecht, and several others—though a Socialist parliamentary party did not yet exist. Except in the ranks of feudal Conservatism, there was on all hands a strong desire that labour should share generously in the first-fruits of unity. Hence a strong disposition was shown to abolish with one stroke all restrictions upon labour combinations, so giving to the working man the right to sell or withhold his labour with just the same freedom with which the capitalist offered or refused employment. When powerful industrialists, like Herr Stumm, a coal magnate of the day, protested against the excessive liberation of labour, they were heard with impatience. Called to state the Government's attitude, Delbrück declared that the time for restricting the right of coalition was past, though he was not prepared to legislate upon the question apart from a general revision of the existing Industrial Codes. So urgent was the Diet, however, that by a large majority it passed a law giving to labour a full right of combination. The Federal Council refused assent, but promised at once to consider the larger question of revising the general position of labour before the law. Months of strenuous work in committee, and long debates in the Diet, resulted in the great Industrial Code of 1869, which served as a foundation for the imposing body of labour legislation which was passed during the succeeding twenty years.

Something was also done to assimilate railway policy and to consolidate the railway system in the federal States. The Confederation took power to build and work railways for military purposes, but for the rest it left this branch of enterprise in the hands of the States, reserving only a general right of control, with a view to unification of rates and charges and the like.

The question of Ministerial accountability came up again, but made no further advance. An undaunted band of Liberals introduced a scheme for the creation of separate federal Ministers for Foreign Affairs, War, the Navy, Finance, and Trade and Industry. Their plea, that the proposal was designed to lighten the duties of the Federal Chancellor, was received by Bismarck with the smiling assurance that his health was good and with due care might be expected so to continue. What was really desired was the subjection of the Government to parliamentary control, and he had thought that this question was already decided. The Diet adopted the proposal by a small majority, though warned in advance that the Federal Council would not endorse it.

During the discussion of the draft Penal Code, which was finally enacted in May, 1870, acute differences of opinion came to light on the subject of the death penalty. When the opponents of capital punishment failed to secure its omission from the code, they asked that it should at least not apply in Saxony and Oldenburg, which had already abolished it. Bismarck opposed this demand in the name of national unity, objecting that he could not agree to signalize the union of the Northern States by creating two classes of citizens—one consisting of several millions of people all too good for the executioner's axe and the other embracing the great multitude for whom that immunity could not be claimed. The death penalty, therefore, stood, though there was a large minority against it.

One of the early acts of the Diet was to make a grant and sanction a loan for the increase of the navy. A shipbuilding programme was prepared, to be spread over ten years, in which time it was hoped that the Confederation would have at command a navy sufficient for coast defence. In 1868 the naval estimates stood at about half a million pounds, an amount increased in the following year to two millions, out of a total budget of eleven and a half million pounds. Unpractical Radicals, grudging such expenditure as unproductive, contended that the most economical way to increase Germany's naval and maritime strength was not to build ships to order, but to invite Denmark and Holland to come into the Confederation.

More delicate, if not more difficult, was the second of the two problems which Bismarck had to face at the close of the war, the relations between the North and the South. Here unfailing sagacity and tact, combined with great patience, were needed. The North German Confederation was a provisional union, and everybody knew it to be such ; the Main frontier was merely a stage on the way to the South, a halting-place at which to take breath before pushing forward again. In the terms of peace offered to Austria's German allies, no less than in his negotiations with the major Power itself, Bismarck had steadily kept the future in view. The States absorbed by Prussia were no longer a source of danger ; from those hostile States which remained independent no cession of territory had been demanded, save in two cases a trivial rectification of frontiers, and the money indemnities imposed were light and entailed no lasting drain upon their resources. Bad blood enough was left, and there had been bad blood between Prussia and her Southern neighbours before : it was only a question of degree.

In remaining out of the Confederation the States of the South, with one exception, certainly did not experience the sensation of the peris who were locked out of Paradise. They were excluded by their own wish, and Bismarck never showed wiser statesmanship than in his steady refusal to press upon them the union which the States of the North had been required to enter. In their eagerness to make entrance easy for them the democrats of the North German Diet had wished to allow them to join by simply declaring their acceptance of the federal constitution. Even in this suggestion Bismarck declined to concur, and it was made a stipulation of the new constitution that admission, if desired, should be on the proposal of the President of the Confederation and in virtue of legislation. Urged from within, invited from without, always his answer was the same: it was not for the Confederation to force itself upon the South; when the South wished to enter, it had only to say so and the door would be opened. "It is open to the Southern States to join hands with the North," he said in September, 1867, "and when they wish it no German statesman will be strong enough to prevent it, or will even desire to see them excluded, but they cannot be compelled." For the present it was his conviction that it was wiser to unify half Germany thoroughly than all Germany incompletely.[1]

Meanwhile, he had done the essential thing: by means of the defensive and offensive alliances of August, 1866, he had made sure that the Southern States should not form alliances out of Germany. By one bold stroke, therefore, he had cut off Bavaria and Würtemberg, Baden and Hesse, from their Austrian ally and equally from any French influence that could be dangerous. Nor did he doubt that if either North or South were ever in peril through menace from the West, they would at once forget past discords and fight together for the common fatherland. "In the event of attack," he said in the constituent Diet on March 11, 1867, "I regard the union of the North and South as absolutely assured in all questions affecting the security of German soil.

[1] Lord Cowley, while British ambassador in Paris, wrote on June 12, 1867, to Lord Clarendon that Bismarck, when in Paris just before, had told him that he "did not want the Southern States and would rather be without them, but that he could not withstand public opinion if the States themselves asked for *annexation*." Of course, it is inconceivable that Bismarck could have said any such thing. There never was at any time either question or possibility of the Southern States being "annexed." Bismarck must have spoken, and could only have spoken, of the "admission" of these States into the already formed Confederation of the North.

No doubt can exist in the South that if its integrity should be endangered North Germany would unconditionally render it fraternal help, and equally no one doubts in the North that we should be assured of the help of the South in any attack upon us."

By the military treaties the contracting parties had mutually guaranteed the integrity of their several territories, and pledged themselves in the event of war to place their entire forces at each other's disposal under the supreme command of the King of Prussia. That meant that Prussia would be able in an emergency to dispose of a force of 800,000 men, a number which would be increased to over a million as soon as the Prussian army laws had come into full operation. The terms of these treaties were published in March, 1867, and created painful surprise both in Vienna and Paris, where they were regarded, with no justification, as a formal breach of the provisions of the Treaty of Prague.[1]

Particularism died last and died hardest in Bavaria and Würtemberg, where the tribal spirit and the attachment to local traditions and institutions were extremely strong and where, in truth, there was much that was well worth being particularist about. In the South, too, lingered still a strong desire for the continuance of close relationships with Austria. From this desire sprang a proposal made by Bavaria and Würtemberg in May, 1867, that the States of the South should severally form with the North German Confederation a new union, which in turn

[1] In a despatch addressed to the Austrian ambassador in Berlin soon after the publication of the military alliances, Count Beust said (March 28, 1867) that while holding that the alliances made impossible the formation of an independent international union of the Southern States, Austria had no protest to make, but accepted the new situation as it was. Two years later (August, 1869), in a speech to the Delegations, he declared that the conventions were altogether incompatible with the Treaty of Prague, a view against which the North German Foreign Office at once vigorously protested. Later he described them as "a masterpiece of treachery." "It has frequently happened in history," he writes (*Memoirs*, vol. ii., p. 23), "that treaties were not kept; but that a treaty (i.e. of Prague) should be broken in anticipation was a novelty reserved for the genius of Prince Bismarck. To sign treaties with the South German States, reducing them to a permanent condition of dependence on Prussia, and then to conclude a few days later a treaty with Austria stipulating for these States an independent international existence—that was indeed the *ne plus ultra* of Machiavellism." In Bismarck's statecraft there was much that is open to legitimate reproach, but here at least reproach is out of place. It was the contemplated *union* of the South German States which was to have an "international and independent existence," and it was still theoretically open to these States to combine in a union of their own if they were so disposed. Moreover, the contracting States accepted the terms of preliminaries of Nikolsburg simultaneously with their entrance into the military alliance.

should enter into a formal alliance with the Habsburg Empire. The Bavarian Minister-President, now Prince Hohenlohe, who had succeeded von der Pfordten at the end of December, 1866, put the idea before Beust, the Austrian Chancellor, who answered that such a proposal could only come from Prussia, and would not further commit himself.[1] Hohenlohe accordingly sounded Bismarck, who welcomed the idea and in the name of Prussia and Bavaria offered Austria an alliance which should guarantee the integrity of her territories. Beust declined the offer, however, not only because it was too early to talk of conciliation with the victors of Sadowa, but because he believed that such an alliance would create a too intimate tie between Prussia and the South, and hence would destroy all hope of Austria ever being able to reassert influence there. He was convinced, too, that such an alliance would be a menace to European peace, by exciting still further the jealousy of France, perhaps to Austria's hurt more than to that of Prussia. In private, Beust spoke of the offer more drastically. Inasmuch as it could have been aimed only at France, he said, it was dishonouring to Austria. "It is scarcely ten months," he said to the Bavarian ambassador, Count Tauffkirchen, "since Napoleon saved Vienna and the integrity of Austrian territory, and yet we are invited to enter into an alliance against France! Never will the Emperor Francis Joseph be induced to commit such an enormity; he will not understand how such a suggestion could even have been made to him."

Beust at that time was brooding over another and a more ambitious plan. This contemplated a formal alliance with France, a cordial understanding with Russia, and as the result the effectual isolation of Prussia. Napoleon might have been quite prepared to welcome an arrangement of the kind, had it been practicable, for Prussia had just administered to him a

[1] Beust writes in his *Memoirs* (vol. i., p. 282): "The excellent footing on which Austria and Germany now (1887) stand is so far from being unwelcome to me that it was I who laid the foundations of it." He says also that on taking office he brought into his new position "neither likes nor dislikes, but only the experiences of my past career." There is little justification for these claims; Mensdorff, whom he succeeded as Foreign Secretary, was so convinced that Beust was bent upon a war of retaliation that he was opposed to his appointment and did his best to prevent it. Later events seemed to confirm his apprehensions. Nevertheless, Beust deserved well of his adopted country. He at once took in hand, and in the face of much opposition carried out, the political reorganization of the monarchy; he reformed the constitution, concluded the dualist compact (*Ausgleich*) between Austria and Hungary, and modified the *concordat* of 1855 with Rome to the benefit of the secular power.

rebuff which showed that he was no longer accepted at the old estimate. This arose out of the non-observance of the provision of the Treaty of Prague guaranteeing to the population of the northern frontier districts of Schleswig the right to declare by *plébiscite* under which rule it wished to live, Danish or Prussian. As there was no disposition in Berlin to give effect to this provision, the Danish Government appealed to France to interfere, and France did so. It was Napoleon's first attempt to exert pressure upon the policy of reconstituted Prussia, and Bismarck determined that it should be the last. Not only was the French ambassador in Berlin informed that no right on the part of France to interfere in a matter between Prussia and Denmark could be admitted, but an inspired announcement was published in the semi-official Press calling public attention to this exchange of communications and declaring that the Government would tolerate no outside meddling in German affairs. The incident increased the hostile feeling against Prussia which was already prevalent in France.

Later in the same year Napoleon gave an unmistakable proof of his desire for closer relations with Austria when, in company with the Empress Eugénie, he visited Francis Joseph at Salzburg (August 18th–23rd). The political significance of the journey to Austria was increased by the fact that he was cordially greeted at Karlsruhe by the Grand Duke of Baden and at Ulm by the King of Würtemberg, and that from Augsburg onward to the Austrian frontier he was accompanied by King Ludwig of Bavaria. Nominally the Emperor went to Salzburg in order to offer condolences to the Imperial family on account of the murder in June of Emperor Maximilian of Mexico (an Austrian Archduke) by rebels. In reality the meeting was of a political character. Count Beust and Count Andrassy, the Hungarian Minister-President, were present, and there were repeated conferences. According to the former, an agreement was concluded to the effect that the two Powers should faithfully observe the stipulations of the Peace of Prague but avoid any interference in German affairs, though Austria was to endeavour to preserve the sympathies of South Germany " by developing a Liberal and truly constitutional system."[1] Nevertheless, the negotiations stopped short of a formal alliance. Napoleon returned direct to Paris without meeting the King of Prussia. On the other hand, when in October Francis Joseph returned Napoleon's visit

[1] *Memoirs*, vol. ii., p. 36.

in Paris he alighted at Oos, near Baden-Baden, where, according to Beust, he had a "hurried and constrained" interview with the King.

While in Germany it was generally recognized that the unity movement could not long stand still, opinions differed widely upon the question how far it was competent for the States of the South to conclude separate treaties with Prussia. It was objected by some that the Treaty of Prague contemplated first some sort of combination amongst these States themselves, and that only after that had been created would union with the North be practicable. The obvious answer to this objection was that there was nothing in the treaty that in the least bound the Southern States to anything at all, since they were not parties to it. All it did was to record in advance Austria's agreement to any separate union into which the States might choose to enter, and inferentially—since such a union was to have "an international and independent existence"—to whatever ties it might wish to establish with the Confederation of the North.

While, therefore, Bavaria contended that the States should either join the North German Confederation together or not at all, Bismarck held that they were perfectly free to do as they liked, yet that it was inexpedient that any of them should be admitted separately. He was particularly determined that Baden should not be allowed to enter first and alone as it wished, for he regarded that State as a far more valuable asset of the unity movement outside than inside the Confederation. For him the chief significance of this provision of the treaty was that it amounted to a warning of "Hands off!" to Austria in all that concerned the future internal development of Germany.

The question was advanced an important stage by the revision of the customs arrangements which the new situation had made necessary, for in withdrawing from the Bund Austria withdrew from all the federal arrangements existing under it. At the end of December, 1866, the Prussian Government had given the requisite notice to terminate the Customs Union, and in the following June the Ministers of the South German States, at its invitation, met at Berlin to consider its future form. There was no great difficulty in agreeing upon a renewal of the treaties, though Bavaria made assent conditional upon the grant to her of certain privileges. More important was the question how the affairs of the union were to be administered in the altered conditions. Bismarck proposed that legislative power in customs questions should be exercised by the new Federal Council and Diet, both enlarged for the purpose by the proportional representation therein of the States of the South, and the latter sitting as a "Customs Parliament." In the past the States of the Germanic Federation had been accustomed to arrange customs questions by means of "Customs Conferences," but at all times with difficulty, owing to the operation of the *liberum veto*, which made it possible for any one of the States to thwart the interests and wishes of all the rest. This veto was to go, and in both legislative assemblies every resolution was to be decided by a simple majority of votes. This plan was approved, and the customs treaty of July 8, 1867, was adopted on this basis, with the stipulation that it was to last eight years, from January 1, 1868, to January 1, 1876.

Nevertheless, the treaty did not pass through the South German Diets without severe struggles, fought on the old battle-cries of particularism and anti-Prussianism. The controversies were all the keener since the military alliances came up for confirmation at the same time. Once more the whole question of German unity seemed to be reopened. The first of the States to confirm the treaty was Baden, where there was a strong sentiment favourable to complete and immediate union with the North. The Grand Duke was enthusiastic in his advocacy of such a union, and he lost no opportunity of urging the Diet to embrace any opportunity of furthering it. As the Customs Union seemed a substantial help on the way, the chambers approved both it and the military alliance with virtual unanimity. Grand-ducal Hesse likewise promptly accepted both treaties.

It was different in Würtemberg, where bitter anti-Prussian sentiments still prevailed. In the Lower Chamber the Radicals and Protectionists united against the Government—the former mainly because of the proposed alliance, the latter because of the new customs arrangements. The deputy Moritz Mohl crystallized the current feeling in a fiery "Warning" ("*Mahnruf*") against the danger of allowing Würtemberg to come under the domination of Prussia. In this manifesto he pictured Swabia as a land richly endowed by nature and favoured by history, its people as the special emissaries of German culture, to whose service it had given Schiller, Uhland, Wieland, and Auerbach, and its State as the embodiment of the spirit of freedom and independence. On the other hand, he represented Prussia as poor by nature, its population divided into two antagonistic classes of arrogant Junkers and downtrodden serfs; he held up the Prussian State to obloquy as the "product of restless conquest, of blood and iron," under which lived a nation "tormented by the oppressive burden of militarism and taxation"; while of the Government he said that it was "omnipotent towards the legislature, despotic towards its federal allies, and disquieting towards all its neighbours." Prussia alone he declared to be responsible for the dissolution of the old Federation, under which Germany had for half a century enjoyed the blessings of peace, and for the bloody civil war which had torn the nation into fragments. Never should Würtemberg, he added, ally herself to such a State: "It cannot protect us: it would shed the blood of our sons for its own purposes." He therefore called upon the nation and the Diet to dissociate themselves both from the military alliance with Prussia and from the Customs Union.

Mohl's manifesto was circulated in tens of thousands throughout the length and breadth of the land, and it powerfully excited political passions. A strong movement of protest was begun, and a national congress of the democratic party, held on September 29th, called for the rejection of the treaties and the dismissal of the Minister (Varnbüler) who had negotiated them. Varnbüler in his defence replied in effect that the treaties were the outcome of facts against which it would be folly to fight. "In the year 1866," he said (October 29th), "there were still two opinions in Germany as to how the German question should be solved. History has decided, and it is useless to ask any longer whether it would have been more desirable this way or that. Austria has been sentenced to leave Germany, and whoever continues to speculate as though this should not have happened is a dreamer." Nevertheless, his words failed to convince, and for a time the treaties had to be put back. Rather than run the risk of losing the Customs Union, however, the Diet in the end approved the action of the Government.

In Bavaria also opinion was divided, and the opposition was strengthened owing to the fact that the Government was in conflict with the Ultramontanes on matters of internal policy. The Lower House of the Diet accepted both the customs treaty and the electoral law for the Customs Parliament—the military alliance did not require legislative sanction—by an overwhelming majority, but the Upper House wished to make its assent conditional upon the reservation to Bavaria of her former special rights as a member of the Customs Union. Such a claim was now out of date, and when the North German Diet had sanctioned the customs treaty, subject to the ratification of all the military alliances, and Bismarck had notified the Bavarian Government that it must choose between accepting the treaty as it stood or being left out of the new Customs Union, here, too, the opposition melted away.

Bismarck was unyielding in the demand that both treaties must be accepted or rejected together, and warned the South German States that if any of them disowned the military alliance he would terminate the Customs Union at once so far as they were concerned. In face of this threat the refractory Diets acquiesced.

To Napoleon the renewal of the Customs Union was a shock: he was surprised that it had been possible to conclude it at all, and doubly surprised that it had been concluded with so little difficulty. His surprise changed into disgust when a little later Baden made formal overtures for admission to the North German Confederation.

The Customs Parliament met for the first time on April 27, 1868. The elections were on the whole very discouraging to the friends of a larger union. Baden, as had been expected, sent a strong contingent of imperialists, but the overwhelming representation of Bavaria and Würtemberg was hostile to any further overtures to the North and particularly hostile to Prussia. Bismarck had expected great things from this meeting of the German States on the common ground of economic interest—it was the mounting-block from which, in his metaphor, Germany was to spring into the saddle—and his greeting to the South German deputies was very cordial. "Here," he said, "you will find brotherly hearts and hands ready to help in every predicament of life." Dr. Simson, in whose blood seemed to run a passion for Presidencies, was once more put in the chair, as before without a division, but acute difference of opinion arose when the two vice-presidents came to be chosen. As a proof of fraternal feeling, the North Germans were willing that these positions should be filled by South Germans, and they accordingly proposed Prince Hohenlohe, the Bavarian Minister-President, as first deputy and Baron von Roggenbach, the late Baden Minister-President, as second. Both men were obnoxious to the Clericals, however, Hohenlohe as an uncompromising enemy of Ultramontanism (though a Roman Catholic himself), and Roggenbach as an enthusiastic advocate of complete national union. Hohenlohe was, nevertheless, elected, but by agreement with the Conservatives the Clericals succeeded in substituting the Duke of Ujest for Roggenbach. A small body of South German (Baden and Darmstadt) National Liberals, supported by their North German colleagues, wished so to colour the address to the King of Prussia in answer to the speech from the throne, as to make it a manifesto on behalf of a fuller national unity. It was soon seen, however, that any such attempt thus to force the pace was premature and could only defeat its own object.

The sentiment still dominant in the South was faithfully reflected by Herr von Thüngen, one of the Bavarian deputies, who declared that while the South was prepared to adhere faithfully to the military treaties, it was not prepared at present to do more. He added: "I will be frank and truthful; I cannot disguise the fact that a majority of South Germans, the mass of the people, are opposed to a closer connection with Prussia. There prevails there a certain distrust, a certain fear, that through a too close association our independence might be prejudiced. If you regard this feeling as unjustifiable, you will at least understand it when you remember that the South German tribes have ever cultivated a great attachment to their institutions and ruling houses, and when you also reflect that with us the great mass of the people are influenced by sentimental feelings and that antipathy begins when their feelings are wounded, as they have been by the Prussian victories." And yet it was a Bavarian deputy, the stalwart democrat Joseph Völk, who in the elation caused by the meeting of the first Customs Parliament uttered the memorable words, "It is spring-time in Germany!" On a division, a combination of Clericals, Conservatives, and democrats defeated the generous design of the imperialists. Not only the unconverted particularists of the South, however, but many warm friends of unity in the North, believed that the best policy was one of vigilant waiting, and that for the present the maxim *solvitur laborando* offered the surest promise of success.

Bismarck accepted the situation as it was, without illusions and without impatience. To General Suckow, the chief of the Würtemberg General Staff, he said at that time (May 11th): "The elections to the Customs Parliament have shown that for the present the South wants to have no further connection with the North save in the form of the Customs Union and the Treaty of Alliance. The North has no reason to require more, for from the strategical standpoint the connection with the South is not for us a source of strength, and politically we have no desire to be merged in the heterogeneous elements of the South, where no one knows whether the particularists or the democrats are Prussia's worse enemies. We are all attached to the national idea, but the calculating politician aims first at what is essential and only later at what is desirable: the house must be first built before there can be talk of enlargements. When the deputies have sat together for a year or two in the Customs Parliament, conciliation will begin, and the South Germans will see that there can be no question of coercion. We are in full sympathy with our South German brothers, to whom we are ready at all times to give our hand, but we neither wish nor have we the right to compel them to take it."

One of the most important acts of the first Customs Parliament was the conclusion of a new treaty of commerce with Austria in place of the treaty of 1865, which had been annulled by the war. The idea of her admission to the German Customs Union was no longer regarded as practicable, but she had still in the States of the South many friends who wished to draw as closely as possible the economic ties between her and the rest of Germany. Prussia, too, recognized the wisdom of a policy of conciliation, and thus it came about that a new treaty favourable to the ejected member of the Federation was adopted on May 11th by an overwhelming vote—246 against only 17. Similar treaties with other States followed.

In closing the Parliament on May 23rd the King of Prussia, as President, reversed the doctrine that "Might is right" in memorable words. "Not the power which God has placed in my hands," he said, "but the rights over which I dispose with my federal allies and the constitutional assemblies of their subjects, in virtue of voluntary treaties, shall now and in the future serve as the rule of my policy."

In spite of their differences, the members of the Customs Parliament gave to the national movement invaluable help. Their very controversies in the end tended to create a greater identity of interest, as more emphasis came to be laid upon the things common to North and South and less upon those that divided them. It is also noteworthy that the spirit of the new customs legislation was from the first favourable to freer trade. Each session duties were reduced or abolished; in particular, two important principles, which were destined to be embodied in the early policy of the Empire, were established—taxation for the purposes of revenue only and the exemption from fiscal burdens of the food and indispensable needs of the people.

Outside Germany the progress of the unity movement was still received with mingled feelings, of which the strongest and most prevalent was a vague mistrust of the final outcome. Officially only one European Power of the first rank can be said to have been cordially disposed towards Prussia and the German movement at that time, and that Power was Russia. However conscious they may have been of the value of a good understanding with Prussia and the new German Confederation in which she was now merged, the attitude of the other leading countries, as represented by their Governments, was either indifferent, suspicious, or hostile. None of them welcomed the appearance of this new political force, menacing to the old balance of power and, as they feared, to the future harmony of Europe. So long as the Bund lasted Austria and Prussia held each other in check, and the rest of the Powers were well satisfied with an arrangement so convenient. Now Austria had for the present fallen into the background, and there had come into prominence a restless and ambitious State, bent on creating a new empire of the Germanic peoples and dominating it. All the instincts of conservatism were opposed to the interloper who had thus broken in upon the scene so abruptly, bringing with him tumults and wars.

At the same time there were still many friends of Austria, in France more than elsewhere, who honestly believed that Prussia's suddenly gained prestige was unreal and would not stand the test of time. They were therefore disposed to rate cheaply her claim to hegemony in Germany, and to assume that as soon as the elation caused by her recent military success had been exhausted she would fall back into a subordinate place in the European concert as sanctioned by the older States, and that the life of Europe would then continue as before. Such men were little concerned to take the new turn of events tragically, or to modify their habitual order of ideas in Prussia's favour.

Not a little of the statesmanship of Europe was bankrupt in ideas, foresight, and courage in the middle of the nineteenth century, when mighty political changes were pending and a great Empire and nation were in the throes of painful birth. " The extraordinary success of the Prussians," Lord Malmesbury wrote after the Bohemian war, "has alarmed all nations." The alarm, if exaggerated, was real in some quarters, but more real and more general was the feeling of disdainful resentment that an upstart Power should have suddenly dared to aspire to eminence without patronage or permission. Prussia had begun to annoy and vex Europe, as Europe had annoyed and vexed the first Napoleon.

No truer appreciation of the events in which Prussia was taking so prominent a part was shown in England than elsewhere, though ties of the most intimate kind had existed between the two countries since the marriage of the Prussian Crown Prince to the Princess Royal in January, 1858. A great political and national transformation, for which the struggles of two generations had been a constant preparation, was nearing fulfilment, yet not a few of the watchmen upon the observation towers at home and abroad failed altogether to understand its significance. There were leaders of British opinion at that time who knew nothing of Germany, nothing of German history, and who hardly dreamed that a German question existed. Historians and men of letters like Carlyle, Stubbs, Freeman, and Kingsley anticipated the coming regeneration of Germany and welcomed it sympathetically from afar, but what is called public opinion is made, not by historians and men of letters, but by politicians—not by the men who write, but by those who talk; and such public opinion upon German politics as existed at all owed its inspiration to these. Almost altogether the sympathies of official England at that time were on the side of Austria, the oppressor of Italy and the one obstruction to Italian unity, a cause to which Germany, like France and England, was yet warmly attached.

The despatches and reflections of German diplomats of the period bear curious testimony to the difficulty which attended their endeavours to interest British statesmen in German affairs, or even to make the unity question intelligible and real to the British mind. Baron Bunsen, the Prussian envoy in London, wrote in July, 1849: "To speak with the English on foreign politics is only worth while on the Roman question. . . . On the subject of Germany the Tories are inimical, the Whigs apathetic, the Radicals alone reasonable." And again (just before the Crimean War): "It is quite entertaining to see the stiff unbelief of the English in the future of Germany. Lord John is merely uninformed. Peel has somewhat staggered the mind of the excellent

Prince by his unbelief; yet he has a statesmanlike good-will towards the Germanic nations and even for the German nation. Aberdeen is the greatest sinner. He believes in God and in the Emperor Nicholas."[1] "One must forget his Continental ideas," said in 1854 Count Colloredo, the Austrian ambassador, "in reading the English daily Press." Recalling his experiences as Saxon envoy in 1854, Count Vitzthum says: "People in England at that time knew nothing at all of what was taking place on the Continent. Only the obscurest ideas of the rivalry of the two German Powers prevailed, and yet therein lay the key to the enigmas of Prussian policy."

Another Prussian envoy, who was already becoming famous, visited London from Paris in June, 1862, and carried away the same impressions. "It was very pleasant there," Bismarck wrote to his wife just afterwards, "but the Ministers know less about Prussia than about Japan and Mongolia, nor are they any cleverer than our own."[2]

It may be said that such opinions—and they might be multiplied—come from sources which are prejudiced in turn; yet they fairly represent the dominant feeling in English political circles at that time. The Press, too, or at least the more influential metropolitan journals, accurately voiced the prevalent antipathy against Germany, and more particularly Prussia. And this antipathy, it must be remembered, existed before Bismarck became the Prussian Minister-President and gave to Prussian policy a moral twist which created against his country a new and more intelligible bias, that thereafter never entirely disappeared.

No one was more painfully conscious of the attitude of mingled disparagement and unconcern held in Great Britain towards Germany and everything German, of the harm which it was doing, and the greater harm which it was certain to do in the

[1] *Life of Bunsen*, vol. ii., p. 189.

[2] To Roon, the Prussian Minister of War, he wrote in the same strain. "People there," he said, "are much better informed about China and Peru than about Prussia. Loftus must write more nonsense to his Ministers than I thought." Disraeli's savage gibes upon certain members of the British diplomatic service contained in a letter to Lord Stanley of August 17, 1866, may be recalled: "I have read Lord Cowley's letter with much interest. Bloomfield's, both handwriting and matter, are those of a greengrocer; Loftus should be the foreign editor of the *Morning Herald*," etc. "Have you heard anything from Mr. Goosey-Gander in Berlin?" he wrote on December 30, 1866. "A pretty instrument to cope with the Prussian Minister" (*Life of Benjamin Disraeli, Earl of Beaconsfield*, vol. iv., pp. 468–9).

future, than the Prince Consort, who included in his censures Ministers and diplomats alike, the former because they did not want to understand, the latter because they would not go to the trouble to discover the facts, though to do so was their one and only duty. Commending a report sent by a consul in South Germany who had gone out of his way to study the German question as it affected the Southern States, the Prince wrote on March 18, 1860: "He evidently takes the means to inform himself, which our diplomatists despise."

Bunsen, in the words already quoted, distributed the blame fairly between the rival parties. Because the Whigs were in power it was apathy which determined the dominant attitude. There were, of course, bright exceptions, both amongst the Whigs and Tories, but the exceptions only made the rule more positive. Stockmar, for example, spoke of Peel in 1850 as having "a good-will, nay, a predilection, for Germany and especially for Prussia," and Bunsen in 1849, with unnecessary exaggeration, described that discreetest of ambassadors, Lord Cowley, as being "as German as myself." So, too, Vitzthum wrote of Disraeli in 1860 that he "in no way shared the indisposition of his countrymen to discuss what are here (in London) known as 'German politics.'" Vitzthum himself was Disraeli's special mentor upon this abstruse subject, yet the slow progress made by his pupil may be judged by the remark of Disraeli's three years later (November, 1863): "Prussia without nationality, the principle of the day, is clearly the subject for partition."

Lord John Russell represented the fine flower of British statecraft in the middle of the century, and no man had a more open mind, yet on his own admission it was only after the shock which Napoleon's rape of Savoy gave to him in 1860—that is, forty-eight years after he entered parliamentary life, twenty-five years after he became a Minister, and fourteen years after he had formed his first Cabinet—that he awoke to the importance of having a policy in regard to Germany. He approached the Prince Consort (March 15, 1860) with a request for "some clue" as to what that policy should be, adding with characteristic candour: "I have hitherto been very unwilling to enter at all into the intimate politics of the German Confederation." In his reply (March 18th) the Prince roughly sketched the main outlines of the German question, but warned that most eloquent of despatch-writers—not perhaps without malice—"Foreign Powers, and England in particular, can do very little good by advice. We ought, therefore, in my opinion, to confine ourselves to inculcating confidence in Prussia at the minor Courts, showing that from her alone can be expected sufficient support and protection, and that the efficiency of that support will be in proportion to their adhesion to her. Of this our diplomatic agents do ever *diametrically* and *systematically* the reverse." [1]

Nevertheless, perhaps of contemporary British statesmen it was Russell who most succeeded in preserving upon this question a clear political outlook in the midst of the prevailing ignorance and prejudice. He not only came to favour German unity, but even to regard the question as one for the Germans alone. Here he differed both from Lord Palmerston and Lord Clarendon. Palmerston had followed the course of events in Germany longer and with a more eager interest, though only up to a certain point, and when he ceased to keep abreast with the march of events his persistent inability to accommodate himself to changing circumstances led him into errors of judgment from which his reputation eventually suffered. As early as 1842 Lord Melbourne complained to Greville of the "aversion" which Palmerston "had inspired not only in France but in all Germany, and said that his notion was that everything was to be done by violence, that by never giving way or making any concession, and an obstinate insistence, every point was sure to be gained." [2]

Equally with Lord John, Palmerston wished to see a strong Germany, as a counterpoise to France and Russia; he knew that a strong Germany would be impossible without a strong Prussia; and for that reason he was willing at a later date to forgive Prussia the seizure of Schleswig-Holstein which otherwise he held to be an altogether reprehensible proceeding.[3] It was Palmerston's habit, however, to have a finger in every European pie; hence he looked for a German unity regulated by the other Powers and was not prepared to allow Germany to transform herself in her own way. Lord Clarendon likewise claimed that before the Germanic Federation could be dissolved the Powers which had helped in the reconstruction of the Continent at the beginning of the century should be consulted as to "the arrangements destined to replace it." Almost generally British Ministers, statesmen, and ambassadors assumed as a matter of course that

[1] The words are italicized in the original as published in Sir Theodore Martin's *Life of the Prince Consort*, vol. v., p. 62.

[2] Conversation of February 11, 1842, recorded in Greville's Memoirs, *Reign of Queen Victoria*, vol. ii., p. 84.

[3] Letter to Lord John Russell, September 13, 1865.

the German house might not be put in order without outside sanction and guidance. The ambassador in Berlin even gravely warned the Prussian Government in 1862 that the pacification of Hesse was a European question, which it would be wise to let alone. At this distance of time such views seem inexcusably foolish and arrogant, but it occurred to few people to reflect that they were either foolish or arrogant then. It is doubtful whether among all the officed statesmen and diplomats of that period there was one man who in knowledge of the true motive forces of European politics, and of German politics in particular, and in perception of the trend of the national movements which were then in progress, equalled the plain-speaking but incomparably shrewd Lancashire cotton-spinner, Richard Cobden.

So it continued even after Sadowa had placed beyond dispute Prussia's right to be regarded not only as a Great Power but as one of the greatest. As late as 1868 Count Bernstorff, the enlightened representative first of Prussia and later of the North German Confederation and the succeeding Empire at the Court of London (from 1853 to 1861 and from 1862 to 1873), had to complain to Bismarck that " the greater part of modern statesmen in England know incredibly little about Germany." The claim to keep Germany for ever in leading-strings had now been abandoned, because it could no longer be substantiated. Yet Clarendon, who by frequent travel made honest efforts to discover for himself at first hand the capital facts of foreign politics, long continued to regard the completion of the work of unity begun in 1866 as merely designed to gratify Prussia's ambition and to place at her King's command an unnecessarily large army.[1] There were still British statesmen, even Foreign Secretaries, who had never troubled even to master the rank of the Prussian Minister who was making Germany and remaking Europe, and two wars were necessary before the British Foreign Office learned to spell Bismarck's name correctly. Foibles of the kind were not comical but tragical, since they were symptomatic of a want of appreciation of the large questions behind. Let there be no misunderstanding: in its dealings with Germany and Prussia at that time England's statecraft was perfectly upright, straightforward, and sincere, from the standpoint of honourable dealing free from any reproach; its faults were culpable ignorance and blindness, and a lack of any appreciation of realities, yet these faults were fatal.

[1] Letter to Lord Lyons, June 8, 1870.

A fatuous notion—not yet exploded—that knowledge of affairs, and especially foreign affairs, comes by intuition, an insuperable prejudice against everything alien to their world of ideas, and a blunt refusal to respond to outside influences led many British statesmen and politicians astray at that great and critical time, with the consequence that the British nation in turn played a short-sighted and ill-considered part. The national movement was not more legitimate or more laudable in Italy than in Germany, yet England's sympathies, freely and generously given in the one case, were to a large extent withheld in the other. It is true that the German struggle for unity lacked the epic moments which appealed to the imagination of a people whose very cradle-song had been a song of liberty, that in it there had hitherto been little that was heroic and much that was weak and ignoble, that the German nation had made few courageous attempts to assert itself, but after every failure to dethrone the reactionary powers which kept it back it had again kissed the rod with servile abasement. Perhaps to that extent it might fairly be said that Germany was herself to blame for the indifference which was felt towards her. No doubt, too, the strong German influences at Court which caused so much resentment in the early Victorian period created prejudices against everything German.[1]

Yet even if it was not necessary, or to be expected, that those whom Germany failed to attract should accord to the national cause sympathy and welcome, it would at least have been common sense to give to it an intelligent understanding and to view it in relation to the entire European situation. But that was not done. Sir Robert Morier did not love Germany and he disliked Bismarck with every reason, yet he understood both as few of his contemporaries did, and he recognized that "the victory of Prussia, ending with the expulsion of Austria out of Germany, would be the greatest boon that could be given to Europe and Austria." The refusal of his countrymen, and above all their political leaders, to make up their minds that German unity was at the door, and to conform their attitude to it, was to Morier a source of poignant mortification and dark foreboding.

[1] The Germans possessed of influence at Court were doubtless in the habit of exaggerating that influence. In a letter of May 15, 1848, Bunsen described Stockmar to Herr von Usedom, the Prussian envoy in Frankfort, as "one of the first politicians of Germany and of Europe, the disciple of Stein, preceptor of Prince Albert, then the friend and private adviser of Prince Leopold, afterwards King of the Belgians, the silent guide of the Court of Great Britain, and the confidential friend both of Lord Melbourne and Sir Robert Peel" (*Life of Baron Stockmar*, vol. ii., p. 260).

The Prince Consort complained to Lord Granville on one occasion that the " principal deficiency " of English statesmen was that they " never looked at any subject as part of the whole." The German question was not merely part, but a large part, of European and of world politics, yet how many Englishmen, in high or lowlier place, conceived it as such ? More or less the same spirit of indifference, now cold, now contemptuous, continued to govern British policy towards the new Power for twenty years, until resolute refusal to recognize facts on one side and equally resolute refusal to have them ignored on the other brought the two countries into a grave conflict over the question of colonial expansion.

CHAPTER VIII

(1867–1870)

THE HOHENZOLLERN CANDIDATURE

MODERN history affords no parallel to the suddenness and completeness of Austria's eclipse after Sadowa and the Treaty of Prague. The Power which had so long dominated Germany, and had spoken for her in the councils of Europe, fell at once into the background. It was not that the war left Austria intrinsically weaker than before, save for the moment, but rather that it had exposed a weakness which already existed, yet had been but little suspected by the outside world, and by Austria herself not at all. Every nation has its mission to perform, the vigorous and the decadent alike : the mission of the former is to go forward, that of the latter to make way for others, and allow them to do the work for which it is unfitted. Austria seemed to have reached the stage of decline in which renunciation and self-effacement are a nation's last remaining virtues. The weight of empire had imposed upon her military strength, statesmanship, and material resources a drain which all were incapable of meeting, and because she had been living upon a past reputation she failed to recognize their insufficiency until it was too late to avert disaster.

Henceforth Austria was thrown back upon herself, and more than ever her politics became circumscribed by Habsburg interests. Driven out of Germany, and now retaining only a narrow foothold in Italy, it was in the East that she was in future to seek the assertion of her influence.

Yet Austria's disappearance from the stage upon which she had so long played the foremost part in the drama of German unity meant only a certain rearrangement of the cast, for the drama itself was to continue a little longer. Now an actor who until lately had been little more than an understudy took the leading place, and the late prompter of the piece aspired to an active *rôle.*

The Hohenzollern Candidature

The relations between Prussia and France were peculiar. Down to the disaster of Sadowa, Napoleon had claimed to occupy the position of an arbiter between the contentious Great Powers of Germany, both of which had in turn been suitors for his good-will and disposed to make large concessions in order to gain it. He indulged in no hollow boast when he claimed that he was the true author of the peace preliminaries of Nikolsburg and hence of the Treaty of Prague, and that he had thus set the limits to Prussia's recent aggrandizement. The war, however, had created a new situation; there was no longer need for an intermediary between Powers of which one had so lately been at the mercy of the other; and both France and Prussia had accordingly to adjust their relationships to an entirely different set of conditions and eventualities.

Of the two, Prussia, in her still uncertain position in Europe, had on the whole the greater cause to seek friendships. In a speech made in the Prussian Lower House on September 1, 1866, Bismarck had said: "The tasks of our foreign policy have not yet been completed. The successes of the army have only increased our stakes; we have more to lose than before, but we have gained nothing at all." Situated as she was, it would have been folly to have sought difficulties, least of all with a neighbour so well able, as it seemed, to reward either good or evil as France. Bismarck, therefore, continued for the present to preserve towards the Emperor the old attitude of deference. Both sides were conscious that the relations between them was that of a merely formal friendship, based altogether on political interest. In a letter written from Nikolsburg on August 10th, Bismarck's confidant, the diarist Abeken, spoke of Napoleon's "flattering speeches," and added: "We pay him back in his own coin." There was this difference, however, between the men who thus dissembled their feelings, that while Bismarck's professions of amity were wholly feigned, those of Napoleon were at least sincere in part and with more ingenuous dealings on the other side might have been sincere altogether.

Bismarck has confessed that down to 1867 he had no reason to believe that France thought of war with Prussia, while he, on the contrary, "always regarded a war with France as an indispensable condition of the national development of Germany." After 1866, when Napoleon had come between Prussia and her victim, his belief in such a war as merely historically inevitable gave place to a conviction that it was an urgent political necessity.

Writing from the midst of the royal and Ministerial circles which had gathered at Ems in the summer of 1867, Abeken, from whom no secrets were hidden, reported (July 27th): " There is a general feeling here that there will never be peace until after a war with France, though every one agrees in thinking that neither Louis Napoleon nor the French nation desires war."

For France it was a task of immense difficulty to accommodate herself to the new conjuncture created by the events of 1864 to 1867, and to determine upon an attitude which, while just to Prussia, should also be safe and advantageous for herself. The question of immediate interest was that of the future relations of North and South Germany. Here one great yet excusable miscalculation vitiated most French speculations and plans—the belief that North and South were so far apart in sentiment and sympathy that union was improbable, and hence that for practical purposes the Southern States might be counted against Prussia in any new combinations which time and events might create. Upon this belief France counted too strongly, making it for a time the pivot of her policy towards Prussia, with untoward results. For the conviction that the two parts of Germany had no desire for union encouraged a disposition to view with hostility any efforts to draw them more closely together.

Looking back upon the course of events, it is superficial wisdom to say that the North German Confederation was bound to have as its sequel the complete unity of the German tribes. No doubt it was, but even in Germany few people believed that the sequel would come so speedily, and there were many statesmen and publicists of the leading rank who still held that a separate Confederation of the South German States was at least a possible alternative. When such uncertainty as to the future prevailed in Germany, it was inevitable that the French mind, with its proneness to rapid conclusions and surface judgments, should misinterpret the signs of the times. There were, indeed, in those days many Frenchmen who contended, with no justification save a boundless credulity, that the Prussian superiority attested by Sadowa was a fiction and that the structure of German alliances built upon it would collapse like a pack of cards before the first strong gust of particularist feeling. Foremost amongst these was Drouyn de Lhuys, the Foreign Minister, whose bitter anti-Prussian sentiment led him to the conclusion that French policy must be directed towards keeping Germany disunited, since an all-German Confederation would only be Prussia enlarged.

It was only a small minority of thoughtful men who, taking accurate measure of the Prussian statesman with whom France had now to deal, as well as of the forces which were at work in German politics, saw clearly that the unity movement could not stop at the Main. The influence of these men was on the side of vigilance and caution. Adolphe Thiers and Émile Ollivier were among the little band of disregarded seers who were firmly convinced that complete unity, though deferred, was certain, and Ollivier, at least, believed that France would serve her true interests by accepting it frankly and generously. Thiers, though his hostility to Prussia was strong and deep, saw clearly the inexorable trend of events, and he showed true prophetic insight in a speech which he made in the *Corps Législatif* on May 3, 1866, just before the outbreak of the Bohemian war. "What is certain," he said, "is that if the war is successful for Prussia that Power will take possession of some of the States in the North and those which she does not annex she will bring under her influence. Prussia will thus have one section of the German nation under her direct authority and the other under her indirect authority; and then Austria will be admitted as a *protégée* in this new order of things. Then, permit me to tell you, there will be accomplished the great phenomenon towards which events have been tending for more than a century; we shall see the establishment of a new German Empire."

Thiers' speech created a powerful impression upon his hearers, and the suggestion in which he epitomized his monitions, that France should protest against the further extension of the German unity movement, justifying her action by the treaties of 1815, had a dramatic sequel. Several days later (May 6th) the Emperor used at Auxerre the significant words, "As for the treaties of 1815, of which we are reminded, I abhor them!"

In the same assembly a year later (March 15, 1867), when Bavaria and Würtemberg were trying to bring Austria back into the German fold, Ollivier combated the persistent unbelief in the permanence of the new Confederation. "The deputy has told us," he said, "that what Bismarck has created will not endure. He is wrong; not only will it endure, but it will develop further. The day will come, sooner or later, but inevitably, when, the Northern Confederation having been definitely constituted, and the South German Confederation having been organized for military purposes on the Prussian system, these two unions will join hands across the Main in spite of the Treaty of Prague."

Unlike Thiers, however, Ollivier frankly repudiated an anti-Prussian attitude, and claimed that the true policy of France was to regard Prussia as a friend until her acts proved her to be a foe. Replying for the Government (March 18th), Rouher repudiated hostility to the German unity movement and avowed his conviction that the attitude of Prussia to France was unprovocative, yet said that if Prussia were to develop aggressive designs against the independence of her neighbours neither France nor Great Britain would be able to look on passively.

This debate had an echo in Berlin, where the constituent assembly of the North German Confederation was at the time deliberating upon a constitution. For the moment this subject was put on one side, and the delegates discussed the European situation. An interpellation was by arrangement addressed to the Government (March 19th) asking whether a promise had been obtained from the States outside the Confederation that they would not enter into alliances which might endanger the safety of Germany or prejudice further unity. Although Bismarck coyly protested that this was an awkward question, he had no hesitation in promptly divulging the defensive and offensive treaties with Bavaria, Würtemberg, Baden, and Hesse.

For Napoleon in particular Prussia's success had been a bitter surprise, and it had thrown him for a time entirely out of his political bearings. In 1863, when the question of German unity seemed to be maturing owing to the quarrel over the Elbe duchies, he had said: "I shall always be consistent in my policy. Having fought for Italian independence and raised my voice for Polish nationality, I shall be unable to entertain other sentiments or obey other principles in Germany." He meant this then, and perhaps he meant it still, but frank acceptance of his own theories was difficult now that the duty of making a clear and unambiguous stand could no longer be evaded. For once his master principles of nationality, equilibrium, and compensations came into a conflict which it seemed impossible to resolve. Each of these principles, standing alone, appeared perfectly reasonable and tenable. What Napoleon too easily ignored, or at least minimized, was the difficulty of reconciling these principles and applying them in conjunction—the fact that any rigorous attempt to realize the principle of nationality on a large scale could only be made at the expense of the principle of equilibrium, and that any disturbance of the Continental equilibrium must bring into play the doctrine of compensations, with all its entanglements and risks.

He had never opposed the German unity movement as such, even though he had ceased to give to it a friendly and ready recognition, from a growing suspicion that in helping Prussia to eject Austria from Germany he had been helping to create a rival Power which might menace the position of France. Hence it was that his influence now, however much he might try to hide the fact behind specious phrases, was bound to be directed towards keeping Germany divided into two spheres of influence, one under the leadership of Prussia, since that could no longer be prevented, the other reserved for Austria, perhaps under his own patronage.

It was one of the greatest disappointments of Napoleon's career that in application to the German question his policy of compensations, to himself so obvious and equitable, failed altogether to work. Incidental reference has already been made to the negotiations, *démarches, pourparlers*—call them what we will—on the subject of territorial acquisitions, which took place on sundry occasions between Bismarck and Benedetti in Berlin and elsewhere, and between Napoleon and his Foreign Minister and the Prussian ambassador, Count von der Goltz, in Paris. The present is a convenient place in which to sum up all that needs to be said further on this subject before it is allowed to disappear from the narrative. The story is, and will remain, an obscure page in the political history of the period, nor is it likely that completer knowledge would make it more edifying. It is obscure for the sufficient reason that on the Prussian side little that is really illuminating was put into writing, so that the authorities upon whom we have to rely are chiefly French. Bismarck's public contributions to the story were for the most part confined to later denials of acts and words of a compromising kind attributed to him by hostile witnesses.

There was a reason for Bismarck's lifelong prejudice against the use of documents in diplomatic intercourse. Documents tell tales : conversations " under four eyes " can take place with the assurance that it is always possible to question the accuracy, and if need be disclaim the authorship, of unguarded confidences which have been inconveniently divulged.[1] Moreover, equivocation is difficult in writing ; sooner or later the time comes when choice has to be made between frankness or silence. That was

[1] This conflict of testimony, as between Bismarck and Lord Granville, occurred in an acute form in 1885 over the question whether the former had recommended the occupation by Great Britain of Egypt. See Chapter XVII.

why Bismarck had no patience with the voluminous epistles of the British Foreign Office, the traditional inscription of whose letters, "Yours in truth and sincerity," must have continually jarred upon his sensitive feelings. It was his belief in the permissibility of equivocation as a fair weapon in diplomacy, and his unwillingness to abandon its use, that led him in the North German Diet to disapprove of the publication of blue books of the English type. For if they were introduced, he said (April 22, 1869), "I should be compelled to write two despatches on the same subject, one intended for practical effect in diplomacy and one which I intended to publish."

How far, then, did Bismarck wilfully deceive Napoleon on the question of compensations? If we would learn his true attitude towards France and the Emperor, we must go to utterances in which he could not be otherwise than ingenuous. Such an utterance is the report which as Prussian envoy to the Frankfort Diet he addressed to his Government on May 10, 1856. Speaking of foreign relationships in general and of those with France in particular, he there said: "Our relations with France for the time being must be such as will allow us at any moment to draw nearer to her without injury or humiliation to ourselves, and that the other Courts may remain under the impression that such a course is open to us." He wrote to his friend Ludwig von Gerlach in the same sense on May 2nd of the following year: "France counts for me merely as a piece, though an essential piece, in the game of political chess. . . . . Courtesy is a cheap coin, and if it does no further service than that of ridding the others of the belief that they are always sure of France against us, and we at all times in want of help against France, that is a great point gained for the diplomacy of peace."

France was, in fact, to be used for Prussia's purposes, yet without any idea of rendering an equivalent. No statesman was cleverer than Bismarck in exploiting the mistakes and weaknesses of his fellow-men, and Napoleon's obsession on the subject of territorial compensations placed in his hands a weapon which he was constantly able to employ to advantage. As early as June, 1850, Napoleon, in a conversation with Count Hatzfeldt in Paris, had tried to win Prussia for an alliance the cost of which was to be paid out of another pocket, for all Prussia was to be asked to do was to agree to the cession to France of Bavarian territory left of the Rhine. Nothing came of the suggestion, but after being abandoned for a long time it was revived in a serious form directly Bismarck came upon the scene.

Even before he had become a Prussian Minister, Bismarck had earned the reputation of a man who showed the greatest moral courage in immoral enterprises. Referring to the idea of the annexation of Luxemburg by France, as a set-off to Prussian acquisitions in North Germany—another project in which Napoleon already took interest—Prince de la Tour d'Auvergne, the French ambassador to Berlin, wrote to the Foreign Minister, Thouvenel, in April, 1862: "The only person I know to whom we could venture to make such proposals is Monsieur de Bismarck." A more impartial witness, Count Bernstorff, complained that in the first years of Bismarck's Ministry (it will be remembered that he took office in the autumn of 1862) there was "a lack of exact information respecting the dealings between the Prussian Government and Louis Napoleon." Even then an uneasy feeling prevailed that Bismarck was committing his country to indefinite obligations which might prove to be indiscreet and unrealizable.

The most cherished of all Napoleon's territorial ambitions was the restoration of the eastern frontiers of France to the limits recognized down to 1815, and this ambition grew the longer he reigned. The outwardly benevolent attitude which he adopted towards Prussia prior to and during the war of 1866 was unquestionably dictated by the hope of attaining or advancing towards this greatly desired goal. Benedetti repeatedly threw out feelers on the subject, and Bismarck never showed reluctance to discuss any new proposition which the French ambassador had to make. Benedetti goes further, and says that the accommodating Minister made counter-proposals of his own. On June 4, 1866, the ambassador reported to Drouyn de Lhuys the substance of a conversation in which he had pointedly asked Bismarck what France would obtain in the event of Prussia being victorious in the then imminent war and annexing territories in North Germany. Bismarck had at once replied that rather than give up Cologne, Bonn, or Mayence, he would "disappear from the political scene," but he "believed it to be not impossible to persuade the King to cede to us the banks of the Upper Moselle, which, joined with Luxemburg, where union with France would be favourably received, would rectify our frontier in a manner entirely satisfactory to us." "I could not tell," Benedetti naïvely adds, "whether Monsieur de Bismarck, in opening his mind to me in this connection without any special pretext, wished to sound me or to let you understand at once through me the concessions which he would be willing to offer you and those which we should abstain from asking of him, but I should not be surprised, since expedients of this kind are habitual with him."

The negotiations at Nikolsburg which followed in July have already been referred to. On the part of France they were pursued with the greater justification since, in Paris, Count Goltz, genuinely convinced of his right to it, was at the time urging Napoleon to press for compensation, though he was of opinion that it should take the form of Luxemburg, and perhaps Belgium, rather than of Rhenish Hesse and the Bavarian Palatinate, as Napoleon wished.[1] The colloquies at Nikolsburg, after Benedetti had communicated the result to his Government and obtained further instructions, led to the preparation of a draft agreement, which he placed before Bismarck on August 5th. By this agreement France was to regain the territories comprised within her frontiers in 1814 which had since belonged to Prussia, and Prussia was also to undertake to obtain for France from Bavaria and grand-ducal Hesse, in return for compensation, their lands on the left bank of the Rhine. On the following day Benedetti supplemented the draft by an interview with the Prussian Minister-President—the interview of which Bismarck gave so highly seasoned a version in the Imperial Diet on May 2, 1871. Benedetti, he said, abruptly appeared in his room, unexpected and unannounced, and presented the ultimatum "Either cede Mayence and the Palatinate or expect a declaration of war!" and was startled when he received the cool rejoinder, "Good, we will have war!" No man incapable of lively flights of imagination can be a good story-teller. Bismarck as a story-teller was incomparable, and he never spoiled the effect of his narratives by any scruple about literal accuracy; the careful student of this fascinating *causeur* knows that he retouched many of his stories for greater effect. Benedetti likewise records the interview, and that it took this very dramatic form is very improbable.[2] The ambassador, we are told, repeated the

[1] Letter to Count Bernstorff, August 28, 1866 (*The Bernstorff Papers*, vol. ii., pp. 246–53).

[2] It is not necessary to labour this point, since Bismarck later caused to be published in the Prussian *Official Gazette* (see L. Hahn's *Fürst Bismarck, sein politisches Leben und Wirken*, vol. i., pp. 510–11) an account of the interview, wherein it was stated that the idea of war as an alternative was suggested by himself ("To the remark of the Minister-President that this demand meant war. . . . Count Bene-

substance of the draft agreement, and Bismarck declined to consider it seriously, but he did so in a manner "*convenable* and *courtois*"—the manner which up to that time the wary Minister had held in all his dealings with Napoleon and France; and compensation in other directions, and naturally out of Germany, was suggested.

Whatever the exact form of words, however, refusal it was, definite and final. Bismarck no longer feared Napoleon, not only because peace had been concluded, but still more because Napoleon had revealed himself to be a weakling. A man who could be put off with mere words, as he had been at Nikolsburg, and so often before, was not likely to cause serious difficulty. Bismarck did not give Napoleon time to reflect upon what he should do, but published in a French newspaper an article in which the Emperor was stated to have demanded from Prussia the cession of Rhenish territory, and to have met with a rebuff. The news promptly came back to Germany, as was intended, and created an angry outcry.

Benedetti himself appears to have reported the conversation to Paris in terms so discouraging that the Emperor now finally abandoned the idea of German acquisitions. He wrote on August 12th to the Minister of the Interior, the Marquis de la Valette: "That convention should have been kept secret, but it has been talked about abroad, and the newspapers go as far as to say that the Rhenish provinces have been refused us. It is evident from the conversation with Benedetti that we should have all Germany against us for a very small advantage. It is important that public opinion should not go astray on the subject. Contradict energetically, therefore, these rumours in the newspapers. . . . The true interest of France is not to obtain an insignificant increase of territory, but to assist Germany to organize herself in the way most favourable to our interests and those of Europe." Benedetti was instructed to ask Bismarck to regard the overture as *non avenu*—a request easier to make than to fulfil.

Wishing to dispel earlier reflections upon his reputation as a schemer against his country's interests, Bismarck seems to have told the Crown Prince about this and other proposals of Napoleon, for the Prince wrote to him on August 9th: "The

detti answered," etc.). Bismarck, however, seldom told a good story twice in the same way; all his reminiscences improved with age and reiteration, and it may be doubted whether, as a rule, his best version was the truest.

evidences of Napoleonic hunger which you have sent me are most remarkable. . . . If Napoleon persists in hankering after the whole left bank of the Rhine, we shall have every reason to be grateful to him for helping us towards the speedy union of Germany under one head."

That Bismarck was ever prepared to assent to the cession to France of either Prussian or Hessian or Bavarian territory is in the highest degree improbable, though up to this time there were countrymen of his in high places, like Prince Hohenlohe, Count Bernstorff, and Herr von Bethmann-Hollweg, who held the contrary.[1] If, however, he must be acquitted of such a design, it is certain that he allowed, and even encouraged, Napoleon to believe that a transaction of the kind was practicable, and made more or less explicit promises to that effect. Certainly the claim which has been advanced on his behalf by some of his admirers that he was really a chaste Joseph, cruelly exposed to the wiles of the French seductress, is too ludicrous for serious refutation. The most plausible defence of his conduct in the matter is his own, contained in a letter which he wrote to the German Emperor on September 10, 1873, when meeting charges of deceit brought against him by the Italian statesman La Marmora. "I could meet the Napoleonic policy," he said, "only by always giving Benedetti and the Italians, who keep nothing secret from Napoleon, to understand that I was quite inclined to stray from the path of virtue, but that my most gracious master was not, and that I must have time to persuade your Majesty. Your Majesty knows that I never attempted to do this, but the French belief that I was working at it was very useful to us."[2]

The infatuated Busch, whose apologies for his hero are usually thoroughgoing rather than discriminating, tells the truth bluntly when he writes that "Bismarck had never held out any distinct

[1] Napoleon said to General Türr in 1867, when told that Bismarck wished for the recall of Benedetti: "I can understand that M. de Bismarck is not pleased with the presence of Benedetti. He has made him too many promises. He is always ready to give away what does not belong to him."

[2] Replying in the Imperial Diet on January 16, 1874, to La Marmora's accusation—made in his book *Un po' più di luce*—that he had been willing to cede to France a portion of the left bank of the Rhine, Bismarck indignantly denied that he had either offered or been willing to give to Napoleon so much as a clover-field of German territory. Several years before (July 29, 1870), in a circular letter to the diplomatic representatives of the North German Confederation, he had summarized his attitude on the compensation question in the words, "I observed silence regarding the demands, and negotiated upon them dilatorily, without on any occasion giving a single promise." Neither of these statements goes as far as his private admission to the Emperor, as quoted above.

hopes to Napoleon, nor yet definitely refused to acquiesce in his wishes, but *had kept him in tow.*" But Bismarck, on his own admission, both deceived Napoleon and lied in doing this. In all these mysterious dealings, however, he was not seeking to sell his country, but France. Napoleon may have been a dull dog to fall into the trap which had been so ingeniously laid for him, but the snare was no more defensible or more sportsmanlike than man-traps usually are; perhaps in this case it was less so, for the snare was set by one poacher in order to catch another. Certainly there is no need to waste tears over Napoleon and his discomfiture. He had engaged in an immoral transaction, and the fact that of the two schemers Bismarck on the whole was probably the less scrupulous does not redeem the sordidness of his own part in the long catena of intrigue. With Bismarck it was the policy that was crooked, with Napoleon the will. One of the most discerning students of character, the Prince Consort, said of the Emperor drastically but truly that he had been "born and bred a conspirator."

Instead of making him more cautious, his failure in the negotiations with Bismarck over the cession of German territory only sharpened Napoleon's eagerness to obtain compensation elsewhere. It was a serious disadvantage of his position as the elected head of a virtually republican monarchy that he was always conscious that the eyes of the nation were upon him, that he held his position by favour, and that he was expected to justify it by furnishing impressive results.[1] He had to reckon also with the temperament of a people which constitutionally had in the course of a century been all things by turn and nothing long, and whose fondness for new things was as pronounced in relation to politics as to *primeurs.* He hated, too, the idea of isolation, not only because it exposed France to possible danger, but because it seemed to indicate political failure and a loss of prestige. If the frontiers of 1814 were not to be won back, an enlargement somewhere else would at least retrieve his position. Prussia's success with the federation of the North German States and the prospect of the States of the South passing under her leadership, if not her control, seem to have suggested to him the idea of gathering under his own wing some of the little borderland

[1] The Prince Consort said to Count Vitzthum in 1860: "Napoleon would like to be Emperor by the grace of God and at the same time *par la volonté nationale.*" Bismarck described his position as "an absolutism based on the sovereignty of the people."

countries—Belgium, Luxemburg, Holland, Switzerland. To the first two of these both Bismarck and Goltz had repeatedly pointed as fairly coming within the sphere of French influence.

Accordingly, barely a week after he had been refused a rectification of his German frontier, Napoleon approached Bismarck again through Benedetti with the request that he would assist him in acquiring Belgium and Luxemburg, regardless of the fact that the independence and neutrality of Belgium were guaranteed by a treaty of 1839, to which France and Prussia, with the other Great Powers, were parties. As Ollivier has shown, a draft treaty was prepared in Paris, and duly submitted by the French ambassador to Bismarck. By it France was to acquiesce in the territorial gains made by Prussia in the late war—in other words, to recognize as accomplished facts which could not be undone—and to offer no objection to the formation of a union of the North German Confederation with the Southern States, while Prussia in return was to help France to acquire the sovereignty of Luxemburg from the King of the Netherlands in return for compensation, and to sanction the military occupation or conquest of Belgium. Bismarck, as usual, listened patiently to all that Benedetti had to say and even discussed the proposals with him, but declined to give a definite promise. Nevertheless, he took care to retain Benedetti's draft, anticipating that it might one day prove useful.

When a little later the negotiations became known to the other Governments interested in the treaty of 1839, Napoleon did not hesitate to declare that the suggestion that he should occupy Belgium came from Prussia and that he had rejected it with indignation. It may be true that the earliest promptings emanated from that quarter, but the apology was none the less a prevarication. This repudiation was followed by a circular letter to the French embassies (September 16th) which was intended to rehabilitate France with the Powers and to remove cause for further alarm in the little frontier States. In this letter M. de la Valette—now acting provisionally as Foreign Minister in place of Drouyn de Lhuys, who had resigned—pointed out that by the advance of Prussia into the ranks of the Great Powers the old traditions and State combinations had been broken down, leaving all countries free to rearrange their associations and make a new start. France, as the champion of the principle of nationality, could not grudge Germany the unity she desired, or make the consolidation of that country a pretext for any indiscriminate accession of territory; she desired no aggrandizement that did not proceed from the voluntary action of the populations concerned.

Henceforth still another corner of Naboth's vineyard was immune from French molestation. Nevertheless, in Bismarck's eyes Napoleon played the fool in the Belgian annexation question, and his fault was not that he wished to commit a crime, but that, having the will, he had not the courage to do it: his was the cowardice of "the unlit lamp and the ungirt loin." Recalling the episode during a conversation with Busch during the war of 1870, he said that the Emperor should have taken Belgium by a bold *coup*, but added that he was ever, and still remained, "a muddle-headed fellow."

Annexations in Germany and Belgium being both beyond his reach, there now remained for Napoleon only one hope, the acquisition of Luxemburg by the prosaically honest method of purchase. It was in regard to this, his final experiment with the policy of compensations, that he believed Bismarck to have treated him most scurvily. Whatever might be said of the propriety of the Emperor's designs in this instance, they were at least open and above-board. In some respects the position of the grand duchy bore likeness to that of Schleswig and Holstein before their annexation by Prussia. Like the Elbe duchies, Luxemburg was connected by personal union with an adjoining kingdom: the King of the Netherlands was its Grand Duke and his brother, Prince Henry, acted as Stadholder. In all internal matters, too, the grand duchy was as independent as the Elbe duchies had been in relation to Denmark. Luxemburg also, like Holstein, had been a member of the old Bund. It was troubled, indeed, by no dispute as to title or succession, yet on the other hand it had to tolerate an arrangement by which the fortress of the capital town was manned until 1856 by a joint Prussian and Dutch garrison, three-quarters being Prussian troops, but since that date by Prussians only.

After the dissolution of the Bund the grand duchy became entirely independent of Germany and was free to go its own way, subject only to the acquiescence of its ruler. The chances of a successful bargain, therefore, were at least favourable to France. Now, at Napoleon's request, Bismarck undertook to advise the King of Prussia to withdraw his troops from the garrison. At the same time he recommended Napoleon to begin an agitation in the country on his own account in favour of annexation, adding that if the Emperor could persuade Holland to part with the grand duchy by sale Prussia would not stand in the way.

Disappointed at Bismarck's coolness in the matter, doubting his sincerity, and fearing also that the scheme would raise in Europe a storm which it would be difficult to allay, Napoleon broke off negotiations for a time. When early in 1867 he reopened the question, it was in the form of an invitation to the Powers to say if they would object to annexation. Russia was favourable, England indifferent, while Austria warned him that the proposal might excite national feeling in Germany and possibly lead to war. Relying upon the support of Prussia—now head of the North German Confederation—Napoleon in March offered to buy out the King of the Netherlands. The King was willing, only stipulating for Prussia's agreement, and on being reassured by the Emperor on this point he accepted the terms of the necessary treaties, and it seemed as if all that remained to be done was to obtain from Berlin a formal endorsement of the transaction.

On April 1st Benedetti waited on Bismarck for this purpose. Suspecting the object of his visit, the Minister put him off with the excuse that he was just about to go to the Diet, where he had to answer an interpellation upon the Luxemburg question. The question which he had to answer—by a well-known trick of parliamentary life it had been arranged beforehand—was this : Had the Federal Government any knowledge that France was angling for possession of the grand duchy ? The answer given by the Chancellor was that he had no reason to believe that a treaty of annexation had yet been concluded, but he could not say the opposite ; in any event, the Government would safeguard the just rights of the German States and populations should they be threatened, and he was sure that it would be possible to do that by peaceable means. Old parliamentarian though he was, Bismarck was not prepared for the passionate outburst which followed. From all sides of the house rose a chorus of protest that France should even have contemplated the appropriation of a " piece of old Germany." After obtaining from the Bavarian Government in the course of the day an assurance that in the event of complications arising with France over the question Bavaria would stand by the Confederation, Bismarck instructed Count Goltz to warn the French Government that in face of the strong national feeling which had shown itself in Germany France would be unwise to take any further public step in the matter, at any rate for the present, and the warning was delivered the same evening. Once more Napoleon found himself checkmated, and by the same hand.

Sybel, whose misfortune it was to have written contemporary history while still under the intoxicating influence of the successful wars of 1866 and of 1870, contends that on Bismarck's part there had been no equivocation : he had given no definite pledge, for nothing had been put down in writing. Napoleon did not take that view, but believed that once again he had been intentionally ensnared and entrapped. Bismarck had advised the Luxemburg transaction and had promised his support ; the King of the Netherlands had given his assent ; the treaty of cession was ready for signature ; yet at the last moment the entire plan was wrecked, as his other territorial plans had been wrecked, by his rival's shiftiness. It looked like a deliberate plot to put France in a false position and damage her credit in the eyes of Europe, and Napoleon told the German ambassador so. Now in disgust he withdrew from the affair, and in revenge for Bismarck's treatment of him determined to challenge Prussia's right to continue to occupy in the name of the dissolved Bund a fortress which was no longer a federal fortress.

Accordingly, on April 15th the French Government invited Great Britain, Russia, and Austria to say whether in their opinion the time for Prussia's withdrawal from Luxemburg had not arrived. The response not being decisive, Czar Alexander II proposed a conference of the Powers with a view to agreement upon a joint guarantee of Luxemburg's neutrality and independence, and the proposal found general acceptance. Prussia made no difficulty, though Bismarck added a black mark to Napoleon's mounting score.[1] The conference met in London on May 7th, and by the 11th a convention had been signed under which the Powers confirmed the settlement of 1839 securing succession to the grand duchy to the house of Orange-Nassau (the royal family of the Netherlands), and assured a collective guarantee of the grand duchy's neutrality. While Prussia undertook to withdraw her garrison from the city of Luxemburg, the treaty stipulated that the fortress should thereafter be converted into an open city, and that no military establishment should henceforth be maintained or created there. Ratifications were exchanged on May 31st. The British delegate had wished the conference to

[1] Three years later, during the Franco-German War, Bismarck said : "I wanted no fighting about the Luxemburg business, for I knew well enough that six wars would come of it."

stop at a declaration that the grand duchy should be neutral in perpetuity and that the Powers would respect its neutrality. It was due to a proposal of the Prussian delegate, Count Bernstorff—acting on the suggestion of his Russian colleague, Baron Brunnow—that the guarantee of Luxemburg's neutrality was given in collective form.

Of all Napoleon's barren hunts for territorial compensation the Luxemburg one was to him the most aggravating, for in this transaction he had really tried to act virtuously. It is not surprising that he should have attributed to the Minister who was able not only to carry to success his own schemes but to wreck the schemes of others a dæmonic power or that he came to see his hand in every one of his reverses. Always in his diplomacy he was haunted by the suspicion that Bismarck was intriguing against him; henceforth in every important move, in every vital decision, his first thought was of the German Chancellor—of what he would think or say or do.

Compelled at last to admit that in Bismarck he had found his master, he seems for a time to have come to the conclusion that to work against him was like working against fate, and that the only safe course for France was to cultivate his goodwill. Explaining in a speech from the throne at the end of the year the policy which he intended that France should follow, he said (November 18, 1867): " In spite of the declarations of my Government, whose pacific attitude has never changed, the belief has prevailed that any transformation of the domestic policy of Germany must be a cause of conflict. This condition of uncertainty must last no longer. We must frankly accept the changes which have been introduced across the Rhine and let it be known that so long as our interests and our dignity are not threatened we shall not interfere with the changes, which have been evoked by the wish of the German nation."

Even now, however, he could not bring himself to accept the view that unity should extend beyond the Main, and it was in this sense that he wished the Treaty of Prague to be interpreted. He wanted the Southern States to be free, as under that treaty they were intended to be, to enter into a union of their own or not, as they pleased, and for the rest to be allowed to go their own way without Prussian compulsion or interference. Secretly he hoped that Austria would still succeed in attaching these States to herself, so creating a counterpoise to the powerful Confederation of the North, though as an alternative he entertained as late as 1868 the crazy idea of the federation of the States with Switzerland. A breath from Lord Clarendon, to whom Napoleon had confided his secret, was sufficient to explode the bubble. The readiness with which the Southern States had entered into a military alliance with Prussia had perplexed and pained him, yet so little does he appear to have abandoned the hope of keeping North and South apart that he could say to the same statesman in October, 1868 : " I can guarantee peace only so long as Bismarck respects the present status ; if he draws the South German States into the Northern Confederation, our guns will go off of themselves."

Yet Napoleon emphatically did not want war, but was profoundly convinced that the interests of France, of the Empire, and, not least, of his dynasty, were bound up with peace. He gave an earnest of his desire for international accord by instituting the great Paris exhibition which was opened in April, 1867. During that festival of peace the lions and lambs of European politics, at his invitation, sat down together at the board of equality and fraternity. Most of the crowned heads of Europe with their Ministers—among the number the King of Prussia with Bismarck and Czar Alexander II with Gortchakoff—accepted his hospitality ; there was a general exchange of courtesies, and conferences of all nations met for traffic in ideas helpful to the progress of mankind.

No Frenchman of the time saw more clearly the drift of events in Germany and the true interest of France in relation to them than Benedetti, who was still serving his country well in Berlin. Throughout the whole of his relationships with the Prussian Court and Government, Benedetti seems to have done his best to promote confidence between Paris and Berlin. He also persisted in believing, even in face of wholesale incredulity and apprehension at home, that Bismarck's policy on the whole was not intended to be hostile to France, subject only to one important condition—that France should not cross Prussia's path. In one of his many despatches on the subject he wrote of Bismarck (January 1, 1868) : " What is his objective, what the end he is pursuing ? It is not to attack us ; I have said it already, and I repeat it at the risk of assuming a great responsibility, because such is my profound conviction ; his aim is to free the Main and to unite the South of Germany to the North under the authority of the King of Prussia, and I will add that he intends to attain it if needful by arms should France openly put obstacles in his way."

Benedetti also, if not a sympathetic friend, was at least not an enemy of German unity, which he regarded as inevitable and legitimate, and he was one of the few Frenchmen of that time who recognized Prussia's strength and the risks which would be involved by a quarrel with her. Accordingly, he had strongly urged upon his Government the acceptance of a policy of conciliation, with candour in avowing and sincerity in applying it, yet warning his Government that if such a policy was rejected France must prepare for war, since war there would be. " The union of Germany will shortly be achieved—should we accept it ? " he wrote. " In that event, let us not disguise the fact that we welcome it benevolently ; let us reassure Prussia ; she will then detach herself from Russia, and the industrial and commercial condition of Europe will recover from its distress. In the opposite event, let us prepare for war without rest, and let us calculate in advance what assistance Austria can offer us ; let us determine our conduct in such a way as to settle in turn first the Eastern question and then the question of Italy. We shall not be too strong if we are to be victorious on the Rhine. The campaign of 1866 has superabundantly shown the dangers of a struggle waged on both sides of the Alps."

Fearing that events beyond his power to control were forcing France and Prussia into a relationship which might only too easily become one of irreconcilable antagonism, and overcome by the old dread of isolation, Napoleon early in 1869 sought to establish his relations with Austria and Italy on a new and firmer basis. In the previous year, Marshal Niel, the Minister of War, had carried, against a hostile Chamber, a moderate scheme of army reform, increasing the field force and reserve both in numbers and efficiency. Unconvinced that France could safely rely upon her own resources and declining for the moment to fall in with a proposal for reciprocal disarmament which was pressed upon him by Prince Metternich, the Austrian ambassador, and Count Vitzthum, the Saxon envoy, Napoleon now conceived the idea of a triple alliance. He opened negotiations with Austria. To Metternich he proposed an unconditional alliance, and was met with the counter-proposal that the alliance should be of a purely defensive character. A draft treaty on this basis was submitted to the Emperor Francis Joseph in March. It pledged the three Powers to take diplomatic action together on every question calling for decision in the East or West, but Austria reserved the right to declare neutrality should France begin a war against Prussia.

Italy was then invited to join, and here Napoleon's overtures led to an equally indecisive result. Victor Emmanuel's first thought was that a formal alliance with France was neither needful nor politic; it was not needful, because his personal attachment to Napoleon justified him in believing that the Emperor, who had done so much for Italy, would not spoil his own handiwork; it was impolitic, because at that time the national feeling towards France was unfriendly owing to her attitude over the papal question. Five years before, by a treaty of September 15, 1864, Napoleon had undertaken to remove his troops from Rome within two years on condition that the King of Italy would not enter. The Pope was to form a volunteer force, composed of Italian Roman Catholic soldiers, sufficient for the security of the Papal State, but to be used for no other purpose. By the end of 1866 the French withdrawal was completed. Nine months later Garibaldi, gathering together his red-shirts, broke out again and marched on the undefended capital. Napoleon went to the rescue, as in duty bound (November, 1867), and, after ejecting the intruders, replaced the French garrison, an act sorely resented by the Italian nation. Although unable to persuade Napoleon to quit the papal dominion at once, Victor Emmanuel agreed to enter into an alliance of a purely defensive character on condition that it should not be directed against Prussia or German unity, and that in the event of war occurring Italy should be able to remain neutral until the French troops had withdrawn from Rome.

Whittled down in this way at both ends, the alliance lost attraction for Napoleon, for it was evident that it would be impossible to count on either of his friends in the very emergency which it was designed to meet, and he therefore let the matter drop and pigeon-holed the draft for future consideration. In the end the three Sovereigns were satisfied with an exchange of assurances that none of them would conclude an alliance with any other State without the knowledge of his two friends.

It is probable that the unwillingness of the rulers of Austria and Italy to commit themselves further was justified by another proof of Napoleon's uncertain judgment which had been afforded a short time before. This was his ill-considered attempt to assert for France in Belgium, in round-about fashion, a controlling economic influence in place of the political sovereignty which had been refused to him. At his instigation, and with his guarantee, the French Eastern Railway Company in the late autumn of 1868 entered into negotiations with two Belgian railway companies, and simultaneously with a Dutch company, for the purchase of their lines, which were in due course to pass under the control of the State. The negotiations led in December to the conclusion of contracts of sale on very liberal terms. No sooner did the affair become known than the Belgian people, suspecting a new design of annexation, raised a storm of protest, and the Government, reflecting the national sentiment, declared in the Second Chamber, after a vehement debate, that in no circumstances would a transaction so contrary to the public interest and so menacing to the country's political independence be allowed to stand. In the following month the British Government also, jealous for the integrity of the neutrality treaty of 1839, made known its hostility to the contract in firm though unprovocative language. The Belgian companies, however, had made a good bargain, and they were not sorry when the French company held them to the contract. On the last day of January the legal formalities were completed, and both parties to the transaction professed to regard the matter as closed. In the meantime national feeling had become still more deeply stirred, so that when the Ministry invited parliament to arm it with a law, having retroactive effect, making any such alienation of Belgian property dependent upon the assent of the Government, the law was voted by both chambers with practical unanimity. Without delay the obnoxious contract was annulled.

Notwithstanding his rebuffs, Napoleon in 1870 came back to the triple alliance idea in another form. Early in that year the Austrian Archduke Albrecht, the victor of Custozza, visited the South of France, and before returning home stayed for some time in Paris, where he conferred with the heads of the army. In a later conversation with the Emperor he suggested a plan of campaign, to meet the eventuality of a war with Germany, according to which Austrian, French, and Italian armies were in that case to march simultaneously on South Bavaria, Stuttgart, and Munich respectively. Napoleon submitted the plan to his generals, who were impressed more by its defects than its merits. They therefore drew up an alternative scheme, and with this General Lebrun was despatched on a confidential mission to Vienna in June. The Archduke was won over, but the last word rested with the Emperor, of whom Lebrun accordingly sought an audience. The result was the polite but decisive rejection of the carefully prepared design ; it was, the Emperor said, an excellent arrangement from the military standpoint, but altogether inexpedient and impossible from the political. In no circumstances, he informed the envoy, would he promise to take part in a war against Prussia, and it was his wish that his imperial friend might be acquainted with that decision. Not without reason did Lebrun, on returning to Paris, report to Napoleon that as an ally Austria was quite unsatisfactory and not to be relied on, a warning which was not taken to heart. It is significant of Napoleon's uncertain attitude towards his Ministers that he never told them of the purpose or the results of Lebrun's secret mission. Ollivier relates that he only heard of the incident by accident from Lebrun, who was ignorant that he, the head of the Cabinet, had been kept in the dark.

A strong reason at that time indisposed the Austrian Emperor to enter into any arrangement which could be interpreted as a sign of hostility to Prussia, for a distinct improvement had just taken place in the relationships of the Courts of Vienna and Berlin. When in the autumn of 1869 it was decided that the Crown Prince Frederick should represent the King at the opening of the Suez Canal in pursuance of the Khedive's invitation to the crowned heads of Europe, the idea was suggested that his journey to the South would afford a favourable opportunity for greeting the Austrian Emperor in his own capital. An inquiry in Vienna as to the timeliness of such a visit was received with unexpected cordiality. No messenger of peace more tactful or more chivalrous could have been chosen than the man who had to the last deprecated war between Prussia and Austria as a war between brethren. He arrived in Vienna on October 7th, and from the moment of his reception at the railway station by the Emperor to his departure the imperial family did their utmost to give the visit the character of a formal reconciliation. Even Count Beust seemed disposed to bury the hatchet. The meeting was recognized in both countries as the beginning of a new era in their relationships, and this impression was deepened by the friendly intercourse which took place between the Emperor and the Crown Prince during their visit to Egypt. The first-fruits of the *entente* was the Emperor's refusal to enter into any binding engagement with France.

The following year, the year of blood *par excellence* of the nineteenth century, was ushered in by earnests of peace and concord on many sides. One of the German historians of the New Empire, Ottokar Lorenz, admits that "It is justifiable to regard as honestly intended Napoleon's professions of peace at the end of 1869 and the programme of the new Ollivier Ministry." The affairs of France had just before passed into the hands of a Government which was sincerely devoted to peace. In the preceding September France had become a constitutional monarchy, and the political and Ministerial changes entailed promised to make still more decidedly for amicable relationships with Prussia and the rest of Europe. On January 2, 1870, the Ministry of M. Émile Ollivier was formed and the career of the "Liberal Empire" began. There was a reassortment of offices, as a result of which Count Daru was given the portfolio of Foreign Affairs and Lebœuf that of War.

One of Daru's first public acts was a proposal that France should invite Prussia to join in a measure of partial disarmament, as a means of relieving the tension between the two Powers and of convincing the rest of Europe that it was their wish and intention to be good neighbours. The Emperor, though sceptical, was not unwilling, but he would not agree to approach Bismarck direct, convinced that that way lay certain failure. "I do not wish," he said, "to make another direct overture. I tried it in 1863, and it did not succeed. I am not opposed to you trying through the mediation of Lord Clarendon, whom I know to be favourable to the idea." Daru accordingly sounded the British Government on the subject, and was gratified to learn that the "commercial traveller for peace" was willing to "risk a snub" in so good a cause. It was a condition of the overtures that Bismarck was not to be told that they were made at the prompting of the French Government. Clarendon discharged his mission with all his accustomed tact, though without the success for which he had hoped. He put the question before Bismarck in a despatch of February 2nd, addressed to the British ambassador in Berlin, Lord Augustus Loftus, in which, after dwelling upon the pacific character of the French Government and the security of Prussia's position, he appealed to him and the King to lead the way towards the gradual abandonment of the oppressive system of large standing armies, which was becoming a serious source of social discontent and a menace to civilization.

Bismarck received the admonition—for such, for all its amiability, Lord Clarendon's appeal was—in good part, and duly returned a courteous reply. This was a regretful refusal to consider the proposal or even place it before the King, on the ground of the hopelessness of persuading him to agree to a course which was inconsistent with Prussia's difficult geographical position and her uncertain relationships with the Powers able to do her evil. Daru regarded it as a gain that Bismarck should have been willing to discuss a topic so alien to his sympathies, and begged Clarendon not to think himself beaten and not to be discouraged, promising that he would shortly give him the opportunity of returning to the charge. In the meantime, Daru declared that he would set an example by reducing the annual levies by 10,000, implying, on the basis of nine years' service, an eventual reduction of 90,000 men.

On March 9th, in a second eloquent letter, Clarendon "fired another shot at Bismarck," though this time with far less hope of effect. The old reasons were repeated in greater detail, but he clinched his case for disarmament by an argument which must have sounded strange in Berlin.

"Count Bismarck will admit," he wrote, "and I am sure that a statesman so liberal and far-sighted will admit without regret, that the people everywhere are claiming and must obtain a larger share in the administration of their own affairs, and that in proportion as they do so the chances of causeless wars will diminish. The people well understand the horrors of war and that they and not their rulers are the real sufferers; they equally understand and will daily become more impatient of the taxation for costly preparations for war which in themselves endanger peace, and I believe that there is at this moment no surer road to solid popularity for a Government than attending to the wants and wishes of the people on the subject of disarmament."[1]

The passage is reproduced not because its force was seriously discounted by the fact that Clarendon's appeal did not imply that his own country was prepared to emulate Prussia in well-doing, though the expenditure of Great Britain on armaments was at that time more than three times that of Prussia, and more than twice that of the entire North German Confederation, but as an illustration of the failure of a very wise statesman to understand that the leading Minister of a military State like Prussia could not possibly be influenced by or appreciate a line of reasoning well suited to the British House of Commons. Nevertheless, at Clarendon's urgent wish, the question this time went direct to the King, who would not hear of disarmament in any form or degree. To the British ambassador Bismarck brusquely hinted that Clarendon's views were those of "a cool friend," were

[1] "Lord Lyons, a Record of British Diplomacy," vol. i., pp. 269, 270.

insular, and made no allowance for Germany's special danger; what would Clarendon say, he asked, if he were told that the peace of the world would be furthered if only Great Britain would cut down her inordinate naval estimates?[1] From that time no more was heard of reciprocal disarmament.

Although Count Daru's proposal had failed, the intentions behind it were sincere; through him Napoleon had given the most convincing proof at his command of pacific intentions. To emphasize this attitude and the friendly disposition of his Government towards Prussia, Ollivier in March sent home a German journalist who visited him with the reassuring message, "There exists no German question at the present time."

Various constitutional changes were proposed in France at this time with the object of bringing the machinery of government into sympathy with the democratic spirit which the new Cabinet represented and Napoleon endorsed. Personal government was to cease, yet not to be superseded by a parliamentary absolutism, for above both the Emperor and parliament the collective will of the nation, as expressed by the *plébiscite* or *referendum*, was henceforth to be supreme. These changes were submitted to a national vote on May 8th. "France desires liberty, but liberty with order," the Emperor had said to the legislature just before. "For order I am responsible. Help me, gentlemen, to endow her with liberty." The substantial issue put to the nation was, Should France henceforth be a liberalized constitutional monarchy? The actual reference upon which a vote was to be taken ran as follows:

"The nation approves the Liberal reforms effected in the constitution since 1860 by the Emperor in conjunction with the legislature and ratifies the resolution of the Senate (*senatus-consultum*) of April 20, 1870."

This resolution of the Senate, as drawn up by Ollivier on the direction of Napoleon, transferred from that body to a *plébiscite* of the nation, to be ordered in every instance by the Emperor, all future amendments of the constitution; it established the Emperor in the exercise of his existing powers as head of the Government, such as the supreme command of the army, the appointment of Ministers, State officials, and members of the Senate, and the right to decide questions of war and peace,

[1] Eight years before (May 8, 1862) Mr. Disraeli, in a speech in the House of Commons, had coined the phrase "bloated armaments," wherewith to emphasize the excessive expenditure of successive British Governments on fleets and armies.

and confirmed the joint powers of the Emperor, the Senate, and the Chamber in regard to legislation.

In their manifestos both the Emperor and the Ministry appealed to the nation in the cause of order, liberty, the security of the Empire, and the maintenance of the hereditary monarchy. " In 1852," ran the manifesto of the Ministers, " the Emperor sought power from the nation in order to secure order ; in 1870 he seeks from it power in order to establish freedom. You are not voting upon the existence of the Empire, but only upon its development on Liberal principles. It is essential to assure our country a tranquil future, so that on the throne as in the poorest hut the son may succeed his father in peace."

The voting was an emphatic approval of the new order and of the men who had introduced it. All the forces of reaction and revolution were whipped up ; Victor Hugo appealed against the Government theatrically in the name of " the citizens of the assassinated republic " ; yet nearly seven and a half million electors voted with yea and only one and a half million with nay. It was a clear and convincing people's vote for a continuance of the even, tranquil, and satisfactory course which national events had taken for so many years. It was significant that there was a majority against the Emperor and the Empire only in the two excitable departments of the Seine (Paris) and the Bouches-du-Rhone (Marseilles), and that the rural population in particular strongly pronounced for the existing *status.* To Napoleon the result of the *plébiscite* was specially gratifying. He had at that time ruled for eighteen years, and he had on the whole ruled well and wisely. Under his government France had prospered greatly ; industry and commerce had expanded ; labour had won a larger reward ; the arts and sciences had received fostering care ; his whole energies had been concentrated upon the development of the nation's material and spiritual resources, and rich fruits had been harvested in every direction. The choice of the French nation in 1852 seemed to have been abundantly justified, and in May, 1870, so far as human foresight could tell, the future of the Bonaparte dynasty was assured. In a word, the Empire seemed firmly established, and it still was peace.

Several changes were made in the Government, of which the effect was to strengthen Ollivier and the Liberal spirit. Count Daru left the Foreign Office, ostensibly on the question of the *plébiscite.* The real reason was that his views on the German question had made difficult his position side by side with Ollivier. He contended that " unity by the fusion of North and South, by what manner soever it might be brought about, even by the will of the populations, would be a disturbance of equilibrium, menacing to our security and one which we should have a right to oppose." Ollivier, on the contrary, " only disapproved of unity brought about violently, without, however, regarding it as a *casus belli*, and I did not believe that my country had a right to forbid a neighbouring nation to order its affairs as seemed to it right." [1] When Daru went, Ollivier himself wished to take the Foreign Office, but Napoleon urged him to concentrate his attention on home affairs, and he agreed. " Ah," he reflected in later years, " if I had known what a plot was brewing ! "

The vacant portfolio was offered to the Duc de Gramont, then ambassador at Vienna, a nobleman of distinction, gifted with all the virtues, yet also not free from the limitations, of his class, and now a man of ripe years. Ollivier describes him as fascinating, witty, in intercourse equable and agreeable, prudent in general, given to viewing affairs in a large way, and impatient of detail—the true type, he says, of the old French aristocrat. Other authorities describe him as quick of imagination, sometimes too quick of decision, and by nature passionate and fiery. The Earl of Malmesbury says he was " vain and impetuous." Count Beust, who knew Gramont intimately, says that " he was in truth a *preux chevalier*, and his one fault was that he was too optimistic and too readily believed in that which he wished to be true." Gramont's diplomatic experience had been rich and varied. As Napoleon's ambassador to Turin and Rome he had witnessed the shepherding of Italy into the national fold by Piedmont, and as his representative at the Court of Vienna he had lived through the events which led to the eclipse of Austria by Prussia. No man in the French diplomatic service was more in touch with the questions then vital to Central and Western Europe. Hitherto he had played no part in party life, and Napoleon regarded it as an objection to his appointment that he had never been a member of either of the Chambers.

If, however, he entered the Cabinet unbound by public acts, all the more firmly was he bound by political prejudices. His special handicap, which he shared with predecessors like Drouyn de Lhuys, Moustier, and Daru, was the idea that for Prussia to attempt to extend her influence beyond the Main would be an

[1] *L'Empire Libéral*, vol. xiii., p. 83.

act of aggression to which France could not be indifferent. He regarded the relationship between the two Powers as fated to grow worse, and he had for some time spoken of war with Prussia as inevitable. Ollivier obtained his promise that he would keep his anti-Prussian bias in the background and loyally carry out the conciliatory policy of the Ministry, and he generously admits that the Duke joined him with a sincere desire and intention to work for the maintenance of peace. Nevertheless, it was not good for France that Gramont's known hostility to Prussia made him *persona gratissima* to the military and clerical parties.

On the last day of June Ollivier declared in the *Corps Législatif* that peace had never been so sure as at that time. Replying to an appeal from Thiers for the pursuance of a consistent policy of conciliation—" If we wish to promote peace," said the eloquent tribune, " we must first cultivate a love of peace and then be very strong"—the Premier affirmed: " The Government has no anxiety of any kind. At no time was the maintenance of peace more assured than now. Wherever one looks no question can be discerned which is capable of creating danger. All the Cabinets understand the urgency of respect for treaties, and particularly of two treaties on which the peace of Europe rests, the Treaty of Paris of 1856, which secures peace for the East, and the Treaty of Prague, of 1866, which secures peace for Germany."

When in that month the War Minister introduced the army estimates for 1871, he announced a reduction of 10,000 in the levy of new men, as Count Daru had promised earlier in the year. Recalling later the Government's action, M. Blondeau, director of the administrative services at the Ministry of War, stated that when in May he asked for a certain vote the Minister made a " lively scene," and declared that " since the *plébiscite* the Government was absolutely bent on peace and there was no anticipation of war." As with the Government, so with the Emperor personally. The Earl of Malmesbury relates a conversation which he had in Paris with Napoleon on May 19th, in which the Emperor " observed that Europe appeared to be tranquil," and he comments : " It was evident to me that at that moment he had no idea of the coming hurricane which suddenly broke out in the first week of June."

In Germany the outlook seemed to be no less tranquil. The States north of the Main had settled down under the new Confederation, and Prussia and Saxony in particular were applying their energies to the advancement of commerce and industry; while the States of the South, far from sympathizing with an aggressive policy, were becoming restive under the military and financial burden already imposed upon them by the alliances, and there had been debates in the Bavarian and Würtemberg Diets on the advantages of a militia as compared with a too costly standing army.

In his speech from the throne made at the opening of the North German Diet on February 14th, the King of Prussia, recalling his hopes of a year before, that "the wishes of the nations and the needs of civilization" would be met by the preservation of peace, said: "It does my heart good to be able to announce to-day that my confidence has been completely justified. Among the Governments, as among the nations of the modern world, the conviction is making triumphant progress that it is the right and duty of every political commonwealth to cultivate public welfare, liberty, and justice independently within its own borders, and that the defensive forces of every country should be used only for the protection of its own independence and not the violation of the independence of other nations." In the Prussian Lower House just before the Radical leader, Dr. Virchow, little suspecting what had been going on behind the scenes, had proposed a measure of disarmament, on the ground that "there seldom was a time when there was so little reason for States to confront each other fully armed." The proposal was rejected, but its discussion showed that the thoughts of politicians were of peace and not of war.

In the midst of an unparalleled calm, a sudden thunderclap shook the skies. There was no immediate storm, but it was a sign that the air was charged with electricity and that a storm was not far distant.

The story of the Hohenzollern candidature for the Spanish throne and of its sequel, the Ems telegram, has been told a hundred times, yet to pass over events so genetic in a history of the war of 1870 would be like ignoring Adam and Eve in a history of mankind. For while other incidents may have been the occasion of the war, it was the candidature episode and it alone that made war possible.

After a long series of sporadic disturbances a real revolution was carried out in Spain in September, 1868, and Queen Isabella II was deposed. A limited monarchy was proclaimed, and pending the choice of a new ruler a provisional Government was formed, with Marshal Serrano as Regent and Marshal Prim as Minister of War but later as Minister-President. In the following February the Cortes were summoned to decide on the new form of government. The assembly proved to be monarchist, like the Ministry, and it was the general feeling that the monarchy should continue but with a new dynasty. The discovery of a suitable successor proved difficult. The throne was offered to the Duke of Edinburgh, but Queen Victoria and her Ministers rejected the idea. Inquiries were made and invitations issued in other directions, but with the same result, for a throne so insecure offered many risks and few attractions. Meanwhile, the republican party was active and making progress, and it soon became apparent that unless a candidate were obtained for the throne speedily there would be no throne left to fill.

Then it was that the idea of approaching a Roman Catholic Prussian Prince in the person of Prince Leopold, a son of Prince Charles Anthony of Hohenzollern-Sigmaringen, occurred, or was suggested, to the royalist party in Madrid.[1] Prince Leopold had been mentioned in Madrid amongst others as an eligible candidate as early as October, 1868, and in the following February his name was publicly advocated by the Councillor of State and deputy Don Salazar of Mazarredo. Between these dates Prince Anthony had made known his opinion that France would never assent to the elevation of a Hohenzollern to the Spanish throne, and had urged that Napoleon's assent should first be obtained. To this course Prim was opposed, and Bismarck, who already had a hand in the scheme, was of the same mind.

In March, 1869, Señor Rancès, the Spanish ambassador to Vienna, visited Berlin for several days and was repeatedly closeted with the King and with Bismarck, who had been quick to recognize the new Spanish Government. Count Benedetti, connecting this visit with the active propagandism which was being made on Prince Leopold's behalf, duly reported the episode to his Government, and was directed to seek assurances that the choice of a Hohenzollern would not be encouraged in Berlin. "The French nation," Napoleon declared, "would never tolerate it, and it must be prevented." Bismarck was away from Berlin at the time, but in his absence Herr von Thile, the Under-Secre-

[1] The point is one of minor interest only, but three sons of Prince Anthony appear to have been concerned in the candidature at different stages of the controversy, viz. Princes Leopold (the eldest), Frederick (the youngest), and Charles (then Prince of Roumania), though it was Prince Leopold who came into public prominence.

tary of State for Foreign Affairs, assured Benedetti on his word of honour that there had been no talk of Prince Leopold as a candidate, that there was no question, and could be no question, of such a choice, and that in his conversations with the Spanish ambassador Bismarck had discussed only the general political affairs of Spain. In April the crown was offered in turn to King Ferdinand of Portugal and Duke Amadeo of Aosta, second son of the King of Italy, and by both was refused. In his desire to divert attention from the only three States able to give to Spain a Roman Catholic Prince of suitable rank, Austria, Bavaria, and Prussia, Napoleon now favoured the recall of Isabella.

In May, however, Prince Anthony was formally sounded as to his willingness to allow his son to accept an invitation, and although he at first declined, it looked as though the contingency feared by Napoleon had come dangerously near. Once more Benedetti was instructed to let Bismarck plainly understand the Emperor's objection to the Spanish crown passing into the hands of a Prussian Prince. Bismarck answered that he had no reason to discuss the question, since the King would in any event disapprove of Prince Leopold's candidature, even if the Cortes invited it, and, moreover, both father and son were against acceptance. Encouraged to frankness by this apparent disclaimer, Benedetti thereupon warned Bismarck that the Emperor was watching the incident with great concern, for it had for France "an interest of the first order."

This warning was given as early as May 11, 1869, and it is of vital importance for the study of later developments, since there can be little doubt that it had a sinister effect upon Bismarck's course of action. Recognizing with what jealousy and hostility Napoleon regarded the idea of a Hohenzollern ruler in Spain, he saw and seized, as he confessed later, the chance of quarrelling with France for which he had been waiting. Let him only succeed in playing his cards with decent skill, and he was sure that the warning would become a threat and the threat lead to actual rupture. As his secretary, Busch, commenting upon the incident, expresses it, Bismarck now "accommodated himself to the situation."

Neither Benedetti nor Napoleon was convinced by the second disclaimer. The reply had been evasive, justifying the suspicion that there were concealed designs behind. In his report to his Government the ambassador wrote:

"If one could unconditionally believe him (Bismarck), everything would be reassuring, but judging by experience, I am disposed to believe that he has not revealed to me his real thoughts. I remarked to him, therefore, that the Prince could not comply with the wish of the Cortes without the King's consent, so that the King would need to prescribe the terms of his decision. Bismarck admitted this, but instead of assuring me that the King was determined in all circumstances to recommend refusal, he returned to his earlier remark that owing to the dangers which would surround the new Sovereign the King would be bound to dissuade the Prince from embarking upon such an adventure. 'Moreover,' he added, 'who knows whether an invitation will come at all or whether so ambitious a man as General Prim will not in the end keep the place for himself ?' He carefully avoided giving me a declaration that the King would in no case permit the Prince to accept the crown, while Thile had assured me of this on his word of honour. It appears, therefore, that Bismarck intends to reserve for the King full liberty of action in any event."

Bismarck may honestly have doubted at that stage whether Prince Leopold would really have a chance of sitting upon the Spanish throne. What is certain—though Benedetti did not then know it—is that he was all the time doing his utmost to further his candidature. It was a species of diplomacy in which he was a practised hand, for he had engaged in it with success only three years before (March, 1866) when he had helped to seat another son of the same Prince on the throne of Roumania, vacant likewise owing to a revolution. In that case it was the right of the Powers to choose a successor, but without giving them time to confer he had urged Prince Charles of Hohenzollern to hurry to Bucharest, not seeking the King's permission, though an officer, and there offer himself for election. The advice was followed, and the Prince was received with acclamations and duly elected on April 20th. Thereupon Bismarck had professed to the ambassadors in Berlin his painful surprise that such an improper proceeding had taken place, and had promised that Prussia would work with the other Powers in any action which they might think fit to take. The Powers duly protested, but Prince Charles was not disturbed, and though his first act had been to call for Prussian officers to instruct his army, his government had succeeded beyond expectations. The fact that the first Hohenzollern candidature had prospered may well have suggested to Bismarck a second venture of the same kind.

For a time events moved slowly in Madrid, though Bismarck's

agents were working there in Prince Leopold's behalf. In the summer a new constitution was settled, and Serrano was confirmed in the regency. The restlessness of the Carlist and republican parties, however, made it necessary to find an acceptable King soon if the monarchy was to be preserved. In September, therefore, a Spanish envoy, Salazar, accompanied by Baron von Werthern, the Prussian envoy at Munich, who played an important part in the candidature drama behind the scenes, waited on Prince Anthony in Switzerland in order to repeat the invitation. Whatever his private wishes in the matter may have been, the Prince prudently showed little enthusiasm, and the only promise he would give was that he might agree to the candidature on being assured by the Spanish Government that his son's election would be acceptable not only to the Spanish nation but to the Emperor Napoleon and to the King of Prussia, as the head of the Hohenzollern house.

Overtures in other directions proving still unsuccessful, Salazar was sent to Germany on the same mission in February, 1870, bearing letters from the Regent both to the King and Bismarck. On the way to Berlin he called on Prince Anthony at his home in Düsseldorf. It was now that the question seriously entered the sphere of Prussian politics. There is no reason to doubt that the King up to this time, and perhaps later, disapproved, or at least did not approve, of the candidature. On hearing now, for the first time, of the project which was brewing, he wrote to Bismarck on February 26th that the announcement was like "a bolt from the blue," declared that he had "not the faintest suspicion" of it, and added: "As you have received details from the Prince, we must confer on the matter, but I am absolutely against it." Having no wish to interfere in a matter so delicate, he now declined to receive the Spanish envoy. All the more cordial, however, was the reception given to Salazar by Bismarck.

The result was that on March 15th a Hohenzollern family council was held on the question. Of this meeting Prince Anthony wrote at the time to his son Prince Charles of Roumania that the King presided, and there were also present "the Crown Prince, we two (Princes Anthony and his son Leopold), Bismarck, Moltke, Roon, Schleinitz, Thile, and Delbrück." Bismarck is concerned to make the point that the council had not a Ministerial character, and leaves it to be concluded that at most a dinner conversation took place. But at least the King's political advisers were well represented, and a formal decision was taken. "The council," Prince Anthony continued, "resolved unanimously in favour of acceptance, which means the performance of a patriotic Prussian duty. After a great struggle Leopold refused. As they want, above all things, in Spain a Catholic Hohenzollern, I proposed Fritz."[1] For a time the negotiations advanced no further.

Seeing that the King still had scruples, Bismarck now took the question more decidedly into his own hands, for he had none. In the spring of 1870 began a series of clandestine negotiations, unknown to the King, carried on between his Minister—partly through two intermediaries—and Prim. His principal agent was Lothar Bucher, a Foreign Office official, who performed much secret service for his chief, and was in later years received into his most intimate companionship, and with him was Major von Versen, an officer of the General Staff. A German historian regrets that more light has not been thrown upon these negotiations. Bucher kept his secrets well, however, and no connected story of his journeys to Madrid and his doings there ever left his pen. Bismarck's *famulus* Busch says the "chief" sent Bucher to the Spanish capital before Easter, with an encouraging letter to Prim, while at home he was plying Prince Anthony with arguments and entreaties to persuade his son to stand.[2] The more, in fact, the Spanish emissaries were discouraged by their efforts in Germany, the more did Bismarck urge Prim and his colleagues in Spain to persist in the Hohenzollern candidature. A gleam is thrown upon dark places by the diary of these feverish days kept by Bismarck's secretary, Abeken. Abeken's letters and notes show that formal negotiations were proceeding between the Minister and Madrid at least from the beginning of May, and that early in June telegrams were passing every day. Then by mischance the unauthorized mission appears to have leaked out, and when the King heard of it he was deeply mortified. Bismarck tried to disclaim underhand work, but the effort was not convincing. On June 20th we find him writing to Abeken, who enjoyed the royal confidence in a high degree, begging him in abject terms to do his best to pacify the King.

[1] *Aus dem Leben König Karls von Rumänien*, vol. ii., p. 72.

[2] "In order to determine the hesitating Prince," Busch writes, "Bismarck sent Lothar Bucher and Major of the General Staff Knorr von Versen on April 3rd to Spain. They were very friendly received there, and sent home favourable reports" (*Tagebuchblätter*, vol. i., p. 30). After Bucher's death on October 12, 1892, his brother, in the course of some recollections published in *Die Grenzboten* (December 1, 1892), recorded the fact that this trusty agent was also sent to Sigmaringen to be the Prince of Hohenzollern's adviser on Bismarck's behalf.

"I beg you to explain the following to his Majesty," he wrote. "I have never carried on any international negotiations without his Majesty's knowledge or consent, nor shall I ever do so. Bucher did not transact anything in Spain, but carried a personal message which I was obliged to give Marshal Prim in reply to a private letter and telegram, the contents of which were known to His Majesty. I did not wish to write, lest my letter should be submitted to the Spanish Parliament, and be there discussed, and I wished it to be as far as possible transmitted in such a way as not to create *by our reserve* an unpleasant impression in Spain. It could only be settled by word of mouth and was difficult to put in writing, and Bucher is one of the few men who know the circumstances and personalities on both sides of the Pyrenees. The answer only amounted to this: that the King's Government cannot undertake to bring influence to bear on the decision of the hereditary Prince, either for or against acceptance, and must therefore let Spain await the Prince's decision. That I did not write, but sent a reply through Bucher, was partly to avoid the harshness which a written answer might convey, and partly, as I said, as a precautionary measure against publicity."

So lame an apology was hardly worthy of a man of Bismarck's resource, but its very transparency appears to have disarmed the King's resentment, for Abeken was soon able to reply that all was again as before. There is no doubt that for once in a way Bismarck had a very bad conscience, not because he had done wrong, but because he had been found out. Only on that supposition is the pique revealed by the closing sentences of the letter comprehensible: "I have withdrawn from the affair, and do not wish to have anything more to do with it. It has caused me work and vexation enough." Perhaps never in the course of his public career, before or after, did Bismarck compromise himself more completely, though he attained his end. Bearing these facts in mind, it is difficult to understand Bismarck's statement to Count Bernstorff at a later date (July 18th) that he "was casually informed in confidence of the Spanish offer by a private person concerned in the negotiations," unless, indeed, the private person was Bucher, his agent.

Nearly two years before, Lord Clarendon, whose political acumen was rated highly in Berlin, had warned the King and Moltke in conversation of the danger of any action which might provoke France, assuring them that if a challenge were offered to him Napoleon would be compelled by the force of military and public opinion to accept it, and that for his own safety he would make war.[1] How Bismarck used this warning—for it cannot have failed to reach his ears—is told by Busch. "Bismarck's plan," he writes of the candidature scheme at this stage, after admitting it to have been a ruse to entrap the French, "had succeeded, unless in the eleventh hour a new impediment should prevent the trap from shutting, i.e. unless the King, owing to his indecisive manner, failed him and allowed the favourable moment to slip by."

But the King, however much he may have been displeased by the underhand manner in which his Minister had been acting, no longer objected to the candidature itself, and he must have given his formal consent before June 22nd, since on that date Abeken, who was with him at Ems, wrote: "The King is satisfied that the hereditary Prince will be acceptable to the Spanish army owing to his having fought in the campaign of 1866." To the threadbare pretence, to which even Sybel gives the support of his authority, that the candidature was a private matter between the Prince and his suitors, another German historian, Hans Delbrück, gives the sufficient answer: "It is certain that no Hohenzollern Prince would have taken such a resolution without carefully inquiring into and taking full account of the royal wishes."

Efforts were to be made to keep the matter quiet for a time, but the fateful choice soon became known. Asked by Prim on July 2nd how the Emperor would receive it, the French ambassador in Madrid answered that the Spanish Government could not have taken a graver step, since it was for Napoleon a humiliation and for the French nation a challenge. Prim excused himself and his Government by the plea that they had been driven to the Hohenzollern as a last resort. The crown had gone abegging long enough, and it was high time to come to a decision. "If we had not seized this opportunity," he said, "it is certain that we should have had either Montpensier or the republic, which I hate like hell." Two days later the Council of Ministers officially adopted the Prince as their candidate, and the formal election was fixed for July 20th.

The candidature proposal, as the Empress Eugénie said at the time, "exploded like a bomb, without warning." So carefully had the secret been kept to the last, that even the Spanish

[1] Letters of Lord Lyons, October 13 and 20, 1868, quoted in *Lord Lyons: a Record of British Diplomacy*, vol. i., pp. 202–3.

ambassador in Paris, Don Sallustio Olozaga, had been unaware of the plot until the Duc de Gramont told him of it on July 4th. The day before the Minister had already telegraphed to the *chargé d'affaires* in Berlin (Benedetti was at Wildbad) expressing the "hope that the Prussian Government was foreign to this intrigue," but directing him to intimate to the Foreign Minister that the "regrettable incident" had created a bad impression in France. To the British ambassador in Paris he had declared at once that rather than see a Hohenzollern upon the throne of Spain he would have France fight both that country and Prussia.

Bismarck was absent from the capital, but his deputy at the Foreign Office, Herr von Thile, the same who was at the council of March 15th, assured the French *chargé d'affaires* that he knew nothing, and that the Government knew nothing, of the incident, which "did not exist for them." Writing of this disclaimer, Bismarck says in his *Recollections*: "The first demands of the French respecting the candidature . . . had been presented on July 4th, and answered by our Foreign Office evasively, though in accordance with the truth—that the *Ministry* (Bismarck italicizes the word) knew nothing about the matter." It was the common fiction of social life translated into diplomatic intercourse: "Madame is not at home," while all the time madame is looking out of the window. Of course the Ministry knew nothing, for the head of the Ministry had not yet formally taken his colleagues into his confidence.

Events of epoch-making moment were in hurried progress, yet so little did the British Foreign Office or its intelligence departments know of or appreciate them, even now, that Lord Granville, who had become Foreign Secretary on Lord Clarendon's death [1] at the end of June, was welcomed by a permanent Under-Secretary on July 5th with the extraordinary assurance that he had never known "so great a lull in foreign affairs," and that "the aspect of Europe was unusually peaceful." Yet upon this very day the British Minister at Madrid, Mr. Layard, telegraphed to Lord Granville the Spanish Cabinet's fateful decision.

France may have exaggerated the danger of a plot which would have put a Prussian Prince, a relative of the Sovereign,

[1] Meeting a daughter of Lord Clarendon in 1871, Bismarck startled her with the remark: "Never in my life was I more glad to hear of anything than I was to hear of your father's death." Perceiving the surprise he had caused, he immediately added: "What I mean is that if your father had lived he would have prevented the war" (*Life and Letters of the Fourth Earl of Clarendon*, by Maxwell, vol. ii., p. 366).

upon the throne of a neighbouring State, whose friendship was necessary to her own safety, though of that she was entitled to judge for herself. Nevertheless, that the candidature was mainly promoted on the Prussian side from political reasons cannot be doubted. Prince Anthony wrote at this time: "Bismarck wishes acceptance from dynastic and political motives, but the King only wishes it if Leopold desires it of his own free will." Whatever the King may have thought, his Minister certainly had very definite ideas of the advantages to be derived from the presence of a Prussian officer upon the throne of Spain. Busch, who knew his patron inside and out, records that Bismarck hoped by this move to make certain of having in the rear of France a friendly State, which, when the inevitable clash came, would "compel France to leave part of her forces behind to cover the uncertain neighbour in the South-west." Such a calculation was entirely in the spirit of Bismarck's policy towards France. Already he had made sure of Russia in the East; he had for several years been busily cultivating the friendship of Austria and Italy in the South, as events proved with consequences disappointing to France; and he was at this moment angling for an ally in British waters. Let Spain be secured, and France would be effectively isolated. The policy of "encirclement," later the cause of so much controversy, had thus been introduced in European politics before the German Empire was established.

In the meantime, Bismarck had set to work the sedulous Busch, who at his inspiration was carrying on a busy Press campaign, of which the object was to convince the country and Europe that France and not Prussia was really at the bottom of the Hohenzollern candidature. The story was even circulated in the newspapers that the French Government had been "aware of the candidature of the Prince of Hohenzollern for months past, that they carefully promoted it, and foolishly imagined that it would serve as a means of isolating Prussia and creating a division in Germany." [1]

Already Paris, always nervous and overstrung, had lashed herself into fury over the deception perpetrated by the truculent Prussian, and the demand was addressed to the Government from all sides that it should require from Berlin the prompt disclaimer of a proceeding which was at once an insult and a danger to France. "Un échec," M. Ollivier had said to Lord Lyons

[1] Busch gives an account of this newspaper propagandism in his *Tagebuchblätter*, vol. i., pp. 31–54.

in January, "c'est la guerre!" Little did French statesmen know how completely they had fallen into the very mood favourable to Bismarck's designs. And now, in a situation which called for the exercise of the greatest caution and circumspection, the Duc de Gramont impetuously blundered into a course of action which placed him at the mercy of his far nimbler and more calculating antagonist. Instead of keeping the question in the channels of diplomacy, he at once took it to the tribune, and instead of appealing to reason he adopted the surest means of stirring up passion.

On July 5th a Council of Ministers, meeting under the presidency of the Emperor, adopted a manifesto, which was read in the *Corps Législatif* on the following day. The Duc de Gramont enjoys the credit of having drafted this document, though Ollivier claims to have given definiteness and vigour to its final form. After an appeal to the good-will of the Spanish Parliament and people, towards whom France had ever shown a friendly disposition, the declaration added:

"We do not believe that respect for the rights of a neighbouring people requires us to tolerate that a foreign Power, in placing one of its Princes on the throne of Charles V, shall disturb to our prejudice the existing equilibrium in Europe, and imperil the interests and the honour of France. We firmly hope that that eventuality will not arise. In order to prevent it we count at once on the wisdom of the German people and the friendship of the Spanish people."

Had the Duke stopped there, it is possible that no harm would have been done. There occurred at this point, however, one of those tempting ejaculations which so often decoy impetuous orators from the path of discretion. For M. G. de Cassagnac now cried out: "And upon our resolution!" Thereupon the Duke continued, as if taking his cue from the suggestion conveyed in these words:

"If it were otherwise, strong in your support, gentlemen, and that of the nation ('It would not fail you,' cried another encouraging voice), we should know how to do our duty without hesitation and without weakness."

So unlike in temper were these words to those which had preceded, that it seems incredible that they formed part of the considered statement. The theory is hazarded that Gramont went beyond his brief, and that the closing menace was a disastrous *impromptu*, suggested by the inflammatory interruptions noted, a response to the psychic influences which surged upon the speaker and for the moment unbalanced his judgment. Salvoes of applause followed the defiant declaration, which reflected so faithfully the mind and temper of the Chamber, of Paris, if not of France.[1] It was in relation to this utterance that Bismarck coined that wise little maxim, "If you want to make a bargain, never threaten." For the speech which elated Paris created corresponding feelings of resentment and anger in Berlin, and made more difficult the diplomatic negotiations which should rather have preceded than followed it.

Perhaps the whole history of constitutional government contains no more lamentable instance of a representative Executive allowing itself to be driven headlong into warlike measures by frantic incitements from the tribune and the street. Writing at a later date, every leading actor in the sorry tragedy—Gramont, Ollivier, Thiers, Benedetti—admitted that Paris for the time went out of her mind. The newspapers did their best to inflame public opinion. With few exceptions they vehemently begged the Government not to moderate its attitude, for only on that condition would an undivided nation be behind it. "The Caudine forks are ready for the Prussians," wrote the *Pays*. "They will have to stoop and pass beneath them vanquished and disarmed if they do not dare to enter the struggle, the issue of which is not doubtful. Our war-cry has as yet elicited no reply. The echoes of the German Rhine are still dumb. If Prussia had used the language spoken by France, we should have been on the march long ago."

The British Government all the time was urging moderation, convinced that France was in the wrong and was putting herself more in the wrong every day. Now, at the Emperor's suggestion, it agreed to use its influence with Berlin, with a view to the simple withdrawal by the Prince of Hohenzollern of his candidature. That seemed the obvious solution of the difficulty, and at this stage the Duc de Gramont asked and wanted no more.[2] The

[1] Ollivier records that on taking his place in the Chamber he said to the deputy Cochery: "You will be satisfied with our declaration; it is pacific, although very explicit." But, however explicit it may have been, the declaration as made was certainly not pacific. Directly it had been read, one of the deputies exclaimed: "It is a declaration of war!" while another added: "It is war already declared!" (*L'Empire Libéral*, vol. xiv., p. 112).

[2] Lord Lyons wrote to the British Foreign Secretary on July 10th: "M. de Gramont told me that I might report to your Lordship (Granville) that if the Prince of Hohenzollern should now, on the advice of the King of Prussia, withdraw his acceptance of the crown, the whole affair would be at an end."

effort was made, but the threat of July 6th rankled in Bismarck's mind, and it was not received with cordiality.

Hitherto not only English opinion but European opinion generally had been decidedly against the choice of the Spanish Cortes, and the Governments of most of the Great Powers were earnestly advising Prussia to show regard for French susceptibilities. At the same time no one defended the Duc de Gramont's rash outburst. Even Count Beust wrote to the Austrian ambassador in Paris on July 11th:

"It is said that France is not the aggressor, and that unless Prussia withdraws the Hohenzollern candidature she will be guilty of provoking war. Let me speak quite frankly. If war should be inevitable, it will be due above all to the attitude assumed by France from the very inception of the difficulty. Her first announcements do not in the least partake of a diplomatic character, but practically constitute a declaration of war against Prussia, couched in terms that have aroused amazement throughout Europe and have justified the conviction that she had made up her mind beforehand to have war at any price."

All this time the Chancellery of Berlin had remained silent, awaiting developments. Events had been set in motion, and it remained to be seen whereto they would grow, and to act accordingly. It was the height of the parliamentary recess, the time of *villeggiatura*, and the capital was empty. The King was recruiting his health at Ems, whither he had gone on June 20th; Bismarck was nursing his nerves at Varzin, the ancestral Tusculum; the rest of the Ministers were at the sea or in the mountains. The time had been singularly opportune for the development of a conspiracy whose success from the Prussian standpoint depended largely upon the creation of the impression that the Government knew nothing about it. After the Duc de Gramont's statement in the *Corps Législatif*, Bismarck had, indeed, written to the German ambassadors in Europe disowning on the part of his Government any responsibility for or knowledge of the candidature negotiations, protesting against the Duke's attack as closing the door to a friendly discussion of the question, and giving due warning that Germany would be prepared to meet any attack from France.

In the meantime French public opinion was more and more being swept into the dangerous swirl of passion, inflamed by injured pride and wounded sensibilities, yet totally unable to recognize that any corresponding sentiment could exist in Germany. Benedetti was still at Wildbad, and there the Duc de Gramont telegraphed on July 7th, directing him to go to Ems, in order to enter into personal relationships with the King. As the temper of the nation, and especially of Paris, had risen, the Duke's conditions had become harder. "The only thing that will satisfy us and prevent war," he now wrote, "is that the royal Government shall disapprove of the candidature of the Prince and require its withdrawal. The matter is urgent, for in the event of an unsatisfactory answer we must anticipate our opponent and begin the movement of troops to-morrow. Should you succeed in persuading the King to revoke his approval of the candidature, it will be an enormous success. If not, it would be war. . . . Therefore, no circumlocution, and no delays! No mission was more important; that you may succeed is my most ardent wish." In a postscript the Duke warned Benedetti against being satisfied with a mere promise that the King would abandon the Prince to his fate and be neutral whatever happened; he must be required to "put right the situation which he had helped to create." Even now, however, the most that the Duke asked was the revocation by the King of his approval.

The King gave Benedetti an audience on July 9th, and after he had protested against the terms and tone of Gramont's declaration in the French Chamber he discussed the question with him affably. He said that he had acted in the matter not as King but as head of his family, so that the candidature was not to be regarded as an affair of State. Benedetti was unable to understand how a Sovereign could thus divide his personality into two parts, nor was the claim compatible with the fact that the King was the head of the Hohenzollern family in virtue of his sovereignty and that his chief Minister and generals had been required to attend the conference at which his approval of the candidature had been given. Nevertheless, while insisting that the Prince had accepted the candidature on his own responsibility, and that he himself had not been in a position to forbid it, the King gave the ambassador reason to hope that if in view of the irritation which had been caused in France the Prince and his father, with whom he was even then in communication, were disposed to withdraw, he would approve their decision. He added that he was expecting word from them any hour, and would communicate with Benedetti as soon as it arrived.

Benedetti concluded from this reply that the King was favourable to renunciation, but that he preferred that the Prince should take the initiative, and so he reported to his Government. Elated by this partial success, the Duc de Gramont advanced his claims still further. "Write me a telegram," he telegraphed to Benedetti next day, "that I can read to the Chamber or publish, in which you will show that the King has known and authorized the acceptance by the Prince of Hohenzollern, and say above all that he has asked that he may confer with the Prince before communicating to you his decision." "If the King is not willing to advise the Prince of Hohenzollern to renounce," the Duke wrote to the ambassador on the same date, "well, it will be war at once, and in a few days we shall be at the Rhine."

Benedetti had a second audience of the King on July 11th, in which he begged him to allay public feeling in France by formally enjoining his relative to withdraw. The King answered that a reply might be expected in twenty-four hours, and if, as was possible, it notified the Prince's withdrawal, he would assent to it. From this statement the Duc de Gramont drew the safe conclusion that the King already knew of the intended renunciation, but that he wished it to be published independently by the Prince, so that he himself might not seem to be capitulating to French pressure. But such a capitulation was exactly what the Duke wanted, and was now determined to have; the renunciation was not only to be complete, but it was to bear the royal seal. Hence on learning the same day how matters stood, he at once instructed Benedetti to "employ all his skill" to obtain from the King himself, without intermediaries, "the satisfaction necessary to soothe the Chambers and public opinion."

That the King was anxious for the abandonment with honour of a scheme which he now saw was fraught with grave danger cannot be doubted. He had written to the Queen on July 7th: "*Entre nous soit dit*, I would be altogether pleased if Leopold were not elected"; and four days later, when the situation had become critical, he wrote to the same: "My cousin is much impressed by the turn things are taking in Paris, but he thinks that I am the one who ought to break off the affair. I have replied that I could do nothing about it, but that I would approve a rupture on his part with joy," adding: "God grant that the Hohenzollern may have understanding!"

In the forenoon of July 12th Prince Anthony sent a telegram to Marshal Prim in Madrid and to the Spanish ambassador in Paris, Señor Olozaga, renouncing the candidature on his son's behalf. Europe breathed freely once more when the good news became known, and for the moment the relief was nowhere greater than in Ministerial circles in Paris. All the more reputable of the newspapers seemed likewise to be pacified. " The candidature of a German Prince for the throne of Spain is set aside and the peace of Europe will not be disturbed," said the *Constitutionnel*, a journal inspired by the Minister of Justice. " We are satisfied. We did not ask more, and it is with pride that we welcome this pacific solution. It is a great victory, which has not cost a tear or a drop of blood."

So thought most members of the Government, and so thought Napoleon himself. Ollivier in particular was elated. " He hastened to M. Thiers on reaching the Chamber," writes Jules Simon. " You were right : we have succeeded. It is peace ! " " Now," said M. Thiers to him, " you must keep quiet." " Be at ease," he replied ; " we have peace, and we will see that it is not disturbed." [1] In contrast to Ollivier's statesmanlike restraint was the rashness of the deputy who in that critical moment called for " guarantees for the future "—sinister words to fall upon the ears of the Prussia-hating Foreign Secretary. Even in excitable Paris the first feeling was one of satisfaction that the threatened war-clouds seemed to have rolled away, and had that feeling been encouraged in high places it is possible that in a few days France might have forgotten the incident and resumed her normal life.

It was now that the Duc de Gramont put the crown to an accumulation of indiscretion. Since the idea that Prussia must be humiliated had gained entire possession of him, he turned every conciliatory act done by the King into a pretext for further pressure, forgetting, as Bismarck himself was soon to forget in turn, that the honour of one country is just as precious as that of another. On the 12th the Duke committed two acts of supreme folly. First he persuaded the Prussian ambassador in Paris, Baron von Werther to write to his King asking him to send an apologetic letter to the Emperor, containing an assurance that he had never intended to offend him or France, and later in the day he obtained the Emperor's permission, after a severe struggle, to the despatch of a telegram to Benedetti directing him to seek from the King a formal assurance that he would not approve of his relative's candidature at any future time. In thus re-opening the dispute after it had seemed to have been so happily settled the French Government alienated the last remnant of

[1] *Souvenirs du 4 Septembre*, p. 161

sympathy felt for it in neutral countries. Lord Lyons, who had all the time been offering the conciliatory offices of his Government, did not hesitate to tell the Duc de Gramont that this new demand was a provocative challenge which would turn against France the public opinion of the whole world.

Benedetti discharged his mission at Ems punctiliously and loyally. Walking on the river promenade in the forenoon of the 13th, he found himself unexpectedly in the presence of the King, who was accompanied by an adjutant. The King greeted him with the words, "The courier from Sigmaringen has not arrived, but here is good news," and he produced a Cologne newspaper containing the news of the renunciation.[1] Benedetti replied that he knew the news already, and proceeded to ask for a guarantee against any future candidature. He has said that he was prepared for the answer which came. "You ask me," said the King, "to undertake an obligation to hold good for all time and all circumstances. Such an undertaking I cannot and dare not give. I must reserve liberty to decide in every case according to circumstances. Certainly I cherish no secret plans, and the matter has given me so much annoyance that I can only wish it settled irrevocably. Nevertheless, it is impossible to go as far as you wish."

After repeating his request with the same result, the Count withdrew. The King had felt humiliated by the pressure put upon him, and his humiliation was increased when a little later Werther arrived from Paris bringing Gramont's demand for a letter of apology. The two affronts decided the King not to receive Benedetti again, though twice during the afternoon a further interview was sought. Nevertheless, he sent word by an adjutant that he approved of his relative's withdrawal, and asked that this approval might be signified to his Government.

All the spirits of mischief and perversity seemed to be ministering to the Duc de Gramont during that July day as he floundered forward in the wrong way once taken and now no longer to be retraced. The King of Prussia's acceptance of the renunciation was emphatic; yet no less emphatic was his refusal to bind himself for all time. Further pressure from France could only be irritating as well as useless, for nothing is more offensive to

[1] He wrote to the Queen on July 12th: "Just now a telegram has come from Colonel Strantz (in Sigmaringen), who announces in veiled words that Leopold withdraws. A stone has fallen from my heart. But tell no one, so that the news may not first come from us."

a man of spirit than the suggestion that he does not mean what he says. Nevertheless, Gramont again telegraphed instructions to Benedetti in the evening of the 13th to " make a last attempt." " Tell the King," he said, " that we limit ourselves to asking him to forbid the Prince of Hohenzollern to go back on his renunciation. Let him but say, ' I will forbid him ! ' and authorize you to write me to that effect or charge his Minister to do it, and we shall be satisfied." In the existing circumstances such suggestions belonged to the sphere, not of diplomacy but of frivolity. But the voices of passion and rancour were egging on the luckless Minister. M. Paul de Cassagnac had only that day dared him to retrace his steps, warning him that if he did " the Ministry of War would henceforth be a Ministry of Shame," and the taunt stung and smarted. Benedetti discreetly made no further attempt to see the King, but conveyed his message through a Minister-in-waiting, with the negative result which he expected.

From the moment that the King had refused the ambassador further discourse, the negotiations passed from Ems to Berlin, from the hands of the King to those of his Iron Chancellor. Bismarck had already asked for permission to wait upon the King, and had received orders to do so. On the 12th he had arrived in Berlin from Varzin, there to break the journey, ill in body and mind, indignant at the insults which the French Government and its diplomacy had heaped upon Prussia during the last few days, and tortured by the thought that if the King were left to himself he might capitulate to pressure and take the issue of war or peace into his own hands. And already Bismarck had determined that there should be war. Before this Werther had reported to him his promise to be the bearer of Napoleon's wish for a letter of apology, and he had angrily ordered him to quit the Paris embassy " on plea of indisposition." The ambassador's act had undoubtedly been gravely indiscreet, for the proper channels for any message of the kind were the French embassy and the Foreign Office in Berlin.

His disappointment was intensified when during dinner, at which both Moltke, Chief of the General Staff, and Roon, the Minister of War, were present, a further telegram arrived notifying the renunciation of the candidature. It seemed as though his deeply laid and carefully nurtured schemes had been frustrated at the moment of apparent success, and, wrathful at the King's weakness, he determined definitely to lay down office and return to Varzin, because " after all the insolent challenges which had gone before I perceived in this extorted submission a humiliation of Germany for which I did not desire to be responsible." Accordingly, he delayed his further journey to Ems, and sent Count Eulenburg there instead, with instructions to state his views to the King. For Bismarck the ensuing night was one of sleeplessness. Next evening the three colleagues met again at dinner—a depressed and dismal company. While they were at table a cipher telegram[1] came from the faithful Abeken at Ems reporting on the reception of Benedetti and the King's reply.

"Count Benedetti," the message said, in the King's words, "accosted me on the promenade in order to demand of me—in the end in a very obtrusive manner—that I should authorize him to telegraph immediately that I pledged myself for all time never again to give my consent should the Hohenzollerns renew their candidature. I repelled him at last, somewhat severely, since one cannot undertake such engagements *à tout jamais.* Naturally, I told him that I had received no news as yet, and that, as he had been earlier informed than I by way of Paris and Madrid, he would see that my Government had again had no hand in it."

Thus far the King's own words. Abeken added on his own account that the substance of Prince Anthony's letter of renunciation had been communicated to Benedetti, but that the King had declined to receive him further. Finally the King asked whether the new French demand and its rejection should not be communicated to the Press—a point left to Bismarck's discretion. It was a temperate report of an annoying incident, written without malice, or any suspicion that it would or could be turned to mischievous use.

The three associates ground their teeth as they reflected that the King had twice in the same day been exposed to insult, and their resentment was aggravated by the thought that neither insult had been repelled with the right vigour. It was clear to Bismarck that Abeken's mild story could not be published as it stood. There was, however, an alternative—to give the substance, but in more telling, more vivacious, more truculent form. That is what was done, and the result exceeded Bismarck's expectations. Sybel says it is puerile to pretend that the Ems telegram was forged. Strictly speaking, there was no forgery and no falsification, only a manipulation of the words and a perversion

[1] It was handed in at Ems at 3.40 and received in Berlin at 6.8 p.m.

of their spirit. What Bismarck, nevertheless, did was so to alter the tone of the despatch as to make innocent language offensive, with the intention of producing a provocative effect upon the French nation.

As to the fact of perversion, the two versions speak for themselves; as to the motive, we have his own admission repeated and gloated over time after time, and finally enshrined in his *Reflections and Reminiscences.* In quieter days Bismarck often told with glee how this witches' cauldron of mischief was brewed. This is the story as taken down from his lips by the adoring Busch: "I told Roon and Moltke how matters stood. Roon was beside himself and so was Moltke; he at once looked old and ill. I asked Moltke whether we were in good form for such a war. He answered that in all human probability we might hope to win. Then, without altering a word, I made twenty words out of two hundred, and read it to them. They said it would have the right effect in that form. 'Before it sounded like a retreat (*chamade*), now it is like a challenge' (*fanfare*). Moltke was all at once young and fresh as before. Now he had his war—his business." Bismarck related at another time how the man whose business was war added: "Let me only lead our army in this campaign, and the devil may then take this pack of bones"[1] (striking his breast). The historian Lorenz speaks of the "delightful story" of this table-talk of the three paladins of the Empire. Nevertheless, it is worth remembering that the jesting, such as it was, sent a quarter of a million Germans and Frenchmen to their deaths.

As despatched, the revised telegram ran as follows:

"After the news of the renunciation (of his candidature) by the Prince of Hohenzollern had been officially announced by the Spanish ambassador to the French Government, the French ambassador in Ems demanded of his Majesty the King that he should authorize him to telegraph to Paris that he pledged himself for all future time never again to give his sanction should the Hohenzollerns return to their candidature. His Majesty thereupon refused to receive the ambassador again, and caused his adjutant in attendance to inform him that his Majesty had no further communication to make to him."

It will be seen that the facts were exactly as stated in Abeken's

[1] General von Blumenthal records in his *Tagebücher* Moltke's remark to him at Nikolsburg in July, 1866: "The struggle with France must be fought out one day, for it is inevitable, but I shall not live to see it."

telegram, but the impression created was altogether different. Whatever he may have felt, the King did not suggest that he had either offered or designed an affront to Benedetti. According to Benedetti there was "*ni insulteur ni insulté*," and when the ambassador left Ems on the following day the King bade him a friendly farewell.[1] Yet the impression given and intended by the altered despatch was that the King had deliberately snubbed the ambassador, and France through him, and had virtually broken off diplomatic intercourse.

Benedetti has been roundly blamed by his own people for his share in the Ems episode, and Ollivier so far inculpates his Ministry, and above all himself, as to find fault with him for not having objected to the demand for guarantees. Never was blame less deserved. It is always difficult to do a bad thing well. Benedetti did his best to fulfil a thankless task, and the failure which resulted was not his, but that of the blundering policy which he endeavoured to carry out from a sense of duty, yet against his better judgment. Gramont charged him at the time with vanity and conceit. "When he looks upon himself he is dazzled," he said. That may have been true, but therein Benedetti was not unique. Incompetent he was not. Ollivier, with all his reservations, has justly said of him: "Harassed by public opinion and by his own anxieties, we spurred him on, urged him to greater energy, and he was wise enough to withstand our impatience and not to endanger by any imprudent step the object he was pursuing." Benedetti was, indeed, wiser on this occasion than the men whose fatuous conduct it was his business to support, though he never endorsed it. In doing this he had for a fortnight, as Ollivier hints, lived a veritable dog's life. In later years he declared that in his opinion the guarantees which he was bidden imperiously to demand at Ems were unnecessary and "conducted us fatally to war." Few impartial critics will disagree, though they will add the saving clause that if France plunged into war Prussia wanted it.

Even if the objective circumstances of the episode of the perverted telegram left any doubt as to Bismarck's sinister intentions, such doubt would not stand against the damning fact that in giving to the words a mordant and inflammatory turn

[1] Nevertheless, it is clear that the ambassador had been at least unduly obtrusive. In a letter written to the Queen on the 13th the King used the words, "As he became increasingly pressing and almost impertinent . . ." ("*immer dringender und fast impertinent*").

he had the excitable populace of Paris in mind. "If the telegram is sent off to our embassies at eleven o'clock," he said, "it will still be announced in Paris by midnight, and . . . will have the effect of a red rag upon the Gallic bull." The effect, both in Paris and Berlin, was what Bismarck desired—in Paris embitterment and fury at Teutonic truculence, in Berlin jubilation and relief that the insult of July 6th had been avenged. "In the streets," says Sybel of the scenes in the Prussian capital next day, "the excited masses swayed to and fro; men embraced one another amid tears of joy, thunderous cheers for King William rent the air."

Events moved fast in those fateful hours. The whole quarrel had developed in a fortnight; it had come to a head in less than a week, and the twenty-four hours following the Ems interview had brought war in sight. Just a week before the Duc de Gramont had said to Lord Lyons that "The voluntary renunciation by the Prince would be a very happy solution of a difficult and complicated situation." Not only had the Prince withdrawn, but the King had approved his act, yet the Duke was not satisfied. How had the problem altered, that a solution which then would have been "very happy" was now no solution at all? It was not the problem, but the Paris populace, that had changed. Before Paris had craved only for Prussia's humiliation; now even that was not enough.

The die had not yet been cast, however, and it lay in the French Government's hand. If the Emperor and his Ministers had been prepared to accept their rebuff, all might still have been well. Had they even taken the elementary precaution of obtaining from Benedetti an independent account of the Ems interview before acting upon Bismarck's offensive version, a rejoinder might have been possible which would have saved their honour and preserved the peace; but the ambassador was not at that stage questioned as to what had actually occurred. A Council of State was held early on the 14th, Napoleon presiding. The Foreign Secretary professed to believe that peace would even yet be maintained, and though the Minister of War, Lebœuf, wished to call out the reserves, he was outvoted. No sooner was the meeting over than Baron von Werther waited on Gramont to report that his unlucky mission to the King had drawn upon him Bismarck's reproof and that he had been suspended. The incident showed that in Germany, too, the signals pointed ominously to danger. At noon the Ministers met again, with the war clamour of the Paris populace ringing in their ears. Lebœuf repeated his demand for mobilization, and on his assurance that Prussia had set the example he had his way.

Already Napoleon had recalled his old panacea for the woes of Europe, a conference of the Powers, but the idea had not found favour. Now it was revived, and a majority of the Ministers clutched at this straw of hope, a reference being drawn up on the spot. The order for mobilization was for the time countermanded. Then came the disconcerting news that Bismarck had notified the Ems episode to the foreign Courts in a way insulting to the honour of France. Council followed council; in the Chamber and in Paris the war-fever increased; even the peace-loving Ollivier was caught up by the waves of passion and flung into eddies too strong for all but the stoutest swimmers. All this time the British Foreign Secretary was making, through the ambassadors in London, Paris, and Berlin, earnest efforts to find a solution for what was at bottom a problem of national pride and honour—the most simple yet most difficult of all political problems—and so to keep the peace.

At the final council held at St. Cloud in the forenoon of the 15th both the Emperor and the Empress were present, and if of all the war-seekers the Empress was the most impetuous, the fact must be laid in good part to the account of her proud Spanish blood. The Emperor's assent was hesitant and unconvinced, yet it was given. There was excuse for him; he had for a long time been ill, and his will-power was undermined by suffering; no longer master of himself, he allowed himself to be overborne and carried away on the crest of a wave of passion. A few days later he wrote to Queen Sophie of Holland: "I did not want this war. I have been forced into it by public opinion," words almost identical with those spoken to Bismarck two months later on the battlefield.

Weighing against each other the factors of unrest and tranquillity in the political situation in France under the new Government, Lord Lyons had written to the British Foreign Secretary on May 6th, before the candidature question was sprung upon Europe: "There is more security against a sudden surprise than there was under the personal Government, but there is also less probability that the Emperor's health and personal views will prevent war." It was not the only time or occasion that the prescience of this acute observer was justified by the event.

In the light of the facts and admissions related above it is not difficult to assign to the chief actors in the two incidents, the candidature and the telegram, their relative responsibility. The Duc de Gramont's diplomatic handling of a situation which from the first was critical disclosed a sequence of blunders as egregious and wrong-headed as were ever perpetrated in the name of statesmanship, culminating in the crime of surrendering whatever remained to him of judgment and sanity to the clamour of an excited populace. In his memorials of the disaster of 1870 Gramont speaks speciously of the course which events might have taken if this thing had been done and that thing had been left undone; yet no less than Ollivier and Benedetti he has to admit that the Cabinet in the end allowed itself to be led into war at the dictation of passions which it was its duty to have controlled.

Great as was the responsibility of the French Ministers, however, the real author of the war was the Prussian statesman who, toiling long and stealthily in secret workshops, had forged a chain of events which closed around France like a destiny and placed her at last in such a position that she was in effect compelled to seal her own doom. The President of the *Corps Législatif*, in his address to Napoleon on July 22nd, used with greater justification than he knew at the time the words of Montesquieu: "The real author of a war is not he who declares it, but he who makes it necessary."

In later years Bismarck was wont to say that the war with France, following one with Austria, "lay in the logic of history." All Bismarck's three wars, indeed, though claimed at the time of their occurrence to be acts of his free will, became in quieter days inevitable, events that were, in his favourite phrase, "in the nature of things." But events only become inevitable because definite causes lead to definite results, and when we speak of the "nature of things" we really mean the nature of the men who govern things and direct events into the channel of deliberate purpose and calculated design.

Bismarck has put on record the reasons which led him to provoke the third and bloodiest of his wars, and it is not necessary to go behind them. "In view of the attitude of France," he wrote at the close of his life, "our national sense of honour compelled us, in my opinion, to go to war, and if we did not act according to the demands of this feeling we should lose, when on the way to the completion of our national development, the entire impetus gained in 1866, while the German national feeling south of the Main, aroused by our military successes in 1866 and shown by the readiness of the Southern States to enter the alliances, would grow cold again."[1] "I was convinced," he says again, "that the gulf which had been created in the course of history between the South and the North of the fatherland by variety of dynastic and racial sentiments and modes of life, could not be more effectively bridged than by a common national war against the neighbouring nation, our aggressor for centuries."[2]

Nowhere is the intrigue by which France was lured into this disaster avowed with colder cynicism than in Busch's recital of Bismarck's table-talk on the subject. He tells how after Austria's defeat Bismarck for a long time took care to humour Napoleon, but only because of uncertainty as to the military strength of France and the readiness of the Southern States to co-operate heartily with Prussia in the event of a struggle. Directly he became satisfied that Prussia had nothing to fear, all scruple vanished. Then his attitude became one of irritation and provocation. He made it his business no longer to stave off war, but so to work on events that it should become inevitable, and above all to see that it was brought about in such a manner that France, while forced to accept Prussia's challenge, would appear to be compromised in the eyes of Europe. Only Busch himself can do justice to the final chapter of this conspiracy.

"Hitherto," he writes, "there was hope in delay, but now there was danger, so that the German statesman was compelled to exchange a policy of postponing decision for one of accelerating the inevitable, and to find a practicable way by which the French, wishful for war but not quite prepared for it, might be so acted upon that they would lay aside reserve, which had been observed by both Governments up to this point, rattle the sword, and issue a challenge, without any previous insult or other urgent occasion being apparent to the rest of Europe. In other words, it was necessary to find the drop needed to make the boiling kettle in Paris overflow; to speak frankly, the French had to be incited, and their foolish fury made it possible to do this in such a way that to the neutral Powers they appeared to be frivolous disturbers of the peace. The foresight and the art capable of constructing and setting such a trap effectively, and finding the best bait for the jealous and haughty Gallic cock, existed in the Wilhelmstrasse at Berlin."

Busch repeats a conversation in which Bismarck is made to

[1] *Reflections and Reminiscences*, vol. ii., p. 88. [2] *Ibid.*, vol. ii., p. 89.

say that "in 1867 he avoided war because he did not judge Germany to be strong enough. In 1870 that difficulty was dispelled; Germany was now sufficiently armed." [1]

[1] Sybel writes in his *History* (vol. vii., p. 237): "In France it is still to-day the overwhelming opinion that Bismarck, thoroughly prepared for hostilities and embarrassed by domestic difficulties, wished to draw Napoleon into a declaration of war; by means of a deeply laid intrigue he deliberately outraged the French feeling of honour, and the Emperor, although insufficiently armed, stupidly fell into the well-prepared trap." Against this view he protests. Delbrück, writing at a later date, says: "The French have been convinced that the Hohenzollern candidature was the work of Bismarck; in Germany it has not been believed, and I myself, like Sybel, protested strongly against that reproach. But events have proved that in this case the reproach of the French was well founded. . . . There no longer exists any doubt that if the first thought came from Spain the candidature itself was the work of Bismarck." From the candidature, however, followed everything else.

Nevertheless, a minor annalist, Wilhelm Maurenbrecher, is so far enslaved to the idea that it is the duty of historians to glorify national policy, regardless of facts, that he could write of the French war as late as 1892: "Germany was in the position of a man who is suddenly attacked by garotters."

CHAPTER IX

(1870–1871)

THE WAR WITH FRANCE

THE French Government having decided on war, all that remained was to justify it to the nation and to Europe, and to wage it with resolution. A manifesto was issued on July 15th in which the events of the preceding fortnight were reviewed and the actions of the Ministry defended in the name of national honour. It ended with the protestation by which, in one form or other, every war between civilized nations has been justified by every combatant: "We have done everything in order to avert war. We now prepare to meet the struggle which has been forced upon us, leaving every one to bear his due share of responsibility." The declaration was read in the Senate by the Duc de Gramont and in the House of Deputies by Ollivier, who added the now historical words: "We have taken upon ourselves a great responsibility, but we accept it with a light heart." [1] All political parties were almost solidly behind the Government. Thiers declared that the Chamber was going to war "sur une question de susceptibilité,"

[1] The phrase has given rise to a, perhaps, unjustifiable amount of controversy owing to the assumption, for which there appears to be no warrant, that Ollivier took the approaching war lightly. In his story of the origin of the war Ollivier gives an explanation of how the words slipped from his lips which seems needlessly forced: he was the victim of an "abstraction oratoire." "Ma démonstration terminée," he writes, "j'eu une de ces abstractions oratoires que connaissent bien les hommes de tribune." Forgetting all the other orators—Thiers, Favre, and the rest—and even the Assembly itself, and thinking only of the brave men who were soon to fall on the battlefield, and of posterity, "je me rappelai les malédictions bibliques sur les impies aux cœurs pesants" (Luke xxiv., 25–6). It was while under the compulsion of these reflections that he said: "Oui, de ce jour commençe pour les ministres, mes collégues et moi, une grande responsabilité. Nous l'acceptons le cœur leger." A voice cried: "Dîtes attristé!" but what Ollivier had said he meant, and he thereupon repeated the words, explaining that by a "light heart" he did not mean that Ministers entered upon the struggle with joy, but that they were free from remorse, and confident in the assurance of a good conscience (*L'Empire Libéral*, vol. xiv., pp. 421–2).

and that torrents of blood were about to be shed upon a matter of form, but his warning was unheeded. The demand for credits was voted by 285 against 6. With the majority voted Gambetta, Jules Simon, and Jules Ferry, and with the minority Jules Grévy; Thiers did not vote, and Favre was absent.

"How was the war received?" asks Benedetti in his memorials of those days, and he admits "With transports of enthusiasm: to deny this would be to ignore a conspicuous truth." In the first frenzy of elation public opinion in Paris insisted that it had driven the Government into hostilities against its will, and the Press declared proudly that this was not the Emperor's or his Ministers' war, but the war of the nation. It was certainly the war of that part of the nation which had for the time gained ascendancy. Though Paris, however, received the call to arms with jubilation, Paris did not faithfully represent France. This was proved by the results of an inquiry made of the prefects, for these showed that opinion in the provinces was greatly divided; only sixteen departments were reported to be warmly in favour of war, thirty-four were as decidedly opposed to it, while thirty-seven were of two minds.

In Germany the war enthusiasm was quite as outspoken, but it was far more real, and the determination to wage it successfully more conscious and more confident. If the cry of Paris was "To Berlin!" that of Berlin was "To the Rhine!" For the third time in six years the stern message "Mobilize!" ran through Prussia, and for the second time within four years the entire German nation was put upon a war footing.

In the northern kingdom the patriotic fervour called forth was not free from arrogance, and behind it was a hatred of France which was perhaps at least as strong as love of Germany, but of the resolution of the great mass of the people there would be no doubt. In the South feeling was less inflamed, yet there, too, it was generally recognized that this was truly a German and not a Prussian quarrel, and that no German State dare stand aside. Writing to the Queen on July 13th, to tell how the Ministers-President of Bavaria and Würtemberg had declared that "if Prussia were attacked all Germany would rise as one man," King William added incredulously: "That is very fine (*brav*)—if only it happens!" Nevertheless, it did happen, for at the call of the blood there was no longer North and South, but one country, no longer a medley of jealous tribes, but a united nation.

Bismarck had in the previous June warned Prince Hohenlohe,

the Bavarian Minister-President, that a breach of the military alliance with Prussia in the event of war with France would be for his country suicidal, since a current of public feeling would result which might lead to its partition between North Germany and Austria. The warning proved unnecessary. Both in Bavaria and Würtemberg, indeed, there were factions which hoped that these States might be able to maintain an attitude of armed neutrality. But neither the military treaties nor the sentiment of the peoples recognized any such equivocal condition ; the Diets promptly confirmed the action of their Governments, and when the Prussian Crown Prince, who was to command the army of the South, visited these kingdoms, bearing with him the fiery cross, he was received with great enthusiasm.

Abroad the feeling towards Germany was more favourable than the feeling towards Prussia had been in 1866. The friendship of Russia, won in 1863 by the Polish convention and since assiduously fostered, now stood her in good stead. The Czar's influence was sufficient to steady both Austria and Denmark and to discourage the efforts of Beust to form an alliance of neutrals for the purpose of moderating Germany's terms in the event of the war going in her favour. It was owing to the benevolent neutrality of Russia and the politic restraint of Italy that Prussia was able to leave her eastern and southern frontiers denuded of troops, just as she had left her western frontier unprotected in 1866 owing to the friendship of Napoleon.

When the die had been cast, France likewise looked about for friends, and met only with disappointment. The ally upon which Napoleon had counted with greatest confidence—the disaffection of the South—having proved a phantom, and Russia being cordially attached to Prussia, only Austria and Italy were possible. To a man driven to desperate straits it did not seem a far-fetched idea that Austria in particular would call to mind with gratitude the friendly dealings of 1866 and would now be willing to convert into a reality the compact which should have been concluded only a year before, yet had been whittled down to a pious exchange of good wishes. Beust readily offered Austria's conciliatory services, but for these Napoleon had no use, knowing that it was now too late for parley. Instead, he sounded the Minister as to the chances of an active co-operation, and urged him as a first step to try to win the Emperor's acceptance of the idea of a European conference.

The Government in Vienna recalled with relief the condition

upon which the proposed alliance of 1869 was to have been contingent, viz. that in the event of a war between France and Prussia Austria, if so disposed, should have the right to remain neutral. Now Austria was so disposed, and no temptation could induce her to take sides. Apart from the fact that the Emperor and his Government had gone far to re-establish relations of confidence and friendship with Prussia, self-interest was altogether on the side of neutrality. It could not be good for Austria that either of the combatants should inflict crushing injury upon the other, and this consideration explained Beust's earlier attempts to prevent a catastrophe. A beaten Prussia, which was at least a possibility, would make Napoleon as much the patron of the Southern States as his uncle had been sixty years before. On the other hand, Prussia's success would mean the union of the South with the North and its permanent absorption in a Germanic empire. From Austria's standpoint, therefore, it was desirable that France and Prussia should continue to hold each other in check; only thus could she hope to retain the small influence in German affairs which still remained to her.

At a conference of Ministers of both monarchies which was held on July 18th to consider Austria's attitude, Beust wished to postpone a decision and for the present to await events, leaving later action to be determined by expediency. Andrassy, however, called for the open and immediate acceptance of a policy of strict neutrality, and he carried the day. Beust's attitude was both irresolute and disingenuous. He was deeply concerned not to offend Napoleon, and on the same day (July 20th) that his Government announced Austria's decision to remain neutral he wrote to the ambassador Metternich in Paris a private letter assuring him that as regards France the neutrality would be benevolent, and that, though a passive friend, Austria would do her best to promote Napoleon's success. In the same letter he urged that France should allow Italy to take possession of Rome directly the French troops were withdrawn. "The question must be settled," he said; "we shall never have Italy sincerely on our side until we have plucked the Roman thorn out of her foot."

Italy was no readier than Austria to forgo the advantages of neutrality. Napoleon urged Victor Emmanuel by all the gods of his fathers to join him, and offered to withdraw his troops from Rome provided Italy would promise to respect the integrity of the papal enclave. The temptation to intervene was not great in the circumstances. The offer simply to withdraw French troops had little value in view of the fact that the King had never concealed his intention of seizing Rome for Italy directly events were favourable. On the other hand, a rupture with Prussia could offer him no profit, and in spite of his personal attachment to Napoleon he could not forget that he had fought side by side with that Power in 1866. After a struggle, more with his military advisers than his own mind, the King similarly decided to keep out of the fray.

Wherever else he looked, Napoleon met with the same disappointment. With a strange credulity he had hugged the hope that all his many efforts on behalf of struggling nationalities—not only the Italians, but the Hungarians and the Poles—would now have their reward in the rally of his political *protégés* to his help. He had to learn the statesman's hardest lesson, that in politics virtue must be its own reward. The only foreign legion that volunteered for his service was a miscellaneous band of adventurous spirits who responded to the call of the intrepid Garibaldi.

Public feeling in England at first and for some time leaned strongly to Germany's side, from a belief that France had wanted war and had wantonly provoked it. It must be remembered that the full story of the Ems telegram was not yet known. That there was widespread sympathy with or understanding of the movement towards a larger unity in Germany may be doubted, though amongst the thoughtful sections of the population the movement had many warm friends. Nevertheless, where it existed the attachment to France, as to a country which had added so greatly to the patrimony of civilization, was marked by great cordiality and outspokenness. The feeling in Germany towards England, on the other hand, alternated between the extremes of heat and cold; it was effusively friendly when the influence of the Government and the Press seemed to favour the German cause, hostile and defiant when for any reason that influence seemed to veer round to the French side. Germany certainly had reason to complain later of a British neutrality which was held to be consistent with supplying her enemy with any and every kind of necessity she required. "We sit by," wrote Sir Robert Morier with the vivacity which prevented his rise in a service in which opinions may neither be strongly expressed nor strongly held, "we sit by like a bloated Quaker, too holy to fight, but rubbing our hands at the roaring trade we are doing in cartridges and ammunition." That was truer for Birmingham and the munition centres than for England at large, but the nation reaped the reproach and venom.

Seldom has a nation gone to war with so little open moral support behind it as the French nation in 1870. The immeasurable incapacity and folly of its statesmanship had isolated France far more effectively than all Prussia's past skilful diplomacy, and is seemed as though now, in the hour of her need, all the intangible forces and influences which Bismarck was accustomed to speak of as the *imponderabilia* of political life were against her and working on the side of a Government and a Minister who, unknown to the world as yet, had planned the struggle and were already counting on the booty. At the last moment the weight of this handicap was still further increased to the disadvantage of France. On July 21st the French Foreign Minister had circulated a strong though somewhat rhetorical indictment of Prussian foreign policy, which was held up to European reprobation as one of systematic aggression and spoliation. Thereupon Bismarck made one of those skilful unexpected moves by which he so often turned the tables upon his opponents in critical situations. Just when France was making this sadly needed attempt to set herself right with Europe, and to allay the impatience with which even the Governments most friendly to her had watched her perverse diplomacy, he produced from his mysterious portfolio and published (July 25th) a document which he had long kept secret, waiting only for a favourable opportunity for turning it to a use proportionate to its importance.

This was the text of a proposal for the annexation of Belgium by France which Count Benedetti was represented to have made to him in 1867. The calculating tactician was no less clever in the choice of time for this surprising revelation than the means of giving it to the world, for he did this, not through his Foreign Office, but through the columns of the London *Times*.[1]

The revelation showed France in a peculiarly unfavourable light, and neutral nations, which had never approved of the Duc de Gramont's violent diplomatic methods, drew back into still greater reserve. To increase the effect created in England,

[1] Some days before the treaty was published Count Bernstorff, the North German ambassador in London, told both Mr. Gladstone and Lord Granville personally of the treaty, and though the communication was supposed to have been made in confidence, Mr. Gladstone was convinced that it was desired that the disclosure would be circulated in the hope that France would be further prejudiced in the eyes of Europe. As the British statesmen would not divulge the alleged plot, Bismarck had to do it himself.

Bismarck telegraphed to the German ambassador in London instructing him to tell the Foreign Secretary that this was only one of several proposals of the same kind, dating from the beginning of the Danish quarrel, by which Napoleon had tried to turn his neutrality to profitable account. " In the interest of peace," said Bismarck, " I have kept secret these proposals and treated them dilatorily." No one had ever suspected Bismarck to be half so virtuous, but there was no doubting the fact that the incriminating draft treaty existed and that it was in Benedetti's handwriting.

Napoleon promptly wrote to his Foreign Minister a letter in which he charged Bismarck with having himself tried to incite France to annex Belgium. Benedetti also replied to the charge of duplicity brought against him, and made out a good case for himself and France, but as Bismarck had had the first word and Europe was in a doubting mood, his repudiations fell flat. He had to admit that a proposal had been put before the Prussian Government in the terms of the draft treaty, but asserted that the incident occurred in 1866 and not in 1867, that its author was Bismarck himself, and that he, as the ambassador of France, had simply acted as Bismarck's tool and dupe. The draft treaty, he said, was the result of repeated verbal negotiations. " Wishing at one of our conversations to keep an exact report of these proposals, I agreed to transcribe them, in some sort, at his dictation." The Duc de Gramont later confirmed this story, and added that Bismarck had invited France to take both Luxemburg and Belgium as early as 1865. He did not say how much earlier Napoleon had planned the same scheme independently. The German Foreign Office, in a rejoinder to Benedetti's counter-charge, did not deny that negotiations occurred with France concerning both Luxemburg and Belgium, but pleaded that they " had been carried on by the Prussian Minister-President with a view to postponing a French attack upon Prussia." That admission alone was a strong point in favour of Benedetti's story. The ambassador was less credible, however, when he tried to acquit his Government of any knowledge of the proposed treaty. Ollivier has since shown that in these surreptitious transactions he acted at the direct instigation of the French Foreign Secretary and with the Emperor's assent.

The revelations were chiefly interesting as throwing a lurid light upon the crooked ways of Prusso-French diplomacy at that time. Europe did not forget in her indignation that two at least are needed to make a conspiracy, and Bismarck was not exculpated. On his own confession he allowed Benedetti to communicate to him the contents of a document of questionable morality, discussed its terms freely with him, induced him to alter them in his presence, and then finally retained the document with the intention of compromising France when it became worth while. Such a proceeding was part of the day's work of a statesman who in the pursuit of his great plans never hesitated, as his secretary, Abeken, said, to employ "oblique and even crooked ways," holding that in politics the end justifies the means, but the reflections which it suggested were not pleasant. In a word, the only difference between the two intriguers was that in plotting with each other, Benedetti was straightforward and Bismarck a dissembler.

The French declaration of war arrived in Berlin on July 19th, and Bismarck said on the following day that it was the only official document which his Government had received from France in the candidature affair.

The revelation of the Bismarck-Benedetti draft treaty pointed to the wisdom of assuring to Belgium, whose position between the contending States offered to both a tempting base of operations, the neutrality guaranteed by the treaty of 1839. The Belgian ambassador in Paris had already given to the French Foreign Minister his Government's promise "to remain faithful to the principle of its neutrality and to fulfil scrupulously all its duties, during the continuance of the war," and the Duc de Gramont had similarly undertaken to "respect the neutrality of Belgian territory on condition that it shall be respected by Prussia." This interchange of pledges having taken place, the Duke resented the action of Great Britain in proposing on July 31st the conclusion of a treaty with both France and Prussia under which that country undertook to defend Belgium's neutrality with all its forces by land and water in conjunction with either of the belligerent Powers, should the other violate Belgian territory. The recent revelations, upon the true inwardness of which few people were able as yet to form an opinion, had disquieted the public mind, however, and neutral countries generally were relieved and grateful when the two treaties had been completed. Similar engagements, arising out of the treaty of neutrality of 1867, were entered into regarding Luxemburg.

Only now did France realize the task before her, obvious though it had been from the first to the rest of the world. Count Vitzthum, asked by Napoleon in 1868 what was thought in Germany of the prospect of a Franco-Prussian war, replied that it was thought to be inevitable. "But do not regard it as an easy work," he added; "it will be a terrible national struggle, in which the Southern States will be involved, and for France the continued possession of Alsace and Lorraine will be at stake." There is no evidence that the warning was taken to heart, either by Napoleon or by his Ministers. Of the latter both Ollivier and the Duc de Gramont say that while they freely discussed the prospects of the war beforehand it occurred to no one to consider whether the military resources of the country would be equal to the strain. Recalling the Ministerial discussions which preceded the declaration of July 6th in the *Corps Législatif*, Ollivier wrote later: "Our first question then was, 'Is our army ready?' And we asked the question simply for form's sake, for not one of us had any doubt as to the reply."

Present and past Ministers of War had given emphatic assurances of the army's absolute preparedness for any ordeal. Niel, though he had not been allowed three years before to carry out in their completeness the military reforms which he regarded as necessary for the country's safety, had said: "Whether we are at peace or war matters not to the Minister of War, for he is always ready"; while Lebœuf was confident that the army, if inferior to that of Prussia in numbers, was superior to it in quality and would prove capable of miracles.[1] When challenged just as the final decision to declare war was taken, Lebœuf still gave the assurance that France was "completely ready," yet he of all men should have known the truth. The Emperor complained to Lord Malmesbury at a later date that he had been "deceived as to the strength and preparedness of his army." Even he, however, was not free from blame.

It was expected that half a million men would at once respond to the first call to arms—no one ever asked where they would come from—and there came just half that number, not too well equipped. As the war advanced this force was greatly increased, though at the time of maximum capacity the force put in the field by France was smaller than that mobilized by Germany at the beginning of hostilities. Not only so, but the administrative and transport managements were chaotic. The railways were few and ill-managed, for little or no thought had been given to the need for co-ordination; large bodies of troops were collected in centres without arms or equipment of any kind; the commis-

[1] Émile Ollivier, *Philosophie d'une Guerre*, pp. 65–66.

sariat system was defective; the fortresses should have been well supplied with stores, but these had been neglected and were totally inadequate. The idea seemed to have been taken for granted that a war with Prussia would for France be a war of invasion, and that the Emperor's armies would merely have to cross the frontier and live on the fat of the enemy's land. Hence it was also that while the officers were provided with maps of Germany they were without maps of their own country. Even in the higher command the same want of foresight came to light, for the strategists had staked the fortunes of war upon one plan of campaign, and when this failed it had no other to fall back upon.

The Prussian military authorities had a far truer idea of the effective strength and efficiency of the French army at that time than the French military authorities themselves, and their estimate of its fighting capacity proved correct. It was this knowledge that led Bismarck to write to a Paris correspondent in 1869: "The opinion should not take root in Paris that we fear a war. A war in itself is always a misfortune, but the view that it would be a greater misfortune for us than for France, and that we have greater cause than France to avoid it, is one which we do not understand here."

When the Emperor joined the army on July 28th, the intention was to take a vigorous offensive and to enter Germany simultaneously in three or four places. The plan was to invade South Germany from Alsace and Lorraine, and had that move been possible at the beginning, it might have changed the entire course of the campaign, for the frontiers were for a long time practically open and behind them was a very insufficient force. Of the three main bodies into which the French forces were divided, under Marshals Bazaine, MacMahon, and Canrobert respectively, with the Emperor as commander-in-chief, the first two concentrated in these provinces. Instead of being across the Rhine before the Prussians were ready, as the Paris newspapers had boasted they would be, the French armies were for a long time unable to move in force. The consequence was that while they were concentrating the Germans hurried half a million men to the frontier and before the enemy was ready for action on a large scale were far into his territory. The French tacticians contemplated only the offensive, but the offensive was never from the first in their hands; and when it had once passed to the invaders it rested in their power to organize and localize the campaign almost as they wished.

Prussia had no need to prepare for the war; she was prepared already, as always when fighting had to be done. The military machinery was in perfect order, and all that was needed was to set it in motion. The combined German forces, instead of falling below the estimates, exceeded them. In the fortnight from the middle of July there had been mobilized a field and garrison force of over 800,000 men, all in perfect readiness, and behind it were reserves of a quarter of a million and the *Landwehr* to an equal number. They were armed with the needle-gun, as in the campaigns of 1864 and 1866, but it proved inferior to the French Chassepot breech-loading rifle.[1] On the other hand, the German artillery was on the whole superior to the French. As a precaution, a sufficient force was left within striking distance of the Bohemian and Danish frontiers, but the great mass of the field force set out at once towards the Rhine. The plan of campaign was to concentrate upon the capture of Paris, as the centre of France; the opposing forces were to be pressed back, as far as possible, in the direction of the less fertile northern departments; and the invaders were to attack without cessation. There were three armies of invasion, as in the campaign against Austria, the first and smallest under General von Steinmetz, the second under Prince Frederick Charles, and the third under the Crown Prince, with whom was General von Blumenthal, as in 1866, as chief of staff. The King himself was commander-in-chief, and in his retinue were Moltke, Roon (the War Minister), and Bismarck. The Chancellor's presence in the field was greatly resented by the Generals, who had not forgotten how he had worked upon the King in the Bohemian campaign, and dictated its end from political rather than military considerations. Before he had entered France the jealous soldiers told him that he was not to attend the councils of war, but mind his own diplomatic business. In the end he minded both his business and much of theirs. More than once the Minister and the Chief of the General Staff quarrelled, and on one occasion the King had to witness an ugly display of their bad temper. In later years Bismarck had many frank things to say of the great strategist, while Moltke avenged himself more cruelly by saying as little as possible about the great states-

[1] "Votre organisation militaire est sublime," Napoleon said to King William after Sedan; and commenting upon the words Roon adds: "Therein lies the root of our military capacity, and not, as is often said, in the needle-gun; for the *chassepots* are far superior to the unimproved needle-gun, as we have found to our cost" (*Denkwürdigkeiten*, vol. ii., p. 467).

man ; in his *History of the Franco-German War* he does not mention Bismarck's name.

Before the end of July the first and second armies had crossed the Rhine, at Coblenz and Mayence, while the third remained for the time in the Bavarian Palatinate. Once more the superiority of the Prussian organization, generalship, tactics, equipment, and *moral* was shown. Nothing had been left to chance, and the fighting machine moved onward with a deadly directness and sureness. The shock of arms began in the early days of August and the first success fell to French troops, which took Saarbrücken. Elated by the trifling incident, Paris began to talk of the illuminations which should welcome the greater triumphs that were to come. The ground won, however, had immediately to be abandoned, and it was not recovered. Battle now followed battle with dramatic suddenness. Napoleon had clung to the idea that South Germany might at the last moment decide not to throw in its lot with the North, even if it did not actively take his side. The fatuity of this speculation was the first of many great surprises which the war was to bring to him. It was in vain that his Government issued a proclamation that the war was not against Germany but against Prussia and the policy of her principal Minister. In the first decisive encounter the French were met and beaten by a force in which Prussian and Bavarian troops fought together. The effect of the German victories of Weissenburg, Wörth, and Spicheren within three days (August 4th–6th) was electrical ; for these successes made any advance of French troops into Germany impossible, and placed it beyond doubt that the war would be fought out in the enemy's territory.

Napoleon kept back as long as possible the news of these reverses, and then made light of them, endeavouring to cheer Paris with the assurance that they would soon be made good. "Tout peut se rétablir," he telegraphed, retreating towards Metz when the Germans had crossed the frontier. But it did not, and now Paris, so lately elated, fell into a panic. Lord Lyons tells how when reports circulated that the Germans would soon be at the gates the Rothschilds and other bankers waited on him to beg that the British Government would intervene and check any further advance of the invaders towards their vaults and counting-houses. In August, blaming the Government for the inauspicious beginning of the war, and clamouring for an efficient Government, the Chamber compelled Ollivier to resign. Napoleon himself did not escape severe censure. At the request of the Empress-Regent a new Cabinet was formed by General Montauban, and in order to appease the populace, which called for wholesale changes, the Emperor resigned the chief command of the army to Bazaine and withdrew to MacMahon's camp.

With slight fluctuations, the course of the campaign continued as it began. Outnumbered and out-generalled, the French, in spite of superb heroism, lost battle after battle, until by the middle of August the Germans were in full possession of the provinces of Alsace and Lorraine with the exception of the two fortified towns of Strassburg and Metz, and these were closely besieged. Their successes of Mars-la-Tour, St. Privat, and Gravelotte, won only at a terrible sacrifice of life, settled the fate of Metz, which was left isolated and beleaguered, its reduction only a question of time and privation. Over 150,000 men, under Bazaine, were cooped up in the fortress, and it was in vain that MacMahon, with an army almost as large, tried to bring relief, for an enemy force of a quarter of a million was on his track.

Meanwhile, in feverish haste General Trochu had put the fortifications and defences of Paris in order for a siege, and not too soon, for by the end of August news reached the alarmed inhabitants that a large army of investment was on the march. Everywhere the French were now on the defensive, hard pressed, and facing desperate odds. The first overpowering disaster of the war came on September 1st and 2nd, when MacMahon's army was surrounded and shattered before Sedan. The French losses exceeded 120,000 men, of whom 17,000 were killed or wounded ; 21,000 were taken prisoners in fighting, 83,000 capitulated, and several thousand more crossed into Belgium. Napoleon surrendered himself with the ill-fated army, and on the following day was taken, a captive, into Germany and lodged in the royal castle of Wilhelmshöhe, outside Cassel.[1] It was the beginning of an epidemic of great surrenders. On September 23rd Toul and on the 27th Strassburg followed suit, an army of 17,000 men falling into German hands in the latter case. Metz, under Bazaine, maintained a brave resistance for a few weeks longer, but despairing of relief and suffering from want of food, it capitulated, after seventy days' siege, on October 27th, and again 173,000 laid down their arms.[2] Four armies had been captured within

[1] Writing to the Queen (September 3, 1870) of his meeting with Napoleon, the King said : " In parting I told him that I believed that I knew him so well as to be convinced that he had not wanted the war, but had been forced into it. He replied : 'Vous avez parfaitement raison, mais l'opinion publique m'y a forcé.' "

[2] In 1873 Bazaine was tried by court-martial and sentenced to degradation

two months, causing Bismarck to declare with heavy humour that if another were taken he would resign office forthwith.

In the midst of these disasters at home a blow was struck at French prestige abroad. Early in the war the French troops had been withdrawn from Rome, and a miscellaneous force of all nations had taken their place. On September 20th, almost on the anniversary of the Franco-Italian Treaty of 1864, guaranteeing the integrity of the papal dominions, Victor Emmanuel entered the city with his army. At one stroke French influence in Italy was destroyed. A touch of irony was given to this final act in the story of Italian unity by the fact that the Pontiff defended his rights with all the tenacity and asperity of a temporal Sovereign.

Already Paris had given a further and more serious sign of its resentment at the inability of the generals to win battles. Lord Clarendon, speculating upon the political gyrations in which the French, whom he knew so well, might next engage, wrote to the British ambassador in Paris on August 31, 1869: "I have an instinct that they will drift into a republic before another year is over." The prophecy or premonition was fulfilled almost to the day. On September 4th, two days after Napoleon was led captive from Sedan to Cassel, a revolution broke out in Paris, the third republic was proclaimed, and the Empress fled to England. The Senate dispersed declaring its unaltered attachment to the captive Napoleon, but the Chamber, which on July 13th had echoed with the cry "Vive l'Empereur!" now decreed the deposition of the imperial dynasty. A Government of National Defence was formed, with General Trochu as President, Jules Favre as Foreign Minister, Léon Gambetta as Minister of the Interior, and General Le Flo as Minister of War. Thiers was urged to take office, but his time had not yet come. France tacitly endorsed the decision of the metropolis.

For a short time the new Executive, which divided itself between Paris and Tours, believed that Germany would be willing to agree to favourable terms of peace now that France had renounced Napoleon. Early in September the King of Prussia was called upon by proclamation to leave the country, and Victor Hugo, in a fervid manifesto, appealed to the fraternal feelings of the German nation. Paper demonstrations of the kind failing, the Executive made formal overtures to the German headquarters,

and death, but the President of the Republic (MacMahon) commuted the sentence into life imprisonment. Confined on an island off Cannes, Bazaine in the following year escaped to Spain and there died in 1888.

now perilously near Paris. Bismarck at first refused to negotiate with them, on the ground that they had no mandate and could bind only themselves. The only legitimate authority was still Napoleon, and he was a captive, disowned by his own people, or at least by Paris. Nevertheless, he agreed in the middle of the month to discuss terms of peace with Jules Favre.

Already there was busy talk of the annexations upon which Germany was to insist, and Bismarck found it expedient to issue a circular letter explaining why territory was necessary. "We cannot seek guarantees for the future in French feeling," said this statement (September 13th). "We must not deceive ourselves; we must soon expect a new attack; we cannot look forward to a lasting peace, whatever the conditions we might impose. It is their defeat which the French nation will never forgive. If now we were to withdraw from France without any accession of territory, without any contribution, without any advantage but the glory of our arms, there would remain in the French nation the same hatred, the same spirit of revenge, for the injury done to their vanity and to their love of power." Four days after the fall of Sedan, Favre (September 6th) had issued a circular despatch to the diplomatic agents of France abroad, declaring "We will not cede one inch of our territory or one stone of our fortresses." It was in this impossible frame of mind that he met Bismarck on the 19th and 20th. Although the German demands were not pressed in their later hard form, France was unwilling to yield anything at all, and the negotiations broke down.

Bismarck had assured a member of the British embassy several days before this that Germany intended to demand only the fortresses of Strassburg and Metz, and not the departments of which they were the capitals. There was, however, no doubt at all that the decision had already been taken on the pressure of the generals to insist at all costs upon the cession of the whole of Alsace and at least part of Lorraine. Warning voices were raised by warm friends of Germany in England against such a measure as certain to exasperate a proud foe and leave open a festering wound, but they were unheeded. A violent change came over the British mind and attitude directly the position of France was seen to be hopeless, and Germany showed signs of an intention to deal harshly with her. Sedan had increased the admiration for the prowess and resource of the invading army, but it also gave rise to the hope that an immediate peace would be offered to the stricken country on favourable terms. When that hope was disappointed there was a strong revulsion of feeling. Sympathy with Germany and the German national movement gave place to sympathy with vanquished France and her efforts to renew herself. There was a strong disposition to blame Napoleon personally for the disaster which had overtaken France, and it was contended that as the Empire had fallen the nation as such ought not to be required to suffer unduly. By thus changing her ground Great Britain at once forfeited the good-will of Germany, yet because she was unable to render France any useful assistance no thanks were reaped in that quarter, and in the end the war left her in disfavour with both combatants.

Mr. Gladstone, firm in his belief in moral influences and the power of eloquent despatches, was even in favour of bringing diplomatic pressure to bear on Germany in discouragement of any annexation against the will of the population concerned. Lord Granville, though more in sympathy with France than was his chief, was opposed to any departure from the principle of strict non-intervention, and no official protest was made. The Queen, however, wrote privately to the King of Prussia entreating him to offer to France such terms as she might accept with honour. " Your name," she said, " will stand yet higher if at the head of your victorious army you now resolve to make peace in a generous spirit." All that the King would promise was that he would be " as generous as my duties towards my own people permit. In shaping the terms of peace I must place in the first line the protection of Germany against the next attack of France, which no generosity will stop." An appeal addressed to the King in October by Empress Eugénie, that he would forgo any claim to French territory as an act of statecraft, and warning him that the contrary course would create enduring hatred, was answered in similar terms.

Even in Germany opinion was then far from unanimous as to the wisdom of claiming back territories which had not been part of Germany for two hundred years, and the Crown Prince, the Grand Duke of Baden, and the Duke of Coburg all warned the King that annexation would be a political blunder, for the Alsatians were passionately attached to France and wished to remain French. The historical case for regarding the cession of Alsace as merely an act of restitution was not a very strong one. It was the impotence of Germany during the Thirty Years' War which caused Alsace, then a mosaic of republics, to seek the friendship and protection of France, a step leading later to complete and amicable amalgamation. Since 1789 no part of France had been more passionately attached to the life and ideals of the common country, with whose glory and greatness its history now became intimately identified. It was an Alsatian who inspired the soldiers of the Revolution with the "Marseillaise," for this unique war-song was originally composed for the troops of Strassburg; and Alsace gave to the first Napoleon some of his best generals and strongest battalions. Bismarck regarded the nationality argument for the return of even the more German of the provinces as merely sentimental and a "professorial idea," and in the attitude which he ultimately adopted on this question he was influenced altogether by practical considerations.

The capitulation of Sedan, combined with the close investment of Metz, Strassburg, and other fortified towns, had created, not only in Germany but in the German Headquarters Staff, the belief that French resistance had spent itself. "The war must really be over now," Moltke wrote home in September; "France has no longer an army." On the contrary, the war was only beginning. Never did a nation show greater fortitude and heroism under reverse than France at that time. Responding to the fiery appeals of Gambetta and the new Executive, the people faced the terrible odds with redoubled determination, and new armies were formed by a *levée en masse* of men of fighting age. For strongly though the German armies had been reinforced by reserves and large levies of partially trained *Landwehr* men, they did not attempt to force a way further into France, with the result that the north-west, the centre, and the south served as recruiting grounds for new forces and as bases for the organization of a new defence. The unorganized and untrained remnant of the nation's manhood, not to be denied the honour of sacrifice, armed itself with such weapons as were at hand, and forming an immense body of *francs-tireurs*, inflicted great inconvenience upon the enemy. Bismarck was for hanging at sight every armed man not in uniform. It would have meant wholesale massacre, but objections based on this ground he brushed aside with the curious plea, "I attach little value to human life because I believe in another world; if we lived for three or four hundred years, it would be a different matter." Terrible reprisals were, in fact, visited upon the irregular combatants.

For a time it seemed as though France had still a chance of

shaking herself free from the enemy's grasp, and as the year neared its close the invading army was no longer as confident of a crushing triumph as it had been after the eastern fortresses had fallen. Three months after his thoughts had first turned homeward, Moltke wrote: "No one will say how long this frightful war will last. An entire nation in arms is not to be underestimated. After New Year we may have a million men against us." Roon, too, who in September had written home from Rheims, "*L'équilibre* has been completely destroyed: is not Prussia's sword to-day the sceptre of Europe?" reflected now: "How, when and where this war will end, God only knows! . . . A little *suffisance* and a little more modesty would be a good thing for many people" (December 10, 1870).

In the consciousness of inflexible courage and determination the French nation for a time clung to the hope, if not of victory, at least of such an honourable peace as would still enable it to buy off the invaders with a money *douceur*, thus speedily wiping off the fair face of France the stain of invasion. If, however, France was under the obligation of honour to continue defence, so was Germany under the necessity of continuing attack and of pressing home her advantage in every direction. After Sedan a bitterer spirit entered into the struggle on both sides. Regarding their enemy's refusal to surrender as mere perversity, and exasperated by the guerilla warfare practised by the *francs-tireurs*, the German generals showed an increasing disposition to inflict upon the French population the worst horrors of war. When Paris was hopelessly closed in, Gambetta succeeded in escaping to Bordeaux; there the Government was reconstituted, and from that safe city of refuge he sustained the spirit of the nation by inspiring manifestos and appeals for "resistance to the uttermost." But unity, enthusiasm, and readiness for sacrifice were unavailing in the lack of the supreme military efficiency towards which Prussia had been working in silence for so many years, and the sequence of disaster continued almost unbroken.

In October Thiers began a round of visits to European Courts and Governments, beginning with Great Britain. He sought to enlist moral influence, not active intervention, on behalf of a peace on moderate terms that should be honourable to France. "He seems come just to do what he can," Mr. Gladstone wrote after meeting him, but what he could do, either in England or elsewhere, was little. Disappointed at the cold *douche* he received in London, he yet proceeded undismayed to Vienna and St.

Petersburg. From the Chancellor Beust—now more wary than three months ago—and the Czar he likewise received much sympathy, but nothing more substantial, and before his return home his Government knew that the only alternatives before it were to make the best terms it could with an exacting enemy or to fight on and take the risk. Faced by terrible odds, the French nation as one man yet chose the better part, and the war continued.

When the new year opened France had still three armies in the field, in the west, north, and east, but their fighting capacity had deteriorated. Everything seemed to depend upon the movements before Paris, whose reduction, in the opinion of the German military council, promised to end the war. The position of the garrison and the civil population became daily more critical as the investment drew closer and the supplies of food decreased. In the forts alone there was an army of a quarter of a million to feed, and behind them was a crowded city of one and three-quarter millions. After a long course of grinding privation, stark hunger at last stared Paris in the face. Every attempt of the garrison to break through the chain of steel which encircled the outer suburbs was repelled, yet the population endured heroically. Finally the invaders recognized that the only hope of bending its stubborn will was to fire on the city. The diarist Abeken claims for Bismarck responsibility for this measure and its execution. He had wanted it, in fact, as early as October, when Abeken wrote from the Prussian headquarters: "The idea of Bismarck opposing the bombardment of Paris because of its works of art or of the splendours of Paris itself is incredibly ridiculous." For some time Moltke disagreed and had his way, though only after violent disputes with the autocratic Minister, whose constant meddling in military matters he resented. Now he agreed that the time had come for rough measures, and the bombardment began on January 5th.[1]

[1] According to Blumenthal, Bismarck, who wished to expedite the fall of Paris from fear that neutral countries might intervene, schemed unblushingly to overcome opposition. On December 7th the Crown Prince showed Blumenthal a "diplomatic telegram" which Bismarck had sent to him from Berlin to the effect that the men in power in Paris urgently wanted the bombardment in order to be able to surrender with honour. Blumenthal believed that the telegram was manufactured. Three days later another telegram came, stating that unless the bombardment was begun at once the North German Diet, which was about to meet, would be enraged, and disorders might occur in Berlin. The King commanded that the military Governor of Berlin should be at once instructed to maintain order at all costs, whereupon Bismarck replied that there had been a misunderstanding, and that there was no need for alarm (*Tagebücher*, date December, 1870).

An attempt, organized by Gambetta, in the middle of the month to relieve Paris by simultaneous movements by the French armies in the field and determined sorties from the forts was frustrated, and, recognizing that all hope was past, Favre obtained permission to open negotiations for the capitulation of the city and the end of the war, and with this object in view he appeared at the German headquarters at Versailles on January 23rd. The French resistance had now been broken down, and it remained to be seen on what terms peace could be bought under the desperate conditions prevailing. After the capitulation of Sedan and the French refusal to accept defeat, the iron entered more deeply into the souls of the invaders. Thiers had seen that when he tried his hand at peace negotiations at the beginning of November. The attempt came to nought, but he "thought he could guess that two milliards (of francs), with Alsace and part of Lorraine, without Metz, would be the conditions of a peace signed immediately."[1] Even those terms the generals were no longer prepared to offer. The conditions of the capitulation of Paris and an armistice were discussed for several days, and on the 28th the agreement was signed. Moltke, at the beginning of the investment, believed that the capital would be reduced in ten weeks, and Trochu himself did not expect that it would hold out so long: the resistance lasted, in fact, four and a half months, and in the end it was hunger and not cannon shot which gave to the besieging army its victory. Four days later came a further misfortune, for on February 1st Bourbaki's army of 80,000 men, hard pressed in the south-east, was led over the Swiss frontier by General Clinchant (who had taken the Marshal's command on his breakdown) in order to escape the greater humiliation of surrender.

When Favre, representing the Government of National Defence, appeared in the German headquarters, Bismarck had bluntly refused to negotiate with the self-appointed Executive, and insisted that peace could only be concluded with the nation as represented by a duly authorized body. The armistice was therefore concluded for three weeks—the Paris forts to be meanwhile evacuated—during which time a national assembly was to be elected, to meet at Bordeaux in the place of the temporary Executive and decide whether France should continue the war or lay down arms.

Gambetta tried hard to secure the return of an assembly that would be willing to support him in the policy of no surrender,

[1] *Memoirs*, p. 98.

but on Bismarck's protest against a too obvious attempt to frustrate the free voice of the nation he resigned. The elections took place on February 8th, and the Assembly met four days later. Thiers, the man who on the fateful 15th of July had incensed the Chamber with the bold declaration, "It is not for any essential interest of France, but owing to the fault of the Cabinet, that we are going to war," was returned by twenty-six constituencies, and he was chosen provisional head of the State with the title Chief of the Executive of the Republic, pending the nation's decision as to the future form of government. Most of the responsible leaders of France now recognized that to defend the national cause any longer by arms was hopeless and that what remained to be saved must be saved by diplomacy, and that speedily. Thiers and Favre, the Foreign Minister, were therefore chosen peace plenipotentiaries, and with a committee of fifteen they at once left for Versailles. At the same time Thiers sent the Duc de Broglie to London to enlist influence there in favour of an honourable peace.

It was clear that the terms of peace had already been peremptorily settled by the generals, and that there could be little opportunity for successful bargaining. Nevertheless, Thiers gallantly contested every demand and gained every concession that was humanly possible. The negotiations lasted from February 21st to the 26th, on which day the peace preliminaries were signed. The terms created intense bitterness throughout France. There was on the Prussian side a feeling that no punishment could be too severe for the vanquished enemy. The French had been beaten, but with obstinate pride they refused to admit it. Their stubborn will must, therefore, be broken, and it could be broken only by the rod of humiliation. There was magnanimity, and even chivalry, in Prussia's treatment of Austria and her only active ally, Saxony, in 1866 ; neither was shown towards France in 1871. France was, in fact, in the least favourable position possible for negotiation. When a show of resistance was made, Bismarck had only to play off Napoleon against the Republican plenipotentiaries, and threaten to restore the Empire, and he had his way.[1] The territories annexed comprised the

[1] Thiers relates how in his negotiations over the armistice question on November 1st Bismarck said to him : "We do not ask anything better than to deal with a proper body representing France and a Government with which we can treat authoritatively ; but we have, if necessary, the choice between the restoration of the Empire, a Republican Government, and even a monarchy other than that of the Bonapartes" (*Memoirs of M. Thiers*, 1870–1873, p. 75).

departments of the Lower and Upper Rhine, the greater part of the departments of the Moselle and the Meurthe, and two districts of the department of the Vosges. Almost the whole of Alsace, with Strassburg, but excluding Belfort, and one-third of Lorraine, including Metz, affectionately described by Thiers as "la ville française par excellence," were cut bodily out of France.

Thiers had fought desperately for Metz, and both Bismarck and the Crown Prince would have renounced it had they had their way. Moltke and the generals were resolute, however, and, having the last word with the King, they carried their point. When in addition Belfort was demanded, Thiers refused, whatever the consequences; whereupon Bismarck said: "Believe me, I have done everything I could, but as to leaving you any part of Alsace it is impossible." "Concede Belfort, and I will sign at once," said Thiers. Bismarck himself was willing enough: the obstacle then, as before, was the Chief of the General Staff. He made urgent representations to Moltke, however, with the result that a little later he was able to say to Thiers: "I have an alternative to propose to you. Which would you prefer—Belfort or the renunciation of an entry into Paris?" Thiers, with Favre's assent, immediately chose Belfort, and so the bargain was struck.

Unquestionably, Alsace had been the great prize from the beginning. When in the middle of August Count von Bismarck-Bohlen was made governor of the province, the Prussian General Staff published a map defining as the limits of his government the very frontiers which later became the frontiers of enlarged Germany. Yet at that time neither Strassburg nor Metz had been invested. It was recalled later how thirty years before (1841) Moltke, speculating upon the outcome of a war on the western frontier, had written that Alsace and Lorraine were for France stolen goods and that though the treaties of 1815 had confirmed her possession of them, should she begin a new war against Germany "we ought not to sheathe the sword until we have obtained our whole right and France has paid us her whole debt."

On the question of the money indemnity Prussia was less intractable. The first sum demanded was eight milliards of marks, and the first counter-offer of France was one of two milliards: by splitting the difference a bargain was struck at five milliards, equal to two hundred million pounds. From this amount thirteen million pounds were deducted to cover the value of the railways in the ceded territories. The first milliard of the indemnity was to be paid before the end of 1871, and the remainder during the succeeding three years, German troops remaining in occupation of the country meantime, but evacuating departments successively as the due payments were made.

Before the Peace Preliminaries could be effective the assent of the Government and Assembly at Bordeaux was needed, and Bordeaux was far away—so far that it seemed unable to realize the hopeless situation that prevailed in the actual field of hostilities or the hard spirit of the victors. There was grumbling for a time and even refusal to confirm conditions so much severer than had been expected. It was only when the two tribunes had taken to Bordeaux a true story of the desperate outlook that the irreconcilable deputies yielded, and on March 1st Favre was able to telegraph to Bismarck that the Assembly accepted the terms, ratifications being exchanged the following day at Versailles. For acceptance there voted 548 deputies, while 106 were against. In the minority was Victor Hugo, who in a dramatic speech prophesied that the " day would come when France would rise again invincible and take back not only Alsace and Lorraine but the Rhineland with Mayence and Cologne, and in return would give to Germany a republic, so freeing Germany from its Emperors, as an equivalent for the dethronement of Napoleon." Before leaving the Assembly the Alsatian deputies recorded their earnest protest against the action of the territories, declaring as null and void " a compact which disposes of us without our consent," and calling upon the people of Alsace and Lorraine to preserve " their filial affection for the France now absent from their homes until the day when she returns to take her place there again."

The territory taken from France had a population of 1,600,000, and comprised the seat of a highly developed and prosperous industry, principally the manufacture of cotton goods and machinery. The printed fabrics of Alsace in particular were famous and superior to any produced in Germany at that time. It was just in the production of artistic goods like these that Germany had hitherto lagged behind, and the advantage of absorbing this province—which was at once a factory and a school—was incalculable. The inhabitants of the annexed territories were given the right to cross over into France and so retain their French citizenship, and during the time allotted a large population, drawn from all classes, exercised this option. "All those who could go went," says a French historian; " those who remained wept in grief that they could not abandon their homes."

Just as after Sadowa the King of Prussia had been eager to enter Vienna at the head of his victorious troops, so now he planned a triumphal progress into Paris, and was willing to abandon Belfort rather than forgo it. The scheme failed, as the earlier scheme had failed, and the quicker wit of the Frenchman was the reason in both cases. Thiers was urgent in his demand that Paris should be spared this humiliation, but consideration for the feelings of a beaten foe was to the mind neither of the King nor his military counsellors. By completing the ratifications on the day appointed for the military spectacle, however, Thiers wrecked the ambitious plan of the royal Commander-in-chief and his generals, to their deep mortification. A large body of troops entered one quarter of the city, but the King was absent.[1] On March 7th the German Headquarters Staff left Versailles, and three days later the National Assembly, fresh from Bordeaux, took its place.

Bismarck's attitude on the annexation question has been a subject of much controversy. It is well known that in later years he took pains to present himself in the light of the moderator, standing between vanquished France and the rapacious generals. That was also the *rôle* which he claimed to have played at the close of the Bohemian war. The diligent student of his life and speeches will, indeed, recall not a few occasions upon which Bismarck endeavoured after the event to disclaim, or minimize his own share of responsibility for, measures or decisions whose wisdom or success became increasingly doubtful with the lapse of time, for with all his greatness Bismarck did not despise popularity, though more than unpopularity he hated failure. Upon the question of the French annexations he found himself constantly at variance with Moltke and the generals, since for him political considerations came first, and these seldom seemed to coincide with the views and requirements of the military experts. There was hardly any limit to the punishment which the generals were prepared to visit upon the beaten foe. They wanted enlarged frontiers and a broken France, caring nothing for the political consequences of excessive severity, while these for the statesman were paramount. "The enemy must be destroyed and under our feet," Blumenthal wrote in his Diary in September; "a Blücher, with his hatred of France, is lacking"; and, still deploring

[1] M. Guizot wrote from Paris on March 4th: "The population of Paris left the Prussian corps to parade through one single quarter of the town in solitude and silence. The Prussians have not seen Paris, and Paris did not go to see the Prussians. Their triumph had no spectators."

Bismarck's restraining influence, he commented as late as February 24th: "Bismarck is carrying on too fine a policy, taking into account matters which do not appear to me to be pertinent. Now it is the foreign Powers, now consideration for the enemy, which must not be mortally embittered, etc. To the simple intelligence of a soldier all this appears comical. The beaten-down enemy must so bleed that he will not be able to stand up for a hundred years: he must be bound in chains which will prevent him from thinking of revenge."

From first to last Bismarck favoured a much smaller cession of territory than the generals demanded, and had he had his way it is possible that no part of Lorraine might have been taken. To the twelfth hour, indeed, he questioned the wisdom of retaining Metz, as being a French city whose inhabitants would be sure to make disaffected German citizens and so cause the new Empire much harm. "I do not like the idea of so many Frenchmen being in our house against their will," he said on February 22nd. He then suggested that it would be far better to accept another milliard of francs instead of Metz. "We would then," he said, "take 800,000,000 francs and build ourselves a fortress a few miles further back, somewhere about Falkenberg or towards Saarbrücken; we should then make a clear profit of two hundred millions." In the following year he told Count Beust at Gastein that "he had opposed the acquisition of Metz because of the disaffection of the inhabitants, and that he only yielded in consequence of the urgent demands of the military authorities, who said that it would make a difference of 100,000 men in time of peace."[1] On the whole, therefore, Bismarck's claim that he was disposed to deal far more gently with France than the soldiers wished appears to be well founded.

Even now that the conditions of peace had been decided and the invaders had carried home the trophies of victory, the troubles of France were not at an end. No sooner had the main body of the investing army withdrawn from Paris than the lawless elements in the populace gained the upper hand, and, reinforced by the demoralized remnants of the National Guard, broke out in wild insurrection on March 18th, and ten days later, having in the meantime taken possession of the government of the city, proclaimed the Commune at the Hôtel de Ville. The outbreak was the result of a concourse of untoward circumstances. Genuine fear that the new republic was in danger, unreasoning resentment

[1] *Memoirs*, vol. ii., p. 260.

that the Prussian troops had been allowed to do what there was no possibility of preventing them from doing—to enter Paris—and the indiscreet administrative measures of friends, irritating a population which had already been goaded past bearing by its enemies, were among the causes of disaffection ; but in addition Paris was overrun by unruly adventurers, native and foreign, ready for any desperate exploit, and the criminal classes were only too ready to add their contribution of villainy to the general confusion. Then the Internationalists saw, in the apparent bankruptcy of the existing political and social order, an opportunity of putting their ideas into practice, and in so doing they made matters worse.

Not until outrageous excesses had been perpetrated upon person and property, until Paris had been the scene of violence and bloodshed far exceeding anything experienced in the worst siege of the war, and rigorous expiation had been exacted from the insurgents—for General Galliffet, who quelled the insurrection, paid the mischief-makers back with interest—were peace and good government restored at the end of May. The interlude of crime and destruction delayed the completion of the peace negotiations, for the Government was driven to obtain German consent to the increase of the forces before Paris beyond the strength stipulated in the preliminaries, and to call in the aid of the returned prisoners of war, who were to have remained interned behind the Loire until the formal conclusion of peace. Before this time Napoleon had been released, and had sought refuge in England for the third time in his fitful life.

The further negotiations over the definitive treaty of peace were continued at Brussels, and at first moved slowly. At one time it seemed as though the Government of Thiers would not prove strong enough to carry out the preliminaries accepted at Versailles, and the German generals were ready to throw back into France at a moment's notice the armies which had been withdrawn ; on April 24th the Federal Diet sanctioned a new loan of eighteen million pounds with that contingency in view. In order to hasten matters, Bismarck insisted that the negotiations should be removed out of the French atmosphere of the Belgian capital to Frankfort, and there the treaty was signed on May 10th.

The losses to the two nations in killed and wounded during this war of seven months have been variously estimated. The latest estimate for France, that of M. Hanotaux, places the number of killed at 139,000 and that of wounded at 143,000, while in addition 339,000 men were treated in hospitals for miscellaneous diseases. Moltke put the German loss in killed, wounded, and missing at 6,247 officers and 123,453 men, a total of 129,000; Dr. Engel, a careful statistician, has since estimated the loss at 45,000 in killed and 83,000 in wounded and missing, or together 128,000; but other estimates run as high as 175,000 and 180,000. Nearly half a million French soldiers were sent as prisoners into Germany; nearly a quarter of a million were prisoners in France; and over 90,000 were interned in Switzerland.

The marvellous recuperative power shown by France after the disaster of 1870–71 must be recalled, since it was indirectly responsible for a renewal of war-alarms several years later. It is common to speak of the war as for France not merely a disaster, which it was, but a *débâcle*, which strictly speaking it was not. A spirit of arrogance and vanity had come over the nation, engendering fatal self-confidence and self-deception, which in their turn had given rise to a false sense both of security and superiority, and caused France to rest in sluggish and enervating content upon the legacies and achievements of the past. Of these things the downfall was complete, but France herself was stronger for the ordeal through which she passed. The spirit of the new France, chastened and cleansed by defeat, was reflected by the words spoken by the President of the Republic, M. Thiers, just after the conclusion of peace: "Our policy is that of peace, equally removed from discouragement as from defiance, moved by the conviction that a reorganized France will be necessary for Europe always, and that only such a France will be able to discharge its duties to the other States and to herself."

The whole energy of the nation was now directed towards the immense task of making good the ravages done by the war, of replacing the wealth sacrificed in works of destruction, and not least of re-creating the army, adding to its virtues of heroism and valour the equally necessary virtues of discipline and efficiency. What France lost by earlier lethargy it gained doubly by concentrated industry. Gambetta gave the nation the inspiration which it needed when he said on June 24th that its motto must be "Le travail, encore le travail, et toujours le travail." And work France did with heart and soul and strength. Unknown and unsuspected stores of spiritual strength were revealed by the supreme effort which was now made by a reunited nation to find its way back to the forsaken paths of prudence, discipline, and self-control. All that the nation possessed of material treasure was likewise contributed to the common stock. In June, 1871, the National Assembly sanctioned a loan of two milliards of francs, and on the day of issue it was subscribed twice over. Bismarck had professed fear that France would not pay the instalments of the indemnity punctually. He was soon to be disabused, and to know that the one wish of the vanquished nation was to hand over the last sou with the utmost speed and be left alone with its sorrow.

By the terms of the treaty the first milliard of francs had to be paid before the end of 1871 and the remaining four milliards within three years of the signing of the Peace Preliminaries. On June 29, 1872, however, a supplementary agreement was concluded, providing for the earlier payment of the instalments and the speedier withdrawal of the alien garrison. The agreement was concluded at the wish of France itself, and as with each payment additional departments were evacuated, its effect was that the hated force of occupation disappeared over the Rhine much sooner than had been hoped or intended. The last instalment was due on March 1, 1875, but it was paid on September 5, 1873. When the French Government invited a loan of three milliard francs to enable the later contributions to be paid, subscriptions came from all the money markets of Europe to an aggregate amount exceeding fourteen times the sum required. The eagerness with which foreign investors were prepared to entrust their treasure to France was eloquent of the faith felt in her power of recuperation, but it also indicated a general conviction that a long period of peace had opened.

Midway in the war an event occurred which further strengthened the friendly relationships between the rulers of Prussia and Russia. The Czar had made it clear both before and during the war that his sympathies were with Prussia and the German cause. Hence, when the Preliminaries of Peace were signed, King William telegraphed to him: "Prussia will never forget that it is due to you that the war has not taken far larger dimensions. May God bless you for it! For ever your grateful friend William." The Czar replied: "I am happy to have been able to show you my sympathy as your devoted friend. May the friendship which unites us assure the happiness and fame of both countries!" In supporting Prussia, Russia had asked for no reward, but that did not mean that one was not expected. A little later Bismarck was able to give a practical proof of his country's gratitude. The war had relaxed the usual regard for international engagements. In August Italy had violently taken possession of Rome; in October Russia declared that she could no longer be bound by the Treaty of Paris of 1856. It will be remembered that this treaty opened the Black Sea to the mercantile marine of all countries, but prohibited the Powers of the littoral from using the sea for ships of war or building arsenals thereon. Far-seeing statesmen had always regarded the prohibition as unwise and unpractical. Lord Palmerston declared, at the time the treaty was concluded, that the irritating stipulations would not last, and he promised them a life of seven or possibly ten years. They lasted a little longer, yet always under protest of Russia, whose movements they were deliberately intended to harass.

The preoccupation of two of the signatory Powers offered to Russia a convenient opportunity for getting rid of the Pontus articles. Accordingly, on October 31st, Prince Gortchakoff, in a circular note to the Powers, repudiated them. The irregularity of the proceeding was pointed out by most of the Governments concerned, but all of them recognized that it was not worth quarrelling about. Lord Granville despatched Mr. Odo Russell to Bismarck in order to sound him, and he, using large latitude, declared that unless Russia withdrew its circular England would go to war, if necessary, without allies. The threat was sheer bluff, though it appears to have been good bluff, or at least Bismarck allowed his visitor to think so, for he immediately proposed a conference on the subject. To Gortchakoff, who, according to Bismarck, loved conferences, since they meant more stars and orders, the proposal was acceptable, and the rest of the Powers welcoming it, this mode of adjusting the question was adopted. The conference accordingly met in London in the following January, and in March a new treaty was signed by which the neutralization of the Black Sea was annulled; henceforth Russia was to be entitled to maintain as large a fleet as it wished in the Black Sea, but the right of Turkey to control the passage of the Bosphorus and the Dardanelles was to remain unchanged, and to that extent the old principle of the *mare clausum* was preserved. Prussia gave to her ally cordial assistance at the conference. It was widely believed that in repudiating the treaty Gortchakoff had acted with Bismarck's knowledge and connivance. The two Chancellors had been in conference in Berlin at the commencement of the war, and it is not likely that a question of such importance to Russia was then overlooked.

CHAPTER X

(1870–1874)

THE NEW EMPIRE

THE remark of Thiers to Bismarck, as he laid down his pen after signing the Preliminaries of Peace, that France had given to Germany unity, spoken though it was in bitterness of spirit, was true. The German Empire was literally created on the battlefield, for not only was it the natural outcome of a war in which all the German tribes fought together against a hereditary foe, but the treaties which brought the States of the South into federal relationship with those of the North were concluded at Versailles, within sight of the ring of German steel which enveloped Paris. It was significant of Bismarck's determination to run no risks, now that the last stage of the struggle for unity had been reached, that he opened negotiations with the Sovereigns and Governments of the still outstanding States immediately the French had shown the first signs of wavering and had asked the price of peace. To those who suggested that this was lightning diplomacy the Chancellor replied that it was necessary to secure the adhesion of the South before there was time for the prevailing enthusiasm to evaporate. Because the treaties which followed were concluded hurriedly, they were faulty, and he admitted it, but now as ever he followed the principle of accepting something less than he wished and being contented with that.

No one doubted any longer that unity would now be completed, yet the acceptance of unity as a foregone conclusion did not diminish the difficulties still in the way—the old sentiment of particularism, nowhere so strong as in the South, unwillingness to surrender any of the substance of political independence, and, above all, jealousy of Prussia and fear of Prussian domination, a sentiment which may have been exaggerated yet which was very real and not altogether without justification. To the removal of these difficulties not merely a resolute will but unfailing tact and resource, and above all an inexhaustible fund of common sense, were needed. Blood and iron had done their part in the rough work of the battlefield, but for the delicate tasks of the council-chamber other and finer weapons were needed.

The principal State to be won over for the larger union was Bavaria; if it could be brought in, the other three States still remaining outside would be sure to follow—Baden, with alacrity, since her ruler had been knocking at the door for admission in vain ever since 1866, and complaining of the discourtesy which had kept him waiting. In truth, a closer union promised for the States of the South great practical advantage, for whereas under the existing military treaties they were entirely without influence upon the foreign policy of the North German Government, yet were virtually compelled to accept its results, and if necessary to place their armies at the disposal of Prussia in defending it, as members of a common federation they would have a direct voice in the shaping of events for whose consequences they would in effect have neither more nor less responsibility than in the past.

Conferences were begun as early as September. Rudolf Delbrück, President of the Federal Chancellery Office and since 1868 a Prussian Minister, who had arranged the commercial treaties of 1862–5, was sent to South Germany to work out the federal problem from the economic side, but the political questions involved were discussed at Versailles, and these created the greatest difficulty. The principal negotiators with whom Bismarck bargained there were Count Bray, Count Holnstein, and Herr von Lutz, representing Bavaria; Baron von Mittnacht and Herr von Suckow, representing Würtemberg; and Herr Jolly and Herr von Freydorff, representing Baden. Baron von Friesen, a Saxon Minister, represented the North German Governments, and Herr von Bennigsen, Herr von Blanckenburg, and Herr von Friedenthal were present as leading spokesmen of the national unity movement.

It is the custom to represent Bavaria as having eagerly responded to the overtures which were now made to her. No idea could be farther from the truth. Even now Bavaria would rather have continued independent had that been possible, and it threw in its lot with the rest of Germany only under pressure of an expediency which was hardly to be distinguished from compulsion. When the first unofficial inquiries were made as to the terms on which this State would be willing to join the North German Confederation, Bismarck was bewildered by the large concessions which were at once demanded. "Bismarck," wrote at the time Prince Hohenlohe, ready though he was for union on terms, "counts on our isolation, and reckons very shrewdly that he will be able to force us in without any concessions." But he had not allowed for the strength of Bavarian particularism. From the smaller forms of that tribal weakness Hohenlohe himself was free, yet he likewise was only prepared for absorption on condition that a large allowance was made for South German idiosyncrasies. "We must arrive as soon as may be," he wrote on February 28, 1869, "at some form of arrangement which guarantees the South Germans the maintenance of their autonomy, their individuality, their kindly, comfortable national life, and at the same time make union with the North possible. Give the South Germans this guarantee, and they will gradually become part and parcel of the great German body politic; without it, never!"

Sir Robert Morier spoke of Bavaria as a State "by itself too small to live and too big to die." Morier could make much better epigrams than that. The real fault of Bavaria was that its head was out of proportion to its body; it was a small State with very much more than the due conceit of a large one. The Bavarian Government began by objecting to the idea of entering the existing Confederation at all, and demanding that it should be formally dissolved and a new start be made. Only thus did it see any guarantee that Bavaria would obtain its rightful position in the larger union now contemplated. For having once been offered by Prussia a preferential position in a reformed Federation, it expected to rank as the equal of that State in the new order of things.

So stiffnecked were the Bavarian ruler and Ministers in the early stages of the negotiations, that the King of Prussia for a time abandoned any hope of bringing in the whole of the South, only stipulating that Baden at least should be allowed to join the States of the North independently. It was only the affability of the Crown Prince, who visited Munich for the purpose of conciliating the sombre-spirited King Ludwig, already in an advanced stage of insanity, and his wavering advisers, that turned the scale.

When Bavaria finally withdrew opposition it was subject to all sorts of conditions, and to the retention of important "reserve rights" which had not been conceded to or claimed by any of the smaller States. These "reserve rights" related to the organization and command of the Bavarian army, the administration of the railways, post and telegraph, the marriage law, the laws of settlement and public relief, and the retention of certain excise duties on beer and spirits, subject to the payment to the Imperial Treasury of a proportion of their proceeds based on the *per capita* taxation of North Germany; in all these matters Bavaria was to retain her old independence. As a concession to dignity also Bavaria and the other South German States, like Saxony before, were allowed to retain their foreign legations and to receive envoys in return, for the transaction of purely local affairs, and Bavaria in addition successfully claimed that her representatives at foreign Courts should in case of need act as deputies for the accredited representatives of the Confederation. An addition of territory at the expense of Baden, which was to be compensated in Alsace, and immunity from contribution to the cost of the imperial navy, on the curious ground that Bavaria had no sea-coast to defend, were among the demands which were refused. There was great rejoicing in Bismarck's diplomatic household when, towards the end of November, the agreement with Bavaria was signed and the reluctant kingdom was safely housed in the Confederation.

The feeling in Würtemberg, which had joined the Customs Parliament in a sullen and defiant mood, proved unexpectedly conciliatory. While the negotiations were in progress the Lower House presented an address to the King declaring its conviction that unity was "a necessity of the German nation deeply rooted in its history" and as good for Würtemberg as for Germany as a whole. Here, again, minor privileges were claimed and accorded. Würtemberg was to retain, like Bavaria, a special position in relation to military questions, there was to be no interference with the postal and railway systems, and the taxation of beer and spirits was to remain as before. Baden stipulated for the last-named concession, but otherwise, like Hesse, accepted the constitution of the existing Confederation virtually without conditions except as to the diplomatic service. Nevertheless, the important concessions made to Bavaria and Würtemberg aroused a strong feeling of resentment in those States, as well as in the larger States of the North, which had not been in a position to bargain with equal success four years before. It followed that any future proposals to modify the constitution in relation to the "reserve rights" thus conceded would be conditional upon the individual consent of the States concerned.

For the rest, the broad basis of the new union admitted of little compromise. The Confederation of North Germany was to be enlarged so as to comprise all the German States, and historical precedent pointed to their organization as an Empire. The jurisdiction of the Federal Government remained substantially as before, and the legislative and executive machinery was also the same with one important exception. This related to the head of the Empire and to his title, a question upon which a long and bitter controversy raged. Here, again, ancient usage, confirmed by the action of the Frankfort Parliament of 1848–9, suggested the restoration of the imperial office.[1] The King of Bavaria and still more his heir were against it, however, fearing that the more the prestige of the Empire was magnified the more would the dignity of the individual States be diminished, a view with which some other rulers cordially sympathized, though none thought it expedient to make an equally open stand. In the end King Ludwig surrendered reluctantly upon this question and his proposal that the imperial office should alternate between the Sovereigns of Prussia and Bavaria.

The King of Prussia was indifferent to the imperial title, and told his Minister that it appealed to him no more than a fancy-dress ball distinction. As, however, the title was necessary and he had to bear it, he wished it to be a real one and accordingly asked to be known as "Emperor of Germany." That title, however, suggested territorial sovereignty, and King Ludwig would not hear of it. "German Emperor" was, therefore, proposed instead. To Bismarck the distinction was one between tweedledum and tweedledee. "What is the Latin for sausage?" he asked his secretaries when they were in the midst of a debate on the subject; and when they began to dispute likewise over *farcimen* and *farcimentum,* he silenced them with "Nescio quid mihi magis farcimentum esset." Nevertheless, as Bavaria preferred "German Emperor" he supported it. Not so the King, who held out until the time fixed for the proclamation of the Empire, with the result that in that ceremony no reference was made to either of the alternatives, but only to "Emperor William." Nor did the King of Bavaria's objections stop here. As he could not prevent the creation of an Emperor, he did his best to restrict

[1] Strictly speaking there was of old neither an Emperor of Germany nor a German Emperor, but a Roman Emperor who was a German Sovereign.

his powers, the King of Saxony helping him in secret, and had he had his way the office would not have been made hereditary in the Prussian royal house ; he declared that if he had known that this would follow he would not have agreed to join the Empire at all.

In this final conflict between South and North the Austrian Chancellor Count Beust was believed to be doing his best to stiffen the resistance of Bavaria and Würtemberg, still cherishing the hope that if these two States kept out of the new Confederation a way might yet be found for an alliance which would put Austria at the head of the union of the South which the Treaty of Prague seemed to contemplate.

In diplomatic negotiations Bismarck, iron-willed though he was, never shut open doors or broke his knuckles against closed ones. Seldom, if ever, did he show greater patience, sagacity, and restraint than in this critical time, when he had to reconcile the most violent antagonisms and to resist pressure from the most influential quarters urging him to break down opposition with a heavy hand. Even the enlightened and Liberal Crown Prince Frederick was in favour of simply laying down the law for the South Germans and forcing it upon them whether they liked it or not. Bismarck is responsible for the statement that now, as in 1866, the Crown Prince wished the title to be not Emperor but King of Germany. " What about the other Kings ? " Bismarck asked him. " They must become Dukes again," the Crown Prince replied. " And if they do not want ? " " They must be made." Altogether there was too much talk of coercion in the discussion of matters that could only be settled, if settled at all, by consent. Bismarck preferred to bend rather than break his opponents. He knew that the mere breath of force would rouse a hostility to union which would spread from the Danube to the Main, not only wrecking his present plan but perhaps undoing the work of 1867, since the adoption of high-handed measures would have justified the worst fears of Prussia's enemies. Now as ever, therefore, he followed the principle of seeking " sure advantages without disproportionately great risks." He complained contemptuously that some Prussian wiseacres in high places, who should have known better, talked as though in dealing with Bavaria Prussia was dictating to a State which had been beaten in war as in 1866, instead of negotiating with one which was now fighting by Prussia's side and whose confidence was essential to German unity.

Thus throughout all the difficult and long-drawn-out negotiations it was Bavaria which demanded the hardest terms, and Bismarck who was the conciliator. Reproached for excessive compliance, his reply was always the same: "We want no ill-humoured but a willing Bavaria." When the special convention with Bavaria was at last safely signed, he said to an associate: "The newspapers will not be satisfied with it, and the man who writes history in the usual way will be able to find fault with our agreement. He may say, 'The stupid fellow should have asked more and he would have got it—they must have given it.' And he might be quite right with his *must.* But what is the good of treaties which people *must* conclude? It was more important to me that the negotiators should be contented with the conditions, and I know that they went away satisfied. The treaty has defects, but for that reason it is all the safer." And so in fact it proved. The opinion of Bavarians in general was that they had made a good bargain and kept all they had a reasonable right to expect, that they might have obtained still more with greater persistence, but that by not winding the screw too tightly their country had come out of the negotiations with profit and credit.

It became known later that many of Bismarck's opponents in those days of empire-building were enemies of his own household. Roon, the Minister of War, was supposed to be fidelity itself, yet in private letters he was at the time satirizing and belittling both the imperial title and the Empire, and so fouling the fruits of the victories which he had done so much to organize. "All the talk is of the coming of the Emperor deputation" (of the North German Diet), he wrote to his wife on December 17, 1870. "Do I rejoice at this new title? Oh, no! I believe, however, that it is an inevitable consequence of the policy which has been followed for years, and that we now can neither wonder at nor complain of it." Like the Prussian feudal Conservatives in general—for he belonged to the landed aristocracy of East Prussia—Roon was not enamoured of the Empire, fearing that it would add importance to the existing Federal Diet, with its democratic franchise and aspirations after popular sovereignty, and would diminish Prussia's status.

The attitude of Bismarck's old party at the time is faithfully reflected in a letter written to Roon by his nephew Moritz von Blanckenburg on November 8, 1870, just after the capture of Metz: "I think of the political future with melancholy. I have talked in Berlin with Itzenplitz, Eulenburg, Wagener, and a large number of Free Conservatives. Even the latter are shocked at the precipitous entrance of Hesse, Würtemberg, and Baden in the Confederation, and regard it as settled that the majority in the new Diet must be completely Laskerized[1] (i.e. Liberalized), since it is impossible to obtain from those States any other elements." Already the Conservatives were scheming for an Upper Chamber, to consist solely of delegates of the Governments, and Roon himself favoured the idea in private.

While thus beset at home by difficulties seen and unseen, Bismarck sought and obtained encouragement in a very unlikely quarter. The Versailles negotiations were still incomplete when he conceived the happy thought of associating Austria with the transformation in progress, hoping thereby to conciliate the South and also to soothe the susceptibilities of the Emperor's Government, which now knew that the last chance of Austria's readmission into Germany had passed away. In a letter of December 14th he informed the Cabinet in Vienna of the impending conclusion of the treaties and reminded it that this movement towards complete unity, which until recently had seemed to lay outside human probability, had proceeded "out of the history and the spirit of the German people," for which reason North Germany, not having sought it, had no right to obstruct or repel it. He assumed that Austria could have no interest in interpreting the Treaty of Prague in a way that would impede the prosperous development of the neighbouring German lands, and added: "We may confidently hope that Germany and Austria-Hungary will regard each other with feelings of mutual good-will, and join hands in promoting the joint welfare and prosperity."

Whatever his personal feelings may have been, Count Beust acknowledged this renewed bid for a fresh start in Austro-German relationships in words which left no doubt that the Emperor was weary of isolation and wanted friendship. This token of a warmer relationship between Courts and Governments but lately estranged gave great satisfaction in both countries, and did much to conciliate the Southern peoples. Already there were speculations as to the possibility of a formal alliance between the new Empire and the dual monarchy, established in 1867.

Only after the Sovereigns had all come into line did a deputation

[1] Eduard Lasker was then one of the most progressive of the National Liberal leaders.

of the North German Diet obtain permission to wait upon the King of Prussia at Versailles in the middle of December with an invitation that he would accept the imperial title, a reminder of the Frankfort Parliament which pleased the constitutionalists. The King received the deputation affably, but took care to remind it that the offer of the crown must come from his fellow-Princes. Then the treaties were referred to the same Diet and the Diets of the States which were to enter the Confederation. They, too, had been ignored so long as the negotiations were in progress, and their assent was asked only as a matter of form. For it is literally true that, as the German historian Lorenz writes, "the establishment of the Empire was in essence the work of diplomacy and the part played in it by Parliament had a merely decorative significance." The North German Diet created no difficulties. It approved almost unanimously the treaties under which Würtemberg, Baden and Hesse were to enter the Empire, and even endorsed the unpopular treaty with Bavaria by an overwhelming majority (195 against 32). Similarly, in spite of much criticism, the Diets of Baden, Hesse, and Würtemberg gave a cordial, and in the case of most of the Chambers virtually unanimous, acquiescence to all that had been done.

Only Bavaria still hung back. There particularism burst forth anew; the Upper Chamber agreed, but the popular House sullenly hesitated; even the Government was halting and apologetic. Defending the treaties, as his duty was, the Minister of Justice, Herr von Lutz, confessed (December 14, 1870) that though the action of the Government had been free, it had also been involuntary—free in that no direct pressure had been applied, involuntary in that the force of events and the danger of isolation made it impossible for Bavaria to stand out. "It is useless," he said, "to cling any longer to the idea of a Great Germany. You have to decide, not to choose. You must accept the treaties." For a time it seemed as though Bavaria was still determined to block the way, and so long as the treaties were not ratified in Munich the King of Prussia refused to accept the imperial crown in Versailles. The deadlock dragged on until late in January, and though the Lower Chamber then capitulated, its acceptance was unwilling and grudging. The requisite two-thirds majority was only exceeded by two votes. The minority for the most part belonged to the Clerical party. So bitter was the feeling against incorporation amongst many Bavarians at that time, however, that they abandoned their nationality and became

Swiss citizens rather than enter a political union in which Prussia was bound to be supreme.

Nothing now stood in the way of the formal offer of the crown to the Emperor-expectant, and this was made in the name of the Princes by the King of Bavaria who, nevertheless, only overcame his last remaining scruples when he was told that the King of Saxony was waiting for his refusal to act as imperial sponsor. In every detail it was a carefully negotiated arrangement. Even the letter conveying the invitation was drawn up by Bismarck and submitted to the King of Prussia beforehand, though as the imperial drama was staged it was represented as the voluntary and single-handed act of King Ludwig.[1]

The final act was the proclamation of the Empire at Versailles, in the royal city where Louis XIV had held his brilliant court, and in the palace which had so long represented the glory of the Kings of France. The inspiring event took place on January 18th, the 170th anniversary of the creation of the Kingdom of Prussia, in the historical Hall of Mirrors (*grande galerie des glaces*) in the presence of the German Princes, many of their leading Ministers of State, and the most notable officers of the victorious armies; no direct representatives of the Diets or of the nation were present. In accepting the crown from his peers, the Emperor said: "We accept the imperial honour conscious of the duty of protecting with German fidelity the rights of the Empire and its members, of maintaining peace, and, supported by the united strength of the nation, of defending the independence of Germany. We accept it in the hope that it may be given to the German nation to enjoy the reward of its arduous and self-sacrificing struggles in lasting peace and within frontiers which assure to the fatherland a security against renewed French attacks which it has lacked for centuries." The outer world little suspected how lightly he took his new rank and dignity and that he had to the last struggled against such a break with the old life of Prussia.[2]

[1] Prince Hohenlohe hints in his Diary that the Bavarian plenipotentiaries obtained their far-going concessions by promising to induce the Bavarian King to propose the acceptance by William I of Prussia of the imperial title.

[2] "I have just returned from the proclamation ceremony (*Kaiserakt*)," the King wrote to the Queen on January 18th. "I cannot tell you how morose were my feelings in these last days, partly by reason of the great responsibility which I have now to undertake, but chiefly because of the pain which I feel at seeing the Prussian title forced into the background. At a conference with Fritz (the Crown Prince), Bismarck, and Schleinitz yesterday I became at last so morose that I was just on the point of withdrawing (i.e. from the imperial office) and transferring everything to Fritz."

The proclamation of the Empire was read by Bismarck, nor could it have been read with right or propriety by any other. For the Empire was his creation, and more than any other man in the brilliant circle he was entitled to share in the honours and jubilations of the hour. He had gained his end in face of enormous difficulties, had gained it by devious ways and drastic means, but therein he had only fulfilled the prophecy with which he entered Ministerial life. Unity had come not by liberty, as the idealists had wished, but by force; the German question had been settled not by Diet majorities and parliamentary speeches, but literally by blood and iron. It had needed three wars to bring the goal within reach; lives had been sacrificed by the hundred thousand, treasure wasted with prodigal hand, countries given over to devastation and ruin; but success had been won, and never did he doubt that the prize was worth the price. Now for twenty years the history of reunited Germany was to be, practically, the record of the same man's efforts for the advancement of his country and the spread of its influence. Survey that history at any point during the period from 1870 to 1890, and the brain and hand of Bismarck will be seen at work, his and hardly any other's. In token of gratitude, his King, now Emperor, gave to his Chancellor the rank of Prince and the estate of Friedrichsruh, in the old duchy of Lauenburg, which, after having been ceded by Denmark to Prussia and Austria jointly in 1864, had passed into the hands of Prussia in the following year.

It was a great day for the Germanic races and for Europe when it could be said that Germany was no longer a fortuitous concourse of impotent sovereignties but a firm and ordered union of States protected by an army which had within four years overthrown two of the strongest of Continental Powers. The only parts of the old Federation left outside the union were Austria and the little principalities of Luxemburg and Liechtenstein. Now it was to be seen whether in the pursuits and emulations of peace the victorious cause of unity would prove to be also the cause of progress and civilization, and the Empire would, in the words of Prince Hohenlohe, one of its later Chancellors, "be an empire of freedom, as well as of prosperity and power." The first effects were not to be mistaken. Instead of becoming more European, the nation thus elevated before all the world became more German; the old cosmopolitanism, which, while a political weakness, had been one of the distinctions of disunited Germany, gradually but surely succumbed to an intensely vivid and powerful nationalism; particularism in Germany gave place to particularism in Europe and the commonwealth of nations. The significance of these changes was to be seen only at a later date.

The first Diet of the new Empire was elected on March 3rd, and met for the first time on March 21st, choosing as its President Dr. Simson, who took the office almost by prescriptive right. The first business was the amendment of the constitution of the North German Confederation in accordance with the treaties which had been concluded with the States of the South. The democrats contended that as Germany had now a new Empire she should have a new constitution as well, and they were in favour of a fundamental revision of the hurriedly drafted constitution of 1867. At heart they hoped that the Empire would be based on a more genuine parliamentary *régime*, with a full Federal Ministry responsible to the Diet. Bismarck, on the other hand, wanted as little alteration as possible, and the majority were with him. The position and prerogatives assigned to the President of the North German Confederation in 1867 were now in substance transfered to the Emperor. The Federal Chancellor became the Imperial Chancellor, but his constitutional position and functions were unchanged. The members of the Federal Council were increased to fifty-eight, Prussia having seventeen seats as before, while Bavaria now received six, Würtemberg four, Baden three, and Hesse three.[1] The members of the Imperial Diet were increased from 297 to 382, and later, owing to the representation assigned to Alsace and Lorraine, to 397.

Apart from the rights reserved to Bavaria and Würtemberg, as already stated, one of the most important changes, introduced as a concession to the larger States, related to the functions of the Federal Council, which was henceforth to have a Standing Committee for Foreign Affairs, consisting of five members, Bavaria, Würtemberg, and Saxony appointing one each and the Federal Council nominating the other two from year to year. Of this Committee Bavaria was given the presidency, while Prussia presided over all the other Standing Committees. It does not appear that the Foreign Affairs Committee proved a very vigorous institution. Upon one notable occasion—in 1875—it was ignored and remained inactive at a time when the issue of peace and war trembled in the balance. For the rest, the legislative power continued to be exercised jointly by the Federal Council, as

[1] In 1911 Alsace-Lorraine received three representatives on the Federal Council.

representing the Sovereigns and Governments of the States and the Diet.

Other important changes related to the consolidation of the defensive forces of the Empire. Born in war as the Empire had been, and enlarged by the incorporation of a slice of France, it was inevitable that military strength and efficiency would be the constant preoccupation of its domestic policy. The military alliances with the South, dating from 1866, had been superseded by agreements which were now embodied in the constitution. Although the Sovereigns of South Germany retained the command and control of their troops during peace-time, the organization of the federal army became uniform in all essential details, such as universal liability to military service, the obligation of the States to contribute in proportion to population towards the peace strength, arming, formation, and command, the training of the troops, and arrangements for mobilization. The constitution fixed the peace strength of the army until the end of 1871 at 1 per cent. of the population of the Empire as enumerated in 1867, a ratio which gave a force of 401,659, a number subsequently embodied in a law having effect for the succeeding three years.

The constitution, as revised, was adopted on May 4, 1871, and but little altered it remains in force to the present day. Its main provisions may be conveniently summarized at this point, the discussion of technical questions being avoided. By the preamble the four States of the South are declared to have concluded with the King of Prussia, in the name of the North German Confederation, "an eternal alliance (*Bund*) for the protection of the federal territory and its rights, and for the promotion of the welfare of the German nation," bearing the name "German Empire."

In territorial and political composition the Empire comprises four kingdoms, six grand duchies, five duchies, seven principalities, and three Free Cities, together with the Imperial Province of Alsace-Lorraine. For the entire federal area the constitution establishes one nationality and citizenship, together with uniformity in the rights and duties deriving therefrom, subject to certain reservations in relation to domicile and settlement and poor-relief.

The principal questions reserved for imperial legislation and regulation are the questions of civil and political rights, migration, domicile and settlement, colonization and emigration, the passport system, insurance, customs, taxation for the purposes of the Empire, commerce, weights, measures, coinage, and the issue of paper money, the bank system, the patent laws, the protection (copyright) of intellectual property, the protection of German trade abroad, the consular service, the railway system (with reservations), maritime and internal navigation, the lighthouse system, the postal and telegraph system (subject to the reserve rights of Bavaria and Würtemberg), the army and navy (as to the former subject to special and general territorial reserve rights), medical and veterinary police surveillance, the Press and association laws, civil law, criminal law, commercial law, and judicial procedure.

The Presidency of the Confederation is a hereditary office vested in the King of Prussia, with the title of German Emperor. Sovereignty, however, is exercised by the federal rulers collectively, as represented by the Federal Council. The legislative organs of the Empire are the Council and the Imperial Diet, and the assent of each assembly, as determined by a majority vote, is necessary to a bill becoming law.

The representation of the federal States in these assemblies is as follows (a State may have as many members as votes in the Federal Council, but its votes must be given together):

	Federal Council.	Imperial Diet.
Kingdom of Prussia	17	236
,, Bavaria	6	48
,, Saxony	4	23
,, Würtemberg	4	17
Grand Duchy of Baden	3	14
,, ,, Hesse	3	9
,, ,, Mecklenburg-Schwerin	2	6
,, ,, Oldenburg	1	3
,, ,, Saxe-Weimar	1	3
,, ,, Mecklenburg-Strelitz	1	1
Duchy of Brunswick	2	3
,, Saxe-Meiningen	1	2
,, Anhalt	1	2
,, Saxe-Coburg-Gotha	1	2
,, Saxe-Altenburg	1	1
Principality of Waldeck	1	1
,, Lippe-Detmold	1	1
,, Schwarzburg-Rudolstadt	1	1
,, Schwarzburg-Sondershausen	1	1
,, Reuss, older line	1	1
,, Schaumburg-Lippe	1	1
,, Reuss, younger line	1	1
Free City of Hamburg	1	3
,, ,, Bremen	1	1
,, ,, Lübeck	1	1
Imperial Province (Alsace-Lorraine)	3	15

The Emperor as such cannot initiate legislation, his assent to it is not required, and he has no right of veto. He promulgates all laws, but in the name of the Empire.[1] In the Federal Council, indeed, he can initiate measures, but only through the Prussian Government, and then he acts not in a German-imperial but in a purely Prussian capacity, and simply exercises the right possessed by every other member of the Confederation. To the Diet he cannot appeal directly at all, but only through the Federal Council or the Prussian members of the same.

In his executive capacity, however, the Emperor possesses important rights and functions. He sees to the execution of the imperial laws, represents the Empire in matters of international law, and in its name declares war and concludes peace, enters into alliances and other political treaties with foreign States, and accredits and receives ambassadors: nevertheless, the assent of the Federal Council (i.e. of all the Sovereigns) is necessary before war can be formally declared, except in the event of an attack on federal territory or coasts, while treaties affecting matters subject to legislation require the assent of both the Federal Council and the Diet. The right to convene, open, adjourn, and close the Federal Council and the Diet lies also with the Emperor, but both bodies must be convened annually and the Council must be convened on the requisition of a third of its votes. While the Federal Council may be convened without the Diet in order to prepare for the work of the session, the Diet cannot be convened separately. Without its consent the Diet may not be adjourned for more than thirty days or more than once during a session; within sixty days of the dissolution of the Diet there must be an election, and within ninety days a new Diet must meet. A resolution of the Federal Council, assented to by the Emperor, is necessary to the dissolution of the Diet before the expiration of its legal terms, as happened in 1878, 1887, 1893, and 1906.

Further, the Emperor appoints imperial officials from the Chancellor downwards and may dismiss them at will. The organization and practically the entire management of the army and navy are his business, and he nominates all officers and officials

[1] Thus an imperial law begins: "We . . . by the grace of God, German Emperor, King of Prussia, etc. . . . ordain *in the name of the Empire after the obtained assent* (*nach erfolgter Zustimmung*) of the Federal Council and the Diet, as follows." On the other hand, a Prussian law begins: "We . . . by the grace of God King of Prussia, etc. . . . ordain *with the assent* (*unter Zustimmung*) of both Chambers."

in those services. He may also declare martial law, should public security require it.

The Federal Council consisted originally of fifty-eight members, every State having at least one seat, but since the admission of Alsace-Lorraine to representation therein in 1911 the number has been sixty-one. The Council possesses a double function, in that it is a legislative and an executive body. In the former capacity, however, it does not correspond to a First Chamber or Upper House, for its members, being the direct delegates of the Sovereigns, are not free to vote as they will, but follow the instructions of their Governments.

As a legislative organ the Federal Council is an absolute counterpoise to the elected Diet. No measure passed by the latter is valid and no resolution adopted by it is binding upon the Imperial Government until the Federal Council has signified its assent, and the same holds good of the action of the Council as against the Diet. Every member of the Council is competent to bring forward and support resolutions, and the President is obliged to allow them to be discussed. As a rule, resolutions of the Council are decided by a simple majority, the President having a casting vote. As the President is the Imperial Chancellor, and as the Chancellor is appointed by the Emperor, this means that the casting vote falls to Prussia. When, however, the Council is equally divided upon a measure relating to the army, navy, or customs and excise, the President may only decide by a casting vote in case this vote be in favour of existing arrangements. When matters not declared by the constitution to be of common imperial concern are under consideration, only the members of the State or States affected may vote. A member of the Council cannot sit in the Diet, but he has the right at any time to appear there and speak in the name of his Government, even though he be in conflict with the dominant sentiment of the Council.

The executive powers of the Federal Council are defined by article 7 of the constitution. It is the business of the Council to decide on (*a*) the proposals to be laid before the Diet, and the resolutions adopted by the Diet, and (*b*) the general administrative regulations and arrangements necessary for the execution of imperial statutes so far as these are not provided for by law, as well as take steps to amend defects that may appear in the execution of the laws and of regulations issued for that purpose. For the more effectual discharge of its functions, the Council forms Standing Committees for the army and fortifications, maritime affairs, customs and taxation, trade and commerce, railways, post and telegraphs, justice, accounts, Alsace-Lorraine, the constitution, and procedure; and in addition there is the Special Committee for Foreign Affairs, whose constitution has already been explained. In each of these committees at least four States in addition to Prussia must be represented. Members of the Confederation who neglect to fulfil their federal duties are liable to the process of execution, which must be resolved upon by the Federal Council and carried out by the Emperor.

The political systems represented by the federal States range, in many gradations of constitutional freedom, from the republicanism of Hamburg, Bremen, or Lübeck to the semi-feudalist systems of the Mecklenburgs. If, however, the constitution allows for this variety of political conditions, it leans far more to the old absolutist traditions than to modern democratic principles. The arrangements which most effectively express these principles are those of the electoral system.

The principle on which the Diet is elected has already been explained—universal (i.e. manhood), single, direct, and secret suffrage, every German citizen who has completed his twenty-fifth year having a vote in the constituency where he resides. There are, however, disqualifications—the military and the navy, both officers and men (though not officials) so long as in active service, bankrupts, also recipients of certain forms of public relief, if received during the year preceding an election, persons who have been deprived of civil rights, and those under guardianship. The second-ballot method of election is followed; unless in the first election a candidate obtains an absolute majority of all the votes given, there must be a further contest (*Stichwahl*) between the two candidates who have received the largest number of votes. The effect in a country having so many parties as Germany is often anomalous. A candidate who heads the poll at the first ballot may be defeated at the second, while his successful opponent will usually owe his return to the votes of other parties than his own, and not seldom to the support of a hostile group which has made a corresponding bargain to its own advantage elsewhere. In the event of a tie resulting, the seat is awarded by casting lots. All elections take place on one day. The official costs of elections fall partly on the Imperial Treasury and partly on the rates.

The Empire is divided into single-member constituencies (" electoral districts "). When the electoral law of the North

German Confederation was passed, the constitution of the Diet was based on the ratio of one member for every 100,000 of the population, though the smallest States—and several had only half the due numerical qualification—were given at least one seat. As there has been no redistribution of seats, the later growth of population has led to great inequality in representation. At the present time the ratio of members is one to every 170,000 of the population. The result is that some States and all the large industrial districts and towns are greatly under-represented. Berlin, the metropolis, for example, still has six members, though on the foregoing ratio it should have twelve. In the smaller States there are constituencies not one-twelfth the size of the working-class constituencies of Berlin. All the efforts of the popular parties to redress such inequalities, however, have been opposed by the Government on the ground that any thorough-going redistribution of seats would transfer the balance of political power to the working classes, and consequently strengthen the already menacing position in the Diet of Social Democracy.

Originally the duration of the Imperial Diet was fixed at three years, but an amendment of 1888 altered the period to five years, as in the case of the Prussian Diet. Measures left uncompleted at the close of a session must again go through all stages, though in the case of an adjournment they are resumed at the stage already reached. In order to its legal constitution and to the validity of any resolution a majority of the total membership (i.e. 199) must be present, but subject to this proviso the principle of an absolute majority governs all divisions, and there is no casting vote. While no legislation can be proposed by the Government without the prior approval of the Federal Council, private members are competent to initiate bills, which the Council may, of course, refuse to accept. The sittings of the Diet are public, and faithful reports of its proceedings are privileged, as are the deputies themselves, so far as relates to utterances within the Chamber. More than once an endeavour has been made to annul these immunities, but on each occasion without the slightest chance of success.[1]

Until 1906 not only was there no statutory payment of members, but members of the Diet were prohibited from receiving "payment or compensation" from any source. It has been shown how the Constituent Assembly of 1867, in debating the North German constitution, contested this provision.[2] In 1873 deputies

[1] See Chapter XII., pp. 467–9.

[2] See Chapter VII., pp. 263–4.

were given free railway passes, but all attempts to introduce the principle of payment of members were frustrated during the Chancellorship of Prince Bismarck, who held unpaid membership to be an indispensable counterpoise to universal suffrage and the ballot. When in 1881 the Progressist party voted compensation of £25 per session to provincial deputies, the Government prosecuted the recipients of this gratuity and obtained a conviction, with the result that the money was declared to be forfeit to the State. The increasing difficulty of securing a quorum of the Diet led the Government of Prince Bülow to capitulate upon this question in 1906. The constitution was accordingly amended, and members have since, in virtue of a special law, been paid at the rate of £150 a year, subject to a deduction of £1 for every day of absence from a plenary sitting or failure to take part in a division taken by names.

The constitution, as already stated, knows only one Minister, the Imperial Chancellor, who can appoint his own deputy. A law of 1878, however, authorized the creation of departments of government (*Ämter*), akin to Ministries in the parliamentary systems of the federal States, each under a Secretary of State. These departments comprise the Foreign Office, the Colonial Office (since 1907), the Admiralty, the Treasury, the Post Office, and those for Justice, Railways, the Imperial Bank, Audit, and the Imperial Debt Commission.

Over the Chancellor, the Secretaries of State, and still less over the Federal Council or its individual members, the Diet has no authority whatever: the utmost it can do is to negative the measures or proposals brought forward by them. One provision of the constitution appears, at first sight, to give the Diet some sort of control over the action of the Chancellor, in that by countersigning all decrees and ordinances issued by the Emperor in the name of the Empire he "thereby undertakes responsibility," a condition, however, which is inapplicable to military ordinances and commands. Yet in reality the responsibility here affirmed is merely of a political, and not of a judicial kind. The Chancellor or Secretaries of State may be interpellated, criticized, and censured, yet all parties combined cannot secure the removal of any one of them unless it be the will of the Emperor that he shall go. "If you strike out my salary," Prince Bismarck told the Diet on December 1, 1885, "I shall simply go to law, and the Empire will be ordered to grant me my salary so long as I remain Imperial Chancellor."

Nor can any Minister be arraigned before either the Diet or any judicial tribunal on account of acts done by him in contravention of the constitution. In this respect the constitution of the Empire marks, singularly enough, great retrogression, in point of principle, from the position adopted in the Prussian constitution of 1850, which gives to either Chamber the right to impeach Ministers for the crimes of breaking the constitution, bribery, and treason.[1] The Supreme Court of the monarchy is supposed to decide such impeachment, though the " special law " which was to have determined the questions of " responsibility, the procedure to be adopted, and penalties " has not yet been passed. The only practical guarantee against the infraction of the constitution consists of the institution of the yearly budget, though theoretically the control which can thus be exercised over the Government is not complete. For a considerable revenue is not voted from year to year, but is permanent, and so, too, is certain expenditure. Further, the constitution allows expenditure to be voted for a longer period than a year in special cases.

The provisions which deal with the amendment of the constitution were intended to make changes difficult. Not only is legislation, implying the mutual assent of the Federal Council and the Diet, necessary, but should fourteen (out of the total of sixty-one votes be given in the Council against any proposed alteration, it falls to the ground. As Prussia alone possesses seventeen votes, she is able, by taking advantage of the full representation on that body to which she is entitled, to veto any proposed change. Moreover, the particular rights of any of the federal States can only be modified with their consent.

The other legislation passed during the first session of the enlarged Diet related to the consolidation of the Empire, the organization of the new machinery of administration, the introduction in the newly federated States of the legislation of the North German Confederation, provision to meet the war expenditure, arrangements for the division of imperial expenditure amongst the States, provision for the war invalids and the survivors of the fallen, the organization of the annexed (or " regained ") provinces, and the disposal of the French indemnity.

After large deductions for common purposes, the balance of the French milliards was divided amongst the States on two

[1] So also in Würtemberg, but in Bavaria and Saxony a majority in both Chambers is necessary to proceedings being taken, while in Baden only the Second Chamber possesses the right of impeachment.

principles—three-quarters proportionately to number of soldiers they had contributed to the war and the remaining quarter according to population. The assignments made applied to such purposes as the restoration of the ravages of war in the army and fleet; the building and strengthening of fortifications on the new western frontier, at Strassburg, Metz, Neu Breisach, and Diedenhofen; provision for the invalids and the relatives of the fallen by the endowment of an invalids' fund of twenty-eight million pounds; compensation for the losses suffered by the shipping trade on land and sea; gifts and loans of money to returned soldiers to help them to re-establish themselves in civil life; compensation to German citizens expelled from France when the war broke out as well as to the towns and villages which had suffered during occupation by the troops; and a handsome grant to the military generals, the division of which was left to the Emperor's discretion. In short, there was compensation of all sorts in all directions, and plenty of money wherewith to pay it. Large sums were also used in the construction and improvement of railways; the railways in the annexed provinces were acquired by the Empire for thirteen million pounds, and one and three-quarter millions more were expended on extensions and improvements. Finally, six million pounds were laid aside in a tower at Spandau, to be held in readiness for the next war.

The fate of the annexed provinces of Alsace and Lorraine excited warm controversy. What should be their status, that of free or vassal territories; should they together constitute a separate federal State; or should they now be attached to one or more of the existing States? The spokesmen of Prussia, led by the historian Treitschke, clamoured for the incorporation of the provinces in that kingdom, and the Federal Council let it be known that it would be willing to accept that solution of the difficulty. On the other hand, there was in the South a strong feeling favourable to the partition of the territories between the adjacent Baden and Bavaria. Against all such proposals of national effacement the populations affected indignantly protested. Not only in Alsace-Lorraine, but in some foreign countries, voices were raised in favour of constituting the provinces a neutral State. It is not likely that the Government ever considered the proposal seriously, but in a speech made in the Diet on May 2, 1871, Bismarck gave the reasons which made its acceptance impossible.

"Another alternative," he said, "would have been to create

a neutral State like Belgium and Switzerland. There would then have been a chain of neutral States from the Baltic Sea to the Swiss Alps, which would certainly have made it impossible for us to attack France by land, because we are accustomed to respect treaties and neutralities. France would thus have had a protective girdle against us, while we should not have been covered by sea so long as our fleet was not equal to that of France. That, however, was a secondary objection. The primary objection was that neutrality is tenable only so long as the population concerned is determined to maintain an independent and neutral position. The population of Alsace-Lorraine, however, in the event of a new Franco-German war, would have joined France again, so that neutrality would have been merely a phantom, harmful for us, but useful for France.[1]

In the end German opinion approved Bismarck's solution, which was that territories which had been won for the Empire by the whole nation should be a common heritage, and a law was accordingly passed declaring them to be " Imperial territory " or an Imperial Province (*Reichsland*). They were not to come under the imperial constitution until January 1, 1874, but power was given to the Emperor, in conjunction with the Federal Council, to introduce the constitution in individual districts in the meantime without consulting the Diet. Bismarck at that time wished to grant to Alsace-Lorraine, by instalments, the largest measure of freedom compatible with the order of the State as a whole, and he had faith that with " patience and good-will " the French would be won over—" perhaps in a shorter time than is now expected." On behalf of the new German citizens he appealed to the nation for " German patience and German love." So far from his mind was any thought of the Prussianizing of the provinces which came into force later, that he protested against any attacks upon their individuality. " During the two hundred years they have belonged to France," he said on May 25th, " Alsace and Lorraine have developed a considerable degree of particularism, in the good old German way, and in my opinion that is the ground upon which we must lay the foundations. It must be our duty to strengthen this particularism. The more the inhabitants of

[1] As late as May, 1889, Signor Crispi sounded Bismarck on the question of the neutralization of the annexed provinces, and received the answer: " The time for neutral States is past. The French Government might agree to it, but not even that would suffice to ward off war. We should no longer be able to threaten France by land, while France would be able to attack us by sea."

Alsace feel themselves Alsatians, the more will they cast off French influence."

On the whole, both the disposition and the intentions of the Diet, no less than of the nation, towards the annexed provinces were at that time kindly and even generous. One of the first acts of the Diet was the decision to re-establish a university at Strassburg, and when the Government proposed to govern the provinces as a Crown colony for the first two years and a half, the Diet reduced the term by a year. It was only when the new administration—Prussian to the core in composition, methods, and spirit—had been set up, that the mischief was done which later made Alsace-Lorraine so grievous a burden to the Empire.

Other projects to which the first Diet devoted itself were a programme of shipbuilding, the establishment of a naval academy at Kiel, and preparations for the construction of the North and Baltic Sea Canal. At that time Moltke opposed the last scheme, contending that the nine million pounds which it was then estimated to cost would be better employed in strengthening the navy. So, too, the coinage was reformed at great cost, a change which coincided with the adoption of the gold standard. In their desire to impose at once a Hohenzollern impress upon the entire life and organization of the Empire the Prussian Conservatives proposed to replace upon all coins the effigies of the territorial Sovereigns by that of the Emperor. Bismarck flatly refused to listen to the idea, and the coinage continued to be issued with a national stamp, as it does to the present day.

Some of the legal and judicial changes which became necessary owing to the unification of Germany, though initiated at once, entailed years of labour. A beginning had already been made by the Diet of the North German Confederation, which introduced within the allied States uniform laws relating to commerce and finance, the conditions of acquiring and of forfeiting federal and State citizenship and domicile, co-operation, and the penal law, and in 1871 these laws were applied to the entire Empire. Between 1872 and 1878 laws relating to civil and criminal procedure, bankruptcy, the constitution of the law courts, the practice and status of advocates, judicial and legal fees, and other legal questions were passed after infinite labour, due to the necessity of conciliating the widely conflicting usage and traditions of many States, and for the most part they came into force in 1879. In the meantime it had been decided in April, 1877, after an acrimonious controversy, that the seat of the new Imperial Supreme

Court of Justice should not be Berlin but Leipzig, and there it was opened two years later. Dr. Simson was appointed the first President, so crowning his unique record for Presidencies. Before this the work of codifying the civil law of Germany had been taken in hand. It was the greatest purely legal task necessitated by the new organization of Germany, and it was not until 1896, after twenty-four years of labour, that it was completed.

The early days of the second Diet witnessed one of those "Chancellor crises" which were to form so familiar a feature of imperial politics in later years. In the spring of 1874 the revision of the military law of the Empire became due. A new Diet had been elected in January, and the National Liberals had been returned in increased strength, forming in the main the Ministerial majority. Nevertheless, the controversy evoked by the question was keen and prolonged. The Government now wished to fix the peace strength of the army definitely at 401,659, without counting officers and men entitled to serve only one year in virtue of educational qualifications, until further legislation should be proposed on the subject. Both the National Liberals and the Free Conservatives regarded the number as excessive, the former proposing as an amendment 360,000, and the latter 385,000. The Progressists and democrats further demanded that the number should be fixed year by year, and contended that unless that were done the budget rights of the Diet would be of no effect. No doubt this was Bismarck's purpose. The hope of making the army and its administration more independent of parliament and its resolutions had been behind the endeavour which he made, when the constitution of the North German Confederation was being drawn up, to reserve for the Executive the right to determine expenditure, while limiting the right of the Diet to the sanctioning of taxation. Therein he had been defeated, but he had succeeded in evading the principle of annual army estimates in the North German Diet and again in the Imperial Diet in 1871 by a compromise under which the peace strength was fixed for a given period. No one supposed, however, that the arrangement would be claimed as a precedent or would be held to justify the invasion of the Diet's constitutional rights which was now proposed.

The Government refused to submit on the question either of time or number, and a conflict, recalling that of 1862–66, seemed imminent. The outlook for the constitutional cause was not hopeful on this occasion, since a large section of the

National Liberal party, while in no doubt as to the gravity of the issue involved, was prepared to sacrifice its principles rather than oppose the Government at such a time on a question of national defence and security. So divided was opinion, that in committee no counter-proposal secured a majority, and the bill was rejected.

Bismarck was ill at the time, and, deeply mortified by what was going on in the Diet, he declared to his bedside visitors that as soon as he could put pen to paper he would resign. The Chancellor's resignations had not up to then been numerous, and when he called "Wolf!" people still affected to be alarmed. The threat was used to excellent effect throughout the country during the recess which followed the rejection of the bill. The result was that the Diet returned to work sobered and penitent; it had had its fling, and was now tractable again. The brave men who a month before had dared to say No now declared that they meant Yes, or shamefacedly said nothing at all. By way of compromise the National Liberals proposed that the peace strength should be fixed for seven years instead of for an indefinite period as the Government desired. This famous "septennate" arrangement was in principle an entire capitulation, and the stalwarts of the democratic party regarded it with the utmost dislike. The essential thing was that it gave the rebellious Ministerialists the opportunity of climbing down gracefully which they desired, and accordingly they grasped at it.

The Government, for its part, was well satisfied to make an apparent concession which was rather an improvement upon its original proposal than otherwise, for it was obvious to every thinking man that, justified by the septennate arrangement, a future Government would demand and expect an increase of the army as soon as the time expired. Accordingly, the bill, so amended, was accepted by a large majority (214 against 123), and the crisis passed away. During the same session the *Landsturm* was reformed by another important law, which encountered little opposition. Hitherto this last reserve had been levied on somewhat arbitrary principles; now it was to form an integral part of the fighting force, and to be organized so as to include all able-bodied men liable to service between the ages of seventeen and forty-two who had not as yet been called to the army or the navy.

These first years of parliamentary life under the new Empire were for Bismarck a time of unceasing anxiety and strain. For the medley of parties with which he had to work, and out of which to form, if possible, the necessary majorities, was formidable in number and represented every variety of political sentiment. The Conservatives, the National Liberals, the Progressists or Radicals, and the Clericals or Ultramontanes represented fairly definite political tendencies, though both North and South had peculiarities of their own. Thus there was in South Germany no Conservative party corresponding to the feudalists of Prussia, for French influence and the absence of the acute social extremes which were a legacy of serfage in the North had to a large degree made its nobles and landed gentry susceptible to democratic ideas. The democrats of Würtemberg, again, proved a welcome source of vigour to their associates of Prussia, who had not recovered from the demoralizing effect of the capitulation on the constitutional question of 1866.

Around the larger groups, however, there was a fringe of minor fractions, organized on sectional or geographical lines. Most of these groups had been elected in order to voice the protests of corners of Prussia or of the new Confederation which were still unwilling to accept the new order of things. There were the Guelphs from Hanover, who had not abandoned hope of the restoration of their shattered kingdom, and still pledged fealty to its blind King. There were Hessians who similarly bore against Prussia the grudge of the disinherited. The Poles already formed a separate party in Prussian politics, and they carried their grievances into the Federal Assembly, where, during the discussion of the new constitution, they made the audacious demand that the Prussian provinces of Posen and West Prussia should not be incorporated in the Empire. The second largest of the centrifugal parties was the contingent of deputies from Alsace-Lorraine, non-jurors, protesters, and irreconcilables, returned to assert their attachment not to new Germany but to old France. Similarly the Danes kept alive memories of the war of 1864 and particularly of Prussia's refusal to carry out the provision of the Treaty of Prague in virtue of which the Danes of the far north of Schleswig were to have been allowed to decide by *plébiscite* whether they would be subjects of the dispossessed King of Denmark or the King of Prussia. An almost unregarded section was that of the Social Democrats, daringly vocal but as yet insignificant in number, for only two deputies had been formally returned as spokesmen of the now rapidly spreading gospel of Karl Marx.

As in the Diet of the North German Confederation, so in the Diet of the Empire, Bismarck had to rely for a majority upon the National Liberals. The feudal Conservatives were ready enough to swell the Ministerial majority when he deferred to their prejudices, but they gave him little help in the establishment and organization of an Empire which they did not want. Few of them were politically enlightened enough to recognize that even from their own interested standpoint it was expedient to identify themselves frankly with the cause of unity. To their restricted minds the only certain results of unity were that the Empire would push Prussia into the background, that an Emperor by the grace of princely election would eclipse a King by the grace of God, and that in the Imperial Parliament Conservatism could not hope to occupy the dominant position which it had enjoyed in the Prussian Diet; and at this price they wished for unity as little in 1871 as their fathers in 1848. In striking intellectual contrast to the typical slow-thinking autocrats from the knights' fees and manors of Eastern Prussia, Pomerania, and the Mecklenburgs, yet equally hostile to the Government, were the little handful of feudalists of the stamp of Blanckenburg—men of the highest character, well born and well bred, eloquent with voice and pen, well informed upon every subject except politics and statecraft, whose patriotism and loyalty were free from any shadow of interested motive. Blanckenburg in particular was a special intimate of Bismarck, whom he admired as a man just as cordially as he hated him as a politician and despised his apparent opportunism. Thrice he was urged to accept the portfolio of Agriculture in the Prussian Ministry—once, at Bismarck's instigation, by the King himself—but he refused from motives entirely honourable: he could not go the way which Bismarck seemed to be going.

Thus it was that in that period of constructive legislation the influence of the Conservatives in general was only harassing and retarding; they gave the Government a certain number of votes, but no moral strength, and even the votes were not always ready on critical occasions. Bismarck used to say that the Junker class never forgave him for having risen out of the mediocrity of his own order and cast off some of its most cherished political traditions. It is certain that they never forgave his advocacy of the cause of national unity, nor yet the peace which he concluded with the Prussian Lower House in 1866 over the budget question, since to them it implied a capitulation to democracy.

Here again, Roon, great though his services to unity, betrayed the obscurantism of his class directly he saw that the German Empire could not be given over to the uncontrolled will of Prussia, and that Liberalism promised to be a greater power in the new Diet than it had been in the old. " Bismarck's policy of Germanization *à tout prix*," he wrote several years later (May 21, 1874), " has made my Prussian programme useless; with it one might have been able to stem the Liberal stream for a time, but it is beyond my power to contend against both." Roon united with a quite vehement personal devotion to Bismarck a strong propensity for saying nasty things about his policy, with which he oftener disagreed than agreed. So far did his distrust of Bismarck's coquetting with Liberalism go that he seems for a time to have entertained the idea that Count Harry von Arnim, at that time ambassador in Paris, would make a good second Chancellor, and the sooner the better.

The Progressists, on the opposite benches, were probably as free as a political party can hope to be from any taint of selfishness, but unhappily they contracted, under the leadership of a series of able but unpractical men, a strong tendency, fatal to success in parliamentary life, to obstinate pedantry and doctrinarianism; and devoted to the cause of unity though they were, they would rather—had the choice been forced on them—have dispensed with the Empire altogether than sacrificed to it one article of their political creed.

The National Liberals, on the other hand, not only formed the largest individual party, but more than any other group brought to the tasks of the Diet, together with sympathy and enthusiasm, the balance and measure of the open, candid mind. In an assembly now increased to 382 members they commanded 120 seats, and thus again held the balance between the more definitely progressive and the openly reactionary parties. Combined with two small groups of Imperialists, one drawn from the Conservative left and the other from the Progressist right wing, the National Liberals formed a powerful middle party of moderate Liberalism, a fortress against which feudalism and radicalism alike flung themselves in vain.

Such was his confidence in the patriotism of the National Liberals that Bismarck was inclined to count too surely on their support, and even to take advantage of their proved readiness to co-operate with him in the cause of the Empire. Never, however, can he be said to have carried the party in his portfolio as was the case with the feudal Conservatives when, in the course of a few years, party fortunes changed and their turn came to receive the Government's smiles and to do its will. Perhaps the cause of durable political progress would have fared better in Germany had the Chancellor been more dependent than he was upon fortuitous political combinations, and had been compelled to pay more dearly for a Liberal support which on the whole was given to him far too readily. Nevertheless, the National Liberals cannot be deprived of the credit of having helped forward the consolidation of the Empire to a degree unequalled by any other political party.

In many respects the new Diet, as it was composed during the early years of the Empire, challenged comparison worthily with the National Assembly of Frankfort, of which it was in some sort the heir and successor—in its truly representative character, its marked capacity, and, not least, the single-minded enthusiasm which most members brought to the discharge of their grave and unexampled tasks. Once more the parliament of the nation proved a faithful synopsis of all the best elements in the life and character of the German races. All the important political groups gave to parliamentary life at that time men of eminence and authority who, apart from their active co-operation in legislative work, and their special services to party organization and discipline, helped powerfully to stimulate and educate the newborn imperial spirit of the nation.

In the National Liberal ranks were found such men as Bennigsen, Twesten, Lasker, and Schwerin-Putzar; in the Conservative parties, Blanckenburg, Bethusy-Huc, Kleist-Retzow, and Friedenthal were conspicuous; in the Progressist party, Bamberger, Waldeck, Schulze-Delitzsch, Richter, and Löwe; in the Clerical, Savigny, Mallinckrodt, Windthorst, Franckenstein, and Peter Reichensperger; while the Socialists had already powerful advocates in the persons of August Bebel and Wilhelm Liebknecht. Among the men who, though for the time immersed in politics, were only in a formal sense politicians, were many scholars and professors of greater fame in the less controversial walks of life—Gneist and Marquardsen the jurisconsults, Mommsen, Treitschke, and Sybel the historians—while men like Bishop Ketteler and Canon Moufang represented the social demands of the age as interpreted by the Church. Of the high standard of ability and oratory which characterized the Assembly, of which he was himself for some years a member, Sybel says, with the enthusiasm of the first-hand witness:

"The years immediately preceding and following the French war indicate a classical elevation of parliamentary activity in Germany such as was never reached before or after. The idealistic trait in German political life had found its full development through the long and fruitless struggle for German unity, then through the vehement struggle for freedom and power in the conflict-time, and finally through the enthusiasm evoked by the realization of the national idea. The ardent enthusiasm did not last long, but it bore a full measure of lasting fruit. In the sections of the nation engaged in politics it had awakened a store of intellectual powers, and in spite of individualistic tendencies it directed these into patriotic channels. The legislatures elected under such impressions comprised so large a number of highly educated, clever, and eloquent men that one might almost have doubted whether the orchestra did not contain too many soloists had they not devoted their undivided strength to the well-being of the State with entire freedom from egoism and heated sectional interests. Their eloquence preserved a happy mean between the rhetorical splendour of a Burke and a Sheridan and the arid commonplace of the purely business debates of later times. Almost always the hearer had the impression that he was in the midst of an intellectual society pursuing idealistic aims." [1]

Political life could not, of course, continue indefinitely at that high level. The German spirit is critical, and criticism is rebellious and disruptive ; and it was inevitable that the time would come when partisanship would gain a prominence in parliamentary proceedings of which the Diet in its early days gave no promise or warning. Yet the ardour and enthusiasm of the first deputies, their devotion and patriotic self-sacrifice, their ambition to spend and be spent in the service of the national cause, now carried to assured victory, tided the Empire safely through all the difficulties and dangers of the critical period of infancy and youth, and their well-wrought workmanship withstood with success and credit the test of later years.

[1] *Die Begründung des deutschen Reiches,* vol vi., pp 284–5.

CHAPTER XI

(1868–1883)

CHURCH AND STATE

The Empire was not a year old before the Government found itself committed to a struggle with ecclesiastical authority which shook the State almost to its foundations, recalling the bitter religious feuds of the sixteenth and seventeenth centuries. This was the struggle with the Roman Catholic Church, nominally over the province of the State and ecclesiastical jurisdiction, actually over the claim of the Papacy to establish in the new Empire an independent dominion, governed by orders issued from Rome. Prussia was the principal scene of this struggle, though the issues which it raised affected all Germany, and few of the other States were able to maintain an altogether neutral position.

As was fitting in a country over one-third of whose population owned allegiance to the Roman Church, the constitution and the laws of Prussia gave explicit recognition to the rights of the confession of the minority. The Protestant or Evangelical Church was the Church of the State and of the dynasty, yet the Roman Church enjoyed equally with it practical liberty and self-government; it shared in the State endowment of religion; and provision was made at public cost for the education of its sons and daughters on confessional lines in school, seminary, and university. The King's position as *summus episcopus* applied only to the Protestant confession, and though appointments made to the Roman hierarchy in the monarchy needed royal confirmation, assent came to be regarded, in course of time, as a matter of form.

Successive Sovereigns, with a tolerance in religious matters which contrasted strongly with their narrowness in political, were not only just but generous in their treatment of the Roman

Church, which was allowed to do its work in its own way with little outside interference. Early in the century Prussia, though a Protestant State, had accredited a permanent envoy to the Vatican in the person of the historian Niebuhr, who had been cordially welcomed there for the sake of his scholarship. There were also personal ties between the Sovereigns and the Roman religion. The second and morganatic wife of Frederick William III was a Roman Catholic, and his son married a Bavarian Princess of the same faith. Always, too, Catholicism had had influential patrons at Court and amongst the territorial nobility of Westphalia, the Rhineland, and Silesia. Thus it came about that Frederick William IV in 1841 agreed to the creation in the Ministry for Spiritual Affairs (i.e. Education and Public Worship) of a special department for the better consideration of questions affecting the Roman Catholics and their Church in Prussia, and the institution was formally recognized by the constitution of 1850. All the members of this department were Roman Catholics, and though originally it was not expected that they would be partisans, they gradually came to regard it as their special function to watch over the interests of the Papacy. Bismarck described them later as " a body of men in the heart of the Prussian bureaucracy who defended Roman and Polish interests against Prussia." During the entire reign of Frederick William IV the Roman Church enjoyed exceptional freedom from secular restraint; the King refrained from interference with the appointment of the clergy, he left the bishops alone, and he refused to tolerate any restrictions upon the religious orders.

That was the state of things when William I came to the throne in 1861, bringing into action new advisers, new principles, and new purposes. In his first speech to his Ministers as Regent in 1858 he had said: " The Catholic Church must be secured in its constitutional rights, but any overstepping of these rights must be resisted," a guarded utterance which seemed to indicate apprehension of coming friction. It was not long before it was seen that a clearer demarcation of the provinces of State and Church was, in fact, intended, and that Cæsar was determined for the future to claim every whit of authority that belonged to him of right. The new spirit was the more irksome to the Roman Church, since it had come to regard State control as a fiction.

When the relationships of State and Church first became strained, however, the immediate causes came from outside. A sequence of unlooked-for events had deprived the Pope of his traditional allies and threatened his temporal sovereignty with extinction. The military defeat of Austria had been a severe blow to the Papacy, for it meant not only the weakening of a State which had for a long time been its chief support, but the rise into prominence of the rival Protestant Power. So closely identified had been Austria and Rome that in 1866 the confident belief prevailed amongst Austrian Clericals that no Prussian soldier who was a true son of the Church would turn his rifle against the forces of so faithful a protector of Catholicism as the Emperor Francis Joseph. Spain, given up to revolutions, had ceased to count as a reliable buttress of the ancient faith. In Italy the national movement had overwhelmed the Pope's temporal dominion, which was now confined to a small corner of the peninsula, and even here his sovereignty was nominal. To trust any longer to France was to lean on a broken reed, for Napoleon, with every desire to be regarded as the special patron and protector of the Papacy, had an increasing crop of difficulties of his own to face. Moreover, French help had been less cordially welcomed by the Pope since the Emperor had shown decided leanings towards Liberalism, upon which he seemed already to have decided to stake the future of his Government and dynasty.

Doomed to growing isolation, pressed on all sides, menaced by enemies and deserted by friends, the Papacy fell back upon itself and decided to rely upon its own inherent resources for the support which was not to be obtained from without. True to its strongest instincts, yet contradicting its own professions, it was to the rock of spiritual authority and not to the shifting sands of temporal power that the Papacy now looked for a firm foothold in a time of danger. By the firmer assertion of his spiritual dominion the Pope, the aged Pius IX, hoped to compensate, and more than compensate, for the loss of his worldly allies.

This was the origin of the papal bull of June 29, 1868, summoning an Œcumenical Council to meet at Rome on December 8th of the following year. The citation stated that the Council was intended to discuss "everything which in these troublous times affects the greater honour of God, the inviolate purity of the faith, the eternal salvation of men, the wholesome and thorough education of the secular and monastic clergy, the improvement of morals, the Christian instruction of youth, the common peace, and the concord of all." Its efforts were particularly to be directed towards the removal of "evils and errors" of all kinds, and the promotion of "piety, honour, integrity, justice, love and all Christian virtues, for the utmost blessing of human society." No formal programme was published, but the Jesuits were early at work, eager to use the Council in the service of their extreme tenets, and long before the first meeting it was known that a determined attempt would be made to secure the uncompromising restatement of Roman Catholic dogma and of its claims in regard not merely to matters of faith and morals, but to public affairs and State action.

In the Encyclical *Quanta Cura* of December 8, 1864, the Pope had issued a Syllabus of Errors, in which the more dangerous of modern heresies in religion, science, and social life, as understood by Rome, were condemned, e.g. religious liberty, Liberalism, the current tendencies in philosophy, freedom of the Press, lay instruction of children, and the claim of the State to exercise supervision over the Church. It was a general declaration of war against modern thought and the political tendencies then in the ascendant. The Syllabus was now to be republished in a more emphatic form, reinforced by the promulgation of a dogma new in the history of the Roman Church, the infallibility of the holder of the Sacred See. Rome, with its eagle vision, incomparable in its clearness and wide survey, saw that what the modern world, rebelling against restraint, needed was not less but more authority, and that in the assertion of authority lay the secret not only of its special advantage over all other religious systems, but of its perennial power. Fortified by this dogma, the vicegerent of God would meet the aggressive movements of a restless age by pointing to the stability and certitude of the unchanging Church, and would win back into the sure ways of faith a generation which trusted more and more to the broken lights of science, philosophy, and free-thought. Above all, his own flock should have security against the enemies of its peace —the security of a "garden walled around" against the insidious intrusions of the world and its intellectual allures.

Without waiting until the Council met, Prince Hohenlohe, then Minister-President of Bavaria, though a devout Roman Catholic, invited the Powers (April 9, 1869) to confer and, if possible, agree upon some common course of action in view of contingencies. Before taking this action Hohenlohe had received from the Munich professor of theology Dr. Ignaz Döllinger the assurance that the episcopacy would be behind him. It was then confidently believed in reflective Catholic circles that the effect of the plot brewing in the Vatican would be to split up the Roman Church into a multitude of autonomous national churches, so realizing Napoleon's gibe or prophecy of "a Europe with twenty popes, every country with its own." Both France and Austria declined to move, on the ground that it was not expedient to anticipate troubles which might not occur. The French Government had, indeed, warned the Vatican that if the dogma were proclaimed the French troops doing service for it in Rome would be withdrawn, whereupon the Papal Foreign Secretary, Cardinal Antonelli, had given the assurance that the dogma had a purely theological significance and bore no relation to secular concerns.

Prussia was disposed to join in any organized action which promised useful results, but equally unwilling to be drawn prematurely into an open conflict. In a letter of instructions which he had sent in March to the German ambassador at the Papal Court, Count Harry von Arnim, Bismarck had said: "How far the bishops are willing or able to go in the maintenance of their rights must be left to their own consciences; all that they can claim is action in the ecclesiastical sphere; the action of the State can only begin when consequences are to be anticipated in the temporal sphere. By premature intervention we should confuse people's consciences and make difficult the position of the bishops themselves." He therefore promptly rejected a proposal made by Arnim that Germany should claim to be directly represented at the coming Council by one or more special envoys or *oratores*, and should protest through them against all resolutions which seemed to infringe the rights of the State. He objected to the first of these suggestions on the ground that a Roman Catholic Council would certainly refuse to accept representatives of Protestant Governments, even if it were expedient to offer them, and to the second because protests of the kind contemplated would be futile unless those who made them were in a position to follow their words by acts. Nevertheless, speaking for Prussia, he let it be understood that while the Roman Church possessed and would continue to possess complete freedom in spiritual matters, any invasion of the sphere of the State would be resolutely repelled.

Bismarck's attitude was thus one of vigilance. He had no desire to enter into a quarrel, but he was determined to resist any attempt to disturb Germany's domestic peace, and perfectly clear in his own mind as to the conditions which would call for and justify interference. As the months passed by his confidence gave place to apprehension. Recognizing at length that if the German States had to act at all it would be wise to act together, he conferred with the Governments of the South with a view to the adoption of concerted measures should the Papacy wilfully tempt reprisals, and in the meantime everything that foresight could suggest was done to warn the leaders of the Church both in Rome and in Germany, and particularly the German bishops, of the danger of yielding to Jesuit pressure. The Prussian Ministry of Public Worship had in August, as Bismarck wrote at the time, " taken pains to exercise a preventive but confidential influence on our bishops."

Before the summer was over, however, he had come to the conclusion, as he wrote on August 11th to Prince Hohenlohe, that the extremists around the Pope were deliberately plotting to " disturb the ecclesiastical and political peace of Europe in the fanatical conviction that the universal troubles which would be caused by dissensions would strengthen the prestige of the Church, basing their expectation on the experiences of 1848, and the psychological fact that suffering men seek dependence on the Church more zealously than those who look to earthly satisfactions." "Without doubt," he added, " we have in our parliamentary legislation, in North Germany at least, an effective weapon wherewith to meet unjustifiable aggression by the spiritual power. But it is certainly better that we should not be compelled to use it, and I shall therefore regard it as a blessing, as well for the spiritual as for the temporal authorities, if a conflict between the two can be prevented by the warnings and precautions to which we have resorted." Above all things he was determined that if there was to be a fight it should not be in Rome, but in Germany, where he felt sure of his ground. " To do battle over Roman Catholic dogmas on Roman soil," he wrote to Heinrich Abeken later, " would be for us like attacking the leviathan in the water ; let it come to land, that is, let the dogma take shape in practical religion, within the sphere of Prussian legislation, and we shall then be masters."

Up to this point there was no sign in Germany that the promulgation of the dogma of infallibility would meet with sympathetic response from either Roman Catholic clergy or laity. All the tokens pointed rather to a revolt against a step which seemed to revive the intellectual tyranny of the Middle

Ages. Not only did a large section of the laity view with alarm the certain conflict between fidelity to the Church and loyalty to the State into which it would be plunged were the Papacy to attempt to invade the sphere of public and political action, but many of the more enlightened of the clergy, and even of the bishops, entertained the gravest misgivings and apprehensions on the subject. In the diocese of Cleves a powerful counter-movement was organized in the form of a collective address to the diocesan. At several of the seats of learning Roman Catholic theologians and other professors conferred, and gave clear warning that the assent of scholarship could not be relied on. On September 6th, alarmed by the growing restlessness amongst their flocks, the bishops with one accord assembled at Fulda, the scene of the labours and the custodian of the remains of St. Boniface, the apostle of the Germans, and hence the Mecca of Roman Catholic Germany, and there drew up a pastoral intended to allay fear and turn away suspicion. Never, they said, could a Papal Council promulgate any " new dogmas which are not contained in the revelation of God and the tradition of the Church, and advance principles injurious to the interest of Christianity and the Church or incompatible with the justifiable claims of the State, civilization, and science, and the legitimate freedom and the temporal well-being of the nations." The assurance was well intended, but it did not go far, for the German bishops could not pretend to speak for the Roman hierarchy as a whole.

The Council had not long been opened before the worst fears of the party of moderation within the Church were realized. On January 3, 1870, a petition bearing the signatures of 369 members called for the promulgation of the dogma. Now Bismarck thought it time to move, and to move vigorously. Two days later he directed Arnim to try to unite the German and Austrian bishops in resistance to so fateful a step before it was too late, and at the end of the month these prelates did, in fact, issue a formal memorial against the dogma as one " lacking authority in divine revelation or the authentic tradition of the Church." This protest they followed by an endeavour to prevent the discussion of the dogma in the Council. An overwhelming majority was against them, however, and the more they protested the more the extremists called for unconditional acceptance. A division was taken in the general congregation on July 13th, when of 601 bishops who took part (out of 692 present in Rome)

451 voted unconditionally and 62 conditionally for the promulgation of the dogma, 88 voted against it, while 91 were absent.[1] Nearly all the German bishops voted with the dissentients. When the final vote was taken at the public sitting of the Council on July 18th all the dissentients with two exceptions stayed away; they had, in fact, returned home the previous day, after having served on the Pope a dignified protest.

On consecutive days two of the most momentous issues in the history of modern Europe were cast upon the knees of the gods. On July 17th France had challenged Germany to military combat; on the next day Germany was committed by the declaration of papal infallibility to an equally vehement struggle with the strongest Church in Christendom.

For the present, however, there was no outward breach of peaceful relationships with Rome. Towards the end of the year the Archbishop of Posen, Count Ledochowski (afterwards Cardinal), even waited on the King of Prussia and Bismarck at Versailles in order to ask German support for the restoration to the Pope of the temporal sovereignty in which he had been supplanted by Victor Emmanuel in September. Although no promise could be given, the reception of the papal envoy was cordial and considerate. Moreover, when in the following March the Empire was established, the Pope was amongst the first of the potentates of Europe to send his congratulations.

Meanwhile, warned by Bismarck's repeated declarations that, greatly though he preferred peace, he was quite prepared to fight the Papacy if challenged, the Clericals prepared for eventualities by organizing their forces. They had already had separate representation in the Diets both of the North German Confederation and Prussia, though it bore as yet no due relation to the extent of the Roman Catholic population. Now they joined hands, and subordinating every consideration, national and

[1] The Dogma as promulgated ran as follows:

"Whence, faithfully cleaving to the tradition received from the beginning of the Christian faith, for the glory of God our Saviour, the exaltation of the Catholic religion, and the salvation of Christian peoples, we, with the approval of the Sacred Council, teach and define that it is a dogma divinely revealed, that the Roman Pontiff, when he speaks *ex cathedrâ*, that is to say, when in exercise of the office of pastor and teacher of all Christians, in virtue of his supreme apostolic authority, he defines a doctrine concerning faith or morals (*de fide vel moribus*) to be held by the whole Church, by the divine assistance promised him in blessed Peter, he has that infallibility which the divine Redeemer willed that His Church should possess in defining doctrine concerning faith and morals; and hence that such definitions of the Roman Pontiff are of themselves, and not from the consent of the Church, irreformable" (*irreformabiles*).

personal, to the interests of their faith, agreed to impose upon themselves the most rigid discipline hitherto known in party warfare. Everywhere Roman Catholics were bidden to think and act confessionally upon all political questions, and they did. In November, 1870, the elections to the Prussian Diet gave the party of the Centre, as the Clericals were called, fifty-four seats, and in the first elections to the Imperial Diet in the following March they captured sixty-three, chiefly in Bavaria and the Western and Polish provinces of Prussia.

In the creation and perfecting of this new weapon of Ultramontanism there were brought into play all the resources of an ecclesiastical system than which none was ever more resourceful in its methods or used its methods with greater effect. Platform, pulpit, and Press—a special party organ was established in January, 1871, with the name *Germania*—were used with immediate success. Fortune also gave to the party a born organizer and leader in the person of Dr. Ludwig Windthorst. Windthorst had been a Hanoverian Minister of State, and hence he brought to his task, both as party organizer and as opponent of the Government, a double devotion, as a convinced adherent of the Clerical cause and as the spokesman of an annexed country, part of which still clung to its dynastic traditions and cherished hopes of the ultimate restoration of its independence. As a parliamentary speaker he was unequalled in his time, and his incisive eloquence added quite as much heat as light to the debates of the Diets of Prussia and the Empire. Bismarck, who feared him as a controversialist, once said of his fiery oratory that " The oil of his words is not of the kind that heals, but that feeds the flames of anger," and he was compelled to admit that the Centre was the only party which had " not been incapably led." Emphatically he was a man whom it was more desirable to count as a friend than an enemy.

Windthorst declared that his party " was not at all confessional," and formally he was right, to the extent that a confessional basis was not publicly avowed, and that no one was required to display a confessional label. In fact, however, the Centre party was composed exclusively of Roman Catholics, and was homogeneous only in its confessional basis, for it included Hanoverian autonomists or Guelphs, Conservatives and anti-Prussians from Bavaria, Poles, irreconcilable Alsace-Lorrainers, and even a handful of democrats who put their Church before their political principles. Apart from questions of religion it inclined in the main towards a progressive form of Conservatism, showing special concern for the interests of agriculture, though here, again, favouring the small farmers and peasant proprietors rather than the large owners.

Bismarck, who saw through the Ultramontane pretence of non-confessional propagandism, professed to regard it as "a monstrous phenomenon in political life" that a whole Church should be converted into a political party, and he pictured the chaos of German national life if all religious communities were to follow this example. It was, however, less the party's confessional basis than fear of its opposition that troubled him. "When I returned from France," he said once in the Prussian Lower House (January 30, 1872), "I could not but regard the formation of this party as in the light of a mobilization against the State, and I asked myself, Will this contentious corps be allied to the Government—will it help the Government or attack it?" That was where Bismarck's scruples really came in; a Roman Catholic party pledged to support the Government would hardly have been objectionable. In reality the sin committed by the Roman Catholics, in thus constituting themselves a separate political force, was that they both represented confessional interests and frankly followed them, while the rest of the Protestants, though divided into many groups, followed confessional interests with equal consistency, but without open avowal. If, therefore, in the struggle which followed Bismarck showed himself to be intolerant, his intolerance was not of the religious order. The strife of confessions as such, like the strife of political parties, left him unmoved so long as the interests of the State were not involved. He was said to have seriously discussed, several years before, the idea of offering the Pope a safe place of refuge in Germany when his temporal friends appeared to be forsaking him, and, however unlikely the idea sounds, there is no reason to doubt that he would have done it if it could have been shown to be in the political interest of the State.

In those days there were many optimistic politicians in the other camps who smiled at the menace of Ultramontanism in German party life, convinced that the confessional basis of the Centre would prove accidental and transient, and that directly the unrest caused by the Vatican Council had disappeared the new organization would be disbanded, or at least would become a normal political party, occupying usefully a moderating influence midway between Conservatism and Liberalism. Few people, if any, suspected that it would one day gain and for years retain a dominating position in parliamentary life, and that successive Governments and Chancellors would be constrained to sue for its support and wait upon its behests.

It was the organization of Roman Catholicism for political purposes that determined Bismarck to do battle without quarter against the Papacy. In this determination he followed one of those sudden intuitions which often guided him aright, yet also often led him into irremediable mistakes. His Under-Secretary for Foreign Affairs, Herr von Thile, told Mr. Odo Russell in 1872 that the Chancellor's decision to fight the Church was so sudden that those around him "could mark the day and hour of the change that came over him like an inspiration." Little did he think that a struggle entered upon so impetuously would prove either so long or so arduous as it did.

What has been said is a sufficient refutation of the idea propagated by some German historians that the restatement of the dogmas of the Roman Catholic Church in 1870 was directly aimed at Germany and particularly at Prussia, and was the Pope's way of avenging the defeat inflicted upon the most Catholic Austrian Emperor at Sadowa. In the event the declaration of the Papacy affected Prussia in a special manner, but only because of the unnatural relationship between State and Church which was part of the Prussian political system and because Prussian statesmanship went out of its way to invite a quarrel, and when the quarrel began chose to fight with the worst possible weapons.

Bismarck used to say that for him the signal for active hostilities was given when in the first session of the Imperial Diet the Centre party attacked the Government for refusing to be drawn into delicate and dangerous controversies likely to endanger the concord and even the cohesion of the newly formed Empire. In the speech from the throne with which the Diet was opened on March 21st the Emperor made the significant statement that the Government had no intention to interfere in the affairs of other States.

Gratifying as the declaration was to the rest of the House, as an assurance that the policy of the new Empire was to be one of peace, it was received with disappointment by the Ultramontanes, as an intimation that Germany was not disposed to assist in the restoration of the Pope to the temporal dominion from which he had been dislodged by violent hands. Bishop von Ketteler, the one episcopal member of the Diet, protested against this doctrine of non-intervention as wrong in theory and unjust in practice. " Hitherto," he said, " it has been regarded as a Christian duty to help a neighbour when his house was in flames," and after drawing the moral, he added: " We do not want to see the Emperor and Pope in antagonism, but united." The great majority of the House agreed with the Government, however, and the address to the Crown, which was adopted by 243 votes against 63, warmly endorsed a policy of abstention, and expressed the hope that " the day of interference in the life of other nations would never occur again under any pretext or in any form."

Bismarck observed with satisfaction the resolute attitude of the Diet, while for the present keeping silence. In his reply to the address the Emperor thanked the Diet for having " perfectly understood my words." It was a second declaration that the Government was determined not to parley with the influences which were conspiring to force upon Germany the undesirable *rôle* of the Pope's advocate and protector.

During the debate on the second reading of the constitution in April the Diet came back to the question. The Centre had proposed to introduce " fundamental rights " similar to those embodied in the Prussian constitution, e.g. freedom of opinion, the prohibition of any future censorship, free right of public meeting and of association for religious as well as other bodies, and above all the " right of the Roman Catholic Church to manage its affairs independently." The historian Treitschke was one of the deputies who vigorously opposed the proposal as outdoing the Frankfort Parliament of 1848. He asserted his favourite doctrine that the State was the sole fountain of right, power, and authority, and that its prerogatives could not be devolved to churches or parties or individuals, for that were to set up rivals to its own throne. " If the Catholic Church," he said, " is to be given the right to regulate its own affairs, that right will put in the hands of any bishop in a small State with a Catholic population a powerful weapon of opposition to the Government." To this challenge Bishop Ketteler replied: " The deputy von Treitschke has begged you not to vote for laws which would make the bishops rebels against the laws of the land. But I will show you a way of avoiding such a danger: do not vote for laws which rebel against the laws of God, then we shall never rebel against the laws of the State."

Much passionate and futile polemic was expended upon this

subject of divine laws and State laws and their respective claims by lay theologians who seemed unconscious that they were bandying phrases which every man interpreted in his own way, and no two men alike. Again the Government refrained from taking part in the debate, for the Diet was doing its work well enough without interference. In the division, Athanasius had again the world against him: for the Clerical proposal was rejected by all the other parties by a vote of 223 against a Clerical phalanx of 54. Nevertheless, its authors were still undismayed. Before long they returned to the attack with redoubled energy, undeterred even by the fact that Cardinal Antonelli, ever eager for peace, had just been induced to disapprove of the formation of a Roman Catholic political party in the Diet.

The resistance of the German prelates to the papal decree had not lasted long. Within a month all had meekly surrendered, bowed the head, and accepted the yoke; Rome had spoken, and for them the issue was decided. Thereafter no body of men showed a greater zeal in fighting the Pope's battles and defending the unpopular dogma against an unbelieving generation than the recanting German bishops.

A preliminary skirmish with the civil power took place in Prussia before the close of the year. In December the Archbishop of Cologne called on the theological professors of Bonn University to declare their acceptance of the dogma on pain of being forbidden to lecture to Roman Catholic students or to exercise priestly functions. The senate of the university complained of this act to the Minister of Public Worship, Herr von Mühler, who promptly reminded the professors concerned that they received their offices from the Government and in that capacity were responsible to it alone. On the same ground the Minister in the following month supported the action of a number of teachers of a Roman Catholic higher school at Breslau in refusing to recant their declarations against the dogma at the bidding of their bishop. Other teachers in Roman Catholic districts, who had been coerced or threatened by their ecclesiastical superiors, were similarly reassured by the reminder that their removal, like their appointment, was the right of the State and not of the Church. The tension entered a more serious phase when in the following April the Bishop of Ermeland threatened to excommunicate all teachers who refused to capitulate to episcopal authority in a matter which was altogether one of intellectual honesty.

The Government replied by abolishing the Roman Catholic Department for Spiritual Affairs (July 8, 1871), a measure of retaliation but also of precaution, a sign that the State intended for the future to be master in its own house. At the same time it publicly declared that though it had offered no opposition to the acceptance of the dogma by bishop, priest, or teacher, it was determined to resist all attempts to force acceptance upon unwilling members of the Church and to protect the victims of coercion in any form. When the bishops protested that the effect of this declaration was to subvert episcopal authority, the Government answered that the prelates might excommunicate as they like, but they must remember that excommunication was a purely ecclesiastical proceeding and that excommunicated teachers were none the less, in the eyes of the Government, as much members of the Roman Catholic Church as before, and had forfeited none of their civil rights.

Already the action of the Government had divided the nation into two parties, the friends and the enemies of the State; in other words, of the Government and the political theories which it represented. Such a cleavage had the advantage that it cleared the air; it showed the Roman Catholics absolutely united, the laity with the clergy, the clergy with the prelacy, the prelacy with the Holy See. Already it was recognized that this was really a struggle between two absolutisms, a political and an ecclesiastical, equally rigid, equally tenacious of their rights.

Hitherto the isolated excesses of the ecclesiastics had been resisted by the aid of existing powers, but these had already proved inadequate. The first exceptional legislation adopted, however, was Imperial and not Prussian. This legislation was directed against the prelates and priests who were systematically using the security of their church walls for a violent agitation which outside would have been promptly checked as illegal. A law passed in December, 1871, made "abuse of the pulpit" (*Katheder*) an offence punishable by imprisonment for a maximum term of two years. The only opposition came from the Clericals, reinforced by a handful of Radicals whose love of liberty was stronger than their dislike of the Papacy and its pretensions.

A little later a step was taken which it was believed might conciliate the Holy See and pave the way for peace at home. In April, 1872, Cardinal Hohenlohe, a brother of the Bavarian statesman, was nominated as Germany's representative at the

Vatican. Far from regarding the nomination as an olive-branch, however, the Pope received it as a shrewd attempt to use against him one of the princes of the Church. The Cardinal had the reputation of being much more German than Roman Catholic in sympathies, and his relation to the head of the Bavarian Ministry, who had taken the lead in mobilizing the European Governments against the Papacy, did not increase his acceptability. Nor was the appointment commended by the fact that it had been publicly announced before approval had been signified by the Vatican. Great was the chagrin in Berlin, therefore, when the Pope informed the German Government through Cardinal Antonelli that in existing circumstances he did not regard as expedient the nomination of a Cardinal to an office so delicate. The Ministerial party in the Diet was indignant at the affront, its Press wrathful and abusive. When, however, Bennigsen declared that so ostentatious a rejection of the hand of peace was an unexampled insult to the head of the Empire, Dr. Windthorst retorted that what was without precedent was the idea of making a politician out of a prelate, and of placing a man who by his office was attached to the inner councils of the Roman Church in a position in which he would be required to serve two masters. "What would you say," he pertinently asked, "if the Pope wished to make the Emperor's adjutant-general his ambassador in Berlin?"

It was in the course of a debate in the Diet upon this question that Bismarck, spurred to defiance by the encouragements of an almost united assembly, used the famous words, which were not to return to him void, "Have no fear—to Canossa we shall not go, either in body or spirit" (May 14, 1872), recalling the abject submission of Emperor Henry IV to Pope Gregory in that historic spot in 1077. Protestant Germany was jubilant, and inscribed the brave words upon many tablets in its public places.

The next step taken by the Imperial Government in the campaign of repression was aimed at a specially insidious centre of disaffection. From the beginning of the quarrel the conviction had been strengthening in Germany that the Jesuits and their propagandism were the source of all the trouble. This conviction led to a widespread demand for a clean sweep of Jesuitism, its organizations, and its institutions from Germany, and petitions rained upon the Government and the Diet to this effect from all parts of the country. It was stated that of Jesuits of foreign nationality alone there were eight hundred in the

Empire at that time. The clamour for the expulsion of the Jesuits had been answered by the Roman prelacy and clergy with an impressive protest against any interference with the existing liberties of the religious orders. The strength of the representations for and against led the Government to refer the question to a special committee whose report—the handiwork of the jurisconsult Rudolf von Gneist—took the form of an elaborate treatise on the history, teaching, objects, and influence of the Society of Jesus. Proceeding from the standpoint of German penology, according to which the treatment proper to undesirable citizens is to pass them on to other countries without so much as asking permission, it was not difficult for Gneist to prove his thesis, viz. that a law should be promptly prepared and enacted forbidding the settlement in Germany of members of this organization and of the congregations affiliated to it unless the legislation of the State concerned expressly allowed it. The report was accepted by the Diet by a vote of two to one, and again most of the members of the popular parties voted solidly with the Conservatives.

As the session was far advanced, the Government proposed a short emergency bill to meet urgent cases, and promised to deal fully with the question in the autumn. The Diet was not in a mood for half-measures, however, and it insisted upon immediate legislation. Accordingly, a bill of three clauses was soon produced, providing that members of the Society of Jesus and the kindred congregations might—which in practice meant should—be expelled from any part of the federal territory, even though they possessed citizen rights. The duty of expulsion was entrusted to the police authority. It was in vain that the speakers of the Centre appealed for a spirit of moderation, and, conscious of the powerful moral force behind them, warned the Government that they were entering upon a struggle in which they could not possibly prove victorious. They spoke to deaf ears, for the idea of force had become an obsession. The bill passed through all its stages in a week, and received the assent of the Federal Council on June 25th. The new powers were at once rigorously enforced; the Jesuit organizations were dissolved, the Jesuits themselves expelled, and fervent patriots cried "Good riddance!" and thought all trouble was now at an end. It was not so, however, for the disappearance of the Order of Jesus only brought to light the existence of other Roman Catholic orders and societies more or less similar to it in character and aims. Until further imperial legislation was possible, therefore, some of the Governments refused to allow either monks or nuns to teach any longer in the schools of their own faith.

At that time there seemed no extreme of coercion to which the excited Protestants were not prepared to go. Germany had just won unity at the cost of a bloody war, and they were not disposed to parley with any party which threatened to weaken the cohesion so laboriously achieved. Forgetting that more than one-third of the population was Roman Catholic, and that the Roman Catholics had borne their full share in the struggle just completed, the adherents of the ascendancy confession raised the cry "No quarter for the Papist faction!" and gave the Government *carte blanche* to assert the supremacy of the State by stern and expeditious measures. There were hot-heads who even contended that just as the Prussian Government had a right to approve the election of bishops presented by the Roman Church, so the Imperial Government should be entitled to approve of the election of Popes. Invited to state his opinion on the question, Bismarck said (June 9, 1873) that the Government would refrain from interference of the kind. Nevertheless, a year before (May 14, 1872) he had issued to the German ambassadors secret instructions to use their influence with the Governments to which they were accredited in favour of joint action with a view to this very object.

In that time of abnormal and excited humours many of the Government's staunchest supporters were found in the ranks of the Radical party, whose whole history had been a protest against Governments which overrode constitutional rights and trampled down parliamentary minorities. Warned by the Clericals that as they had suffered in the past so their turn to face the rod might come again, they scoffed incredulously. "There must be created for a time a Ministerial dictatorship!" said a leading deputy of the Prussian Diet, Professor Rudolf Virchow, a man who during all his public life had been fighting dictatorship in the name of Liberalism and freedom. It was a phrase used by Virchow which stamped this conflict between State and Church with the name under which it has gone down to history. "The contest," he said, "has taken the character of a great cultural struggle" (***Kulturkampf***). In no constitutional country is the tyranny of catchwords so great as in Germany. Had not the struggle been consecrated by that unhappy phrase, it is possible that it might not have appealed to the nation with the overwhelming force it did or have been waged in so bitter a spirit.

The Vatican was not indifferent to the storm which was now so furiously raging in the North. So long as the German prelates and clergy appeared to be holding their own the Pope refrained from open interference. With the passing of exceptional laws, however, he broke silence. In an address to a deputation of German pilgrims he said of Bismarck, on June 24, 1872: "The first Minister of a powerful Government, after victorious exploits in the battlefield, has put himself at the head of this persecution. I have told him that a triumph without moderation cannot be of long duration, and that a triumph in a struggle against truth and the Church is the greatest of follies. Who knows," he said in conclusion, "whether the little stone may not soon be loosened from above which will shatter the foot of the Colossus?"

While the Imperial Government was thus vigorously applying coercion in the Empire at large the Governments of some of the leading States were following its example within their own territories. In Prussia a beginning was made in December, 1871, with the introduction of a bill to remove the schools altogether from clerical control. It was ostensibly directed towards the discouragement of the Polish movement in Silesia and West Prussia, but it was intended to strike a blow at Clericalism throughout the kingdom generally. It affirmed that the supreme supervision of all public and private schools belonged exclusively to the State, reserved to the State the sole right to nominate and remove the local and district school inspectors, and in effect aimed at depriving the clergy of all confessions and churches of any influence, other than that expressly delegated to them by the State, in the schools of the people. Bismarck euphemistically described the object of the bill as simply to compel Prussian subjects who had not hitherto spoken German to learn to use that language. The inclusion of the State clergy in a general prohibition was designed to avoid the appearance of exceptional legislation, but it aroused such vehement resentment amongst the feudal Conservatives in the Upper House that the bill had for a time to be withdrawn.

Before it was reintroduced a change was made in the Ministry of Public Worship, which prepared the way for a more systematic and resolute policy of repression. Herr von Mühler, who had held the office hitherto, was an uninspired administrator of somewhat wooden mind, one of those safe public officials who are warranted to walk in the straight ways of mediocrity, to make no mistakes due to courage, and to be guiltless of accessibility to new ideas. He was not the man to grasp novel situations with a strong hand, and above all he was not a political fighter, and it was a sturdy combatant that Bismarck needed by his side in the task which he had undertaken. So little enamoured of coercion was Mühler, that in the Council of Ministers he had opposed the introduction of the School Inspection Law, though it was his duty to expound and defend it in the Diet. His wavering and ambiguous attitude and his general inability to rise to the occasion had won for him general distrust, and in January, 1872, the opposition against him took the form of a vote of no-confidence so unmistakable that he at once resigned.

His successor was ready in the person of Dr. Falk, an old parliamentarian free from strong party ties, a man of marked capacity, uniting with a practical mind a wide knowledge of affairs and great strength of purpose. Avowedly he took office with the one object of asserting the rights of the State as against the new claims of the Roman Church. "I shall never impede the full and free movement of the Church and the ecclesiastical organizations," he said (January 30th), "but where it is necessary to protect the rights of the State against these organizations I shall resolutely repel all unjustifiable pretensions." There was no mistaking the spirit and the intentions which lay behind this declaration: a new policy was impending—the policy of "Thorough." In order to prevent misunderstanding, Bismarck added in the same debate that he was in complete agreement with his new colleague.

Falk's first move was to take up the School Inspection Bill again, and see what he could make of it. Reintroducing it in an amended form, he had the satisfaction of seeing it accepted on first reading by the House of Deputies. In the House of Lords the Evangelical Conservatives were still as much opposed to it as the Ultramontanes were in the Chamber below, and once again its fate for a time hung in the balance. Deserted by his friends, Bismarck lost patience. Adjuring the pillars of State and society in the select assembly to "occupy themselves with realities, and to show now the confidence in the Government which they had shown in the past," he ended with a threat that even were a wholesale creation of peers necessary in order to carry the bill, he would not hesitate to create them. The warning proved sufficient: the cave which had been forming collapsed, and the bill became law. Put into operation the law did not prove nearly so revolutionary as had been feared. Most of the school inspectors of both confessions remained in office, though State inspectors were appointed in the Polish districts.

How badly Bismarck took the defection of the Conservatives appears from letters of the period. Disaffection had been brewing even before the Empire, which the feudalists did not want, became a certainty, and with its establishment it became a slumbering revolt. Moritz von Blanckenburg wrote to his uncle, the Minister Roon, as early as January, 1870: "The opposition of the Conservatives against Bismarck is making rapid progress; one might even call it embitterment." Roon replied to this letter: "Politically I, too, belong to the Conservative Opposition, for I will not be led against my will with my eyes bound when I do not know where I am going." Bismarck knew of the rising tide of opposition, for he had his agents and eavesdroppers everywhere, and received their reports now in his official residence, now (and more often) at Varzin. What now caused the revolt to break out again more vehemently was the spectacle of a Prussian and an Imperial Government being carried on with the assistance of the Liberal groups, for the alliance had to be paid for, if not extortionately, at least in Liberal coin. One of the obnoxious measures given to the popular parties, in acknowledgment of favours past and to come, was the District Government Ordinance of December, 1872, which was to do for rural administration what Stein's Municipal Ordinance of 1808 did for urban government—to abolish an oligarchy and place local government upon a broad popular basis. First rejected by the Upper House, this measure was only passed after the dissolution of the Diet and the dilution of the obstructive Chamber by the creation of twenty-five new peers. Following in the wake of the School Inspection Law, this measure exhausted both the patience and the fidelity of the feudalists, who ever since the introduction of constitutional government had been so intimately identified with the Ministry that they had come to regard it as no less intimately identified with themselves, and the breach with Bismarck which resulted lasted for some years.

The next step in the quarrel with Rome was to try direct conclusions with the prelates, who had hitherto acted as though they and not the King's Ministers wielded the power of the State, and had set at nought the civil authority in a way that in the King's Ministers would have been treason. A beginning had been made in January, 1872, with the chaplain-general of the forces, who had forbidden a chaplain of the Cologne garrison to use a church which served likewise for separatist Catholic services, though directed so to do by the Minister of War. The Minister's remedy was simplicity itself; he abolished the chaplain-general's office. Other military chaplains who obeyed their bishop's orders rather than those of the military authorities were dismissed. The Bishop of Ermeland had already made himself specially notorious. One of his acts had been to forbid Roman Catholics to have any intercourse with their excommunicated brethren. Now Dr. Falk warned him that such boycotting was a direct infraction of the Prussian Common Law, and that unless it were withdrawn he would be suspended from his see. The bishop invited the Minister to address his letters to the Pope, and on being again asked whether he was prepared to obey the law of the land he replied with a refusal to give any undertaking of the kind. Thereupon his salary was suspended. The Archbishop of Cologne had pronounced the "greater ban" upon several Roman Catholic professors of Bonn University who had declined to accept the dogma, and when the Government refused to remove them from office, had forbidden attendance at their lectures. For the present nothing more could be done by administrative measures to remedy the intolerable situation created by conflicts like these; all the more, therefore, did the Government feel the need for stronger powers, and these were now created.

At the end of 1872 Bismarck's health had broken down under stress of work, and still more of disappointment and chagrin at the defection of those who should have been his staunchest supporters. In a letter to Roon he complained in December that he was surrounded by enemies. "I am in disfavour with all the members of the royal house," he wrote, "and even the King's confidence in me is declining. Every intriguer has his ear." In the bitterness of his isolation he appears for a time to have contemplated total retirement, but on reflection he saw the danger of handing over foreign affairs to a successor lacking his knowledge and experience. He therefore offered to retain the Chancellorship and the portfolio of Foreign Affairs if the King would relieve him of the office of Prussian Minister-President. To this course the King agreed, and Roon accepted the vacated post at the beginning of 1873, retaining it until October, when Bismarck again took up the double burden.

In resigning the Presidency of the Ministry, Roon also laid down the office of Minister of War, which he had held since 1859. The reason given for his retirement was ever-increasing physical infirmity, and his age—for he was now over seventy—seemed to justify the plea. His letters show, however, that he was also dissatisfied with the direction which domestic affairs were taking, and was unable to keep abreast with Bismarck's violent transformations, particularly as revealed by the development of the *Kulturkampf*. "Tired out as I am," he wrote to Blanckenburg at the time, "I feel incapable of stemming and forcing back the onrushing flood. By my assent to the District Government Ordinance and the May Laws I have shown that I have abandoned the Conservative standpoint of 1848, and sincerely desire to see rational developments. But I have no breath, either physically or metaphorically, for being rushed."

When Roon went, the Conservatives lost all restraint. By the use of Court influence, the value of which they nevertheless seemed to exaggerate, by a violent Press campaign, and by backstairs intrigues of many kinds, they made a desperate attempt to undermine Bismarck's position, and to create in the public mind the conviction that Count von Arnim was really the man whom the country now needed. Nor was Arnim slow to accept his friends' estimate of his abilities. Bismarck nipped the plot in the bud by promptly disgracing the aspirant to his office. Causing Arnim to be recalled from the Paris embassy on the ground of contumacy and neglect to give to the Government's policy due support, he wound the wayward diplomat in toils which held him the more securely the more he struggled to free himself, until at last he was undone.[1]

Bismarck felt keenly Roon's defection at a critical moment, when troubles were threatening him at home and the foreign situation had suddenly taken an alarming aspect. "By your retirement," he wrote to him (November 20, 1873), "I am left alone, for you were the only sympathetic spirit amongst the Ministers. The remnant of the old stock that remains is good for nothing. Office will henceforth be lonely for me, and the more so the longer I remain. The old friends are dying or changing into enemies, and one does not make new ones. As God will! Your vacant sofa seat in the yellow council-chamber

[1] See Chapter XV.

will never be filled again, and I shall never see the void without reflecting, 'I had a comrade!'"[1]

On retiring, Roon had addressed to his colleague a generous and fervent valediction (October 12th): "Let me call to you out of a full heart, 'Adelante, adelantador, atrevido!' ('Forward, ever forward, brave hero!'), and beseech God's blessing on your further prosperous and grandiose endeavours." Nevertheless, with recovered freedom he still cultivated close association with his old feudalist friends, and retained to the end an attitude of detachment, amounting at times to covert hostility, towards the Government and its policy, though his hands were never soiled by intrigue. "It would only be justifiable," he wrote on April 18, 1874, when Bismarck's enemies were conspiring to compass his downfall, "to make Bismarck impossible, or to create difficulties for him if there were a better man to put in his place. But where is there such a man? Moltke? He would not be likely to agree. Manteuffel? Him I regard as quite impossible, though I prefer not to give my reasons. Who else is there? I know absolutely none. Whatever may be said, therefore, against Bismarck, or rather against his political devices, I should still regard it as a great misfortune if he were to be compelled to retire owing to illness or intrigue. I regard him as necessary so long as I can find no better man, and I know of none. The political hotspurs who would like to overthrow him do not know what they want."[2]

Meanwhile, the struggle with Rome developed. For the present Prussia had still the scourge in hand, and the flagellation of the rebellious clerics was far from completed. In January, 1873, Dr. Falk further justified his appointment to office by introducing a series of four drastic bills which later were passed as the "May Laws." The first of these laws took from the bishops much of their disciplinary power, and made it an offence punishable with fine or imprisonment for any servant of the Church either to impose or to threaten penalties in matters not of a strictly religious character. The second related to the education

[1] The first words of Uhland's song "Der gute Kamerad" (Roon's *Denkwürdigkeiten*, vol. ii., p. 607).

[2] *Ibid.*, vol. ii., pp. 631–2. Bismarck says in his *Reflections and Reminiscences* (vol. i., pp. 328–9): "Without my will and to my regret, chiefly through gossip-mongering, there came to be in Roon's last years not exactly a coldness but a certain distance between us, and on my side the sense that my best friend and comrade had not confronted the lies and calumnies which were systematically circulated about me as decisively as I hope that I should have done if his case had been mine."

of the clergy, which was now placed entirely under State supervision. Henceforth the clerical office might be filled only by Germans who had undergone a prescribed course of liberal training; the entire organization and curriculum of seminaries and other institutions for aspirants to the office were subjected to State control; the bishops were required to notify to the Government all intended clerical appointments, and the Government was to have a right of veto upon them. The effect was not merely to raise the standard of qualification for the priesthood—a right proceeding done in the wrong way—but the priest was made for practical purposes a State official. This intrusion of the secular power in a sphere in which the Roman Catholic Church had never tolerated interference was not made more acceptable by the fact that the law was applied equally to the Protestant confession.

A further law facilitated secession from the Church. Henceforth all that was necessary was for the dissentient to declare before a local judge that he wished to withdraw—a short-sighted measure, which in later years cut deeply into the cohesion of the State Protestant Church. The fourth of the May Laws, besides limiting and subjecting to State control the ecclesiastical discipline to which Roman Catholic clergy were amenable, brought it under regular and prescribed procedure, and provided for appeal to the ordinary courts of law.

During the discussion of these laws it was found that some of their provisions were contrary to the constitution, but that discovery was not allowed to be an obstacle; the constitution was promptly amended and the laws were then duly passed. In the Lower House a few Conservatives of the staunch religious type were not able to support the Government in these revolutionary changes, but all were approved by the usual majority of two to one. In the vote of the Upper House the Conservatives were in a majority, and fearing that this attack upon Romanism would react injuriously upon the Protestant Church, they for a time withheld assent. Only after Bismarck had again threatened to elect new peers did they surrender. To his sorrow, it fell to the arch-feudalist Roon to defend the May Laws against his own political associates.

When the enactment of these new laws was seen to be certain, the bishops met once more at Fulda to take courage and devise counter-measures. After a week's conference they adopted an address to the Government declaring their determination to obey the laws of God, as they understood them, rather than those of men; in other words, to set the secular power still at defiance. "No Catholic Christian," they said, "could acknowledge these laws or voluntarily obey them without the gravest violation of his faith." The Government's answer to this challenge made it clear that the laws would be enforced without compunction.

Feeling in the Protestant parts of the country now had worked itself into a kind of frenzy, and there was no longer any question of moderation or mutual concessions, no longer any fair weighing of right and wrong. If the Roman Catholic bishops and clergy were obstinate, rebellious, and provocative, the great mass of Protestants, clerical and lay, were intolerant, implacable, and vindictive. The "No Popery" party, lashing itself into fury, had armed itself for an old-fashioned fight in the old-fashioned way, and bigotry ran riot. The few Protestants who remained sane in the prevailing dementia, and refused to join in the general hue and cry against the rival confession, were attacked almost as viciously as the Ultramontanes themselves, and branded as enemies of their country and the State. Yet the inevitable effect of coercion upon the persecuted Church was to strengthen its cohesion. In the elections to the Prussian Diet in November, 1873, the Ultramontanes gained thirty-two seats and became the second strongest party in the Lower House, while in the elections to the Imperial Diet in the following January they increased from sixty-seven to ninety-two.

Having entered upon a policy of repression, one measure created the need for another, for by the very act of coercion new difficulties and problems were created. One of these arose out of the wholesale sequestration of bishops and clergy. One of the first of the dignitaries of the Church to suffer was the Archbishop of Posen, Ledochowski. His salary was withdrawn at an early stage in the quarrel, but as he was not dependent upon the State treasury he continued to administer his diocese as before. Called upon to vacate the see, he refused and was prosecuted, and as on conviction an impossible fine was imposed upon him, he was imprisoned for two years. The Archbishop of Cologne and the Bishops of Treves and Paderborn, after incurring fines to the amount of some thousands of pounds, similarly passed from six to eight months in gaol; if upon some of the prelates this ignominious punishment did not fall, it was only because they fled the country. As with the bishops, so with the clergy; prosecution, imprisonment, and sequestration were their common portion. Yet bishoprics and benefices whose occupants had been removed by the Government were not held to be vacant by the Roman Catholic Church, since it did not recognize the right of a secular power to invade its jurisdiction. As, therefore, the patronal authorities in such cases refused to appoint either successors or substitutes, it was necessary for the State to devise arrangements in order to prevent large sections of the Roman Catholic population from being deprived of religious ministrations. This was the origin of a law passed early in 1874, providing for the administration of vacated offices.

About this time Bismarck let it be known in Rome that peace was possible if the Pope wished for it. Cardinal Antonelli declined to take the first steps, however, conscious that the Prussian Government was engaged in a futile struggle and that time was on Rome's side. The struggle, therefore, continued. A further Prussian bill to make civil marriage obligatory was introduced in March, 1874. The measure was repellent to the consciences of many deputies and of a large number of citizens favourably disposed towards the Government and its policy, but it had been made necessary by the repressive laws which had gone before. For inasmuch as many of the sequestered clergy, as in conscience bound, continued to perform the duties of the sacred office of which the State had nominally deprived them, it followed that in the eyes of the law the official acts done by them—and amongst them the performance of the rite of marriages—were illegal. The civil and social confusion thus created could only be remedied by separating the civil from the ecclesiastical sanction of the marriage contract and regarding the former only as valid and necessary.

As a member of the Second Chamber of the Prussian constituent Diet of 1849, Bismarck, then at the threshold of his public career, had protested against making civil marriage an article of the constitution, on the ground that to do so would "weaken in the national mind the sense of religion and of the religious tie of marriage, degrade the office of the clergy, and subordinate the Church to a bureaucracy." As late as 1868 he had repeated his objection to such a worldly innovation. Though still heartily disliking this measure, it became his duty to propose it, under pressure of circumstances which were far stronger than his convictions. "I believe," he said, "that the State needs this law as a measure of defence, and I am resolved to defend it, like much else that does not commend itself to my personal convictions and especially those of my youth." Like the facilities given for withdrawing from the State Church, this measure, too, was to prove a doubtful blessing to Prussia. Undoubtedly it has had all the ill results predicted of it by Bismarck in 1849, with others like to them ; an increased tendency to dissolve marriage by divorce, and even in certain classes of society to dispense with marriage altogether, may be attributed in large measure to the secularization of the marriage ceremony.

A year later (February 6, 1875) the principle of civil marriage was applied to the whole Empire, though not without strong opposition from a number of State Governments which were not convinced of its necessity. In the meantime the Imperial Diet had passed a law (May, 1874) to prevent the exercise of ecclesiastical functions by unauthorized persons. Under it, contumelious ecclesiastics might be assigned to definite places of residence, might be deprived of the citizenship of their States —a penalty which disqualified them from being citizens of any other German State—and even be expelled from the Empire if they dared to exercise office or functions of which they had been deprived by the secular power.

While thus Bismarck's hand lay heavily upon the Ultramontanes at home, his eyes had been fixed anxiously upon their associates in unfriendly France. There a new spirit had reigned since the nation had recovered from the first depression caused by the disasters of 1870–71. During the first two years of the Republic it fell to Thiers to direct the policy and organize the will of the chastened nation, and he devoted his energies undividedly to the one purpose of healing the wounds wrought by war and internal discords. With that end in view he discouraged ideas of revenge, and strove to concentrate the nation's mind upon its own regeneration, as a goal to be reached only by the severe discipline of moral earnestness and strenuous devotion to public and private duty. The purging of his Government of elements which he believed to be hostile to national unity brought about in the spring of 1873 a combination against him of the various groups which represented the old monarchical traditions and attachments, and in face of a vote which, though it left the Ministry with a small majority, was yet too emphatic to be ignored, he resigned the presidency on May 24th, and was the same day succeeded by Marshal MacMahon.

During MacMahon's term of office a reactionary spirit set in ; the Monarchists and Clericals, who had bided their time, made common cause and gradually gained the upper hand. Embittered by the repressive laws which were being enforced in Germany against their Church and co-religionists, the Ultramontanes in particular embraced with vehemence the spirit of revenge. Roman Catholic bishops gave to the movement their support, and a well-disciplined Press and a profuse literature popularized the idea in every nook and corner of France. Berlin took alarm, and when repeated remonstrances to the Government had no effect, Bismarck caused the German ambassador in Paris to direct its attention to certain French laws which would enable the authorities to check and suppress agitations of the kind, and to hint that if the powers at command were not used the conclusion would have to be drawn that there was no desire to discourage these agitations.

Veiled threats of this kind proving equally ineffectual, Bismarck in January, 1874, instructed Arnim to do his utmost to induce the Government to join in the Prussian struggle with Rome. The papal pretensions, he pointed out, were a source of danger and of possible political convulsion for all States, but for France in particular to tolerate them would be to destroy any hope of peaceable relations with Germany, or, indeed, with the rest of the world. The French Government was asked, in fact, to bring its policy into line with that of Prussia and the German Empire, and so to lessen for Bismarck the increasing weight of his domestic difficulties. Again the desired response was lacking.

In the midst of his campaign of repression Bismarck himself had a taste of vindictive violence. On July 13, 1874, while at Kissingen taking the cure, he was shot at and slightly injured by a half-witted journeyman cooper of Magdeburg, a Roman Catholic whose brooding over the Church and State struggle had brought him to the verge of insanity. His assailant was sentenced to fourteen years' penal servitude. An attempt was made to fix upon the Clerical party responsibility for the crime, but without the slightest justification. The only effect of the outrage was to increase Bismarck's popularity greatly, and to harden the resolve of the Protestant part of the nation to persist in the policy of coercion. In December, in order to make the breach with Rome complete, the embassy to the Vatican was suspended. A little later Bismarck even tried to persuade the Italian Government to agree to the revision of the Law of

Guarantees with a view to curtailing the Pope's liberty, but Italy had no wish to fight Germany's religious battles, and the suggestion was not entertained.

An attempt to intervene in the dispute made by the Pope early in 1875 led to new reprisals. A papal letter of February 5th, addressed to the Prussian bishops, declared null and void all Prussian laws which denied and sought to undermine the divine sanction and authority of the Roman Church. The publication of the letter was proscribed in Prussia, and newspapers which reproduced it were confiscated and their editors and publishers prosecuted, whereupon a Clerical deputy read the document in the Prussian Lower House, a device which legalized its appearance in print as a fair report of parliamentary proceedings. In April the Prussian Government replied with the Bread-Basket Bill, a measure which suspended all grants by the State to the Roman Church in sees whose bishops and clergy refused to promise obedience to the laws of the land. The bill was promptly passed with the usual majority. A law followed repealing the articles of the Prussian constitution which guaranteed independent government to the Protestant and Catholic churches and their substitution by the provision that these churches and all others should henceforth be regulated by the laws of the State. Effect was given to this change by a law relating to the administration of the estates of Roman Catholic communities. It provided that a church council consisting of from four to twelve persons should be formed in every parish under the superintendence of the bishop, to administer the Church funds. The first disposition of the bishops was to ignore this law like the other, but on reflection they decided to accept and work it rather than see the estates of the Church pass under the control of State officials, which was the alternative to the formation of local councils.

The last of the Prussian exceptional laws was one passed in May, 1875, dissolving the religious orders and congregations, with the exception of those engaged in the nursing of the sick. It was stated in justification of this measure that between the years 1855 and 1873 the number of members of these organizations had increased from 913 to 7,992.

It is unnecessary to follow the course of the quarrel in the other States in detail, for while the vigour with which it was waged and the weapons used by the State Governments differed greatly, the issues in the main were the same everywhere. The position in Bavaria was peculiar, for while there the Government disputed Rome's pretensions not less earnestly, though with greater moderation, than in Prussia, the Diet was under Ultramontane influence. The Bavarian bishops and clergy were unanimous in accepting the dogma of infallibility and in the resolution to exact compliance from the entire body of the laity, and, relying on the traditional strength of their position, they did not anticipate serious opposition. The Government had forbidden the promulgation of the dogma without royal permission, yet the bishops acted in defiance of the prohibition, and coerced, penalized, and excommunicated right and left. Some of them declared to be null and void every oath which involved a pledge contrary to the Roman Catholic faith as lately expounded. If, they said, the State placed itself in opposition to the pretensions of the Church, the duty of obedience and loyalty, either in official or soldier, lapsed. Divided in will and fearing the results of an open breach with the national Church, the Government temporized as long as possible, but the example of Prussia and the Empire eventually compelled it to move. In Bavaria, too, contumelious bishops were removed from their sees, and the vacated offices remained unfilled, while many of the clergy were sequestered.

In Würtemberg there was far less upheaval, partly because the Roman Catholics formed a small minority of the population, partly from the greater spirit of accommodation peculiar to the Swabians. In Baden, two-thirds of whose inhabitants were Roman Catholics, the Government acted with a high hand, and besides severely repressing clerical excesses, it offered recognition and support to the separatist Catholic communities, which were enabled to form a number of churches. In Hesse, where Bishop von Ketteler headed the clerical revolt in its early stages, a series of laws modelled on the Prussian May Laws was introduced. In relation to the schools the Government improved on Prussia's example, for it excluded the priestly orders from any share in their management and facilitated the conversion of confessional into "simultaneous" schools.

At an early stage in the quarrel a counter-movement, aiming at the defence of the Roman Catholic faith against the new claims made on behalf of the Papacy, took root in several parts of the country. Its adherents called themselves Old Catholics, and the impetus came from Munich. Here Döllinger early raised the flag of revolt, and his fellow-protesters at the university rallied to his support with an address of congratulation endorsing his protest against the "unchristian tyranny" which the bishops of Germany were seeking to impose upon the consciences of free men. The bishop of the diocese replied by excommunicating the daring theologian, upon which his colleagues elected him to the rectorship of the university. This assertion of independence in the headquarters of German Catholicism was as unpleasant for the heads of the Church as it was unexpected by them. When a mass meeting of Catholic citizens of Munich adopted a written address of protest to the King, the bishops and clergy replied by excommunicating all whose names could be identified. Embitterment increased when a Munich non-juring professor was refused absolution at death and burial with ecclesiastical forms was forbidden. Public opinion now indignantly called upon the Government to hold a more resolute attitude, and the prevailing discontent led to a change in the Minister-President. The display of mingled intolerance and tyranny shown by the ecclesiastical authorities in Bavaria gave to the Old Catholic movement just the publicity and stimulus which it needed.

Döllinger had for many years occupied a unique position as the advocate of a free Catholic Church of Germany. More than twenty years before, at a Roman Catholic Congress of 1848, he had sketched the outlines and organization of such a church, and it was understood that he would have been willing to be its Primate. Into the movement which seemed likely to realize his dream he threw the full weight of his personality and influence. In September, 1871, a general congress of Old Catholics was held at Heidelberg, where, together with a few of the clergy, a large body of laymen, many of whom bore names well known in scholarship and in academic circles, gathered from all parts of Germany. The idea underlying the movement was not merely to preserve the Roman Catholic Church from a new superstition, but to purge it of Jesuitical influence and of all hindrances hostile to nationalism and national aspirations. The result of the congress was a decision to constitute a separate church. Later, at Cologne, a bishop was chosen in the person of Dr. Reinkens, a former professor of Catholic theology at Breslau; the necessary administrative machinery was created; a constitution was drawn up; and arrangements were made for the organization of parishes. The bishop was ordained by a Dutch Jansenite prelate, and besides being allowed to take the oath to the King of Prussia, the Diet of that country voted his salary. The

Governments of Baden and Hesse formally recognized him as the bishop of the Old Catholic communities in those States, and that of Bavaria would have done the same, had it had the constitutional power, but in default it allowed him to visit the separatist churches and to hold confirmations. In all these States the Diets made grants towards the stipends of the Old Catholic clergy, and placed churches at the disposal of the new communities.

Nevertheless, propitious though the beginning of the Old Catholic movement was, it never reached formidable proportions. Many communities were formed in the South and in Prussia, but they were all small, and everywhere it proved easier to establish churches than to obtain priests. In Bavaria the ratio was one priest to fifteen churches. The movement, in fact, represented only the intellectual protest of a minority of the educated Catholic laity; it lacked a deep spiritual foundation, it created no religious or moral stirring, and the common people in general held aloof. At the time of its maximum strength, in 1878, the adherents of the Old Catholic Church did not exceed 52,000, and four years later, when the quarrel with the Church was nearing a settlement, they had fallen to 35,000.

For six years repressive laws fell upon the Roman Catholic Church and its leaders in Germany like the murrain upon the Egyptians; in Prussia alone twelve exceptional laws of various kinds were passed in four years. Thereupon, having, as they hoped, paralysed the power of Rome, the Governments, both Imperial and State, hoped for peace. So thoroughly had the net of coercion been drawn around the Church, that it seemed as though nothing more remained to be done but to gaze upon its futile and impotent struggles and wait until, in abject submission, it should sue for release. If systems of coercion worked like machinery, the system devised during the *Kulturkampf* would have been perfect. What the Government forgot was that it was attacking men and women in the most sensitive part of their being, their feelings and consciences—attacking them over matters and relationships which to the vast majority of Catholics were as precious as life and as sacred as death, their religion and the tie of the believer to his faith and Church. The Roman Catholic bishops and clergy may have been obstinate, lawless, and despotic, yet at least they were honest and believed that they were obeying a sanction higher than that of men. Hence, the consequence of persecution was that, instead of making mere misdemeanants of the clergy, the Governments made of them martyrs, and instead of cowing the laity, they roused in it a resentment which rallied it whole-heartedly to the side of a cause which, intrinsically, was by no means free from reproach.

But still the repressive laws were not obeyed. The consequence was that by 1877 eight archbishops and bishops had been removed from their sees in Prussia, leaving only four in office, three had been removed in Bavaria, in Baden one, and in Hesse one. Half of the bishops in Germany had been displaced, and had sought asylum in other countries. "All went abroad," says a German historian of the time, faithfully reflecting the uncharitable spirit which had gained the upper hand, "where they properly belonged." Hundreds of clergy were similarly removed, many being imprisoned, and a far greater number of officers and servants of the Church of minor grades were deprived of their employments and livelihood. Many loyal Catholics returned in 1871 from the French war, in which they had gallantly fought for their German fatherland, only to be exiled and compelled to take refuge in the very country which but lately they had left as victors.

As with the servants of the Church, so with its institutions and agencies. Colleges and schools were suppressed; societies and organizations were dissolved; and churches were closed by the hundred. The whole organization of the Church was dislocated; its ministrations were in many parishes entirely suspended, and in a larger number seriously curtailed. The infant was left unbaptized; the marriage rite was performed by stealth; the dying were deprived of the solaces of their religion and were left to go upon the last journey without the *viaticum*. The condition of things created in England at the dissolution of the monasteries in the dark sixteenth century was repeated in Protestant Germany in the enlightened nineteenth. Those who suffered most were not the prelates and priests, but the common people, who understood little of the questions in dispute, never gave a thought to the political aspect of the papal power, and were unable to appreciate the high-flown theories of the State put forward by the parliamentary advocates of the policy of coercion, but who knew by daily experience that their beloved Church was in hostile hands, that their temples were defiled and the priests whom they revered were persecuted and torn from their side. Bismarck was never weary of declaring that the struggle which he was waging with Rome was "not a confessional but a political struggle," but the distinction—to him, perhaps, clear enough—did not lessen the religious animosity and bitterness of those who encouraged and applauded him, or alleviate to his victims their hardship and suffering.

To such depths of pettiness and spite did the anti-Clerical agitation go, that in 1874 the historian Heinrich von Sybel, then professor at Bonn, formed a fanatical association whose elevated mission it was to spy into the public and private life of State officials in every town and village in the Rhineland—Landrats, Mayors, school inspectors, clergymen, teachers—and denounce to the Government those who were deemed to be wanting in loyalty to its repressive measures. Bismarck welcomed and used the information yielded by this despicable inquisition until revelations of blackmail, levied by a more than usually sordid agent, discredited the organization and its works, and he then suddenly knew it no more.

For a time the strength and self-consciousness of the new Empire seemed to be justified by this relentless assertion of its will. It was left for the next generation to learn by bitter experience that in binding in chains the Church of the minority the nation bound itself more strongly than it knew in slavery to the omnipotent State in whose name the work of repression was done.

Nevertheless, there was something amiss with the imposing system of coercion, and of this the proof was seen in its failure. For it produced results contrary to those expected of it; those whom it was intended to overawe became only bolder and more defiant; and at the very moment that the policy of repression appeared to have reached its maximum effort it was reversed. Bismarck's correspondence shows that when, at the end of 1877, Count Henckel von Donnersmarck was mediating between him and Gambetta in Paris and elsewhere, trying to win the then dethroned tribune for an anti-Clerical policy,[1] his Government was limbering up its guns and prepared to seize any pretext for beating a retreat.

Attempts at reconciliation were first made by Rome in 1878. Within the first five weeks of that year three of Italy's foremost men passed away—first La Marmora, the ill-fated general who led the Italian army to defeat in 1866; then Victor Emmanuel, the unifier of the kingdom; and on February 7th the Pontiff himself. Pius IX was succeeded by Cardinal Pecci as Leo XIII,

[1] See Chapter XV.

a man of suaver temper, not less jealous of the rights of the Sacred Cure, but more diplomatic in asserting them. Diplomatic intercourse had ceased between Rome and Berlin, but through Bavaria the new Pope notified his election to the German Government in a message in which he begged the Emperor to restore concord in the place of strife, and so strengthen the loyal devotion of his Roman Catholic subjects to his person. "Our soul will never have quiet," he wrote, "so long as ecclesiastical peace has not been restored in Germany." The Emperor, in a cordial reply, invited the Pope in turn to persuade his flock to obey the law, since disobedience was the cause of all the Empire's woes.

The exchange of courtesies did not go further at the time, but it had achieved a valuable purpose: silence had been broken. Feelers after peace were soon afterwards put forward on both sides, first through intermediaries, leading gradually to informal negotiations, which passed through every gradation of suspicion, caution, and incertitude before they reached the stage when practical statesmen could take them in hand. For while both State and Church were fully persuaded that the quarrel had lasted long enough, neither wished to concede too much.

The Pope wanted the Falk Laws to be repealed bodily. That would have been a complete surrender to Clericalism, and an implicit admission of the papal right to dictate to the State which laws it should reject and which retain. The demand was therefore refused. At the same time Bismarck let it be known that, though the laws themselves would have to remain, there were ways of softening and even of evading them. But what was the Pope willing to offer in return? Loyal obedience to the laws must be yielded by the clergy in any event, but a mere promise to that effect would not be sufficient; there must be some guarantee of good conduct. A guarantee which might be acceptable was the recognition by the Pope of the legalized duty of bishops to notify in advance to the Government all intended appointments to the clerical office—the much-discussed *Anzeigepflicht*—a duty which, as has been shown, carried the complementary right of the Government to object to appointments so proposed. So protected, the civil authority would at least be able to convince itself that the aspirants for clerical office were men of loyal and law-abiding character. After much wavering, in which the negotiations at times seemed in danger of shipwreck, mutual concessions were offered on these lines: the Prussian Government was to obtain a dispensatory power to whittle down the Falk Laws in practice, and to offer a hope of permanent modifications at a later date, while the Pope was to be bond for the good behaviour of the hierarchy in Germany and to accept without reserve the obligation of pre-notification. The desire for peace having thus been practically avowed, further progress on the same way was merely a question of method and time. Upon one thing Bismarck was determined: the Roman Church should never again be restored to the privileged position which it had enjoyed in Prussia from 1840 to 1870.

In August, 1878, Bismarck himself, while at Kissingen, had begun negotiations with Cardinal Marsella, the papal nuncio at the Bavarian Court, who had been empowered by the Cardinal-Secretary Franchi to treat with him. The bargain proposed and virtually agreed to was that in return for the recognition of the bishops' duty to pre-notify clerical appointments the German Government would be willing to resume diplomatic intercourse with Rome. Franchi's sudden death interrupted these negotiations, and his successor, Cardinal Nina, lacking his pacific spirit, was not in a hurry to resume them. Nevertheless, there was no longer any doubt as to where events were tending when in July, 1879, Dr. Falk resigned office. In taking leave of the Prussian Diet, which had supported him so well, he said that after having fought the Clericals for seven years he was not the man to have charge of a policy of peace and conciliation, nor was it likely that his opponents would willingly receive olive-branches from his hand. When Falk resigned, eight of the ten Prussian bishops had been removed from their sees, 1,400 clergy sequestered, and all the Catholic seminaries closed. He was succeeded by Herr von Puttkamer, by marriage a relative of the Chancellor.

In the following September Bismarck at Gastein resumed with the Pro-nuncio Jacobini the negotiations which were suspended at Kissingen. The Vatican had stiffened in the meantime; now it asked for the unconditional repeal of the May Laws and in return offered little. Bismarck said that the recognition by the Pope of the obligation of pre-notification was a *sine quâ non* of an agreement, but, that conceded, Germany would be willing not only to resume diplomatic intercourse but to do much more to efface the effects of the religious war. All that the Pope would promise was that he would "allow" clerical appointments to be notified to the Government; he subsequently added that even this unsubstantial concession was conditional upon the practical abandonment of the May Laws. Bismarck was still willing, and offered, to obtain for the Prussian Government dispensatory powers in virtue of which the laws, while continuing in force, might be treated as nugatory, but this concession did not satisfy the Vatican, which now displayed a double portion of the Chancellor's stubbornness. Despairing of success, Bismarck, after a sharp exchange of letters, abandoned negotiations and determined to introduce such ameliorative measures as the interests of the Roman Catholic population required, without for the moment seeking any concessions in return, a proceeding which amounted to an unconditional surrender.

The retreat had made such progress by April, 1880, that Bismarck wrote to Prince Reuss, the German ambassador in Vienna, who was mediating between the Government and the Holy See: "So far it is we who are showing practical overtures; the police and legal prosecutions have been stopped, as far as the law allows of it; we have imposed silence upon the public prosecutors and the police, so far as we have been able, and we intend to propose laws which will allow us to do this on a larger scale." He complained in particular that the Centre party, both in the Imperial and Prussian Diets, was as implacable as before.

The first legislative harbinger of the new policy was seen in the following month, when a bill was introduced in the Prussian Diet empowering the Government at discretion to fill vacant benefices and restore sequestered priests in disregard of the stipulations of the May Laws of 1873, and to allow the orders which were engaged in the care of the sick to carry on their work as before. A further proposal that the King should be able to reinstate bishops who had been removed by judicial procedure was abandoned in face of strong opposition. After radical amendment, the bill was passed in July. How serious were the evils which it was designed to remove may be shown by the fact that during the first six months of its operation nearly a thousand parishes, with a population of two million souls, were again supplied with priests. During the same year most of the vacant bishoprics were refilled, and the State grants towards their maintenance were renewed. Diplomatic intercourse with the Vatican was also resumed.

Bismarck was known to be a consummate opportunist, but even the blindest of his admirers were greatly perplexed by this quick and thoroughgoing change of front. The cool deliberation with which this unemotional statesman entered upon the quarrel with the Church was only equalled by the *nonchalance* with which he withdrew from it. To judge by the suddenness with which, once its futility was recognized, he lowered his flag, it might have seemed as though the bitter war of the creeds had been a huge pretence, a mere stage fencing match and not a mortal duel. Yet all the time he was careful to make it clear that he had not changed his opinions upon the questions at issue, but was influenced altogether by considerations of expediency ; he wanted peace, and was prepared to pay the necessary price. The party hacks and servile journalists of the day bravely went to his assistance. These men, who had hitherto defended the Government's policy of coercion as the quintessence of political wisdom, were now required to prove that conciliation and not force was true statesmanship, and their versatility and resource proved equal to the task.

While, however, Bismarck had a genuine desire to pacify Rome and so to end a quarrel which was morally exhausting, and good neither for the Governments nor the State, another and a more worldly consideration had all the time been influencing him. The majority upon which he had hitherto depended threatened to break up. For a new and altogether different problem, the reform of fiscal policy, had come to the front, and already it was apparent that if headway was to be made with it he would need the help of other allies. The National Liberals, who had stood staunchly by him since 1867, showed signs of wavering, for the economic changes contemplated were wholly at variance with their convictions. On the other hand, the Conservatives had already signified their readiness to give the Government hearty support in any attack upon the existing Free Trade system, and it seemed at least likely that the co-operation of the Ultramontanes, with their strong leaning towards the interests of agriculture, might be had for a price, payable only in Canossa coin.

The only uncertain question was, Would the Conservatives and Clericals agree to work together ? That question was now answered for him satisfactorily by the two parties themselves. The Conservatives had never liked the repressive laws, and least of all those which struck at ecclesiastical authority. They had also a genuine fear that the war against Rome would prove to be a war against religion in general, and they were confirmed in this fear by the vigour with which the democratic parties, the traditional enemies of the Church and the open champions of free-thought, threw themselves into the fight on the Government's side. More than once it was only the strength of old traditions which had prevented them from making common cause with the Ultramontanes, who, whatever their political misdemeanours, still stood for religion and the authority of the Church. As early as 1876, recognizing the value of an alliance with a party, now a hundred strong, with whose general outlook they had so much in common, the Conservatives made formal overtures for an alliance, and these were favourably received. Upon the coalition which followed Bismarck's power rested for many years, and with a change in the Ministerial majority came an entire change in the spirit of legislation, for it was soon seen that under the Conservative-Clerical *régime* the masters would be the servants and the servants the masters.

It is not necessary to follow through all its stages the progress to Canossa. At every shrine on the irksome way the travel-worn pilgrim made some new oblation of piety and of penitence ; each one a law removing some disability, assuaging some hardship, or recanting some pretension rashly claimed and never effectively asserted. The displaced bishops were restored to their sees ; all the vacant benefices were refilled, often by priests who had not yet undergone that perfect system of State education which was to turn the Romanist cleric into a good German, indisposed again to place the Church before the State ; the closed churches were reopened and their ministrations resumed ; the duty of pre-notification was renounced in the case of the assistant clergy whose appointments were revocable ; the State grants impounded under the Bread-Basket Law were paid back with interest ; the admission of foreign priests was again sanctioned ; and five years after Dr. Falk's retirement most of the surface wounds and sores wrought upon the body of Catholicism seemed to be closed and healed. Another and less bigoted Minister of Public Education, Dr. von Gossler, had in the meantime (1881) superseded Puttkamer, who was given the congenial portfolio of Home Affairs, carrying with it the duty of administering a new repressive law directed against Socialism and manipulating the elections. A visit of friendship made to the Pope in December, 1883, by the Crown Prince Frederick delighted the German Protestants almost as much as the Catholics, and seemed to seal the new bonds of amity.

The ultra-Protestants objected vigorously to the readmission of the orders, but Bismarck brushed all such resistance aside.

In adopting legislation for the conciliation of a large section of the population, he said with provoking candour, the prejudices of a small minority must be disregarded; it was sufficient for him that the Roman Catholics themselves stipulated for this concession. That had always been his principle in negotiating with opponents. "In concluding peace with foreign Powers—Austria, France, Denmark," he once said, "I never asked myself the question why do they press this or that claim; I simply recognized the fact that they did press it."

It was a habit of Bismarck to attribute to his colleagues and subordinates the blame for legislation which experience showed to have been ill-considered and mistaken. Hence the time came when he tried to fasten upon Falk responsibility for the laws bearing that Minister's name. He admits frankly that he enjoined upon Falk a policy of reprisals, but pleads that he did not prescribe the precise methods or pretend to accept in all details the measures which were, in fact, applied. He accuses Falk of a psychological misconception of his task and of the means which he employed in endeavouring to accomplish it. "The blunder was made clear to me," he has written, "by the picture of honest but awkward Prussian gendarmes with spurs and trailing sabres pursuing dexterous and light-footed priests through back-doors and bedrooms." [1]

This endeavour to make a scapegoat of a Minister whose chief fault was that he did his master's bidding not half-heartedly but only too well has been endorsed neither by friend nor foe. The fact remains that Bismarck's compunctions came after the event, when the policy of hardness had proved a failure. He is far more credible when he declares that he never regarded the May Laws as permanent, but as exceptional measures devised to meet an exceptional situation, weapons of war intended for use only so long as hostilities lasted, and that sooner or later he contemplated their abandonment. "When one believes that one is on the eve of war," he said on one occasion in reference to these measures, "and lays in stores of melinite and other explosives, one does not for that reason regard such materials as a permanent part of one's household furniture."

On which side, then, did victory rest in this bitter struggle between the spiritual and the secular power? It seemed at

[1] *Reflections and Reminiscences*, vol. ii., p. 130. For a specially apologetic utterance on the subject see his speech in the Prussian Lower House on January 24, 1887.

the end that both sides were left almost as at the beginning. That meant, however, that the secular power had been beaten. In offensive warfare that side is the loser which fails to realize its objective; the laurels lie with the side which is able to hold its own successfully. That is what the Church had done. One of his ablest and at the same time most discriminating of his biographers, Erich Marcks, says of Bismarck's action in provoking the *Kulturkampf* that "When he entered upon it he did it in the spirit of the great realist, exaggerating the intellectual and underestimating the ecclesiastical forces behind the State and the nation." Without injustice to Bismarck, one might go further and say that he made no allowance at all for the fact that in fighting the Roman Church he was fighting a spiritual as well as a political antagonist, and that he failed altogether to grasp the truth that in warfare between mind and mind force has seldom, if ever, proved a successful weapon.

Hence it was that the State emerged not stronger but weaker from the futile struggle, for it had taught the Church its power and made of it an enemy with which there could be no hope of permanent peace. This was perhaps the bitterest disappointment which his defeat brought to Bismarck. When the Centre party was formed he professed to doubt its permanence, and even when the struggle was suspended he still cherished the belief that with the disappearance of the causes which gave to the party its *raison d'être*, its influence, and even its confessional character, would disappear. Here he entirely failed to appreciate the profound influence upon the national mentality and temper of the bitter feud for which he more than any other man was responsible. Never again were tolerant relationships between the two great confessions restored. Their position henceforth was to be that of an armed truce, each side ever suspicious, vigilant, *en vedette,* and ready for any sudden call to arms.[1] At the close of his life, Bismarck had to revise his earlier hopeful judgment. He wrote in 1893: "The conflict which has been waged from time immemorial between priests and kings cannot be brought to a conclusion at the present day, and in Germany least of all."

[1] Cf. Prince von Bülow: "The Centre is the strong bastion built by the Roman Catholic section of the people to protect itself from interference on the part of the Protestant majority" (*Imperial Germany*, p. 154).

CHAPTER XII

(1848–1888)

SOCIAL DEMOCRACY

WHILE the struggle with the Roman Catholic Church was still in progress domestic troubles of another kind had been thickening. Not for the first time, but with greater urgency than before, the working classes were claiming a more tolerable place in the new Empire which they had helped to create. Socialism had been proclaimed to them as a gospel of hope and cheer, and they were welcoming it with the enthusiasm of men to whose lot the powers ordained by God had long been singularly indifferent.

If the student of sociology knows nothing else with certainty, he knows that it is seldom possible to point to any one event or point of time and say of a great cultural movement, " In this way it had its origin ; from that day dated its commencement." The current of modern German Socialistic thought had many tributaries, and the sources of these tributaries must be sought in different gathering grounds. What is known as the social question—using the phrase in its narrow sense as connoting the problem of labour and its place in economic life—was of later date in Germany than in England because the conditions which created it were there of later origin. When the economic revolution following upon the introduction of steam power and machinery and the consequent institution of the factory system of production had for practical purposes been completed in England, Germany was still leisurely jogging along in the old-fashioned eighteenth-century ways. The German working classes had to pass through the same transition as the English, but its severity was tempered to them by the experience of the older industrial country and by the humaner sentiment of the age. The change to a new industrial order, when it began, was also slower, and it never became so complete.

Two conditions essential to the success of the factory system of production are capital and concentration of population, and in Germany generally these conditions have never existed to the same extent as in England ; even if the little kingdom of Saxony be regarded as an exception, it is only partially so. In the middle of the nineteenth century Germany was more an agricultural country than England had been in the middle of the eighteenth. It is estimated that one-half of the population was then directly engaged in agricultural occupations, and that industry employed little more than one-third. Similarly, Germany has not until quite recent years been a country of large overcrowded towns. Even as late as in 1871 three-quarters of its population ranked as "rural," and nearly two-thirds lived in rural communes containing less then 2,000 inhabitants. The predominance of agriculture gave to the home industries a far more prominent place than they had ever taken in England, while, owing to the more equal distribution of population in small communities, the handicrafts and the system of petty enterprise generally have retained even to the present day much of their old vigour and importance.

Nevertheless, from the second quarter of the century forward the steady progress of capitalist enterprise created a large displacement of labour. Thus spinning machinery gradually crushed out home employment in the cotton, linen, and woollen trades ; the power loom similarly displaced the hand loom, turning the weaver, usually for his good, from his unhealthy workshop-bedroom into the factory, where he was not under the same temptation to work by night as well as by day ; gas, supplanting the tallow candle, made the chandler superfluous ; railways displaced road carriage and deprived the cartwright of much of his work. These and similar transformations were typical of a large and widespread dislocation of industry. In some parts of the country this dislocation created for a time acute misery. One of the most important centres of the home industry in Prussia was Silesia, whose cotton and linen weavers underwent great privation owing to the introduction of machine power in the early 'forties. When in 1844 the sufferings of these people found expression in violent outbreaks, the Government intervened to suppress disaffection with a severe hand, but did little to remove the underlying evils. The Silesian industry was further injured after 1846 owing to the fact that the King, who had never been sympathetic to the population of republican

Cracow, agreed in that year to the permanent incorporation of this City State in Austria, ignorant, as the Government afterwards acknowledged, that Cracow was the principal market for Silesian textile goods.

In no Continental country is the social conscience more awake in the present day than in Germany; in none was it more somnolent than in the middle of last century. At that time labour knew the State far more from the repressive than the benevolent side. The political reaction which set in with the promulgation of the Carlsbad Decrees of 1819 was still in flood, and the severe measures taken against democratic movements had led to the forcible or voluntary exile of many men who should have been the leaders of the popular cause. The emphatic response given by Germany to the French revolution of 1848, however, shook the Governments out of their lethargy. With the popular demand for political rights were mingled more or less definite demands for the amelioration of social conditions. It was inevitable that the popular disaffection of the time should have brought the Sovereigns and the Governments under a common condemnation. The withholding of constitutional rights from people who had never possessed them would not alone explain the vehemence of the outburst which then threatened thrones, and converted monarchs for a time into humble suppliants for their subjects' indulgence. The working classes instinctively associated their condition with the political systems under which they lived. The King who claims to be absolute must at least be prepared to meet the responsibilities inseparable from such a claim, and failure to do so makes his position an anomaly and his assumptions an imposture. Proceeding from that assumption, without arguing it, the workers were led to identify the evils from which they suffered with the system of government under which they lived and the Crown which was its emblem. How closely economic demands were interwoven with political at that time was shown by an "open address" to Frederick William IV of Prussia which was published broadcast by the factory workers and handicraftsmen of Berlin in March, 1848, when revolution was knocking at the doors of the royal castle. The very moderation of its language emphasized the reality of the grievances from which the petitioners suffered.

"Most exalted King," said this document, "the workers of every grade venture to address a petition to you in these hard times; it is for the speedy relief of the workers' great need and security for the future. We therefore humbly beg your Majesty to appoint a Ministry for Labour which shall be composed only of employers and workpeople elected by their peers. Such a Ministry will alone be able to ascertain the true reasons of the oppressed condition of the people, to ameliorate their lot, to protect the State against the dangers which threaten it, and to guard the property and lives of all against imminent destruction."

Among the demands advanced by the proletariat of that time were the systematic organization of labour, State provision of work for the unemployed, co-operative associations, higher wages, and shorter hours of labour. When two months later a crowd of some thousands of labourers stormed the entrance to the Ministry of Commerce in Berlin, it was to demand not a constitution but work, and when, instead, alms were offered to the leaders, they were rejected with indignation.

At that time constitutions were given and parliaments created where they did not exist before, yet to the movements and aspirations of the working classes the Radical and Liberal parties, absorbed in political controversies, gave neither sympathy nor a bare hearing, for the proletariat had no votes, and politically it was therefore of no consequence. Moreover, individualism, which had kept back social legislation in England, was now in the ascendant in Germany, and the cry of the Radical politician was only for economic liberty.

One of the foremost members of the individualistic school was the parliamentarian Schulze-Delitzsch,[1] who had at that time a considerable following amongst the Radicals. Conscious though he was that much was not right with an industrial system that doomed so large a section of the population to poverty, his remedies were nevertheless simplicity itself. Let men work diligently, live frugally, and save unceasingly, and all would be well. The fault was in themselves that men were underlings. He taught the comfortable doctrine that capital, intelligence, and moral behaviour were the chief conditions of the workers' advance in social well-being. If a man had not the first, he should cultivate the others all the more, and so restore the balance. Where, however, individual ability and industry proved unavailing then co-operative effort might be tried, but such effort must be based on self-help, for nothing must be done that could

[1] Hermann Schulze, of Delitzsch, in Prussia, the hyphenated name being appropriated in order to distinguish him from other holders of a common patronymic, a common device in Germany.

in any way weaken the spirit of self-reliance or deflect the State from its true purpose, which was to keep order and guard the security of life and above all of property. The forms of co-operation approved by Schulze included credit, loan, deposit, and similar societies or banks, societies for providing their members with raw materials, warehouse societies for the sale of their industrial products, stores for the sale of food and general commodities, and sickness and provident societies, though the last he favoured grudgingly. Schulze in general copied the principles which had been followed by the co-operative movement in England for many years, though he placed these principles upon a more scientific basis and was altogether bolder in his application of the co-operative idea.

The co-operative movement at once attracted the more prosperous section of the working classes, though, as in England, its immediate developments were all on the distributive side. The artisans and smaller *entrepreneurs*, who stood on the thin dividing line between a condition of independence and one of economic servitude, were attracted by an idea which seemed to offer to them a reasonable hope of holding their own against the attacks of the factory and of capitalism. To the masses of the toilers, however, co-operative schemes brought neither relief nor hope.

In the meantime, many influences had acted upon the working classes from abroad. German artisans, in their wanderings to France, Switzerland, and England, found themselves transported into a new and larger world of ideas, and what they learned by intercourse with their comrades in these and other countries they gave back to their own circles at home. They learned especially how backward was the political and social position of the German workman in comparison with that of the working classes of England and France. While the English workman, if discontented with his wages or conditions of labour, could bargain with his employer on equal terms, and lay down his tools if so disposed, such a liberty was unknown in Germany. Because "strikes" were forbidden the word itself had no equivalent in the German language at that time, and it was found necessary to borrow the English word and respell it. It was 1865 before the idea of strikes was first openly advocated in Germany by a cigar-maker named Fritzsche, who formed an association of his trade associates for the purpose of fighting capital by this hitherto untried weapon. Two years later freedom of association was conceded by the North German Diet, and it then became possible to organize strikes on a larger scale.

The time came when the short-sightedness which had, by means of narrow franchises and fraudulent systems of representation, excluded the proletariat from any share in the political life of the nation avenged itself on the Governments and the parties which monopolized legislative power. Refused influence in parliament, the leaders of labour determined to form a party outside, independent of all existing political groupings. A new popular movement, having at once a political and a social side, was begun, and it speedily took root in the towns. Until the beginning of the 'sixties the working classes had not been organized as an independent class, either politically or professionally. In so far as they took part in politics it was as an appendage of the Radical party, which was able by their help to assert a predominant position in the Prussian Diet, for the first and only time in its history, during the constitutional conflict of the years 1862 to 1866. There was a time when the Radical party, had it but shown an intelligent interest in the welfare of labour, might have prevented the secession which took place later. Only when the working classes had found themselves, however, did the middle-class political parties think it worth while to go in search of them, but then it was too late.

It was at this time, and in this atmosphere of social ferment, that there came into sudden prominence a striking personality who was destined to impress himself strongly upon the life of his generation and powerfully help forward the collectivist movement. This was Ferdinand Lassal or Lassalle (as he preferred to call himself), whose pyrotechnic flitting across the national stage between the years 1860 and 1864 will remain always one of the most romantic episodes in German social history. Born at Breslau in 1825, the son of a prosperous merchant, Ferdinand Lassalle was originally intended for a commercial career, but being sent to the university, he there studied philosophy and law, and he eventually chose the advocate's calling. In his later life his attention was divided between law and politics, with a leaning towards the latter. A diary kept by him in the years 1840 and 1841 shows that even as a youth of fifteen, when his political maturity was that of a man twice his years, he had determined to devote his life to the democratic cause; it also shows that the spirit of revolt was in his very blood and marrow, an expression of the protest of the rarer part of his race against centuries of oppression. He was not fifteen when he wrote, "I would not even shrink from the scaffold could I but once more make of them (the Jews) a respected people. Oh, when I yield to my childish dreams it is ever my favourite fancy to make the Jews, armed, I at their head, free!"

He would rather have been a Christian than a Jew, an aristocrat than a *bourgeois,* but as he could not alter his position in life he would at least one day make the ruling classes tremble. Still as an adolescent in years—for he was only twenty-three—he took part in the revolutionary movement of 1848, coming into association at the time with Karl Marx, Friedrich Engels, and other democratic leaders who were later to become famous. For inciting the populace of Düsseldorf to armed resistance to the Government, when the Prussian National Assembly was forcibly dissolved in November of that year, he was arrested and luckily escaped with imprisonment for six months. His defence at the trial ranks still as a masterpiece of acute legal argument. It was called a speech, though in fact it was not spoken at all, for Lassalle had had it printed in advance, and copies had been circulated even before the trial came on, on which account the elaborate defence was taken as said. Alexander von Humboldt wished to intercede with the King on the prisoner's behalf, but Lassalle refused him permission, and when he heard that a free pardon had been sought on his behalf the arrogant youth wrote to the King to say it had been done without his knowledge and that he would not accept it.

Eager to be in the full current of national life and to find for his talents a wider sphere, wherein he might win the recognition for which his soul craved, he obtained through Humboldt the King's permission to settle in Berlin, and thither he removed in 1857. In Berlin he played for a time a more or less dilettantist part in political life. Already he was judged to be a man of brilliant parts but of divided purpose. He had done some clever political writings, and had dabbled in philosophy, but he was better known as a graceful man of the world, with plenty of money at his disposal, who took life easily, and had no reason to quarrel with fortune. At that time he could not have been regarded, by any stretch of imagination, as a serious social reformer. Amongst the friendships which he made about this time was that with Lothar Bucher, a reformed revolutionary of 1848, who was settling down into respectable ways and was destined to enter the service of Bismarck and eventually to be his confidential friend. In 1861 he contemplated the founding of a "big newspaper," and he writes to Marx, still a refugee in Paris, to ask if a capital of 10,000 thalers (£1,500) would be sufficient, and if he would be willing to join in the venture. Marx appears to have favoured the idea, and Lassalle accordingly sought for him the benefit of the political amnesty which was proclaimed on the accession of William I, in order to enable him to live in Berlin. A Liberal Minister, von Schwerin, was short-sighted enough to refuse the request.

The Liberal party in the Prussian Lower House was then on the threshold of the fateful constitutional conflict over the budget question, and it was in addresses to Liberal ward meetings in Berlin on the absorbing question of the day that Lassalle came to the front as a popular leader. A man of vehement convictions, he did not spare the Ministerial constitution-breakers, and his bitter attacks upon the Government led to a prosecution on the charge of incitement to social antagonism. He emerged from the trial with flying colours, for though he was sentenced to four months' imprisonment the sentence was reduced on appeal to a small fine.

From politics he next extended his survey to social reform, and it was in this sphere that he made his special mark upon the movements of his time. The working classes were then still, as we have seen, as sheep without shepherd and without fold. There were in all the large towns working-men's associations of a local character, pursuing social and educational aims, but there was no central organization voicing their common interests. During the summer of 1862 the leaders of the Labour party at Leipzig succeeded in forming a representative committee for the purpose of establishing such a national organization. A preliminary meeting was held in Berlin in October, but the organizers were unable as yet to agree upon a basis of action: they were not even sure whether the association ought to be political or non-political, and if the former, whether independent or a section of the existing Progressist or Radical party.

While this doubt remained, a *deus ex machinâ* came forward in the person of the lawyer-politician. On April 12th, Lassalle had addressed a Berlin labour association on labour politics and aims, and the address was at once published with the title "Labour Programme." Schulze-Delitzsch had been preaching to the working classes the saving virtues of self-reliance and self-help by co-operation. Lassalle, with his Hegelian love of antithesis, leaped to the idea of co-operation with the help of the State. The idea was not, of course, new; Louis Blanc and Proudhon had popularized it in France already. What was new in Germany was Lassalle's practical application. With ruthless dialectic, he tore to pieces the entire fabric of Schulze's scheme of salvation by individual effort. In arraigning Schulze, however, he indicted the Radical party to which he belonged, with its arid programme of liberties which never materialized into bread and butter, free labour and free competition which gave the workless man no employment, and its insistence upon the blessedness of the free exercise of personality for men whose personalities were distorted out of human semblance by the hard pressure of economic forces and social fate. All such ethical values were to Lassalle figments and falsities. He stormed at the intellectual dishonesty of politicians who strove to conceal behind fine phrases the inherent rottenness of an industrial system which already was economically and morally bankrupt. The Israelites were not more remorselessly ground down by Pharaoh than the helots of modern capitalism by Ricardo's "iron law of wages," according to which the rate of remuneration under competitive conditions tended inevitably to fall to the level of bare subsistence. The only hope of the labouring classes was to slip the yoke of private bondage, claim the State as their protector, and with its help become independent producers through a system of national co-operation, which was to be financed by national funds.

Meanwhile, the project of a national labour organization had been suspended. The *brochure* containing Lassalle's programme coming now before the notice of the Leipzig constituent committee, they invited its author to expound his views in greater detail. Lassalle answered in an "open letter," in which he developed a bold programme of political and economic reforms to be realized by the working classes as an independent party. The effect upon the Leipzig committee of this new pronouncement was powerful, but not yet decisive. The committee had been in communication with Schulze-Delitzsch, who at their request had similarly propounded his own gospel of social reform, consisting mainly of the old platitudes about self-help and co-operation. Before choosing between the two programmes they invited Lassalle and Schulze to debate the whole question in public, and the rivals talked at each other during two days before a conference of 1,300 delegates of working-men's associations, which met at Leipzig in May, 1863. Lassalle carried the meeting with him and won an overwhelming vote of approval. His specific for the economic uplifting of the working classes was still as before the formation of co-operative Productive Associations by the help of State funds, but recognizing that this could not be done unless the workers first captured the State machine, he coupled with this proposal a demand for universal suffrage, which was to be a step towards genuine popular government. It was a new conception of the State as an institution that might and ought to do something more for them than tax them and make them into soldiers. In germ his programme was thus that of the later Social Democratic party, to the extent that political measures were to pave the way for economic, but on the other hand Lassalle accepted both nationalism and monarchy as presuppositions of his scheme. The statutes of a national organization to be known as the Universal German Working Men's Association were adopted on May 23, 1863, and Lassalle was chosen as the first president.

For twelve strenuous months Lassalle threw himself into the organization of this Association with all the ardour of an intense nature. He travelled the country restlessly, addressing meetings, receiving deputations, forming societies, and everywhere converting his hearers by the rush of his enthusiasm, the strength of his conviction, and the magic of his impulsive personality. They had never heard of Louis Blanc's workshops or of Fourier's phalansteries, and therefore could not know of their failure. It was enough that this wonderful mesmerist told them that Schulze-Delitzsch and his self-help were out of date and that he and his Productive Associations would convert the existing system of private enterprise, with all its one-sidedness and its extremes of riches and poverty, into a comprehensive national partnership in which all men would have enough and no man would fare better than his neighbours. The common people, above all, heard him gladly; he was the object of their frantic ovations; processions greeted his coming and benedictions accompanied his going. Lassalle must have been far freer from vanity than he was had his head not been turned by this surfeit of faith and adulation. It was turned badly, for Lassalle's vanity was as boundless as his ambition.

What was the secret of the singular influence upon the masses of this remarkable man? It cannot be found altogether in the political or social doctrines which he proclaimed to them, for these were not new. A democratic franchise and genuine popular government had been the aspiration of the German nation long before the Frankfort National Assembly brought them so near to realization in 1848. Not one of the vital ideas in Lassalle's economic programme was his own. He had taken his "iron law of wages" from Ricardo, and had also been anticipated by the warm-hearted Prussian landowner and philanthropist Heinrich von Thünen (1783–1850), who had laid down the proposition that the capitalist can always maintain labourers and enjoy the fruits of their labour for the price of their bare life, and as a practical protest against this idea had worked his own estate on the profit-sharing principle. Similarly, the idea of co-operation in production with State help, with the entire working apparatus through which it was to be realized—the normal workday, the labour tickets, and the rest—had been borrowed from his learned contemporary and friend Rodbertus, with whom he was in active correspondence.

Lassalle's distinction lay in his ability to transmute the vague theory of the study into a tangible substance which common minds could lay hold of, to make the ideal seem real to men who had neither the time to pursue nor the mental grip to apprehend abstractions. His purely political utterances impress one more by their pointed common sense than by any special profundity. Here was seen his happy faculty for appropriating the commonplace phrases and formulas of inferior minds and giving them back to the world in more attractive form. Many a reputation is built up on the same slight foundation, with even slenderer material, in modern political life, where half the game is that a man shall be able to give to platitudes the appearance of originality, and above all do it better than his rivals. And if this had not been sufficient to assure success with the crowd, Lassalle was a born tribune, a consummate controversialist, and a master of the whole armoury of rhetorical resource. Moreover, he adapted his oratory to his hearers, and therein showed genius. The heavy Liberal politician, as a rule a confirmed pedant, spoke down to popular audiences—the Conservative politician ignored them altogether—in turgid periods, like a pedagogue rather than a party leader, delivering his message with faultless, gramophonic accuracy and indifferent whether the result were praise or blame. Lassalle addressed his hearers as a man to men, and he spoke for effect; his rivals talked books to the masses; his was the utterance of a living soul. Doubtless he had a very decided consciousness of his superiority to the people whom he sought to attract to his banner, but he was too prudent, too wary, too calculating to betray it. He boasted, indeed, that in every line he wrote he was "armed with the learning of his century," but, like a shrewd man of the world, he remembered that scholarship is not for the popular platform. He could soar to heights of sheer eloquence, but his strength lay in his power to identify himself with the common people, to speak to them in their own tongue, to traffic with them in their own mental currency. It was this characteristic, combined with his fire and magnetism, his geniality and approachableness, which caused him to fascinate and inflame the thousands who had hitherto been chilled by aloofness and disdain.

He was unquestionably a demagogue, a special pleader, and even to some extent an actor, as both demagogue and special pleader always are, yet all his rhetorical arts and wiles were only means to an end, the advancement of a great public cause which was intensely real to him. When he entered public life he may not have been conscious of a call to be a social regenerator, yet it is certain that before long he developed a social conscience of a very genuine order, and when allowance has been made for much exaggeration and not a little false sentiment, due to race, temperament, and the artifices of controversy, his writings and speeches may be accepted as the faithful expression of a true and generous sympathy with the workers and an earnest desire to befriend them.

Though he made no public avowal to that effect, Lassalle was conscious as his agitation proceeded, and as he came more and more to grasp the largeness of the problem which he had raised, that his Productive Associations were capable of only a very partial success, and that private capitalism was so strongly entrenched in its positions that only a great social and political convulsion would dislodge it. He did not advance far enough in his agitation to make positive attacks upon the institution of private property, but his acute study, ***The System of Acquired Rights***, might well have been intended to serve as a prolegomenon to Karl Marx's ***Kapital***, which appeared six years after it.[1] The argument of the book is that rights, and amongst them the right of ownership, are entirely historical in character and hence are

[1] *Das System der erworbenen Rechte*, Lassalle's most scholarly work, was published in 1861, and the first volume of Marx's *Das Kapital* in its original (German) form in 1867.

transitional and fugitive ; each and all have been created by law, and the breath which has made may, with equal right, unmake them. Stated thus, the proposition, like many other propositions equally far-going in their implications, is not so unreasonable as to excite alarm ; the point of importance lay in its application. That Lassalle would have hesitated to advocate the abolition of private property or anything else had the success of his great scheme depended on it may be doubted, for he was by nature a rebel, and the tribute paid to him upon his tombstone as "the thinker and fighter" is truer than posthumous tributes usually are.

But even had he not been confronted by the power of vested interests, Lassalle came to doubt whether his Productive Associations would, after all, prove the universal specific he had represented and perhaps had once believed them to be. His correspondence with Rodbertus shows that he was growingly conscious of the superiority of the system of collectivism propounded by that profounder and more original thinker, and that, had it been possible, he would have staked his faith upon it more readily than upon his own. And ultimate success apart, it is certain that there never was a moment in which the ambitious scheme had the slightest chance of adoption on a large scale. Lassalle himself was so modest in his expectations that he appears to have contemplated an enterprise financed by a State loan of five million pounds—the capital of a medium-sized joint stock bank in the present day. He brought his project before the notice of the Prussian Government, and in conferences with Bismarck, then Minister-President, convinced that unsentimental statesman, if not of the practicableness of his proposals, at least of the policy of encouraging them. Although public money was not invested in Lassalle's scheme, the King was persuaded to make a grant out of his private purse towards the organization of Productive Associations. Probably the encouraging glances thrown upon the scheme from above were not altogether unconnected with a hope that it might split the democratic party, and divert the attention of the working classes from the constitutional struggle then in progress, if not win for the Government active allies in that unlikely quarter. Certainly the Radicals did not forgive their old associate for his unkindness in having, at a critical moment in the history of the popular cause, divided the interest and energy of the democratic forces.

With the aid of funds raised in various ways, a number of

associations were formed, but they did not live long, and it is interesting to recall the fact that, like the parallel industrial partnerships which had been established in France some years before on co-operative principles, the only co-operative enterprises which seemed to thrive were those formed in simple trades requiring neither a high degree of technical skill nor a large amount of capital, and that the larger the scale of experiment the less favourable were the conditions of success. It was found also that the members of established associations, which, after doing hard pioneer work, had succeeded in gaining a foothold, were reluctant to admit new workers on equal terms.

The key to Lassalle's personal influence—a key of many wards—has been suggested. Wherein, then, lay his significance and value for the German Socialist movement and his special service to the working classes ? His mind was in the highest degree assimilative, but it was not creative. Nor does his fame as a social reformer rest upon any practical achievements. Of his social and political ideas, indeed, not one proved practicable for his generation, or has been realized since. With his death his Productive Associations drooped and died, while his " Universal " Association was soon swallowed up in a more militant movement.

His value was chiefly suggestive and stimulative. First, it was his merit to have made the social question itself real to a nation which hitherto had been prone to ignore its practical claims. For more than half a century before him there had been a direct line of social philosophers, from Fichte onward through Heinrich von Thünen, Karl Marlo, Heinrich Gall, Rodbertus, and others, who had been speculating on the position of the labourer in society, his relation to his circumstances and surroundings, and groping their way towards conceptions of economic conditions based on greater justice and offering the promise of social harmony. Lassalle brought these theories of social reform out of the dim atmosphere of the study into full daylight ; ideas which had been the monopoly of the scholar he made the intellectual stock-in-trade of the workshop, the platform, and the market-place.

It was he also who first gave to the working classes of Germany self-consciousness, taught them to feel, think, and act together, and implanted in their minds the idea, which in later years became fruitful in a singular degree, that they must work out their own salvation, and hence that independent organization as an estate apart was the only key that would open the door of fate behind which lay for them the promise of a larger life and a fuller civilization. As appendages and hangers-on of the dominant political parties they might, indeed, hope to receive such boons as their patrons, influenced by interest or fear, might choose to dole out to them. Only, however, by organizing themselves as a separate party and resolutely going their own way, regardless alike of blandishments and temporary disadvantages, would they be able to wrest from society the full recognition and rights which were their due.

More truly than any other man Lassalle may be claimed as the father of the modern German labour movement. Not only so, but he was the herald of modern State Socialism. At a time when the Prussian tradition of State solicitude for the weaker members of society had almost died out, when individualism was arrogantly boasting of its victories, and the Radicals were busily propagating the dangerous idea that the State was a necessary evil, to be endured but no more, Lassalle restated the forgotten doctrine that the State represented the nation's collective will and that its highest function was to advance the public good. His advocacy of co-operative production by the help of State funds familiarized not only the working classes, but the ruling classes and the Government, with the root idea of modern State Socialism, and so made easier the advance begun on these lines twenty years later.

And so it may be said that Lassalle's principal legacy to his generation was an influence and an inspiration rather than a completed scheme of social regeneration. He, who was no idealist himself, gave to the German working classes new ideals which have carried them far, and will carry them still farther, in the struggle for greater economic independence and higher culture. Not only so, but those for whom he worked are conscious of their indebtedness to this gifted man, who, though not springing from their midst, came so near to them, and it is a true and creditable instinct which has led them to observe as the birthday of the Social Democratic movement the day upon which he publicly expounded in Berlin the first systematic German programme of labour claims and aims.

In order to follow the later developments of German Socialism it is now necessary to go back some years, and take up the threads of a movement which for a time ran parallel with that created by Lassalle. If Lassalle may be regarded as the father of German

Socialism, another German, Karl Marx (1818–1883), was the father of International Socialism; and, like Lassalle, Marx also was a Jew.[1] The son of an advocate of Treves, in the Rhineland, Marx first studied law, but early in life he drifted into journalism. It was the time of the reactionary terror in Prussia, when every political journalist carried his own halter in his pocket, and when in 1843 his journal criticized the Government too drastically it was suppressed. Marx thereupon removed to the freer atmosphere of Paris, and there lived for several years in close fellowship with Heine and other political outlaws, writing much, and working out schemes for the conquest of the German proletariat.

It was in Paris, too, that he met another exiled compatriot, Friedrich Engels, with whom he concluded an intellectual and political partnership which was to last until his death. In collaboration with Engels he drew up in 1847 the famous Communist Manifesto with its invocation "Proletarians of all countries, unite!" which was destined to be the rallying cry for his later International agitation, and his was the first signature.

After the revolutionary movements of 1848, in which he had given the German insurgents a helping hand, Marx settled in London, which henceforth remained his home. There for some years he worked quietly on an epoch-making book which, while revolutionary in conception and purpose, was to win the admiration of friend and foe alike, only emerging from his literary haunts at short intervals in order to take part in new propagandist endeavours on behalf of the democratic cause. ***Das Kapital*** was written in German, and the first of its two volumes appeared in 1867. Because he wrote in England, Marx's illustrations are largely drawn from the life and conditions of English industry and labour as he studied them in the middle of last century. Some German critics of the later Social Democratic movement have in consequence maintained resentfully that this movement was a gift from England. The contention is ludicrous. What is true is that many of the early German propagandists of the Socialist cause—next to Marx, the best known are Weitling,

[1] Maxime Ducamp in 1886 told Prince Hohenlohe of a conversation he had had with Marx, who had said that "the International and its party recognized no separate nations, but only mankind." To a defence of nationalism, Marx answered angrily: "Comment voulez-vous que nous avons du patriotisme, nous qui depuis Titus n'avons plus de patrie?" It is perhaps no accidental fact that many of the best-known leaders of the German Socialist movement have belonged to the brilliant but cosmopolitan and disruptive Jewish race; two have been mentioned, and others were Singer, Arons, Fischer, David, Bernstein, and Stadthagen.

Engels, and Liebknecht—for the most part driven from their own land by repressive laws, in enforcing which German Governments never thought of the interests of other countries, sought England's hospitality, used England as a laboratory for their study and research, and so came to regard that country as a second and kinder fatherland. But always German Socialism was indigenous and racy of the soil. No other nation could have produced a system of thought so ponderous and pedantic, and so little in harmony with human nature and actuality.

Powerful as was the Communist Manifesto as a declaration of policy, it was many years before it bore practical fruits. Only in 1862 was a serious concerted endeavour made to organize the adherents of the International idea for aggressive work. The London World Exhibition of that year offered the opportunity. London had in the meantime become a centre of traffic in Socialistic thought. The exhibition drew thither ardent social reformers from continental countries, and the exchange of opinions led to a desire for closer international co-operation in the spread of Communist doctrines. The wish took practical shape in 1864, when at a congress representative of many nations, held on September 28th, a committee was appointed to draw up the statutes of an International Working Men's Association. Of this organization Marx became the head, and its direction on Communist lines became the principal occupation of his later political life. He had already gathered round him a band of enthusiastic disciples who, imbibing his ideas and spirit, were now ready to carry the new evangel from England, where it failed to gain a foothold, to Continental countries. The head council of the International was located in London, but each country had its own central committee and general secretary, whose duty it was to organize local associations and federate them in district unions.

One of the most devoted of Marx's followers was Wilhelm Liebknecht, a journalist who had proved his attachment to the democratic cause in 1848, and had been expelled from Prussia with so many other inconvenient politicians. When William I came to the throne in 1861 a Liberal political amnesty was proclaimed, and Liebknecht took advantage of it and returned to Germany. Now he founded with others the *North German Gazette* as a republican organ, but left it when it fell into Government hands. Had he been like-minded, he might, with Lothar Bucher and a few other accommodating democrats of the time, have made peace with autocracy and ended his days in a comfortable Civil Service post. Liebknecht's character, however, was of the stern stuff of which martyrs are made. His idea of setting the world right was to turn it upside-down, yet with all his extravagances he was a truly honest man. One of his colleagues described him as "a fanatic with all the good and bad sides of one." A man of singular unselfishness, no leader of the German Socialist movement spared himself less or identified his interests and life more completely with those of the working classes. He was not a profound thinker, and he did not write much, but as a public agitator for the Socialist cause his fame was both national and international. It was Liebknecht whom Marx sent to Germany in 1865 in order to assist the cause of Internationalism there.

Lassalle had thrown away his life on August 31, 1864, in a love duel, an act of physical suicide which might have been impossible had not moral suicide long preceded. The tragedy brought the productive partnership movement almost to a standstill, and the momentum lost was never regained. The Working Men's Association continued for a time, but its "universal" character became more and more a fiction. The best of leaders would only have been good enough to follow in the footsteps of so consummate an organizer and so daring a propagandist, but Bernhard Becker, whom Lassalle had named in his will as his successor in the presidency, was a pompous mediocrity, without either talent or character. When after three years Becker gave place to J. B. von Schweitzer, it was too late to arrest the decay that had set in owing to bad leadership and internal dissension.

The International thus came on the scene in Germany at a time specially favourable to its success. Liebknecht had no sooner entered upon his attempts at fusion, however, than he once more found himself in conflict with the authorities. In 1865 he was again expelled from Prussia, an act of unwisdom for which the Government was to pay heavily. For Liebknecht took refuge in Saxony, and it was there and then that he made the acquaintance of a man who was to become the most famous protagonist of German Social Democracy. This was August Bebel (1840–1913), a wood turner, the son of Roman Catholic parents, hitherto a good monarchist and a parochial politician of the mildest type. Then a young man of twenty-five, he was fourteen years Liebknecht's junior and his inferior in education and in grasp of economic questions, yet he proved himself from the first an apt and enthusiastic learner. Bebel was then the president of a working men's improvement association in his native town, and was so far from having imbibed definite Socialistic notions that he opposed Lassalle and his project of productive associations. Liebknecht brought him out of his obscurity, opened his mind to the large social issues which faced the modern world, and set the parochial politician on the way for becoming a cosmopolitan statesman.

In 1867 the North German Diet came into existence, the creation of a universal, equal, and direct franchise, and to it five Socialists were elected. Liebknecht and Bebel were among them, Bebel sitting for a Saxon constituency, still as a delegate of the orthodox People's Party, unconscious of the larger field of activity which awaited him. Under Liebknecht's influence the Leipzig wood turner was won over to the cause of International Socialism, and though it was the elder man who gave the impetus to the movement in Germany, it was Bebel who now captured the working classes for it. As a delegate to a congress of working-men's associations of the Lassalle type held at Nuremberg in September, 1868, Bebel proposed the acceptance of the International programme as approved by the Geneva Congress of 1866. The proposal was adopted, but against the opposition of some fifty of the delegates of the nationalist persuasion, who in protest withdrew from the proceedings and forthwith formed an independent congress on the old lines.

The great significance of the step taken at Bebel's instigation lay in the fact that the German Socialistic movement now for the first time entered a political channel. The earlier labour organizations, like the workers' improvement and educational associations, the trade unions, and even to some extent the Lassalle productive associations, had eschewed political agitation as a hindrance rather than a help to the cause of labour. Henceforth political aims took a leading place, and the labour movement became more and more closely identified with republicanism. In August, 1869, the first Social Democratic congress for all Germany was convened jointly by Liebknecht and Bebel. It was held at Eisenach, and 372 delegates (representing 150,000 organized workmen) attended, nearly one-third of them being old followers of Lassalle. The Lassalleans had hoped to dominate the congress and bring back their erring brethren into the nationalist fold, but as soon as they saw the strength of the new party they again withdrew and conferred alone. The majority now formed the Social Democratic Working-men's Party on International lines, and adopted an elaborate programme of political and economic demands. The Lassalleans remained aloof for six years longer, but the fusion of the two parties was completed at a congress held at Gotha in May, 1875. The alliance was cemented by the adoption of a new programme, by way of concession to the party absorbed. The Gotha programme likewise contained both a political and an economic side. The economic side was intended to conciliate the Lassalle party and the political to satisfy, in so far as satisfaction was possible, the extreme anti-nationalists. Being thus a compromise, the programme disappointed as many as it pleased. Marx regarded it as illogical, fallacious, and unsound, and in a letter to his friend Bracke even condemned it as " thoroughly contemptible and demoralizing to the party." Liebknecht, who probably at heart agreed with his master, obtained possession of this incriminating document, and kept it secret for many years, until it could no longer do harm. Good or bad, however, the Gotha programme held the party together until 1891, when the congress of Erfurt revised it.

In the meantime the Lassalleans had entered into a prosperous partnership. The Socialist movement was running stronger than ever ; its organization covered the country ; and it could boast of twelve political newspapers, as well as minor publications, with an aggregate subscription list of 100,000. In the elections to the Imperial Diet two years later the Socialists put forward 175 candidates, fully three-fourths of whom were known as " counters," and appealed for votes solely in order to register the party's voting power in the constituencies. The number of votes recorded for Socialism was 493,000 as compared with 352,000 in 1874, while the seats captured increased from nine to twelve.

A crisis in the history of the Socialist movement was now reached, for at this point the more or less passive resistance which had hitherto been offered to it by the Governments gave place to a policy of systematic repression. A great change had come over the temper of the working classes under the influence of the militant doctrines of the International and the violent advocacy of its propagandists. More and more Socialism had taken the form of class warfare. It became an article of faith with the party that the existing social order must be superseded before the working classes could hope for any amelioration of their lot, and the employment of forcible measures was commonly advocated. There was even much loose talk of revolution. Perhaps to most of the leaders revolution meant merely a fundamental transition, to be wrought by peaceful means, but others were prepared for violent changes, and said so. A small party, convinced that no useful compromise with German autocracy was possible, boldly preached the Paris gospel of 1871, 1848, and 1789. Liebknecht, one of the most vehement advocates in the extreme wing of the party, to whom, however, much might be forgiven by reason of the vindictive persecution which he had to endure, frankly accepted Bismarck's reproach of sympathy with violence, and declared: "Socialism is simply a question of power, to be decided not in parliament but in the street and on the battlefield, like any other question of power." Yet he added at once that the Socialists had learned the doctrine that might is right from Bismarck himself.

In 1876 Bismarck decided that the time had come to oppose the further advance of a movement which had become dangerous to the State. He had watched its growth for a long time, marking with alarm its decline from the innocent Socialism on a monarchical basis which Lassalle had preached and in which he himself had for a moment taken a more than platonic interest. His contemporary sayings, when in France the Empire gave place to the Republic in September, 1870, would appear to indicate his apprehension even then as to the effect of the new political order upon the larger Continental monarchies. At a later date he said that he became for the first time conscious of the danger which threatened Germany when in the first session of the Diet in 1871 the Socialist deputies had lauded the Paris Commune. "That appeal to the Commune was a ray of light upon the matter, and from that moment I regarded the Social Democratic elements as an enemy against which the State and society must arm themselves."[1] Already in that year he had endeavoured to induce

[1] On May 25, 1871, when the excesses of the Commune were at their height, and the Palais Royal, the Hôtel de Ville, the Prefecture of Police, Government offices, museums, theatres, railway stations, and even churches, were burning, Bebel declared in the Imperial Diet: "The eyes of the entire European proletariat and of all in whose breasts breathes a spark of liberty and independence are turned to Paris. And though at the moment Paris is crushed, I would remind you that the struggle in Paris is only an outpost skirmish, and that before many decades have passed the battle-cry of the Paris proletariat, 'War to palaces, peace to the cots, death to want and sloth!' will be the battle-cry of the entire proletariat of Europe." Two days before this a conference of the German Socialist party had formally voted sympathy with the Paris Commune and the cause for which it stood.

the Governments of Europe to combine in resistance to the common enemy of their peace, and in the following year he had supported Spain in a proposal that the Powers should suppress the International Association, as the root of the evil.

Both of these attempts had failed in the absence of agreement; England in particular refused to depart from her traditional standpoint, which was that so long as the strangers within her gates obeyed the laws of hospitality there was no good justification for ejecting them. Busch, the revealer of so much of the secret political history of the period, says that Bismarck's motive in proposing international action on the Socialist question was not fear of Socialism at all, though that was the standpoint which Busch was bidden to emphasize in his Press articles on the subject, but rather a wish to keep Russia still isolated from France, by prejudicing the latter as the land of the Commune, and also to win Austria more firmly to Germany's side.[1] As ever, Bismarck's motives were probably complex, yet it need not be doubted that a genuine apprehension as to where the International and its propagandism might lead influenced him greatly.

Failing thus to bring about international action, Bismarck turned his attention to possibilities of action at home. In 1874 he proposed an amendment of the Press Law which would have made the encouragement of illegal acts or of disrespect for the law an offence punishable by long imprisonment. The Diet resented that attempt to revive the evil memories of Carlsbad and to manacle again an institution whose freedom had been so lately won, and the matter rested for a time. Two years later he proposed to amend section 160 of the Penal Code so as to make it an offence to incite, either by word or writing, to acts of violence or to attack the institutions of marriage, the family, and property. But the Diet as then constituted was still unfavourable to attacks upon liberty, even in the name of *raison d'état*, and this proposal was likewise rejected as inconsistent with the imperial constitution, which guaranteed to all German citizens the right of free thought and free speech. Windthorst, the spokesman of the Ultramontanes, declared: "If the Minister of the Interior and his colleagues have no better means of dealing with the Social Democrats, and these people are really as dangerous

[1] Beust relates that at his interview with Bismarck at Gastein in 1871 he proposed the establishment of an "Anti-International" Society, whose action was to be independent of the Governments, and he adds that Bismarck agreed. Nothing came of the idea.

as they are represented, then may God help us!" A sense of partnership in suffering made the Clerical leader tender to the grievances of the Socialists. To him it was far more important to know in what respects the Socialists were right than to ferret out their heresies. Let error, he said, be combated with truth, and above all let the Government remove the consciousness of injustice and so dry up the springs of discontent.

Two more years passed before Bismarck again attempted coercive measures. In the meantime the German Social Democrats had at the Ghent Internationalist Congress (September, 1877) subscribed to a manifesto in which the working classes of all lands again, as in 1848, proclaimed blood brotherhood, and vowed to use "every political measure which can lead to the emancipation of the proletariat." In the following year an event occurred which seemed to justify drastic action. On May 11, 1878, a half-witted tinker of Leipzig, named Hödel, a convicted thief of low character, fired a pistol shot at the Emperor in the Berlin Park. He missed his aim, but the attempt sent a wave of horror and indignation through Germany. The first thought of the reactionaries was to exploit the crime as the foul fruit of Socialist agitation. Hödel professed to be a Social Democrat, and from this fact they drew the conclusion that regicide was a recognized part of his party's programme. It was in vain that the Socialists disclaimed responsibility for the crime, and pointed to Hödel's earlier connection with the Christian-Social party, then in high favour.

Bismarck had long been waiting for the opportunity of applying to the new political movement his specific of physical force, and now the justification seemed to have come. It is said that on hearing of Hödel's crime his first exclamation was, "Now we have them!" At once he sent word from his retreat in Varzin that a law against Social Democracy should be immediately prepared. It was ready in two days, and after endorsement by the Federal Council was laid before the Diet by the 20th.

Conceived in such haste, the bill proved to be badly drafted, and in Bismarck's absence it was just as badly defended in the Diet by advocates who were only half-hearted in their work. The first provision set forth that "publications and associations following the aims of Social Democracy may be prohibited by the Federal Council," subject to subsequent approval or disagreement by the Diet. It was pointed out, however, that so wholesale an embargo upon the aims of Social Democracy was absurd, inasmuch as many of them were found on the programmes of the loyal and patriotic parties. To the Conservatives this objection was pure pedantry, and they were for passing the bill without discussion in any form the Government wished. The thoughtful section of the House, however, declined to allow itself to be stampeded in a moment of panic, and the bill was rejected by 281 votes against 57, without reaching the committee stage. The majority consisted for the most part of National Liberals, Progressists, and Clericals. The Socialists had not taken part in the debates. Observing how the wind was blowing, and assured that the Government would be more easily beaten without their help than with it, they declared it to be inconsistent with their dignity to take part in the discussion of a "law which constituted an unexampled attempt upon popular liberty," and discreetly remained silent. The Government prorogued the Diet in pique, yet admitted its decision to be prudent and just by promptly announcing that the defeated proposals would not be proceeded with.

Once again, however, events played into Bismarck's hands, though with a cruel irony. No sooner had the Diet refused to entrust to him the weapon against violence which he demanded than a further crime was perpetrated which both confirmed his attitude and confounded his opponents. On June 2nd a second attempt was made on the life of the aged Emperor, again in his capital and within sight of his palace. This time the would-be assassin was not a crazy youth, but a man of thirty years, a doctor of philosophy and a farmer. This man, by name Nobiling, awaiting his victim at the top window of a house in the Linden Avenue, fired two shots at him as he drove past, wounding him in the arm and neck, though not dangerously. Followed into the room by an infuriated crowd, which had rushed indoors from the street, Nobiling turned his still smoking weapon against himself with better effect, for the shot inflicted injuries to the brain, which brought on unconsciousness, and in this condition he lingered for several months, until death cheated the gallows of its due. The Emperor bore the blow bravely, suffering more in spirit than body. Recalling on the last day of the year the fate which had befallen him, he wrote in his Diary: "The physical sufferings were not to be compared with the pain that sons of Prussia should have perpetrated a deed which at the close of my life was doubly hard to overcome, and has darkened my heart and mind for the rest of my days."

Bismarck was now in no mood for temporizing with a reluctant Diet. Apprehensive that it could not be trusted to endorse the drastic measures which the occasion called for, he persuaded the Federal Council to dissolve it, and new elections took place on July 30th. In the meantime, the Crown Prince had been charged with the representation of his father in affairs of State. The result of the elections was the return of a Diet entirely pliable to the Chancellor's wishes. In the previous year the Conservatives of North Germany, comprising the feudalists, had joined with those of the South and formed the German Conservative Party. The blend was not a good one, but it secured greater unity of action, and as a result the confederates gained thirty-eight seats, while the National Liberals lost twenty-nine, the Radicals eleven, and the Socialists three.

A revised bill for the repression of Socialist excesses was introduced on September 9th, and its success was assured from the outset. Bismarck took charge of it, and the speeches which he made in the course of the debates on its several readings deservedly rank amongst his most remarkable political utterances. They were also important as foreshadowing the era of social legislation which began several years later. Throughout the discussions the Chancellor carried with him the overwhelming sentiment of the Diet, and public opinion in the country was equally on his side. It was in vain that the Socialists protested; the bill was passed on October 19th by 222 votes against 149, the majority including all the Conservatives and National Liberals, with several Progressists; while the entire Clerical party, still in antagonism against the Government on the Church question, and most of the Progressists voted in the minority. With a true insight the Radical leader Richter declared, as a parting shot at the bill: "I fear Social Democracy more under this law than without it." The Socialists received the result with defiance, warning the Government that repression would rather benefit than injure their cause. The law was to come into force at once.

The Socialist Law, which though first passed for a period of two and a half years, was destined to remain in operation for ten, prohibited all endeavours aiming at the subversion of the existing State and social order, or otherwise dangerous to public peace and concord. Meetings, festivities, and processions having the same objects might be dissolved or forbidden by the police authorities. Socialistic agitators might be imprisoned, refused residence in given areas, or expelled from the country, while printers, booksellers, colporteurs, owners of lending libraries, and innkeepers who promoted Socialist propagandism might be refused permission to carry on these occupations. The public circulation of Socialistic publications in any manner was made illegal. The penalty for infraction of the law was imprisonment or heavy fine. The most drastic weapon forged by the law, however, was the power given to the Governments to proclaim within given towns or districts a "minor state of siege," a condition entailing a rigid police surveillance over political agitation of all kinds, over public meetings, the sale of newspapers and publications, and the sale and use of arms. In a word, within a large and important sphere of her public life Germany was transferred from the civil to an arbitrary police jurisdiction. Bismarck never passed laws which were intended merely to adorn the statute book, and the Socialist Law was at once vigorously enforced. From the first prohibitions rained upon the Socialists like the plagues of Egypt—prohibitions of political associations, of trade unions, of newspapers. Amongst the newspapers whose career was promptly cut short were the party organs *Vorwärts* and *Zukunft*; but intellectual property is independent of time and space, and the suppressed sheets soon appeared abroad in the old guise and found ready admission into the country. Before the law was passed Liebknecht had declared defiantly, "We shall remain just as we are." That prophecy proved only true in part. A hue and cry was raised against the luckless leaders of the party, who were harried from town to town and from State to State like felons. The central executive lived for a long time a nomadic life, never certain of security in a new abode, wherever chosen, and ready to strike its tents at a moment's notice. Agitation became surreptitious and subterranean, and until the comrades were able to accommodate themselves to the new conditions and improve their methods it was seriously checked. Yet in the end zeal and devotion triumphed over all difficulties; with leader and follower alike it became a point of honour to stand by the cause and see it safely through the evil days. After a year of diligent repression the Government had to confess that the impression made upon the movement was insignificant.

Meanwhile, in the hope of checking Socialist propagandism still further, an attack had been made upon two of the most valued immunities of parliamentary deputies. The imperial constitution provided that no deputy might be arrested or imprisoned for any offence during session except with the assent of the Diet, unless he were taken while committing the act or on the day following. When, therefore, a letter was read to the Diet in February, 1879, in which the Berlin President of Police asked for permission to arrest two members who perversely continued to attend its sittings notwithstanding that notices of expulsion from Berlin had been served upon them, angry cries of "The constitution!" were raised. The idea of using the Socialist Law for the purpose of preventing members from attending to their parliamentary duties strained the patience of all but the feudal Conservatives, and the permission sought was promptly refused.

The second attack upon the constitution was even more daring. Free speech having been denied to Socialists in public meeting and party print, an attempt was made to deprive them of it in the Diet. It was easy for the police authorities to silence public agitators by expelling or imprisoning them; what they could not do under the exceptional law was to prevent Socialist deputies from talking to their hearts' content from their places in parliament or the party newspapers from publishing the speeches so made, however violent and provocative, for these rights were secured by the constitution. Outside, the free speech of a Bebel or a Liebknecht was at the mercy of any police inspector who chose to regard his words as injurious to social harmony; in the Diet both Government and Speaker were powerless to prevent the open avowal of the most outspoken Socialism. That was one of the safeguards of free parliamentary discussion, introduced into the constitution not without protests from reactionaries at the time, and now destined to convert the Diet into a city of refuge for the political outlaws when able to claim sanctuary nowhere else. Now this valued right was challenged. In March a bill was introduced at Bismarck's instigation giving the Diet power to punish by censure, obligatory apology, or expulsion for a fixed period any deputy who abused his parliamentary position, such disciplinary measures to be applied by a committee of thirteen. It was also proposed that the Diet should at its discretion sit *in camera* and suppress the publication of its proceedings. This power was to be exercised for two years. Members debated the Muzzling Bill for three days before rejecting it, but it never had a moment's chance of success. Even the Chancellor was at last reduced to the necessity of apologizing for it. During the same session the Berlin police sought the Diet's approval of the arrest and prosecution of one Socialist deputy (Hasselmann) and the expulsion from the metropolis of another (Fritzsche) on account of an offence against the Socialist Law of the previous year. This proposal likewise was warmly resented, Gneist, the constitutional historian, leading the attack against it, and was negatived. In January, 1882, a Socialist deputy was arrested at Stuttgart during session in violation of the constitution, but as a result of an interpellation he was promptly released.

The provocative policy followed by the Government led to retaliatory measures. There had always been in the Socialist ranks a section favourable to violent measures. Now the advocates of force asserted themselves, and under the leadership of Johann Most and Wilhelm Hasselmann they urged, at a secret conference held at Wahren, in Saxony, in September, 1879, that the movement should frankly aim at revolution. Most had just established the journal *Freiheit* in London with the motto "All measures are lawful against tyrants," and in it the man who had been wont to harangue the working-men of Berlin on the theme "Think and thought will conquer" now proclaimed the sole efficacy of dynamite and the bomb. The Wahren conference decided to adhere to constitutional methods, and from that time the physical force party went its own way. A year later, at a conference held in Wyden, in Switzerland, Most and Hasselmann were disowned, and there was a formal split.

Early in 1880 the time came for renewing the Socialist Law. The Government was not able to report hopefully upon the results of its policy of repression. It had used its exceptional powers rigorously, but the only visible effect had been to force agitation underground, compel the Socialists to change the character and centres of their organization and agitation, and to make out of simple working-class leaders martyrs and popular heroes. The Government wished for the renewal of the law until April, 1886, but the Diet would not go beyond three years. The majority in its favour was larger than before—191 against 94—though in a smaller House; this time thirteen Clericals voted with the Government.

The assassination of Czar Alexander II in St. Petersburg by Nihilists on March 13, 1881, convinced Bismarck that he was still dealing too mildly with a movement which at any time might lead to regicide at home. The Emperor urged him to try once more to unite the European Governments in a common plan of action. "The chief thing," he wrote, "is to induce England, Switzerland, and France, which have hitherto offered asylum to the perpetrators of political murders, to enact laws for putting an end to this mischief." In other words, these countries were to alter their criminal laws to suit the necessities of Germany and Russia, to make themselves accomplices of methods of government of which they could not approve, and to assume responsibility for their evil effects. Bismarck opened negotiations, and with his encouragement the Russian Government invited the principal States to confer at Brussels. The three Eastern Empires agreed, but the two Western Powers and the minor States declined, and the conference was not held. The small result of a great design was that Germany and Russia concluded an extradition and dynamite treaty and agreed to assist one another in combating the enemies of their peace and order, just as they had done at the time of the Polish rising in 1863.

In October of the same year the Diet was re-elected, with results discouraging to the Government. Free trade had in the meantime been abandoned without a definite national mandate, and the fiscal issue overshadowed all other questions, with the result that there was a strong movement to the left. The Conservative parties were decimated; the National Liberals went into the contest divided over the question of Protection, and one-half of their former seats went to the Radicals; the Clericals largely increased their strength; and even the Socialists regained the ground lost in 1878. The Socialist gains were accompanied by a large decrease of votes; but this was to be explained by the difficulty of putting forward candidates and generally of fighting elections at a time when voters who avowed attachment to Socialism risked both liberty and livelihood. Two years later anarchism showed its face in Germany, first in the form of a dynamite outrage in an Elberfeld restaurant in September, 1883, and at the end of the same month of an attempt to blow up the imperial family on the occasion of the festive inauguration of the Niederwald monument on the Rhine. The Niederwald plot was devised with astonishing clumsiness, and the evil designs of its authors were brought home in the course of a long trial to three of them, of whom two suffered the capital penalty and the other was sentenced to imprisonment for life.

The effect upon the Government and the police authorities of these crimes was to redouble their vigilance and rigour, and no quarter was shown to Socialist advocacy in any form. Leader after leader was imprisoned, until the parliamentary party had dwindled into a handful, while known agitators were unsparingly harried across the frontiers. The labour leaders who to-day fill Ministerial portfolios and sit in Kings' houses, who promulgate political programmes from their armchairs and direct popular movements through the telephone, have little conception of what the life of the German Socialist pioneers was half a century and even a generation ago, of the persecutions they had to endure, of the sacrifice and privation required of them every day and hour. Many of them, driven from their fatherland, wandered for years over Western Europe, homeless and friendless, seeking brief covert wherever it might be found, yet followed everywhere by the sleuth-hounds of a vindictive police system which lorded it in the seat of justice. They may have been fanatical, their ideas confused, their methods violent, their speech rude and provocative; yet at least these men were in their way idealists, upright in purpose and desperately in earnest, and they literally pledged their strength and hearts' blood to a cause which to them stood for justice and right-doing. Yet again, as in the case of the struggle with the Roman Catholic Church, repression defeated its own object. The Socialist movement still grew, merely accumulating in the time of restraint a force which, when set free, was to give to it a new and stronger momentum.

In May of 1884 the Socialist Law was prolonged. The Centre, without whose support a majority in its favour was impossible, was divided, Windthorst, its leader, being against further repression, of which he thought that both the Roman Catholics and the Socialists had had sufficient. The Government now would not accept amendments, however, and it was only by a unique feat in cross-voting—many Radicals supporting the law and many Clericals opposing it—that the requisite majority was obtained. The extension was for two years. In 1886 the Government wished to prolong the law for five years, but again the Diet adhered to two, and the same proposal was made with the same result in January, 1888, when the law was renewed for the last time.

INDEX

Index

Index

Index

Index

Index

Index

END OF VOL. I.